Praise for

DEMAGOGUE

An Amazon best histor
A *Christian Science Monitor* best

"Tye captures 'Low Blow Joe' in all his shambolic inglorious-
ness . . . The result is an epic exposé that . . . will leave [readers]
shaking their heads over the rise and fall of the greatest demagogue in American history, with the possible exception of the [for-
mer] White House incumbent."
— *Boston Globe*

"The fullest account yet of the crusading junior senator from Wisconsin . . . The rigor of [Tye's] research ensures he goes far beyond
the caricature to give us a portrait of nuance and depth."
— *Wall Street Journal*

"*Demagogue* does an impressive job of shedding new light on Joe
McCarthy, but the more light is shed, the more repulsive he appears. 'The more we learn,' Tye writes, 'the fewer heroes this story
has.'"
— *Christian Science Monitor*

"Tye has produced a compelling and rich biography that will become the new authoritative text on its subject."
— *Los Angeles Review of Books*

"[A] vivid chronicle of the ascent, reign, and decline of Joseph Mc-
Carthy."
— *National Book Review*

"*Demagogue* is a beautifully written, richly researched tragedy, a morality tale in three acts. In the end, it proves that most demagogues, like the legendary emperor, usually have no clothes. And it's not a pretty sight to behold."

— *New York Journal of Books*

"An interesting, readable account . . . New material from McCarthy's personal archive adds interesting and colorful detail to what has previously been known."

— *Life and Liberty*

"Tantalizing."   — *Milwaukee Journal Sentinel*

"In an age when we see the resurrection of Senator Joe McCarthy's tactics — exaggeration and lies, guilt by association, the smearing of political opponents, and above all the acquiescence of enablers who know better — Larry Tye's *Demagogue* is a gripping, essential read. Drawing on records newly unsealed after sixty years, Tye explains how McCarthy's fearmongering caught fire, offering timely insight into the rise of bullies and what is required to defeat them."

— **Samantha Power, former US ambassador to the United Nations and *New York Times* best-selling author of *The Education of an Idealist***

"For many contemporary readers, Joseph McCarthy is a done and dusted relic for the history books, but Tye (*Bobby Kennedy*, 2016) brings him back to ferocious life . . . Tye is an even-handed reporter, tracking the truth of stories advanced by both McCarthy's devotees and detractors . . . This is a must-read biography for anyone fascinated by American history, and every reader will blanch at its events' resemblances to today's fraught political conflicts."

— ***Booklist*, starred review**

"Larry Tye's *Demagogue* nails the defining biography of Joe McCarthy. I grew up a Cold War kid watching it all on television. I thought I knew it all, but Tye makes it real. To understand Donald Trump, you have to understand Joe McCarthy first, and Tye's your guide."
— John Kerry, special presidential envoy for climate and former US secretary of state

"Tye has written a fabulous, can't-put-down examination of one of the most dangerous politicians in American history. But *Demagogue* is more than a biography — it's a warning of the peril we are facing."
— William Cohen, former US secretary of defense

"Written in a straightforward, judicious style . . . a definitive biography that will stand the test of time."
— *Library Journal*

"[A] sure-handed account . . . searing and informative portrait of [Senator Joseph McCarthy] and his specific brand of self-aggrandizing demagoguery."
—*Publishers Weekly*

"Meaty narrative . . . a timely examination of a would-be savior whose name remains a byword for demagoguery."
—*Kirkus Reviews*

"As the demagogue [formerly] in the Oval Office — mentored personally by McCarthy's unscrupulous disciple Roy Cohn — asserts monarchical authority, it has never been more urgent to have Larry Tye's definitive answers to the questions: How did Joe McCarthy get power in America? And how was he brought down?"
— Daniel Ellsberg, nuclear defense analyst and author of *The Doomsday Machine*

"Tye takes us, step by step, as one of America's most dangerous right-wing populists learns how to use fear and deception to vault his way into power and threaten our country's most basic rights. The lessons for today are all too clear."

— **Steven Levitsky, coauthor of** ***How Democracies Die***

"This well-crafted, deeply researched study of Joseph McCarthy and McCarthyism reveals the awful consequences of demagoguery in America and its toll on our democracy. Tye provides not only untold history, but an essential primer for the times of Trump. We cannot ignore the lessons revealed in Larry Tye's narrative.

— **John W. Dean, former Nixon White House counsel**

"Larry Tye's deeply reported *Demagogue* accomplishes two essential tasks at once. As first-rate biographies do, it lifts Joe McCarthy from stereotype to vivid flesh, while also using the past to illuminate the present.

— **David Maraniss**, **Pulitzer Prize–winning author of**
A Good American Family: The Red Scare and My Father

"Fueled by a trove of newly uncovered documents, *Demagogue* charts the legacy of Joe McCarthy, reviled master of the political smear, through the malign tutelage of McCarthy henchman Roy Cohn and directly to Donald J. Trump. A must-read."

— **Richard Ben-Veniste, assistant Watergate special**
prosecutor and author of ***The Emperor's New Clothes***

"Larry Tye's razor-smart and riveting account is a timely, and dismaying, reminder of how hard it is for American politics to turn on a demagogue who exploits our fears. Joe McCarthy left few profiles in political courage in his wake."

— **Tim Naftali, former director of the Nixon Presidential**
Library and coauthor of ***Impeachment: An American History***

"There couldn't be a more fitting time for Larry Tye to revisit the history of Senator Joe McCarthy. Based on new archival findings, *Demagogue* tells the story of one of the notorious senators in congressional history, a legislator who destroyed lives, shattered reputations, and damaged institutions until he eventually did himself in."

— **Julian Zelizer, author of *Burning Down the House:*** ***Newt Gingrich, the Fall of a Speaker, and the*** ***Rise of the New Republican Party***

DEMAGOGUE

DEMAGOGUE

THE LIFE AND LONG SHADOW
OF SENATOR JOE McCARTHY

LARRY TYE

Mariner Books
Houghton Mifflin Harcourt
Boston   New York

First Mariner Books edition 2021
Copyright © 2020 by Larry Tye

For information about permission to reproduce selections from this book, write
to trade.permissions@hmhco.com or to Permissions, Houghton Mifflin Harcourt
Publishing Company, 3 Park Avenue, 19th Floor, New York, New York 10016.

hmhbooks.com

Library of Congress Cataloging-in-Publication Data
Names: Tye, Larry, author.
Title: Demagogue : the life and long shadow of Senator Joe McCarthy /
Larry Tye. Other titles: Life and long shadow of Senator Joe McCarthy
Description: Boston : New York : Houghton Mifflin Harcourt, [2020] |
Includes bibliographical references and index.
Identifiers: LCCN 2019024932 (print) | LCCN 2019024933 (ebook) |
ISBN 9781328959720 (hardcover) | ISBN 9781328960023 (ebook) |
ISBN 9780358316619 | ISBN 9780358315087 |
ISBN 9780358522485 (pbk.)
Subjects: LCSH: McCarthy, Joseph, 1908–1957. | McCarthy, Joseph, 1908–1957 —
Influence. | Anti-communist movements — United States — History. |
Legislators — United States — Biography. | Subversive Activities — United States —
History — 20th century. | United States. Congress. Senate — Biography.
Classification: LCC E748.M143 T94 2020 (print) | LCC E748.M143 (ebook) |
DDC 328.73/092 [B] — dc23
LC record available at https://lccn.loc.gov/2019024932
LC ebook record available at https://lccn.loc.gov/2019024933

Book design by Margaret Rosewitz

Printed in the United States of America
DOC 10 9 8 7 6 5 4 3 2 1

Joseph McCarthy Papers accessed through the Department of Special
Collections and University Archives, Marquette University Libraries.
Access granted by permission of the donors. Excerpts from the diaries of
Reed Harris used by kind permission of Donald Harris. Selections from Jim
Juliana's unpublished memoir used by permission of the Juliana family.

To Dorothy Rubinoff Tye, my mother, earliest editor, and enduring inspiration. She turned a joyful 101 while I was completing this book, but did not live to see its publication.

CONTENTS

Preface   1

A Joe McCarthy Chronology   11

Author's Note   15

  1. Coming Alive   17

  2. Senator Who?   65

  3. An Ism Is Born   114

  4. Bully's Pulpit   188

  5. Behind Closed Doors   244

  6. The Body Count   300

  7. The Enablers   341

  8. Too Big to Bully   372

  9. The Fall   447

Epilogue   475

Acknowledgments   483

Notes   487

Bibliography   523

Index   571

DEMAGOGUE

PREFACE

THIS IS A BOOK ABOUT America's love affair with bullies.

Front and center is "Low Blow" Joe McCarthy, one of the most reviled figures in US history. It's not often that a man's name becomes an ism, in this case a synonym for reckless accusation, guilt by association, fear-mongering, and political double-dealing. In the early 1950s, the senator from Wisconsin promised America a holy war against a Communist "conspiracy so immense and an infamy so black as to dwarf any previous such venture in the history of man." While the conspiracy and infamy claims were a stretch, the body count was measurable: a TV broadcaster, a government engineer, current and former US senators, and incalculable others who committed suicide to escape McCarthy and his warriors; hundreds more whose careers and reputations he crushed; and the hundreds of thousands he browbeat into a tongue-tied silence. His targets all learned the futility of taking on a tyrant who recognized no restraints and would do anything—*anything*—to win.

"To those of you who say that you do not like the rough tactics —any farm boy can tell you that there is no dainty way of clubbing the fangs off a rattler or killing a skunk . . . It has been a bare-knuckle job. It will continue as such," the farm-bred soldier turned senator delighted in telling audiences about his hunt for pinkos and Reds. "I am afraid I will have to blame some of the roughness in fighting the enemy to my training in the Marine Corps. We weren't taught to wear lace panties and fight with lace hankies."

But this is more than the biography of a single bully. A uniquely

American strain of demagoguery has pulsed through the nation's veins from its founding days. Although Senator McCarthy's drastic tactics and ethical indifference make him an extraordinary case, he was hardly an original. He owed much to a lineup of zealots and dodgers who preceded him — from Huey "The Kingfish" Long to Boston's "Rascal King" mayor James Michael Curley and Michigan's Jew-baiting radio preacher Father Charles Coughlin — and he in turn became the exemplar for nearly all the bullies who followed. Alabama governor George Wallace, Nation of Islam minister Louis Farrakhan, and Ku Klux Klan Grand Wizard David Duke tapped the McCarthy model, appealing to their countrymen's simmering fears of imagined subversions even as they tried to escape the label of McCarthyism. All had big plans and glorified visions in which they played the crowning roles.

Now that we at last have access to the full sweep of the records on Joe McCarthy's transgressions, we can see that his rise and reign also go a long way toward explaining the astonishing ascension of former President Donald J. Trump. While some seek comfort in the belief that Trump's election was an aberration, the truth is that he was the latest in a bipartisan queue of fanatics and hate peddlers who have tapped into America's deepest insecurities. In lieu of solutions, demagogues point fingers. Attacked, they aim a wrecking ball at their assailants. When one charge against a manufactured enemy is exposed as hollow, they lob a fresh bombshell. If the news is bad, they blame the newsmen. McCarthy was neither the first nor the last, but he was the archetype, and Trump owed much to his playbook.

The playbook invariably is the key. It transformed Joe McCarthy from a crank to one of the most menacing men in modern civilization. Armed with a similar blueprint, Donald Trump rose from sideshow to contender to commander in chief. Neither was sure of the formula in advance — bullies seldom are, but they can sense in their bones how to keep the pot simmering and know when they achieve a critical mass. Suddenly and shockingly their scattershot bile is gaining traction and lacerating countless noncombatants. Americans, or enough of them to matter, actually believed that McCarthy had the list he claimed of 205 Communists lurking at the State Department. And that Trump's Mexican wall would make the United States safe. Was it simply through endless, mind-numbing repetition that these fictions became facts?

Candidate Trump boasted to supporters in 2016, "I could stand in the middle of Fifth Avenue and shoot somebody, and I wouldn't lose any voters." Sixty-two years before, polling pioneer George Gallup penned a chillingly similar prediction about Joe's minions: "Even if it were known that McCarthy had killed five innocent children, they would probably still go along with him."

At the time when McCarthy drafted his poisonous script, few people knew the Wisconsin native's full story. America got its best look at the single-minded senator in his public and prodigiously publicized hearings, when he targeted alleged Soviet infiltration of the Foreign Service, the Voice of America, and, in a step too far, the mighty US military. "Have you no sense of decency, sir, at long last?" the Army's special counsel famously asked him on live television in the spring of 1954, echoing what much of the nation was thinking by then. Americans would have been asking a lot sooner, and reached a quicker tipping point, if they had witnessed the secret hearings McCarthy was holding. It turns out that only a third of his conspiracy hunting happened in public sessions; evidence of the rest, filling almost nine thousand pages of transcripts, was kept under lock and key for half a century.

Those records, unveiled by McCarthy's successors in 2003 and never before closely examined, reveal in disturbing detail that when the subcommittee doors slammed shut, Chairman McCarthy came unhinged in a way unimaginable to most Americans. He ceased even pretending to care about the rights of the accused, whom he summarily declared guilty. He held one-man hearings, in violation of long-standing Senate tradition. When he was absent, his poorly trained, sophomoric staffers leapt in to badger witnesses on his behalf. It is true that he ferreted out a handful of leftists, but most were indictable more for youthful idealism and political naïveté than for the sedition and treason of which they were accused. He searched in vain for a big fish—his own Alger Hiss or Julius Rosenberg—and targeted fellow lawmakers who dared challenge his shakedowns. And he grew nastier still after lunch, where he routinely washed down his hamburger and raw onion with whiskey. Here, in executive session, when he thought nobody was looking, this snarling senator showed his unvarnished essence.

If that is the darker-than-we-knew side of Joseph Raymond McCarthy, there is also an untold tale of the beguiling charm with which he seduced the Badger State and much of America. Snippets of the private Joe — the relentless yet riveting sycophant, incongruously generous to those he had just publicly upbraided — have filtered out over the decades, but these generally came from unreliable sources bent on either shielding or savaging the senator. Now we have his unscripted writings and correspondence, military records and wartime medical charts, love letters, financial files, academic transcripts, and box after box of other personal and professional documents. Joe's widow donated them sixty years ago to his alma mater, Marquette University, and they were made available, for the first time, to this author.

These papers and others reveal a figure far more layered and counterintuitive than the two-dimensional demagogue enshrined in history. Just three years before he launched his all-out crusade against Russian-style communism, McCarthy was taking courses in the Russian language and assuring his instructors they were playing a role "in the furtherance of peace and understanding among the people of the world." Later, when his Red-baiting was going full steam and his favorite target was Harvard University — McCarthyites called it the "Kremlin on the Charles" — Joe and his wife, Jean, were troubled by the beating that Harvard physicist Norman Ramsey was taking on the Sunday morning TV show *Meet the Press,* as reporters goaded the professor into defending the university against Joe's brickbats. As soon as the show was over, the McCarthys invited Ramsey to a dinner party; he came and stayed for three and a half hours while McCarthy feted him, charmed him, and offered him a job, which he declined. "I'm not sure that we convinced him," Jean recalled of their evening with the scientist, who, three decades later, would win the Nobel Prize. "But I'm sure he left agreeing that Joe doesn't have horns." Ramsey volunteered a different takeaway: "At that time there was some speculation that

McCarthy might become president or even a dictator. After our evening together I concluded this was no threat from McCarthy alone but might be with him and his wife together."

Jean, who shared Joe's zeal, was twice as disciplined, and out-lived him by twenty-two years, assembled her own illuminating take on her husband's outer and inner lives in the form of an un-published manuscript titled "The Joe McCarthy I Knew." James Juliana, a former FBI special agent and Joe's lead Senate investi-gator, likewise spent the years after McCarthy's death organizing his files into a memoir he never got around to publishing before his own death in 2013. Jean's and Jim's families made their recol-lections available for this book. Daughters and sons of McCarthy victims did the same with their loved ones' painful reminiscences, told in private oral histories or personal letters. Bethesda Naval Hospital, meanwhile, opened for the first time, to this author, its records on Joe's treatments from early in his Senate career to the day he died there, all of which confirm some long-held theories about his health and demise while upending others. And the US Marines, the Federal Bureau of Investigation, the Central Intelli-gence Agency, Marquette University, the Russian Foreign Ministry, and other institutions and individuals central to Joe's life recently unveiled files that weren't accessible to earlier McCarthy biogra-phers.

Even as I was poring through those collections — along with everything ever written on Joe in books, newspapers, magazines, and yellowing government files — I was racing to reach aging Mc-Carthy friends and colleagues, as well as his enablers and casual-ties. They, together with their survivors, helped me unwind his tangle of contradictions. Months before Leon Kamin died, the eighty-nine-year-old psychology professor said that being targeted by McCarthy left him "unemployable in the United States." Reed Harris, a Voice of America executive whom McCarthy denounced for his campus activism and leftist politics two decades before, wrote in a journal he left to his children that his days testifying be-fore the Wisconsin senator were "the toughest and saddest week of my life, but in a way it also was the finest. For I was able to stand up to McCarthy." And Bronson La Follette told me that his father, former senator Robert "Young Bob" La Follette, "committed suicide instead of being called before McCarthy's committee . . . [H]e was very, very agitated."

Yet Ethel Kennedy, who got to know the Wisconsinite after he gave her husband, Robert, his first real job, saw a very different side of the senator. The public may have thought McCarthy a "monster," but he actually "was just plain fun," she says. "He didn't rant and roar, he was a normal guy." Sometimes she and Bobby would visit Joe at his Capitol Hill apartment, bringing along their toddler Kathleen. Joe "just wanted to hold her. We'd be talking and then he'd say something to her," remembers Ethel. "I have had that kind of bond with somebody else's baby and so I understand that it can happen. It's like falling in love."

Examining all the fresh evidence of McCarthy's official excesses and his behind-the-scenes humanity makes him more authentic, if also more confounding. Today, every schoolchild in America is introduced to Joe McCarthy, but generally as a caricature, and parents and grandparents recall the senator mainly with catchphrases like witch-hunter or with a single word: evil. The newly disclosed records let us shave away the myths and understand how the junior senator from Grand Chute rose to become powerful enough not just to intimidate Dwight Eisenhower, our most popular postwar president, but to drive legislators and others to take their own lives. Pulling open the curtain, we find Senator McCarthy revealed as neither the Genghis Khan his enemies depicted nor the Joan of Arc rendered by friends. Somewhere between that saint and that sinner lies the real man. He was in fact more insecure than we imagined, more undone by his boozing, more embracing of friends and vengeful toward foes, and more sinister.

These documents and testimony tell us one more thing that is unsettling, at least for McCarthy's most zealous detractors: they borrowed too many of his techniques, too eagerly accepting as truth things they couldn't have known or that they simply got wrong. The gay-bashing senator was not, as rumor had it, himself gay, nor did he skim from his patrons to make himself rich. And despite repeated claims that he never exposed a single Communist in the government, he did, although nearly all were small-time union organizers or low-level bureaucrats, and there weren't nearly as many as he boasted. Most twenty-four-karat spies had slipped away long before Joe joined the hunt. The more we learn, the fewer heroes this story has. Dwight Eisenhower surely wasn't one, as his brother Milton made clear in his early and futile pleas that the president take on the bullying senator; neither was Secretary of State John Foster Dulles, although his CIA director brother Allen came closer when he refused to bend to Joe's threats. Even Edward R. Murrow, who has been cast in movies and mythology as McCarthy's public executioner, came to the battle late and said himself, "My God, I didn't do anything." Some call it just punishment that McCarthy the mudslinger fell victim to his own methods of smear. I find it ironic, and sad, that this senator's inquisitions first muzzled America's political left, then, once he and his ism had themselves been blackballed, undercut legitimate questions about security and loyalty. That McCarthy crippled anticommunism at least as much as he did communism was the singular thing that both Communists and anti-Communists accepted as fact.

I seek not to redeem the Wisconsin senator but rather to unmask fanatics and fabricators on all sides in a way that presents a truer, more fully dimensional portrait of a figure so central to the narrative of America. Shameless opportunism may have inspired McCarthy's anti-Communist jihad, yet by the end he had willed himself into becoming a true believer in the cause and even cast himself as its messiah. He didn't invent the dread of an enemy within that permeated the United States during its drawn-out face-off with the Soviet empire, but he did channel those suspicions and phobias more skillfully than any of his fellow crusaders. In the process, he shattered many Americans' faith in their government, trust in their neighbors, and willingness to speak up. While his reign of repression lasted barely five years, that was longer than any other demagogue held our attention, and at the height of his power fully half of America was cheering him on.

I have always been drawn to Joe McCarthy's story as an object lesson in what this country was like in the 1950s, the decade of my birth, and I became more intrigued while researching my last book, a biography of Bobby Kennedy. McCarthy offers a barometer of the '50s much the way Kennedy does for the '60s, although of a darker kind. Both were cultural icons as well as political ones, with Bobby's unruly locks and riotous crowd appeal pushing the press to brand him the Fifth Beatle, while McCarthy's table-thumping bravado was what Americans seemed to want in the midst of a frightening stare-down between superpowers. Both, too, unapologetically embraced their Catholic and Irish roots, and were eager to take on and if need be shame the political establishment. The stories of Kennedy and McCarthy share one more thing: each had an ideological idiosyncrasy that was easy to miss but was central to his character. In Bobby's case, it was the way this liberal icon was nurtured on the rightist orthodoxies of his dynasty-building father and started his public life as counsel to the left-baiting McCarthy. McCarthy's transformation was in the opposite direction, from flaming New Dealer to the frostiest of Cold Warriors. That Bobby embraced Joe as an early mentor speaks volumes about McCarthy's magnetism.

I have tried to judge McCarthy by the standard of his tense times, rather than by more recent insights about just how wobbly the Soviet empire was, and to give the senator the benefit of the doubt he seldom gave his victims. While I focus on the decade of McCarthy's life in Washington, I return repeatedly to his bedrock origins in Wisconsin for deeper understanding. Only by examining the nuances of his pilgrimage — it was neither a straight line from liberal to conservative nor so simple as a prince turning into a frog — can we pare away the historical fictions and see this unorthodox political figure as human and plausible.

Before the era of Trump, even a groundbreaking biography of Senator McCarthy might have seemed like a chapter of American history too painful to revisit, one with little relevance to a republic that had outgrown his appeals to xenophobia and anti-establishmentarianism. An autocratically inclined Russia might unite behind the ironfisted Vladimir Putin, and an Italy that had lined up behind flag-waving Benito Mussolini could be lured in again by the anti-globalist Five Star Movement, but surely this would never happen in the judicious, eternally fair-minded United States of America. After the 2016 election, nobody needed reminding that this had become a story of our time. To make sense of Donald Trump's rise, reporters swarmed into America's heartland to interview his angry white believers. Another vital way to understand what happened is to look back at the bully who set the guideposts. Cross out the name Joe McCarthy in the vitriolic transcripts of his hidden hearings, and it's easy to imagine we are listening to our forty-fifth president.

There is one more through-line that connects McCarthy's story to Trump's. It is Roy Marcus Cohn, an attorney who, while only in his twenties, already was a seasoned Red-hunter. Cohn served as McCarthy's ingenious and imperious protégé. Thirty years later, this petulant front man became Trump's bare-knuckled preceptor, channeling the senator's playbook to the eventual president.

As gut-wrenching as their tales are, McCarthy and his fellow firebrands offer a heartening message at a moment when we remain desperate for one: every one of those autocrats — James Michael Curley and George Wallace, "Low Blow" Joe McCarthy, and truculent Donald Trump — fell even faster than they rose, once America saw through them and reclaimed its better self. Given the rope, most demagogues eventually hang themselves.

A JOE McCARTHY CHRONOLOGY

- **November 14, 1908:** Joseph Raymond McCarthy is born in Grand Chute, Wisconsin, the fifth of seven children of Bridget Tierney McCarthy and Timothy McCarthy, modest farmers and the offspring of Irish and German immigrants.

- **Spring 1923:** Joe graduates from the Underhill School in Grand Chute, a single-room schoolhouse with one instructor for eight grades. He is a strong enough student, and is needed enough on the farm, that he completes grades seven and eight in one year.*

- **1924–1929:** Using $65 he earns in farm work, the teenager builds an impressive poultry business, only to lose it less than five years later to an intestinal parasite and his overly ambitious expansion.

- **Spring 1930:** Managing to finish four years of work in a single, breakneck year, Joe graduates from Little Wolf High School in Manawa, Wisconsin, with his principal proclaiming him "the most ready for college [of any student] I ever had."

- **Spring 1935:** He graduates from Marquette University Law School, having earned his undergraduate and law degrees in five years, while making money washing dishes, cooking short-order at restaurants, filling in as a janitor at a nightclub, and working as many as twelve hours a day at a Standard Oil station.

---

* The year of his graduation is uncertain, given different stories Joe told and others repeated, and the fact that the Underhill's records weren't saved when the school closed.

- **Spring 1935:** The newly minted attorney sets up his first law practice in Waupaca, Wisconsin, then early in 1936 he is wooed away to join Mike Eberlein's practice an hour away in Shawano.

- **1936:** Joe launches his first bid for public office, running as a Democrat for district attorney and declaring himself an "authority on poultry raising" and a "militant New Dealer." He loses badly.

- **1939:** He wins the next office he runs for, circuit judge, beating a twenty-four-year incumbent in a bared-teeth campaign.

- **1942:** Six months after the attack on Pearl Harbor, Joe secures a commission as a first lieutenant in the Marine Corps and serves in the South Pacific as well as stateside over the next twenty-nine months.

- **Summer 1944:** Still in the Marines, Joe challenges incumbent Alexander Wiley for the Republican nomination for US senator, losing nearly two to one. Precisely when he converted to the GOP is uncertain, although his reason for doing so in heavily Republican Wisconsin is transparent.

- **1946:** He runs again for senator, this time barely beating the incumbent, Senator Robert La Follette Jr., for the Republican nomination, then in November trouncing Democrat Howard McMurray.

- **1947–1949:** During his early years in the Senate, McCarthy makes friends with big business by opposing public housing and pushing to end the rationing of sugar. His sharp-elbows approach earns him the enmity of fellow senators, including many in his own party.

- **Spring 1949:** Joe takes up the case of the Nazis convicted of the Malmedy Massacre, the bloodiest slaughter of American soldiers during World War II.

- **February 1950:** Speaking at a Lincoln Day Dinner in Wheeling, West Virginia, Joe salvages his political career by launching a crusade against alleged Communist subversion, charging that the State Department is riddled with Reds.

- **July 1950:** A Senate subcommittee led by Maryland Democrat Millard Tydings issues a report blasting Joe, calling his charges of Communist infiltration "a fraud and a hoax." He is undeterred, branding the partisan review a whitewash.

- **November 1950:** McCarthy leads a deceitful and successful campaign to unseat Senator Tydings that sends this clarion message to his foes: sign on, stand aside, or beware my battering ram.

- **December 1950:** The senator assaults muckraking columnist Drew Pearson in the cloakroom at Washington's posh Sulgrave Club, a move that sends Pearson and the wider media a message like the one he'd sent Tydings: take me on at your peril.

- **June 1951:** Joe delivers a speech in the Senate placing General George Marshall, the secretary of defense and former secretary of state, at the epicenter of "a [Communist] conspiracy so immense and an infamy so black as to dwarf any previous such venture in the history of man."

- **January 1953:** With Republicans in control of Congress and the White House, and Joe easily winning reelection, he transforms from gadfly to powerbroker as he takes over as chair of the Committee on Government Operations and its even more influential Permanent Subcommittee on Investigations.

- **September 29, 1953:** Joe marries Jean Kerr, his most trusted adviser and longtime staffer, at St. Matthew's Cathedral in Washington.

- **1953–1954:** Joe holds hearings probing alleged Communist influence everywhere from the State Department and the Voice of America to the Government Printing Office and the US Army.

- **Fall 1953–Spring 1954:** Edward R. Murrow goes after McCarthy in national TV broadcasts that will become legendary, although enterprising print journalists were, as Murrow acknowledges, doing the same thing long before Murrow.

- **Spring 1954:** Joe's putting the Army in his crosshairs is a step too far for President Eisenhower, the US Senate, and the American public — especially when it looks like he is more interested in protecting an unpaid staff consultant who is trying to evade military service than in investigating alleged subversion. At the start of the

Army-McCarthy hearings his popularity is at 50 percent; by the end it plummets to 34 percent.

- **June 9, 1954:** The Army-McCarthy hearings reach an emotional climax when, out of the blue and beyond any bounds, McCarthy verbally attacks a young associate of Army special counsel Joseph Welch. Seemingly near tears, Welch asks the senator, "Have you no sense of decency, sir? At long last, have you left no sense of decency?"

- **December 1954:** By a margin of 67 to 22, the Senate denounces its Wisconsin colleague for having treated fellow members with contempt in 1952 and again in 1954. It isn't surprising that all forty-four Democrats present vote against Joe. But so do twenty-two of forty-four Republicans and the Senate's sole independent.

- **1955–56:** With Democrats reclaiming control of the Senate, and Joe ostracized after his condemnation, he turns up at work less often, shows signs of depression, and begins drinking more heavily than ever.

- **January 1957:** Joe and Jean adopt five-week-old Tierney from the New York Foundling Hospital. "I don't know very much about babies," Joe tells friends, "but I'm crazy about this one."

- **May 2, 1957:** At the young age of forty-eight, Joe dies at Bethesda Naval Hospital from what his doctors say is acute hepatitis and what doctors today, looking at his medical records, say was alcohol withdrawal and the DTs.

AUTHOR'S NOTE

I use the present tense in quoting people I interviewed, the past tense in quoting those whose words came from earlier writings and recordings. I employ terms like "Negro" and "Indian" when writing about the eras when that was how Blacks, Native Americans, and others referred to themselves.

1

COMING ALIVE

TAIL GUNNER JOE.

It was the perfect nom de guerre for this pugilistic Marine as he launched his first run for statewide office in 1944 — casting himself as a World War II warrior fending off Japanese Zeroes as his crew navigated the perilous skies near their Pacific islands, and a GI Joe keeping safe pint-sized Jacks and Jills back in the Badger State. This battle-tested veteran knew not just how to command attention with his very name, but how to offer up the kind of unflinching, stabilizing leadership that postwar Wisconsin craved.

And it worked, at first. Joe's campaign literature touted his handle and his heroism, and so did the newspapers. "Appleton Captain Has Triple Exploit While Off Duty," screamed a headline in the *Racine Journal Times.* "Chauffeured by three different pilots, the former Wisconsin circuit judge shed his judicial restraint to strafe Jap ground positions with 4,700 rounds of ammunition after the planes he rode in had dive bombed an enemy anti-aircraft emplacement, plastered a Jap bivouac area, and knocked out a field gun shelling American troops on Bougainville. Although normal flight schedules send dive-bomber pilots and gunners into combat only two or three times a week, Captain McCarthy showed no ill effects from his three-in-one exploit." No wonder voters swooned.

Over time, however, the accolades turned to acid. The *Capital Times,* a southern Wisconsin competitor of the *Journal Times,* indicted McCarthy for "phony war heroism." He was a desk jockey, not an airman, his press critics insisted. When he did tag along with a bomber squadron, the shooting he did was primarily with a camera taking surveillance pictures, the only bullets he fired were at coconut trees, and the sole enemies he dodged were fellow soldiers incensed that he was puffing up his record. His medals attesting otherwise had been awarded as the result of political pressure. Any feats of glory were a candidate's fantasy. Marine files, reported America's most widely read columnist, Drew Pearson, "fail to show any record of combat missions." So broadly accepted was this topsy-turvy version of his military record that NBC would mockingly title its made-for-TV movie on McCarthy *Tail Gunner Joe,* informing anyone who didn't already know that Joe was a fraud as a war hero and so much else.

Seventy-five years later, it turns out that McCarthy — pegged by history as a chronic liar — was actually telling the truth about this formative chapter of his biography. His political enemies fabricated their own rendering of his war record in order to bring him down, just as he said they had.

We know that from his personal diaries, compiled while he was in the service and buried in the Marquette University Archives. They confirm that while his official assignment was as a landbound intelligence officer, he repeatedly volunteered for combat. At sea, that meant going on submarine patrols ("somewhat of a thrill the first time"). When he got to his island base in the South Pacific, he took to the air on dangerous missions anytime he could. ("Have been on 12 strikes to date — had the plane hit no. of times but lucky.") His candor about himself ("getting a bit homesick"), his superior officer ("he must learn to act his age"), and a political ally back in Wisconsin ("acts like a nearotic [sic] woman during menopause") suggests the diary is an authentic day-by-day chronicle never meant to be shared. It also demonstrates that his hyperbole came naturally, long before he became a politician.

Convincing backup for Joe's version comes in the form of thirteen letters to McCarthy from Marines who served with him in the Pacific theater and, after the war and at Joe's behest, answered in writing the doubts raised by journalists and other detractors. Some described Joe framing reconnaissance pictures from the rear gunner's seat, which put him in danger but didn't involve discharging a weapon; others testified that on many missions, he was precisely the tail gunner he claimed to be. "While I was Operations Officer of this squadron Captain McCarthy participated in several combat dive bombing strikes against enemy held airstrips, towns, and supply and ammunition dumps, as rear seat aerial gunner for me and for other pilots in the squadron. His reason for doing this was to experience the same problems and tension that confronted pilots and gunners," wrote Major E. C. Willard. "Capt McCarthy's participation in these attacks was beyond the call of duty since his assignment as intelligence officer did not require engaging in combat [flying] in any capacity."

Another serviceman, Duane Faw, wrote Joe, "I remember that my gunner, Val B. DeSpain, showed you what to do in the rear seat, and how to load the ammunition . . . I distinctly remember that you strafed the area with the .30 cal. guns in the rear seat both after the dive and during the strafing run." While describing himself as "on the opposite side of the political fence" from McCarthy, Faw, who would rise to brigadier general, added that "this doesn't change the truth." E. G. McIntyre, too, recalled Joe flying combat strikes as a rear-seat gunner, writing, "I do know that you did want to go on more strikes than you did but [were prevented] from doing so by the commanding officer as he considered you were more valuable as a live intelligence officer than a dead gunner."

As for why those and other missions didn't show up in Marine Corps logbooks, making it easy for reporters to conclude they didn't happen, another officer told Joe that "any flights that were made by you and other intelligence officers were kept 'off the record' as much as possible, since it would have been a hell of a mess trying to explain to the commanding general what you were doing in a combat plane in case there would have been an accident."

If journalists had actually had access to official military records, the way Pearson and others maintained they did, they would have seen even more substantiation that McCarthy was a real tail gunner and a legitimate war hero. Records at the National Archives show that his ratings by superiors generally ranged from "very good" to "outstanding," the highest classification. A letter from the Navy's Board of Decorations and Medals in 1952, when McCarthy hater Harry Truman was president, said that after carefully reviewing the evidence for and against, the board recommended going ahead with awarding him an Air Medal, four Gold Star medals, and a Distinguished Flying Cross. A quarter century later, when CBS told its derisive version of the tail gunner story, the armed services again took a close look and concluded, "The only portion of the script that can be confirmed from documentation is that Marines served as escorts and pallbearers for the [McCarthy] funeral ceremony in the Senate chambers. The remainder of the script relating to his service in the Marine Corps is either misleading or incorrect."

How, given all of this, could critics have gotten things so wrong? Much of the redeeming information has become available only recently, and journalists back then took whatever they could get, often from fellow soldiers who didn't like McCarthy or Pentagon leakers who fed misleading pieces and bits. It's also true that doubters in the media and beyond were out to stop him. But Joe sabotaged his own credibility by embellishing so much. For example, he entered the Marine Corps as a commissioned officer, not the buck private he later claimed. He lied about his leg wound, which he said was sustained in combat when it actually happened during a riotous hazing ritual. He was based on Pacific islands that had been largely secured before he arrived, resigned his commission while the war was still raging, and ignored Marine edicts by orchestrating his next political campaign in between combat missions. He spun his wartime exploits to get precisely the press attention that he yearned for from home state papers. And while most of his service buddies acknowledged his bravery, they were at least as appreciative of the beer, gin, and fresh meat that "Father Mac" procured. He even adorned his military tent and truck with "MCCARTHY FOR US SENATOR" signs.*

The lessons were simple even if they never sank in with Joe McCarthy: Stretch the truth often enough and not only will people never trust you, but even you will have trouble remembering what

---

* Ed Nellor, a journalist turned McCarthy aide, said Joe admitted lying about some details of his war record: he "used to laugh about it." Thomas Reeves interview with Nellor, June 6, 1979, WHS.

is real. Malign people enough and they will fight back in kind, with evidence as half-baked as yours. It's the dilemma of all demagogues: they can't help lying and smearing.

While Joe would spend most of his adult life at the center of America's political and cultural maelstrom, he entered the world on an isle of calm in the US heartland.

Grandfather Stephen Patrick McCarthy established the family's foothold in America in the mid-1800s. A native of Ireland, Stephen made his way to Wisconsin's Fox River Valley, where farmland was so cheap he could buy 160 acres for $600. The pioneer in him would have found this untamed hinterland of waterfowl and white bass more appealing than his first and more subdued landing spot in rural New York. Irish were welcome enough in the Appleton area that they'd already carved out a colony amidst settlements of transplanted Germans, Dutch, Scots, and New Englanders.* The timing of Stephen's journey to America, like that of so many migrants, was determined by calamitous circumstances in his homeland. Staying in County Tipperary during the Irish Potato Famine might have meant joining the million of his countrymen who were starving; instead, he joined another million in exile. Even though the Wisconsin acreage he had bought sight unseen included a large swath of swampland, the hardworking farmer coaxed enough from the pink loam to be able to bring his mother over from Ireland and to marry Margaret Stoffel, a daughter of Bavaria whose parents farmed the land across the road. Together they would raise six boys and four girls, never guessing that one of the clan would write their surname into infamy.

Timothy, the third of Margaret and Stephen's brood, spoke with his father's Irish brogue and stayed on his parents' farm, inheriting 143 acres in the rustic township of Grand Chute. In 1901 he followed his father's example by marrying a neighbor, Bridget Tierney. Her father and mother were both Irish immigrants, al-

---

* How many people were moving in and out of McCarthy's hometown of Grand Chute is made clear by US Census data: of its 619 residents in 1850, only 89 were born in Wisconsin, and only 102 of those 619 were still in Grand Chute in 1860; http://www.apl.org/node/251.

though her family was a bit more prosperous than the McCarthys. "Bid" was four years younger than Tim, and, as all who met the pair noticed, she was taller, chunkier, and less handsome than her husband, who stood just five foot eight and was a wiry 150 pounds. The couple would share child raising, which was almost as unusual for Irish Americans then as Tim's teetotaling. The "old man," as the kids called him, carved out farm operations as his domain, and he got his children to do his bidding by persuasion, never by spanking. Bid was the family balance wheel, dispensing practical advice about baking and homemaking as well as homespun philosophy. "Dog bite Indian once, dog's fault," she would counsel. "Dog bite Indian twice, Indian's fault." Tim's advice was more bare-bones: "Don't forget to say your prayers."

The latter admonition reflected a devotion to their Roman Catholic heritage that Tim and Bid would pass on. Every Sunday they rode their buckboard — and later the Dodge — seven miles to St. Mary's Church in Appleton, the same as their parents and other Irish neighbors. Fellow worshipers called it "lovey-dovey" the way Bid and Tim held hands as they headed to their pew. They would do the same thing later on the Lord's Day when they walked the farm, surveying their oats, barley, and dairy cows.

Wisconsin farm families ran big, and the McCarthys already had four at home by the fall of 1908. On November 14, with help from a midwife, Bid delivered the biggest of her babies, Joseph Raymond. He came at an opportune moment, soon after the family had moved from a cramped log cabin to their white clapboard house with eight rooms and two porches. Electricity and indoor plumbing would come later. So would privacy; for most of his youth Joe shared a bedroom with Howard, the brother he stayed closest to and named as his beneficiary. There was no mistaking the McCarthys of Grand Chute for the likes of the lace-curtain Kennedys of Hyannisport and Palm Beach, but if some dismissed Joe and the rest of the McCarthys as shanty Irish, so be it. It was one more chip he would carry proudly on his shoulder all his life.

Over the decades, biographers have cherry-picked the facts of Joe's beginnings, like they did with every aspect of his life, offering spins that depended on whether they were foes or fans. The first to attempt a full-blown sketch was Jack Anderson, columnist

Drew Pearson's sidekick, who started out as a McCarthy pal but had changed sides by the time of his 1952 collaboration with Wisconsin researcher Ronald May. In Anderson and May's rendering, the early Joe foreshadowed everything evil that he was to become. He was a big-chested, short-armed ugly duckling who was bullied by his father and brothers and pampered by his mama. "Young Joe," Anderson added, "wore overalls instead of diapers, shucked corn instead of playing with blocks, and learned to pitch hay long before he learned to pitch baseballs . . . And when [his older brothers] beat him up, he would run crying across the yard to the house — to his mother — for comfort and protection. Then Tim would scold his wife for mothering Joe."* Historian Arthur Herman sought to set that record straight in his apologia, published forty-eight years after Anderson and May's indictment. Joe's early life, Herman tells us, was "simple," with "homey, rural values," and the conviction "that success was a matter of hard, physical work and that people who grew up on farms had a built-in advantage over those who didn't." If he stood out at all, says Herman, it was because "Joe McCarthy impressed everyone with his tireless capacity for hard work and infectious enthusiasm for whatever came to hand."

In reality, the young Joe McCarthy was no more a Tom Sawyer than a Huckleberry Finn. But he was the most talented and good-looking of Tim and Bid's seven children, no question. Not one of the others matched his fierceness or his love of fun, none had as many friends — or enemies — and he was the only one the rest saw as a standout, even a prodigy. He was one-quarter German, but it was his Irish ancestry that Joe embraced. Holding on to bits of his father's and grandfather's Gaelic accent although he was two generations removed from the island, Joe had black Irish looks, with

_____

* One sign of Anderson's intent was the early titles he and May were contemplating for their book — *Wild Man from Wisconsin,* or *The Hairy Ape* — which eventually yielded to the toned-down *McCarthy: The Man, the Senator, the "Ism."* Anderson acknowledged in an interview with a later biographer that he and his collaborator had fudged their identities in doing interviews for the book — Anderson by suggesting he was a friend of Joe's when he no longer was, Ronald May by claiming to be a reporter for UPI when his only tie was a brief one and in the past. Drew Pearson Papers, LBJL; Wisconsin Newspapers File, Robert Fleming Papers, WHS; and Reeves interview with Anderson, November 19, 1976.

hazel eyes, thick brows, and mats of black hair on his head, chest, and back. At five foot ten and a half and 160 pounds (he never exaggerated his weight but sometimes added lift, saying, "I am five feet eleven and a half inches—six feet if I stretch"), he was a more imposing physical presence than Tim. He also was more combative, soaking up the boxing lessons his father gave him as he was turning twelve, challenging his brothers or the German neighbor kids to duke it out, and generally inflicting more lumps than he absorbed. "After he was able to walk," his brother Howard would recall, "Joe always knew how to take care of himself."

His siblings refused over the years to comment on their controversial brother's politics, but all would stay close to him and most offered telling memories of his boyhood. "He was always exploding on something. At the dinner table, if we had company and there was some discussion, the rest of us kids were afraid to talk. But not Joe. He'd always speak up, no matter what the subject might be," recalled younger sister Anna Mae. Older sister Olive marveled that Joe "was always reading library books," especially Old West novels.* He was "awful friendly" in a way that made it appear from the start that he was running for something, said his brother Steve. Howard, born a year and a half after Joe, knew him best: "Joe was like any other kid, except that he was generally three steps ahead of them."

Sometimes that gumption—friends called it "push"—posed problems, like when he couldn't keep his mouth shut or his body still. He wolfed down his food and managed just a few hours of sleep at night. Given a chance to ride his older brother Steve's motorcycle, he crashed into a corncrib and broke his ankle. He talked younger brother Howard into testing a pair of toy wings Joe had designed by leaping from an elevated hayloft, which seemed like a great idea until Howard tumbled to the ground unconscious. Antics like those were laughed off by saying Joe had "ants in his

---

* In later years, friends would remark on how little he read—no Shakespeare, no Hemingway, not even Will Rogers, whose common touch he aspired to. "I don't think he ever read a book cover to cover," said Appleton pal Urban Van Susteren. Pamela Marshall interview with Van Susteren, 1968, WHS.

pants" and was "full of beans"; today he'd likely be diagnosed as hyperactive and impulsive, and be treated medically.

That penchant for practical joking, and poor sense of proportionality, created a challenge when Joe enrolled at the Underhill School. The single-room schoolhouse used orange crates to make up for the shortage of real desks, and it had one instructor for eight grades totaling thirty students, a third of whom were named McCarthy. Rather than let this McCarthy upend her classroom, his teacher allowed him to progress at his own speed, which was fast enough that he completed seventh and eighth grades in a single year. Then, like his siblings and most other children on farms, he decided that seven years of school were all he needed and all his family could afford, given the cows that needed milking and crops to be picked. No matter that Bid and Tim hoped their boys would attend not just high school but college.

Timothy and Bridget did dream big, but those aspirations fell within the limits of their experience, and perhaps their appraisal of their children's potential. It is said that every American mom believes her child can grow up to be president, but not Bid McCarthy, whose son came closer than most. Joe confided years later to journalist pal Fulton Lewis that he was glad his mother didn't live to see him make it even to the US Senate. "The height of her pride," Lewis remembered Joe saying, "came when he was elected Justice of the Peace. That, he said, she could comprehend. That was within the scope of her world. The idea of being a Senator would frighten her. It was too big."*

Less than a year after Joe graduated from Underhill, in the thick of the Roaring Twenties, the fifteen-year-old decided to strike out on his own, a would-be entrepreneur. Using $65 he'd earned by helping an uncle, Joe rented from his father an acre of land and started to build from scratch a chicken farm. It turned out he had a knack, along with a willingness to do the grunt work of rising before dawn on frigid days and sweltering ones to feed his birds,

---

* Bid and Tim would have been less unnerved by what their other children ended up doing. Howard became a farm auctioneer and real estate agent, Stephen and Anna Mae mill workers, Bill a truck driver. Olive managed a bakery when she wasn't raising her kids and working for Joe. Mary Ellen, the eldest, died young.

wring the necks of any that ate their own eggs, and perpetually scrape the poop from his pens. By the time he was sixteen, poultry magazines were touting him as the boy tycoon of the chicken kingdom. By eighteen, he had increased his realm to two thousand hens and ten thousand broilers, along with a fixer-upper truck to cart his eggs to stores in the Fox River Valley and his birds all the way to Chicago. Bid was delighted at Joe's successes, but was so alarmed at the prospect of her teenage boy visiting the home of Al Capone and the Mob that she insisted on accompanying him on his first trip, her first time traveling beyond Wisconsin.

Joe made quite a sight in big cities and even small ones, this thickset farm boy with a slight stutter and an overblown swagger. Mocking him, however, carried a price. "He was always alone. He was a hick—he wore bib overalls—and we were little smart-alecky kids," recalled journalist Edwin Bayley of the day half a century before when he ran into Joe in Appleton, where he'd come to sell eggs. "We'd yell at him and he'd yell back. The teasing was mostly good-natured, but we enjoyed it because there was something dangerous about Joe. He'd lunge at us, and we'd run. I can't remember how we knew his name, but we did."

Back on the farm Joe continued to push, too far and too fast. First he overloaded the truck, scattering broken crates and traumatized birds across the highway when he took a bend without slowing. Then he bought more breeders than he could manage. "He overexpanded," said sister Anna Mae. "He just had too many [chickens] to take care of." Finally, after one of the endless cold nights in his stuffy chicken house, he contracted a virulent flu that kept him in bed for weeks. He hadn't wanted to admit to his family that he needed help, and had tried to get by on the cheap by hiring local youths to tend the flock, with disastrous results when an intestinal parasite struck. Five years into his dream, at the not-so-young age of twenty, everything was gone—his birds, his money, his humble empire.

But he came away with a wealth of hard-won wisdom. He was becoming a connoisseur of people, especially the backwoods, European-sprung, culturally cautious kind that future generations would label Middle Americans. He took those lessons to Cashway, a local chain of groceries, first as a clerk at its Appleton store, which used to buy his eggs, then thirty miles east to the smaller community of Manawa, where Joe was named store manager. He put his enterprise to the test by making his the only grocery to stay open after sunset, every day but Sunday, and hosting community gab fests that proved so alluring that even rival grocers dropped by. He let customers wait on themselves rather than relying on the grocer to gather items on their list, which was the practice back then. Olive ("Sis" to him) came to work as his clerk, and the two lived in a local boardinghouse. Other stores would purchase six watermelons at a time and a crate or two of peaches; Joe stretched his profits by buying at bulk discounts — fifty watermelons and twenty crates of peaches. He won over old ladies with flattery and an extra potato, men by making clear he shared their disdain for the "know-it-alls" from the city, and teenagers just by paying attention. Few noticed how bashful he was around young women. And he earned the gratitude of local farmers whose chickens were struck by a diarrhea epidemic, going coop to coop to share his hard-earned expertise on how to fight the offending heat, worms, or bacteria.

Add it all up, and his bosses were hearing just the sound they'd hoped for: *ka-ching*. A mere two months into the job, Joe had the largest sales volume of Cashway's twenty-nine stores even though his was the smallest. He managed that not by following the company's playbook but by rewriting it.

He was savvy enough, however, to understand the limits of where Cashway could take him and the expediency of going back to school, the way Bid and Tim had hoped. His plan was to make it through high school in just two years, then try for college. "The age differences between the freshmen and myself caused me to plan to get it over quickly," he explained matter-of-factly. At the ripe age of twenty in the fall of 1929, he persuaded Leo Hershberger, principal of Little Wolf High School in Manawa, to give him a chance. A new system let kids work at their own pace, the way he'd gotten used to at Underhill. Students could decide how high they wanted to reach, with the most difficult assignments giving them a shot at an A and the easiest earning at most a C. Passing oral and written exams let them move to the next subject. Three weeks in, Joe was so far ahead he was excused from the classroom and allowed to work on his own. He was up at 5 a.m., put in twelve-hour days six days a week, and was back at the books on Sundays after church. It paid off: by Thanksgiving he was a sophomore, by mid-year a junior, and by Easter he was doing the work of a senior and proving that even his ambitious two-year plan wasn't bullish enough. "The teachers were swell," he said, "and gave me special instruction after school, and at noon, and at night."

His return to school cost him his job at Cashway, but he earned money as an usher at a local movie house. He also taught boxing for an hour a day until the younger kids learned how hard he could punch. He ran, hiked, and played basketball. His freshman classmates elected him vice president, even though he was with them for just a quarter of their year and was seven years older than most. The junior class nominated him as Manawa's "most loveable man." By the end he was a legitimate city celebrity, and his comings and goings made it not just into the local newspaper but onto the front page. The *Milwaukee Journal* also took notice of the lovable four-years-in-one whiz kid, noting that he had "enlisted the support of the school's entire teaching staff" and that "the youth's records indicate that he didn't 'fall down.'"

His records indicated a lot more than that. He made the honor roll with grades that were, on average, just over 90. He scored an "excellent" in school citizenship. Hershberger wrote in the remarks section of Joe's permanent file that "he did not pass off subjects by exams. He waded through and actually covered the work by will power, unusual ability, and concentrated work!!"*

What his transcript couldn't reveal was the price he paid by hot-footing it through. There was no time for art or music, writing for the school newspaper or trying out for theater productions. The manic cramming he did in study hall let him finish his courses but left little time for just hanging out with fellow students — or with teachers. High school is where young people can learn to think rigorously, write creatively, make social connections, and work out

---

* His Little Wolf records also show him scoring an off-the-charts 205 on a Terman IQ test, which would be high in the genius range if it was using the conventional scale.

their identities in ways that help them navigate the world. But that would have taken time Joe didn't have.

To Hershberger, what mattered wasn't what he missed but all that he managed. "We kept telling the teachers, 'Don't baby him. Don't help him more than you have to but make him earn what he's got,'" said the principal, who made his prodigal pupil the centerpiece of the 1930 graduation ceremony as the proud McCarthy clan looked on. "Joe in one year did more real honest to goodness work . . . than the average person does in four." Was he ready to graduate? The educator of forty-six years didn't hesitate, pronouncing Joe "the most ready for college [of any student] I ever had." No part of his youth would be mythologized more than his high school year, and yet this McCarthy feat was grounded in fact. He was, in Hershberger's words, "the irresistible force who overcame the immovable object" and "a true American." Underhill's boy in a hurry now was Little Wolf's man on a mission.

Joe's college career reportedly started with a white lie. He knew there was just one school for him, Marquette University, which was run by the Society of Jesus, was in the core of Wisconsin's biggest, most vibrant city, and promised not just a good education but an affordable one. The Milwaukee college looked especially attractive in 1930, when it was spiffing up for its Golden Jubilee. With his top grades at Little Wolf and glowing recommendations, there was only one obvious impediment: a question on the application asking, "Did you attend four years of high school?" The answer, in Joe's case, was an uncomplicated no. The response on his application, however, was yes.

Or so said Leo Hershberger, the Little Wolf principal, in a story repeated over the decades by esteemed biographers and respected journalists. At first, Hershberger fingered Joe as the one who fudged. Later versions had it that the principal did it on McCarthy's behalf—leaving blank that critical question, saying Joe had done "four years work," or answering yes and instructing Joe to keep it secret "until after you've completed the first quarter and shown that you can do the work."* There are two holes in those

---

* When he got to Marquette, Joe never made a secret of the fact that he'd finished

narratives, which have been used to blacken Joe's college career. First, there was no actual application question asking whether he had completed four years of high school. And second, the "certificate of graduation" form that Hershberger signed said specifically that Joe had attended Little Wolf from September 1929 to June 1930, which was a single academic year.*

Hershberger isn't alive to explain whether he was misquoted, he misremembered, or he intentionally skewed the facts. The first explanation seems unlikely, given how many writers said the same thing, on the basis of independent interviews. The last seems equally implausible, since Hershberger took such pride in his star student and, elsewhere in those interviews, did all he could to strike down other misconceptions about Joe's time at Little Wolf. Most probably he remembered incorrectly the events that he didn't start recounting until he was in his sixties, twenty years after Joe's graduation, and that he continued recollecting, with modifications, into his mid-eighties. That his warm feelings for Joe were reciprocated became clear years later when Senator McCarthy gave his former principal a fountain pen set inscribed "TO L. D. HERSHBERGER The Father of McCarthyism." Whatever the truth, the result, as with the tail gunner saga, was to give lethal ammunition to Joe's enemies.

When he landed at Marquette in September 1930, Joe was nearly twenty-three, four years older than most of his classmates.

---

high school in record time. Just the opposite. "Joe made his high school credits in one year of study so that he could enter Marquette," the *Marquette Tribune* reported in 1931 in a two-sentence item. "Boxer Completes Prep Studies in One Year," *Marquette Tribune*.

* Further confirmation that Marquette knew from the start Joe's four-years-in-one high school background came twenty-three years later, in a letter from George E. Vander Beke, Marquette's registrar and director of admissions. McCarthy's dusty admissions files showed that the then-senator had "completed 16 units of high school work by attending the Little Wolf High School for 1 year and earning most of his work by correspondence." The registrar continued, "It is likely that Mr. McCarthy was admitted on Adult Special basis since he was 22 years old at the time of his enrollment. This means that he had 2 years to prove himself capable of carrying college work before being accepted as a candidate for a degree." The letter concluded, "Mr. McCarthy was a good student while attending Marquette University." Vander Beke to Edward J. O'Donnell, May 11, 1953, Marquette University.

His academic focus was no surprise: engineering, the sort of fact-based, practical training that made sense for a farm-born fortune seeker, especially with the country mired in a depression that cost one in four wage-earning Americans their jobs and that made more adventurous careers seem irresponsible.* But his performance was average at best. He earned in his first semester three C's, two B's, and a single A. The next three terms were worse, with two D's, twelve C's, five B's, and two A's. More to the point, Joe found that his mind wasn't suited to the disciplined, precise mode of an engineer. It was true then and would be more apparent later, which explains why he lasted just two years in the College of Engineering before switching to the law school.†

Law was a better fit with his verbal and social skills, although even there his grades were so-so. Over the three years from 1932 to 1935, he scored an 80 average, a full ten points lower than in high school and just three points above the minimum needed to graduate. He certainly didn't distinguish himself in his studies on morality, either in the engineering school, where he earned a C in Applied Ethics, or in the law school, where his grade in Legal Ethics was 79. He never made it onto the law review or the law school honor roll. Blame that partly on his breakneck pace at Little Wolf, where it was impossible, in a single year, to get the scholastic grounding his classmates received in their four. Or maybe it was his parallel whirlwind routes to undergraduate and law degrees, which normally took a total of seven years but, thanks to an accelerated option at Marquette, Lightning Joe managed in just five.

---

* The aptest reflection of the sour state of America's economy and its politics at the time came from Babe Ruth, who, asked whether he realized that his record-breaking $80,000 contract would eclipse President Hoover's $75,000 salary, quipped, "I know, but I had a better year than Hoover."

† Joe told a Wisconsin journalist that he was persuaded to switch to law by his two roommates, who were law students. That may be true, or it may have been a way to disguise how poorly he was doing in engineering. Karney, "The Irresistible Force Overcomes the Immovable Object," *Wisconsin State Journal.*

He was in almost as much of a hurry in college as he had been in high school. Marquette encouraged students to spend three to four years in college before enrolling in the law school, but Joe entered after just two years and a summer in engineering, then spent the normal three years at law school. Marquette transcripts and *Law School Announcements, 1932–33.*

None of that bothered young Mr. McCarthy. High school had simply been a steppingstone to college. Law school was a means to a sensible degree — his sights were fixed at first on patent law — and Marquette was the right career-focused, non-theoretical institution to provide it.* In primary and secondary school as well as college, he had put in the hours needed to skip grades and get by; in law school he again did what it took to pass his courses, but no more. That meant finishing classes in the morning, seldom studying during the semester, and barely knowing his way to the law library. Classmates described him as a phantom whom they rarely saw and scarcely remembered. Before exams he would sit in a study group with "real students," close his eyes, and silently absorb the back-and-forth, recalled Charles Hanratty. That propelled him through law school but ensured that, despite his likely being smarter than everyone around him, he never was what anyone would call a student of the law. McCarthy "knew very little when he got here, and very little when he left, but got through on his memory," one professor observed.

Joe juggled a series of jobs in law school, relishing his image as a working-class stiff. He washed dishes and cooked short-order at restaurants, and filled in as a janitor for "Dirty Helen" Cromwell at her unhallowed nightclub. He worked as many as twelve hours a day at a Standard Oil station, for the kingly wage of thirty-five cents an hour plus tips. He could peddle anything door-to-door, from flypaper to window caulking. Selling his blood brought in $25 per pint, a boxing bout $50. It is unclear, however, whether the plasma, the sparring, or any of the rest was really necessary. His annual tuition was just $225, or about $4,200 in today's dollars, less than a tenth of what Marquette law students pay now. Engineering was even more of a bargain at $210 a year. And Joe had help, even if that fact never made it into his bootstraps narrative. "I make no provision for my son, Joseph McCarthy, for the reason that I have expended a rather considerable sum for his education," Tim would write in his will. Brother Bill was perpetually lending Joe money, and Steve likely did too, to help their only sibling who

* The state-sponsored law school in Madison was where more scholarly Wisconsinites went, if they could get in.

made it to college.* Joe told a fraternity brother that the proceeds from the sale of his chicken farm aided in paying not just for college but also for his sporty roadster. Jack Pankratz says his family lore held that his father, Hugo, who was Joe's barber in Appleton, went to church with the McCarthys, believed in his young friend, and "had given him some money to go to school. I don't know how much."

However much money Joe had, from whatever source, it didn't all go to tuition. Thomas Korb, who was a year behind him in law school and worked for a competing filling station, said he and Joe would attend classes until noon, pump gas until midnight, then head to a saloon, with McCarthy generally arm in arm with Mildred Byrnes, a striking redhead with whom he had an off-again, on-again relationship at Marquette. When it was off, Korb said, it didn't take Joe long to find another, equally pretty girlfriend. Hanratty called him "a man's man" with "gals by the dozen." He was successful enough in the dating jungle to be marked as a "wolf," according to another chum, Gerald T. Flynn. But Flynn's wife, Mary, said that wasn't the kind of animal most girls wanted to meet. Marie Brissone, a friend Mary fixed up with Joe, reported back that McCarthy had "as many arms as an octopus" and she didn't want to see him ever again.

Joe's other after-hours obsession during college was gambling. It didn't matter where the bets were made — at a Louisville horse track, in front of a slot machine in Biloxi, or back in Milwaukee dealing the cards for games of cribbage or sheepshead.† Poker was his game of choice, and hands were dealt throughout the night at his fraternity, Delta Theta Phi, where the radio stayed tuned to *Amos 'n' Andy* or Benny Goodman. Most games featured five or six players, but "on occasion after the game would break up, he and I would play two-handed poker until our 8 o'clock class,"

---

* Bill later asked Joe to help get a friend appointed as a lowly clerk to the 1948 Olympics, and Joe went to extra lengths to oblige because "this is the first time in twenty years that he has asked me for any favor. On the other hand, I have been imposing on him periodically." Letter from Joe to Al Lindley, September 3, 1947, unprocessed files, MUA.

† Sheepshead is a trick-taking card game popular in Wisconsin and similar to skat, with anywhere from two to eight players.

recalled Francis Reiske. While most players nervously inspected each new card that was dealt facedown in seven-card stud, Joe would cheekily bet without looking, raise, then shove everything he had into the pot. He loved kicking up his own adrenaline while wracking his opponents' nerves. The goal wasn't the payout but the chance to play the swashbuckler. When he won, much of his jackpot would go to buying everyone Cokes and sandwiches.

Joe lived at the fraternity house, a large white structure on West Wisconsin Avenue that was later converted into the offices of a law firm. Members refurbished the building and hired a housemother to cook lunch. The frat hosted beer bashes that often included faculty, even though it was a Catholic campus and Prohibition was still in effect. Joe generally stopped after two or three mugs. He showed less restraint when it came to the mischief-making part of Greek life, like when he and his co-conspirators borrowed the huge urns in front of a nearby apartment building to serve as ashtrays in their house. Still, Joe found time to call his parents regularly from the fraternity house telephone. He'd affect a brogue — "Mither" and "Fither" — prompting his Delta Theta brothers to ask how recently he'd gotten off the boat. He never forgot his roots on the farm and further back in Ireland, and he remained sensitive about being less educated and sophisticated than his pampered classmates, all of which contributed to what Korb saw as a "fantastic" inferiority complex at the core of Joe's personality.

Boxing offered another indicator. Intramural matches like his attracted hundreds of passionate fans, with Joe competing first as a middleweight, then a heavyweight. He was more of a roadhouse brawler than a studied puncher, better at attacking than defending, with a roundhouse right that could deck an opponent. "Joe McCarthy had dynamite in both hands," raved the *Marquette Tribune*. Concession was out of the question, as there seemed no limit to the beating he'd swallow. Once he got so bloodied that his opponent wanted to end the bout, but McCarthy, grinning, yelled, "Come on! Come on!" Hence the nickname Smiling Joe. His skills were impressive enough that he was asked to coach fellow students, working to build their confidence much as he had in high school and giving up smoking to set an example. Images of Joe unleashing haymakers in the boxing ring would prove irresistible over the years to foes, friends, and journalists, as a metaphor for Joe's letting fly with wild accusations in the political arena. But there was a less obvious lesson Joe learned in the ring: no matter how savagely you worked over an adversary, after the bout there were no grudges. It was, after all, just a game.

McCarthy didn't expressly engage much with world or national politics during his time at Marquette. He likely wouldn't have recognized Mahatma Gandhi, *Time* magazine's Man of the Year Joe's freshman year, or known that Joe Stalin was launching a campaign of collectivization and repression that would claim 25 million lives. But Steve Swedish, a piano player who got to know Joe when he was performing in the dining room of Milwaukee's elegant Schroeder Hotel, said even then McCarthy was sounding warnings of the perils of homegrown communism: "Steve, you have no idea what danger we're in . . . how the Communists are infiltrating . . . I have a feeling that they're just creeping into everything like a cancer." Presumably, politics also was on Joe's mind one morning when he and a fellow law student, on one of their visits to the Milwaukee city council, listened to a series of monotone speeches on topics as scintillating as streetlights and sewers. "If that's the best they can do, they ought to be kicked out," mused McCarthy, adding offhandedly that someday he'd like to be governor or senator.

Joe did take his first steps toward public life while at Marquette when he ran for president of the Franklin Debating Club. He'd already established himself as a fearless if not especially big man on campus by offering to arm-wrestle anyone for money and showing how he could sharpen his straight razor on the palm of his hand. Still, he lost the debating post to fellow law student Charles Curran. Not long after that, the two faced off again for the freshman class presidency, and each agreed to cast a gentlemanly vote for the other. When the race ended in a dead heat, the dean suggested drawing straws, cutting cards, or flipping a coin to determine the victor.* Joe, however, insisted on a runoff, which he won by two

---

* Law school classmate Charles Hanratty says he and other McCarthy pals stuffed the ballot box on Joe's behalf in the first round, leading to nearly twice as many votes being cast as there were students in the class. Reeves interview with Charles Hanratty, July 24, 1975.

votes—his own and his rival's. Curran confronted Joe, who explained that "he had worked so hard trying to convince his classmates that he was the best candidate, that he finally convinced himself."

The story ends there in most histories of McCarthy, with him proving himself brazenly unscrupulous and wantonly narcissistic. But Joe was steadfast as well as shameless, which Curran had learned shortly before, when his father died: "As soon as Joe heard of his death, he came over to my rooming house to see if he could assist me in getting to the train for the trip home. On the day of the funeral, Joe borrowed an old Model 'T' Ford and drove to Mauston to attend the funeral. I am sure that he had to either borrow the money for the gas or go without some needed requirement such as food." To Curran, as to many others, the Dr. Jekyll side of Joe's character eclipsed any Mr. Hyde tendencies, and the two stayed friends forever.

Joe's years at Marquette also left a mark when it came to religion. Bid and Tim had impressed upon their children the importance of their Catholicism, and the Milwaukee Jesuits reinforced that message. Joe took four semesters of theology courses, as required for Catholic engineering students. He earned A's in the first two, Natural Religion, which focused more on philosophy than on doctrine and explored how God shows himself through reason along with revelation. He did less well in Social Justice–Sacraments, getting a B the first semester and a C the second. The Marquette Jesuits back then described him as dutiful and deferential but also joyful. What stuck with McCarthy, however, was his church's opposition to communism, and its Index of Forbidden Texts. Books were banned if they contained material deemed to be heretical, salacious, or just not good for Catholics to read, and a list of Marquette students who did read them was forwarded to the archbishop every semester. Such tabulations, which had been around since the Protestant Reformation in the sixteenth century, were discontinued by Pope Paul VI in 1966.

Still, we should not attribute too much of who Joe became to his instruction on the Jesuit campus, said Donald F. Crosby, a Jesuit historian who devoted an entire book to McCarthy's relationship with the church. "His Marquette experience," wrote Crosby, "seems less an exercise in formation at the hands of the Jesuits than simply a stop on the way up the ladder to political success."

Joe was reaching for the next rung within hours of receiving his diploma in June 1935. Classmate Charles Hanratty drove with him to the state capital, where both would be sworn in as lawyers. They got there in Joe's new Ford, with six new suits hanging in the back, but the only answer Hanratty got when he asked how Joe could afford everything was "none of your business." They didn't stay long in Madison, leaving the day of the swearing-in for Waupaca, which isn't far from where McCarthy had gone to high school in Manawa, and where he'd already leased a law office with his name in the window. Again, Hanratty asked Joe, "Where did you charge this, you bastard?" Again, no answer.

The unfledged attorney's bare-bones workspace was in a large stone building on Main Street, surrounded by a beauty parlor, the Waupaca Abstract & Loan Co., and two dentists, one of whom shared Joe's waiting room. His living situation, also boarding with a dentist, was equally spartan. After hours he amused himself with softball (he was error prone) and swimming (he could barely tread water), along with girls and poker (he bragged that he'd mastered both). Joe's strategy for taking home the biggest pots was exquisite: bluff so much that when he really had a strong hand, the other disbelieving cardplayers would cheerfully match round after round of his raises. Other times he won by cheating—not for the money, which he'd return, but for the thrill. If he had to choose between a girl and a game, the latter won, as his friends learned one weekend at Ben Johnson's bar. Joe had invited a date up from Milwaukee, then left her in the front room while he lingered over his cards in the back. By 4 a.m. she'd given up. Joe merely grunted, "She knows the way home."

Joe no longer took out just the best-looking girls but also the youngest. And they weren't all single, said Andrew Parnell, a Marquette-trained lawyer practicing in Appleton. McCarthy wasn't necessarily after sex—"I never heard him mention it"—but he liked looking good at parties. The only way Parnell could explain that blend of arrogance and indifference was that Joe thought he talked to God.

McCarthy showed a more endearing side of himself at Waupaca's annual baseball fundraiser. Fielders were mounted on donkeys, prodding their animals to follow the ball so they could field it, while hitters had to ride a donkey to each base. But when Joe batted, his burro wouldn't budge. Proving himself equally stubborn, he lifted the two-hundred-pound donkey and carried it to first base. The crowd roared, and Waupaca attorney Edward Hart, laughing as he retold the story forty years on, deadpanned, "Joe was a very strong farm boy."

McCarthy didn't drink much in those days, Hart added, but when he did, he could be oblivious to the consequences. That was the case when the two lawyers were collaborating on a trial. Just before facing the jury, Joe had a couple of drinks. Hart was dumbfounded. Imprudent behavior like that may have been one reason why Joe's law business was slow to build, despite his keeping his lights burning on shopping nights. Another, said retired lumber executive Walter Jolin, was that local attorneys were jealous, sniping that he was a boy wonder and declining to refer clients his way. The result: during his first nine months as a lawyer, he handled just four cases, all civil, all settled out of court, and all together earning him an income of $771.81 in 1935, which would be $14,000 today. But spending less time on the law left more for the schmoozing that Joe loved, and that would become invaluable for the career he was plotting. He signed up with the Junior Chamber of Commerce, Lions Club, and Waupaca County Bar Association. If there were tickets to sell or fundraisers to promote, Joe volunteered. He again taught kids boxing and launched a Matt and Mitt Club to encourage older men to stay fit. He even agreed to chair the Harvest Day Committee, where the single perk was picking the Harvest Day Queen. All of which got Joe's name around and had Mike Eberlein inquiring about him in February 1936, just eight months after McCarthy arrived in Waupaca.

Eberlein was a seasoned and successful trial attorney from Shawano, an hour north of Waupaca. He said he'd been impressed by Joe's performance in the courtroom, but that was Mike's kind of brassiness. In reality, he was hard-pressed to fill an opening in his office. The two exchanged banter, with Eberlein entreating, "Why don't you close up this dive and come to work for me?" Joe: "Why don't you close up that dump of yours and come down here and work for me?" In truth, only one of the solicitors had a practice that was making money, so — for a less than princely offer of $80 a month plus a percent of the work he brought in — Joe packed his bags, rented a room at Mrs. Edith Green's boardinghouse, and days later was at his desk at the firm of Eberlein and Larson. By that time he was not just a registered Democrat but a New Deal partisan, which his new boss hoped would double the practice's political appeal, since Eberlein was northeast Wisconsin's Mr. Republican.

The local newspaper in Waupaca found the political contraposition amusing, publishing words whose irony it couldn't have anticipated: "'When I move to Shawano,' murmured Joe McCarthy unhappily, 'I'll have to make hasty transition from a Young Democrat to a Young Republican.' So, just to add a dash of zest in the life of Mike Eberlein's new hired man, we carefully padded his brief case with a couple copies of the 'New Masses,' a recent edition of the 'Daily Worker,' and a vest pocket size 'Das Kapital.'"

It didn't take long for Joe to become known in his new community. He reminded the men of the Shawano Lions Club that tarnishing the innocent meant "miscarriages of justice." He wrote unsigned editorials for the steadfastly Republican *Shawano County Journal,* with each earning him five dollars. And, just five months after arriving, he jumped into the race to be the Democratic candidate for district attorney in 1936, declaring himself an "authority on poultry raising" and a "militant New Dealer." At the same time he stepped up his party activity, serving as chairman of the local Young Democrats, fundraiser in chief for President Franklin Roosevelt's county organization, treasurer of the county Democratic Party, and dispenser of New Deal largesse in and around Shawano. Never passive, he attacked the platform of Republican presidential nominee Alf Landon, calling it "brainless, halfbaked, cockeyed pleas." Joe would vote for FDR three times and believed that voters would be crazy not to stick with the president, "every drop of whose blood and every faculty of whose mind and body is devoted to that great noble, unselfish task . . . of serving all the American people."

He started his own campaign for Shawano County district attorney on an upbeat note, suggesting he was an "ordinary farm boy" and that the county could save $1,500 a year by making the DA's office part-time. He also designed a free traveling billboard by painting "ELECT JOE MCCARTHY" on the side of his car. When those positive approaches didn't work, Joe went nasty. His pamphlet accused the incumbent, the Progressive Party's Louis Cattau, of holding a second job despite a local ordinance specifically forbidding that. In fact, as Cattau pointed out in a newspaper ad, that second "job" was secretary to the County Fair. "McCarthy's charge was devious, exaggerated, and tardy," University of Wisconsin history professor Michael O'Brien concluded. "But Cattau's action had indeed violated the spirit of the ordinance and probably its letter."

On Election Day, Cattau trounced McCarthy, 6,175 to 3,422, but Joe did manage to best the Republican candidate, Ed Aschenbrenner, who drew just 2,842 votes. Joe learned three essential lessons from his initial post-college defeat. First, withering attacks were the way to put your opponent on the ropes, where a relentless fighter like Joe wanted him. Second, newspapers would print without confirmation almost anything a would-be candidate said, which in Joe's case included a page-one puff-up of his own legal résumé and boxing and wrestling prowess. Lastly, and most convincingly, Joe saw that he couldn't win as a Democrat in that GOP swath of Wisconsin, but neither could he appear too opportunistic in abandoning the party of his father and uncles, nearly all of the rest of Irish America, and his own earlier pledges of allegiance. So after that race for district attorney, he quietly pulled back from his Democratic activism, expediently sat out the next election, and determinedly started scouting out a political office free from partisanship.

Grover Meisner, a stalwart Shawano Democrat who'd campaigned alongside McCarthy in 1936, watched those maneuverings with a mix of wonderment and suspicion. Joe confessed to him that "if you want to get anywhere in politics, you've got to feed the public what they want to hear and not what you believe." McCarthy did that so artfully, Meisner added, that he could "make you believe blackbirds were white." Edward Hart, who'd had his eye on McCarthy even longer, decided that "Joe lived in a different moral universe. He asked himself only two questions: What do I want and how do I get it?" Other lawyers in the area had names for guys like Joe, calling him everything from a four-flusher (a poker term meaning an unsuccessful bluffer, which he wasn't) to an ambulance chaser. (When he heard about an accident he did rush to the home or hospital, hoping to persuade the victim to sue.)

He was spending more time now on Main Street than in his law office, glad-handing friends and strangers alike, and dropping in on local businesses to salute the cleaning lady and secretary. He raised money for the Boy Scouts, Red Cross, and Holy Name Society, and told a gathering of the Junior Women's Club that, no matter what they had been taught (or what he would say in his later America First incarnation), Americans were no more special than any other nationality. The Joe McCarthy who showed up in the Eberlein office was poor as a church mouse, recalled Mae Voy, Mike's secretary, but he had "a heart as big as a hotel." He would clean and press old suits, then deliver them to the poor. And he was willing to bare his vulnerabilities, showing Mae the tiny scars near the bridge of his nose — disguised by eyeglasses — where his perpetually running sinuses had been drained from the outside.

Early in 1937 Eberlein decided that Joe was worth the investment for his legal and PR skills, and more than doubled his salary to $2,500. Yet knowing how clueless Joe was about holding on to his money, Mike dispensed half at the start of every month and the rest in a lump sum at year's end. "He had a poor business head," Eberlein explained. "If he ever saved a cent, it would be a surprise to me." The incremental payments might have worked if Joe, by now a chronic debtor, hadn't borrowed against his escrow. Still, at the start of 1938, the signs on the windows and door were repainted to read "EBERLEIN & MCCARTHY."

At twenty-nine, Joe already was five years beyond the median age when American men of that era wed for the first time. While that wasn't his way, he did make it as far as engagement twice during the early years of his career. His first fiancée was Mary Louise Juneau, a dark, statuesque coed at Milwaukee's Mount Mary College, who would later, after a failed marriage, reveal that she was a lesbian. The other engagement was to Maybelle Counihan, a short, attractive Irish American nurse from Milwaukee who moved to Appleton because of Joe and remained his friend longer than the others. There were simply too many entrancing and available women to stay focused on any one, and he still had ants in his pants.

Joe's single-minded ambition, then as always, was to prove himself at the ballot box, and it didn't take him long to find the perfect office for which to aim. Circuit judges were elected on a non-partisan basis, which meant less focus on Joe's Democratic roots and his contemplated Republican makeover. Terms were six years, which meant less worry about having to run again soon. A judge's $8,000 salary would have meant a substantial raise, even after being named a partner in his law firm. Only two things stood in his way. To begin with, his benefactor and mentor, Mike Eberlein, also aspired to that office. And the incumbent officeholder, who'd been there twenty-four years, routinely trounced all challengers, in part because he was, in the words of Joe's hometown paper, "a judge of unassailable integrity." Joe didn't care about Eberlein's aspirations and he didn't consider his friend real competition, noting that "Mike has one of the finest legal minds in the state. But he's also the worst politician in Wisconsin." McCarthy didn't even bother to tell Eberlein before announcing his bid in late December 1938, when his senior partner read about it in the newspaper. While Joe says it was he who quit Mike's firm, it seems clear that Mike ordered Joe to take a leave, a demand born out of pique along with fear of a conflict of interest should Joe win. Over the years, Eberlein's candor about what happened diminished in direct proportion to Joe's increasing political muscle. "He never even mentioned Joe again," recalls Cody Splitt, an Appleton lawyer who worked alongside both men.

As for the sitting judge, Joe knew that taking on an entrenched fixture like Edgar Werner was just the attention-getting gambit that could catapult a backcountry chicken farmer not just to the circuit bench but to the legitimacy he thirsted for. Joe waged the same kind of two-tiered campaign he had for DA, starting on the highest and longest road. He bought a fresh-from-the-factory 1939 Oldsmobile, on credit, and added a newfangled Dictaphone that he could power up from the car's generator. Then it was off on a tour that would have exhausted even intrepid barnstormers like Satchel Paige and Dizzy Dean. Navigating frozen country lanes, Joe stopped at least once at nearly every farm in the three-county judicial district. He talked sick chickens with farmers and jollied housewives by insisting their cherry pie was the best ever to cross his lips. He'd wave at barns and pastures, on the likelihood a shy farmhand was there, peeking through the boards. "When I first noticed him," said one grizzled homesteader, "he was outside petting the dog. By the time I got to the front door, he was handing my daughter a lollipop, and then Indian-wrestling with my boy." Joe never breached the topic of the election, although he did ask after the farmer's ailing horse. "He acted as if it was the saddest thing in the world that my mare was sick. And he promised he'd do all he could to help."

Joe let his hosts see that he wasn't a loathed city slicker. Back in his Olds, before he forgot, he'd dictate a letter for his secretary to type, complete with the first names of the farmer and his bride, their arm-wrestling son and the daughter with the lollipop, and the sick mare. On the eve of the election every family got a postcard reminder, with a photo of a freckled boy waving his baseball mitt next to the caption "Let's Play Ball." The right picture, he knew, conveyed more than any political rhetoric could. "It wasn't McCarthy's fault if the recipient thought the boy was his son," reported the *Saturday Evening Post*. "The message on the card urged the housewife to shanghai her husband and get to the polls early." Thankfully for Joe, nobody compared all the scrawled postcards to discover they were written in different hands. They had been penned on the q.t. by Joe's sisters and brothers, his poker pals, Shawano housewives and high schoolers, and fellow residents of Edith Green's rooming house. And nobody suspected that the expensive campaign had been financed in part by a generous loan from Joe's most faithful booster, "Fither" Tim McCarthy.

It was direct mail before most Americans recognized what that was, and it stood out even more when compared to Werner's complacency. The veteran judge haughtily assumed that his long record of service would be enough to beat this brash upstart. Joe took nothing for granted. His gladiator instinct had him looking for ways to hammer the incumbent, and he took his cue from a recent campaign in Shawano, in which an old judge had been taken down over the issue of age. Werner made an especially tempting target because, while he was a relatively spry sixty-six, he had inflated his age earlier in his career — to convey gravitas — making himself variously four or six years older. Joe trumpeted the oldest figure, implying that the pompous and eccentric judge was also a doddering liar. Joe rarely referred to his opponent by name or office, instead drumming in that he was "my 73-year-old opponent." Werner's protests accentuated that his age was a legitimate issue, the way Joe knew they would. For good measure, McCarthy charged that Werner, having earned as much as $200,000 during his decades in office, had grown rich by bilking farmers and laborers.

He was nearly right on the matter of money, but at the same time misleading. On an annual basis over the years, Werner made a relatively modest $7,250. He was technically right, too, on the judge's evolving birthdates, but it was cheeky for him to be throwing rocks, given the glass house he would soon inhabit. Joe's certificate of death showed he was born on November 14, 1909. So did his draft card — he signed it under a line saying "I affirm that I have verified above answers and that they are true" — along with his medical records at Bethesda Naval Hospital and year after year of listings in the *Congressional Record* and *Who's Who in America*.* And his campaign literature in his first bid for the Senate subtracted a second year from his age. But the definitive record, his birth certificate on file at the courthouse in Outagamie County, Wisconsin, confirmed that he came into the world a year sooner, on November 14, 1908. The *Chicago Daily Tribune*, which always liked him, gave him the benefit of the doubt when it revealed the discrepancy, noting the day after his death that "McCarthy, himself, apparently was confused as to the year of his birth." Who spawned that confusion, and when, is unclear, but his hometown paper used his real age in stories about this race for circuit judge.

---

* His *Congressional Directory* biographies, like everything else, evolved, saying in 1947 that he'd applied for enlistment "as buck private and was later commissioned," but dropping those details in 1949. By 1950 his entry was down to two-and-a-half lines, compared to the sixteen-and-a-half lines in 1947.

(It later joined the pack in getting it wrong, with some papers so befuddled they varied his age within the same story or sliced two years instead of one from his life.) Why the deception? He never said, but he may have taken to heart his own one-man youth campaign against Werner.

McCarthy's relentless messaging got through to Wisconsin voters that spring. Those who appreciated a kick-'em-in-the-nuts type of candidate could feel comfortable with Joe; so could those who wanted a farmer in the dell. Enough of both combined to topple the long-serving judge who'd once looked invincible, with Joe drawing 15,160 votes, Werner 11,154, and a third candidate, a municipal judge, 9,071. While Joe won just 43 percent of the ballots cast, the *Appleton Post-Crescent* called it "one of the most astonishing upsets in the history of the Tenth judicial circuit" and "surprising to even his most ardent supporters." The gambit had played out just the way he had pictured and was a piece in what was becoming a pattern. It started with his youthful chicken empire, continued through four years in one at Little Wolf and a series of small triumphs at Marquette, and culminated with his seizing the judgeship he coveted.

Dr. A. J. Werner considered his father — who died suddenly six years after losing the election — McCarthy's first victim. "He not only drove my father to his grave but turned longstanding family friends against our whole family," said the Appleton dentist. "It was amazing how one man (McCarthy) could wreck the reputation of a man loved and honored in this community."

Judge Joe toasted his selection as not just deserved but historic. At age thirty, he was the youngest circuit judge ever elected in Wisconsin. Or so he claimed, as did reporters and biographers, although it wasn't true. (Charles H. Larrabee was elected at age twenty-eight in 1848, the year Wisconsin was admitted to the Union.) Even more improbably, Joe claimed to be the youngest circuit judge ever elected in America, saying he had read that in a magazine. Yet McCarthy's very youth, and his lack of both textbook and courtroom experience, raised a more critical question: What kind of jurist would he be?

No great shakes, if legal prowess was the measure. His pictures in the paper showed him newly bespectacled and presumably clear-sighted. Watching him in action, however, made it plain that the rookie judge didn't know the finer points or even the broadest strokes of the law, said Andrew Parnell, who often practiced before him. He compensated by being "smart, like a crook is smart," and by studying at night a new three-volume set on the rules of evidence. Self-promoter was the image that came to mind for Robert Harland, who edited the law review when Joe was at Marquette: "It's maybe old fashioned now to think that if you're going to be a judge, you're going to be a judge and not think about running for governor or some other crap." The gaps in Joe's legal lexicon were glaring, and his everyday vocabulary was meager, said John Wyngaard, a reporter and columnist for the newspapers in Appleton and Green Bay. McCarthy overused terms like "vicious" and "inconceivably inconceivable," and quizzed Wyngaard about the proper use of other idioms, then he absorbed like a sponge the phrasing Wyngaard proposed.

Urban Van Susteren saw and heard what the others did — even more, given how much time he spent in Joe's courtroom as his divorce counsel* — but he had a different take on it. Judge McCarthy, he said, had an instinct for justice if not for rules, and for people if not issues. His mind was "lightning quick," added Van Susteren, who was equally fast and even more idiosyncratic. "He knew so little, but what he knew he knew so well."

The circuit courts played a consequential role in the life of Wisconsin, overseeing the patchwork of county, civil, and municipal courts and handling everything from grisly murders to breached contracts. Convinced that justice delayed was justice denied, Joe went full throttle as he took control in the resplendent new Outagamie County Courthouse. There was a backlog of some 250 cases when he arrived, so he logged twelve-hour days, sometimes hear-

---

* The divorce counsel was an unusual part-time posting — required by law, appointed by the judge, and paying a modest $1,500 a year. By statute, the counsel could influence everything from how much alimony was required to which parent got to keep the children; in practice, the job involved a clerk-like processing of decrees. Van Susteren, who later served as a circuit judge himself, became Joe's campaign manager and best friend. Feinsinger, "Divorce Law and Administration in England," *Wisconsin Law Review*.

Urban was the father of TV news personality Greta Van Susteren.

ing cases past midnight and through weekends. During one stretch he managed forty trials in forty days. Wherever in his geographically dispersed circuit the lawyers were ready, Joe would be there to rubber-stamp out-of-court settlements.

The backlog was gone within months. Most cases now were disposed of in thirty days or less, and 70 percent were resolved without trial. The numbers looked good, but the whispers suggested they'd come at a price. Chester Roberts and his estranged wife were frustrated after a half-year wait for their local court to hear their divorce case so they circuit-shopped it to Joe, who just two days later granted the final decree. Was that a courtesy extended because Roberts was head of the Milwaukee County Young Republicans? Was the McCarthy courtroom a divorce mill — and a magnet for the politically connected? And what about the way Joe swapped benches more than any judge around, sitting in circuits far and wide — was that all about sharing meals with politically wired barristers and scribes? Yes, yes, and yes, opined biographers Jack Anderson and Ronald May. Judge Joe was "providing himself with an expense-paid means of becoming known from one end of Wisconsin to the other . . . Justice took off her robes and put on a track suit." The *Milwaukee Journal* agreed, saying that Joe's judicial behavior showed "an astonishing disregard for things ethical and traditional."

Carpers like those were right on the facts but wrong in their verdicts, countered Van Susteren, the divorce counsel. Sure, Joe could do a divorce in under ten minutes, and he did hundreds. And yes, his cronies flocked to his court. But that's simply how things were done in that judicial world, and none of Joe's divorce decisions was appealed. As for any implication that Judge McCarthy would take a bribe, Van Susteren shot back, "Never." McCarthy had other defenders. Attorneys who practiced before him, especially younger ones, loved that he was not just speedier but less hidebound than most jurists. "You could call on him any time if you had a problem. Joe was full of vitality, piss, and vinegar," said Francis Werner (no relation to Judge Edgar Werner). "He opened the courtroom windows and let in a little fresh air."

The recklessness he displayed at the poker table carried over into his life as a judge. He was drinking more now, and hiding it better. He still was quick to pick a fight and loath to admit a mistake, but he had more tolerance for criminals and less for the jaundiced legal system. Feeling sorry for a woman who killed her mean-spirited husband, he slipped the jailer $10 to supply her with the cigarettes she longed for. Feeling bad that a drunk driver he'd imprisoned, then released, was working at a saloon, he wrote with this counsel: "I do wish you would not make it any more difficult for yourself and everyone concerned by working in a tavern where you certainly will do considerable drinking unless you are a superman." Another time he voiced doubts shared by everyone in his courtroom when a doctor defended as "reasonable" what he'd billed a patient hurt in a car crash. Addressing the plaintiff's lawyer, Joe mused, "Every time a doctor comes in here, he tells me his patient was seriously injured and his bill was reasonable. I'm still waiting for the day when a doctor comes in and says, 'No, my patient wasn't hurt so bad, and my bill was way too high.'" Pitch perfect.

There wasn't as much time as he'd have liked for vacations during those years, but driving back with friends from a short trip to Wisconsin's North Country, Joe insisted on stopping at one roadhouse after another for a drink. "I told him that either I drive or we weren't getting back into the car. He was in no mood to be challenged, so he said, 'Fine, screw you,' and just drove off, leaving us stranded in the middle of nowhere," recalled Francis Werner. "All our baggage and our house keys were in the car. It took us hours to hitch home, and even then we were locked out. Well, my wife and I just wrote him off . . . A few days later, Joe called and talked us into meeting him for dinner at a restaurant in Appleton. When we got there, the table was filled with wine and flowers. Joe was like that. He'd do something nasty and then make it up to you. He couldn't stand to have people stay mad at him."

In 1942, Joe spent twelve days presiding over a stockholder battle in Racine, two hours south of Appleton. He was sharp on the bench, and sharper still at the Elks Club, a gambling hot spot where his games would start at midnight and end in the early morning. The bluffing began before he pulled up his chair, as he tried to convince tablemates that he was a novice cardplayer when in fact he was a master, winning $2,000 over the course of the trial. One night, in the middle of a hotly contested game, word came that the jury in the stockholder case had reached a verdict. Not a problem: Joe and the lawyers he was playing with put their cards in their pockets, headed to the courtroom to hear the decision, then reconvened at the Elks to finish the hand.

The case that offered the most resonant testament to his record on the bench involved Appleton's Quaker Dairy Company. It was selling milk at a rock-bottom price that delighted its customers but violated a state edict aimed at protecting dairy farmers. When the Department of Agriculture sued, Joe took a series of injudicious steps. First he ordered Quaker to obey the law, then he suspended his own injunction. The price support law was about to expire, he explained, so Quaker's illegal act might soon become legal. His novel reasoning stemmed from his belief that holding the trial the state wanted would be "a waste of the court's time." Or at least that's the way those who were there remembered it. No one could say for sure because Joe had ordered his court reporter to "tear out the remarks." When the stenographer balked, Joe picked up the record and removed the offending page.

The Wisconsin Supreme Court quickly let McCarthy and the world know what it thought of his behavior. "It is not for a judicial officer to exercise a discretion or a decision which is the function of the legislature," chided Chief Justice Marvin Rosenberry. What McCarthy had done constituted "an abuse of judicial power." And covering his tracks by destroying his notes was "highly improper." McCarthy, who reveled in his image as an outlaw, got the last word when that court sent the case back for a rehearing. He again sided with Quaker Dairy. The state's push for higher prices made it the enemy of the people, he said, while Quaker — and by implication the judge who sided with it — were tribunes for the poor. The case dimmed Joe's standing among legal intellects but elevated it in the body politic. It was a trade-off he made with relish.*

Barely three years into Joe's judicial term, the Empire of Japan sucker punched the United States of America, unleashing a crip-

---

* Decades later, Quaker Dairy president Ben Cherkasky's son weighed in with his own verdict. Ben and his cronies "devised a scheme" and "got McCarthy involved," says Bill Cherkasky. "All these things that happened were, as far as I know, maybe unethical, maybe illegal." Author interview with Bill Cherkasky.

pling assault on the naval fleet at Pearl Harbor and letting loose a stampede of American boys raring to pound back. Judges like Joe, however, were deemed to be doing their part already, and most watched from the sidelines with nobody doubting their manliness or their patriotism. That was not enough for Joe McCarthy. He believed in public service, which was one reason he'd run twice for office at Marquette and two more times soon after graduation. He also was unabashedly ambitious, which had him eyeing Carl Zeidler, the wunderkind mayor of Milwaukee, who could someday be a rival for statewide office and who, in early 1942, scored page-one headlines by enlisting in the Navy. There was always more than one thing driving Joe, and now it was defending his country *and* one-upping his imagined opponent. The way to do that, he reasoned, was to sign on with the most hallowed of the armed services: the leathernecks of the US Marines.*

McCarthy's enlistment produced his first wartime fib. "I went down and was sworn in as a private . . . I never did apply for a commission," he told reporters later, although in actuality he wasn't a private and he did apply, two days before the first headline appeared. He repeated that phony version over the years, including in the *Congressional Directory,* calling himself a "buck private" to underline that he'd gotten no special favors in accepting the lowliest of military ranks. His military records, however, make clear that in June 1942 he did ask to be made an officer, that he was appointed first lieutenant that July and reported for active duty in August, and that the Marines were thrilled to have him, even at the comparatively advanced age of thirty-three. Submitting his ap-

---

* Urban Van Susteren says he planted the idea of Joe's joining the Marines, telling him that would make him an even bigger hero than Zeidler. Unlike Zeidler, McCarthy didn't resign his office when he signed up for armed service. He says he offered his resignation to the governor, who turned it down.

Robert Lorge says Joe helped persuade his father, Gerald, who was determined to be an Army Ranger, to become a leatherneck instead. "If you want to go kill some Japs," McCarthy told Gerald Lorge, "you oughta be a Marine. Because you're tall, you're a leader." Gerald later became a state senator, serving for thirty years, and Robert was the GOP nominee for Senate in Wisconsin in 2006. Reeves interview with Van Susteren, November 25, 1975; McCarthy deposition, September 26, 1951, *Drew Pearson v. Joseph R. McCarthy et al.;* and author interview with Robert Lorge.

plication on official Circuit Court Chambers stationery let everyone know he was Justice Joe, not just some average Joe. It worked: a mere two days later his file was forwarded to the Marine Corps commandant. "This applicant is considered as possibly the most outstanding applicant for commission that has applied to this recruiting office during the past year," Major Saxon W. Holt Jr., officer in charge at Marine headquarters in Milwaukee, wrote in his cover letter. "His acceptance by the Marine Corps should result in favorable publicity in this area."*

Journalists would gradually unmask those embellishments, and newly released files from the Marine Corps and the Marquette archives confirm that his media critics were right in their conclusions, if not in all the specifics. But those records also make clear that Joe wasn't trying to duck his duty. "Mr. McCarthy, expressed a strong desire to serve with troops in combat," noted Holt. Months before, Joe launched a fusillade of confidential letters to Marine Corps headquarters saying he was willing to take a leave from or even resign his judicial office, and to serve without pay, if they would please, please take him. "I am not concerned with whether I enter as a private or as a commissioned officer," he wrote. "Having no dependents, I can get along quite well on a private's pay." That documented flag-waving, done with guile yet without fanfare, would have made an even more compelling narrative than Joe's fairy tale. But his impulse to embroider was irresistible.

He gave in to it again while explaining how he fractured his left foot and burned that leg in a way that bred foul-smelling, stinging infections. He'd hurt them "while helping to remove a pregnant woman from off a submarine," he told a crowd at the Shawano Club. No, wait, he'd injured them when a dive-bomber "ground-

---

* It did result in favorable publicity from the start, with the press showing up to watch Joe preside over a Milwaukee courtroom — in full Marine uniform — a day before reporting for duty. The text and picture in the *Milwaukee Journal* made clear that the young judge was entering his service as a commissioned lieutenant.

A decade later, when he was under fire from journalists for allegedly exaggerating his military service, Joe asked the Marines to check his files. "The records fail to indicate any enlisted service," Brigadier General R. H. Ridgely Jr. wrote back. "Man in Uniform Is on Bench," *Milwaukee Journal;* and letter from Ridgely to McCarthy, November 13, 1953, NPRC.

looped, overturned and burned. He got out of the wreckage in time," he informed a *Saturday Evening Post* reporter, "and, refusing medical attention, headed for the Intelligence shack to make his report." A home state newspaper said his wounds came "in line of duty in the southwest Pacific" and were bad enough that he was "in a military hospital" and was "expected to remain there about eight weeks." Sometimes he blamed the Japanese, and said their shrapnel — ten pounds of it — was embedded in his damaged limb. To other audiences he insisted "there wasn't a Jap within 300 miles when it happened," nor was he carrying around any shell fragments. His earthiest answer came when Urban Van Susteren asked. Joe lifted his foot, pulled down his sock to expose his scar, and pronounced, "There, you son of a bitch, now let's hear no more about it." His most restrained rendition was under oath: "Oh, a minor — I forget what it was. I did suffer some minor injury."

In truth, he was seriously injured, but it happened six hundred miles away from, and ten weeks before, his first combat assignment. The USS *Chandeleur* was ferrying his squadron to the Pacific Islands on a voyage notable for what didn't happen — no German submarines, no Japanese bombers, not even a general quarters alert. The skipper thought things were so safe that, on June 22, 1943, he authorized seasoned Shellback troops to stage the traditional initiation for Joe and other Pollywogs who'd never before crossed the Equator. Shave your heads, they were told, then put on your pajamas and take off your shoes. "Rank meant nothing, of course, as we were paddled, soaked with hoses, speared by the electric trident, and generally abused," reported one novitiate who asked to go unnamed. Joe had nearly survived his hazing when, walking down a ladder with a bucket strapped to his right foot, he slipped. His other foot caught a lower rung and he fell backwards. "Three bones were broken," the friend said, "and I watched them put a cast on his foot. It was either then, or that night when we were drinking together, that Joe said to me, 'Don't tell Maybelle I broke my foot in this silly way.'"*

---

* In his official report on the incident, Joe's commanding officer deadpanned, "On 22 June 1943 Captain McCarthy suffered a broken and burned foot and leg. He however refused to be hospitalized and continued doing an excellent job as

The fracture wasn't the worst of it. When it was time to remove his cast, the medical corpsman used acetic acid instead of vinegar to soften the plaster. The acid burned Joe's leg, leaving a substantial scar that was a long time in healing. A month later he complained to his diary, "The burns on my leg acting up a little but the broken foot coming along O.K.," and two days after that, "Dam infection in my leg acting and stinking up."*

Most maladies during his war years, and there were plenty, are documented in his Marine Corps records. He arrived with a history of sinusitis going back to when he was eleven, and had had a tonsillectomy in 1929 and an appendectomy in 1936. His hairline was receding now and his waistline expanding. (The scales showed him at 199 pounds, which was forty more than he'd weighed on the farm and thirty more than when he'd been healthy.) During his second year in the Pacific that list ballooned to include myositis (inflamed muscles), cellulitis (a bacterial skin infection), and scoliosis (curved spine), along with stomach distress, shortness of breath, and ongoing lower back pain.† He reported to sick bay often enough, with symptoms his doctors couldn't explain, that they reached for terms like "loss of energy," "nervous," and "tense," which seemed more suited to mental than physical disorders. His diary around that time also talked about how the unrelenting swelter and clamminess were taxing "to the point you feel your ambition slowly draining away." None of that was uncommon in a battle theater as unforgiving as the Pacific, with unwholesome food, chronic dehydration, little chance for sleep, hard-to-navigate terrain, monsoon rains, and a seesawing between extreme terror and acute boredom. His complaints hinted at malingering, or maybe battle fatigue, but the medics concluded it was "not misconduct."

Intelligence officer, working on crutches." Letter from E. E. Munn to commandant, February 11, 1944, series 17, MUA.

Maybelle was Maybelle Counihan, his Irish American flame from Appleton by way of Milwaukee.

* Joe would later say that some of his medical records were missing, including ones with a chart showing "scars and marks." Marine Corps Records, series 17, MUA.

† Arch supports helped when he was in the Marines. He later wore elevator shoes that he said were meant to compensate for the shrapnel in his knee but more likely were intended to ease an aching back and make him seem taller.

After they looked him over and let him rest, he typically was "discharged to duty," although once he was transferred to a Navy base hospital "for treatment and disposition."

His official overseas assignment was to debrief returning pilots so their next missions could be more on the mark, but in practice he often was in the thick of the battle himself, and not just in the skies. "The day Batdorff got hit with shrapnel when the Japs were throwing mortar on to the strip, you and Bill Weir, Cropley and I were all in the same foxhole, sweating it out," wrote Major Robert "Ric" Barvoets, who served alongside Joe in the South Pacific. Another letter testifying to Joe's willingness to engage the enemy came from a fellow soldier in Marine Scout Bombing Squadron 235 identified only as "Coop": "I took the mess cook named Helmuth Aab — Who could ever forget the name — and you were riding in the same section perhaps with Pat Casey, and Aab was so afraid he never got off a shot while you set some sort of record and completely emptied the twin 30's. I particularly remember the pilot commenting that he couldn't get you to stop shooting and was afraid you would burn out the guns. Incidentally, Aab is not recorded in my log either." Not all who served with him were fans. Master Sergeant Jerome Wander told a McCarthy biographer that Joe was "an opportunist" who wanted a combat record to spruce up his political résumé, flew mainly milk runs, and angered his pilot-hosts who preferred an experienced gunner to a wannabe one.

In the end, did he deserve his eleven medals, commendations, and ribbons? No other member of the military has ever had that question asked about him as often as Joe McCarthy. Two presidents, Truman and Eisenhower, surely would have relished the chance to prove him a fraud, even if that meant second-guessing the senior officers who approved the citations.* Given the way McCarthy's combat flights frequently were kept off the books, there is no way of knowing definitively whether he had enough to qualify for each of his honors. The way his own tallies climbed over

---

* One embarrassment in Joe's file was that a card inserted while he was a senator to indicate his reserve status in the Marines happened to be colored pink, the shade Joe would use as shorthand for Communist-leaning. The military apologized for that color choice, saying it was purely by chance. Letter from Brigadier General W. J. Scheyer to Joe, June 26, 1951, NPRC.

the years — from fourteen to seventeen to thirty-two — rightfully raised eyebrows and hackles. But the newly unveiled letters from Joe to his squad mates asking them to tap their recollections and logbooks suggest a serious effort to assemble evidence. Its aim was transparently self-serving — to refute those accusing him of fraud — but in the process it filled in missing facts. Joe concluded that he was on thirty different bombing flights in 1943 and 1944, during fourteen of which he experienced antiaircraft fire. Targets ranged from gun positions and pillboxes to enemy convoys, ammo dumps, bridges, and airfields. "Note," he wrote, "that many of these targets were clearly outside of simple intelligence missions."

Further confirmation that his awards were deserved came from his Marine Corps bosses. "We fought together on Guadalcanal, Bugaineville [sic], and Munda in the South Pacific. Mac was a captain and the squadron intelligence officer. And believe me, he was certainly no coward. He was a brave Irishman. And he did a great job for us. He was a hell of a man," Major Glenn Todd, Joe's commanding officer, told a reporter years later. "Mac didn't give a damn about any medals. But he came up with the log book and I wrote him up for the two Air Medals. Now, I knew Mac was hot politically and you can be damn sure when I made those recommendations I didn't want to do anything that would bounce . . . At that time you could get credit for any kind of mission. But where Mac was concerned, I only counted those missions he got fired on or dropped bombs."* The Marine Corps's highest-ranking officer

---

* In a series of letters to McCarthy biographer Thomas Reeves in 1977 and 1978, Todd went back and forth on whether Joe overcounted his combat missions. "I can't say Joe did not fly 32 missions," he wrote in one missive. In another he said, "There is *no* possibility Mac could have flown 30 missions." What he was sure of was that he hadn't recommended Joe for the citation he got from Navy Fleet Admiral Chester Nimitz: "I believe Joe wrote his own citation and got the group, wing, or strike command to forward it to Admiral Nimitz." Letters from Todd to Reeves, April 19 and October 15, 1977, and April 27, 1978, WHS.
  Reeves went a step further, saying that Joe apparently forged Todd's signature on a recommendation letter to Nimitz, and that Joe didn't fly the thirty-two missions he claimed or even the twenty-five required for his Distinguished Flying Cross. Walking out on a thinner limb, Reeves concluded that Joe's Flying Cross, the most hallowed of his medals, "was clearly unearned and was granted with the collusion of top Marine Corps officials, who were fully aware of his actual service record." Reeves, *The Life and Times of Joe McCarthy,* 48 and 51–52.

agreed, telling the secretary of the Navy that, despite the lack of written records, "it is the opinion of this Headquarters" that "McCarthy participated in combat flights in addition to those used as the basis for the recommended awards."

Others defined heroism differently. Real valor would have been staying home rather than signing up, according to Arold F. Murphy, chairman of Wisconsin's Board of Circuit Judges. "I still believe you are making a mistake and that the important judicial business of your circuit is going to suffer by your absence from the Bench," Murphy wrote McCarthy a week before he was commissioned. "Oftentimes great courage is required to hold fast to an extended duty even though it be less colorful than another opportunity to be of service." Two years later Gerald Jolin, an Outagamie County judge and Joe's friend, suggested that Murphy's fears were being realized: "There has been another murder in the County and which is to be tried in your Court and again the need for your presence on the bench has become acute."

Neither Jolin nor Murphy nor anyone else could have known what Joe really was thinking during those years, but now we do, courtesy of his wartime diaries. Some entries were whimsical, painting his Pacific Islands as a paradise, not the war zone they were: "This would make a perfect health resort—Dr's bitch because no one ever in dispensary. Exercise & sun during day— plenty sleep at night." Joe also found plenty to complain about, starting with the food: "Some of the men irritated by the fact that the Merchant Marine is eating fresh meats fruit & butter and we [have] something called Spam but isn't." Most but not all native customs were alluring: "Over at Malaita [in the Solomon Islands] the moral code is extremely strict—penalty for rape or seduction —death—the offending parts are then cut off, sun dried and hung before the hut of the deceased as a warning to others." If his spelling and grammar were irregular, he can be excused: many of his notes were scrawled under combat conditions, and Joe had hurried through his schooling in reading and writing.

He had fine-tuned his hyperbole, however, and it helped him describe the blood being shed around him. "We are located between Jap lines and our artillery which makes it interesting—especially before dawn when they start to duel . . . Tonight is supposed to be

D night for the Japs—an all out attack . . . Hope we hold the little bastards," he wrote in March 1944. "Some sergeant used AA
searchlight on a low overcast as a reflector—lighted up the Japs
like day—slaughter—saw over 100 hanging on the wire the next
day—such is war." Entries make clear that, while the Japanese already had evacuated such strategic enclaves as Guadalcanal and
the Aleutians by the time Joe got there, they were still entrenched
on other islands and his duty was still dangerous.

What would become McCarthy's trademark antipathy toward
the military brass was born during his own armed service. For
starters, he felt it took far too long to transport him and his mates
from Hawaii to the battle zone. He also resented the military's ongoing sugarcoating. "Raid: Japs version: '2 photo planes over wake
both shot down.' Army Version: '24 tons of bombs unloaded on
wake—all planes returned—no injury to personnel,'" he wrote in
his journal on May 18, 1943. "Shit! Who the hell do those mental
midgets think they're fooling & why?" Two months later he railed
again: "Oranges, Lemons, Limes, Coconuts—fruit aplenty here—
all going to waste—almost as bad as the rest of the terrific waste
encountered each day—food, materiel, men. Incompetence of
rank stifling much of our war effort." Most irritating to him were
the inter-service rivalries: "Sometimes wonder if we are fighting
the same war as the Navy & Army. Last week went over to Havana
Harbor to try to buy a few of the Navy's Surplus of 11,700 cases of
beer—pissmires—finally got a few cases after a lot of crotch kissing."

Being overseas didn't keep Joe from gambling, with one diary entry indicating "to Sydney for week again—70 winner[s] on
races."* He also kept by his cot a little black book filled with addresses of girls from LaGrange, Missouri, to Chicago and Los An-

---

* Even in a war zone, Joe could sniff out a poker game. "I was on a Convair out of
Chicago and seated next to a man who identified himself as an official of a large
Wisconsin corporation," Darrell St. Claire, assistant secretary to the US Senate,
recalled three decades later. "He said that Senator McCarthy, as a Naval officer,
had regarded himself as quite a heavy poker player and hearing of this game on
another island, had himself flown over to take part in it. My seat mate was also a
part of that poker game, knew McCarthy, and took something like $2,800 from
him, and for this he got an IOU from Senator McCarthy. He then told me, 'If you
can get it from him and know him well enough to do so, I will give you half.' I am

geles. And he managed a side business of procuring not just beer, and not just from the Navy. He had medicinal brandy, canned turkeys, pineapple juice, and other items his fellow Marines longed for and for which they were willing to pay richly. It was a three-man syndicate. Joe bought the contraband from, among others, British and Australian seamen. John "Jocko" Kidney ferried it on his seaplane to an American base, where Jerome Wander handled the distribution. It made the trio momentarily flush and the troops staggeringly happy, Wander recalled years later. Then Joe and Jocko got into a bloody fistfight over how profits would be divvied up, and all deals were off.

As his diary attested, Joe never lost his empathy for fellow soldiers: "Major Bill O'Neal a really good guy blew up with all his crew in a T.B.F. [torpedo bomber] making a forced landing at Munda. Killed about 15 in all and destroyed 6 planes by the blast. Got to look up his family for sure when the war is over — maybe can help the kids get a job or something." A confidential letter from one of his majors to the Marine Corps commandant noted that Joe was "continually acting as personal advisor to the Squadron personnel." But again, McCarthy couldn't resist adding his own strain of schmaltz to the facts. "My task at night was to write home to the young wives, to the young mothers," he would tell an American television audience years later, "with the hope that we might be able to make the blow fall less heavily." And for anyone who missed the message, he would affect a slight limp as a reminder that he too had suffered a wartime blow.

His Marquette archives highlight one more task that Joe devoted himself to when he was overseas: feeding his own hunger for higher office, no matter that the armed services had a bell-clear ban on political activity. "No member of the land or naval forces, while on active duty, will use his official authority or influence for the purpose of interfering with an election or affecting the course or outcome thereof," Secretary of War Henry Stimson and Navy Secretary Frank Knox ordered. Forbidden activities, they added,

---

not sure that the debt was ever paid." Darrell St. Claire OH, December 16, 1976, US Senate Historical Office.

included "participation in political campaigns, the making of political speeches, the publication of articles, or any other public activity looking to the influencing of an election or the solicitation of votes for himself or others."

First Lieutenant McCarthy targeted the next office to aim for while he was still in training stateside. He and a buddy at Camp Lejeune got seventy-two-hour passes and flew to Washington, DC. Joe referred to the capital as his future home, Leo Day remembered thirty years afterward, and said he wanted to see what it looked like. The two also visited their home state senator, Robert La Follette Jr., chatting about everything but politics.* In fact, as Joe shipped out to the South Pacific, it wasn't La Follette's seat he was lusting after — not yet — but that of Republican Alexander Wiley, the junior and weaker senator from Wisconsin, who was up for reelection in 1944.

Several factors convinced McCarthy that the time to at least get his name recognized across Wisconsin was now, even though he was eight thousand miles away in a war zone. Allies in the state capital were quietly repealing a statute making it a felony for a judge to seek another office. Carl Zeidler, his feared rival from Milwaukee, was gone, initially reported missing and later confirmed to have perished when his merchant ship was sunk by a German U-boat. Joe also had more money than ever, thanks to investments that netted him more than $40,000 ($600,000 in today's dollars, and twice what Joe was giving up in judicial salary). His profits were partly a matter of booming wartime markets, partly his own financial savvy and his willingness to tap colleagues and friends for stock tips. Joe tried to disguise the windfalls — along with his spending more than the legal limit of $5,000 of his own money for electioneering — by not filing a state tax return in 1943. He also said that his father, brother, and brother-in-law had contributed amounts that defied logic, given his recent jackpot and their meager incomes.†

---

* The next stop on that trip was Baltimore, where, after a night of heavy drinking, Day said he and Joe somehow ended up at the Waldorf Astoria Hotel in New York. Neither recalled how they got there. Reeves interview with Leo Day, February 11, 1977.

† A campaign document showed this stream of supposed donations from How-

So from his perch in the Pacific theater, he silently stage-managed his campaign for senator from the American heartland. Surrogates back in Wisconsin mailed him newspaper clippings, lists of contributors, and bills for everything from radio ads to staff salaries. "Sis" again quit what she was doing to devote herself to her little brother, this time spearheading the addressing of 800,000 McCarthy for Senate letters. He mailed in his campaign filing and searched out soldiers from Wisconsin, unofficially asking for their votes. Joe had handed over most of his investment profits to Gerald Jolin, the Outagamie County judge who was steering his election finances, but he thought Jolin was doing a lousy job. "Campaign picture back home unpleasant," now-Captain McCarthy confessed to his diary on December 26, 1943, a day when most soldiers were waxing sentimental about a Christmas away from home and family. Three months later he worried that "Jolin was very much of a disappointment. Mental & moral stature questionable." But when stories on his wartime injuries and exploits started appearing in Wisconsin papers, he perked up, tracking down Marine public relations officer Penn Kimball, waving a sheaf of clippings Kimball had helped generate, and gushing, "This is worth 50,000 votes to me."*

---

ard McCarthy, who made his living auctioning farm equipment and had never earned more than $4,000 a year in net taxable income: $5,100, $5,000, $5,500, $2,500, and $1,800. Tim McCarthy, meanwhile, made so little that he paid state taxes only one year ($2.62 in 1919), although after he died, Wisconsin authorities said he should have paid $68.08 more over the years. Campaign Records, series 23, MUA; and *Life and Times of Joe McCarthy*, 55.

Syndicated columnist Drew Pearson suspected there was another source for Joe's campaign cash: Al Capone's older brother Ralph "Bottles" Capone, who operated the family's legitimate bottling and beverage businesses and was named by the Chicago Crime Commission as Public Enemy Number Three when Al was Number One. Similar rumors would resurface over the years, sometimes linking Al to Joe. Joe's Marquette files show he knew just what Pearson was hearing and saying about him. Capone File, Fleming Papers; Pearson column, January 17, 1951; and Pearson File, series 14, MUA.

* Kimball speculated later that he was the inspiration for Joe's tail gunning. McCarthy had asked him to gin up a story for home state papers, Kimball recalled, "and I said, 'Joe, there's an old rule in the newspaper business that [a reporter] can't write a story unless you do something. Now you are sittin' around and you are a nice fellow but you are not doing anything.' And he came back to me a few days later and he told me that 'I've been talking to my squadron leader and he said

Those activities didn't just violate Army rules; they were a breach of the Wisconsin Constitution. "No justice of the supreme court or judge of any court of record," the charter read, "shall hold any other office of public trust, except a judicial office, during the term for which elected." State law said essentially the same thing, and showed it meant it by making any violation a felony. The point, as bar association codes of ethics spelled out, was that blind justice and blind ambition don't mix, and judges should avoid even the appearance of a conflict of interest created when they are nominated to another office.

Joe seemed torn on the ethics of politicking while he was a soldier and a judge. On the one hand, he told the Wisconsin League of Women Voters it would violate military regulations if he were to "take any position publicly on political issues" (it actually would have violated his precept to duck difficult issues), and he gave back money his stand-ins had solicited from lawyers for fear that was "viciously improper" for a judge. (He didn't mention the illegal donations he himself was making.) Yet propriety—and subtlety—went only so far. In Wisconsin, voters were reminded he was doing his duty by his campaign letterhead: "Committee to ELECT Captain JOSEPH R. MCCARTHY of the US Marines to the UNITED STATES SENATE." On the Pacific Islands, "MCCARTHY FOR US SENATOR" posters were plastered across two trucks and a jeep in Joe's squadron, and writing on his tent announced, "HEADQUARTERS, MCCARTHY FOR US SENATOR." (Fellow soldiers countered with a good-natured ribbon of their own: "Protect the coconut trees—Send McCarthy back to Wisconsin.")

He rationalized his violation of state laws by reasoning that they would kick in only in the unlikely event he won, at which point federal law would trump any state restriction. As for the Marine Corps rules, during his years in uniform he never ceased to influence the elections they told him not to, although he did take the

---

that it would be ok for me to ride in the rear seat of the dive bombers and to make some direct observations as an intelligence officer' . . . I said, 'Well, that sounds promising, why don't you do it.'" From the film *The Real American: Joe McCarthy* (2011).

secretary of war's ban seriously enough that he stumped as quietly as he knew how.

That made his relations with journalists tricky. He needed and wanted their help introducing himself to Wisconsinites, but didn't want them to expose his long-haul campaigning, the money he was funneling through his family, or the disinformation he was spreading about being a buck private and injuring his foot on the battlefield. His best-kept political secret was when and why he had flipped from unflinching Democrat to unwavering Republican. It may have been as long ago as his 1936 race for district attorney, or as recently as just before the intelligence officer formally announced for the US Senate in April 1944. There never was a formal proclamation of the switch in loyalties — more like whispering it in the middle of the night when he hoped nobody would notice. He would later tell reporters that he delighted in having it both ways, being a Republican with a Democratic name. Part of his reason for running that year's abbreviated campaign against Wiley seemed to be to get balloters and bosses used to his new partisan label. He knew that party mattered less than personality, but he also knew that in Wisconsin, being a New Deal Democrat made most voters unwilling even to listen.*

Things weren't always easy with the Marine Corps, either. For the most part the corps was his enabler — willing to give him a commission even though he hadn't given up his elected office, to accept his count of combat flights, and to ignore his rum-running and other get-rich-quick shenanigans. After all, the press Joe was getting generally reflected well on all leathernecks, just as Major Holt had predicted when recruiting him. That's also one reason why the Marines would eventually promote him to major, then lieutenant colonel. But there had to be limits, especially when he was so blatant about his politicking. As he was heading back to America just before his Senate primary in the summer of 1944, the military finally balked. "You shall not, while enroute to the United

---

* Pinning down the moment when he made the party switch is rendered more difficult by Wisconsin's nonpartisan voter registration, in which there is no option to name a party when you sign up, and voters can cast ballots in any party's primary election.

States, or after arrival in the United States, participate in a press conference, talk to reporters, or talk over the radio except after consultation with and clearance of the subject matter by a public relations officer of the Navy or Marine Corps," his commanding general wrote in an unusual if not unprecedented admonition.*

All his behind-the-scenes and overt campaigning didn't help much in Wisconsin. Wiley beat him nearly two to one in a drubbing reminiscent of his race for district attorney eight years earlier. But Joe focused on the fact that he drew nearly eighty thousand votes, twice as many as the third-place finisher, and he won the three counties in his judicial district. As in his quixotic race for district attorney, the point in running had been for voters to get to know him so that later he could zero in on a race he could actually win. No sooner had he lost than he was offering to help Wiley in the general election campaign, with the senator pointing out just the "keymen" he would like Joe to solicit. Jolin, meanwhile, was pointing Joe toward another Senate election in two years and advising him to be ready to fight even rougher: "I suggest that you immediately start cooking up a new and unique approach to the voters . . . Fairness and logic are not ordinarily the stuff out of which campaign issues are manufactured, and the fire of ambition burns in other bellies besides those of Grand Chute farm boys."†

---

* Five years later, as a senator, Joe helped rescue the Marine Corps. The Army had drawn up a plan that would have effectively eliminated it as a combat service. Senator Paul Douglas, the Marine Corps' key defender, was told that if he made a public show of shaking hands and chatting with McCarthy, whom he despised and who despised him, Joe would not just back Douglas and the Marines but would get four of his Senate pals to do the same. "I never knew why Joe wanted this public recognition from me in view of his known feelings about me," Douglas said afterward. "But apparently he did, and that ultimately saved the Corps." Douglas, *In the Fullness of Time*, 346–48.

† If a judge like Jolin weighing in on politics and counseling against fairness was a borderline breach of ethics, another figure offering behind-the-scenes advice went beyond any borders for his profession. "The essential point is that you got a good vote — the highest vote of a loser — in spite of the mistakes and the pitiful mismanagement," John Wyngaard, a political columnist in Madison, wrote in one of his series of private letters to McCarthy. "You mention gratitude for my small contributions toward the campaign in its late stages. As it turned out it didn't amount to a whole lot, although I think it demonstrates what can be done when a publicity man turns his mind to it."

But Wyngaard was a journalist, not a PR man, and while his statewide read-

By the end of 1944 it was clear that Joe had had enough of the Marines. He had served patriotically, but the next year he was up for reelection as judge, and campaigning long-distance was simply too hard. He was stationed in California now and knew that if he stayed in the military, he might be shipped overseas again early in 1945. He asked for a four-month leave to get his court in order, let his injured foot heal, and, while this went unstated, take stock of his political standing. The corps said no. The base commander on his review panel wanted to grant the leave, reasoning that McCarthy "is not in a key position and can be easily replaced." But the director of aviation was against it, saying, "Should he desire to resign, such a request would receive favorable consideration." He made that request, and the Marines granted it, just before Joe's fellow leathernecks back in the South Pacific stormed the islands of Iwo Jima and Luzon in two of the deadliest battles of World War II. By the time his resignation took effect on March 29, 1945, Joe, now thirty-six, had spent a full year serving his country abroad and just over twenty-nine months on active duty.

His first day back on the bench, he showed up in full military dress, much as he had his last day there. Only now he was wearing not the single silver bar of a first lieutenant but a captain's dual bars. And now he was not just Judge Joe but Tail Gunner Joe.

---

ership expected impartiality, he apparently had something different in mind, as he wrote to Joe: "We talked long ago about the time that I shall want to finance a country home for my family. When that time comes I shall almost certainly be obliged to call upon you or someone like you to pave the way to some credit. If you feel that I have done you a favor, perhaps we can see that it is returned at that time. I have great faith in your ability to accumulate shekels, and to arrange for credit." Whether McCarthy ever helped Wyngaard with a loan is unclear, but Joe did become godfather to one of John's daughters. Wyngaard, in turn, generally lauded Joe in print, labeling him a "political Horatio Alger," although in later years they had little contact. Wyngaard letter, August 26, 1944, unprocessed files, MUA; George Greeley OH, WHS; and Wyngaard, "Madison," *Green Bay Press-Gazette*.

2

SENATOR WHO?

SELDOM IN AMERICAN HISTORY HAS a state election had national consequences as monumental as Wisconsin's did in 1946, trading one of the Senate's most enlightened and honorable statesmen for its most ignoble. How that happened is only partly the story of Joseph McCarthy wresting away the seat, although that is the time-honored version. What really happened is that Robert La Follette Jr. surrendered it.

The La Follettes were to Wisconsin politics what the Lees had been in Virginia, the Tafts were in Ohio, and the Kennedys would become in Massachusetts: powerful to the point of royalty. The pompadour-wearing patriarch Robert La Follette Sr., known as "Fighting Bob," served as district attorney, congressman, four-term US senator, and, in 1924, the combative presidential nominee of a national Progressive Party, which he launched to further his ambitions. His younger son Philip was a three-term governor, implementing in Wisconsin many New Deal programs before President Roosevelt could do so nationally. Lacking his father's oratorical fire and his brother's to-the-manor-born presence, the decorous and deliberate Robert Jr. seemed the least likely of the trio to matter when, upon his father's death in 1925, he finished first in a special election to fill that seat. At age thirty, in the shadow of his father's name and his brother's promise, he became the third-youngest senator in US history.

"Young Bob" defied the handicappers. Chairing one of the most productive investigating committees ever, he unmasked company-sponsored violence in the coalfields of Harlan, Kentucky, and established as fact the horrors of farm worker life depicted in John Steinbeck's novel *Grapes of Wrath*. Anyone who collected unemployment compensation owed him a debt. Same for Social Security recipients. Big business detested him even more than his father and brother, while civil libertarians, labor unionists, New Dealers, and FDR hailed him as their champion. In 1928 he set a statewide record that still stands in Wisconsin, winning reelection with 85.5 percent of the vote. President Roosevelt was such a fan that he considered tapping him as secretary of state, Supreme Court justice, vice president, and even as his White House successor, all despite the fact that Young Bob was neither a lawyer nor a Democrat, and, before Pearl Harbor, he had railed against Roosevelt's attempt to pull America into the war in Europe. By the time La Follette announced his bid for a fifth term in 1946, after forty years of that Senate seat's being held in family hands, he looked to outsiders like as sure a thing as there is in politics.

The first sign of trouble came with his pick of political parties. Early in 1946 he formally disbanded the moribund Wisconsin Progressive Party, which he'd co-founded with his brother and under whose banner he'd run in the last two elections. He rejoined a Republican Party that, minus its progressive wing, had moved rightward. That upset the Democrats, who were begging for his help in building a party capable of competing in Wisconsin. It also alienated organized labor, which had always sided with the Progressives, had been instrumental in Young Bob's earlier wins, and now saw the Democrats as its best alternative. Angriest of all were conservative Republicans — self-styled "Stalwarts" — who wanted Robert back even less than he wanted to return. They were hellbent on keeping their party ideologically pure and on toppling, once and forever, the loathed La Follette dynasty.

That intraparty turmoil created just the opening a disrupter like Joe thrived on and which he'd been plotting to fill during his sleepless nights in a Marine tent in the South Pacific. Looked at one way, an ex–New Dealer like him was an impossible long shot to trip up the party-hopping La Follette or sate the GOP's hunger for a true-blue conservative. But Joe was a master of spin, selling himself not just as a war hero with a judicial temperament but, in the words of *The Nation* magazine, as a cipher "whose strategy was the simple one of taking any position that La Follette opposed." He also was busier than ever between bench hearings, stealthily building bridges to grassroots Republicans, and especially to youthful ones. It was this burgeoning network of Young Republicans, led by Joe's fittingly named friend Loyal Eddy, which he saw as instrumental to winning over the grayer and stodgier Republican Voluntary Committee.* Unlike the official party, the RVC had no statutory spending limits, was free to back candidates in the primary, and was under the thumb of anti–La Follette conservatives.

If the RVC was the door to the Stalwart kingdom, "Boss" Thomas Coleman was the keeper of the key. A handsome, gracious industrialist, the fifty-two-year-old Coleman had been drawn to politics by his principled conservatism and his abhorrence of the La Follettes. He knew 1946 offered the best shot at Young Bob. Yet a meeting in late 1945 with Judge Joe convinced him the Appleton roughneck—in the state capital they called him "that rube judge from upstate"—was the wrong man to take it. "Joe, you're a nice guy and I like you. But you're a Johnny-come-lately in Republican politics," Coleman told McCarthy as they sat in the English Room at Milwaukee's elegant Pfister Hotel. "If you work as hard as you have been working and gain more support, you may have a chance some time in the future." Sipping his bourbon and water, Joe calmly replied, "Tom, you're a nice guy and I like you. But I got news for you. When that convention is over next year, Joe McCarthy will be the Republican-endorsed candidate for U.S. Senator." Coleman wasn't impressed, at least not then, barking back as he departed, "What you need is some self-confidence."

McCarthy backed up his big talk. He crashed RVC meetings in seventy-one cities and towns, urging delegates to the May convention not just to endorse candidates for the primary, which they didn't have to do, but to back him for Senate.† He headed to Wash-

---

* At age thirty-seven, Joe himself was ineligible for membership in the Young Republicans, whose upper age limit was thirty-five. His solution: say he was thirty-five. *Life and Times of Joe McCarthy*, 68.

† He'd opposed any RVC endorsements two years before, when he knew the group would back his opponent, incumbent senator Alexander Wiley. One col-

ington to lobby Wisconsin's Republican lawmakers. And on the eve of the Oshkosh convention, he muscled aside his two strongest competitors for the conservative mantle, either of whom Coleman would have preferred. He took a direct approach with Walter Kohler Jr., son of a former Wisconsin governor, scion of the plumbing products empire, and a veteran who'd recently gotten divorced. Seeing that failed marriage splayed across the front pages during a campaign wouldn't be easy to take, Joe advised. "Who would do a thing like that?" Kohler asked. Joe: "I would."* In the case of ex-governor Julius Heil, Joe exercised the kind of bluff he'd fine-tuned at the poker table. The chunky governor turned businessman was chatting up delegates over drinks when, one after another, they confessed that while they'd like to support him, "all the boys seem to be strong for that upstart McCarthy." Which was just what Joe had told the handpicked group to say to Heil, who, after a sleepless night, announced he wouldn't be running for senator after all.

With the field cleared of its establishment favorites, Joe was the only candidate remaining with a prayer of unseating La Follette. So the RVC-Stalwart delegates yielded to the McCarthy-made inevitability, giving him 2,328 votes compared to 298 for his remaining opponent, a barely known lawyer from Milwaukee. This master of the political upset had won the first of three rounds in the battle for the US Senate.

Round two was a one-on-one against La Follette in the Republican primary. "I am glad to see Bob come over and fight in my own backyard," Joe told reporters, as if La Follette was the only one hurdling party fences. "The fight will be very rough, but clean." McCarthy kept his promise at first by sticking to the issues, although newly available transcripts of his speeches make clear that his stances evolved so often they were impossible to

umnist labeled Joe's new focus on Republican ideological purity "political Aryanism." O'Brien, *McCarthy and McCarthyism in Wisconsin*, 60.

* When Joe told that story to journalists, Kohler, who was later elected governor, denied it. Years later he said, "McCarthy was a very devious character . . . It's entirely possible that he may have told some newspapermen that he said that, so he would get the credit for saying it without actually having said it — credit or debit, whatever it was." Kohler OH, 1971, Columbia University.

parse. To maintain the postwar order, he told Young Republicans in early May, the world needed a workable United Nations that kept out countries like Switzerland, which couldn't be peace-loving because it hadn't fought during World War II. To forge effective armed services, America needed to break down the "almost insurmountable social barrier between commissioned officers and enlisted men" (an interesting remark from a commissioned officer), to erect a sensible system of jurisprudence to replace "the alleged justice of many of the military courts that smelled to high heavens" (a charge he'd repeat and that would be repeatedly disproven during the Malmedy Massacre hearings), and to abolish all political appointments to the naval and military colleges. (His attempt to infuse politics into military appointments would, years later, speed his undoing.) He ended the speech by railing—in a way he knew Tom Coleman would relish—against two national Democrats, liberal senator Claude Pepper of Florida and President Harry Truman. "Such men in positions of power are viciously dangerous," Joe said. "They must be removed; they can be removed; and by Heaven they will be removed."

On Memorial Day, the recently returned warrior argued against overseas interventions like those he'd fought in, and for isolationism: "We can better serve the world and world civilization by reserving most of our energies and our thoughts for our own problems. Too much of America's mind is centered on Europe's problems to the neglect of our own." A month later he was warning that "one can pick up votes by attacking Russia but it would serve only to destroy our nation for, even if victorious, we could not survive the tremendous economic and social upheaval which would accompany another war." By that fall's general election campaign, he had veered left and was accusing the Democrats of advocating what he himself had been pressing for: that "we should completely withdraw from Western Europe and allow the 350 million people in that area to be dominated by Soviet Russia—and that we should likewise do the same thing where the hundreds of millions in Eastern Asia are concerned." Keep listening, he seemed to be saying, and you'll find a position you like.

He had promised to fight clean, but his free-swinging style ensured some punches would land below the belt. La Follette, Mc-

Carthy told voters, was a "gentleman from Virginia" who'd "sat out" the war. Joe's point was plain: his country squire competitor with pearl-gray spats and slicked-down hair had lost touch not just with the common American but with the heartland he was supposed to represent. Joe offered a striking contrast, as spelled out in his ads asserting that he'd "resigned his job to enlist as a PRIVATE in the MARINES," that "he and millions of other guys kept YOU from talking Japanese," and that "TODAY JOE MCCARTHY IS HOME. He wants to SERVE America in the SENATE. Yes, folks, CONGRESS NEEDS A TAIL GUNNER." So what if much of it was untrue? McCarthy, we know now, never resigned his judge's job, he never was a buck private, and La Follette never lived in the run-down house in Virginia that he had sold two long years before.

And the mud kept flying. The behind-the-times incumbent, his challenger insisted, had an anti-farm record that betrayed his farm state constituents. He was an ally of New Dealers who were bound and determined to "destroy this nation from within." The roughest and least fair of his charges were that La Follette had used his influence to win federal approval for Milwaukee radio station WEMP, of which he was a part owner; had earned $50,000 from the investment; and had done all this at a moment that made it war profiteering. This assault was like the "gentleman from Virginia" one in two respects: it stretched the facts (federal approval came before Bob was a station owner, and his $50,000 profit was nearly identical to what Joe himself earned as a windfall from wartime investments), and La Follette looked guilty when he didn't answer. Damage done.

Once an admirer of the La Follettes, Joe had learned from Fighting Bob and Young Bob how effective it was to target eastern elites — grain dealers, railroad magnates, bankers, even munitions merchants — saying they were out to screw beleaguered midwesterners. But while both sprang from populist roots, La Follette–style Progressivism offered a litany of carefully crafted remedies, whereas McCarthyism, even in that nascent stage, meant scapegoating and belittling, with little restraint and few solutions. And while it remains an enigma how the same state could spawn such mismatched sons as Tail Gunner Joe and Young Bob, Wisconsin politics always had two strains. A liberal lineage made it the first state to grant public workers the right to unionize, and a rightward lean made it the first to rein in those and other union powers. In 1911 Wisconsin elected America's first Socialist to Congress, in 1919 it was the first to ratify the women's suffrage amendment, and in 1921 it pioneered an equal rights law for women. But the state also evidenced a deep-seated nativism, and its Republican Party was so strong that, in 1925, Democrats held none of the thirty-three seats in the state senate and only one of ninety-nine in the assembly. Even the La Follettes were Republicans for twenty-eight of their forty years holding that US Senate seat, although they never were the "regular" type Joe claimed to be.*

To break that hold, McCarthy showed that he could outhustle as well as outtalk this most cerebral, least pugnacious of the La Follettes. Joe's campaign mailed out 750,000 copies of booklets titled "The Newspapers Say" and "The Press Speaks," with gushing copy and flattering photos of him in uniform or perched in the rear gunner's seat, machine gun ready. He also revived his 1939 penny postcard offensive. Pensioners, along with students from Appleton's Lawrence College, earned half a cent a card filling in addresses they extracted from telephone books and county directories. One side of the mailer bore a picture of Joe, the other the admonition "Your vote Tuesday will be greatly appreciated, by Joe McCarthy." While the stamps were bought at the Appleton post office, the campaign was so suspicious of its Democratic postmaster that the 500,000 cards were mailed from as far away as Milwaukee.

It wasn't just his stamp lickers who were working overtime in 1946. Some of the thirty pounds he'd put on since his boxing weigh-ins at Marquette came from the never-ending Friday night fish fries, where he'd never forget a name or forgo a hand. By the end of the summer Joe had logged 33,000 campaign miles

---

* Joe's hometown of Appleton was an especially conservative outpost, as it would show in 1964. While Lyndon Johnson was capturing the White House in a landslide, Joe's friend Barry Goldwater won nearly 53 percent of the vote in Appleton, the biggest Wisconsin city in his column. That same year, George Wallace found it the perfect setting to kick off his white-backlash campaign for the Democratic presidential nomination. And for two generations before that, Appleton was a sundown town, the name given to communities where Negroes were allowed during the day but unwelcome after sunset. *Wisconsin Blue Book*, 1966; and email to author from Matt Carpenter.

and worn out two cars. One day in particular became part of that election's lore, as recorded by America's favorite magazine. "He got up at 5:00 A.M. in Marinette, in Northeastern Wisconsin, and started driving toward Superior, in the northwest, 250 miles away, where he had a radio speech scheduled for 5:00 P.M. and a public appearance at 8:30 P.M.," the *Saturday Evening Post* reported. "In the first 100 miles, driving over rutted roads, McCarthy had four blowouts. He left his car in Rhinelander and took passage in a small passenger plane for Superior . . . Over Butternut the plane developed an oil leak and landed in an oats field. He hired a taxi-cab to finish the dash to Superior; its engine coughed out at Ashland. McCarthy, who had learned to fly small planes in the Solomons, borrowed one from a lawyer he knew in Ashland and flew it himself to Superior. He missed the radio date, but spoke at the public meeting."

Cody Splitt, a young law student who chauffeured Joe around the state, seventy years later recalls her effort to console him: "I said, 'Oh, Judge, you know, I wouldn't worry about this whole thing . . . if you don't get to be senator, you'll still be a judge.' Well, he looked at me and said, 'My god, don't you know the difference between being a judge in a county and being a United States senator?' . . . That was Joe. He had his eye on the target."

The barnstorming "Flying Badgers" covered any towns or cities that McCarthy couldn't. Three days before the primary, more than one thousand of the Young Republicans quietly climbed into three airplanes and 208 automobiles, dispensing campaign propaganda to every Wisconsin community with more than five hundred people and to each fairground. While the booklet promoted all of the Stalwart-backed candidates, Joe was front and center. A cynical newspaper columnist called it "Operation Kindergarten," but organizers were closer to the mark when they labeled it a "statewide vote attack."

Those efforts cost money, and the once reluctant Tom Coleman was there to help. Some bills he and the RVC paid themselves. For others, they enlisted fellow corporate big shots who set up, for that purpose, the kind of McCarthy Club that remained active throughout his career. Altogether the McCarthy forces spent more than $50,000 on the primary campaign, nearly four times La Follette's

$13,000 and closer to the norm for California than Wisconsin. Joe especially appreciated his deep-pocketed backers since he'd let his early success in speculating go to his head, and bankers made him huge loans with less collateral than they'd have required from an investor with less clout. The upshot was that, by the end of 1945, his once flush finances were in ruins and he owed the Appleton State Bank $169,540.70.

Impressive as those exercises were, none would have been insurmountable if La Follette had put up even a modest campaign effort instead of a white flag. The thrice-elected incumbent failed to anticipate or reverse the defection of organized labor to the previously moribund Democratic Party. He failed to account for all the Democrats who would cross over in this open primary to vote for McCarthy in the misplaced hope that he would be easier than La Follette to beat in the general election. And he failed to foresee how hard the only Democratic candidate, former New Deal congressman Howard McMurray, would pound him. Dredging up the senator's anti-interventionist past, McMurray let loose with hyperbole nastier than McCarthy's. "La Follette spent five years before the war voting for Hitler," McMurray charged, adding, "If a man had to sell out his civilization to get votes he should not represent a free people in a democratic society." Could this senator, esteemed by his colleagues in Washington as one of the great men of the Senate, in fact be a Nazi quisling?

Young Bob was just fifty-one at the time, but he waged his campaign like an old man—and a weak one. It was partly that, like many of his supporters, he took for granted the magic of the La Follette name in Wisconsin and didn't take seriously enough the upstart McCarthy or the muckraking McMurray. Yet alarms had been sounded. "Frankly, Bob," campaign coordinator Glenn Roberts wrote in May 1946, "our leaders have a feeling that perhaps you do not care too much for them. Perhaps I do not put this well, but they long to shake your hand and to have you slap them on the back and say hello." After all that time living in Washington when his father was senator, and as a senator himself, he was as out of touch with his Midwest base as Joe made him out to be. His feeble public excuse for staying away from Wisconsin that spring was that he was too busy passing a once-in-a-generation congressional reorganization act. The bill was as important as he said, but he could have headed home to secure his political future during the month-and-a-half gap between the time the Senate passed the measure and when the House took it up.* More believable was what he was telling friends: that he thought he would lose and didn't much care. "I've been in the Senate representing Wisconsin for 20 years," La Follette explained wearily to William Benton, then assistant secretary of state. "If the people at home have decided they don't want me, then I'm ready to quit."

His miserable health helped explain that lassitude. When he was at the University of Wisconsin, a serious viral infection prevented him from finishing his degree. The same bug, plus emotional strain, kept him in bed and out of World War I. As he aged, he suffered phlebitis, an inflammation of the leg that produced a blood clot. A strep infection caused swelling around his eyes, nose, and cheeks, while his other maladies included diverticulitis, bursitis, mild diabetes, and ongoing pain in his neck, hip, and shoulder. He may have had coronary heart disease. (He said yes; his doctors said perhaps.) Underlying it all were a recurrent depression, too much drinking, and ongoing marital troubles. Bob La Follette never liked campaigning and now was even more reticent, especially against a hard-boiled political brawler like Joe McCarthy, who landed blow after blow against his opponent without any counterpunching.

When the senator finally did come home, six days before the election, he took to the airwaves and public podiums to position himself as a moderate: "The Communists want Bob La Follette's scalp because I am not far enough to the left to suit them. The Colemanites have been attacking Bob La Follette because I am not far enough to the right to suit them." The way forward, he concluded, is "the Middle Way, the American Way." It was a strategy that could have worked if he'd begun earlier—and had kept his mouth shut about the governor's race. Instead, he jumped in

---

* The Legislative Reorganization Act of 1946 sought to reverse the wartime flow of power from Congress to the White House, and while it failed to do all that La Follette hoped, it gave the Senate and House more control over the federal budget and greater oversight of the executive branch.

with a late endorsement of his friend Ralph Immell, who was challenging incumbent governor Walter Goodland. That turned Goodland's boosters against him in the last hours of the campaign and dumbfounded the governor, who had been urging Tom Coleman to drop his support for McCarthy and get behind La Follette.

On primary day, McCarthy's victory was more of a shock than it should have been. Two thirds of voters stayed home, the way they usually did in a non-presidential year, with some confused by a primary that had been moved from April to August during the war years. Given all that McCarthy had done right on the campaign trail—from outhustling, out-organizing, and outspending his opponent, to convincing voters it was time to give a say to returning soldiers like him—the biggest surprise was how close La Follette came. The final tally was 207,935 for McCarthy and 202,557 for La Follette, with Joe's slender edge coming in Milwaukee, a labor stronghold that had been La Follette territory. But in elections as in boxing, it's not the margin that matters but whose hand is raised at the final bell. Joe had won a Republican nomination that he would later call the sweetest political triumph of his life.*

There was a general election ahead, and this onetime chicken farmer knew not to count on a full nest until the eggs were laid. Joe immediately set out to attack his Democratic opponent's patriotism in a way intended to define him for the majority of the

---

* La Follette explained the most embarrassing political drubbing of his life with a storyline he knew the media would love. He said that Communists in the US labor movement—angered by his attacks on their beloved Soviet Union—persuaded fellow members to abandon him in favor of a candidate who, ironically, would become America's number one Soviet basher. The truth was that the Reds had modest influence among Wisconsin unionists, they expended little effort attacking La Follette, and they did even less to boost McCarthy. Unionists as a whole, and especially in the labor stronghold of Milwaukee, did back away from La Follette, but it was generally to support the Democrat, McMurray.

Another tempting narrative is that, before the primary, Joe was wishy-washy on communism, and possibly even pro-Red. It gained traction when, in response to a reporter's asking how he felt having gotten a boost from the Communists, Joe was reputed to have responded, "Communists have the same right to vote as anyone else, don't they?" The New York Post reported that in a 1951 series, Anderson and May repeated it in their 1952 biography, and it has become part of McCarthy lore. But Joe's denial that he ever uttered those words gains credence from the fact that there is no evidence of the remark appearing in a newspaper or anywhere else back in 1946, when he supposedly said it.

Wisconsin electorate who had never heard of Howard McMurray. The fuzzy-headed political scientist was being aided by "the communist dominated" political arm of the labor movement, a McCarthy fundraising letter claimed. It was, ironically, the same claim made against Joe in the primary, and in both cases it was true but not nearly a difference maker. McCarthy also trumpeted that McMurray had been endorsed by the Communist *Daily Worker* newspaper, which again was accurate, although equally convincing was McMurray's counter-claim that while he had neither solicited nor seen the endorsement, "if I have the support of the Daily Worker, I certainly repudiate that paper and their whole tribe." In his favorite smear, McCarthy called McMurray "communistically inclined," a phrase he never defined but one his listeners knew must be bad. Joe wasn't alone in tapping the fear of communism as a political bludgeon; the US Chamber of Commerce, the Roman Catholic Church, and lots of Republicans were doing it too. And the previous March, in a speech in nearby Missouri that signaled the onset of the Cold War, British prime minister Winston Churchill coined the frightening metaphor of an Iron Curtain to describe the schism between East and West. Parts of central and eastern Europe already were under Soviet dominion, Churchill warned, with the Communists making inroads in Germany, Italy, Greece, and Turkey. "Whatever conclusions may be drawn from these facts — and facts they are — this is certainly not the Liberated Europe we fought to build up," the English leader told his American listeners. "Nor is it one which contains the essentials of permanent peace."

McMurray punched back in ways that the more courtly La Follette hadn't. Far worse than any ties he might have to the left, McMurray said, was McCarthy's backing by American Action, a far-right group with a million-dollar war chest filled by *Chicago Tribune* publisher Colonel Robert McCormick and his industrialist cronies, and his consuming focus on electing a Congress of America Firsters and anti–New Dealers. Joe initially professed ignorance of the endorsement, and even of the organization. "I know nothing about American Activities, Inc., if that's its name," he said. "If it is the old America First group, I want no part of it." Yet understanding that much of his base embraced precisely that noninterventionist ideology, he deftly tap-danced, adding, "If it is organized to fight communism as they say, I welcome their help in defeating communists and those who are communistically inclined like McMurray."

The Democrat was helped by a press that, taken aback by McCarthy's come-from-nowhere primary win, had suddenly gone digging into Joe's background. What about those quickie divorces for his political pals and the destruction of an embarrassing court log? Was McCarthy dodging income taxes he owed the state? How could his family members cover his campaign bills when they could barely cover their own living expenses? Had those questions been asked earlier, La Follette might have gained the traction he needed to overcome McCarthy's narrow margin of victory, as repentant reporters understood. And what about the American Bar Association code admonishing judges against running for political office—a question the *Milwaukee Journal* now took so seriously that it printed in full the ABA ethical canon?

Joe's glib answers—that the state supreme court had cleared him of the constitutional ban on judges running for other offices, and that he wasn't bound by ABA ethics since he wasn't a member of the national or state bar associations—satisfied campaign crowds but not journalists or legal authorities. W. T. Doar, a member of the Wisconsin Board of Bar Commissioners, did his own investigating and found a copy of a state bar proceeding from 1946 showing "that there is a fellow named, Joseph McCarthy, Appleton, Wisconsin, listed as a member. That must be 'Slippery Joe.'" That revelation came more than two years too late to help McMurray, whose bid to brand McCarthy "Two-Job Joe" never caught on. Wisconsin's high court, meanwhile, had in fact held that federal law trumped state when it came to guidelines for US senators, although it later added that McCarthy had "violated his oath as a circuit judge and as an attorney at law" and deserved "just censure." Thankfully for Joe, the latter court judgment, like Doar's, came in 1949, and not when voters were casting ballots in 1946. As he had in the Quaker Dairy case in 1941, Chief Justice Rosenberry let Joe walk away without punishment and able to twist the court's words into a vindication. "We thought the only thing to do was to censure him," Rosenberry told a reporter later, adding that "it didn't seem a matter worth disbarring him over." But the chief justice's ruling reinforced Joe's conviction that he could remain above the law. He made light of Rosenberry's reasoning, saying all it amounted to was "it was illegal — Joe was a naughty boy, but we don't think he'll do it again."

One reason why he hadn't wanted to give up his judgeship — which was supposed to be nonpolitical as well as nonpartisan — was that he knew the advantages it could offer in his bid for state-wide office. Letters he exchanged with lawyers mixed talk of cases pending before his court with references to the impending Senate primary. Shirley Foresman, his judicial secretary, wrote to attorneys and others on behalf of the campaign as well as the court. Joe himself never saw the need to demarcate his roles as jurist and candidate, using his courthouse stationery to solicit campaign funds and using his judicial travel as an election tool. "I have been doing a great deal of speaking — fence building for 1946," he wrote his buddy Van Susteren early in 1945. "The work in Circuit Court is at a minimum, which gives me a lot of time to beat the bushes throughout the state."

Joe also blithely ignored the boundary between truth and falsehood, as his correspondence from that era makes clear. In a 1945 missive to a Roman Catholic seminary in Malaya, he explained that he "was discharged in March of this year because of injuries received in a plane crash." Two months later he laid out for Van Susteren his financial high jinks: "I gave Lawler your check in the amount of $1912.00 and then stalled him on the balance with the story that you had sent me government bonds which were not properly signed and that I had to send them back to you, hoping that in the meantime the stuff would get back up above 32½. However, he started to get uneasy while the stock was still at 31½, so I gave him $700.00 and told him to change it to a margin account." Slippery Joe indeed.

McCarthy got an assist during his general election battle from the unlikeliest of sources, his vanquished primary rival Robert La Follette Jr. As one of the first respected liberals to sound an alarm about both Soviet aggression and the growing influence of the US Communist Party, Young Bob had enormous credibility on the issue. He put that on the line by publishing in *The Progressive* magazine slashing attacks on left-wing Democrats, unionists, and others who, "like vermin," were "prostituting liberalism for their own devious purposes." He never mentioned McMurray, but he didn't have to, since everyone understood, and pro-McCarthy newspapers reprinted his articles. La Follette hadn't forgiven McMurray's primary campaign barbs, and while he never had liked McCarthy and never would, he liked McMurray so much less that on November 5 he cast his ballot for the man who had dethroned him.

Two thirds of Wisconsinites did the same. It helped that 1946 brought a Republican tidal wave, the way midterms often do for the party that's out of the White House. (Democrats lost fifty-four seats in the House, eleven in the Senate, and the control of both branches for the first time since 1932.) It helped Joe, too, that the Badger State was so deeply Republican. (The GOP had been in control for nearly a century, Democrats wouldn't truly compete for another decade, and Progressives were gone forever.) The final tally was 620,430 for McCarthy and 378,772 for McMurray. Joe had finished first in an eye-popping seventy of the state's seventy-one counties and won all three rounds in the fight of his life. His rise from chicken farmer to small-town attorney to US senator at the age of thirty-nine was the kind of rags-to-ruling story that would have impressed Fighting Bob, who took twelve years longer to make it to that sacred seat in the US Senate.

Joe's most luminous days as a senator came just after he rocketed into Washington, before he was even sworn in. He arrived as a slightly dazzled rube. His youthfulness alone made him a standout —ten years younger than the average incumbent, twenty-five compared to the typical committee chairman. Most senators had done an apprenticeship in the House or at some other posting more likely to steep them in the machinations of the Capitol than a back-country judgeship.* But most also were shopworn captives of old guard Washington, with Joe vowing not just to infuse fresh blood but to be the stouthearted spokesman for all the veterans who had

---

* Like Joe, Richard Nixon and John Kennedy used their World War II service in the South Pacific as launching pads for their political careers, and like him, the two of them were elected to Congress in 1946. But even Kennedy and Nixon, who would both rise to the White House, began in the lower chamber, not as a senator like McCarthy.

just rescued the Free World from the Nazis and their Axis allies. The unwritten Senate code then was that new members should comport themselves like children, being seen but not heard. Yet nearly everyone was curious to hear from this farm-bred freshman from Wisconsin who had come out of nowhere to vanquish the venerable Young Bob La Follette. And so they would, sooner than anyone dreamed and before the new Congress convened.

They could have gotten an opening glimpse of how against the grain and off-color their new colleague would be had they been on his train as it pulled into Union Station, bringing him to Washington for the first time since his election in the fall of 1946. An exhilarating era was dawning, with Air Force Captain Chuck Yeager about to break the sound barrier, inventor Edwin Land ready to click his first instant Polaroid picture, and Jackie Robinson gearing up for a barrier-breaking debut with the Brooklyn Dodgers. Asked by an aide for what he hoped would be a quote-worthy reflection on this novel universe, Joe offered, "Oh shit, it's raining."

McCarthy was never one to admit he was wowed, or to tread quietly. Still a senator in waiting, he phoned the White House and said he'd like to talk to President Truman about the coal strike that was crippling the economy and had darkened the Capitol building. Try back when you're a real lawmaker, the president's operatives advised. Undaunted, the next morning he summoned fifty news-hungry journalists to discuss the same topic, one he hadn't thought much about but knew would get people's attention. Before he could say a word, one of the pack asked the question likely on the minds of all: "You're a new man here. Why did you call a press conference?"

The question was a fair one, but Joe was a step ahead, knowing that if he offered something dramatic, even these hard-bitten Capitol Hill reporters would nibble. So with a "let's get down to business," he spent the next thirty minutes explaining why the government should draft union president John L. Lewis and his 400,000 mine workers into the Army. "That's the only way to settle this strike," the Marine turned politician lectured before shifting to the most original and least constitutional part of his plan. "If Lewis failed then to send his men back to work, he would be subject to an Army courts-martial [sic]. In wartime, courts-martial penalties range up to and including the death sentence." Nobody took his proposal seriously — "You mean you would line up men like John L. Lewis and have them shot?" an incredulous reporter asked — but they gave him ink anyway. His remarks appeared not just in the *Washington Post* but in the *New York Times,* including in the jump of the lead story on page one on December 6, 1946.

It was Joe's perfect platform. As a senator elect, he could say whatever he wanted without having to follow through or be subject to reproach by colleagues. "I don't claim to be any smarter than the next fellow, but I do claim that I work twice as hard and that's what I intend to do in Washington the next six years," McCarthy told the *Milwaukee Journal,* whose top editors still were smarting over their failure to endorse the senator he had unseated. Yet the reporter assigned to cover his debut was cheerleading, in awe at how, after a fourteen-mile hike through the backwoods with his assistants, "the former marine captain and Marquette boxing coach, fit and trim at 198 pounds, was jauntily out in front of his panting companions." As for his policy prescriptions, this scribe's rose-tinted crystal ball revealed the moderation of a liberal Republican. McCarthy was for removing "stifling government control" and cutting the civilian federal workforce by two thirds, but also for responsible government planning and a federal minimum wage. As for our relations with the Soviet bear, the just elected senator insisted he was all for compromise: "Russia does not want war and is not ready to fight one. Stalin's proposal for world disarmament is a great thing and he must be given credit for being sincere about it."*

---

* Joe was not just interested in speaking about Russia; he wanted to speak Russian. To that end he shelled out $200 early in 1947 to the School of Slavic Languages, and another $316 later that year. He also wrote to the head of the school applauding his part in "the furtherance of peace and understanding among the people of the world." He explained to others that he was learning the language so he could go *mano a mano* with Joseph Stalin in case he got a seat on the Foreign Relations Committee, which he didn't. He also didn't have a facility with languages or time to learn. Russian Lessons File, series 21, MUA; Pilat and Shannon, "Smear, Inc.: The One-Man Mob of Joe McCarthy," pt. 2; and Reeves interview with Tom Korb September 6, 1975.

Not everyone was enthralled by his call for international cooperation and even global governance. Pointing to his lack of experience in foreign policy, edi-

Press coverage didn't come easily or by chance, with ninety-six senators and 433 congressmen jockeying for attention.* But few of them had Joe's grasp of journalists' deadlines and inclinations. He would shrewdly position himself at the opportune place and time with just the right storyline or quote. He donated blocks of hard-to-procure Dairy State cheeses to the National Press Club bar and cooked for eight female correspondents from the Senate press gallery a fried chicken and hot biscuits dinner, flying the fryers in from Wisconsin. That goodwill campaign paid off. *Newsweek* shaved two years off his age and gushed about his claim that the next six years would be "twice as exciting as shooting up Lever Bros.'s coconut trees in the Solomons." *Time* fell into line regarding McCarthy's birthday and his upbeat persona, calling him "Wisconsin's jovial Republican." *Washington Post* columnist Marquis Childs, soon to become a biting critic, for now gave him the benefit of the doubt. While the proposal to draft Lewis "has a shocking sound," Childs wrote, "it comes out of the same sense of frustration that millions of Americans feel as they see the productive machine slowly brought to a standstill."

Nobody in the press corps was closer to Joe in those early days than Jack Anderson, legman for the widely feared columnist Drew Pearson. "McCarthy made himself available to us as a source . . . At my prompting he would phone fellow senators to ask what had transpired this morning behind closed doors or what strategy was planned for the morrow. While I listened in on an extension he would pump even a Robert Taft or a William Knowland with the handwritten questions I passed him. This blot upon senatorial honor was for a reporter a professional coup of high rank and I rejoiced in it, prying out of McCarthy every last morsel of confidential information," recalled Anderson. "Had it not been for the hours I would put in conducting unfruitful interviews with unco-

---

torial writers at the conservative *Chicago Daily Tribune* declared derisively, "The great world awaits Mr. McCarthy. We trust that he will pursue his new senatorial opportunities to make its acquaintance. The wide-eyed wonder will all be his." "Senator McCarthy and the World," *Chicago Daily Tribune*.

* There were only forty-eight states at the start of the 80th Congress, with Hawaii and Alaska not yet in the Union. And because of a death and a resignation, the House had just 433 members, two short of the full complement.

operative senators in order to cover McCarthy's tracks, he would have been exposed as a traitor to the Club and appropriately exiled; as it was, he was never identified."

Part of what attracted Anderson and the others was McCarthy's Mr. Smith Goes to Washington counterpoint to the patrician titans of the Senate. He listed his address in the telephone directory, next to his number: Emerson 3-0867. His only jewelry was a wristwatch with a plain leather strap. "For a member of the 'world's most exclusive club' in the status-conscious 1940s, he was refreshingly unpretentious," said Anderson, who five years later would author the most scathing of the early biographies of the senator. "Teetering back behind the great block of his government-issue senator's desk, he would hold rump court in his shirt sleeves and not infrequently in his undershirt. He was comfortably old-shoe. The traditional outlets for foppery — clothes, accessories, dinner menus, wine lists — tempted him not a bit."*

Publicity was Joe's alpha and omega. Yet while the goodwill generated by his biscuit baking and secret dispensing lasted longer than it should have, there were limits. After he was sworn in, reporters began to sense he wasn't delivering what he had promised or they had predicted, although most took years to wise up. The first suspicions surfaced during his dogged bid to kill controls on the production and sale of sugar, which, like other precious commodities, had been rationed during the war. The public was sick of rations, a message made clear when it dubbed the Senate class of '46 the "Meat Shortage Boys." Even more frustrated were producers in states like Wisconsin, where beet sugar was big business and farmers longed for a free market that would let them charge higher prices. Joe, they decided, was their tribune, which was natural.

What was unusual to anyone who didn't know him was how he went about his advocacy — with teeth bared and truths forsworn. In the middle of a mind-rattling floor debate over sugar produc-

---

* Anderson wrote for McCarthy at least one populist speech on farm policy even as he was writing about the senator as a journalist. Today that would be a firing offense at most news outlets; back then it was more common, and fewer considered it a conflict. Pilat, *Drew Pearson: An Unauthorized Biography,* 25.

tion claims, Joe delivered a dispatch that seemed to settle the matter. "Within the past 10 minutes I have received word from the Department of Agriculture that they have gone over the figures which we have been submitting," he assured his colleagues, his words flowing with the *rat-a-tat* of the machine gun he had manned during the war, pressing forward on his feet as if to take flight. Cuba had completed its harvest. It was a bumper crop. And the Truman administration now was admitting we were awash in the white gold. His bulletin seemed to settle the matter, and would have had it not been a fairy tale. Senator Charles Tobey had just made his own call to the Agriculture Department, to Secretary Clinton Anderson himself, who had authorized the New Hampshire Republican to report "unqualifiedly" that, no matter how Senator McCarthy chose to interpret production numbers, "there is no more sugar available for home consumption." Never one to back off, Joe lit into the very Agriculture Department that minutes before he had said deserved the final word: "I do not give a tinker's dam what Secretary Anderson says about the matter. The sugar is here." The dismissive tinker's dam would be added to Joe's list of favorite expressions of outrage, and Tobey, who chaired the powerful Committee on Banking and Currency, on which Joe sat, would add himself to the growing register of Senate insiders alarmed by this freewheeling freshman.

The more telling question about McCarthy's passion for lifting inventory controls on and ending rationing of sugar was whether it was driven by his constituents' financial interests or his own. As always, Joe's complicated web of pecuniary relationships and his penchant for prevarication made it difficult to know. A stack of letters to and from his banker and his brother reveals that he was back playing the stock market, and again losing. While his hometown bank and its obliging president, Matt Schuh, came through with $75,000 in loans, this time Schuh insisted on more than Joe's tumbling stocks as collateral. Conveniently, an equally friendly lobbyist for Pepsi-Cola, Russell Arundel, signed a note for $20,000.* Joe also was seen socializing with Pepsi president Walter Mack Jr. "It

---

* After he bought a tiny island off the coast of Nova Scotia, the whimsical Arundel named his land the Principality of Outer Baldonia and crowned himself prince.

is an interesting coincidence," Senator Tobey said at a closed-door GOP caucus in 1947, "a very interesting coincidence that the language of [McCarthy's decontrol] bill is strikingly similar to the text of Mr. Mack's testimony before the Banking and Currency Committee. Maybe the Senator can explain that."

Arundel denied any quid pro quo. The loan, he said, was made for reasons of friendship rather than influence peddling, and as a Pepsi bottler rather than a manufacturer, he broke with his parent company in that he liked sugar rationing, which let him charge more for scarce soft drinks. Joe was even more direct in denying any payments from Pepsi. "No," he told a pair of journalists who asked about it. "But I got to know Walter Mack very well and I understood why Pepsi-Cola had to push hard for more sugar while a rival like Coca-Cola could coast on previously-arranged supplies." Congressional investigators who looked into these matters years afterward weren't convinced. "His acceptance of a $20,000 favor from the Washington representative of the Pepsi-Cola Company at the very time he was attacking the Government for its manner of handling sugar control," they reported, "makes it difficult to determine whether Senator McCarthy was working for the best interests of the Government, as he saw it, or for Pepsi-Cola."* In the end, Washington insiders offered their verdict by adding a nickname to Joe's lengthening list: "Pepsi-Cola Kid."†

Housing was his other preoccupation during his inaugural year in the Senate. The dramatic slump in construction during the Depression, together with 9 million returning veterans needing a

---

* John Moore, who oversaw the probe, went several steps further in questioning McCarthy's ethics: "Preliminary investigation indicates that Senator McCarthy launched a severe attack upon the purchase of Cuban sugar by the Army in the Fall of 1947; that the charges were groundless; that they were made without attempting to secure the facts from those in possession of the facts; and, finally, that they may have been inspired by Walter S. Mack, Jr., President of the Pepsi-Cola Company, in an attempt to deter the Army from continuing its sugar purchasing program for the prevention of famine in Germany, Japan, and Korea." Memo from Moore to Subcommittee on Privileges and Elections, June 3, 1952, US Senate, Subcommittee on Privileges and Elections, *Investigations of Senators Joseph R. McCarthy and William Benton.*
† Told about this nickname, Pepsi lobbyist Arundel countered, "Well, he's not my kid." *Life and Times of Joe McCarthy,* 123.

place to live, spawned the worst housing crisis in US history. Some battle-scarred GIs were crammed in with relatives, while others sought shelter in Quonset huts, trailers, coal sheds, and tent cities reminiscent of the shantytowns that went up after World War I and helped bring down President Herbert Hoover. Joe proclaimed that unless his fellow vets got the housing they deserved, "the whole Congress should resign." Brave words, but the question was how. The Truman administration wanted the government to clear slums, underwrite loans, kick-start construction, and build half a million publicly owned units. The buck-stops-here president from the heartland wasn't the only one. Conservative darlings of the Senate Robert Taft and Allen Ellender joined with New Deal hero Robert Wagner to push a warlike home-building mobilization known as the Taft-Ellender-Wagner bill. The housing industry, which had welcomed government help in digging out of the Depression, said okay to clearing slums but insisted that any replacements be scoped out, built, and owned not by a distant federal government but by private developers working with city planners. Joe obligingly agreed.

As he'd done with sugar controls, he launched his home-building crusade with a power grab that challenged Senate norms and Senator Tobey. A joint House-Senate committee was being formed to study the postwar housing crunch "from A to Z" and draft a solution. McCarthy had proposed the formation of this powerful body and wanted to chair it, but so did Tobey, who outranked him. Seniority was Congress's Golden Rule, but Joe maneuvered to schedule the deciding vote for a mid-August day when he knew Tobey's supporters would be away. The New Hampshire lawmaker left his sick wife to attend, armed with proxy votes from his absent backers, but Joe knew he had a majority of those physically present and won a ruling to disqualify the proxies. Tobey had seen fellow senators play hardball but not this kind of dirty pool. "This comes with little grace from you. You, who dared to use proxies time after time in the Senate Banking Committee, sometimes when you didn't have them," Tobey shouted at McCarthy. But like most demagogues, Joe was shameless. He got his bloc to elect an unknown and easily manipulated House member as chairman and inserted himself as vice chair, a position that gave him undisputed control.

"This child is born as a result of malpractice," Tobey railed. "I hope the forceps didn't hurt it."

Joe traveled thirty thousand miles across the country, taking testimony on housing policy from 1,286 witnesses and working as hard as he'd promised the *Milwaukee Journal* he would. What stood out here as elsewhere was not his conservative proposal, which was defensible even if it was the identical one being pushed by the powerful real estate lobby. His trademark was the way he demonized those who disagreed, in this case the president and the majority of senators who believed in a modest role for government-backed housing and rent controls. He kept witnesses waiting if they favored public housing, then jumped on them like a prosecutor would. And he made clear that public housing projects were "breeding grounds for Communism" and "deliberately created slum area[s], at federal expense." Fresh from a visit to Rego Park Veterans Housing Project in Queens, he pronounced that "this housing was built over a garbage disposal area. Wives of veterans were wading in mud up to their ankles to hang out the washing. I myself saw four dead rats. Gas from the garbage was seeping up through the mud and slime. Baby carriages were up to their hubs in mud." While the tenants appreciated any spotlighting of their problems, they rightfully charged that McCarthy was "interested not so much in seeing to it that the veterans are provided with a place to live, but with arousing sentiment against continuing the very vital program of public housing."

McCarthy's business-chummy approach won. Truman signed the bill in August 1948, saying something was better than naught. Mayor Francis Wendt of Racine, a rooter for public housing and for the La Follettes, was less forgiving. "The homeless people of Wisconsin can thank McCarthy for keeping them homeless," he said. Then he added his own to the list of sobriquets for his home state senator: "water boy of the real estate lobby."*

---

* Never one to cede the last word, Joe shot back that Wendt was the "Pinko mayor of Racine." Later the senator got serious, disputing the notion that he'd sold out his brothers in uniform by siding with the real estate lobby. Other bills of his, he pointed out, ensured that the government paid half the costs of homes for the roughly 1,500 veteran paraplegics, and provided additional compensation to wid-

That characterization took on new resonance in March 1949, when Joe unveiled a thirty-eight-page booklet he'd crafted for the Lustron Corporation, maker of the all-new steel-paneled prefabricated homes that claimed to "defy weather, wear, and time." The purpose of his article, the senator said, was to explain "in four letter words" the housing aid available to veterans and others. He declined to say how much he'd been paid, calling it "embarrassingly small" and adding, "I have to split it with 10 people who helped me." Very little of what he told the press that day was true. His contract paid him ten cents a copy for the first 100,000, then five cents for successive copies, with a guarantee of $10,000. That added up to $1.43 per word, or substantially more than the $1 per word that Winston Churchill was getting for his long-anticipated memoirs. Lustron didn't come to him; Jean Kerr, Joe's assistant and eventual wife, made a hard sell to the company in the fall of 1948. While insisting he didn't believe in ghostwriters, he would concede that the real researchers and writers here were two high-level federal housing aides, along with Jean (who says the senator rewrote nearly everything she submitted). Joe entered the $10,000 payment on his 1949 income tax return, which was a year late, and he made clear that all of it came to him. While he professed to have produced an easy step-by-step guide for consumers, what was published was too long (thirty-eight pages) and too dense (trying to explain the congressional machinations behind the housing bill) to be of any value to a typical homebuyer.

Its usefulness to Lustron, however, was apparent. Company president Carl Strandlund saw himself as the Henry Ford of premade homes. Now he had the imprimatur of a powerful US senator to make a case not just to homeowners but, by implication, to a federal government that already had loaned the company $37 million and was being asked for more. While Joe's name was only over his article, not on the rest of the ninety-four-page sales screed, his was the only byline in the table of contents, and the casual reader might assume that Joe had written the whole thing. Strandlund admitted that he had "purchased the name of the Sen-

ows and children of veterans who died in the Second World War. "Smear, Inc.," pt. 7; and letter from Joe to Roy Matson, December 3, 1948, WHS.

ator" and wasn't concerned about what, if anything, Joe had written himself. Lustron never did get the extra government money it needed to survive. With each home costing the company more than it charged, Strandlund had to shut down after selling just 2,500 of the hundreds of thousands of production-line houses he'd dreamed of.

As he had with Pepsi, Joe insisted his Lustron alliance was perfectly legal, and he was correct. But he again missed the point. His pamphlet acknowledged that he'd used his government position and payroll to do the writing, saying it was "based on information gathered by United States Senator Joe McCarthy of Wisconsin, in the course of his research and investigation as Vice-Chairman of the Joint Committee on Housing." He had the right to vilify public housing and cheer for-profit companies, but he was on much shakier ground when he shared in those profits, especially from a company that depended on federal loans. Joe was hungry to get the Lustron money so he could pay down his debt to the Appleton bank, but ever the plunger, he instead doubled down by buying more stock. Clyde Foraker, the federal court receiver in Lustron's bankruptcy case, would later call the $10,000 payment "unethical" and surmise, "I'll bet he wouldn't have gotten it if he hadn't been [a] United States senator."*

Joe's tone deafness regarding conflicts of interest was understandable. In the 1940s, Congress had no financial disclosure rules, ethics committees, or worries about outside income. But even by those sparse standards, Joe trespassed legislative ethical boundaries just as he had the legal profession's and the military's. Driving him now was the urgent need for cash, and his search for scapegoats took him back to his 1944 campaign. "While I was overseas," he wrote, "not only without my consent but against my definite orders, some of my very well-meaning friends who were in charge of my campaign spent practically all of my assets." He also was paying off back taxes and an old debt to the Appleton Loan and Finance Company. To stay afloat, he took out fat loans from two executives

* Jean responded for Joe on this one, saying, "It's interesting that nobody thought this 'unethical' until the Senator started to expose Communists in government." Academic Requests, unprocessed files, MUA.

with direct interests in his work as a senator—Victor Minahan, editor of the *Appleton Post-Crescent* and *Green Bay Press-Gazette,* and Frank Sensenbrenner, an influential Wisconsin Republican and former president of paper colossus Kimberly-Clark. Whatever borrowing he did never seemed enough, as his Marquette files reveal. "[I have] a total fixed monthly expense of $1062.25. My monthly salary check, after income tax deductions, amounts to slightly over $1,090.00. I have been averaging an additional three to four hundred dollars a month for speaking," Joe pointed out in a letter to Sensenbrenner. "This barely covers the living expenses down here, etc. For these reasons I had hoped that I could impose upon you and a couple of my other good friends whom I have had to call upon, to ride this out with me until the market recovers."

He also imposed on business mogul and philanthropist Walter Schroeder, whose twenty-five-story hotel at the corner of Fifth and Wisconsin was a Milwaukee landmark. "I have just received a letter from Tom Korb to the effect that you had cancelled a rather sizable hotel bill which we ran up during the campaign. It is perhaps needless to say this is very greatly appreciated," McCarthy wrote Schroeder just after his election as senator. "This bill was rather embarassing [sic] for a number of reasons—not the least of which was that I would have had to violate the election law in order to personally pay for the rooms in view of the fact that they were used as campaign headquarters. Also, since the election I have had to put the names of my creditors into a hat and each pay day pull out a name and the lucky man gets the money."

Financial entanglements like those led journalists and political foes to logically suggest a cause and effect with the special interests he championed, which went well beyond soda pop and metal homes. He pushed to cut appropriations for public power and supported Taft-Hartley and other labor laws that tied the hands of unions. He backed the St. Lawrence Seaway linking the Great Lakes to the Atlantic Ocean in part because shipping interests backed it, and delighted home state dairy farmers by fighting to keep the tax on rival oleomargarine. He befriended the rich by voting to slash their taxes (he promised to support even bigger percentage cuts for the poor), voted to rein in spending generally and especially on education (unneeded federal money, he argued, meant unwanted federal control), and was for cutting spending for "countries devastated by the war" as well as the National Cancer Institute (the Senate agreeing about the latter but not the former). None of this should have been surprising for a Tom Coleman–style conservative, although on issues like public housing he stood to the right of right-wing paladins like Robert Taft and New Hampshire's Tobey, an America Firster long before Joe. It was partly that Senator McCarthy had talked himself out of the New Deal ideology that proved a political nonstarter for him in Wisconsin and into the Stalwart mindset that had sent him to Washington. It also may have been the case, as two *New York Post* reporters wrote in their seventeen-part series on him, that "it is easier and personally more advantageous to string along with the haves rather than with the have-nots of this world."

But he reveled in proving his critics wrong, especially anyone who tried to pigeonhole him. Such was the case when he backed the moderate Harold Stassen for president in 1948 not just against liberal New York governor Thomas Dewey but also ahead of two proven conservatives, the buttoned-down Senator Taft and flamboyant General Douglas MacArthur. Joe's foreign policy at that point was moderately internationalist and surprisingly bipartisan. But his choice was more about people than politics. Stassen was a friend with ties to McCarthy's Senate aides, whereas Taft had opposed Joe in supporting public housing. As for MacArthur, whom Joe would later court, he was allied with Philip La Follette, which was reason enough to be wary.

On the offense as ever, McCarthy sought to advance Stassen's cause by dragging down MacArthur. First, he said in a campaign letter, there was the question of age: "Twice before we have had Presidents who became physically weakened during their term of office and both times it had very sad results for our country. The most recent case was that of the last term of President Roosevelt who was physically worn out at Yalta during his conference with Stalin, with very bad results. Woodrow Wilson got tired out at Paris, and we lost the peace after World War I. General MacArthur," who was sixty-eight, "would be much older than either of these two men were . . . That is why I believe that we should give the General his well-deserved hero's acclaim and retirement when his job is done and not try to have him undergo the strain of years as President of our country in this difficult time." Then there was the matter of MacArthur's divorce, an especially sensitive subject in Joe's home state, where a third of the population was Catholic. "He was first married in Florida to Mrs. Walter Brooks of Baltimore, who now lives in Washington, D.C.," Joe reminded voters. "After she divorced him in Reno, Nevada, he was remarried in New York City."*

Senator Joe's performance was easier to evaluate than Judge Joe's. He had won a victory on housing, but at enormous cost. He'd so enraged his fellow senators that when the Republicans lost their majority in 1948, the incoming Democratic chair of the Banking Committee said he'd take the job only if Joe were booted from the committee.† "He is a troublemaker," explained Senator Burnet Maybank. "That's why I don't want him." Truman, meanwhile, pointed to McCarthy's watered-down housing bill as part of an assault on the "do-nothing" 80th Congress that helped the president stage one of the greatest upsets ever in winning reelection over Governor Dewey. And in the wake of that '48 victory, Congress passed a bill that resuscitated the public housing program that Joe had branded a breeding place for radicals.

Lots of groups did their own rankings of the hotheaded freshman. Organized labor scored him ninth from the bottom among labor-friendly senators, tied with Taft. Columnist Drew Pearson banished him to a class of what he called "dunce caps," with a grade of E. McCarthy "came to the Senate with more publicity

* Giving a deposition in a lawsuit three years later, when he was under oath in a roomful of young attorneys, the senator offered a decidedly different verdict on the general's fitness: "I think he is a much younger man in terms of stamina than anyone in this room . . . I think Douglas MacArthur would be plenty young enough to be President of these United States." At other points McCarthy called MacArthur "the greatest American ever borne" [sic] and "the greatest military leader since Genghis Khan." McCarthy deposition, October 5, 1951, *Drew Pearson v. Joseph R. McCarthy et al.*; and attachment to letter from Robert Fleming to Hugh Morrow, November 2, 1951, Fleming Papers.
† That was not just embarrassing; it meant losing a seat on one of the most powerful committees in the Senate in return for one of the least useful for Wisconsinites, the Committee on the District of Columbia. His other committee, Expenditures in the Executive Departments, also seemed like a sleeper until Joe made it famous.

build-up than any colleague," Pearson wrote, "but fizzled faster." No matter how much he hogged the spotlight, he mattered so little at this early stage that when in 1949 *Pageant* magazine asked Washington's leading print and radio correspondents to name the best and worst senators, Senator McCarthy barely warranted mention, tying with two others for twenty-second on the list of the lowest rated.

A consensus was building: his career as a senator was more than just undistinguished; it was a train wreck. Even his fellow Republicans saw him as a gasbag and a pretender. Joe had seen silver linings even when he was trounced in his bids for district attorney and to unseat Senator Alexander Wiley, but now he was shaken. At the end of 1948 he wrote a friend at the *Wisconsin State Journal*, Madison's Republican paper, complaining about an editorial in the rival *Capital Times* "setting forth just what a reactionary bastard McCarthy was." Attached was Joe's thirteen-page letter to another friendly editor outlining his stands on critical issues. Two aspects of the missive were notable: his need to prove he wasn't a heartless right-winger, and a racist remark near the end. "Some teachers," he wrote, "are now getting salaries lower than a darky could get with a shovel and a hoe." Like his later anti-Semitic slurs, this affront reflected the casual bigotry of the era more than a dark side of Joe, or so insisted his colleagues and friends.

The fact was that in that letter and elsewhere, Joe was lashing out at enemies — in the press, the Democratic Party, the Communist movement — with no recognition of his own bad behavior. Newspapers actually were attacking him less and ignoring him more. Three years after toppling a Senate icon, Joe was at risk of becoming a nobody — his and every demagogue's deepest dread. Just two years before, the *Milwaukee Journal* had said he "has the strongest personal political 'machine' of any Wisconsin politician." Now that machine was breaking down and his political future looked bleak. He wouldn't face the voters again until 1952, but already would-be challengers were mocking him. "I think I could take Wiley" in 1950, one prominent Wisconsin Republican told newsmen in 1949. "But I'll wait for the easy one in 1952."

▪ ▪ ▪

Jean Fraser Kerr had already proven her professional worth in everything from ghostwriting the Lustron pamphlet to the political navigation she offered when Joe seemed lost, as he so often did. But her appeal went beyond policies or prose. It was her legs and lips that had convinced a glamour girl sorority to crown the blue-eyed brunette its beauty queen and a journalism fraternity to name her "Miss Type Face of 1948"—and that got the attention of Senator Joe McCarthy, a Don Juan with ex-girlfriends everywhere from Milwaukee to Washington.*

Jean was born in Washington, DC, to Scottish immigrants in 1924, when Joe was fifteen. Unable to afford college, she attended secretarial school, then got a job with an ad agency, where she wrote copy for radio and saved her nickels. When she had enough, she enrolled at George Washington University and, in 1946, won $150 for her essay "The Promotion of Peace Among the Nations of the World."† Attracted to magazine writing, she transferred to the Medill School of Journalism at Northwestern University, where she minored in political science and took courses in Russian history. It was on a sweltering July morning in 1947 that she first visited McCarthy's office on Capitol Hill for a lunch date with one of his secretaries. "In walked a big, broad-shouldered Irishman with a happy face and a certain swing to his walk. This was the Senator," she recalled years later. "He said hello as if we had always known each other and sailed into his private office." Joe, meanwhile, was raving to a pal, "God, she's beautiful." That evening her secretarial friend called to offer her a job with the senator. She accepted, then changed her mind the next day when an internship she had applied for came through. When she ran into Joe later

---

* Ray Kiermas, who managed Joe's Senate office, got to observe that womanizing up close and offered this verdict: "Like Jesus, he loved them all." Reeves interview with Kiermas, March 17, 1977.

† This was one in a series of student papers showing that Jean, like Joe, started life as a liberal even if she ended it as an equally militant Cold Warrior. Another essay called for America to broker a deal between the warring Chinese Nationalists and Communists by convincing "both sides in China of the justice and ultimate gain that lies in unity." Later, sentiments like these from State Department officials were enough to make her husband scream treason. "Our Stake in Future Peace—China Today," November 26, 1945, series 24, MUA.

that summer, both were nervous, though he managed, "Don't forget you have a rain check on that job with me."

Once she headed back to Northwestern at the end of the summer, their story is best told in his love missives and her reminiscences, both gathering dust at the Marquette archives. Joe wired in April, "AM COMING INTO CHICAGO ON THE NIGHT OF MAY 4 AND HOPE YOU ARE FREE. AS I RECALL, YOU OWE ME A BEER AND I WANT A CHANCE TO COLLECT." Then this from Western Union a week later: "COMING IN BY PLANE. WILL CALL YOU ABOUT 8:30 OR 9:00. HOPE YOU ARE FREE TO HELP ME CELEBRATE STASSEN'S VICTORY IN OHIO."* She had a date and said dinner wouldn't work; he called back the next morning and she agreed to lunch. "I had such a good time that I never looked at my watch," she said later. "When I finally did make a dash for Evanston and dinner, the house mother bawled me out proper for being late."

Jean didn't have nearly the dating history that Joe did, but she was in demand and had been engaged, three years before, to a young ensign named Benjamin Semple Chase. Her letters to him make clear he wasn't paying enough attention. "Perhaps it's I who soaked in more champagne and moonlight than was good for me that night," she wrote, "for our present state is not at all what I would expect from the man I intended to marry." After the engagement was called off, others tried, but by graduation time there was nobody to keep her in Chicago. So she headed back to Washington to see whether Joe's rain check was still good. He didn't flinch, and had a first assignment waiting: write a booklet for metal housing maker Lustron. She did it, but found it "boring and tedious."

Jean laid out her version of their early relationship in her unpublished memoir and in rare interviews. She rejected Joe's endless entreaties to mingle romance with business, and he pretended to accept that. Too often to be convincing, he'd find himself so busy during office hours that he couldn't review her research. So night after night he showed up at her mother's house, where they went over the work, and he invariably would be invited to

---

* Stassen didn't win, but he did capture 43 percent of the primary vote in Ohio, not bad considering he was up against home state senator Robert Taft.

stay for dinner. Joe even started bringing along his specialty, venison meatballs wrapped in grape leaves.* When he knew Jeannie
was at home with a date, he'd telephone every quarter hour asking, "What's the matter? Hasn't he got the price of a movie? Can't
he take you out to dinner?"† But as his pushy romancing started
showing results, he pulled back a bit, letting her know "there is no
place in my kind of life for a wife. I can't work at politics if I have
to call home every half hour, and if I can't stay away from supper when I want to." He eventually learned to convey his message
more gently: "How would I feel, with all these people out to get
my scalp, if I had a daughter at high school—how would *she* feel?
Do you blame me for not getting married?" If friends were around,
he'd mug and respond, "I've been begging this girl to marry me every day for the past two years. She won't have me!" Joe and Jean
each had a fiery personality; their romance would burn hot, then
suddenly cool off. During those chilly interludes, Jean would date
other men and Joe would profess not to care.

That may have been because he was doing the same thing. Joe
dated other women during his early Senate years, before Jean
came into the picture, and did again when they were on the outs.
"To say he was a rough diamond was a misnomer in the sense that
he was never a diamond. He was rough," said John W. Hanes Jr., a
friend who worked for the State Department. "He brought a succession of floozies, usually, out with him. If he didn't, he was making passes at everybody in the house, including my sister." At one
dinner party, Hanes added, Joe showed up with a buxom young
woman and "disappeared upstairs and screwed her on the hostess'
bed . . . He didn't even take the damn counterpane off. The hostess
said she was never going to have him in her house again."

Another factor that kept Jean and Joe apart early on was religion. Jean was raised Presbyterian, but the more Sundays she
spent with Joe, the more she embraced his Catholicism until finally she converted. "Gradually, as I came to understand the Cath-

* The "venison," those who knew said, actually was chain store chuck. Trohan,
Political Animals, 250.
† Liz Brown, Jean's good friend, noted that the guys who were there when Joe
called "would never show up again. Maybe they were afraid of being investigated." Book notes, unprocessed files, MUA.

olic faith and began to see how much his faith meant to him, in a quiet, basic way—like breathing or eating—I saw a new side to Joe," she wrote in "The Joe McCarthy I Knew," her unpublished memoir. "Behind the warm, happy, bubbling personality, behind the kidding and the humor was a serious man, a purposeful man whom God had endowed with an extremely keen, absorbent and discriminating mind and the drive to make right what was wrong."

Jean had it right about Joe's faith. It was heartfelt, but he set the terms, not the church. For years he quietly mailed $50 a month to Catholic missionaries he'd met in the South Pacific. He seldom missed a Sunday service or a chance to confess, but wouldn't be caught dead lighting candles or attending a Holy Name Society breakfast. Friends describe tripping over him in the dark as he knelt to pray; others recall taking him from Sunday mass to a crap game at the Hotel Schroeder that lasted until Monday afternoon; and he refused to travel—even in an elevator—without his money clip bearing the image of Saint Thérèse, the patron of missions. Father Donald Crosby, whose book probed the ties between Joe and his church, concluded that "few Catholic politicians ever made less public display of their religion than did Joe McCarthy." And while Crosby worried that "McCarthy thought that going to Sunday Mass (as well as getting baptized, married, and buried in the church) was all that Catholicism stood for," the author conceded that Joe "observed these functions with a fidelity that would have brought joy to the heart of many a Catholic pastor."

Among Joe's touchstones with his faith were the words of his Marine Corps chaplain, which he recited regularly in the years that followed: "If you young men, regardless of whether you live for four or five hours or whether you may live for forty or fifty years, if you will remember two fundamental truths—two fundamental truths every religious group has been teaching since the beginning of time—you will remember, one: there is a God who is Eternal, two: each of us has a soul which is immortal—then you will do an outstanding job, not only for yourselves, but also for your country."

That earnestness also animated his Pied Piper relationship with children. He wouldn't have one of his own until later in life, but in his younger days scores of kids saw him as their rules-defying uncle. Thirteen-year-old Agnes Buckley cherished eating water-melon with him in the backyard, and remembered Joe giving her a nickel and joking that she should call him when she was nineteen. Peter Voy, whose mother was Mike Eberlein's secretary in the Sha-wano law office, also called him Uncle Joe. "If your dad hadn't been such a good-looking salesman," Voy remembers Joe saying, it might have been Joe he was calling "Dad." All Dirk Van Susteren wanted was a cap pistol when he stopped by McCarthy's Washing-ton office with his dad, Urban. Joe's secretary had one waiting for him, and when he opened the senator's door, Joe was kneeling be-hind his desk with two cap pistols of his own, blazing back.

Senator McCarthy knew the names of elevator operators and guards whom most senators never noticed, insisting they call him Joe, which they did. A Negro woman working in the takeout sec-tion of the Senate cafeteria liked him enough to double the meat in his sandwiches. His Senate frank, which let him mail packages for free, carried the informal "Joe" McCarthy in place of the Joseph R. that had been his trademark. Yet even as he curried an every-man image, increasingly he referred to himself in the smug third person.

He was also palling around with Washington's A-list of political players, most notably FBI director J. Edgar Hoover. "Dear Edgar: I just want to take this opportunity to thank you again for the very fine day that Jeannie [and I] spent with you on Memorial Day. We both enjoyed the day thoroughly, as I am sure you know, and cer-tainly appreciated your thought in inviting us," Joe wrote in June 1949. As if "Edgar" wasn't a friendly enough greeting, the senator crossed that out and handwrote over it "Boss." By then, Hoover had shown how much he cared for this young lawmaker by re-peatedly asking him to Harvey's Restaurant, Washington's power dining hub, and to the Bowie Race Track in Maryland, where they bet on the ponies and watched the races from the director's pri-vate box.* There were official favors, too — offering Joe the cher-ished slot as graduation speaker at the FBI National Academy,† ap-

* McCarthy's secretary knew his code: "Going to Naval Hospital" meant sneak-ing off to the racetrack. Oshinsky, *Conspiracy So Immense*, 56.
† Hoover made clear just how valued that speaking slot was in his invitation let-

pearing alongside him during an interview with a Wisconsin radio station, and instructing the local FBI office to entertain the senator when he was visiting Phoenix. The affection was mutual. Joe called the FBI "the only bureau in Washington that gets the highest praise from everyone," adding that "many of us feel you should have more men in the FBI at this time."

Joe acted as if such relationships were the most natural thing in the world, but he hadn't lost sight of how far he had come. In 1947, at an especially swank cocktail party in the Capitol, the freshman lawmaker stood in the corner with a friend reflecting on the big shots whose hands he'd been shaking: "I wonder what these people would think if they knew I once raised chickens." Whether or not they would have cared about that, some might have been shocked at how, rather than finding a place of his own in Washington, he was camping out college-style in a small room he was renting from his office manager, Ray Kiermas. Underwear was piled up under the bed, and pants were wedged under the mattress in hopes of removing the wrinkles. "Whenever we move to a new home we tell him the address on moving day," said Kiermas. "He comes there that night instead of going to the old place." While Joe didn't mean to be insensitive, he was to Ray and even more to his wife, Dolores. On the eve of one of their moves, he told her he'd invited a few people to dinner, and persisted although she explained that the dishes were packed. That night eighteen journalists turned up. She unpacked, then repacked, everything that was needed. Joe thought nothing of it: "Everyone sat around on crates and had a fine time." Van Susteren compared him to "a stray dog. He'd stay three days at one place, three at another, and four at another. He'd sleep on the couch, on the floor, on the porch — it didn't matter at all to him."

Joe made it back home more regularly than most senators. He no longer had a house in Wisconsin, so he stayed at the Apple-

ter, saying that previous speakers had included the commandant of the Marines and the secretary of the Navy, a Supreme Court justice, and three more senior US senators. Still, McCarthy declined, saying he'd do it if Hoover really wanted him to, but he would prefer to take a rain check. Hoover, in another sign of their strong bond then, readily assented. February 3, 1948, letter from Hoover to McCarthy and February 13, 1948, memo from Hoover to senior staff, pt. 6 of 28, MFBI.

ton Hotel, in the Van Susteren basement, or with his sister Olive Kornely. "The press showed up, and all this entourage of people," remembers Olive's son Kelly. Joe had big hands, the backs of which were carpeted with hair, broad shoulders, and an expression that was "half between a grin and a smile." Kelly also talks fondly of Zeke, the English bulldog Joe won in a poker game, then bequeathed to the Kornelys. With both of Kelly's parents working, Zeke spent his days lounging at the sheriff's office; on weekends he lay in the road, perhaps sensing that cars would give a wide berth to Senator McCarthy's dog; in campaign season he was decked out with McCarthy signs. "When Zeke died," says Kelly, "there was a big obit in the local paper."

The paper ran a much longer obituary, naturally, when Timothy McCarthy died in 1946, just as his son was launching his second run for the Senate. Tim's estate documents show that he was one of Joe's financiers, lending $10,000 just as Joe was gearing up his expensive campaign for judge in 1938, and another $10,000 in 1945, after Joe's first bid to be a senator and before his next one. The McCarthy patriarch didn't have it easy at the end, paying seventy-four visits to the hospital in his last month. Although Tim was seventy-nine, Joe thought he could be saved, and he rushed in a specialist from Milwaukee. He'd felt the same way when his mother died five years earlier, saying an inept physician had killed her. Tim's estate was unusually large for a modest farmer — $21,127.21 ($315,000 in today's dollars), nearly half of which was a promissory note from Joe due to be paid in 1948. Noticeably, the senator was not named an heir, with his father explaining that he'd already helped Joe pay for school and that Joe "has requested that I make no provision for him in my last will."*

Despite his air of rugged virility, Joe's own health was far from 100 percent, as his closely guarded files at Bethesda Naval Hospital make clear. In 1948 alone he was in and out of that hospital for "acute pain" in his left scrotum (a kidney stone that passed), an aching lower back and heels (elevator shoes helped), and gastrointestinal cramps (which temporarily eased). The stomach dis-

---

* The estate documents listed the addresses of his children and grandchildren, with Joe's as Hotel Appleton.

tress, his doctor reported, traced back ten years and "at present it follows each meal and requires [a] teaspoonful of baking soda for relief." He'd had diarrhea for twenty days before checking in to Bethesda in December. He also reported "bleeding gums which become sore at times." Worst of all was the "frequent recurrent chronic" sinusitis. Three operations hadn't cured it but had produced "a mess" of damaged bones and scar tissue, and left him coughing up into handkerchiefs a "thick, purulent discharge" of mucus. Doctors' favorite remedy for whatever ailed him was the still fairly novel wonder drug penicillin, which helped with some things and was worthless for others, and their favorite way to relieve his pain was with high doses of morphine, codeine, Demerol, and other potent narcotics, as was the fashion. He'd stay in the hospital for at least several days and sometimes a week or more.

The record keepers were seldom explicit about Senator McCarthy's mental health, which is not surprising for that era or this celebrity patient. There are, however, clues. One is phrases like "generalized malaise" and "extreme fatigue" that showed up in doctors' memos. There also was a notation, on a file diagnosing him with pneumonia, that he really was sick and that his using the military's medical services was "not misconduct." It was as if someone were questioning whether his frequent hospitalizations were a way of shirking his duty, the same way they appeared to be when he was with the Marines in the South Pacific. Another thing his records establish is how sleep-challenged he was. That was clear not just from what he told his doctors but from the high doses of powerful sedatives like pentobarbital prescribed during his overnights at the hospital.

Loyal Eddy, the Republican activist who bunked with Joe during their travels, saw up close those ailments and the quirks they spawned. Joe had asthma and couldn't stand to have a window open, Eddy said. "He was a nervous wreck, up and down all night. Whenever I shared a room with McCarthy I said goodbye to sleep." The senator's breathing issues help explain why he couldn't stomach smoking or smokers.* Tom Korb recalled visiting him in the

---

* He had a way of dealing with cigar smokers when he was with them in a car. "Hey, let me take a puff of that," he would say. "Maybe I'll get to like it." He'd then

hospital early in 1949, when he was recovering from surgery on his rib cage and back. From then on, he said, Joe had a rightward twitch of his neck and head, and suffered a dull pain that had him perpetually reaching for aspirin.

To the outside world, he still seemed a tough, barrel-chested Irishman, reminding movie fans of Hollywood's Irishman in residence Pat O'Brien. Joe sported snap-brim hats and off-the-rack double-breasted suits in deep blue, though by noontime they usually were wrinkled and stained with sweat. The senator's neckties seldom matched his jackets or his pants, the pockets of which were stuffed with scribbled notes. His nose had a crimp put there by a line drive in a baseball game during his youth. Steak remained his favorite food, "cremated" in a way sure to offend beef lovers. His hands were habitually interlaced, squeezing hard across his stomach, which a reporter who followed him surmised was "to get rid of excess energy. He speaks softly but fast, the words emerging like slugs from a machine gun equipped with a silencer."

His drinking remained a problem, although some friends unconvincingly maintained that it was just an act and that he would nurse a single drink over an evening while letting people think he was a two-fisted carouser. He also was still playing poker, despite efforts by Senator Clinton Anderson of New Mexico to talk him out of it after seeing how reckless he was. He "fared even worse at gin rummy," said Anderson, the former secretary of agriculture whose advice on sugar rationing Joe had scoffed at. "To his credit, however, he showed great determination. He asked the Library of Congress to send him every book on the game. He then phoned Oswald Jacoby, the noted card expert, and asked him to come to Washington to give him lessons. Jacoby declined, but he gave McCarthy the name of a reformed card shark to help him master gin rummy. Before long, a gleeful McCarthy was telling me how he was taking [Senator Robert] Kerr for large amounts of money," Anderson added in his memoir. "I attribute the improvement to his discomfort at being so frequently humiliated by his colleagues . . .

---

fling the cigar out the window. Days later he would send the bereft smoker a box of cigars. Harris, "The Private Life of Senator McCarthy," *American Weekly*.

Periodically, McCarthy would come up to me and say, 'I really got him bloodied last night, Clint,' and to inform me exactly how much he had won from Kerr." Joe won almost enough to retire on during one game of gin rummy in Houston. He thought the stakes were five cents a point when his opponent meant five dollars. When Joe was way ahead, he was asked for one more game, double or nothing; Joe agreed to that, and to doing it again, then to one last time. His foe finally won and said, "Whew — think of that — one game for $300,000." Joe, who presumed he'd been playing for $3,000, was outraged, according to Senator Anderson, who told the story to *Washington Post* publisher Philip Graham, who repeated it to a Milwaukee journalist.

Samuel Shaffer, a *Newsweek* correspondent, saw a different side of Joe, the side that dreaded being alone in the evenings. "Guess who?" the senator would say when he phoned. Shaffer: "Oh, come off it, Joe. What's on your mind?" McCarthy: "I'm lonely. If you and your wife aren't busy, I'd like to come over and watch some wrestling matches on your television set." Shaffer, unenthusiastically: "You can watch wrestling in the den. I'll shut the door, if you won't mind." The senator would drop by, the reporter added, and "I'd set him up with a few beers or scotches, and he did just what he said he wanted to do: watch those fixed wrestling matches which used to pollute the airwaves in the early days of television."

The more famous Joe become, the more old friends and colleagues were asked to account for him. Andrew Parnell, a lawyer and judge who'd known Joe going back to Waupaca and Shawano, was flummoxed. You can't explain it, Parnell said, you can simply describe it.

Relegated to the status of backbencher less than halfway through his first term, Joe thirsted for a new cause that could salvage his career. The one he picked — as apostle for the Nazi perpetrators of the bloodiest slaughter of American soldiers during World War II — would, more than anything he had done previously, define him for fellow senators and anyone else paying attention.

The event that triggered this drama began just after midday on December 17, 1944, in the ice-encrusted fields on the Belgian side of the German border near the medieval city of Malmedy. America and Great Britain had the Wehrmacht in a tightening vise, but Hitler had plotted an audacious counteroffensive in which his troops would crash through enemy lines, capture the port of Antwerp, and isolate American and British armies. The Führer had a special role in mind for his elite Waffen SS, who idolized Genghis Khan, lived by a code of silence, and were under orders to totally annihilate the enemy.* That frigid day outside Malmedy, a battle group of the First SS Panzer Division Bodyguard Adolf Hitler overwhelmed a contingent of lightly armed US troops. It was one of the earliest encounters of the costliest of campaigns known as the Battle of the Bulge, and by mid-afternoon the GIs' only option was to raise their white flags. After accepting their surrender, the Nazis mowed down most of the Americans with machine guns, crushed the skulls of others with their rifle butts, and burned out those who sought refuge in a nearby café. Earlier that day, outside the nearby town of Honsfeld, Johnnie Stegle was randomly selected from a line of captives by an SS soldier who summoned his best English to yell, "Hey you!" before raising a revolver to the American corporal's forehead, killing him instantly. By day's end, the toll exceeded one hundred and fifty, with eighty-four murdered at the deadliest of those encounters: the ill-famed Malmedy Massacre.

The stories of Stegle and the others might never have been told if everyone had perished, but fifty Americans played dead or overcame their wounds and were later able to recount the fate of their executed compatriots. The memory of the massacre galvanized Allied troops in the last months of the war, after which the Americans tracked down seventy-five of the culprits, from generals to rank and file. Their trial that spring and summer of 1946, in the former concentration camp in Dachau, Germany, was the most intensely followed of the era. It assembled into one case twelve alleged war crimes committed over the course of a month, in the same general area, resulting in the deaths of 350 unarmed American POWs and a hundred Belgian civilians. All but one of the de-

---

* This SS regiment's nickname—Blowtorch Battalion—told its story. It had burned two villages, killing all their inhabitants.

fendants were pronounced guilty, with forty-three condemned to death and twenty-two to life in prison.*

The Allied narrative saw Malmedy as a metaphor for Nazi heinousness and American justice. The frozen corpses of the slaughtered had been retrieved and carefully autopsied. Intrepid investigators gathered evidence and conducted in-depth interviews of survivors from both sides. Prosecutors laid out a vivid portrait not just of this act of barbarity but of the modus operandi of the SS, the most savage of Hitler's war makers. The nobility and burden of the enterprise would be captured in the popular 1961 film *Judgment at Nuremberg*, one of whose stars was the same Marlene Dietrich whose USO tour had been scheduled to take her to Honsfeld the day after the GIs were massacred there.

An alternative telling of the story arose during and after the proceedings, however, that made it the most controversial war crimes trial in US history. This new version flipped the script and cast as malefactors the Army investigators, prosecution team, and military tribunal. It alleged that the German prisoners had been cruelly tortured—interrogators were said to have kicked their testicles and wedged burning matches under their fingernails—and that confessions were compromised. The US side was out for vengeance, this theory held, which shouldn't have been surprising, given that some of the investigators were Jews. Yes, war was brutal, but any atrocities committed in the frozen forest of the Ardennes that afternoon in 1944 should be laid at the feet of the generals who issued the orders, not the troops who followed them. Yes, America had won the war, and it was imposing a classic victor's justice. The primary spinners of this replacement narrative were the chief defense attorney, the convicted perpetrators and their ex-Nazi supporters, US peace activists, American and German journalists, and the junior senator from Wisconsin.

Three years after the verdicts, the Army appointed a three-man commission to try to sort out the conflicting renditions. That spawned more lurid news accounts of alleged coercion of testimony and mistreatment of inmates, which led the Army to name

---

* Charges were dismissed against Marcel Boltz when it was learned he was a French citizen. He was returned to France, then released.

yet another review panel. With political pressure building, the Senate convened a special investigatory subcommittee chaired by Republican Raymond Baldwin of Connecticut, with two Democratic members, Estes Kefauver of Tennessee and Lester Hunt of Wyoming.* Senator McCarthy, who'd been intensely interested from the start, was allowed to sit in as an observer, a role that he would exploit and that the committee would rue.

Joe's interest in Malmedy grew out of an earlier and broader fear that the Germans were being mistreated in the wake of the war. It was an unusual posture for a returning GI, although he'd fought only the Japanese, never the Nazis, and was himself one-quarter German. During his 1946 Senate bid, he'd charged that of the 100,000 Germans captured at Stalingrad, "over 40,000 have died from ill treatment and lack of food." He was equally harsh in condemning the French, saying that "over 100,000" former German soldiers "are today dying in France from starvation and mistreatment." And while it was a step too far for many to think that the US armed services might take revenge on their former enemy, Joe had made clear in both his wartime diary and his 1946 campaign how little use he had for America's military brass. He in fact understated the case regarding the Russians, overstated it for France, and never made any specific charges of abuse or reprisal by Americans. But Jean said his intent throughout was noble. "Joe felt this was a brand of 'justice' that could be turned against us in the future," she wrote in her memoir, which gave voice to sensibilities he couldn't or wouldn't share publicly. "This was not a popular opinion to hold." It was his willingness to stake out an unpopular stand like that, Jean added, that made her fall for Joe.

With Joe, however, it never was that simple, and domestic pol-

---

* The subcommittee makeup was unusual in that a Republican was named chairman even though the Democrats controlled the Senate. McCarthy would say that was part of a setup to ensure a friend of the Army was in charge. But historian Steven Remy, who pored through the hearings transcripts, German and American press coverage, committee staff papers, and counterintelligence reports, concludes that Baldwin "was a principled moderate who respected evidence and the truth and stood up to a willfully ignorant bully [Joe McCarthy] in his own party." As for whether the hearings were fair, Remy answers with "an unqualified yes." Remy email to author.

itics also factored in. People with Germanic roots held sway in forty-one of seventy-two Wisconsin counties, and while it's unfair to assume they'd have supported the perpetrators of the massacre, there was widespread concern that all Nazi soldiers not be tainted as butchers. John Riedl, managing editor of the *Appleton Post-Crescent,* told friends that he was the one who'd talked Joe into attacking the Malmedy prosecutors, convincing him that German American farmers would thank him. But Joe, who came from that farm country, didn't need coaxing.

A more troubling theory popular with his critics is that McCarthy's actions regarding Malmedy were driven by anti-Semitism. They found plenty of grist for their mill in Joe's own words. Les Chudakoff, his lawyer, was "a hebe." A Jewish businessman Joe suspected of cheating him was "a little sheeny," and, years later, he repeatedly referred to a Jewish staffer he disdained as "useless, no good, just a miserable little Jew."* Then there was the backing McCarthy got from notorious Jew-haters like radio commentator Upton Close and America First Party founder Gerald L. K. Smith, and the backing he gave fascist activist William Dudley Pelley.† Joe liked to shock friends by pulling out his copy of Hitler's *Mein Kampf,* calling it inspirational or saying, "That's the way to

---

* It was common if not excusable to use anti-Semitic expressions like "sheeny" and "Finklestein" when Joe was growing up in Appleton, said Edwin Bayley, a reporter at the *Milwaukee Journal* who also was raised there and wrote a hard-hitting book on Joe's relationship with the press. Later, similar slurs were common among Joe's closest friends. Tom Korb said that two of Joe's Jewish staffers "were certainly as kike as could be." One of those he was referring to, Roy Cohn, himself referred to media magnate S. I. Newhouse as "Jewhouse." Reeves interviews with Edwin Bayley, July 7, 1977, and Korb; and Sherrill, "King Cohn," *The Nation.*

† While publicly denying any association with the likes of Close, Joe's private files show him retracting that denial. "A favorite smear, of course, is to claim that a man is anti-Semitic," he wrote the radio commentator. "I am sure you will understand that it would be entirely beyond my task to make an investigation of you or any other commentator to determine whether or not the charges against you were true or merely a typical smear. Suffice to say—I know nothing about you which I would call anti-Semitic." Letter from Joe to Close, August 8, 1950, series 14, MUA.

As for Pelley, founder of the right-wing Silver Shirts, Joe was one of six senators to support parole for the seditionist, who'd been sentenced to fifteen years. *Jewish Life,* May 1950.

do it." Most of that was ambiguous enough to explain away, but now, those looking for evidence of an anti-Jewish bent had it in spades. Why else would this one senator among ninety-six crusade to save the worst of Hitler's shock troopers? Why single out the German-born Jewish investigators who, he said, "intensely hate the German people as a race" and had formed what amounted to a "vengeance team?"*

The truth, those who knew him say, is that Joe didn't really have it in for Jews. He had too many Jewish friends and staffers to make it plausible that he did, and he boosted Israel while decrying Soviet repression of Jews. Notorious xenophobe Agnes Waters went so far as to accuse the senator of being a "crypto Jew" and saying McCarthy was a pseudonym used to disguise his Jewish surname. He certainly knew how to hate, but he wasn't that kind of bigot. He simply lacked the filter to keep his language civil or to screen out the misanthropes among his enablers. Urban Van Susteren was willing to call out McCarthy when he thought he was wrong, including with his use of the expression "hebe," but he insisted that his friend found anti-Semitism abhorrent.

Whatever drew him to the Malmedy drama, once he got involved he convinced himself that what he was saying was not just right but righteous. He was standing up not for Nazi assassins but against retributive justice. The fuel for his fury came in packets of letters airmailed or hand-delivered from a parish priest, an ex-Nazi lawyer, and others in the American zone of a divided Germany, along with friends like Milwaukee industrialist Walter Harnischfager. They laid out the allegations of abuse and insisted the prisoners get clemency. Joe bought the claims, which also were sent to—and generally ignored by—other members of Congress. He championed the proposed pardons. And he wasn't about to take a back seat as he cross-examined witnesses and dominated the proceedings that he was supposed to be observing in

---

* Later in the hearings Joe did a blatant about-face: "We have often heard the claim made which I have always felt there was no foundation for" that "the non-Aryans who suffered persecution in Germany and were forced to leave Germany have carried a feeling of vengeance toward the whole German race." US Senate, Subcommittee of the Committee on Armed Services, Malmedy Massacre Investigation, 608.

the spring of 1949. One measure of that sway was that McCarthy's name turned up in the hearings transcripts 3,586 times, compared to 3,504 for Chairman Baldwin, 619 for Senator Hunt, and 331 for Senator Kefauver.

While he preferred to be the one asking questions, he was subjected to his own grilling by military lawyers and investigators as well as subcommittee senators. How could he be so sure about the *Progressive* magazine's allegations of crippling abuse when the article's author said that he hadn't written it and that much of it was exaggerated? What about McCarthy's other "sources," who, on the stand, were recanting their tales of tortured prisoners and biased investigators? It quickly became clear how ill-prepared the Wisconsin senator was, in contrast to the thoughtful experts he was challenging. His case in tatters, Joe turned without missing a beat to what would become his default position whenever he was cornered: his adversaries were two-faced, and a lie detector could prove it.

"I think you are lying," he told Lieutenant William Perl, the chief Malmedy investigator and a Zionist who credibly claimed to have rescued forty thousand European Jews during the war. "I do not think you can fool the lie detector. You may be able to fool us." Perl, a psychologist as well as an attorney, had already made clear he wasn't intimidated by McCarthy or the polygraph, agreeing to subject himself to the test but wondering, "Why [have] a trial at all? Get the guys, and put the lie detector on them. 'Did you kill this man?' The lie detector says 'Yes.' Go to the scaffold. If it says, 'No'; back to Bavaria."

Joe knew the subcommittee would say no to his lie detector demand because members rightfully doubted the machine's accuracy and because fairness would dictate giving the test not just to the interrogators but to the SS inmates, who were highly unlikely to accept. His polygraph bluff gave McCarthy an excuse to storm out of the proceedings. "I feel that the investigation has degenerated to such a shameful farce that I can no longer take part therein and I am today requesting the expenditures subcommittee chairman to relieve me of the duty to continue," he told Senator Baldwin and the others. The truth is that neither the Expenditures Subcommittee nor anyone else in Congress had ever pushed him to sit in on the Malmedy proceedings or was fazed that he was quitting. But the always eager press did care, and so, even before he addressed his fellow senators, he was ready with a news release blasting his colleagues. "I accuse the subcommittee of being afraid of the facts," he said. "I accuse it of attempting to whitewash a shameful episode in the history of our glorious armed forces."

Baldwin, the former three-term governor of Connecticut who had been talked into serving as chairman, responded with the understatement that was characteristic of him and a contrast to his Badger State colleague: "The chairman regrets that the junior Senator from Wisconsin, Mr. McCarthy, has lost his temper and with it, the sound impartial judgment which should be exercised in this matter." Baldwin, who would later serve as chief justice of Connecticut's Supreme Court of Errors, might also have noted the irony that one of the Senate's and the nation's most outrageous liars would become a champion of the lie detector.

This tail gunner, however, was irrepressible. When the subcommittee wrapped up its Washington hearings, it decided to see for itself the scene of the murders and the men accused of them, which was unusual and impressed everyone but Joe. He said America's treatment of the Malmedy prisoners made it "guilty of adopting many of the very same tactics of which we accuse Hitler and Stalin." He condemned the Army for "brutalitarianism." And he challenged the integrity of two of the three members of the Malmedy subcommittee, Baldwin and Kefauver, saying they had been professionally associated with lawyers they were investigating. His colleagues were becoming used to this brash freshman's grandstanding but not to his getting this personal. The full Armed Services Committee took an unorthodox action of its own, unanimously approving a vote of confidence in Baldwin. We "take this unusual step," they explained, "because of the most unusual, unfair, and utterly undeserved comments" made by McCarthy. Signing the measure were such lions of the chamber as Lyndon Johnson, Harry F. Byrd, William F. Knowland, and Styles Bridges, Joe's future Senate soul mate. Everyone but Joe got the point.

The subcommittee, meanwhile, doggedly pursued its mission. It had interviewed 108 witnesses, from the SS perpetrators and their defense team to investigators, prosecutors, judges, religious leaders, and others on all sides. Everyone Joe had asked it to talk to it did, and it had extended him the unusual courtesy of letting a nonmember cross-examine witnesses. Prisoners were checked out by Public Health Service doctors and dentists, looking for any signs of abuse. And in its final report, the subcommittee criticized the military on matters ranging from the mock trials it used with a fraction of the prisoners to elicit confessions or soften up suspects ("a grave mistake") to the use of mass trials that lumped officers together with subordinates ("they should be indicted and tried separately"). It was even more plainspoken in its primary conclusions: There was little if any beating, kicking, or other brutalization of prisoners. They'd been given plenty of food, water, and medical attention. Their trials were fair. And, most important in explaining why such charges had been raised, then re-raised, the subcommittee said they had sprung from a coordinated campaign of misinformation involving ex-Nazis and possibly Communists in Germany, along with an "extreme" pacifist organization in America.

That Senate verdict notwithstanding, the military was already moving to defuse the public controversies in West Germany and the United States. Some of the death sentences of the SS murderers had been commuted and the rest would be. By the late 1950s, all the prisoners would be freed. One of the last to walk out of prison, in December 1956, was *Obersturmbannführer* Joachim Peiper, commander and namesake of the SS unit that mowed down the surrendering GIs in the fields near Malmedy.*

The narrative that America had reason to apologize for its handling of those murderers has persisted for three quarters of a century, thanks in part to the legitimacy conferred on it by the most outspoken member of the US Senate. Some McCarthy defenders would go so far as to view Malmedy as a precursor to US mistreatment of Iraq War detainees half a century later, and to see the Abu Ghraib whistleblowers as following in Joe's shadow. A recent book-length treatment of the Malmedy misdirection, drawing on newly declassified documents, at last sets things straight. "Former National Socialists and their apologists have shaped our knowledge

---

* Peiper was murdered in France twenty years later, most likely by former members of the French Resistance.

of the Nazi dictatorship, the war, and the Holocaust," writes European history scholar Steven Remy. "That its construction came at the cost of a more substantial measure of justice for Nazi Germany's victims should be acknowledged as one of the darker legacies of World War II and the Cold War." Colonel Burton Ellis, the chief Malmedy prosecutor and one of McCarthy's favorite targets, was equally incensed at the distortions of history when he looked back three decades after the hearings: "It beats the hell out of me why everyone tries so hard to show that the prosecution[s] were insidious, underhanded, unethical, immoral and God knows what monsters, that unfairly convicted a group of whiskerless Sunday school boys."

Joe's miscasting of the SS prisoners as the aggrieved, and the US military as the aggressor, had practical consequences. Germany's left-wing press and the Anglo-American right echoed his words and used them to inflame readers against the US military occupiers. McCarthy was also widely quoted by amnesty advocates and the mainstream press in West Germany, which considered him a hero and a crusader for the truth. "I have seen persons bent on murdering me, persons who murdered my companions, defended by a United States senator," Virgil P. Lary Jr., a field artillery lieutenant who escaped the massacre by pretending to be dead, told reporters in 1951. "I charge that this action of Sen. McCarthy's became the basis for the Communist propaganda in western Germany, designed to discredit the American armed forces and American justice."

But Malmedy was just a warm-up act. Even as Joe's behavior surrounding the massacre was muddying the historic record, it illuminated the kind of scorched-earth senator he would become. Falling for conspiracies and failing to vet propaganda would continue to be flaws, and he was always game to ratchet up the charges he was spoon-fed. He fine-tuned his skills at dishing to the press, instinctively grasping its hunger for fire-eating phraseology like "whitewash" (it appeared twelve times in the record under Joe's name), "moron" or "moronic" (four times), and "lie detector" (seventy-four times by or in response to him). He also sensed that making his SS "clients" younger made them more sympathetic, so while the youngest were eighteen, McCarthy went from referring to them as "18 and 19" to "a 15- or 16- or 17- or 18-year old boy." Discrediting one of his accusations might send him into momentary retreat, but he'd soon resurrect the indictment, then claim vindication when there was none. His favorite targets were Democrats, but Senator Baldwin learned that Republicans weren't immune and that Joe didn't care about the Senate's previously inviolable rules of decorum. The Connecticut lawmaker had decided before the Malmedy hearings to resign his Senate seat, but the verbal brutalitarianism he suffered at McCarthy's hands made him happier to go and convinced his biographer that he was "the first victim of 'McCarthyism.'" That was a mantle many would claim, from Edgar Werner to Robert La Follette and Howard McMurray.*

The Malmedy hearings were the first time *New Yorker* columnist Richard Rovere encountered McCarthy, and he was riveted enough that ten years later he would write a book on the senator. Joe offered to show the writer the documents that had convinced him Baldwin and others were covering up the truth about abuse of the SS inmates. "I read rapidly through what he gave me. Then I read it a second time, more carefully. When I'd finished the second reading, I was certain that the Senator had selected the wrong document," Rovere recalled. "He kept handing papers across the desk to me . . . None of them seemed to advance his argument by very much, but then he was no longer claiming very much for them . . . I read here and there in the Army files, and told McCarthy that, perhaps because of my ignorance, I was unable to see any holes in the Army's case. 'Of course you don't,' he said. 'Naturally, they're going to make out the best case they can for themselves. You wouldn't expect them to spill the beans in their own records, would you?'" Asked if he wished to see more records, Rovere said, "I thought I'd skip them. I thanked the Senator for his courtesy and left.

"I was not aware then of having been switched, conned, and double-shuffled by one of the masters."

---

* With so many claiming to have been Joe's first casualty, Jean would turn it into a joke, saying her falling for his nonstop courting made it clear: "I was the first victim of McCarthyism." Book notes, unprocessed files, MUA.

3

AN ISM IS BORN

THE CAUSE THAT WOULD SALVAGE his political career and ignite a home front holy war came to Joe McCarthy like a bolt of lightning. He was on his way to that dreaded Republican sacrament, the Lincoln Day Dinner, before a hotel ballroom packed with moneyed matrons and mine operators, in a Democratic stronghold that McCarthy aides called Wheeling, West-by-God Virginia.* But Democrat or Republican, Wheeling, Waco, or Walla Walla, America was in a tizzy that winter of 1950. Six months earlier, US spy planes had confirmed that Russia, too, had an atomic bomb. Two months after that, Mao Tse-tung and his troops remade Nationalist China into Red China. A month before Joe took to the podium in West Virginia, accused Soviet spy Alger Hiss was convicted of perjury; nine days before, President Truman defied his advisers and announced he'd build the H-bomb; and a week before, officers from Scotland Yard arrested atomic espionage agent Klaus Fuchs. The morning of his Wheeling speech, part five of a ten-day series in the *Chicago Daily Tribune* laid out the threat from the godless, ruthless Soviet empire and, creepier still, from pinkos lurking behind every pillar in our own out-of-touch State Department. With things so scary that school kids would soon be instructed how to duck under their desks to escape a nuclear blast, there had to be somebody to

---

* The dinner is an annual celebration of the birth of Abraham Lincoln, the first Republican president, and is a key fundraising tool for state and county parties, generally featuring a speech by a GOP luminary.

blame. Joe arguably was less well versed in foreign policy and Russian statecraft than anyone in the US Senate in 1950. But nobody was better at reading America's pent-up fears and feeding them.

"While I cannot take the time to name all the men in the State Department who have been named as active members of the Communist Party and members of a spy ring," Joe told his Lincoln Dinner audience that night of February 9, "I have here in my hand a list of 205 . . . a list of names that were made known to the Secretary of State as being members of the Communist Party and who nevertheless are still working and shaping policy in the State Department." It wasn't the first occasion where this senator had whipped up the specter of an enemy within, nor was he the first to try. But this time he grasped something earlier treason-shouters hadn't: that counting and naming the actual traitors had a frontier justice allure. No matter that the paper he was clutching didn't justify his numbers or fill in his list. Nor that he'd waited until the last minute to decide which speech in his briefcase to deliver, the Red-baiting barnburner or a snoozer on national housing policy. When fellow lawmakers denounced his anti-Communist crusade as a hoax and him as a charlatan, he brazenly doubled down on the broadsides. Abe Lincoln was surely turning somersaults in his tomb, but Joe McCarthy had the issue he needed to snatch the limelight he craved.

Or did he? That wasn't entirely clear the morning after his Wheeling fusillade, when the only paper that reacted was the one in Wheeling, which splayed its story across page one under the headline "M'Carthy Charges Reds Holding US Offices."

But Joe was just getting going, and the press caught up fast. That afternoon, another thirty-three papers ran in their Friday editions a short wire service story laying out McCarthy's claims. And that weekend the upstart senator had four more speeches to deliver, each an opportunity for an explosive escalation. At the Denver airport, he bade Secretary of State Dean Acheson to phone him for his list of the department's "bad risks." He'd have shared it right there with them, he told the assembled journalists, but unfortunately he'd left it in his bag on the plane. In Salt Lake City he withdrew his offer to newsmen and added a caveat for Acheson: before he could see Joe's names, the secretary must "show his sincerity" by giving Congress any information he had on the "communistic activities" of department officials. Finally in Reno, two days after his Wheeling blast, Joe wired the White House, urging Harry Truman to intervene personally and warning that "FAILURE ON YOUR PART WILL LABEL THE DEMOCRATIC PARTY OF BEING THE BED-FELLOW OF INTER-NATIONAL COMMUNISM."

Instead of letting it go or passing it on to the FBI, the pugnacious president penned a hot-blooded response: "This is the first time in my experience, and I was ten years in the Senate, that I ever heard of a Senator trying to discredit his own Government before the world . . . I am very sure that the people of Wisconsin are extremely sorry that they are represented by a person who has as little sense of responsibility as you have." While that note was never sent, the State Department showed no such restraint. A spokesman, taking the senator's bait, smugly told reporters that his agency "knows of no Communist party members" in its ranks. "If we find any they will be summarily dismissed." A simple denial, but it legitimized Joe's bomb-throwing and, in an era when newspapers defined the news, it helped drive 355 more stories the next week, everywhere from Boston to Butte.

Journalists' heads were spinning as they tried to keep track of what the Wisconsin Republican had been saying during his whirlwind tour. Was it 205 spies at the State Department, as Joe was reported to have said in Wheeling, or fifty-seven, as he went on to say in Denver, Salt Lake City, and Reno? And had he ever really said 205? He denied it, attributing the confusion to scribes following the early typed version of his speech rather than what he had hand-edited and ad-libbed. There was conflicting evidence from journalists and others who were there, and some of their stories morphed over time. So did Joe's, depending on whom he was addressing and whether he was under oath. Sometimes it was fifty-seven, other times 205, and, at least twice, 207. WWVA, the local Wheeling radio station, broadcast the speech, then erased its tape the way it always did. The Marquette archives might have settled the mystery but instead only deepen it: one archived version of the "enemy within" speech shows a typed "205" crossed out, with "57" handwritten in the way Joe said he had done; another copy may suggest a bid to rewrite history with "57" (along with other revisions) typed free of edits, as if that was what he'd meant to say from the start; a third version has some but not all changes typed in. All that is sure is his uncertainty.

Joe confused matters further by constantly changing his definition of the traitors he had allegedly uncovered among the striped-pants, Ivy League–pedigreed diplomatic corps. In Wheeling, his list included "members of the Communist Party." In Denver it was "bad risks." By the time he got to Salt Lake City, his tally had shrunk from 205 to fifty-seven, but all of those were pinned with the more damning label of "card-carrying members of the Communist Party." His flipping and flopping was aided by the fact that the intrepid reporters covering him, like Frank Desmond, who wrote that inaugural story for the Wheeling paper, didn't have the background in foreign affairs or the long experience with McCarthy's fact stretching that Capitol Hill correspondents did. Had they — and had they insisted on seeing the letter he was waving that first night — the story might have ended there. It was a perk of the backwater, and press savant that he was, Joe would cash in on it repeatedly by leaking his most ruinous, least substantiated charges as far away from Washington as possible.

The truth was that members of the Communist Party USA hadn't carried membership cards in years, and the last thing any streetwise spy would do was to bear an ID or affiliate with a party that would blow his cover. The muddling over counts and definitions was a calculated distraction. Joe didn't have the names he claimed. He had no numbers that meant anything. If there were undercover agents in the State Department, Senator McCarthy didn't know who they were or how to find out. At this early stage his behavior was not just a ploy to misdirect his audiences but a case of his own confusion, and it was inevitable given the ham-handed way his speech had been assembled.

Who actually wrote the speech that launched McCarthyism? The senator intended that winter of 1949–50 to hire as his speechwriter Jim Walters, author of many stories at the conservative *Washington Times-Herald* purporting to expose hidden Communists, but he mistakenly signed up another journalist at the paper,

George Waters. Waters was delighted but incapable, so he enlisted help from two veteran journalists, Ed Nellor and Willard Edwards. Edwards had written more on the topic than any other journalist in the nation and offered his clippings, while Nellor drafted the bulk of the speech. The result was a clip job — partly cribbed from Congressman Richard Nixon's recent speech to the House attacking Alger Hiss, with paragraphs borrowed from an Edwards newspaper story, and some recycled from speeches by Joe himself. While the term "Cold War" had already been in the national lexicon for three years, seldom had a national leader been as clarion clear that America was losing that war not because it wasn't the strongest nation on earth, but because of Judases in its midst. "Today we can almost physically hear the mutterings and rumblings of an invigorated God of War. You can see it, feel it and hear it all the way from the hills of Indochina, from the shores of Formosa, right over into the very heart of Europe itself," McCarthy told the 275 members and guests of Wheeling's Ohio County Women's Republican Club. "The one encouraging thing is that the 'mad moment' has not yet arrived for the firing of the gun or the exploding of the bomb which will set civilization about the final task of destroying itself . . . The reason why we find ourselves in a position of impotency is not because our only powerful potential enemy has sent men to invade our shores . . . but rather because of the traitorous actions of those who have been treated so well by this nation."

The address was the most consequential of McCarthy's life and era, and one of the most carefully parsed in political history. Yet the only line anyone remembers — counting the infiltrators at the State Department — was buried in the middle. It was an afterthought that, even as he was delivering it, Joe realized had to be the centerpiece. The number 205 came from a three-and-a-half-year-old letter from then Secretary of State James Byrnes, who said that his screenings had turned up damaging information on 285 employees, but that only seventy-nine had been terminated. For Joe and his speechwriters, that left a simple matter of subtraction, with no consideration of how many had been fired in the intervening years, or who was a Communist as opposed to a fascist, felon, homosexual, or other category the department deemed untrustworthy. And the McCarthy gang couldn't even get the computation right, making famous the figure of 205 when it should have been 206.

The genesis of fifty-seven, Joe's favored number, was equally sloppy. In mid-1947 a House Appropriations subcommittee started poring through State Department files, looking for security risks among applicants as well as employees. It cast its net widely and problematically — looking for everything from whites befriending Negroes to State Department workers playing bridge with their counterparts at the Soviet embassy — and found 108 suspicious cases, of whom fifty-seven were employed as of March 1948. Joe was leaked a copy of this so-called Lee List — named for Robert E. Lee, the ex-FBI agent who led the investigation — and he changed its meaning to suit his purposes that Lincoln's Birthday weekend in 1950. The employees from 1948 became employees "at present," without anyone checking to see whether they still were working there. Possibly disloyal staffers had been randomly elevated to confirmed Communists. The senator also neglected to mention evidence that might prove him wrong, in this case that the Appropriations subcommittee believed that the State Department had the situation in hand, or that the FBI had probed and cleared more than half of the fifty-seven while the rest were being reviewed.* As for the names he said he had in his hand that night in Wheeling, there were none in the Byrnes letter or the Lee List.†

He all but confessed that he'd been winging it when he met with a pair of reporters in Reno the weekend after Wheeling.

---

* A note in the Marquette archives — apparently from Lee himself, written sometime after the Wheeling speech — cautioned that "it is important to remember that this is *not* a list of 108 Communists, fellow travelers or even Security Risks. Rather it is a series of illustrations of deficiencies in the Department of State that were referred to in the substantive report . . . As a matter of fact some of these individuals are listed to show that they are good loyal Americans qualified for employment but were *not* employed while others of a questionable nature were . . . Likewise it must be remembered that the information was as it appeared as of the date of examination of the files. Thus it is conceivable that subsequent information proved the original data in error." Lee Report File, series 14, MUA.

† Joe told the *Milwaukee Journal*'s Harry Pease — presumably in jest — that the number fifty-seven came from the bottle of Heinz 57 ketchup at his speakers' table. Willard Edwards says it probably came from Edwards's articles. Wells, *The Milwaukee Journal*, 369–70; and Gold, "McCarthy Without Paranoia," *The Washingtonian*.

Frank McCulloch of the *Reno Gazette* and Edward Olsen of the Associated Press left Joe's Saturday evening speech in awe of how he'd worked the crowd with incriminating innuendo that stopped just shy of calumny. Afterward they invited the supersonic senator to unwind with them at the rooftop bar of Reno's most elegant hotel, the Mapes. Between bourbon and waters, the journalists pressed for facts. Did he really know about fifty-seven party members, and were they traitors? "I'm not saying they're Communists," McCarthy hedged. Why, the Wisconsin lawmaker wanted to know, couldn't these reporters understand him when his audience clearly had? They weren't cowed: Could Joe produce the list, or was this another bluff? Sure, he said, digging into his pocket but coming up empty, the way he had at the Denver airport. "At the end he was screaming at us that one of us had stolen his list of Communists," Olsen remembered years later. "He lost his list," McCulloch added, "between his eighth and ninth bourbons." Hotel owner Charlie Mapes warned that unless the three quieted down, they'd have to go. "The man just talked circles," Olsen added. "Everything was by inference, allusion, never a concrete statement of fact." Nearly seventy years on, McCulloch recalls Joe drunkenly conceding, "Hell, there ain't no list."

The senator had a more sober lunch at the popular Moy Toy's Chinese restaurant in Milwaukee the next Saturday with a trio of journalists from the *Milwaukee Journal*. He'd just completed his dizzying circuit from Wheeling to Denver, Salt Lake City, Reno, Las Vegas, Los Angeles, and Huron, South Dakota, and the home state reporters were even more insistent on getting the facts straight than their colleagues in Nevada. "The three of us used everything but the third degree in trying to get some hard evidence," recalled editorial writer Paul Ringler. "We cajoled, we pleaded, we insulted. Finally I said, 'Joe, I don't believe you've got a goddamn thing to prove the things you've been saying. It's all a lot of political hogwash.'" Pounding the table, McCarthy shot back, "Listen, you bastards. I'm not going to tell you anything. I just want you to know I've got a pailful of shit and I'm going to use it where it does me the most good."

It wasn't only that cavalier willingness to lob grenades — or ma-

nure — that made McCarthy "odd," said Clinton Anderson, the former agriculture secretary and by now a Democratic senator from
New Mexico. It was that "he treated his own action as if it were
nothing more than boyish mischief." Willard Edwards, author of
the *Chicago Daily Tribune*'s ten-parter on the Red menace, agreed:
"Senator McCarthy was irresponsible in the way that an over-
grown boy is careless when his size belies his years. In some respects he never grew up." Jean Kerr, not surprisingly, saw Joe differently — as a patriot, not a panderer, willing to stand up not just
to Communists in government but to a sneering press corps and
skeptical friends. "I drove him to the National Airport" for the trip
to Wheeling, she wrote in her memoir. "On our way, as we passed
the Jefferson Memorial, he said to me, 'Now don't be upset when
you read the papers after this. I'll probably be smeared from hell to
breakfast.' I did not know what he meant. But I soon found out."
Upon his return, Jean added, "he had not been back in Washington an hour before one of his closest friends started dressing him
down. 'What's going on McCarthy[?] I don't get it. You're smarter
than that. Why? You've ruined yourself politically. I suppose you
knew that. Why? Why did you do it?' It was true. Joe had invited
political trouble."

Defiant though he was, Joe himself realized that while he
might get away with vague hyperbole in his initial accusations, he
would eventually have to produce actual numbers and names. So
he tapped old friends and new, starting the week after Wheeling.
"He called me shortly after he returned to Washington from Salt
Lake City to ask whether, as a result of my work on the [Alger]
Hiss case, I had any files on communists in the State Department,"
recalled California congressman Richard Nixon, who, unlike Joe,
had come to Washington in 1946 with real anti-Communist bona
fides. "I told him he was welcome to look through whatever files
I had. But I urged that he be especially careful about facts . . . He
thanked me warmly for my advice and said I had made an important point. As the months went by, however, he continued to strike
out indiscriminately."

Congressional investigator Lee knew even more about Communists in and out of the government, and in the days after Wheeling,

he too was summoned by McCarthy. The investigator was shocked when Joe asked, "Who the hell is Earl Browder?" (Browder ran the Communist Party USA from 1930 to 1945 and remained its best-known adherent.) "Joe simply got carried away," said Lee, who liked the senator. "You couldn't control him."

The press was essential to McCarthy, not just in amplifying what he said but in quietly supplying him with facts. And no media conglomerate would do that more than Hearst. "Joe gave us a call not too long after the speech," said the senator's pal William Randolph Hearst Jr., "and you know what — he didn't have a damn thing on that list. Nothing. He said, 'My God, I'm in a jam . . . I shot my mouth off. So what am I gonna do now?' Well, I guess we fixed him up with a few good reporters." His search for "fresh stuff" and "something sensational" even took him to his soon-to-be nemesis Jack Anderson. McCarthy "had 'hit the jackpot,' he said, and had gotten hold of 'one hell of an issue,'" Anderson wrote later. "But he needed all the help he could get in building up his files on Communist infiltrators. 'You guys must have leads that would help me,' he said. He was aware that spy stories, like organized-crime stories and Ku Klux Klan stories, were a speciality of ours."

Joe's most important call was to Washington's best source on spies: the FBI. Director J. Edgar Hoover had his staff help his friend gather any dirt it could, which turned out to be a lifeline for this first-term senator whose party was out of power, who held no powerful committee postings, and who was a pariah to the few senators who noticed him. But the savvy FBI boss also gave Joe what a Hoover aide called "unshirted hell" for his inventions, knowing they could compromise the bureau's own search for Commies. The agent who would become the FBI's head of domestic intelligence was skeptical from the get-go. "We gave McCarthy all we had, but all we had were fragments," said William C. Sullivan. "We didn't have enough evidence to show there was a single Communist in the State Department, let alone fifty-seven cases." McCarthy, Sullivan added, "did grave damage to national security in the sense that reflective men said if this is anti-Communism I want none of it."

What mattered in the end wasn't whether Washington insid-

ers or professional anti-Communists swallowed Joe's names, numbers, and cases, but that enough ordinary Americans believed he
was on to something. Sooner than he'd dreamed, he had the headlines he wanted, along with a movement that carried his name. He
had flown into West Virginia amazed that the stewardess recognized him, then gave a performance that would introduce every
schoolchild in the nation to the brawling senator from Wisconsin.
His Lincoln Day Dinner talk was a natural extension of the playbook he'd tried out during his run for class president at law school
and perfected in the race for circuit judge. The tactics of McCarthyism, like Joe McCarthy himself, were self-created although not
original — the big bamboozle with scant proof; narratives that were
deliberately distorted and told with a shaking fist; remaining a step
ahead of fact-checkers while never recanting anything. He said he
was sounding an alarm to an American nation that was sleeping
through a Russian death threat. "We have to pick out cases that
make sensations," he argued, "and use these to rouse the people."
In reality, the prairie fire had been waiting to burn, and Joe willfully struck the match.*

His longtime executive secretary Mary Brinkley Driscoll read
those cues better than anyone, but out of loyalty she didn't whisper
a word until the senator was dead, and then only to her brother,
the esteemed television newscaster David Brinkley. "I asked Mary:
'What did he have in his hand [in Wheeling]?'" Brinkley recalled
decades later in his autobiography. Mary: "He had a few scribbled
notes to use in his speech . . . mostly about housing for war veterans." David: "Did he have two hundred and five names?" Mary:
"No." David: "Where did he get that number?" Mary: "He made it
up." When he saw the headlines his talk was generating, McCarthy
"was nearly insane with excitement. He clutched the newspapers
and ran around the Senate office shouting, 'I've got it, I've got it!'"
Mary told her brother. "He thought he had the issue he needed to

---

* Everyone had a favorite analogy for what McCarthy had unleashed in Wheeling.
Republican senator Charles Potter, who would take on McCarthy but only after
it was safe to do so, said, "At that moment, a poison pellet was dropped into our
society and the fumes would never entirely blow away." Potter, *Days of Shame*, 46.

make him into a great political figure and to guarantee his Senate seat forever."*

The dictionary definitions of demagogue and McCarthyism are strikingly similar. Both involve gaining power by playing to emotions and passions, then fanning those prejudices by flinging accusations. Both tap overblown oratory, simplified logic, and outright untruths to plant discord and seize power. Both appeal to the populace (*demos* means "people" in Greek) and aspire to lead (*agogos* means "leading"), but seldom in the uplifting way the ancient Greeks had in mind. The line isn't always bright: one man's populist champion (think Malcolm X or William Jennings Bryan) often is another's jawsmith. But history has a way of sorting out the real bullies, like it did with Joe McCarthy.

To understand McCarthy as demagogue, it helps to look at the worst of his precursors. Worldwide there were scores whose names still beget shivers, from the Third Reich's Adolf Hitler to the Republic of Uganda's Idi Amin Dada. The Greeks gave us histrionic Cleon of Athens, who argued for killing every adult male in the conquered city of Mytilene and selling their wives and children; although the Athenians quickly realized the savagery of his decree and reversed it, a thousand prominent men were put to death without trial. The Romans had their own version in Julius Caesar, who waged unsanctioned wars, exploited his countrymen's anxieties, and helped topple the Roman Republic even as he was assembling the Roman Empire, and whose very name became a synonym for emperor or dictator. McCarthy's critics compared him to those and other tyrants, which might have been fair with regard to his self-promoting methods but stretched too far when it came to murderous results or even grand designs.†

---

* David Brinkley and his sister "were unable to discuss her work," he wrote, "because I so detested McCarthy that whenever his name came up in our conversations I routinely pronounced him to be what he was, a loudmouthed liar . . . Mary tried to defend McCarthy, and this always led to an angry, shouting argument. In time we had to agree that to avoid ugly fights we could never mention his name. Our agreement held until he died." Brinkley, *David Brinkley: A Memoir*, 112.

† It wasn't just Dwight Eisenhower's brother Arthur who would publicly compare McCarthy to Hitler, but also Eleanor Roosevelt, Drew Pearson, Republican senator Ralph Flanders of Vermont, Democratic senator Hubert Humphrey of

While America thought it was immune from despotism like that, it had produced its own unmistakable and irredeemable parade of bullies, all of whom Joe had at least heard of. Open societies are in fact uniquely susceptible to such mob sensibilities, whereas autocrats can squash them. "The true theater of a demagogue is a democracy," author James Fenimore Cooper recognized in 1835. The demagogue "calls blackguards gentlemen, and gentlemen folks, appeals to passions and prejudices rather than to reason, and is in all respects, a man of intrigue and deception, of sly cunning and management, instead of manifesting the frank, fearless qualities of the democracy he so prodigally professes . . . He who would be a courtier under a King, is almost certain to be a demagogue in a democracy."

Among the earliest made-in-the-USA demagogues was Congressman Lewis Charles Levin, a leader of the appropriately named Know-Nothing Party, who in the mid-1800s became a mouthpiece for xenophobic anti-Catholicism, and especially anti–Irish Catholicism. Fifteen years later, President Andrew Johnson singled out different scapegoats, railing against establishment elites and newly freed slaves. "Pitchfork Ben" Tillman used his time as South Carolina's governor and senator to replace the racially progressive Reconstruction laws that unnerved Johnson with a Jim Crow segregation system that whites in the Palmetto State called Redemption. Ma and Pa Ferguson were elected twice each as Texas's governor early in the twentieth century, dazzling the electorate with a homespun wit that to many compensated for their alleged acceptance of bribes. (He was impeached, she was dishonored.) Black nationalist Marcus Garvey and Senator Theodore Bilbo of Mississippi both made combustible appeals to resettle America's Negroes in Africa — Garvey to empower them, Bilbo to expel them. In the 1930s, when fascists and militarists were seizing power in Germany, Italy, Japan, and elsewhere, America produced its own variations in William Dudley Pelley's Silver Shirt Legion, George

---

Minnesota, former Harvard president James Conant, columnist Marquis Childs, *Capital Times* publisher William Evjue, the deputy leader of Britain's Labour Party, officials of the Soviet Foreign Ministry, and Hjalmar Schacht, Hitler's minister of economics.

E. Deatherage's Knights of the White Camellia, the Reverend Gerald L. K. Smith's America First Party, and Fritz Julius Kuhn's German American Bund. Catholic priest Charles Edward Coughlin, the father of hate radio, reached an audience of 30 million with his pro-fascist, anti-Semitic venom until FDR (Coughlin said that stood for Franklin Double-Crossing Roosevelt) and the Vatican drove him off the airwaves in 1939.

What that all-American rogues' gallery had in common was the impulse to exploit the circumstances of their times, whether it was resentment over a crumbling racial hierarchy or anxiety about economic upheaval. All professed to be men or women of the people, and each used flattery, manipulation, and enchantment to attain his or her disguised ends. None felt bound by constitutions, social norms, or any other rule. Coughlin, the Fergusons, Tillman, and the rest understood, as a matter of instinct in service of ambition, just how effective it was to sow divisions in the population. Who the straw man was didn't matter. It could set white versus black, gentile against Jew, poor opposing rich. Lies, bombast, and fearmongering were just the tactics. The underlying strategy was us against them, and it was no accident that we were in the majority.

The label "demagogue," like "McCarthyism," was and is used so often that it loses its ability to alarm. But monocrats are real and frightening, as Huey Long made clear in the early 1900s. This champion of the little man and defier of the new industrial order emerged from the hill country of Louisiana to bewitch and bedevil wide swaths of the nation. As governor, the Democrat smashed his Democratic as well as Republican opponents, amassed dictatorlike powers, delivered unheard-of public benefits to one of America's poorest states, and inspired Robert Penn Warren's Pulitzerwinning novel and its movie adaptation, both titled *All the King's Men*.

Long had learned what made people tick from his days as a traveling salesman, when he could peddle lumber to lumberjacks. He brought that fluent tongue with him to the governor's mansion in Baton Rouge. "They say they don't like my methods. Well, I don't like them either," he grumbled about Louisiana lawmakers. "I'd much rather get up before the legislature and say, 'Now this is a good law; it's for the benefit of the people, and I'd like you to vote for it in the interest of the public welfare.' Only I know that laws ain't made that way. You've got to fight fire with fire." His game plan, he explained, was simple: "Always take the offensive. The defensive ain't worth a damn." As for the charge that he was a tyrant, he protested, "A man is not a dictator when he is given a commission from the people and carries it out." Flash forward twenty years and you'd swear you were listening to Joe, not Huey.

Long was the one politician who frightened FDR, who called him "one of the two most dangerous men in America" (the other being General Douglas MacArthur). The appeal lingers even today of his "Every Man a King" motto and a "Share Our Wealth" manifesto that guaranteed every family a "household estate" of $5,000 — enough for a home, a car, a radio, and other "ordinary conveniences" — along with an ensured income of $2,500 a year. By the time of his assassination in the fall of 1935, Long was a US senator and was planning a third-party challenge to Roosevelt that couldn't have won but that FDR worried might swing the election to the Republican.

The lesson from Huey Long and the others couldn't be clearer: demagogues are universal and eternal.

If America's tradition of rabble-rousing offered one model for Joe McCarthy, its history of anticommunism offered another. The venom he unleashed at Wheeling wasn't America's first Red Scare. It wasn't even the beginning of the most recent one. Americans had been unnerved by communism since the Bolshevik Revolution in faraway Russia in 1917, and that fear reached home two years later, when a breach in the Socialist Party of America bred the Communist Party USA. The loathing came naturally: egalitarianism, democratic socialism, class struggle, and other founding precepts of communism and Marxism were the antitheses of democracy's and capitalism's free markets, multiple parties, and individualism. Central casting couldn't have supplied a more horrifying face for those anxieties than Joseph Stalin, a murderer of millions whose self-proclaimed goal was international revolution and whose true purpose was global dominion.

Logic, however, can't explain everything. The same way the Jew embodied for Hitler a psychotic fear of the alien and un-Aryan, so the Communist was for American xenophobes and their political bedfellows a threat to the status quo and to patriotism itself. If the poor and the lazy got more, the way the Reds wanted, there would be less for the rich and hardworking. Early anti-Communists insisted they were defending democratic values, and sometimes they were; just as often they were attacking what seemed foreign, an about-face made easier by the fact that the Communists who turned up in the American press were often the unwashed of eastern Europe. And usually Jewish. Nuance was lost and irrational connections followed — that Communist meant Stalinist, and that all party members and fellow travelers must be spies and anarchists.

One of America's smartest and most internationally oriented presidents, Woodrow Wilson, planted the seeds of suspicion during World War I. Worried about real and fantastical divided loyalties of immigrants from Germany, Ireland, and Italy, he railed in his 1915 State of the Union address against hyphenated Americans who "poured the poison of disloyalty into the very arteries of our national life." His warning seemed to be borne out in 1919, when anarchists mailed or hand-delivered bombs to American business executives and government officials, including two aimed at the Washington home of newly appointed attorney general A. Mitchell Palmer. (The second bomb blew up the front of his house, along with the bomber, and shook up neighbors Franklin and Eleanor Roosevelt.) Organized labor, meanwhile, was staging strikes everywhere from the shipyards of Seattle and steel mills of the Midwest to the Boston Police Department. That steamy summer, race riots broke out in more than thirty cities. The country, it seemed, was splitting at its seams, and someone had to be held to account.

Palmer started plotting the government's counterattack that same summer. He created a General Intelligence Unit at the Bureau of Investigation, precursor to the FBI, and turned it over to twenty-four-year-old Justice Department lawyer J. Edgar Hoover, who'd proved his steel during the war by running a program that imprisoned suspected aliens without trial. Hoover and his Radical Division quickly gathered any dope they could find on sixty thousand political dissidents. The temperamentally moderate but politically ambitious attorney general was in a vise: a unanimous Senate and overwrought media were demanding action to quell the unrest; the president suffered a nervous breakdown and a paralytic stroke that fall which left him unable to decide; and while Hoover had supplied the list of dissidents he'd asked for, Palmer didn't want to overreact. That changed the night of November 12, 1919, two years almost to the day after the Bolshevik Revolution. Working with local police, Hoover and his agents launched raids in eleven cities and arrested a thousand purported radicals. Some were beaten. Many were guilty merely of being Russian or of being in a building that housed political groups, and 199 were deported on a ship that reporters dubbed the Soviet Ark. Two months later there was a second roundup, encompassing triple the number of cities, netting four times as many arrests, and often depriving suspects of the standard rights of a warrant, a lawyer, and a phone call home.

Public, press, and political support for the Palmer Raids at first was robust. "If I had my way," said a beaming Massachusetts secretary of state Albert Langtry, "I'd take them out in the yard every morning and shoot them, and the next day would have a trial to see whether they were guilty." But Palmer and Hoover overplayed their hand. As May Day approached, they warned that radicals were aiming to launch a reign of terror timed for the workers' holiday. Whether or not they believed that, no uprising materialized, and Palmer's White House ambitions were dashed. Wilson's actual successor, Senator Warren Harding, pronounced the death knell for that Red Scare (some called it "Palmer's Reign of Terror") in August 1920, a year after it began. "Too much has been said," declared Harding, "about Bolshevism in America."

The anti-Communist fervor fell dormant, but it never disappeared. Neither did Hoover, who was promoted to bureau director in 1924. Elected officials understood the appeal of the Bolshevik defamation campaign and would revive it when needed. And the public continued to see communism as evil, as a Gallup poll found in 1938: asked to choose between fascism and communism, 61 percent preferred the former. While 97 percent of respondents said they believed in freedom of speech, only 38 percent felt that right extended to Communists.

It was against this background that the House of Representatives in 1938 formed the Un-American Activities Committee

(known later as HUAC and at the time as the Dies Committee).*
Martin Dies, a Texas Democrat and the first chairman, vowed to
devote equal attention to right-wing subversives as to left, but that
never happened. The Ku Klux Klan largely escaped scrutiny, as
did groups like the German American Bund, which would advance
the German cause in the United States until America's entry into
World War II. From the start, Dies's preferred enemies were the
New Deal and the Communist Party; the former, he insisted, was a
Trojan horse for the latter. The chairman's uncertain record in unearthing Commies was apparent in his failure to sniff out his own
colleague Samuel Dickstein, the Democratic congressman from
New York who co-chaired the precursor to the Dies Committee
and — operating under the apt code name "Crook" — was himself
on the payroll of the Soviet spy agency.

Dies was McCarthy's spiritual father, pioneering nearly all
the techniques Joe would use to ferret out Communists. The tall
blond Texan loudly named names, hundreds of them, and coined
the parlance of the anti-Communist movement with phrasing like
"soft" on Russia and "coddling" Communists. He assembled six
hundred file cabinets with a million index cards of gossip on un-
American goings-on, and listed as possible Communist fronts 280
labor groups, 438 newspapers, and 640 organizations, including
the Campfire Girls and the Boy Scouts. He zeroed in on figures he
knew would draw attention, demanding the resignations of Franklin Roosevelt's labor secretary Frances Perkins, interior secretary
Harold Ickes, and adviser Harry Hopkins, all central figures in the
New Deal. "These satellites range in political insanity from Socialists to Communists," Dies said, "with the common garden type of
crackpots preponderating." (FDR blasted back by branding Dies's
attacks "flagrantly unfair and un-American," while Harry Truman
later called HUAC "more un-American than the activities it is investigating.") Dies probed organized labor as well as Hollywood,
and estimated that the "subversive element" included 7 million
Americans out of a population of 130 million. He also captured
the public's imagination, with an astounding 83 percent of Ameri-

---

* The special committee became permanent in 1945.

cans saying they knew of his work a year after his committee was launched. Of those, 52 percent agreed with his choice to zero in on domestic Communists, compared to just 25 percent who wanted to target the American Nazis whose overseas compatriots were overrunning the capitals of Europe.

And it wasn't just Dies. Congress passed a dizzying series of measures to keep Communists out of the country and out of the government. The 1939 Hatch Act denied federal jobs to anyone belonging to an organization advocating the overthrow of the government. The 1940 Smith Act required non-citizen adults to register and be fingerprinted. Six years later, the so-called McCarran rider gave the secretary of state the authority to fire from the department anyone he labeled a risk. Crackdowns based on beliefs rather than actions defied basic American principles of justice. So did letting bureaucrats rather than judges decide. Not to be outdone, the executive branch launched its own repressions. Starting in 1940, government agencies could ask the FBI to investigate employees suspected of disloyalty, and the FBI retrained its sights from bank robbers and white slavers to pinkos and Reds. This crackdown against the left happened not during the Cold War but as America was about to jump into a world war against Nazi Germany, Fascist Italy, and the Empire of Japan, countries whose threat originated on the opposite side of the ideological divide. Communist Russia, by contrast, was poised to become our confederate.

In the wake of that war, Harry Truman found himself in two separate predicaments. First, he was under attack from both sides of the congressional aisle. Republicans, who in 1946 picked up enough seats to win control of the House and Senate for the first time in fourteen years, were accusing him of abandoning Chiang Kai-shek and his Nationalists in China and failing to root out the Communists from the New Deal, the Fair Deal, and the State Department. At the same time, the Henry Wallace left flank of his own party complained that he was too tough on the Russians and wasn't trying hard enough to get along with Stalin. The Missouri-bred president should have been bulletproof to both attacks. No Republican program matched the Truman Doctrine in bolstering countries under assault from Soviet-backed insurgents, and no other Democrat had taken as bold a step toward international harmony as his Marshall Plan to rebuild Europe. He had green-lighted a thermonuclear weapon, revived the draft, and helped create NATO. But it cost him: to win congressional and public support for expensive remedies like the Marshall and Truman plans, he had to exaggerate the Communist threat and propose remedies he knew were excessive.

The second bind for Truman was that during and after World War II, Washington was infused with spies, not just from the Soviet Union but from our other major wartime ally, Great Britain. Both war-ravaged nations worried that the newly empowered United States would turn on them — Russians for the obvious reason that they were hungry to spread communism around the world, and Britain for the less justified fear that we would train our anticolonial rhetoric against history's biggest colonizer. Americans know Roald Dahl as the author of best-selling children's books like *Charlie and the Chocolate Factory;* fewer know that he was feeding American secrets to Winston Churchill and other English leaders. Truman could have opted to sound an equivalent SOS about the infestation of spies from both foreign lands, but politics demanded he pick sides and decreed that the Soviets — who were expanding their empire while Britain's was contracting — would draw the shorter stick.

On March 21, 1947, the president launched the most sweeping peacetime security screening measure ever. It was called the Loyalty Order, and mandated checks on the nearly 5 million federal employees and applicants. Review boards were set up in every agency, with the FBI investigating anyone suspected of being a Communist or any other brand of subversive. At first an employee could be fired only if there were "reasonable grounds" to believe he or she was disloyal. That was later loosened to "reasonable doubt."* To aid the boards and the bureau, the attorney general prepared a list of subversive organizations that started

---

* During the Truman program's six years, 4.8 million current or would-be employees were screened, and 26,236 were subjected to a full-fledged FBI investigation. Of those, 16,503 were cleared, 6,828 resigned or withdrew their applications, and 560 were fired or turned down for jobs on the grounds of loyalty. Lewy, *The Federal Loyalty-Security Program,* 4.

with eighty-two, grew to 299, and included the Jewish Culture Society and United Negro and Allied Veterans of America. While it painted with a broad brush groups supposedly sympathetic to communism—nobody explained why such sympathy was a threat when the Communist Party was legal—the ledger was then used by local and state officials, school boards, private employers, and, more than anyone else, Joe McCarthy to crush the groups and anybody who'd ever been a member, no matter how young they were or how short their association. The slightest step out of line spelled doom.

As a senator, Truman had chaired an investigation committee that would become even more famous, under a slightly different title, when Joe McCarthy took it over a decade later. As president, Truman told himself his loyalty order was a way of heading off more draconian measures advanced by House and Senate Republicans. The truth was that those screenings tarnished not just Communists but liberals and freethinkers, and history would judge him appropriately harshly. "It is unfortunate that McCarthyism was named teleologically, from its most perfect product, rather than genetically—which would give us Trumanism," wrote Pulitzer Prize–winning journalist Garry Wills. "In 1947 the President not only cooperated with these [investigative] committees, but gave them the means to grow powerful."*

The nation, meanwhile, was taking its cues from Washington. In Hollywood, studio bosses put out word they wouldn't knowingly hire Communist actors, screenwriters, directors, or musicians; later, to ensure they didn't make a mistake, they consulted *Red Channels,* a broadcast industry blacklist published by anti-Red stalwarts.† You could also detect the difference in what was screen-

---

* Wills was not the only one claiming that McCarthy wasn't the most deserving anti-Communist to have the movement bear his name. Others argued for McCarranism, to honor Pat McCarran, the Nevada Democratic senator who'd been on the case longer and had more legislative clout; Diesism, a tongue-twister recognizing the HUAC chairman; Cohnism, after Joe's soon-to-be staff director Roy Cohn; or, most fitting, Hooverism, celebrating the FBI director who outlasted all of them.

† *Red Channels* named 151 actors, actresses, writers, musicians, playwrights, and others with alleged ties to communism—from musician Pete Seeger to movie star Edward G. Robinson—who it said shouldn't be hired. Most of those names

ing at theaters: one study found that 28 percent of films had a serious social bent in 1947, compared to just 18 percent in 1949 and 11 percent in 1950. The American Legion and Chamber of Commerce were on the warpath, too, while the Congress of Industrial Organizations was on the defensive, purging Communists from its leadership and expelling Red-dominated affiliates. Mickey Spillane's hard-boiled private eye Mike Hammer was doing his own housecleaning: "I killed more people tonight than I have fingers on my hands . . . They were red sons-of-bitches who should have died long ago, and part of the gang who are going to be dying in the very near future unless they get smart and take the gas pipe. Pretty soon what's left of Russia and the slime that breeds there won't be worth mentioning and I'm glad because I had a part in the killing."

Gallup calibrated echoes like those and found that, in 1948, 22 percent of Americans wanted to deport Communists living here, 4 percent to "shoot them, hang them," and 1 percent to "let them rave, but watch them." That toxicity worked its way down to children, and through their chewing gum, no less. A 1951 series of bubble gum cards featured a "Children's Crusade Against Communism" that spelled out the "savage warfare" of Mao Tse-tung, introduced Olga and Ivan, a "typical Russian family" who "are told where to work, where to live and what subjects they must master at school," and exhorted kids — in bold red-and-black lettering — to "Fight the Red Menace." A year later in Wheeling, "subversive" gumball machines were seized for doling out trinkets bearing what was said to be Communist propaganda and turned out to be educational briefs on UN member countries, in Russia's case: "U.S.S.R., population 211,000,000. Capital, Moscow. Largest country in the world."

Were these appropriate reactions or overkill? There is evidence for both. Communism did pose a bigger domestic challenge to America in the 1940s than at any other time before or since. Membership in the Communist Party USA swelled from 7,500 at the start of the decade to a peak in 1947 of 82,618 — and J. Edgar Hoover estimated there were ten fellow travelers for every one

came from McCarthy friend J. B. Matthews, and most of the funding was from another McCarthy supporter, Alfred Kohlberg.

who formally signed up. The US party wasn't the independent organization it claimed to be but an appendage of the Soviet apparat. Russia had demonstrated its depravity in 1939 by signing a short-lived nonaggression pact with Hitler and, longer-term, by borrowing the Nazis' techniques of oppression.

Then there were the spies. In the spring of 1945, several staffers at the journal *Amerasia* were charged with unlawful possession of sensitive government documents and were suspected of passing them to the enemy. That fall, a clerk at the Soviet embassy in Ottawa defected, muttering to reporters that "it's war, it's Russia," helping unmask two Soviet spy rings in Canada, and kindling suspicions that would eventually expose a series of US traitors who were leaking atomic secrets. By the summer of 1948, Washington was on the edge of its seat as it listened to spy queen Elizabeth Bentley—who once filled her knitting basket with rolls of microfilm—tell all about dozens of her former couriers in arms. More riveting, and more alarming, was converted Communist spy Whittaker Chambers's revelation that he'd hidden in a hollowed-out pumpkin secret documents passed to him by Alger Hiss, a State Department official who became a poster child for the effete leftists conservatives abhorred and who was convicted of perjury for denying his ties to Chambers.

We now know even more. In the mid-1980s, word began to filter out about Venona, a US counterintelligence project that had been monitoring Soviet cables since 1943, and in 1995 the government officially divulged the secret it had kept for half a century. The decrypts made clear that some 350 Americans had been spying for the Russians, and their network may have been wider. "There was a problem of Communist subversion in the US government, and of Communist espionage," says John Earl Haynes, a retired historian at the Library of Congress who, with his colleague Harvey Klehr, has plumbed the Venona documents more thoroughly than anyone else. "It was a serious problem and needed to be dealt with."

Other developments, however, argued that the threat never was as deep or as dire as claimed by early Cold Warriors like Dies and Hoover. Declared Communists made up a microscopic 0.06 percent of the US population—0.6 percent with Hoover's inflation index — and they lacked the clout to elect even one of their own to Congress. While the Soviet Union did control the levers of power in the CPUSA, most members were drawn by its struggle for justice and against fascism, not by any allegiance to Moscow. Most also had abandoned the party by the end of World War II, although even a brief flirtation meant trouble when loyalty checkers asked not just whether they were currently a member of the Communist Party but whether they'd ever been. Some exchanges lumped into the spy charges, including in the *Amerasia* affair, may have been innocent and the information overdue for declassification, although the mishandling of the case fueled conspiracy mongers like McCarthy. By 1949 Hoover's G-men had squashed the worst of the spy nests. Truman's loyalty tests had rooted out most security and loyalty risks, the labor movement had realigned its leftward tilt, and an anti-Communist consensus prevailed among liberals and Americans generally. After 1949 there was just one more major spy case — that of Julius and Ethel Rosenberg, alleged masterminds of a nuclear espionage network — although it was the most frightening of all.

We understand now that by the time of Joe's Wheeling speech in 1950, "the problem was actually well on the way to being solved," says Haynes. "He really was engaged in what amounts to shooting the wounded." It wasn't that the Russians didn't want to recruit spies to replace those uprooted by the FBI. But by the dawn of the Cold War "the Soviet Union had lost much of its appeal even to young radical intellectuals alienated by the materialism and injustices of American society," said KGB experts Christopher Andrew and Vasili Mitrokhin. "It was deeply ironic that when McCarthy's self-serving campaign against the Red Menace was at its height, Soviet penetration of the American government was at its lowest ebb for almost thirty years."

Where was Joe McCarthy during that earlier and all-important phase of the hunt for subversives in the 1940s? He wasn't a major player, or even a recognizable bit one. He did speak out on the Communist threat earlier than is generally recognized, and more often, although not in ways that indicated that he had anything original to say or that it would become the centerpiece of his Senate career.

He went on the attack in his 1946 general election race, using the specter of communism to bludgeon his Democratic opponent, Howard McMurray. Most press coverage focused on the charge that McMurray was "communistically inclined," raised at a candidates' forum in mid-October, but Joe's Marquette files show him wading in two weeks earlier. He vowed at an unidentified campaign forum to "clean the communist element out of the union movement," and advocated "that every communist be immediately discharged from the federal payroll . . . If the Russians want a communistic form of government that is their business, not ours. But when communists come into this country and propose to destroy our form of government, then that is our business, the same as though some of our people went over into Russia and attempted to destroy the Russian form of government." Ouch.

He returned to the issue in his first year as a senator, in his first set of Lincoln Day addresses. While his main focus was on alleged postwar mistreatment of prisoners, he scolded the leaders of the wartime Allies — President Truman, British prime minister Clement Attlee, and Soviet premier Stalin — for leading the world down a perilous path. "The history of America is written around certain principles of liberty, justice and equality, and unless we return to those principles the day of reckoning for this [nation] will most certainly come. Unless we return to those principles, then some day there will come true the words of that [unnamed] poet who said, 'And the savage from afar shall stand on the broken arch of the bridge of the golden gate and guffaw at the ruins of a Western civilization,'" McCarthy intoned in a speech in Oklahoma delivered almost exactly three years before his West Virginia tribute to President Lincoln. Joe stuck with the theme in a speech in Boston that March, warning the Clover Club of the special threat to Ireland posed by the "vicious, underhanded tactics of the Communists." In April he argued in a radio debate that the way to address the threat was to outlaw the Communist Party. He even worked communism into his condemnation of public housing, which he said was a breeding ground for rats and Reds.

His most blistering attack against Communists came in November 1949 and was both a settling of scores and a hint of what lay ahead. The *Capital Times* of Madison was "the Red mouthpiece" for the Communist Party in Wisconsin, according to an eleven-page release that the senator mailed to every media outlet in the state. The *Times*' city editor, Cedric Parker, he charged, "was at one time a member of the party and was closely affiliated with a number of Communist-front organizations." Parker had in fact flirted with communism years before, but now there was convincing evidence that he and the paper were as anti-Communist as the rest of the country. Joe wasn't fooled. "If a fowl looks like a duck, walks like a duck, swims like a duck and quacks like a duck, then we can safely assume that it is a duck," McCarthy's three-thousand-word statement asserted. No need to mention that he had singled out the *Capital Times* because it had devoted more column inches than any other newspaper in the land to exposing matters ranging from Judge Joe's quickie divorces to Senator McCarthy's mangled and dodgy finances. Whatever his motivations, Joe understood that his attacks against the paper generated more positive publicity than anything else he had done since he came to the Senate.

Jack Anderson knew that Joe had a history of Red-baiting, but he wove a more romantic foundation myth of the senator's anticommunism. Building on a column by Drew Pearson, Anderson sought to graphically reconstruct a 1950 dinner Joe had at Washington's swank Colony restaurant with Father Edmund Walsh, dean of Georgetown's School of Foreign Service, and two other prominent Catholics. Joe desperately needed an issue. What about rallying support for the St. Lawrence Seaway? Joe: "That hasn't enough sex." How about a pension plan that covers all aging Americans? Joe asked. Too expensive, his friends advised. Finally Walsh offered, "How about Communism?" Joe loved it: "The government is full of Communists. The thing to do is hammer at them." And, as Anderson wrote, "His three fellow Catholics went away with the feeling that the sincere McCarthy would do his country a service by speaking out against the Communist fifth column." The author then imagined what might have been had Walsh and the others jumped at Joe's idea about a universal dole for old folks: "Joe McCarthy might well have gone forth, in all his aggressiveness, to win for himself a pedestal in the pantheon of fighting liberals."

The evening get-together did happen, a month before Joe's speech in Wheeling. The avidly anti-Communist Walsh probably did urge Joe to play a more active role on the issue, whether or not he used the words attributed to him. And shortly after the meeting Joe did ask one of his speechwriters for a talk on subversion in government. But compelling as the conversation might have been, it wasn't the born-again moment suggested by Anderson and all those who have repeated it. Joe didn't need Father Walsh to point him to an issue he'd been talking about for three years. It was the wild reaction to his stem-winder in Wheeling — not the words of an aging Jesuit — that convinced him of the political hay he could make from it. The Colony restaurant version was embraced with special zeal by those who wanted to link McCarthy's campaign to the conservative Catholic Church, and was roundly rejected by Catholics eager to be free from that taint.*

Joe's awakening may have begun more than a decade earlier. Tom L. Cahoe knew him in Appleton before he became a judge, and the two would walk together in the woods while Cahoe hunted rabbits. "Once when we came in from rabbit hunting and the windmill was broken down, I sat on the water trough and Joe pumped water by hand. At that time he said to me, 'Tom, you mark my word, the communists will take over this country without firing a shot.'"

President Truman was intrigued enough by the roots of McCarthy-style anticommunism that he asked his staff to trace them. Major General Robert Landry, a presidential assistant, assembled in 1949 a 170-page memorandum that went all the way back to the Salem witch trials and concluded that McCarthyism was the latest

---

* Whatever role Walsh may have played in drawing Joe into the anti-Communist movement, there is no question that he did just that with a young Dwight Eisenhower. Walsh's three-hour lecture to Ike's class at the Army War College in the winter of 1928–29 "marked the beginning of the Cold War, even though it would be many years before the Communist-Freedom struggle would acquire that label," the future president wrote in an uncompleted and unpublished book on the Cold War. DDEL.

incarnation of an ignorance that regularly ravaged the body politic. The tome was trimmed by another aide, summarized by a third, then handed out by Truman to anyone he met who was confused by the Red Scare.

Joe's own take on the story cast him not as an unscrupulous crusader but as a reluctant savior, although there were new facts and a new flair with each retelling, not unlike with his explanations for his accelerated high school career and his war wounds. His favorite version assigned the role of mentor to Secretary of Defense James Forrestal, who had invited him to lunch just after he arrived in Washington in December 1946. "Before meeting Jim Forrestal I thought we were losing to international Communism because of incompetence and stupidity on the part of our planners," Joe recounted six years later in his tract *McCarthyism: The Fight for America*. "I mentioned that to Forrestal. I shall forever remember his answer. He said, 'McCarthy, consistency has never been a mark of stupidity. If they were merely stupid they would occasionally make a mistake in our favor.' This phrase struck me so forcefully that I have often used it since." Forrestal wasn't around to add to the story, or contradict it, having died in 1949 in a presumed suicide when he fell from a window on the sixteenth floor of Bethesda Naval Hospital, where he was being treated for depression.

Joe told Jean that an incident involving the Russian fur trade had alerted him to the Red Menace. Amtorg, the Soviet trading agency, was a front for smuggling in Russian spies and smuggling out US dollars, Joe said. When he tried to legislate a ban on Russian fur imports, the State Department blocked him. Wink, wink. A more likely explanation is that Joe was protecting Wisconsin's fur farmers and the department was protecting American fur buyers. Later, he told the editors of *Cosmopolitan* magazine that his concerns about communism sprouted upon his return from Marine duty in the South Pacific, when he resolved to put the "faces and names" of government traitors "on the front pages of every American newspaper" — and that his speech in Wheeling grew out of "an unlimited amount of research covering the background of the architects of disaster for America and success for Russia." The former is at least possible; the latter explanation is belied by the way he winged it in Wheeling.*

A more complicated and captivating rendering was the one he gave the hyperbolic Roy Cohn, McCarthy's aide in his second Senate term. It was just before Thanksgiving 1949 when three men came to Joe with a one-hundred-page FBI report laying out what they said was the full story of Communist subversion at the State Department and elsewhere. Nothing had been done with the document in the two years since it was completed, and nothing would, the mysterious trio were convinced, unless they could find a senator to take it public. Having tried three other Republicans, who refused, they were down to their last hope. McCarthy took the report home, devoured it, and, Cohn said, "He told me later, 'After a couple of hours' sleep, I got dressed and went to the office. I had made up my mind—I was going to take it on. It was fantastic, unbelievable. Take any spy story you ever read, any movie about international intrigue, and this was more startling.' The first telephone call McCarthy made that morning was to one of the group. 'I got him out of bed,' McCarthy recalled, 'and told him I was buying the package.'"

And "why, quite specifically, did Joe McCarthy 'buy the package'?" Cohn added in his biography of his mentor. "I believe he did so for two reasons: The first was patriotic. He was worried about the threat to the country posed by the Communist conspiracy, and he decided to do what he could to expose it. Secondly, I am sure he saw the dramatic political opportunities connected with a fight on Communism."

Cohn was half-right. McCarthy had found his issue and it was political dynamite. But if it had sprung from public spiritedness, or he'd sensed the drama in advance, he wouldn't have come to

* The most concise and honest of Joe's renditions dates to April 1950, ten weeks after Wheeling. Over highballs, a young woman asked, "Senator, just how long ago did you discover communism?" McCarthy: "Two and a half months!" Woltman, pt. 1 of "The McCarthy Balance Sheet," *New York World-Telegram.*

Wheeling with a backup speech on housing. He wasn't convinced he'd picked the right one until he saw the firestorm it ignited.*

As soon as Joe landed back in Washington after his Lincoln Day tour, he promised to enlighten fellow senators about the spies in their government. He magnified the drama by telling colleagues and journalists it could take as long as five hours to lay out his charges, but all he really had was a deck of characterizations from the Lee List that he had reshuffled to disguise his reliance on re-cycled cases that were two years old. Even then, he couldn't resist embroidering. A suspect who Robert E. Lee said was "somewhat left of center" became, in McCarthy's telling on the Senate floor, "communistically inclined"; Lee's "inclined toward Communism" was McCarthy's "communistic connection and beliefs"; while what was to Lee a "member of the Communist Party" was amped up by McCarthy to "not only very active as a Communist, but . . . a very dangerous Communist." Joe denied, then affirmed, having used the number 205 — or was it 206, which he also mentioned? As for identifying those on the Lee List or others, McCarthy didn't and couldn't. For now all he had were numbers with no names to match, although he suggested a more high-minded motivation for keeping what he knew to himself: "If I were to give all the names involved, it might leave a wrong impression. If we should label one man a Communist when he is not a Communist, I think it would be too bad." While conceding that his information was nei-ther new nor complete, Joe's rendering sacrificed not just nuance but fairness. Even William F. Buckley Jr. and L. Brent Bozell, two young conservatives who wrote a book-length defense of their fa-vorite senator, managed to count thirty-eight instances of exag-geration that night for which "McCarthy deserves to be censured."

Had Senate Democrats simply let Joe drone on to a nearly empty chamber, it might have become clear that his bulging brief-case contained no meaningful facts and that he was a bloviating pretender. Instead, they chose to go toe-to-toe with him, helping

---

* A less forgiving McCarthy biographer, Richard Rovere, saw his subject's motive more clearly when he called him "a political speculator, a prospector who drilled Communism and saw it come up a gusher. He liked his gusher, but he would have liked any other just as well." Rovere, *Senator Joe McCarthy*, 72.

make him into a martyr the same way President Truman and the State Department had after Wheeling. By the time the rare evening session wrapped up just before midnight on February 20, 1950, Majority Leader Scott Lucas had challenged McCarthy sixty-one times. Democratic Caucus secretary Brien McMahon butted in another thirty-four. Neither had learned yet the futility of taking on an opponent with Joe McCarthy's blend of wit, whimsy, and mendacity. He'd learned early that there was no worse a penalty for a big lie than for a little one, but that only the big ones drew a crowd, so he told whoppers. Nor did his rivals appreciate that, backed into a corner, Joe could transform himself into either a pit bull or a lamb, whichever would get him out of his particular jam. In the Senate chamber that night he claimed the high ground and painted Lucas, McMahon, and the rest as ignoble partisans. "All I am doing," he pleaded, "is presenting enough of the picture so that I hope both the Democratic side and the Republican side will forget politics and help clean house. I think this is something in which we cannot think of politics as usual."

Samuel Shaffer, the *Newsweek* reporter who'd been watching him from the start, said taking on this senator was "like trying to pin down a blob of mercury." Most of Congress, he added, "not only underestimated Joe McCarthy but had failed to measure the temperature of the nation. The issue of Communists-in-government took hold in the country. It was not only the kooks who saw conspiracies everywhere. Patriotic organizations were quickly caught up in the hysteria."

McCarthy's grandstanding roiled the White House as much as the Senate. The year 1950 had started out swell for President Truman. America was uncontested as the world's superpower and the economy was roaring, with new cars costing just $1,500, new TVs $250, and, thanks to the new plastic cards from Diners Club, both could be bought on credit. Nevertheless, the president couldn't go a day without hearing another unsettling report about the unruly senator. Meeting McCarthy's demand to make security files public could "place in jeopardy the lives of confidential sources," result in "an injustice to innocent individuals," and let real spies "flee the country," Attorney General J. Howard McGrath warned. Democratic senator Millard Tydings of Maryland pushed back, telling the president it was vital "for your own welfare, for the welfare of the country and lastly for the welfare of the Democratic party" that he and other lawmakers see the sensitive documents so they could answer McCarthy's charges. Truman eventually charted a middle course, letting several senators — not including Joe — have a look, but only at an FBI abstract of the raw data in one key file, with a military guard looking on. (Joe said the files had been "raped" of their original and incriminating content.) The president from Missouri also hit hard at the junior senator from Wisconsin, calling him "the greatest asset that the Kremlin has" and saying his move to sabotage traditionally bipartisan foreign policy "is just as bad in this cold war as it would be to shoot our soldiers in the back in a hot war."

The normally straight-shooting Truman, who never did acknowledge his role in fertilizing the soil that sprouted McCarthyism, wanted to have it both ways. At the same time the president was insisting that McCarthy was bluffing and didn't have any inside information, his cabinet was desperately trying to ferret out the moles who had given Joe that information. In the case of a suspected leak at the Civil Service Loyalty Review Board, for instance, Democratic National Committee chairman William Boyle Jr. confided to FBI agents that "if we can satisfy ourselves as to the identity of the person giving the information to McCarthy we will fire him outright."

The FBI was in a dither, too, as Joe's own FBI files confirm. There was no way Hoover would stand up for the State Department. The record is full of his cryptic notes accusing top department officials of "passing the buck" and warning that "we have to be forever alert to fast ones from State." But the bureau also was disconcerted to learn that Joe had been "using the old list Bob Lee had." The sharing of secrets, those files make clear, was mutually enriching, with McCarthy giving information to as well as taking it from Hoover and his minions. Hoover is revealed here at his Machiavellian best — or worst — doing the bidding of his bosses, the attorney general and the president, even as he was coddling a senator he'd been warned might be committing "theft, embezzlement, and unlawful removal of Government documents."

Joe's own office could barely keep up. The hyperkinetic senator not only wanted to accomplish a lot but also wanted it done lickety-split. (When he wanted to show he was serious, he'd admonish his deputies, "Stop assing around.") In the six noisy and frantic weeks since Wheeling, his staff had been transformed from a sleepy collection of double-dipping journalists and Wisconsin hangers-on into the vanguard of an international counterintelligence operation. Nobody better reflected that changeover than Don Surine, the six-foot-four tough-guy aide who oversaw investigations and was the primary conduit for leaks from the FBI. Surine worked for the bureau from 1939 to 1950, starting as a clerk, rising to special agent, and, the day before McCarthy's West Virginia speech, getting fired for fraternizing with a hooker during a probe of white slavery. He said the contact was innocent and blamed a "stuffed shirt" supervisor; Hoover countered that his firing was based on his "gross misconduct" and "complete disregard of Bureau rules and regulations," and not for the first time.* Whatever he said publicly, Edgar was quietly telling Joe to hire Don, which he did.

Joe was mysterious about how many staffers he had, where they were based, how much they earned, and who was paying. By the spring of 1950 it was estimated there were fifteen investigators; eventually there'd be fifty, scattered from Washington to Taipei, Paris, Calcutta, Los Angeles, and Geneva. Columnist Drew Pearson said that one McCarthy staffer, a New York attorney and former Navy Intelligence man, worked out of the office of Brooklyn Dodgers owner Walter O'Malley. Some Joe paid from his own pocket or from funds he solicited, and most were housed in three rooms jam-packed with desks and file cabinets outside his personal office in Room 428.† He already was getting a thousand let-

---

* Jim Juliana, another FBI agent who would later work for Joe, offered a more graphic version of why Surine was booted from the bureau: "He was working in white slave cases, prostitution, and ended up screwing a prostitute. They caught him." December 25, 1997, interview, JJP.

† Three months after Wheeling, Joe wrote *Look* magazine executive James Milloy, "The other night after the Gridiron Dinner you and a couple of our mutual friends indicated an interest in being of some financial assistance in the present anti-Communist fight . . . I have one project now which is extremely important and could yield phenomenally good results if we could get someone to underwrite the necessary cost." One cost *Look* did underwrite was the salary of its reporter

ters a day, a number that would grow to five thousand (and require a special US Post Office truck to deliver them), and many came with bank checks or cash and coins ranging from $1 to $50 (along with at least one Social Security check).* Willard Edwards of the *Chicago Tribune* said Joe sometimes wedged the money into his pocket or bet it on the commodities market. With rich benefactors also kicking in, there eventually would be enough to pay off Joe's $45,000 Appleton bank loan as well as the $14,000 he borrowed from Frank Sensenbrenner, the powerful Wisconsin Republican who ran Kimberly-Clark. Ray Kiermas, his office manager, thought that one McCarthy account contained at least $125,000 ($1.3 million today).†

While she didn't have a title that indicated it, Jean Kerr was the focal point of Joe's brain trust. She lacked Surine's law enforcement training and his bluster, but she was defter, a better writer, at least as ambitious, more political, and less combustible.

Ed Nellor, whom it lent to Joe as a speechwriter. Nellor thought it improper, but no more so than when another of his bosses, radio broadcaster Fulton Lewis Jr., did the same thing later. Memo from McCarthy to James Milloy, May 29, 1950, unprocessed files, MUA; and Reeves interview with Nellor, May 7, 1977.

* Some mail intended for Senator Joe McCarthy ended up in the office of liberal congressman Eugene McCarthy of Minnesota. When the congressman flagged the mistake, the *Milwaukee Journal*'s Robert Fleming said, the senator told him, "We've got so much of it here, you just keep it." Joe, meanwhile, insisted that with his letters, "about 99.5 percent" were supportive. *Conspiracy So Immense*, 160; and Stuart, "The Controversial Senator Contends His Tactics Are Both Practical and Fair," *New York World-Telegram and Sun*.

† The summer after Wheeling, Joe severed his affiliation with Zabel, Wolf and McCarthy, the Milwaukee law firm he'd joined the previous summer. In a letter to partner Adam Wolf, Joe said having his name on the firm's letterhead and door hadn't helped him or them financially. He proposed cutting ties because, he said, "I know that when the Administration is through fine-tooth combing my own past life, it will start on all of the members of the firm, past and present, and pick up anything that could be twisted to make it sound [derogatory] and then use it in the current smear fight against me." If reporters or others asked why he was leaving, Joe suggested lying: "Tell them the decision was made months ago when I discovered I would be unable to get back [to] spend any time in the office."

Before Joe joined, the firm had successfully defended him when the Wisconsin bar commissioners tried to remove his law license for refusing to resign his judgeship when he ran for Senate in 1946. Gossip columnist Drew Pearson believed the firm had links to the Capone mob of Chicago. Letter from Joe to Adam Wolf, June 13, 1950, series 14, MUA; and Drew Pearson Files, LBJL.

She grounded Joe when he got in over his head, which he did all the time, and was the one female employee who felt comfortable calling him "Joe," rather than "Senator," at least in private. It was true that the senator tended to follow the advice of the last person he talked to, and increasingly that was Jean. She also was a true believer even in those earliest days, when Joe wasn't and the staff needed one.

"A visit to the McCarthy lair on Capitol Hill is rather like being transported to the set of one of Hollywood's minor thrillers," the columnist brothers Joseph and Stewart Alsop wrote in the *Saturday Evening Post*.

> The anteroom is generally full of furtive-looking characters who look as though they might be suborned State Department men. McCarthy himself, despite a creeping baldness and a continual tremor which makes his head shake in a disconcerting fashion, is reasonably well cast as the Hollywood version of a strong-jawed private eye. A visitor is likely to find him with his heavy shoulders hunched forward, a telephone in his huge hands, shouting cryptic instruction to some mysterious ally. "Yeah, yeah. I can listen, but I can't talk. Get me? Yeah? You really got the goods on the guy?" The senator glances up to note the effect of this drama on his visitor.

Befitting his new celebrity, writers bestowed on Joe a new nickname: Hawkshaw, after the stage and comic book character Hawkshaw the Detective. The senator generated his own theatrics by regularly striking his telephone mouthpiece with a pencil, which he said jarred the needle off any concealed listening device. Another favorite gimmick was turning on the tap in the nearby bathroom to generate white noise aimed at throwing off bugs planted in his office. Even as the State Department feared that McCarthy was spying on it, he worried that he was the target of eavesdroppers. Such scenes seemed silly, the Alsops added, but they reflected a troubling reality: "Washington is rapidly becoming a town in which no man entirely trusts another."*

---

* Don Surine said the only silly thing was how the Truman administration was "trying to nail me" — putting him under twenty-four-hour surveillance and hav-

The staff's most consuming job was gathering leaked information and managing the network where it originated. Joe's best source remained the FBI, with information flowing from the near-weekly lunches he had with Hoover and from abstracts prepared by agents and handed over to Surine. Other dossiers were made available in full, as suggested by the stacks of FBI material in the Marquette archives marked "Security Information" or "Confidential," along with notes from the director himself on suspected subversives. A memo from Jean to Mary Driscoll, the senator's secretary, read, "These are my notes from FBI files on various individuals." Another document, prepared by the State Department on Far East Policy, had a note in pencil reading, "DO NOT EXPOSE PHOTOSTAT BECAUSE ITS MARKINGS WOULD REVEAL SECRET SOURCE." Hoover delighted in using McCarthy to further his own hunt for Communists, but he was determined not to get caught or to alienate Truman, Acheson, or his nominal boss, Attorney General McGrath. So anytime he could, the FBI chief disguised the leaks to look as if they had originated in agencies like the Civil Service Commission. In one instance of hoodwinking, Hoover actually had the bureau lead an investigation into who at the commission might be leaking.

That wasn't all the wily FBI director did. McCarthy hired so many ex-agents that his Senate office would be christened the Little FBI, and the bureau offered up its best Communists turned whistleblowers to bolster Joe's cases. The agents in charge of crime records helped McCarthy aides write speeches. Assistant Director Lou Nichols schooled the senator to hold his stories until just before press deadlines, so reporters didn't have time to solicit rebuttals, and to avoid difficult-to-prove phrases like "card-carrying Communist." McCarthy showed his appreciation by taking aim at Hoover's enemies, especially the Central Intelligence Agency, and backing the bureau's requests to Congress for more men, money, and legislated powers.

---

ing his phone tapped by five different agencies. But that scrutiny might have been warranted if, as journalist and McCarthy staffer Ed Nellor charged, Surine "was a ferret" — swiping documents left and right. Reeves interviews with Surine, April 7, 1977, and Nellor, June 6, 1979.

Hoover wasn't alone in showing loyalty to Joe in these early days, or in flouting codes of ethics and criminal statutes. McCarthy bred bad behavior in nearly everyone. Insiders at the CIA and in the armed services passed top secret and encoded documents to the senator; the snitch generally was a secretary or clerk, but on occasion it was an admiral, a general, or an intelligence chieftain. The Post Office sprang its own leaks, as did the Bureau of Internal Revenue, the Civil Service Commission, and the agency McCarthy despised most, the State Department. In the name of safeguarding security, these officials spilled the country's securest facts and files. Reporters were supposed to be looking for disclosures, but many were themselves sources, feeding their best dirt to Joe. So vast was this network of informants that it got its own name: the Loyal American Underground or, for short, the McCarthy Underground. His web extended beyond US shores to Germany, Switzerland, and other overseas outposts. Speechwriter Ed Nellor estimated there were twenty thousand distinct leads, most from reliable informants but some from what he called nuts. People stopped him and other McCarthy staffers on the street to hand them documents or called to say they'd left folders in a nearby phone booth. Sifting through them — and working them into the five hundred or so speeches that he drafted — meant putting in up to eighty hours a week. That "almost ruined my health," recalled Nellor, although Joe himself was inexhaustible.

McCarthy meant it when he said he'd go to jail rather than divulge his tipsters. The *Milwaukee Journal*'s Robert Fleming felt the senator was just as sincere, although less in touch with reality, when he said, "Bob, I sometimes think that everyone with a story to tell is coming to me. I sometimes get 20 tips a day. Senators, government workers, career people, the public, crackpots all shove information at me . . . Just think, Bob, about the responsibility. If we should make a single mistake, after the work we've done, we could ruin a man. That's why we have to be so damned careful, and [do] so much investigating, so that some crackpot doesn't fool us or someone doesn't trap us into a phoney case." As to who had the last word on all that vetting and assembling, Joe told Oliver Pilat of the *New York Post* that, while information flowed in from "hundreds" of people on the claims he presented to the Senate, "no one prepared any of the cases for me. McCarthy prepared his own cases."

His focus was necessarily on Washington, but Joe couldn't wait to get out of the capital, away from the bloated bureaucrats, and fine-tune the stump speech he'd test-run in Wheeling. The McCarthy road show was full of well-orchestrated trumpet calls and hullabaloo: a color guard, marching band, priest, and the Pledge of Allegiance set a solemnly patriotic tone. The senator would arrive late enough for the on-air and in-person audiences to be antsy, but not yet angry, giving bear hugs to those within reach. Then he'd take the stage, hands clasped above his head like the boxing dandy he'd been. Bodyguards manned their spots and an overstuffed briefcase appeared at his side. His opening sentence nearly always was the same: "It's good to get away from Washington and back here in the United States." And he meant it, because he was a man of the country and because he was in such demand when he got back from West Virginia — shuttling in one six-week stretch from Passaic to Chicago to Atlantic City, with three appearances in between on *Meet the Press* — that his speaking fees were reaching four figures.

The speech also was cookie-cutter. A skunk story made plain whose side he was on:

> When I was a small boy on the farm, mother raised chickens. The eggs and meat furnished groceries and much of the clothing for our family of nine. We lived fairly close to the woods, and weasels, snakes, and skunks would steal the baby chicks from beneath the mother hen and kill them. One of the jobs which my three brothers and I had was to dig out and destroy those killers. It was not a pleasant job — and sometimes we did not smell too well when the job was finished. But the skunks were dead and the chickens alive. A much more dangerous and smellier breed of skunk is now being dug out in Washington.

General Telford Taylor, one of McCarthy's most eloquent critics, offered this response to the skunk story: "There is no point to a skunk hunt in which the hunter permanently absorbs the odor of the animal. Furthermore, when this happens the hunter's olfactory apparatus becomes desensitized and indiscriminate, so that he can no longer distinguish between skunks and other more useful and attractive creatures . . . The victim of this kind of hunting will not be the skunk, but the American eagle."

After Wheeling, Joe's message was all Commies, all the time. We'd already lost the so-called Cold War, he would tell listeners, with the Soviet orbit having expanded from 180 million to 800 million people in just six years. "This," he said, "indicates the swiftness of the tempo of Communist victories and American defeats in world war III." Then he fingered specific "traitors" and "fools" in the State Department, with their "master plan" of "hitting Communists at the front door with a silk handkerchief while they beat the brains out of your friends at the back door." Just when the crowd might be tempted to tune out over his historical minutiae, he reeled them back in with hyperbolic phrases like "the big gangster in the Kremlin." In the end, the senator pleaded, it was up to the president to "stop your whistle-stop campaigning and come home . . . Come home, Mr. Truman, and fire the Pied Pipers of the Politburo. Fire the headmaster who betrays us in Asia. Fire the collectors of corruption, those prancing mimics of the Moscow party line in the State Department."

Props added to the performance, especially when Joe waved in the air a stack of papers and proclaimed, "I hold in my hand the proof." It was convincing, the way it had been in Wheeling, no matter what he really held in his hand. The senator loved it and his audiences loved him, nearly to a person. But Jack Anderson found one skeptic who said McCarthy's "proof" called to mind the story of the rabbit trapper who said his quarry had escaped up a tree. When friends questioned him, he answered, "Yessir, that rabbit certainly did climb a tree. What's more, my dog had to run up the tree to catch him. And if you don't believe me, I'll show you the tree."

The reporters covering his speeches had the same questions those hunters did. They wanted to see the evidence Joe brandished yet seldom revealed. They printed his long and changing lists of little-known names — from Asia expert Haldore Hanson to UN planner Esther Caukin Brunauer and her Navy chemist husband, Stephen, and from Spanish colonel and composer Gustavo

Durán to scholars Harlow Shapley and Frederick Schuman — but seldom had time to probe their backgrounds or, as Hoover had anticipated, even to get their response to that first and most damning story branding them knaves and traitors. When they did raise convincing doubts, as all of them did, Joe simply moved on to the next name.

The Democrats who ran the Senate were in a quandary about how to handle their rogue colleague. Majority Leader Lucas had tried cornering him and watched Joe fight his way out. So Lucas, McMahon, and the other party bosses did what senators do when they're stuck: appoint a blue-ribbon panel, in this case the Subcommittee on the Investigation of Loyalty of State Department Employees. That was a mouthful, and everyone shortened it to the Tydings Committee, after Chairman Millard Tydings.* Democrats were convinced that the Marylander — a soldier, attorney, and author who'd served four years in the House and twenty-three in the senior chamber, where he'd earned a reputation as an anti–New Dealer, balanced budget conservative, and goad of the Senate — was just the maverick and tough guy to expose Joe McCarthy as the snake oil salesman he was.

The Tydings Committee launched its hearings on March 8, 1950, a month almost to the day after the Wheeling screed. Joe grabbed control from the start. He wasn't a member, but it was his claim of a Communist-infested government that provided the rationale for the proceedings, and Tydings eagerly ceded center stage to McCarthy, certain he'd flop. Instead, he delivered a triumphant performance if not the evidence he kept promising. Joe himself was the first witness and the dominant one, and it was his accusations that determined who followed him to the stand. Senator McCarthy testified and prosecuted, dazzling spectators and giving journalists the page-one stories they cherished. "The Tydings Committee had an enormous role to play," wrote one scribe, "yet the mad force of mad circumstances compelled them to sit and listen for days and weeks and months on end to a poolroom politician grandly seized with an urge to glory (and soybean fu-

---

* Nicknames aside, the Tydings Committee was just a subcommittee.

tures) reciting facts that were not facts, about State Department employees who were not State Department employees."

Joe's opening target was an instructive one. Dorothy Kenyon was, at sixty-two, a lawyer, a former municipal judge in New York, a liberal activist, and a last-minute selection by McCarthy, who was desperate for a live body to show his colleagues while his staff scrambled to match names to the Lee List numbers he'd been citing. He chose Kenyon, he said, because she was "in a high State Department position getting about $12,000 a year who belongs to 28 organizations that have been listed by the Attorney General and by various senatorial and House committees as subversive or disloyal . . . It is impossible for any normal individual, of normal intelligence, to be so deceived that they can act as sponsors for 28 different Communist-front organizations. I might say that I personally would not be caught dead belonging to any one of the 28." Then, using his "walks like a duck" standard, the senator announced his verdict that "the Communist activities of Miss Kenyon are not only deep-rooted but extend back through the years. Her sponsorship of the doctrines and philosophy of this ruthless and Godless organization is not new."

He had a point in wondering why the State Department had never bothered to ask Kenyon about all her memberships before naming her as the US representative to the League of Nations and United Nations commissions on women. But he once again went too far on the basis of too little legwork. He inflated the number of groups Kenyon belonged to that were on the attorney general's list (four, not the nine Joe claimed), how many of her memberships continued *after* the attorney general published his list (just one, the National Council for Soviet-American Friendship), how many distinguished Americans belonged or had belonged to that council (Albert Einstein, Charlie Chaplin, and a collection of congressmen and senators), and how many groups he presented evidence on (twenty-four, not the twenty-eight he announced).* The State

---

* Lists compiled by the attorney general, HUAC, and the FBI were, as their corroborating files show, based on innuendo along with facts and didn't always prove someone was a Communist. Proving that, in turn, was a long way from showing he or she was a spy.

Department, meanwhile, pointed out that it no longer had any affiliation with Kenyon, her UN term having just expired.

Still, Joe might have escaped unscathed from his first naming
if the one he picked wasn't such a convincing witness. McCarthy, Kenyon told journalists, was "an unmitigated liar" and "a coward to take shelter in the cloak of Congressional immunity," which
shielded lawmakers from civil suits for anything they said from the
floor of the House or Senate. She was even clearer with the Tydings Committee. "I am not and never have been, a Communist,"
she declared. "I am not, and never have been a fellow traveler. I am
not, and never have been, a supporter of, a member of, or a sympa-
thizer with any organization known to me to be, or suspected by
me of being, controlled or dominated by Communists . . . My faith
in people and my impulse to fight for them is my religion and it is
the light by which I live. I also believe that it is America. There is
not a Communist bone in my body." Joe, for reasons not explained,
wasn't in the committee room for Kenyon's self-defense, but senators who were seemed struck by her sincerity as well as her elo-
quence. Conservative Republican Bourke Hickenlooper of Iowa,
who cross-examined her in McCarthy's absence, concluded by assuring her, "I haven't the least evidence, nor do I have any belief,
that you are subversive in any way."

To McCarthy, the Kenyon case would be a forgotten footnote
in his crusade against communism. Asked why he had singled her
out, he said that it was "not because Judge Kenyon herself was important . . . I took a typical case to show just what being 'cleared
by the Loyalty Board' meant. Unfortunately, it happened to be the
case of a lady." For Kenyon, McCarthy's incriminations didn't end
her activism—she would file briefs for the ACLU and the NAACP,
promote the desegregation of New York City schools, and battle
against the Vietnam War and for feminism—but it did ensure that
no officeholder would again nominate her for a public posting. For
Joe's friend Willard Edwards of the *Chicago Tribune,* the Kenyon
episode was an augury of the chaotic frenzy to come. "I've never
known a more disorganized person, much less senator," said Edwards. Joe "never knew at 9 P.M. what he would be doing at 10
A.M. the next day."

Kenyon quickly fell from the headlines as McCarthy offered a much more tantalizing prize: a man with State Department connections who had been Alger Hiss's boss, and who was, in Joe's words, "the top Russian espionage agent in this country." Who cared whether or not a lowly ex-judge was a fellow traveler, or about the scores of other cases Joe would present, not one of which, according to Senator Tydings, was a proven Communist, not to mention a traitor? A master of intrigue as well as superlatives, Joe identified his super-spy to fellow lawmakers but would only whisper about it off the record to reporters. Then, on March 26, he broke his own blackout, slipping the name to Jack Anderson, who passed it to his boss, Drew Pearson, who let his radio listeners across the nation in on the secret. At that point, as Anderson recalled, "Joe sat back and waited for the explosion. The result was a front-page story in every newspaper in the land; the name of the 'top Russian spy' was Owen Lattimore."*

That was a surprise to the press, who'd never heard of the fastidious political science professor from John Hopkins, and to Lattimore, who at the time was on a United Nations mission to Afghanistan and wired back, "DELIGHTED HIS WHOLE CASE RESTS ON ME AS THIS MEANS HE WILL FALL FLAT ON FACE." It seemed a surprise even to McCarthy, who first called Lattimore a "pro-Communist," then upgraded him slightly to an "extremely bad security risk." Suddenly the senator was staking his reputation on Lattimore's being the master of all spies, boldly proclaiming, "I am willing to stand or fall on this one." After the name became public,

---

* Herbert Fierst thought McCarthy meant him. The diplomat recognized from the nameless description that he was case number one on McCarthy's version of the Lee List, and a newspaperman told him that the senator's about-to-be-named top spy "is probably going to be you!" Fierst recounted. "So I hung around the news ticker the following day in the State Department, as McCarthy had his press conference. Lo and behold, he came up with the name that, in my ignorance, I had never heard of before, Owen Lattimore." Years later Fierst met Lattimore and told him, "I was glad it was somebody other than myself!" That, Fierst added, was "the way things went in those days. It was very exciting to be in the government, but also there were some very tense times." Association for Diplomatic Studies and Training, Foreign Affairs OH Collection, July 16, 1996.

Anderson and Pearson, meanwhile, chose to ignore the other half of Joe's gothic tale — that four Russian spies had been dropped on the US coast by a submarine, then went straight to Lattimore for instructions. *The Man, the Senator, the "Ism,"* 177.

Joe, his staff, and outside anti-Communists scrambled around the clock to come up with a justification.* He also shifted the onus to the president, calling on Truman to "put up or shut up" by opening to lawmakers Lattimore's FBI files. The president reluctantly did so, again with the understanding that McCarthy wouldn't be among those getting an off-the-record peek. And just five days after Pearson broadcast Joe's "top spy" accusation, Joe was backtracking without admitting it. "I fear in the case of Lattimore, I may have perhaps placed too much stress on the question of whether or not he has been an espionage agent," McCarthy told his fellow senators, as if it were someone else who had raised that puffed-up charge. "Forgetting for the time being any question of membership in the Communist Party or participation in espionage, I would like to deal briefly with what this man himself advocates and what he believes in."

It was a weaselly performance that upset even the arch-isolationist, ardently anti-Communist senator from Nebraska, Kenneth Wherry, a Republican and McCarthy stalwart. "Mac has gone out on a limb and kind of made a fool of himself," Wherry told an associate, who repeated it in testimony to the Senate. "We have to back him up now." (Embarrassed by the disclosure, Wherry would deny having said any such thing.)

That backup came not from Wherry but from an ex-Communist named Louis Budenz, who hated his former comrades at least as fiercely as Wherry, McCarthy, and fellow whistleblower Whittaker Chambers did. Budenz had spent nearly three thousand hours enlightening the FBI on all he knew, yet he was reluctant to thrust himself into the spotlight offered by Joe. McCarthy, however, was willing to issue a subpoena if needed, as he explained in a telegram to Budenz: "I KNOW THIS WILL INCONVENIENCE YOU SOMEWHAT BUT AM SURE YOU REALIZE THE TREMENDOUS IMPORTANCE OF GETTING BEFORE THE COMMITTEE AND THE PUB-

---

* The Marquette files include reports on Lattimore prepared by Alfred Kohlberg, a longtime friend of Chinese Nationalist leader Chiang Kai-shek and enemy of Lattimore, and by Joseph Zack Kornfeder, a founding member of the US Communist Party who in the 1930s became virulently anti-Communist. Kornfeder wrote a twenty-nine-page manifesto titled "The Case Against Owen Lattimore, Troubadour of Soviet Imperialism."

LIC INFORMATION SUCH AS THAT WHICH YOU HAVE." Now the witness was here, and before a record crowd of seven hundred jammed into a hearing room designed for three hundred, he was ready to ensure that Joe stood rather than fell on the Lattimore charge. At this moment of reckoning, Joe demonstrated his gambler's confidence and his boxer's cockiness when, on the way to the session, his car passed a group of kids playing ball in the street. "The ball rolled in front of the car and Joe got out and began tossing it around with them," said Wisconsin buddy Urban Van Susteren. "I remember thinking, 'God, for a guy whose ass is on the line, he's awfully loose.' But Joe was always that way."

Budenz wasn't quite the savior Joe counted on. At first he identified Lattimore as a Red. Then he conceded that he didn't know for certain but was only making assumptions based on what he recalled others saying years before. He testified that he'd seen documentary evidence, but unlike Chambers, he hadn't saved it in a pumpkin or anywhere else. He explained that he hadn't mentioned Lattimore before because he hadn't gotten around to it, but had been planning to, soon. Yes, it was true that the *Daily Worker* had attacked Lattimore, but that was part of a calculated strategy with people the paper embraced, to "praise them with faint damns." (One biographer stamped this "guilt by dissociation.") What about the McCarthy allegation that Lattimore was America's top-drawer traitor? "To my knowledge," Budenz said, "that statement is technically not accurate." Budenz was all over the place in a way that called to mind Joe himself, and it produced the same result among listeners — convincing them that with so much smoke, there must be a fire someplace.*

But there never was any fire with Lattimore — not the kind Mc-

---

* Questions about Budenz's own behavior should have raised doubts about the credibility of his finger-pointing, according to Jack Anderson: "While married to one woman, Budenz had lived with a second for several years. A third female showed up with him on various hotel registrations in Connecticut, Pennsylvania and New York. In the wake of all this there were three illegitimate children, a trail of forged hotel registrations and a divorce on grounds of desertion ... He faked a marriage date in his self-penned *Who's Who* biography; stumbled lamely, in the timeless manner of errant husbands who are ambushed, through interrogatories about his incontinent past; and even took the Fifth Amendment about some of his trysts." Anderson, *Confessions of a Muckraker,* 202.

Carthy was alleging. Hoover's FBI and the Red-hunting Senate Internal Security Subcommittee both doggedly examined every record they could find, but turned up no proof that the China expert was a spy for the Soviets or the Chinese, or a member of the US Communist Party. He had been an apologist for the Russians in early writings that defended Stalin, and might even have been the "conscious, articulate" propagandist that the Internal Security Subcommittee called him. He did the same for the Red Chinese, convinced as he was of the corruption and incompetence of Nationalist leader Chiang Kai-shek, whom he had seen up close during eighteen months as President Roosevelt's emissary to the Chinese leader during World War II. But when it came to McCarthy's slurs against the professor, the emerging consensus was best expressed by retired brigadier general Elliott Thorpe, the counterintelligence chief who had delivered an unheeded warning about the Japanese attack on Pearl Harbor: "I have never, in my experience as an intelligence officer, heard a man so frequently referred to as a Communist with so little basis in fact." Even so, the Justice Department was under such pressure from the public and the White House that it brought in a hardhearted young prosecutor named Roy Cohn, who won a seven-count indictment against Lattimore for lying to the Senate. A federal judge listened, then rejected the charges.

Lattimore's real crime, history suggests, lay in his early sympathies for the Soviets and his later conviction that America could woo Mao Tse-tung away from Russia's orbit. While Lattimore had never been a State Department employee, McCarthy ensured he'd never again be hired as a consultant. As with Kenyon, it wasn't a risk any public official could dare run. In Lattimore's case, his students were blacklisted, former secretaries lost their jobs, and in 1963, America's leading China scholar left Johns Hopkins to become head of Chinese studies at Britain's insulated and isolated University of Leeds. His experience, Lattimore said, convinced him that "McCarthy is a master not only of the big lie but of the middle-sized lie and the little ball-bearing lie that rolls around and around and helps the wheels of the lie machinery to turn over."

Like many of Joe's witnesses, Budenz would eventually go to work for the senator, producing reports on topics like the changing face of communism.

That ability to spin the truth would inspire poetry from an army of McCarthy biographers and profilers, with Richard Rovere crowning him the "champion liar . . . He lied in his teeth and in the teeth of the truth; he lied vividly and with a bold imagination; he lied, often, with very little pretense to be telling the truth." The Alsop brothers lyrically observed that McCarthy was "the only major politician in the country who can be labeled 'liar' without fear of libel." (Less lyrically, McCarthy referred to the brothers as the "Allslops.") A fourth journalist, Time's Thomas Griffith, offered the most compact judgment on the senator: "Over his grave should be written the simple epitaph: THE TRUTH WASN'T IN HIM."

The extent to which Joe relished his role as a disrupter, if not quite a liar, is reflected in a joke that he was told, then retold: When Secretary of State Dean Acheson died, he found Saint Peter barring the gate to heaven. "You can't come in here. Go through the door at the end of the corridor," Peter said. Acheson did, and found himself up to his neck in a ditch filled with feces. In the distance, Acheson sighted Owen Lattimore. Acheson: "We're sure in trouble." Lattimore: "This is nothing. Wait till Joe McCarthy comes through in his speedboat!"

The Lattimore case marked a watershed in the life of the Wisconsin senator and his country. He'd named enough names by then, and stirred up enough bedlam, that it prompted the professor to reach beyond his own circumstances to warn senators about "the shadow of McCarthyism" that "hangs over the whole procedure of our public life." For most Americans, that was the first time they'd heard the expression "McCarthyism," although five weeks before, editorial cartoonist Herb Block had minted it in the Washington Post. (The satirist, known as Herblock, pictured a terrified GOP elephant being pushed by party leaders to stand atop a tottering platform labeled "McCarthyism.")* Other early adopters were columnist Max Lerner, the liberal New Republic, the Communist Daily Worker, and Webster's Dictionary.†

* McCarthy kept a file on Herblock, including a list of countries that had received reprints of his cartoons on communism. Series 14, MUA.
† Webster's Third New International Dictionary was the first with the courage to list "McCarthyism," in 1961, along with words like "beatnik," "drip-dry," "jew,"

Whoever christened it, most agreed on the meaning of McCarthyism. It implied more than being anti-Communist, and stigmatized that earlier, more fact-based movement. It didn't start with Joe or end when he did, although he was so hypnotic an apostle that it took his name instead of that of Hoover, Nixon, Dies, or any of the other more provident and plodding Red-hunters of the era. It smeared targets like Kenyon and Lattimore for their opinions more than their behavior, and shattered careers even when the mud didn't stick. So great was the threat of subversion, McCarthyites said, that the sanest option was to suspend normal democratic processes like the rights of the accused to know the charge, to face one's accuser, and to be presumed innocent. The new tools of character assassination were indictment by sneaking suspicion, trial by accusation, and guilt by association. The best test of patriotism was conformity. Fabrication underlay the entire enterprise, with outsized untruths peddled like pixie dust and Ponzi schemes. Corroboration could be assembled after the bombs had been tossed and names named. At its nub, McCarthyism meant browbeating, and Joe was America's bully in chief.*

Attacks like those made Joe's defenders even more resolved to rally around him and the movement. They saw him as a true patriot, rooting out enemies in our midst. Any restrictions on freedoms were tolerable and unavoidable. Any arm-twisting was necessary to wake the nation, and a government job, after all, wasn't a right but a privilege. Any sinning by Joe was venial, paling next to the mortal sin of Marxism. While critics railed against guilt by association, boosters said more fitting labels would be bad security risk by association and guilt by collaboration. "As long as McCarthyism fixes its goal with its present precision," authors Buckley and Bozell argued, "it is a movement around which men of good will and stern morality can close ranks." The senator himself was wounded by the eponym, attributing it to the Communist Party

---

"jap," and "schlemiel." The stodgier *Oxford English Dictionary* didn't follow suit until 1976.

* Book publisher Sol Stein, a McCarthy critic, had a less forgiving definition in the film *The Real American:* "McCarthyism is the brouhaha that surrounded the nonsensical accusations of a drunk who happened to be a United States Senator and who happened to have a good platform."

and Owen Lattimore, then spinning warmer definitions. "In my State, McCarthyism means fighting communism. People write in all the time saying they wish there was more McCarthyism," McCarthy said. He liked even more this rendering: "McCarthyism is Americanism with its sleeves rolled [up]."*

The two sides agreed on one thing: how extraordinary it was, just three months after its unveiling in Wheeling, that a crusade named for a former chicken farmer from the heartland was dominating the conversation across America. Joe was better known now than any of his fellow senators and almost as famous as that other McCarthy, the redheaded talking dummy Charlie. Nearly every state had its own mini–McCarthy inquisition. And the ripples extended beyond our borders. France, Italy, and Belgium were captivated by McCarthy's charges of subversion at the State Department. They were scared stiff that "the United States is likely to go over to Russia," in Drew Pearson's words, "leaving Western Europe out on a limb." In the Far East, meanwhile, the sense was "that the U.S.A. is near revolt."

Important critics both at home and abroad felt compelled to weigh in. "I think that I have done as much against the communists as McCarthy has done for them," Winston Churchill would tell Richard Nixon, adding with a grin, "Of course, that is a private statement. I never believe in interfering in the domestic politics of another country."† Ernest Hemingway didn't hide behind third parties, writing directly to Joe, "You are a shit" and "[I] would knock you on your ass." Eleanor Roosevelt was more polite, by a smidgen: "What I think of Senator Joseph McCarthy can hardly be put into words."

Composer and lyricist Edgar Leslie did manage to find the

---

* Ed Nellor said he was the one who coined the "McCarthyism is Americanism" catchphrase, adding that it didn't work and that the word "McCarthyism" deeply affected the senator: "It killed him." Reeves interview with Nellor, June 6, 1979.
† Churchill did of course weigh in, inserting a willfully anti-McCarthy passage in Queen Elizabeth's broadcast 1953 coronation address. "Parliamentary institutions," the new monarch said, "with their free speech and respect for the rights of minorities, and the inspiration of a broad tolerance in thought and its expression — all this we conceive to be a precious part of our way of life and outlook." Brownfeld and Hennessy, "Britain's Cold War Security Purge," *Historical Journal*.

words — but his were of praise, sung adoringly if not memorably or frequently to the tune of "Battle Hymn of the Republic":

This is a land of freedom and when communists appear,
They represent a menace we must recognize and fear;
So get behind the movement of the modern Paul Revere
His truth is marching on.

Chorus:
FALL IN LINE WITH JOE MCCARTHY
FALL IN LINE WITH JOE MCCARTHY
FALL IN LINE WITH JOE MCCARTHY
His truth is marching on.

What the senator's critics and even his boosters failed to see, because his rhetoric remained so consistent, was that Joe had changed since that Lincoln Day tour. He began as a gamesman and carpetbagger but quickly became a true believer and missionary. A slapdash cry for attention had become a transcendent calling. It is impossible to pinpoint just where or when it happened, although it may have been in the Senate chamber that evening in February when Scott Lucas and the Democrats boxed him in. You don't know or believe in anything, they said, and they were right, but just for the moment. It didn't take long for the actual zealots to rally around their Richard the Lionheart, giving him an agenda and a dogma. The same way he'd embraced his earlier transformations from engineer to lawyer and from Democrat to Republican, so now this consummate shape-shifter more and more believed his own rants about the State Department being chockablock with Communists. It was a new and starring role worthy of his silver screen hero, macho man John Wayne.*

• • •

---

* The feeling was mutual, with Wayne later joining *Wagon Train* hero Ward Bond as co-chairs of the Hollywood for McCarthy Committee. And when Joe died, Wayne wrote, "I thank God we had Joe in our government, and that I could call him friend." *The Life and Times of Joe McCarthy,* 430; and note from Wayne, May 8, 1957, series 24, MUA.

Communists were Joe McCarthy's favorite bogeymen but not his only ones. Homosexuals were another focus, one fraught with opportunity as well as peril for the bachelor senator. And much as he was playing an essential role in perpetuating the Red Scare, he also utilized his trademark tactics and strategies to ignite and sustain what became known as the Lavender Scare.

The threat, as McCarthy shouted it, was that homosexuals working for agencies like the State Department were living closeted lives, petrified they might be exposed, and were therefore prime targets for blackmail by Soviet spymasters.* That logic seemed compelling to the department itself, which announced that in recent years it had accepted the resignations of ninety-one employees in the "shady category." In case anyone was unclear what that meant, which few were, the undersecretary of state added, "Most of them were homosexuals. In fact, I would say all of them were." By that reasoning as to what made a public official vulnerable, there was a bull's-eye on the back of a big-time gambler like Joe, who rolled up debts that even casual acquaintances knew about. And if his gaming didn't make him a mark for extortionists, his boozing might.†

---

* Ironically, the most compelling instance of that vulnerability to blackmail occurred when J. Edgar Hoover successfully threatened to unmask various homosexual bureaucrats unless they became his informants. Dean, *Imperial Brotherhood,* 166.

† Walter Trohan, Washington bureau chief for the *Chicago Tribune,* had a different worry about McCarthy's liability to blackmail: "He just couldn't keep his hands off young girls. Why the communist opposition didn't plant a minor on him and raise the cry of statutory rape, I don't know." The FBI reportedly had a file backing up Trohan's suspicions. Maintained on "an unusually strict, need-to-know basis" by Hoover's longtime secretary Helen Gandy, "it allegedly concerned McCarthy's involvement with young girls. Very young girls," wrote Hoover biographer Curt Gentry. "Former close personal friends of the senator were quoted in the memorandum as cautioning other friends that they should never leave McCarthy alone in a room with young children, that there had been 'incidents.' The two affidavits allegedly concerned such incidents, both involving girls under ten years of age. Nor was this gossip restricted to the upper levels of the FBI. CIA Director Allen Dulles was said to possess similar, if not the same, information, which, even while the CIA was under attack by McCarthy, Dulles was too much of a gentleman to use." Trohan, *Political Animals,* 250; and Gentry, *J. Edgar Hoover,* 434.

It was bedroom behavior, however, that grabbed Joe's attention in the weeks after Wheeling. Homosexuality was not just a stigma then but a curse. Even the high-minded *New York Times* used loaded references like "perverts," and few people knew anyone who admitted to being one of them. McCarthy took time away from his hunt for Communists to zero in on a "notorious homosexual" known to haunt the men's room at Lafayette Park in Washington, and who was arrested there by the Metropolitan Police for disorderly conduct. While he'd resigned his job at the State Department, he now held a high-paying post at the CIA. Why, McCarthy wanted to know, wasn't he fired from his first job, and why would either agency hire "a very, very unusual" man like him when "we have so many normal people, so many competent Americans . . . It certainly gives the country an odd idea of the type of individuals who are running things down here."*

The CIA man wasn't alone. A homosexual translator at the State Department "had extremely close connections with other individuals with the same tendencies," and another group of gays there had "rather unusual mental twists." Both cliques, the senator said, were not just sexual deviants but were tied up with communism. Was there a link between their perversions and political orientations? "One of our top intelligence men in Washington" thought so, Joe reported. "He said, 'Senator McCarthy, if you had been in this work as long as we have been, you would realize that there is something wrong with each one of these individuals. You will find that practically every active Communist is twisted mentally or physically in some way.'" Joe concurred, saying, "There is certainly something wrong with this group. I might say that the new security officer has recommended that they get rid of all that type of individuals regardless of whether they are shown to have any communistic connection or not."†

---

* That CIA official thought he'd be able to keep his job when, according to a then secret CIA report, he "frankly [admitted] his homosexuality" and therefore was less susceptible to blackmail. CIA director Allen Dulles was "inclined to keep him on, but bowed to the threat that McCarthy would make hay of this." CIA FOIA Archive, www.cia.gov.
† McCarthy missed the opportunity to unmask an even bigger scandal, according to George Tames, a *New York Times* photographer back then. "I had it in my

If he'd had his way, "that type of individual" would be gone from the press, too, starting with Joseph Alsop, a newsman who was a closeted homosexual, a military hawk, and an unrelenting McCarthy critic. "I think [Alsop] should expect that I may publicly discuss any of his mental or physical aberrations which I see fit," McCarthy wrote Alsop's boss at the *Saturday Evening Post*. While Alsop never backed off, the *Post* did, publishing no more of the articles that Alsop pitched on the senator. The lesson McCarthy should have drawn from Alsop's case was that homosexuals could be morally resolute in withstanding Soviet blackmail bids. Alsop would do just that when Russia's secret police photographed him having sex with their male undercover agent, then futilely attempted to recruit the journalist to spy for them.

In fairness, Joe was not the first to sound the "homosexuals can't be trusted" alarm that cost thousands their jobs, and, while he never dropped it entirely, "homo-hunting" never became a centerpiece of McCarthyism despite its crowd appeal.* He never explained why, but his reasons were partly self-protective. Unmarried at forty-one, he knew there were doubts about his own sexual prowess and preference. We know now how widespread the whispers were. Drew Pearson had in his files allegations of McCarthy sodomizing one man and kissing another on the lips; while he didn't publish the rumors, he apparently shared them with *Las Vegas Sun* publisher and editor Hank Greenspun. "It is common talk among homosexuals in Milwaukee who rendezvous at the White Horse Inn that Sen. Joe McCarthy has often engaged in homosex-

---

power to make Joe a hero and to get him off the hook, because the task force that the State Department had put out to investigate his charges of homosexuals in the State Department was headed by a homosexual. Nobody knew it, but the way I knew it was simply because I had subleased an apartment from this man," Tames recalled decades later. "I would get these mysterious phone calls from various people, and sailors knocking on my door at all hours of the night. It doesn't take an Einstein to finally realize what was going on. This man apparently was a practicing homosexual. But I didn't say a word. I sat there, playing God, I guess, and enjoying it, as to whether I should blow the whistle or not." Senate OH Program, 1988.

* Just how appealing gay-bashing was became clear in the 25,000 letters addressed to Joe's office after those early hearings. Only a quarter had to do with Reds; the rest, as a newspaper reported, "are expressing their shocked indignation at the evidence of sex depravity." Johnson, *The Lavender Scare*, 19.

ual activities," Greenspun wrote after McCarthy attacked him as a liar, smuggler, army deserter, and ex-convict. The Las Vegas newspaperman also described Joe's gait as "a little to the left of manly," said he'd take a female date to a party only to leave with "some Gay young blade," and reported that "the persons in Nevada who listened to McCarthy's radio talk thought he had the queerest laugh. He has. He is." Gamesman that he was, Greenspun couldn't resist a last sneer. Playing on the familiar slogan that Schlitz was the "beer that made Milwaukee famous," he tagged McCarthy "the queer that made Milwaukee famous."

When the charges grew loud enough, the FBI launched an investigation, telling Joe as it did. "Senator McCarthy said he hoped I would make the inquiry in such a manner as if he were a perfect stranger and I did not even know him," wrote J. Edgar Hoover. The bureau's main focus was a letter from an Army lieutenant, who said, "When I was in Washington some time ago, [McCarthy] picked me up at the bar in the Wardman [Hotel] and took me home, and while I was half-drunk he committed sodomy on me." The missive, Hoover concluded after his agents talked to everyone involved, was "entirely a fake," written because "the homosexuals are very bitter against Senator McCarthy for his attack upon those who are supposed to be in the Government." That same motivation may have been at play with other charges the bureau investigated, then dismissed. Throughout, Hoover was sensitive to what he called "the delicacy of the matter," instructing his senior staff that "it was imperative that no steps be taken that might lend the possibility of this becoming known to the press before the investigation was completed." (Hoover and his G-men were especially eager to track down and squash even more rampant rumors that it wasn't just the senator who was a "sexual pervert" but the FBI director too.)

Was the gay-bashing senator himself gay? The gossip was constant and lurid, with tales of him having affairs with one man in Wausau and another in Milwaukee, and becoming entangled with young bellboys and elevator operators. And it wasn't just what he did but whom he affiliated with. Charles Babcock, a young war veteran who organized Students for McCarthy clubs during the 1946 Senate campaign, then handled veterans' issues in Joe's Washington office, was arrested by the District of Columbia vice squad in the same park and on precisely the charges that Joe had found scandalous when they involved the CIA employee. While he may not have realized Babcock's sexual preferences, he couldn't deny knowing those of his eventual chief of staff, Roy Cohn. Greenspun admitted years later that he'd been using the standards of McCarthyism in branding Joe "a faggot. Maybe he was. He was as much a homosexual as the hundred homosexuals he said worked in the State Department, which he never produced. It was fighting the devil with fire."*

Thankfully for Joe, the judge who mattered most, J. Edgar Hoover, applied more forgiving standards. The FBI boss kept his pledge to stay quiet, which saved his friend McCarthy while giving Hoover the leverage he sought over every politician in Washington. Babcock was fired and forgotten. Joe encouraged press coverage of his romance with Jean and, when that was in a trough, of his liaisons with broadcast journalist Martha Rountree and *Washington Times-Herald* publisher Ruth McCormick "Bazy" Miller. While no one will ever know what he did in his bedroom or others', Urban Van Susteren probably was right when he labeled as "pure horseshit" the notion that McCarthy was a homosexual. "If a man wants to suck another man's cock, so what?" Van Susteren once told his friend. Joe shuddered, then growled that *"nothing* was more revolting to him than that."†

Anti-Semitism was another issue that surfaced, again, in that career-defining year of 1950. It too arose through his haphazard choice and oafish handling of his victims. Anna Rosenberg was such a star when she worked for the War Manpower Commission and other agencies during World War II that General Eisenhower

---

* The Marquette archives suggest both sides used more fire than anyone knew. His friends as well as his enemies apparently planned to use lie detector tests to bolster their version of whether Joe had had male sexual partners. Memos to Joe from Karl Baarslag, November 5, 1954, and from Gomillion Detective Agency, February 28, 1953, series 14, MUA.

† Years later, Wisconsin reporter Dion Henderson was out drinking with Joe in Milwaukee when they "stopped for another drink at the Mint Bar, near the Auditorium. He was raising the glass to his lips when someone said, 'Did you know this was a hangout for queers?' In the same motion, Joe threw the drink over his shoulder and rushed out." Bayley, *Joe McCarthy and the Press*, 74.

made her the first female recipient of the Medal of Freedom and President Truman bestowed on her a Medal for Merit. When the Korean War was gearing up, Secretary of Defense George Marshall tapped her to raise the troops needed to fight there, protect Europe, and safeguard the home front. Never had the Defense Department offered such an influential posting to a woman. Even more unlikely, this slip of a woman was a Hungarian-born, liberal-leaning Jew. Within a day, an army had mobilized to oppose her nomination, uniting enemies of the New and Fair Deals, racial desegregation, world Zionism, current and past presidents, and the Nuremberg verdicts. It wasn't just her gender and ideology that enraged them but the conviction that anyone named Rosenberg was ipso facto a Soviet spy. Marshall realized a fight was inevitable but hadn't anticipated the intensity of the resistance. Naming Anna Rosenberg, he conceded, was either "my biggest boner or a stroke of genius."

Joe should have known better than to sign on with screwballs like Rosenberg's opponents, some of whom denied Jesus Christ was Jewish. As early as his 1946 campaign, the senator had heard about Gerald L. K. Smith (who would warn his followers to "keep the Zionist Jew Anna Rosenberg from becoming the dictator of the Pentagon"). He met and seemed impressed with the Holocaust-denying Ku Klux Klansman Wesley Swift, who had founded the Swift-worshiping Church of Jesus Christ Christian (and would instruct his congregants that Rosenberg was not merely a "Jewess" but "an alien from Budapest with Socialistic ideas"). McCarthy trusted the notorious liar Ralph DeSola when he swore he'd met Rosenberg at a gathering of the Red-friendly John Reed Club. (He had met *an* Anna Rosenberg, of which there were forty-six listed in New York directories, but as the FBI knew all along, DeSola's Anna was living in California now and wasn't being nominated for anything.) While he was an instinctual people person, Joe was an increasingly indiscriminate judge of character. He listened to a callow staff eager to please him and a coterie of professional anti-Communists out for scalps, rather than to the Republicans on the Armed Services Committee who joined Democrats in unanimously okaying Rosenberg's nomination. The upshot: doubters once again wondered how this veteran of the Malmedy debacle could be so oblivious to the evil that had recently decimated the Jewish people. Was he after all an anti-Semite? In the end, Joe was again forced to do an about-face, not just ending his bid to defeat Anna Rosenberg but voting to confirm her.*

Rosenberg was shaken by her experience, saying, "I was almost [Marshall's] Dreyfus case."† Recognizing that he was the one McCarthy and his collaborators were really after, Marshall ordered his staff to prepare a study on how smears could be used to bring down innocent victims like Rosenberg, Lattimore, and Acheson, all of whom the general had defended. The nine-page report was titled "Character Assassination" but could as easily have been called "McCarthyism."‡

Marshall, a former five-star general of the Army who masterminded Allied military operations during World War II, was right about his being the next big target. McCarthy already had maligned Marshall's boss Harry Truman as that "son of a bitch," his cabinet mate as "Red" Dean Acheson, and Marshall himself as a diplomat who "did much to lose the war which as a soldier he had done much to win." Nobody was immune. But no one could have anticipated how much further this senator would go in blackening the man the president called the "greatest living American." In a speech delivered to the Senate on the afternoon of June 14, 1951, McCarthy placed Marshall at the epicenter of "a conspiracy so immense and an infamy so black as to dwarf any previous such venture in the history of man." The assault, which ran to sixty thousand words, was an onerous undertaking even for as ornery a politician as Joe, as he confessed later: "[I] recalled the advice given me by some of my friends before I gave the history of George Marshall. 'Don't do

---

* Arnold Forster, general counsel of the Anti-Defamation League, believed that while Joe might not be anti-Semitic, "there was scarcely a professional American anti-Semite who had not publicly endorsed the senator." Judging by Joe's own standard of association, juries would have unanimously pronounced him guilty. Powers, *Not Without Honor*, 262.
† France's 1894 conviction for treason of Captain Alfred Dreyfus is a universal symbol not just of injustice but of anti-Semitism.
‡ Joe insisted, "I don't smear anybody. I expose things that need exposing, that's all. And I won't let the Communists and pro-Communists scare me into quitting." "The Controversial Senator Contends His Tactics Are Both Practical and Fair."

it, McCarthy,' they said. 'Marshall has been built into such a great hero in the eyes of the people that you will destroy yourself politically if you lay hands on the laurels of this great man.'" Yet McCarthy bulled ahead, excoriating Marshall for caving in to the Kremlin, vilifying him for selling out a free China and a free Poland, and upbraiding him for weakening "our will to resist evil." The general turned Secretary of State turned Secretary of Defense knew just what he was doing. "If Marshall were merely stupid, the laws of probability would dictate that part of his decisions would serve this country's interest. If Marshall is innocent of guilty intention, how could he be trusted to guide the defense of this country further?" McCarthy wondered. "We have declined so precipitously in relation to the Soviet Union in the last 6 years. How much swifter may be our fall into disaster with Marshall at the helm? Where will all this stop? This is not a rhetorical question: Ours is not a rhetorical danger. Where next will Marshall carry us?"

Joe's speech cited as sources everyone from Winston Churchill to General Omar Bradley. But as Marshall's biographer pointed out, it "lifted statements out of context, added comments in quotations that were not in the original, omitted qualifying sentences, included rhetorical speculations by unnamed Democrats as to why Marshall went wrong, and cited as fact unproved charges made from various hearings. The State Department later compiled the actual complete statements from the various sources cited, which lauded the man their hacked-off sections had been spliced together to condemn."

Recognizing that most of the speech was a recycling of Republican charges against Roosevelt and Truman, and the rest was the slander of an icon, Democratic senators boycotted it.* A handful of Republicans came and fewer stayed. Joe asked for and got a short recess that let him eat a sandwich and drink a glass of milk. Then he was back to the scholarly-sounding stretching of facts that he may have been reading for the first time, since they were assembled by conservative journalist Forrest Davis, then edited by Jean,

---

* It also was a recycling of charges that Senator William Jenner had leveled a year before against Marshall, calling him a "front man for traitors" and a "living lie." Pogue, *George C. Marshall*, 427.

Don Surine, and other staffers. Finally, the senator tired as even Jean and Don left the chamber; after nearly three hours he began skipping pages, then stopped reading altogether and inserted the remainder into the *Congressional Record*. Later, he published an expanded version of the speech in a thin book, under his own byline, called *America's Retreat from Victory: The Story of George Catlett Marshall*. He was so convinced that it would sell that he ordered 25,000 copies, giving the publisher as collateral two hundred shares of Seaboard Air Line Railway Company stock and seven hundred of Four Wheel Drive Auto Company.

Marshall pretended to be unfazed about being accused of treason, saying that if he responded, "I would acknowledge something that isn't true, that McCarthy's accusations are worthy of defense. There is no necessity for me to prove my loyalty to the United States; I have lived that loyalty every day of my life." Then the general told a time-tested joke he said was the best retort to the dirt the senator was dishing: "As the street cleaner said to the elephant, 'that's enough out of you.'" But while Marshall had learned to disguise his fierce temper, his actions were telling. He resigned three months after the McCarthy jeremiad, which was longer than he'd originally planned to stay but not as long as Truman wanted. After fifty years of government service, the seventy-year-old general was left to tend his gardens and exercise his horses.

Others were less restrained. *Collier's* told its 3 million readers that "this speech sets a new high for irresponsibility in a senatorial career distinguished mainly for its extravagant accusations," adding that no "American who is both sane and honest can believe that George Marshall or Dean Acheson is a traitorous hireling of the Kremlin." As for how Republicans should treat their obstreperous colleague, the magazine offered this headlined suggestion: "Why Not Spank Him?" Leverett Saltonstall, Joe's GOP colleague from Massachusetts, did give Joe a verbal paddling, albeit years later, calling the denunciation of Marshall "sickening, simply disgusting." Even Van Susteren, normally an apologist for Joe's bad behavior, said this episode was *"indefensible . . .* It makes me sick."

McCarthy's attack on the secretary of defense was partly a case of throwing red meat to the Republican right, which blamed Marshall for Truman's firing of its favorite five-star general, Douglas MacArthur. But the conservatives who had questioned his treatment of Marshall fell back into line when Joe zeroed in on the most loathed of his front-line prey in that post-Wheeling period: syndicated columnist Andrew Russell "Drew" Pearson. Pearson's eight weekly "Washington Merry-Go-Round" columns were printed in six hundred daily and weekly newspapers with a combined circulation of 40 million. Every Sunday night in that Golden Age of radio, 20 million listeners pulled their chairs and sofas around the two-foot-high Philco console, the brown Bakelite dial carefully tuned to the blend of news and gossip delivered staccato fashion on *Drew Pearson Comments.* No correspondent in America wielded more clout than the mustachioed Quaker from Pennsylvania. Nobody was a more faithful heir to the Progressive Era's muckrakers or did more to beget the Watergate Era whistleblowers. And from the late 1940s through the mid-'50s, no public figure aroused Pearson's ferocious ire more regularly than the finger-pointing senator from Wisconsin.

Pearson penned fifty-eight columns on Joe in the months after Wheeling, all scathing. "This writer, who has covered the State Department for about twenty years, has been considered the career boys' severest critic. However, knowing something about State Department personnel, it is my opinion that Senator McCarthy is way off base," he wrote in February 1950. "The alleged Communists which he claims are sheltered in the State Department just aren't." Three weeks later Pearson was back, blasting Joe for a "witch hunt," saying he "has disrupted our entire foreign service," and reporting that "Republicans consider this a calamity." And the columnist didn't stop there, revisiting Judge McCarthy's tax troubles, short-order divorces, and near disbarment. By April, Drew was branding Joe "another Huey Long. Like the Louisiana Kingfish, Joe McCarthy has an engaging manner, great personal charm, tremendous energy and an insatiable desire for putting headlines ahead of public welfare." The Merry-Go-Rounder was relentless, and his audience wasn't just the public but journalists who were too busy or too browbeaten to do muckraking of their own.

Pearson divined in McCarthy a witch-hunter who couldn't

snare a witch—precisely the sort of faker he'd spent his career ferreting out.* The columnist was a Washington player who, for the sake of a better story, didn't hesitate in allowing his legmen to misrepresent themselves to unsuspecting officials or otherwise bend the rules. Yet while columnists were less bound by journalistic neutrality than beat reporters, Pearson felt compelled to remain bipartisan, if only because his writings appeared in more Republican papers than Democratic ones. His exposés also generally were on target, and his prey almost always deserved whatever he hit them with. That's what kept readers coming back to his column for an unheard-of thirty-seven years, and what kept Drew coming back to Joe. He published rumors he could pin down, and leaked to Greenspun or held as future fodder less substantial ones on topics as explosive as McCarthy's sexual preferences and his alleged ties to the Al Capone gang.† The columnist even had a paid informant in Joe's Senate office, passing information to Pearson until the setup became too costly. Likening his boss to Don Quixote, Jack Anderson said, "McCarthyism was to him the ultimate windmill, the clear and present danger."

The obsession was mutual. McCarthy kept tabs as well as files on Pearson, partly because of the columnist's reach in Wisconsin and across the land. But there was more to it. Drew had started out evenhanded and at times friendly, and Joe fed juicy tidbits to him and his sidekick, Anderson. The journalist's turning on the senator was, in McCarthy's Irish-tough world, an unpardonable breaking of faith. He also saw Pearson as an exemplar of the Washington establishment he detested and an archenemy of his Middle America. What irked Joe most was that Drew seemed to be the one press

---

* His critics came up with endless colorful metaphors for Joe's Red-hunting—saying that he was like a blindfolded man flailing away in a roomful of bats, that he wouldn't recognize a Communist if he tripped over one in a well-lit closet, that he couldn't find a Red in Moscow's Red Square on May Day, and that he didn't know Karl Marx from Groucho Marx. Morgan, *Reds*, xiii; "Smear, Inc."; and *McCarthy and the Press*, 68.

† Pearson did publish at least one reference to Capone and McCarthy, telling "the income-tax story of gangster Charlie Fischetti, cousin of Ralph Capone of Mercer, Wisconsin, at one time a McCarthy political booster." Ralph "Bottles" Capone Sr. was Al's older brother and a Chicago gangster in his own right. Pearson column, January 17, 1951.

person he couldn't easily counterattack the way he did Joe Alsop the queer or Cedric Parker the Commie. Pearson was married, and bled red, white, and blue, with a longer, deeper anti-Communist résumé than the senator.* And he didn't scare.

Joe was seething — and plotting. He kept by his bedside a baseball bat with *"Drew Pearson"* carved into the wood, next to a sledgehammer bearing the legend *"for Drew Pearson only."* During a drinking bout, a friend of Pearson's overheard McCarthy and his entourage musing about the pros and cons of "bumping Pearson off" versus "a little permanent mutilation." Weeks later, at a Gridiron Club Dinner, the senator greeted the columnist, "Someday I'm going to break your leg, Drew, but for the time being I just wanted to say hello."

Talk turned into action on December 12, 1950, the eve of Pearson's fifty-third birthday. Louise Tinsley Steinman, the daughter of a wealthy newspaper publisher, was hosting an intimate dinner dance at Washington's posh Sulgrave Club. She didn't tell Joe that she had asked Drew, or vice versa, as was her mischievous wont. McCarthy greeted Pearson with an offer to get him a drink and the assurance "I am really going to take you apart on the Senate Floor." Pearson sniped back, "Joe, how is your income tax case coming along . . . How long are they going to let you stay out of jail?" Then, according to Drew, Joe called him "a God damned son of a bitch," said "come on outside," and, in Pearson's words, "gouged me as hard as he could, so that an intense pain shot through my head and staggered me for a moment." Steinman tried to calm the ruckus she'd orchestrated, telling Drew's wife, Luvie, "to dance with [Joe] and, you know, sort of flirt a little to prove that Drew had married A Real Woman."

There was a lull, but as the party broke up, the combatants met again in the cloakroom. Drew claimed he reached into his pocket for tip money, at which point Joe "pinned my hands down, swung me around, and proceeded to kick me in the groin with his knee . . . He said, 'Keep your hands out of your pocket; no fire-

---

* In 1946 Pearson broke the blockbuster story about a ring of Soviet spies in Canada who might have made their way across the US border and were spilling atomic secrets.

arms, no guns' . . . He kicked me a second time, and we stood there, he saying, 'Take that back about my income taxes.'" That's when Richard Nixon showed up. McCarthy, seeing his anti-Communist confederate, landed a head-snapping slap on Pearson with the commentary, "That one was for you, Dick." Nixon pushed the pair apart, admonishing, "Let a good Quaker stop this fight." But Joe "broke loose and swung on me with the flat of his hand," Drew said, adding, "It didn't hurt. It was just a little bit of a sting . . . I guess McCarthy is not the great Marine pugilist that he says he is." As for any return punch, Drew said he was manacled by the morals clause in his radio contract: "I was toying with the idea of whether to come back at him or just take it, and I took it."

Joe offered different and shifting versions of the face-off that had every Washington tattletale tittering. In a letter to the editor of the *Saturday Evening Post,* Joe said it was Drew who was the aggressor and he'd tried to turn the other cheek, ignoring the columnist "until he followed me down to the cloakroom, at which time he made a statement to the effect that if I dared to make a speech against him, he would 'get me,' and boasted that he had never failed to get anyone he went after." As the threats continued, said Joe, Pearson "started to place his right hand in his coat pocket. I had heard that he carried a gun, which I frankly did not believe, but I could not take any chance, so I grabbed his right arm with my left and pinned it to his side so he could not reach any further into his coat pocket. I slapped him on the side of the face until he withdrew his hand from his coat pocket. I checked his pocket and found he did not have a gun—that he was bluffing as usual." (*Post* editors gave Drew the final word: "The only thing that's true about Senator McCarthy's version of the incident is that we were both at the same party.")

In a second telling, under oath in a deposition, the senator related this story: "I got an Elgin watch several days later inscribed 'For combat duty on the 13th of December above and beyond the call of duty.'* Well, this wasn't very rough combat service. My big

---

* Joe joked that the anonymous benefactor in Missouri who sent the watch must be Harry Truman. Journalist George Reedy, who heard about the Sulgrave episode from Joe, said the glee with which he described it—in a high-pitched voice

difficulty was to avoid hurting Drew." And in a letter to Jean, Joe described what happened when he arrived at a luncheon with Senate colleagues two days after the dustup with Pearson: "You would have thought I had just guaranteed perpetual life and perpetual time in office to each Senator there. They all greeted me as a greatly beloved and long lost brother. John McClellan [of Arkansas] was perhaps the most enthusiastic — said that it carried him back to the days his daddy used to talk about, when men were men. Just what the hell they think was manly about kneeing and slapping that puke of a Pearson, I don't know."

Three days after the Sulgrave encounter, McCarthy gave Pearson an even fiercer pummeling, this time on the Senate floor and with a well-exercised tongue. Just before his speech, he told Anderson what he had in mind: "Jack, I'm going to have to go after your boss. I mean, no holds barred. I figure I've already lost his supporters; by going after him, I can pick up his enemies." Joe called Drew "one of the cleverest men who has ever prostituted one of the noblest professions — a man, who, in my opinion, has been and is doing an infinite amount of damage to America and all of the institutions of our form of government." Then he quoted damning remarks about Pearson from a bipartisan lineup of congressmen and senators, a union leader, President Truman, and Drew's ex-mother-in-law, who supposedly called him a "child cheater" as well as "vicious and perverted." While "it appears that Pearson never actually signed up as a member of the Communist Party and never paid dues . . . that has not in any way affected his value to the party," the senator said. "He has always consistently and without fail launched a campaign of personal smear and vilification against any man in public life who has stood against any plan of socialization in this country." It was just the kind of slurring that Pearson had charged McCarthy with, as Joe knew. He also knew his critics had been taunting him for hiding behind his

---

with a teenage giggle — brought to mind a boy who just pulled up a girl's skirt. Utah senator Arthur Watkins, who would later play a central role in Joe's undoing, on this occasion approached his colleague to say, "Joe, the newspapers differ as to where you hit him, but I hope both accounts were right." Reeves interviews with Van Susteren, March 16, 1981, and Reedy, May 12, 1976; and Pearson column, December 15, 1954.

congressional immunity as he slandered others, so here too he tried to turn the tables on Pearson: "If Mr. Pearson wants to waive his own special, self-created kind of immunity . . . I shall be glad to repeat this, if he will submit the request in writing—and will tell me where and when he wants this repeated off the floor of the Senate."

What to do with this dangerous pressman? Joe knew just the thing: boycott the underwriter of his radio show. The American people "can notify the Adam Hat Co., by actions, what they think of their sponsoring this man," McCarthy said. "It should be remembered that anyone who buys an Adam hat, any store that stocks an Adam hat, anyone who buys from a store that stocks an Adam hat, is unknowingly and innocently contributing at least something to the cause of international communism by keeping this Communist spokesman on the air."

Anderson recalled running into McCarthy again just after the speech, "swinging through the doorway with a buoyant stride, as though he had just accomplished the Lord's work. He saw me and stopped: 'I wasn't talking about you, Jack,' he said." The newsman "fumbled for something appropriate to say and again came up dry. 'I see you're wearing a red tie, Joe,' I mumbled. 'Maybe you ought to investigate yourself.' He moved on with the lofty resignation of one whose gallantry is uncomprehended. As he passed out into the December night, he put on a gray Fedora which I recognized —an Adam hat, size 7⅜, presented to him a year before by Drew Pearson."*

McCarthy didn't let up, with seven Senate speeches in seven weeks that included calls for Pearson's prosecution. He was right about some things. One assistant whom Drew belatedly fired, An-

* Just how energized Joe was by the Pearson attack was apparent in his letter to Jean, who was away from Washington recuperating from an injury: "I asked Mary to send you a copy yesterday air mail special—thought you might enjoy it. Perhaps you can use it instead of a blood transfusion . . . I understand the radio and the press quite generally covered the remark about Adams Hat, which is the one I think will damage him the most. It also will put some of the other advertisers on notice not to hire Commie commentators or they may be labeled also. I would say from the standpoint of public relations, slapping his face and giving the speech were rather successful. How much it will cut him down to size remains to be seen." Letter from Joe to Jean, December 16, 1950, series 24, MUA.

drew Older, was a Communist like Joe said. Another, David Karr, denied it vehemently, as did Pearson. We now know that Karr did in fact work for Soviet intelligence, but not until the 1970s, a generation after McCarthy inaccurately branded him Pearson's KGB controller. More recently, it has been suggested that Pearson's earliest collaborator, Robert Allen, was a paid covert informant for Russia, although he may have been duped, and what he passed on had limited value. Joe also had information that he threatened to use on how, at the age of seventeen, Drew was arrested for indecent exposure in Reidsville, North Carolina, after he and a black co-worker were caught prancing naked after midnight near where they worked. The judge accepted their explanation that they were taking an innocent sponge bath following a night of grimy labor, but an investigator McCarthy sent to look into it decades later reported that "upon advice of his attorneys Pearson is said to have claimed he was merely taking a bath, while the officer said there was no water any place around." Joe never went public with his suspicions, but he couldn't resist describing Pearson with no-need-to-explain adjectives like "degenerate" and "perverted."*

Joe landed his most crushing blow against this adversary, and by extension against any journalist tempted to take him on, by the attack on his paymasters. Shortly after his call for a boycott, Adam Hats announced it was canceling its sponsorship of Drew's radio show, which paid him $250,000 a year ($2.5 million in today's dollars). The hat company's insistence that its decision had been made before Joe's Senate speech didn't keep him from claiming credit or the world from seeing it as cause and effect.† While Pear-

---

* Joe also was getting tips about Pearson's finances, including a 1951 note from Robert Barker, the chief investigator for a House committee, saying, "Pole Cat Drew has been hollering about your tax returns. I thought perhaps you would like to see his: Here they are for twelve years — 1932 to 1943." In addition, Barker gave Joe an FBI file on David Karr, while another friend fed the senator a secret report prepared for Pearson by a detective hired to dig up dirt on McCarthy. The sleuth had told the columnist about Charles Babcock's arrest with other "queers," and called the young aide "McCarthy's protégé." As their battle heated up, Joe would encourage the attorney general to indict Drew on espionage and other charges. Pearson File, series 14, MUA.

† It *was* cause and effect, and Adam's suggestion otherwise was "sheer nonsense," said the Anti-Defamation League's Arnold Forster, an up-close observer. "The in-

son found other underwriters, none were as long-term or gold-plated as the hatmaker. The columnist tried to strike back in kind, filing a $5.1 million suit against McCarthy and his allies alleging that he'd suffered a huge financial blow (he had), that he had endured major pain and suffering from the Sulgrave attack (he probably did), and that Joe and his cronies were to blame (a claim there was no chance to test because Pearson withdrew his suit three years later, without explanation).

Drew had counted on public figures and fellow journalists to rise to his defense, but almost none did, not even his former friend and fellow gossip monger Walter Winchell. A month after Pearson broke with McCarthy, Winchell formed an alliance with the senator that lasted nearly until the end.* President Truman seemed to speak for all those who let Drew down when, having seen a transcript of Joe's upbraiding of the columnist, he said, "I hope they both kill each other off." Later he added a postscript: "The only good thing McCarthy ever did was to knock down Drew Pearson."

Interestingly, Joe hesitated about dressing down other high-profile figures, even if they were easy targets. The clearest case was theoretical physicist Albert Einstein, who had helped the Allies win World War II by pressing President Roosevelt on the urgency of building an atom bomb before the Nazis did. The Nobel laureate was an avowed Socialist, a pacifist and gay rights advocate, a Jewish German refugee, and a sufficient worry to the FBI that it kept a 1,449-page file on him. That was enough for Joe to write the professor into the draft of a speech to the Senate in Octo-

---

tent on both sides to renew," Forster said, "was clearly understood by both sides. In the middle of negotiations the company routinely sent its November 15th notice to Pearson that the contract was to be terminated at the end of 90 days. It was McCarthy's boycott *alone* that changed his sponsor's mind." Klurfeld, *Winchell,* 145–46.

* Winchell had his own version of his split with Pearson, saying Drew phoned him after the Sulgrave attack "and said, 'What are you going to do about that sonofabitch?' 'Not a thing,' I said. 'It's not my table. Where am I going to put it? In the Hearst papers? Over King Features Syndicate—Hearst-owned? They are on McCarthy's team!'" That very night, Winchell added, Pearson exacted revenge by reporting on his radio broadcast, "Many people are wondering about Walter Winchell's peculiar palship with gang chief Frank Costello!" Drew, Walter added, "immediately went on my Ingrate List. The End of a Beautiful False Friendship." Winchell, *Winchell Exclusive,* 256–57.

ber 1950 on Communist infiltration of the scientific profession. "I don't challenge the legal right of Professor Einstein to be a Communist, a fellow traveler, or just a plain political dope. It is his legal right to select any of these categories," Joe planned to say. "Albert Einstein is one of the great scientific geniuses of all time. On the other hand, it is clear that Albert Einstein has grossly abused the privileges which he has been accorded by the gift of American citizenship. Despite the fact that Einstein is a refugee from Hitler's murderous totalitarianism, he has on many occasions supported the causes of Stalin's even more brutal totalitarianism, ever since his arrival in the United States."

That wasn't all. "Einstein has been affiliated with not less than 27 Communist front organizations. These affiliations, taken in their entirety, constitute a close and active *collaboration* with Communists. This is not a case of guilt by remote or accidental association," read the McCarthy text, which had been crossed out in dark pencil with a pink note saying "cut from Atomic Scientists speech." Joe's undelivered Einstein remarks ended with this line of poetic vituperation: "The clichés of the rabble-rousing soapbox Socialist pour from his pen as easily as his cosmic equations."

Did he hold back for fear of being accused again of anti-Semitism, or because a staffer cautioned temperance when it came to the revered genius? Joe never said. What we do know is that his worries about Einstein were reciprocated. "America is incomparably less endangered by its own Communists than by the hysterical hunt for the few Communists that are here," Einstein wrote as the congressional hunts for Reds quickened. As for his own politics, the scientist asserted, "I have never been a Communist. But if I were, I would not be ashamed of it." And he advised colleagues who were called to testify before legislative panels probing communism to refuse, even if it meant "jail and economic ruin." Joe got the last word: "Anyone who advises Americans to keep secret information which they may have about spies and saboteurs is himself an enemy of America."

Republicans were torn. Most recognized early on that McCarthy was an irresponsible bomb slinger, but they were heartened that he was aiming mainly at Democrats and was arming Republicans with a potent electoral issue. Most also had been chasing Communists long before McCarthy stumbled onto the cause, although more politely and productively. So they held their noses and publicly encouraged him to keep hurling.

Nobody embodied the push-pull better than Senator Robert Taft, the Ohio Republican and unchallenged leader of his party's conservative wing. Taft resented Joe for having backed Stassen instead of him in the 1948 presidential primaries, for challenging him on public housing and other issues, and for his boorish defiance of every norm and protocol sacred to this scion of the Senate. Taken by surprise with the Wheeling diatribe, he confided to one friend that McCarthy "doesn't check his statements very carefully and is not disposed to take any advice so that it makes him a hard man for anybody to work with, or restrain." To others, he called the Wisconsinite's performance "perfectly reckless" and prophetically pronounced that Joe had "made allegations which are impossible to prove which may be embarrassing before we get through."

But there was a reason Taft was called "Mr. Republican." Donning his partisan persona, the civil libertarian senator found a stream of rationalizations for his rights-bashing colleague. Although Joe hadn't unmasked any Communists yet, Taft said a month after Wheeling, he ought to "keep talking and if one case doesn't work out, he should proceed with another one." When President Truman vilified Joe, Taft accused the president of "libeling . . . a fighting Marine who risked his life to preserve the liberties of the United States."* Two weeks later he ventured onto even thinner ice: "Whether Senator McCarthy has legal evidence, whether he has overstated or understated his case, is of lesser importance. The question is whether the Communist influence in the State Department still exists." Taft's prevaricating was perhaps best explained by a Washington acquaintance: "McCarthyism is a kind of liquor for Taft. He knows it's bad stuff, and he keeps taking the pledge. But every so often he falls off the wagon. Don't ask me

---

* Asked at a press conference whether he'd libeled the senator, Truman asked back, "Do you think that is possible?" *Conspiracy So Immense*, 144.

why. I only know that he doesn't like it and can't stay away from it."*

The only Republican to take a firm stand against McCarthy was the Senate's only woman, Margaret Chase Smith of Maine. It would be her proudest moment in the chamber and one for which she would pay dearly. Smith had met McCarthy years before at a dinner party and she was charmed. The two shared a skepticism about Dean Acheson and communism, and Joe not only named her to the investigations subcommittee where he was ranking Republican but also touted her as a future vice presidential nominee. Wheeling was her breaking point. "The more I listened to Joe and the more I read the papers he held in his hand, the less I could understand what he was up to," she said looking back. "One day Joe said, 'Margaret, you seem to be worried about what I am doing.' I said, 'Yes, Joe. I want to see the proof.'" McCarthy: "But I have shown you the photostatic copies." Smith: "Perhaps I'm stupid, Joe. But they don't prove a thing to me that backs up your charges."

On June 1, 1950, mimeographed remarks in hand, Smith was heading for the members-only train that would take her from her office to the Capitol when she ran into Joe. "Margaret," he said jauntily, "you look very serious. Are you going to make a speech?" Her: "Yes, and you will not like it." Him, smiling: "Is it about me?" Her: "Yes, but I'm not going to mention your name." Him, frowning: "Remember Margaret, I control Wisconsin's twenty-seven convention votes!"

On the Senate floor, Smith said she wanted to discuss with her colleagues "a serious national condition" that made it "high time for the United States Senate and its members to do some soul-searching—for us to weigh our consciences—on the manner in which we are performing our duty to the people of America . . . Those of us who shout the loudest about Americanism in mak-

---

* *Life* magazine, owned by the ardently anti-Soviet Henry Luce, was outraged by what Taft was doing. "If Houdini were a suspected Communist he couldn't get near a sensitive government payroll today. In short, *Communist infiltration of government is no longer a legitimate worry*," the magazine declared in an editorial that called on Taft and his supporters to "renounce and repudiate all political connections" with McCarthy. "Taft and McCarthy," *Life*.

ing character assassinations are all too frequently those who, by our own words and acts, ignore some of the basic principles of Americanism: The right to criticize; The right to hold unpopular beliefs; The right to protest; The right of independent thought." While saying that "the nation sorely needs a Republican victory" in the November elections, she added, "I don't want to see the Republican Party ride to political victory on the Four Horsemen of Calumny—Fear, Ignorance, Bigotry, and Smear." Finishing her opening remarks, and trying to settle what she'd concede was a fluttering stomach, the ordinarily cautious Smith read a "Declaration of Conscience" that called for civility and bipartisanship and was co-signed by six moderate Republicans.*

It was a fifteen-minute act of gallantry and grit, one that Joe listened to silently from his desk two rows behind Smith's. But the recriminations were quick and stinging. Columnist and McCarthy friend Westbrook Pegler called her "a Moses in nylons" who "took advantage . . . of her sex." Others suggested that the two had been romantically involved, or she'd wanted to be, and that the speech was personal revenge. Joe had the most cutting quip, calling Smith and her co-signatories "Snow White and the Six Dwarfs." His words were reinforced by splenetic action. Using his authority as ranking Republican, in 1951 he dumped Smith from the subcommittee he'd named her to, replacing her with a friendlier Richard Nixon. He let her know not in person but in a note slipped under her office door. After reading it, she tried to phone McCarthy; told he was busy, she left this message: "I fully realize that kicking me off the Investigations Subcommittee is an act of vengeance." Message delivered—and received.

Smith also had her defenders, starting with Democratic senator Paul Douglas of Illinois, who walked over after she delivered her

---

* The six senators were Charles Tobey of New Hampshire, Irving Ives of New York, Edward Thye of Minnesota, Robert Hendrickson of New Jersey, George Aiken of Vermont, and Wayne Morse of Oregon. Only Morse, Smith said, never retreated or repudiated his support. That was being unkind to Hendrickson, who withstood tongue-lashings from McCarthy, and perhaps too kind to Smith herself, who, once the Korean War broke out, embraced not just Joe's anticommunism but some of his unforgiving tactics. Smith, *Declaration*, 10–11; and author's interview with and emails from Gregory Peter Gallant.

declaration, tenderly grasped her hand, then, voice choking and eyes tearing, silently retreated. Days later at a luncheon, President Truman told her that her remarks were "one of the finest things that has [*sic*] happened here in Washington in all my years in the Senate and the White House." Most satisfying of all in that era of glass ceilings, statesman and financier Bernard Baruch said that if a man had delivered the same rebuke Smith did, he'd be the next president of the United States.

While the Democrats loved seeing Republicans squabble among themselves, they still couldn't figure out what to do with McCarthy. They'd counted on Senator Millard Tydings to rein him in, but that strategy had problems from the get-go. The mandate of Tydings's subcommittee was "to conduct a full and complete study and investigation as to whether persons who are disloyal to the United States are, or have been, employed by the Department of State." Tydings, who had to be asked twice before he took the job nobody wanted, defined a mission he preferred rather than the one he was handed. He knew there was no gain for a Democratic senator in harassing a Democratic administration's State Department, and that HUAC and other congressional committees already had done that. So instead of investigating the diplomatic corps, he investigated its chief accuser. Tydings's goal was unmistakable: to show that everyone outed by Joe McCarthy already was out or innocent.

Starting the month after Wheeling and finishing two weeks after Independence Day, Tydings compiled 1,498 pages of testimony and another 1,024 of documentary evidence. Everyone was allowed to have a say, but few minds were changed. McCarthy badgered Kenyon, Lattimore, Rosenberg, and others he said were unpatriotic, and received as gospel the testimony of professional anti-Communists like Budenz. Democrats did the same in reverse. The State Department's word on the reliability of its loyalty reviews and the innocence of its staff was good enough for Senator Tydings. That was mainly a matter of politics, but the surveillance system really had been beefed up as much as it could be in a democracy that cherishes freedoms of association and speech. Joe was playing politics as well, saying that his job was to provide clues rather than polished briefs, with the onus on Tydings and the White House to determine who was a spy among the officials he'd named. His supporters credit him with pinpointing 124 potential security risks, at least eighty of whom were still at the State Department.

In that back-and-forth, Joe once again showcased his wizardry at bending rules and controlling the conversation of a subcommittee on which, as with Malmedy, he didn't sit. When witnesses testified in public, he accused Democrats of shaming them. When senators finally closed their doors to hear his charges, it was Tydings, not McCarthy, who was accused of hiding while Joe became a hero by leaking to the press. He cast himself as David standing up to the Goliaths of the State Department, the White House, and the inner sanctum of the upper chamber as personified by the senator from Maryland.

Tydings, meanwhile, turned out to be neither the statesman nor the warrior that his colleagues believed him to be. He relished a good fight but had never experienced a street brawler like Joe McCarthy. Worse yet, the Maryland senator surrendered the moral high ground by appearing one day on the Senate floor with a record player. He claimed he had a recording that would prove Joe had used the controversial 205 figure he'd denied uttering in Wheeling. It was Tydings's version of McCarthy's "I hold in my hand" ruse. The recording actually was of a later interview on a Salt Lake City radio station. Had his fellow senators called his bluff, it would have proved nothing other than that Millard was Joe's match as a gambler and dissembler.

The subcommittee's final report, released five months after Wheeling on July 17, ran to 313 pages and 350,000 words. It examined McCarthy's numbers, names, and corroborating witnesses, rejecting all of them. Joe had no lists. There were no spies. Dorothy Kenyon wasn't a Communist or disloyal; Owen Lattimore wasn't a traitor, top-level or otherwise.* "We are constrained fearlessly and frankly to call the charges, and the methods employed to give them ostensible validity, what they truly are: A fraud and a hoax," Tydings and his fellow Democrats wrote. "They represent

---

* Lattimore and Kenyon were among the lucky few vindicated in the Kafkaesque world of McCarthyism, where accusations were page-one news and not many targets were publicly cleared of wrongdoing.

perhaps the most nefarious campaign of half-truths and untruth in the history of this Republic." No courtly Senate-speak there. Nor here: "For the first time in our history, we have seen the totalitarian technique of the 'big lie' employed on a sustained basis. The result has been to confuse and divide the American people." Joe had also sought to confuse and divide the subcommittee with "an organized campaign of unwarranted and unfair vilification without parallel in the history of congressional investigations," the majority report said, including "repeated charges that we were attempting to 'whitewash' the State and Justice Departments." There was a thin hope of isolating Joe from the two Republicans on the panel, but even that was dashed when the Democrats upbraided that pair for failing "to attend subcommittee sessions with any degree of regularity."

The searing language split the Senate in two. Every Democrat endorsed the Tydings report, while every GOP member — Margaret Chase Smith included — voted "nay." Democrats whispered that Republicans were privately laughing at McCarthy, which many were. Republicans said the transcripts were missing key pages favorable to McCarthy, which was true at first, and that the Democratic report was one-sided, which it was. "The fact that many charges have been made which have not been proven," GOP senator Henry Cabot Lodge Jr. wrote in his thirty-four-page minority report, "does not in the slightest degree relieve the subcommittee of the responsibility for undertaking a relentlessly thorough investigation of its own." FBI director Hoover, meanwhile, chose the day the subcommittee findings were unveiled to announce his arrest of atomic spy Julius Rosenberg, homing in on the Democrats' headlines as he knew he could. Ignored in the infighting were a pair of interesting recommendations by the subcommittee: to create a presidential commission to thoroughly study the whole federal loyalty program, which Joe wanted, and to rethink whether members of Congress should continue to be immune from lawsuits for libelous charges made from the floor of their chamber, which was aimed squarely at depriving Joe of such a shield.

Joe knew before it spoke what the subcommittee would say and was ready with a blistering rejoinder. "The Tydings-McMahon report is a green light to the Red fifth column in the United States," he said. "The most loyal stooges of the Kremlin could not have done a better job of giving a clean bill of health to Stalin's fifth column in this country." McCarthy borrowed from the tribunal's condemnation of him to censure it for a report that "is gigantic in its fraud and deep in its deceit." As charged, he'd already branded the Democratic-led proceedings with his trademark comeback, calling it "Operation Whitewash." Jack Anderson figured this was simply more McCarthy flimflam; the senator assured the columnist, "No, no, no. This is the real thing, Jack. This is the real thing."*

In the end, the hearings and findings elevated McCarthy and left Tydings exhausted and deflated. Joe hadn't proved his charges, but the former country judge knew he didn't have to. He wasn't out to prove guilt beyond reasonable doubt, but only to raise doubts and raise hell. It was the president and State Department who were on trial and the safety of the nation that seemed at stake. Rather than humiliating or muzzling McCarthy, the Tydings Committee had given him a wider stage and a louder bullhorn to name his names. Joe had stood the ground he'd staked out in Wheeling and somehow made himself look more like the aggrieved than an aggressor. His murky cause had become an article of canon for Senate Republicans. His audience never was fellow senators, or even the reporters in the gallery, but the chicken farmers and grocers with whom he'd grown up. Ask God-fearing people anywhere who their white knight was in the crusade against the Red Menace and there no longer were ifs or buts: it was that battle-ready Leatherneck, Jousting Joe McCarthy.

---

* Conservative journalist Ralph de Toledano wrote Joe that August proposing a ten-part series titled "Whitewash Inc.: The Story Behind Joe McCarthy and the Tydings Subcommittee Investigation." He said he'd pitch it to the Hearst chain and to King Features, but it apparently never was published or even written. Letter from de Toledano to Joe, August, 28, 1950, unprocessed files, MUA.

4

BULLY'S PULPIT

IF WHEELING WAS WHERE SENATOR JOE McCARTHY made himself the most divisive man in America, Baltimore was where he became the most feared.

Joe couldn't forget a slight, and none of his colleagues in Congress had maligned him more than Millard Tydings, who publicly branded him a faker and called his holy war a mirage. Nobody made as tempting a target, either, for the farm-raised McCarthy. Tydings was among the Senate's richest members (by marriage) and the most pontifical (by not knowing when to muzzle himself). His tailored suits, *comme il faut* diction, and baronial estate on the Chesapeake Bay made it easy for Joe to lampoon him as a soul mate of "Red" Dean Acheson, "Traitorous" George Marshall, and the rest of the Foggy Bottom set. No matter that Tydings's rise from a one-room schoolhouse and a job with the railroad was truer to Horatio Alger, and less adorned, than McCarthy's. Joe was the one framing the narrative, and in his rendering it was Man of the People McCarthy versus "Milord" Tydings.*

With the who decided, the focus switched to how. McCarthy "was so preoccupied with Tydings," reported one person close to

---

* At a party at the Van Susterens', Joe was overheard referring to Tydings as a "sheep-fucker." The barnyard reference was a sign of how much he despised the Maryland Democrat, and of how boorish his language had become. "One listener," a *Washington Star* reporter wrote, "clocked him at four unprintables in just three minutes." Reeves interview with Dave Brooker, August 10, 1976; and "Benton-McCarthy Feud," *Washington Star*.

the Wisconsin senator, "that he'd sit by the hour figuring out ways to get revenge." Joe realized what usually mattered most to politicians was their reelection. Taking on a four-term incumbent like Tydings, whom even Franklin Roosevelt had done his damnedest to topple but couldn't, seemed pointless, which is why the only Republicans running against him in 1950 were D. John Markey, a former hat and shoe salesman, and John Marshall Butler, a realtor turned lawyer whose primary qualification was his made-for-the-Senate name. For McCarthy, those long odds made the race just the attention-getting gambit to bolster his claim that a silent majority of Americans believed in his anti-Red evangelism. The Maryland senator's blows against him had drawn national attention, and Joe knew his public was itching for him to counterpunch. So just days after the Tydings Committee unleashed its blistering report, Joe was huddling with Butler, arming him with every weapon McCarthy knew could win elections even before Butler won his own primary.

Step one was assembling the brain trust, and Joe had just the people. Who better to steer the media campaign than Bazy Miller, publisher of the *Washington Times-Herald,* niece of right-wing newspaper magnate Colonel Robert McCormick and sometime McCarthy sweetheart? She was soon huddling with Joe's more regular girlfriend Jean Kerr, McCarthy investigator Robert Morris, candidate Butler, and Joe himself, who was, in the words of his Senate colleagues who would later probe the election, "a leading and potent force in the campaign against Senator Tydings." McCarthy endorsed Bazy's choice to head the campaign, Jon M. Jonkel, a Chicago public relations man whose appointment broke a Maryland law requiring that in-staters be in charge. The Wisconsin senator made three personal appearances in Maryland and went on the radio. He turned over to Butler his anti-Tydings speeches and cartoons, and shifted the focus from bread-and-butter issues like taxes to whether the incumbent was "protecting Communists for political reasons." And Joe's Senate staff—from his investigators and administrative assistant to his secretary and clerks—managed the essentials of the campaign, including research, press outreach, and ferrying money from Washington to Baltimore.

Money has always been the animating element in politics, and Joe by then had a deep-pocketed network willing to contribute wherever he directed. With funds flowing in from Oklahoma and Texas, Maine and Minnesota, the campaign was able to spend a total of $75,000 ($804,000 in today's terms). What later caught the attention of congressional investigators wasn't just the huge amount raised for a statewide race but the fact that it was five times the limit set under the Federal Corrupt Practices Act. Much of that money wasn't reported to federal officials, as required, until after the campaign, and after the Senate had set up a special subcommittee to unearth the truth. Jonkel would be the fall guy, pleading guilty to six charges of violating spending laws, although he got off with a fine, not the twelve years he could have spent in prison.

Two contributions were especially interesting. One — for $10,000 — came from the archconservative Bentleys, Alvin and his blonde, azure-eyed, about-to-be-ex-wife Arvilla, whom everyone called Billie. Joe transferred that money to a friend, who invested it not in the battles against Communists or Tydings but in soybeans, where it turned a profit of $17,354.30. When congressional investigators started asking questions about the money, Billie took off to Nassau, traveling under her maiden name, Mary Peterson, then darting spy-like in and out of trains and planes at prearranged signals, with the arrangements made by her escort and soon-to-be new husband Harvey Matusow, an aide to McCarthy. "Later I found out that Billie's main worry, as well as McCarthy's, was that, if she were placed under oath on the witness stand, she would have to tell of the more than $75,000 that she had put at McCarthy's disposal in the 1950 election campaign," Matusow said. "I was only too happy to oblige and help spirit Billie out of the country . . . I talked with Joe McCarthy and informed him that all was well, that he need not worry. Joe thanked me and showed great signs of relief.

"I must admit that I would not be telling this story if the statute of limitations had not expired," Matusow added. "Billie is now safe from any prosecution which could have been brought against her. All her help to McCarthy was done because of her desire to help McCarthy's anti-Communist cause."*

---

* While she initially was a big Joe fan, Billie Bentley soured on him when he

The second eye-catching donation to the Butler campaign was from Clint Murchison, a Texas oil magnate and underwriter of right-wing causes. "Having watched the actions of Mr. Tydings and the Un-American Activities Committee, I decided that I could possibly be of some service to the citizens of the United States by going up into Maryland and defeat[ing] the gentleman in the coming election. I therefore sent up a man from Texas who, in my opinion, is the most astute political organizer in the United States. The net result of his visit is enclosed, and he advised me to put my money back in my pocket," Murchison explained in a letter to conservative radio host Fulton Lewis Jr., a copy of which went to Joe and is preserved in his Marquette archives. The oilman's sleuth reported that Colonel McCormick of the *Chicago Tribune* was pulling campaign strings, "entirely under cover of course," with Joe traveling to Baltimore to deliver "a rousing speech Sept. 22nd in which he said that Tydings had 'Coddled the Communists' and in which he was bitter against the national administration." Interesting as that stealth campaigning was, Murchison's agent concluded that it wasn't enough to oust the entrenched Tydings. The Texas tycoon trusted his investigator — but he trusted McCarthy more, and gave one check for $5,000 in his name and another in his wife's, neither of which was reported until after the election, and both of which were made out to Jonkel rather than Butler.

Joe's rallying the troops for his own election wouldn't have been unusual, but a vengeful blitzkrieg like this against a fellow senator was unheard of. The McCarthy forces were slugging lower and harder than Tydings knew how to, and Joe had barely gotten going. He laid out "instructions for filling out post-cards" that echoed those he'd used on his campaigns, and his staff helped address and mail half a million of them to voters. Jean and others

---

didn't pay her back what he'd borrowed. "I talked with Mrs. Bentley about meeting with you the next time she was in Washington, and she has expressed an unwillingness to do so. I told her of your version of the note and as to that she disagrees," her Washington lawyer Joseph Rafferty wrote the senator in 1956. "She has asked me to write you again to request that the note be paid or some arrangements made to pay it over a period of time. Otherwise, the unpleasant task has been assigned to me to send the note to an attorney in your State for appropriate action." Letter from Rafferty to McCarthy, April 20, 1956, series 20, MUA.

also helped prepare more than 300,000 copies of a four-page tabloid called "From the Record," which described itself as published
and paid for by Young Democrats for Butler. That, congressional
investigators would conclude in 1951, was "a false front organization." The eighteen charges made against Tydings — from undermining American war aims in Korea to underwriting a lecture tour
by Owen Lattimore — contained "misleading half truths, misrepre-
sentations, and false innuendos," according to the bipartisan Senate probe. As for the back-cover photograph that made it look like
Tydings was enjoying a tête-à-tête with Earl Browder, the former
Communist Party boss, that was an artful fake. A recent picture of
Browder had been merged with a twelve-year-old photo of Tydings smiling as he watched election returns in 1938, when he was
on his way to a third term.* Publishing the doctored picture, the
subcommittee said, "was a shocking abuse of the spirit and intent
of the first amendment to the Constitution." While Jean claimed
that "there are no lies about Mr. Tydings in this tabloid" and insisted that the Maryland senator had indeed coddled the Communist leader, Joe conceded that the photograph went too far. On the
whole, however, he called the Butler-McCarthy effort "one of the
cleanest campaigns in the country."

The Butler drive that Joe masterminded did worse than merely
rattling skeletons and slinging mud. There was also the matter
of the midnight ride. In the early morning of the day before the
election, trusted McCarthy investigator Don Surine and two cronies picked up William Fedder, a forty-year-old Baltimore printer
who'd been hired to reproduce and distribute Butler campaign literature, and took him for a spin. Worried about the money he was
due, Fedder had gotten Butler to write a letter offering his "personal assurance" that payment would be made. The printer called
his six-hour car ride a virtual kidnapping, in which he was get-

---

* While the photo was identified as a "composite," the subcommittee said it "was
so prepared as to create an immediate impression to the viewer that it was an
actual photograph of the individuals pictured." Few likely noticed the composite descriptor; fewer knew what it meant. Butler's campaign treasurer, after the
fact, characterized the composite as "stupid, puerile, and in bad taste." US Senate, Subcommittee on Privileges and Elections, Maryland Senatorial Election of
1950, 7 and 21–22.

ting "sicker by the minute" as the McCarthy crew strong-armed him to sign a statement saying Butler owed him nothing. Tydings offered a similar version, characterizing it as "a story of Chicago gangland transported into Maryland." But Surine and his compatriots were sure Fedder was scamming them by pocketing money meant for distributing the campaign material — and they insisted their mission was aboveboard: "to pick up and mail addressed post cards." The subcommittee didn't trust either side. It wondered why Fedder, who had access to a phone several times during the night, didn't call the police. As for Surine, the probing senators first noted that he "was at the time acting with the knowledge and consent of his employer, Senator McCarthy." They added that the McCarthy men's explanation "for their activities on this occasion is not convincing; and it is the opinion of this subcommittee that the 'picking up and mailing of addressed post cards' was not the only purpose of their mission."

The day after that now famous outing, Maryland voters rendered their verdict: 53 percent pulled the lever for the unknown aspirant Butler, 46 percent for the seemingly unsinkable Tydings. It was a landslide and an earthquake. A series of factors were in play. The midterms were a slap at the increasingly unpopular President Harry Truman, as well as at Maryland's Democratic governor, who was driven to defeat by his unpopular sales tax. Tydings had become as out of sync with Maryland as Young Bob La Follette had been in Wisconsin in 1946, and had alienated critical blocks of blacks, unionists, and local politicos. And while an anti–New Deal, pro–balanced budget Democrat like Tydings might sell in Alabama and even Virginia, more liberal Maryland wasn't buying. Even with all of that, the biggest inspiration to Butler, and the incumbent's ball and chain, was Joe McCarthy. "One lighted match might have sufficed to singe Tydings's reputation; McCarthy ignited a scorching election campaign," said Tydings biographer Caroline Keith. "McCarthy salted every wound and fostered unity among unlikely allies."*

---

* Tydings wasn't sure how to react to his loss. He tried being philosophical, telling a journalist that McCarthy "probably saved my life because if I had stayed in the senate, I'd have worked myself to death." But then he made it clear how much

What happened in Maryland aroused sufficient indignation in the Senate that two Republicans and two Democrats were appointed to a special subcommittee that held two months of hearings and, nine months after the election, issued a blistering report. At the same time Butler was conducting a "front street" campaign on a "decent plane," the senators said, "non-Maryland outsiders" were conducting a "back street" operation. "It might be an exaggeration to call this 'back street' campaign a 'big lie' campaign. But it certainly is no exaggeration to call it a 'big doubt' campaign . . . The Butler campaign manager, Jon M. Jonkel, himself characterized the heart and theme of the campaign strategy as 'exploiting the doubt.'" Once again, senators were abandoning their gentlemen's league politesse to chastise their inveterate tormenter: "Any sitting senator, regardless of whether he is a candidate in the election himself, should be subject to expulsion by action of the Senate, if it finds such Senator engaged in practices and behavior that make him, in the opinion of the Senate, unfit to hold the position of United States Senator." Yet once again they named Joe only by implication, alluded to the appropriate punishment but didn't try to impose it, and could agree only to study how future Senates might purge members who committed such "acts of defamation, slander, and libel." In this case, the timidity was the price of getting Republicans on the subcommittee to sign on, something that Tydings himself had failed to do a year before.

Joe, who turned down three invitations to testify, was used to being taken to the woodshed by fellow lawmakers. "As long as puny politicians try to encourage other puny politicians to ignore or whitewash Communist influences in our Government, America will remain in grave danger," he said in familiar language.* But this time the outrage was feigned. He was proud of what he'd done,

---

he resented McCarthy and wanted to see him defeated, saying, "I'll give money to help anyone, Republican or Democrat, who has a chance to win." Tydings File, Fleming Papers.

* On the one hand, McCarthy had a point when he charged that subcommittee members were biased against him from the start. The two Democrats could be expected to sympathize with Tydings, while the Republicans were Margaret Chase Smith, author of the anti-McCarthy Declaration of Conscience, and Robert Hendrickson, who signed it. On the other hand, finding senators who were neutral on McCarthy was increasingly challenging.

calling it "perfectly proper for the President or anyone who is interested in the welfare of this country to go in and try to defeat a Senator whom he considers bad for this country." He was grateful to the subcommittee for crediting him with a back-street blueprint worthy of that Renaissance master of politics and power Niccolò Machiavelli.* He especially loved the way the press portrayed him as his paramount enemy's political executioner, with the *New York Times'* chief congressional correspondent writing, "Essentially, Senator McCarthy beat Senator Tydings in Maryland, though the successor to the office was the new Republican Senator, John M. Butler."

The message of this commotion-creating anti-Communist was barefaced: sign on, stand aside, or beware the battering ram.

The shadow of McCarthyism spread well beyond Maryland during the 1950 midterms. He received two thousand requests to speak, which was more than for all the other senators combined during that election. Republicans may not have liked him any more than Democrats did, but they held their noses and, in fifteen states, asked him to cast aspersions on their behalf. "Only by 'mucking' can we win," one GOP leader told a reporter. "And only a mucker can muck." Republican Senator John Bricker put it less delicately in a story McCarthy liked repeating: "Joe, you're a dirty son of a bitch, but there are times when you've got to have a son of a bitch around." He mucked SOB-style for his ideological bedfellow Everett Dirksen in Illinois, urging the large crowds he drew to oust Democratic majority leader Scott Lucas, who was number two on his enemies list. Electing Dirksen, Joe said, would be "a prayer for America."† In Florida, he was all in for conservative Democrat

---

* Contemplating whether it would be better to be feared or loved, Machiavelli concluded, "The answer is, of course, that it would be best to be both loved and feared. But since the two rarely come together, anyone compelled to choose will find greater security in being feared than in being loved." McCarthy would have delighted when the *New York Times* used nearly identical words in describing him: "He has not accomplished his position of power in the Senate by being admired there; on the whole, he has accomplished it by being feared there." Machiavelli, *The Prince,* 60; and White, "What Motivates Joseph McCarthy," *New York Times.*

† The McCarthy Club in Wisconsin, organized by Tom Korb and others close to Joe, took as its motto the nearly identical "A Vote for McCarthy Is a Prayer for

George Smathers and adamantly against incumbent Claude "Red" Pepper, who he'd been warning for years was "viciously dangerous." And from North Carolina and California to Idaho and Utah, McCarthyism, if not McCarthy, was front and center as voters decided. When Joe's picks won in those states and others, pundits didn't look deeper to see that it often was local issues that had made the difference, not Joe McCarthy. To the press, the public, and his Senate colleagues, Joe had proven himself the very thing he claimed to be, a slayer of dragons.* "There was a time, only a few months ago, when many Republicans in the Senate quietly arranged matters in the daily routine so as never to pass close to the desk of their colleague, Joseph R. McCarthy of Wisconsin," William White wrote in the *Times*. "The desk of Senator McCarthy of Wisconsin is not, these days, avoided very often by his Republican associates. 'McCarthyism,' be it an incomparable epithet, is simply today a very considerable force in the Congress of the United States. And it seems to be here to stay."

Nothing happened by accident. Matusow, the ex-Communist turned professional witness who worked for the senator, recalled suggesting, "Joe, why don't you have one of your newspaper friends write an article about you? One that pictures you as a human being, a guy who gets along with children, and is friendly with people in general?" Leaning back in his chair and mulling over the suggestion, McCarthy finally gave an answer that would have resonated with demagogues of any era: "No, Harvey. That wouldn't be any good. Because as soon as my enemies see me as

America." It took as its co-chairman Steve Miller, a cheese broker from Marshfield, Wisconsin, who was a bedrock conservative, a political neophyte, and a Jew, with the last the main reason he was selected. A fundraising letter to affluent Jews noted, "You may be interested to know that Steve Miller, President of the McCarthy Club, is also a member of our faith and will especially welcome your support." Michael O'Brien interview with Carl Thompson; and letter from Alfred Kohlberg, September 11, 1952, series 23, MUA.
* Sixty-four years later, two political scientists did look deeper, finding that "some candidates McCarthy targeted did worse than expected, just as many candidates did better . . . The politicians of the 1950s seem to have misread McCarthy's campaign strength, crediting him with more political influence than he actually had. Their subsequent fear of McCarthy and failure to stand up to him may have generated a self-fulfilling prophecy that awarded him undue power." Berinsky and Lenz, "Red Scare?," *Public Opinion Quarterly*.

anything but the villain with three horns who spits fire, I'll lose my effectiveness."

Jean never saw Joe as a devil, but she hadn't yet embraced him as the angel she later would. For now, she seemed more committed than he was both to the cause and to their up-and-down relationship. That romance seemed to be ebbing in November 1950, when Jean headed off without Joe to the Royal Hawaiian Hotel in Waikiki.

As with everything surrounding the McCarthys, speculation raged as to why Jean was leaving Washington and with whom. Was it, as Matusow said, with Billie Bentley, and to make Jean unavailable to the subcommittee probing the Tydings campaign? Was it simply a matter of taking the vacation she'd had to delay the previous summer when she was working to unseat Senator Tydings, as Jean said? Or could it have been, as alleged by a detective hired by Drew Pearson and whose report was leaked to McCarthy, that Jean was pregnant? She may have regretted that she wasn't, and she certainly needed time away from work and was eager to avoid any congressional inquiry that could embarrass Joe. Whatever inspired her trip, FBI director Hoover wanted to make sure that once she arrived she got "every possible courtesy," as he made clear in a wire to his senior agent on the island.*

Rather than safeguarding her, her FBI escorts left her crippled, albeit unintentionally and temporarily. "Two of the Special Agents of the office and I were showing Miss Kerr one of the nicer private homes on the Island, and at approximately 6:30 p.m., after dark, we were leaving this residence to return her to the hotel so that she could fulfill a dinner engagement," wrote agent in charge Joe Logue. "I was escorting Miss Kerr down an outside stone stairway leading to the garage and parking area of this residence, and

---

* Hank Greenspun, as always, had his own unlikely and unflattering theory. Jean, he wrote, "was observed in tears at the Washington Airport when Joe put her on the plane, but it was also observed that she brushed him off when he tried to kiss her goodbye." According to the newspaperman, she'd found out Joe was a homosexual, "which occasioned the tearful breakup and the hurried trip to Hawaii. Joe wasn't heartbroken at the separation. He was fearful of exposure by a furious woman." Greenspun, "Secret Lives of Joe McCarthy," *Rave*.

both she and I tripped and fell over an unbarricaded ledge, falling some four or five feet to the asphalt parking area at this residence." Whether they were trespassing wasn't made clear, but Jean was lucky that the damage was limited to a fractured hip. She was luckier still that the FBI ensured she got the best doctors and checked on her medical insurance, watched over her during her time in the hospital and a convalescent home, brought her gifts over Christmas and confirmed she had a good view of New Year's Eve fireworks out her nursing home window, and when she was ready to head home eight weeks later, the bureau got her the necessary stretcher and wheelchair.* Less lucky were two of the agents with her when she fell, who Jean said were transferred by an angry Hoover.

Joe kept in constant touch with Jean during her ordeal, directly and via Hoover, who, in this honeymoon period of his and Joe's relationship, made it his business to please the powerful senator. Hoover also was determined that the press shouldn't find out about those three-way communications. When columnist Jack Anderson inquired about what had happened with Kerr, and whether the way she was treated reflected a special bond between McCarthy and Hoover, Hoover assistant Lou Nichols denied it: "I told [Anderson] that we steered a middle of the road course with everybody and merely did our duty." Hoover scribbled at the bottom of Nichols's memo, "This fellow Anderson & his ilk have minds that are lower than the regurgitated filth of vultures." For once Hoover may have been right, given the theory being advanced

---

* Jean told a slightly different version of the story in notes for her unpublished memoir and in an interview with Victor Lasky for an article he called "The Gal Who Married Joe McCarthy," which apparently never made it into print. The accident, she said, happened when she was leaving the home of an agent and his wife, because "lights failed on the steep unprotected curving steps from the house." She and her escort "mistook the last unguarded stair landing in the darkness for the driveway." The broken hip, which wasn't healing right and required months in a cast, combined with upcoming hearings on the Maryland election, led to "depression and discouragement" and marked the "WORST YEAR SHE EVER LIVED."

She wanted to testify before the Maryland panel, Jean added, but her doctor at first forbade it. "Weeks later," Lasky wrote, "she hobbled in and testified, her first venture out of home since the accident." Lasky, "The Gal Who Married Joe McCarthy," unprocessed files, and "The Joe McCarthy I Knew," series 24, MUA.

by Anderson's boss, Drew Pearson, as to what was going on between Joe and Jean. Drew "heard reports that Joe was unfaithful and was favoring Martha Rountree (of 'Meet the Press') and Bazy Miller. [Jean] then said she was going to get even by talking about the Maryland campaign," Pearson's lawyer Warren Woods told journalist Robert Fleming. "Woods offered records of McCarthy's long-distance telephone call[s] to show that Joe called Hawaii every day or two for two weeks, says Jean was finally pacified, and again is a faithful and capable assistant."

Just how faithful, and whether she still was his assistant, were matters Joe raised doubts about in one of his letters to Hawaii:

> Since having dictated this I got your "My Best" letter and talked to you twice over the phone last nite. I get the definite feeling that you may have developed a new heart interest. If so I don't blame you but wish you would let me know just what the status is. Your suggestion that you quit as of Dec 22 disturbed me. I hope you continue in the office regardless of what you may have developed as a new interest . . . We want you back here anyway — even if you fell in love with an F.B.I. man with hair.

How badly he wanted her back in Washington was clear from Joe's letter written just before she left Hawaii, when he offered to contact the president of Northwest Airlines to make the arrangements and to fly to Chicago to meet her for the trip from there to the capital. Then he thought better of that: "I know *The Washington Post* and Pearson will get hold of it and try to make it sound like something sinister, etc. As you know, I don't give a damn what they have to say about McCarthy, but think it might be embarrassing for you, your mother, etc., if they wrote a story about McCarthy traveling from Chicago with his 'secretary.' If they said '*Research Analyst*,' it would be o.k., but am afraid they would not do that."*

---

* There was one more twist to the Hawaii episode. Joe had been determined from the start that Jean get all she was owed from the insurance company — for doctor and hospital bills, lost wages, and pain and suffering.

Two years after Jean flew home, Joe also was eager to file a claim against the wealthy Hawaii homeowner in whose yard she had fallen. As part of that process, Joe asked for and received the FBI's help in tracking down the unnamed

Joe's own health was slipping as his national crusade gained traction. His sinus troubles hadn't let up, and he was coughing more, sometimes to the point of choking. The twitch migrated from his head to his hands. In the winter of 1951, just as hearings on the Maryland campaign were about to start, he had a major sinus operation that kept him in the hospital for two weeks. He was back for two more procedures in 1952, another on his sinuses and the second to repair a herniated diaphragm. The hernia had presented itself in the form of the severe indigestion he'd been suffering for years. A diet consisting of too many hamburgers dripping with melted cheese, accompanied by milkshakes or apple pie topped with vanilla ice cream, didn't make it easy to stay in fighting shape or help his stomach pains.* His temporary solution had been to swallow handfuls of baking soda, up to three pounds a week, washed down with warm water. In the summer of 1952, doctors performed the hernia operation he should have had months if not years before. Joe emerged minus a rib and with a two-foot-long scar that started in his belly, ran beneath his arm, and ended at the top of his shoulder. But as his doctors reported, "he was able to enjoy food for the first time in years and proceeded to gain 15 lbs."

When anyone questioned his health he'd reply, "Rubbish! I'm in excellent shape. I have no intention of retiring, and I expect to live forever." Then, grinning, he'd add, "But maybe you'd better not repeat that — it might depress too many people!" As for the rib that was removed, Joe said it was used "to patch up a chaplain's jaw; he'd had his own blown off in Korea. After he got well, he wrote me a note saying, 'Now, I won't be responsible for what I say!'"

Liquor made things worse. He was consuming more of it now,

---

homeowner, who he knew had insurance and he worried might evade the three-year statute of limitations. Letter from Joe to Jean, December 16, 1950, series 24, MUA; and letters from D. M. Ladd to Hoover, February 24 and 27, 1953, pt. 6 of 28, MFBI.

* Nearly every meal and snack, winter or summer, included extra-strong iced tea. Sometimes he'd call it "Irish tea," seemingly proud that it was black, strong, and, unlike Irish coffee, not spiked with alcohol. "The Private Life of Senator McCarthy"; and Cohn, *McCarthy*, 258.

in ways everyone who spent time with him noticed. Matusow remembered meeting Joe in Appleton at the Van Susteren home,
where he was a regular guest, and where Urban was happy to join
him in his cups. It was after midnight, Matusow recalled,

> and [McCarthy] was raking in the money in a fast game of sheeps-
> head . . . Joe had just drained the last drop of whiskey from his
> glass. I suggested we get more. He said: "Well, you can put it this
> way—Yes." With that he pulled a $20 bill out of his pocket and
> sent me on my way. The party broke up about 4 a.m. Whiskey
> and guests were gone. Joe was in his undershirt. "I'll show you
> my scar for a quarter," he offered, referring to the incision made
> during his operation. I flipped him two bits. He hoisted his un-
> dershirt and proudly displayed a scar which almost divided him
> in two.* As I was about to say good night, Joe saw me to the
> door and handed me a hundred-dollar bill. "Go buy yourself a
> new suit, but, you son of a bitch," he swore, "if you tell anybody
> I gave it to you, I'll . . ."

He was a friendly lush, but only apologists denied his heavy
drinking now. He did it mainly in the evening and at liquid lunches.
His favorite daytime spot was the Grill Room of the Carroll Arms
Hotel across from the Senate Office Building, where his preferred
table was always waiting and his typical order was two double
martinis. Sometimes he'd begin his day with a stiff one. "He would
gulp down a water glass filled with Scotch in one swallow and
then chase it with bicarbonate of soda. As his drinking escalated
he would eat a quarter-pound stick of butter, which he claimed
helped him hold his liquor," wrote journalist and author David
Halberstam. "He was, said his old friend from Appleton, Ed Hart,
'the town drunk in businessman's clothes.'" Every reporter who
covered him had a story—of Joe finishing off in the morning the
warm remnants of last night's cocktail, or making inroads into a
bottle of brandy before Sunday morning mass. Assigned to write a

---

* Urban's son Dirk, who was McCarthy's godson, was so intrigued by Joe's scar
that he invited neighborhood kids by to see it. Joe obliged, and suggested that the
boy charge his pals ten cents each. Reeves interview with Dirk, August 9, 1976;
and author interview with and emails from Dirk.

day in the life of the senator, Loren Osman arrived at 7 a.m. at Milwaukee's Schroeder Hotel to find him lying nude on the bed, swilling a pitcher of martinis. Thanks to an unwritten press edict that boozing and philandering were excusable behaviors, stories like those never made it into the papers.

While he'd often disguise his drinking by quietly spiking his orange juice or milk, or filling a medicine bottle with bourbon, at other times he almost boasted about it. It was part of the persona he was cultivating, of an undershirt-wearing hail-fellow you'd want to get a drink with or introduce your kid sister to. "He encouraged photographers to take pictures of him sleeping, disheveled, on an office couch, like a bum on a park bench, coming out of a shower with a towel wrapped around his torso like Rocky Marciano, or sprawled on the floor in his shirt sleeves with a hooker of bourbon close at hand," said biographer Richard Rovere. "Where other politicians sought to conceal a weakness for liquor or wenching or gambling, McCarthy tended to exploit, even to exaggerate, these wayward tastes. He was glad to have everyone believe that he was a drinker of heroic attainments, a passionate lover of horseflesh, a Clausewitz of the poker table, and a man to whom everything presentable in skirts was catnip."

Joe also wanted people to think of him as the prizefighter he might have been, especially when it came to his bouts with Tydings and other Washington power brokers. "It was not, I imagine, without some such image in mind that he acquired his swaggering, shoulder-heaving walk and his ballplayer's slouch; that he cultivated a five o'clock shadow with almost cosmetic care," observed Rovere. "He liked to be known as a politician who used his thumbs, his teeth, and his knees, and I suspect he understood that there is a place for a few such men in our moral universe."*

It was an act for Joe, and he thought others understood that. When they didn't — when, out of the spotlight, they wouldn't shake his hand or didn't appreciate his overfamiliarity — he seemed not to comprehend. That happened with the socialite Alice Roosevelt

---

* His perspiration wasn't pretending. He could sweat through three shirts (all white) in a day, along with a suit (mostly blue) and a tie (which seldom matched his suit or socks). Reeves interview with Dion Henderson, July 20, 1977.

Longworth, who had recently been with Joe at a dinner party and, on their next meeting, was jovially told he would henceforth address her by her first name. "The trash man can call me Alice, and so may the clerk in the store and the policeman on the beat," Longworth retorted, "but *you* may *not* call me Alice."

The reaction was even frostier when he shared an elevator in the Senate office building with the famously prim Secretary of State Acheson, whose scalp Joe had been seeking ever since Wheeling. "'Hello, Mr. Secretary,' he said, and stuck out his hand," Acheson wrote later. "Instinctively I took it, simultaneously recognizing his much-cartooned, black-jowled face. Flashbulbs exploded as the doors slid shut. Neither of us spoke during our few seconds' ride. 'What happened in the elevator?' the press asked him. 'Neither of us,' he replied, 'turned his back on the other.' It was a smart trick and, of course, got him on front pages across the country." For his part, McCarthy wondered about Acheson, "What the hell is the matter with him?"

That is the question many were asking about Joe as he went on his rampage against Acheson, Marshall, and the rest of his lists of traitors and fellow travelers. Eminent psychiatrists rendered their diagnoses based on nothing more than observing his public behavior. One review, Rovere reported, "stressed the elements of classical paranoia in McCarthy's actions: life was a series of conspiracies." A second zeroed in on "his basic insecurity, self-doubt, and self-contempt." Other armchair analysts insisted that Joe, as an aftereffect of his hospital stays, had become addicted to the morphine generously administered there. Van Susteren countered that if there had been such an addiction, "We would have seen the needle marks . . . Joe was just not the kind." This closest of Joe's friends had heard all the rumors and, looking back years later, laughed off most of them. "At least," said Van Susteren, "they haven't blamed McCarthy for Kennedy's assassination."

For someone who was the subject of so many rumors about his own health, Joe might have been more careful in dropping hints about others, especially the president. But that would have required a restraint he didn't possess. So in April 1951, Joe told a convention of furniture sellers that Harry Truman's momentous decision to fire General Douglas MacArthur had been clouded by "bourbon and Benedictine," adding, "Most of the tragic things are done at 1:30 and 2 o'clock in the morning," when aides like Acheson have "had time to get the president cheerful." Did he agree with his fellow Republicans who were demanding Truman's impeachment? reporters gathering around his hotel washbasin wanted to know before Joe got to the convention hall. McCarthy didn't hesitate: "The son-of-a-bitch should be impeached."*

No politician in America understood better than Joe McCarthy how the press worked and how to manipulate it. He knew reporters wanted their stories on page one, and he was a daily drama man who could put them there more than anyone except the president. He memorized the late-night deadlines for morning newspapers and the late-morning ones for afternoon papers, and he met those, but just barely, intentionally leaving writers no time to ferret out the other side or read through his supposed evidence. He pioneered the morning press conference to announce the afternoon press conference, which got him extra headlines like this: "NEW MCCARTHY REVELATIONS AWAITED IN CAPITAL." His mimeographed handouts included phrases like "top Russian spy" that were ready-made for bold captions and story ledes. Understanding the profession's internal dynamics let him twist them to his ends, the way any well-schooled saboteur would.

He also appreciated the behind-the-scenes machinations of the

---

* Truman tried turning the other cheek, even when Joe disparaged his wife, Bess. But in a private moment with Vice President Alben Barkley, the president recounted the fable of a dog who misbehaved so badly that its owner put a "clog" on its neck to keep it from biting. The canine foolishly thought it a badge of honor. "Men often mistake notoriety for fame, and would rather be remarked for their vices and follies than not be noticed at all," said Truman. The story, he added, "seems to describe certain ballyhoo artists we both know." Fried, *Men Against McCarthy*, 155.

Joe would bring to mind a different image of a dog for Senator Paul Douglas. When the Illinois Democrat was running for reelection in 1954, he got a close-up look at the contradictory McCarthys. First the Wisconsinite viciously attacked him, but when Douglas got back to Washington, he recalled in his memoir, McCarthy "shook hands heartily and assured me that he was delighted by my reelection. Joe was that kind of fellow. He was like a mongrel dog, fawning on you one moment and the next moment trying to bite your leg off." Douglas, *In the Fullness of Time*, 251.

wire services. Most papers didn't have Washington bureaus, or ones in the burgs like Reno and Wheeling where he was planting his charges. The wire services, by contrast, were everywhere, with callow reporters who earned considerably less than their counterparts at the big dailies. Their bosses were loath to challenge the consensus of neutrality among client papers, so they covered McCarthy's claims straight-up, like they would those of a trustworthy lawmaker. And competition among the three wires — Associated Press, United Press, and International News Service — was even fiercer than among newspapers, which meant sacrificing time-intensive fact-checking and doing anything to land an exclusive. For Joe, that yielded just what he wanted — perpetual coverage with practically no perspective. "We'd fight to get a two-minute beat on a new name, and Joe McCarthy rode this. We were trapped by our techniques. If he said it, we wrote it," admitted Charles Seib, an INS reporter who later became ombudsman for the *Washington Post*. "That simplistic, gee-whiz reporting, with its phony objectivity, did as much to raise Joe McCarthy from a bumbling unknown to a national menace as the craven behavior of his fellow senators and the White House." George Reedy, who was with the competing UP, said that "talking to Joe was like putting your hands in a bowl of mush. It was a shattering experience, and I couldn't stand it. Covering him was a big factor in my decision to quit newspaper work."

The most surefire way to dominate the conversation, Senator McCarthy realized, was to get the press to accept his premise: that there were Soviet spies in the State Department, with the only questions being how many and who. There must be — right? — if an esteemed newspaper like the *Baltimore Sun* was running headlines like "McCarthy Has New Evidence" and the *Kansas City Star* was blaring "Knows Names of 57 Reds." No one knew that's not what the headline writers meant, that the stories under the header laid out a more nuanced reality, or that what the titles implied turned out to be untrue. "There were flat statements in the headlines where the fact in the story was merely a charge," said Ed Bayley, who later studied the behavior of the McCarthy-era press and at the time was part of it as a political reporter at the *Milwaukee Journal*.

"McCarthy was a dream story," said Willard Edwards of the *Chicago Tribune,* Joe's favorite paper. "I wasn't off page one for four years." Neither were other reporters who covered the crusade. In just the first month after the Wheeling kickoff, there were a dozen page-one stories in the *Baltimore Sun,* sixteen in his hometown paper in Appleton, thirteen in Madison's *Capital Times,* and eight each in the *Wall Street Journal, Washington Times-Herald,* and *Memphis Commercial Appeal.* That was the kind of coverage generally reserved for ax murderers and heads of state, and it continued for four years. Making page one in the morning paper, meanwhile, almost guaranteed that the story would be repeated verbatim over the radio and, increasingly, on television. Joe had become a name brand.

Joe also was a Master of the Revels, making it fun for journalists who played along. He used signals so the writers who covered him regularly would know there was whiskey waiting in his room. "Glad to see you, talk with you later" meant "Don't eat too much because we'll go out for supper later and shoot the breeze." Clasping his hands over his head like a boxer meant "Give me a few minutes and come up and tell me I've got a phone call from Washington; I've spent enough time shaking hands with the people here." Reporters were drawn like moths to an evening of good tips and good liquor. He promised Dion Henderson, an AP correspondent who was writing a not-so-flattering novel patterned after the senator, that he'd denounce it from the Senate floor if that would boost sales.

To McCarthy, all this was the natural order. "I'm one of the men placed in the watchtowers to try and guard this nation. When I find that someone is bad for this nation, that consistently he does things good for Communist Russia, then my duty is to expose him and let the American people know what he stands for," he said in a radio interview. In a more candid moment, he told a pair of visiting wire service reporters, "If you want to be against McCarthy, boys, you've got to be a Communist or a cocksucker." Then he sat back in his office armchair and laughed as he took another swig from his medicine bottle.

If Joe rewrote the rules of politics and press, his minions acted as if there were none. "I also had made up my mind that I would place in the [Senate] record a statement of 'the number of Communists working for the New York *Times* and *Time* magazine.' I had previously discussed this with Senator McCarthy and it had his approval," Matusow said. "Once the 'facts' were in the record McCarthy knew that he could accuse the *Times* and *Time* of being pro-Communist. And we would both make headlines . . . My statement was based on twisted facts. It could not be disputed, nor could it have been completely dismissed. I couldn't name names, but I didn't have to. There were enough people, like McCarthy, who insisted that there were Communists employed by *Time* and the *New York Times*."

Reporters who crossed the McCarthy tribe might feel the battering ram that had flattened Senators Tydings, Lucas, and Pepper. Joe dispatched his investigators to dig up dirt on reporters covering him closely and critically like Phil Potter of the *Baltimore Sun,* whom he threatened three or four times to subpoena but never did. With the Associated Press's Marvin Arrowsmith, it was less about what he had written than what he might. "I know you've got six kids, Marv, and I don't want to kick about your work, so I hope there is no reason to do so," Joe told him. It was surely not a coincidence that when Oliver Pilat tried to talk to his pal Arrowsmith about the McCarthy series Pilat was co-writing for the *New York Post,* the AP man not only said no but also asked, "As a personal favor, will you please tell no one that you called me about McCarthy."

Miles McMillin, a columnist and editorial writer at the *Capital Times,* remembered when hecklers had put Joe on edge during a speech to service clubs in La Crosse. "When I got up to ask a question, Joe blew up. 'Get him out!' he yelled. 'That's a representative of a Communist newspaper.' Those Rotarians and Kiwanians surrounded me and shoved me out the door." Another time McCarthy incited a crowd at an auditorium in Shorewood, a plush suburb of Milwaukee, by directing his venom against the *Milwaukee Journal.* Fifty women marched to the orchestra pit, where reporters were sitting, yelling, "Get the *Journal* reporter!" and "Where's the *Journal* reporter?" Ed Bayley recalled, adding, "I was the *Journal* reporter, but I didn't say so." McMillin came to the rescue, saying he was from the *Chicago Tribune,* which he knew the ladies cherished. "In the confusion that followed," said Bayley, "I slipped past them and out a side door. McCarthy's comments about the press had been very restrained that night, but it didn't take much to get his supporters worked up."*

Other McCarthy defenders phoned the *Journal,* calling whoever picked up a Communist. J. Donald Ferguson, an editorial writer later elevated to editor, suspected that the senator's spies were rifling Ferguson's wastebasket for anything incriminating. He ensured they got what they wanted, regularly scribbling blood-and-thunder notes on what he'd like to do to McCarthy and tossing them in his trash can. He also gave this instruction to one of his reporters after McCarthy intercepted an embarrassing missive: "Don't write any more letters. Use the telephone, and if you think that's tapped, take a plane. But don't write letters."

As he had with Drew Pearson, Joe called on his supporters to make life financially miserable for his critics. He went after the *Capital Times* as early as 1949, telling the Madison Shrine Club, "When you expose a paper as being communistic, then I believe that businessmen should never send in a check for advertising. When any man pays a nickel for a newspaper, he is contributing to the communistic cause." With the *Milwaukee Journal,* the strategy was not to "break" the paper, Joe confided to the *Journal*'s Robert Fleming. "I don't know that I can cut its profits at all . . . But if you can show a paper as unfriendly and having a reason for being antagonistic, you take the sting out of what it says about you. I think I can convince a lot of people that they can't believe what they read in the *Journal.*"

His concern about the *Journal* was understandable. By the early 1950s the paper was acting like the secret police, with Fleming and others staking out the senator 24-7 whenever he came to Wisconsin. "If he landed by airplane, we were at the airport. If he came by train, we were at the railroad [station], and we kept notes of who he spoke to, who he stayed with, and that sort of thing," recalls Bob Wills, a *Journal* reporter who went on to become editor

---

* In a later phase, Joe punished the *Journal* by banning its reporters from his press conferences. That backfired when other journalists stuck up for the paper, filling in its reporters on what they'd missed. *Joe McCarthy and the Press,* 135.

of the rival *Sentinel.* "Covering McCarthy was a cause . . . When we heard he was going to be naming a group on television that night, or radio, we would, the members of the staff, would often get together, have a party, and listen."

The *Post-Standard* in Syracuse felt McCarthy's full fury. In 1951 the paper ran a scathing editorial accusing Joe of hiring a man named Charles Davis to frame the US ambassador to Switzerland, John Carter Vincent, by sending him a phony telegram that made it look as if he had ties to Communists. And that wasn't all. McCarthy had framed Tydings with a fake photograph, the paper said, and taken money from the Lustron Corporation for an article he hadn't written. "McCarthy," the editorial concluded, "is a disgrace to the United States Senate." The *Post-Standard* was wrong on enough specifics that it had to back down, paying McCarthy a settlement of about $15,000 and, more to the senator's savoring, publishing what it called a correction but amounted to a surrender. While its original blast was "written in good faith," it said, a series of statements "nevertheless proved to be untrue and unfair to Sen. McCarthy." History makes clear the paper was more right than it realized about McCarthy's close ties to Davis, his willingness to pay for information, and his claim of authorship of the Lustron pamphlet.

The senator went after *Time,* too. The publication, owned by magazine magnate Henry Luce, had at one time backed McCarthy, but in October 1951 it labeled him a demagogue on its cover and in a four-page story accused him of "hitting low blow after low blow" and "bamboozling audiences." Its sister publication, *Life,* was even harsher, accusing him of "groin-and-eyeball fighting." Joe fired back fast, accusing *Time* of "degenerate lying" and urging businesses to stop buying ads. While the admen didn't bite, Luce did. He'd assumed that by mid-1951 McCarthy was "on the skids"; hence his tough-talking letter to Joe in November saying, "You feel TIME hasn't lived up to those principles [of fairness] in its treatment of you. TIME feels you haven't lived up to those principles in your campaign against Communism." Not long after he sent it, however, he realized the senator was "more popular and powerful than ever," said Luce biographer W. A. Swanberg. "The Lucepress withdrew to a safe distance. It played the issue very cautiously as the weeks went on, avoiding any suggestion that Joe might be dangerous, now and then slapping his wrist or patting his back and taking the general line that McCarthy was a needed balance against Truman's softness on communism."* Score another knockout for Smiling Joe, who was having the time of his life.†

While *Time* and the *Post-Standard* backed off, McCarthy's call for a boycott of the *Milwaukee Journal* just made the paper angrier. "We wonder," mused an editorial in September 1950, "whether the senator's friends shouldn't persuade him to see a psychiatrist." When the *Washington Post* asked tough questions, Joe accused it of "moronic thinking." But that paper, too, persisted, the way it would during Watergate and into the era of Trump. It published the dogged news coverage of reporters Alfred Friendly and Murrey Marder, hard-hitting editorials, and cartoons by Herblock that made McCarthy ever more apelike and menacing (and made Jean cry). "McCarthy's fraud was apparent from the start," Block wrote. "Since the spring of 1950 no time was too early to speak up about him, and there was no time when colleagues in his party or in the Senate could not have smacked him down."

That was easier for a star cartoonist to do and say than for a vulnerable beat reporter like Arrowsmith or Marder. A conscientious, straight-arrow reporter like either of them became "a straight-jacketed reporter," said media critic Douglass Cater. That in turn meant that few if any reporters pointed out that fellow scribe Willard Edwards had given Joe the grist for his Wheeling speech, that Chiang Kai-shek's lobbyists were feeding him material on Owen Lattimore, or that the senator's most spectacular wit-

---

* Luce's retreat was especially apparent at *Life*. Less than a year after it called McCarthy a "liability and a danger, both to the Republicans and to the nation," it was splitting hairs — saying McCarthyism was only a "venial sin" whereas "Communism is a mortal sin. Contemporarily, Communism is the Great Sin Against Humanity." "Taft and McCarthy" and "Recalling All Liberals," *Life*.

† Another media legend, publisher Joseph Pulitzer of the *St. Louis Post-Dispatch*, backed down in the same way. In a cascade of memos over four years, he asked his editors to be nicer to Joe and the Republicans. They found ways around him until, in 1954, a frustrated Pulitzer went from beseeching to ordering: "I must ask that the words 'McCarthy' or 'McCarthyism' or any oblique reference to either shall not appear on the editorial page without my specific approval." *Joe McCarthy and the Press*, 139–42.

nesses often were the least reliable. In their bid to be detached and neutral, as every journalism student is taught to be, political reporters became instead stenographers, echoing Joe's rants. "The advent of McCarthyism has thrown real fear into the hearts of some — fear of what a demagogue can do to America while the press helplessly gives its sometimes unwilling co-operation," Cater wrote four months after Wheeling. "Perhaps Joseph McCarthy, Senator from Wisconsin, is not that demagogue. But who knows? One greater than McCarthy may come."

It was Joe's attack on George Marshall that pushed the *New York Post* to assign two senior reporters to a top-to-bottom exposé of the senator's career and tactics. Called "Smear, Inc.: The One Man Mob of Joe McCarthy," the series ran over seventeen parts. "The basic fact about Joe McCarthy is that he has been getting away with murder. He has been getting away with it because too many newspapers and too many politicians have been afraid to fight him," editor James Wechsler wrote in an introductory commentary. The *Post* wasn't the first to take on McCarthy, but nobody else devoted as much ink to him, blending unflinching reportage with McCarthy-style vituperation. Communists ironically helped elect him and the fascist fringe backed him, according to the series, which labor unions reprinted and circulated nationwide. "The simple truth is that what Ponzi was to finance and fortune-telling is to science, Joseph McCarthy is to politics." Joe wasn't amused. A week after the last article ran, he told a Senate panel that Wechsler and his wife had been members of the Communist Party and that, while they claimed to have left, he had his doubts. And the McCarthy archives at Marquette show that someone was leaking to the senator endless pleas for interviews that the *Post* reporters were mailing out, including one that explained, "I'm in the process of writing a piece on the way Sen. McCarthy used you as a sacrificial goat."

When the press attacked him, Joe said he was soothed by the quote from Abraham Lincoln hanging over his desk: "If I were to try to read, much less answer, all the attacks made on me, this shop might as well be closed for any other business . . . If the end brings me out all right, what is said against me won't amount to anything. If the end brings me out wrong, ten angels swearing I was right would make no difference." And when Joe couldn't beat a reporter into submission, he tried seducing him. In 1951 he offered the intrepid Edwin Bayley a job, saying he'd pay him twice whatever the *Milwaukee Journal* did. "How could you think I'd work for you after what I've written about you?" Bayley asked. McCarthy: "That doesn't matter. If you worked for me you'd write it different." Reflecting on the exchange later, Bayley said it "seemed to me to demonstrate his cynicism, or at least his lack of seriousness."

Yet Joe seemed to mean it when he denied that his tormenting of individual journalists meant that he was a threat to a free press. "Every once in a while a lawyer or a judge has to be prosecuted on criminal charges, but does anybody raise the cry that the legal profession thereby is endangered? Awhile ago we had an Army officer who was sent to jail for a crime he'd committed. But did that mean the Army was being persecuted?" the senator asked, shaking his head in rebuttal. "I don't get this menace-to-freedom-of-the-press stuff."

Some media outlets stooped to the same low and juvenile tactics that Joe had used. The editor of a labor journal registered his lowercase stature by writing his name "joe mccarthy." (The official Soviet party paper *Pravda* would follow suit.) In Manhattan, Kansas, the *Mercury-Chronicle* ordered all its stories about McCarthy onto page three instead of page one, robbing story editors of their rightful discretion. Writers compared him to Joseph Stalin, Genghis Khan, Joseph Goebbels, and, most of all, Adolf Hitler. "Like Hitler," wrote journalist and author Richard Rovere, "McCarthy was a screamer, a political thug, a master of the mob, an exploiter of popular fears. He used the fear of Bolshevism as Hitler used it, with the difference that Hitler described Communism as a revolutionary menace to the state, while McCarthy described it as a conspiracy that had already achieved some of the ends it prized the most." The venting felt good, but the words were so scalding they sacrificed not just the truth but any chance of winning over anyone still on the fence about the senator.

Other papers tried more subtle fixes. The *Milwaukee Journal* offered bracketed inserts that unspun Joe's charges. When he said, for example, that Owen Lattimore had "long been referred to as the architect of the state department's Asiatic policy," an insert explained, "State department officials and three former secretaries of state have denied that Lattimore played any part in forming policy." One story included fifteen paragraphs of such clarifications and corrections. At the *Denver Post,* editor and publisher Palmer Hoyt at first believed McCarthy's charges, then started to suspect he was "shooting from the hip," and finally concluded the senator was "outrageous." In a 1953 memo to the managing editor, Hoyt authorized reporters to call a liar just that when they knew it to be the case, and told copy editors to include a line like "McCarthy Charges Today" over each new accusation. In a speech explaining his worries, Hoyt said, "It is necessary for newspapers to function more sharply, more adequately than ever before. And, believe me, there is nothing wrong with this country that repeated strong dosages of the facts will not correct. Even McCarthyism will melt away before this treatment."

One of the last to abandon the just-the-facts approach and embrace interpretive writing was the *New York Times,* which knew firsthand the sensation of being in McCarthy's crosshairs. When the paper finally decided stronger medicine was needed, it ordered that if Joe's charges made page one, so should the story if they were disproved. Richard Johnston of the *Times'* Chicago bureau, who handled much of the McCarthy coverage, said that "while it was a burden and a trial for some of us, it was a joyous thing for Joe at all times. I finally came to the conclusion that in the strictest sense of the word he didn't understand a goddamn thing he was doing except that it was getting him a lot of notoriety and this he loved."

He may have believed that there was no such thing as bad publicity, but Joe could not bear ridicule. That was clear when he secretly investigated and publicly tongue-lashed the cartoonist Herblock, and again when he spoke at the University of Wisconsin in May 1951. After the senator called General MacArthur the "greatest military leader since Genghis Khan," his audience booed, then laughed. Joe dismissed them as "braying jackasses," then left, saying he had to be at an important meeting in Washington. The most trenchant mocker was cartoonist Walt Kelly, whose *Pogo* strip in 1953 introduced a deranged wildcat named Simple J. Malarkey, modeled after the fire-breathing lawmaker from Wisconsin. More people learned about McCarthy from *Pogo* than from editorials, with the strip appearing in almost five hundred newspapers and Kelly's books selling 30 million copies. The gun-toting Malarkey was the most vicious character to venture into the Okefenokee Swamp, and he remade the Audible Boy Bird Watchers Society into the Bonfire Boys, then the Jack Acid Society. McCarthy "was a great source of material. I got some of my funniest lines right out of his speeches as reported in the *Congressional Record*," said Kelly. As for his decision to wade into politics, Kelly explained, "It is my obligation not only to remind us how youthful and brainless we are, but also within the same framework to hold out hope for the future."*

With Kelly against him, along with eight of the top-ten prestige newspapers and the best newsweeklies, Joe had a point when he grumbled about an anti-McCarthy cabal. What he didn't say was that at least as many reporters, editors, and publishers were colluding *with* him. He could count on favorable stories, along with assistance digging up names to name, procuring and coaching witnesses, and drafting speeches. Those he turned to most often were Wheeling speech writers George Waters of the *Washington Times-Herald* and Ed Nellor of *Look* magazine, former FBI agent Lawrence Kerley of the *New York Journal-American,* Hearst reporter and former *Daily Worker* staffer Howard Rushmore, radio broadcasters George Sokolsky and Fulton Lewis, and old friend Willard Edwards of the cheerleading *Chicago Tribune.* Their work might

---

* While Kelly initially received surprisingly little pushback from client papers, when the pressure mounted, he started penning two versions of the strip — one with controversial characters like Malarkey, the others what he called "Bunny Strips" with inoffensive rabbits telling dumb jokes. Black, *Art of the Swamp,* 224.

As *Pogo* was belittling McCarthy, Robert Walker, Helen Hayes, and Paramount Pictures passionately endorsed his cause in their film *My Son John,* in which the title character's mother condemns him after learning he has been consorting with a woman who may be a spy. President Truman's attorney general rendered an equally jingoistic verdict at about the same time against the world's most recognizable film star, Charlie Chaplin. In London for the world premiere of his movie *Limelight,* Chaplin, a British citizen, was told he wouldn't be readmitted to the United States unless he agreed to be interviewed about his leftist politics. He didn't return to the country for twenty years.

not be read or heard in Washington salons, but it turned up in many of the same households across Middle America that were enjoying *Pogo*.

It helped that several of America's most powerful media barons were on Joe's side. Colonel McCormick, the *Tribune*'s publisher and WGN radio station co-owner, had been there from the beginning.* Even more influential were the heads of the Hearst empire, editor in chief William Randolph Hearst Jr. and CEO Richard Berlin. When Joe needed guidance with names and numbers after Wheeling, Hearst reporters served as his technical staff. When the Tydings Committee blasted the Wisconsin senator, sixteen Hearst papers at once branded it "the most disgracefully partisan document ever to emanate from the Congress." Says Berlin's son Richard Jr., "There was a wonderful symbiosis between Joe McCarthy and the Hearst press," with the latter intent on selling newspapers and the former great at making news. While Hearst told his editors to render their own judgments on covering McCarthy, those editors believed in the crusade and at times outdid the crusader (endorsing, for instance, the construction in outposts like Wyoming of wartime detention centers for Communists and their friends). "McCarthy remained in the news through the Tydings aftermath," say Hearst biographers Lindsay Chaney and Michael Cieply, "largely because the Hearst press kept him there."†

Initially one of Joe's staunchest defenders, Willard Edwards eventually became disillusioned and could pinpoint the moment his doubts mushroomed:

> Some of the staff came to me and asked me to write a speech for Joe. They had a good solid case about the infiltration of the National Labor Relations Board — people with Communist leanings, Communist propensities, etc., all those words we used those days when we didn't have actual proof that they were

* Not known for his modesty, McCormick named his radio station WGN for his paper's motto, World's Greatest Newspaper.
† Adela Rogers St. Johns, a counselor to two generations of Hearsts, said later, "We didn't know he was a drunk. If McCarthy hadn't been an alcoholic the whole story would have been different, because we had the material but he kept blowing it. He'd get drunk and say things he shouldn't." Tuck, *McCarthyism and New York's Hearst Press*, 75–76.

Communists. I did it reluctantly. I deliberately understated it. My lead was: "I rise to present evidence demonstrating the existence of Communist leanings among a number of officials of the NLRB" . . . [Joe's] lead was: "I rise to present evidence that the NLRB is honeycombed with members of the Communist Party." That was his great flaw — exaggeration. If the Communists had wanted to pick someone to attack them, they couldn't have done better.

The European press offered its readers an alarming view of the Wisconsin senator. "The McCarthy story seems to come only as one part of a larger story that the London *Economist* calls 'the national hysteria [and] red witch hunts that mark the national life of America today,'" *The Reporter* magazine noted in the spring of 1950. "And little by little, month by month, the citizen of Paris or Rome who looks at America feels more and more confused as to where this great country is going, and where it is leading others."

In Russia, where the stakes were higher, the coverage evolved. His debut in major USSR publications came a month after Wheeling, when he was lumped with other Red-hunting senators as "a cross between [a] group of clowns in a circus arena and amateur night in a madhouse." As the months went by and he supplanted the others, the big Russian publications stopped portraying Joe as a simpleton and started seeing him as an "inspiration" to reactionaries and, later, as "Satan's most potent weapon." Their American Communist counterpart, the *Daily Worker,* gave him saturation coverage, with close to two thousand often hyperbolic stories between 1947 and 1957.

Privately, Soviet diplomats were struggling to understand the McCarthy phenomenon, as reflected in the now open files of the old USSR embassy in Washington. "The overwhelming majority of loyal Americans condemn the methods of McCarthy, rooted in Hitler's tyranny," reads one representative letter. Others try to follow how McCarthy was being received by Republicans, Democrats, labor unions, and the Catholic Church. Despite such vitriol, it's surprising how infrequently the senator and his crusade appear in these files. The Politburo was less concerned about him as a threat to its spy network than as a reflection of the rightward drift of American politics. He was "one of the more such crazy Americans, who [were] trying to fight communism," explains Sergei Khrushchev, whose father, Nikita, ran Russia during a critical phase of the Cold War and who emigrated to the United States in 1991. "So many [anti-Communists] were before him, starting with Winston Churchill, that the people of the Soviet Union [didn't pay much attention] . . . It was Winston Churchill, it was Hitler, Mussolini, and [then] McCarthy."

Love him or hate him, journalists here and everywhere gave Joe what every politician and bully relishes: attention. He'd mastered the print media especially, the way Roosevelt had radio and Eisenhower and Kennedy would TV. But what did the reporters who covered him day in and day out think of him? They were generally loath to say since they were supposed to be impartial, but 128 Capitol correspondents responded to an anonymous poll by *Pageant* magazine in 1951. "Pugnacious Joe McCarthy, 41, had no competition for the title of No. 1 'worst' U.S. Senator (three out of four votes—almost double those of his nearest competitor)," the magazine announced in what was a momentous shift from his twenty-second-worst standing in a similar survey in 1949. "In McCarthy's case, the correspondents' reasons for their choice were given with considerable vigor. Some of them: 'His record is reason enough to consider him the most ignorant and vicious member of the Senate.' 'As a Senator his disregard for personal rights and freedoms make him an extremely dangerous man.' 'A shrewd and dangerous exploiter of uninformed prejudice.' 'A demagogue who has introduced McCarthyism (the technique of the Big Lie) to split the country.'"

Joe was used to getting ripped in the press. The only opinion that mattered to him was the one reflected at the polls on November 4, 1952, Election Day. His supporters loved that he'd made an enemy of the mainstream press. And rather than splitting the country, he was counting on uniting it behind his anti-Communist crusade and having Wisconsin voters send him back for a second term of discomfiting his too comfortable fellow senators.

The timing of the vote worked both for and against him. On the one hand, he was reaching giddy oratorical heights, embraced everywhere he went as the Pied Piper of the patriotic brigade. The Democrats' war in Korea was a stand-in for the broader Cold War, with America and its South Korean allies battling Chinese as well as North Korean troops, both armed by Russia. But US strategies and tactics were ill-defined and shifting. The fighting was so up and down that a barren ridge called Mount Baldy would change hands eleven times, fifteen hundred Americans died near there each week during the peak of fighting, and the battle-hardened general Dwight Eisenhower despaired that "men are stupid." Commander in chief Truman was a lonely lame duck, with Adlai Stevenson, an even less popular Democrat, carrying the presidential banner against Ike, who was so universally admired that either party would have embraced him as its nominee. And yet rather than enjoying the free hand that circumstances would have suggested, Joe the investigator was himself under investigation again. His tormenter this time was a Connecticut senator smart enough to have been offered a Rhodes Scholarship, ambitious enough to have turned it down to make his millions in advertising, and angry enough that he wanted Joe not just censured, the way Tydings had, but subjected to the Senate's nuclear option: expulsion.

"There is one act of hypocrisy which most offends the deepest convictions of the Christian conscience and also the American spirit of justice and fair play. That act is to put the brand of guilt on an innocent man," Democratic senator William Benton told the Subcommittee on Privileges and Elections in the fall of 1951, just a year before voters would render their verdict. "I submit that there is no one who has erred more recklessly and maliciously in this respect than Senator Joseph McCarthy. Let us now remember the words of Isaiah: 'Woe unto them that call evil good and good evil.'" Joe turned to the book of Exodus for his eye-for-an-eye-style riposte. Even as it was probing McCarthy at the instigation of Benton, Joe pushed the subcommittee to simultaneously probe Benton for what McCarthy said were his Communist sympathies and financial improprieties. And in a TV interview, the ex-pugilist tried to cut his new rival down to size by dubbing him "Little Willie Benton, Connecticut's mental midget." Few were distracted, as it was apparent that it was McCarthy, not Benton, who was on trial.

The subcommittee wanted Senator McCarthy to defend himself in person, but it refused him the right he demanded to cross-examine other witnesses. He never actually said he wouldn't testify, but the only time he showed up before his colleagues was to blast Benton, preferring to mount his defense through a series of blistering letters to the subcommittee chairman. The only reason he was being investigated was that he was investigating communism, he charged in one, adding that "it is an evil and dishonest thing for the Subcommittee to allow itself to be used for an evil purpose." In another he made fun of the fact that his persecutors' "star witness" had been committed to "an institution for the criminally insane." (The witness, Lustron competitor Robert Byers Sr., wasn't in fact a star, and while he'd apparently had a breakdown, he was never judged criminally insane. Senator McCarthy made no reference to the history of mental illness of his own lead advocate, Daniel Buckley, a former subcommittee staffer and later McCarthy aide who, with coaching from Joe's team, issued a press release saying he'd resigned because he "was expected to substantiate Senator Benton's charges and to discredit McCarthy at the expense of the truth.") Asked repeatedly why he himself refused to testify, Joe explained, "I don't answer charges, I make them."*

That was just part of the backstage madness surrounding the subcommittee. McCarthy critic Margaret Chase Smith was on the panel, then nudged off in favor of a McCarthy ally. Democratic senator Guy Gillette chaired it until, faced with threats by McCarthy to campaign against his reelection, he resigned. So did two other members. Democrat Thomas Hennings, the new chairman and now one of just three members, took a bender cruise through the bars of New York, then spent weeks trying to sober up, with help from Drew Pearson and Mrs. Hennings. Hennings learned firsthand how intimidating Joe could be when he got a letter suggesting that he too resign — because "the general public will have little confidence in a committee report censuring McCarthy for fighting Communists when one of the members of the Committee

---

* Given how many times Joe was quoted saying that same thing, journalist Robert Fleming asked if he in fact had. Joe: "Of course not, and if I did, I'd be a fool to admit it." McCarthy Gossip File, Fleming Papers.

is on the payroll of the *St. Louis Post-Dispatch* and whose law partner is representing in a criminal action one of the 11 top Communists who were convicted for treason."

Benton, meanwhile, was convinced that his phones were tapped, his tax records had been leaked to McCarthy, and his personal safety was so imperiled that he ordered his chauffeur, an ex-prizefighter, to ensure nobody was following him. It wasn't pure paranoia. The Marquette archives make clear that McCarthy investigators *were* poring over every bill the Connecticut lawmaker had ever filed and every speech he'd ever made, along with unsupported gossip about his sexual preferences surfaced by the Loyal American Underground. George Sokolsky, Fulton Lewis, and the House Un-American Activities Committee were scouring their files too. It was war, and the fighting Marine was enlisting every available ally and weapon. Unable to disprove the message, Joe once again went after the messenger. In this case, the Democratic-controlled subcommittee surrendered the moral high ground when its chief counsel, acting on his own, got the Post Office to turn over the names and addresses of every first-class correspondent with McCarthy, Jean Kerr, and Don Surine.

During their back-and-forth with the subcommittee, Benton borrowed a page from the McCarthy playbook to tease him. He offered to waive his senatorial immunity and dared Joe to sue over any of the accusations made during Benton's thirty thousand words of anti-McCarthy testimony. Having painted himself into a corner, Joe filed a $2 million libel suit against his Connecticut colleague, the first time anyone could remember one senator suing another and one more in Joe's string of legal battles. "I consider this lawsuit as a means of pinpointing the contest between America and the Communist Party," he wrote his adversary. When he eventually dropped the claim, McCarthy said it was because his lawyer had been unable to discover a single person in the whole United States who believed Benton's charges. Benton and his backers again called McCarthy's bluff, running newspaper ads under the banner "WE BELIEVE BENTON," and generating 1,400 signed responses of people willing to testify. Van Susteren said the lawsuit never was aimed at a payout, just a payback. Every morning when Benton was shaving, Joe hoped the Nutmegger would look in the mirror and imagine having to fork over $2 million to the man he hated most. And that would make him sweat.*

Joe himself had nothing to sweat over in his primary campaign in 1952. The Republican he feared most was Governor Kohler, but party leaders at the state and local level adamantly opposed Kohler's running. McCarthy suddenly had become their favorite son and the party's most sought-after keynote speaker and productive fundraiser. Kohler wasn't a fan, but he was a realist: "I've seen tears come to people's eyes and they [kissed McCarthy's] hand when he was campaigning. He was that much of an emotional mover. Too bad, but that's the way it was. I mean, no politician should ever evoke that kind of response, I don't believe." That left as the main challenger Leonard Schmitt, a former Progressive and longtime thorn in the side of Stalwart Republicans like Tom Coleman. Schmitt faced a double whammy: Joe raised more money and had a bigger on-the-ground organization, while labor unions and other natural allies skipped his primary to vote in the closely contested Democratic one. The result was a slaughter, with McCarthy topping Schmitt 515,481 to 213,701. The primary turnout was the largest in state history, with Joe getting eighty thousand more votes than the combined totals for all the other candidates, Democrats and Republicans.

The Democratic nominee, Thomas Fairchild, was a soberminded former attorney general and one of the only Democrats in Wisconsin with a track record of winning statewide. He also was as temperamentally different from McCarthy as La Follette had been, making this campaign seem, in the words of one analyst, "like a staid minister scolding the town rowdy."† Fairchild's strategy was to move the debate from Joe's preferred Reds-in-Washing-

---

* Even as he was fending off the subcommittee, Joe was being investigated by the Bureau of Internal Revenue on old questions about who in his family had loaned him money and how much. "Don't give any of those investigators any information at all. They are entitled to nothing," he wrote to his brother William. "They are ... trying to go through the fakery of saying they want to see your records and books ... knowing all the time that they have no right to do this." Letter from Joe to William, June 26, 1952, series 20, MUA.

† Half a century later, Fairchild would say he'd viewed McCarthy as "a potential American Hitler," but that passion was missing when it could have helped. Thomas E. Fairchild Lecture, April 19, 2002, University of Wisconsin.

ton focus to staff-of-life concerns like the price of milk, the cost of education, and the incumbent's opposition to Social Security. Fairchild had plenty of money, strong support from unions and the big newspapers in Milwaukee and Madison, and a liberal and Democratic base that, unlike in 1946, knew just who Joe was and why he had to go. Joe also campaigned less, and less aggressively, than he had in 1946, at first because of illness and later because he was busy campaigning in other states. What Fairchild and his supporters lacked was the conviction that he could slay the bully.

Joe's base, by contrast, believed in him then and forever. John Oakes, a member of the *New York Times'* editorial board, got a feel for that loyalty after spending a month in Wisconsin in the fall of 1952. "He's against communism — and we're against communism," explained one farmhand. "Besides, if he wasn't telling the truth they'd 'a' hung him long ago." A tavern keeper in Milwaukee said, "Perhaps he isn't much of a Senator but he's a real fighter. He may be a stinker — but he's a Wisconsin stinker." Others told Oakes that it felt like the choice was between Joe McCarthy and Joe Stalin. To a demagogue, there are always just two alternatives — themselves or disaster. Wisconsin's demographics also helped McCarthy. It wasn't just that Republicans had dominated state politics for a full century, but all the Germans, Scandinavians, and Catholics were predisposed toward him too. So was Wisconsin's large bloc of Polish Americans. "You can hardly find a politician among the Poles of Milwaukee's South Side who doesn't believe that many of his normally Democratic constituents voted for McCarthy in the primary because they were against 'Yalta,' against the Administration that 'sold Poland down the river,'" Oakes reported. "'Yalta! Yalta!' exclaimed one Polish-American leader who is all out for McCarthy. 'Many people here don't know if it's the name of a man or the name of an overcoat. But they do know they're against it and so is McCarthy and that's the way they voted.'"

This Senate race, the most closely watched in the country, offered a home for every slice of the electorate. There were Republicans for Fairchild and Democrats for McCarthy. A "stop McCarthy" movement that called itself "Operation Truth" staged a series of gatherings across the state, while a 136-page pamphlet prepared by a seventy-five-member Citizens' Committee on Mc-

Carthy's Record was more in-depth and professional-looking than the brochure Joe helped assemble in Maryland but every bit as anti-McCarthy as Joe's was pro-Butler.* Edward Morgan, the chief counsel of the Tydings Committee, bolstered the Fairchild bid by telling a TV and radio audience that Joe, "in a mad effort to justify his charges of Communists in the state department," had taken to the Senate floor reading from a document that was "an out and out forgery." But McCarthy had most Wisconsin newspapers behind him editorially, and his name appeared in stories three and a half times more often than Fairchild's. (The ratio was nearly five to one when it came to page-one headlines.)† Hollywood A-listers ranging from Cecil B. DeMille to Louis B. Mayer helped the incumbent raise interest and money. Celebrity newsmen Westbrook Pegler and Fulton Lewis pushed their fans to donate more, painting their friend the senator as broke (he wasn't anywhere near) as well as sick (he was, with two surgeries that political season).‡ Money "was pouring into McCarthy headquarters from all over the country," reported Matusow. "A full suite on an upper floor was devoted just to handling the mail from the Pegler column. The average letter contained a dollar or two, but a few Texas letters went as high as a thousand. People from all over the forty-eight states were mailing money into Wisconsin to get Joe reelected."

---

* It wasn't just conservative journalists who crossed professional lines into politics. The Citizens' Committee report was written by Miles McMillin of the *Capital Times* and Edwin Bayley of the *Milwaukee Journal*. Jack Anderson and Ronald May also did their part, rushing into print their hypercritical biography of McCarthy a month before the election, when it could do the most damage. The book, a best-seller, "was aimed at providing the scattered anti-McCarthy movement with a complete arsenal under one cover," Anderson bragged. Reeves interview with Bayley; and Anderson, *Confessions of a Muckraker,* 254.

† That trend was especially pronounced in the last week of the campaign, when McCarthy's name appeared in headlines 665 times in newspapers circulating in Wisconsin, compared to Fairchild's 112. As for page-one stories, McCarthy headlined 209 of them, Fairchild just thirty. *Joe McCarthy and the Press,* 104–5.

‡ Joe's Marquette archives include detailed notes on what kind of help specific reporters could be counted on to provide. Pegler "will help in his column." George Sokolsky was a "great one in contacting other people to do jobs." And Bob Hurleigh, news director of WGN Radio in Chicago, was "the Fulton Lewis of the midwest; will help on his radio program at any time." McCarthy Club 1952, series 23, MUA.

Aldric Revell, the political reporter and columnist for the *Capital Times,* best captured how entrenched Joe had become in just six years: "To wage a campaign on the issue of McCarthyism is to strengthen the McCarthy forces, since reiteration of this word rings a Liberty Bell in the minds of the uninformed." It was futile, he added, "to fight emotionalism with rationalism." Public opinion analyst Samuel Lubell interviewed Wisconsinites and concluded that two factors explained their support for McCarthy. One was the demand that "we clean up these Commies at home with our boys dying in Korea." The other was Irish German Joe's popularity in German, Irish, and other communities that had questioned the US entry into World War II.

Campaigning wasn't without risk for a combative candidate like Joe, even in his home state. He stayed away from open windows for fear of assassins and kept a loaded revolver in his desk drawer. Albert Shortridge, a Milwaukee County sheriff's deputy who doubled as his bodyguard during the 1952 campaign, confirmed that there were dozens of threats. One time he was walking with the candidate down a corridor when he heard a door open a crack; a man hiding there had a club. Another time, at Marquette, a flashbulb exploded. Shortridge jumped, but Joe "never even flinched. He just kept on walking." His philosophy, the senator told a friend, was "He who does not live dangerously does not live at all." Van Susteren put it more graphically: "He had no shit in his pants."

He put that outlook to the test in Nevada. His appearance there was supposed to boost the election prospects of Senator George Malone, who was in a tight race for reelection, but the fighting Irishman from Appleton zeroed in on an old enemy in the audience, the *Las Vegas Sun*'s Hank Greenspun. "I wish his name was not Greenspun because he is a disgrace to a great race of people," McCarthy said referring to the Brooklyn-born publisher's Jewish heritage. "So if you want, and you're [the] people of Nevada, I don't think you do, but if you want this Greenspun-ism, you can have it and you can keep it, but I think you'd like to send him back to where he belongs . . . I think he should be allowed as much time as he wants on this stand to explain his position when I get through speaking. I will be glad to usher him to the stand myself." When the senator was through, the newspaperman took the stage, but Joe departed, saying, "I invite you to, if you care to stay, to listen to the editor of the local *Daily Worker*. Personally I'm not staying." It was classic Joe, spewing venom but stopping short of slander, whipping up his crowd then heading out the door. While many of his followers exited with him, some stayed to listen. "I challenge him to come debate with me about these things! He ran! He ran like the skunk on his farm in Wisconsin!" said Greenspun, a bomb thrower in his own right. "I just thought when he invited me up to the platform that he was going to stand here and discuss it with me in the true American fashion! But he ran! He ran like he does all over! That's all."

Raucous tactics like those alarmed at least one candidate Joe tried to help that election year. Prescott Bush, a buttoned-down Republican running for a Senate opening in Connecticut created by the death of McCarthy foe Brien McMahon, appeared with McCarthy at a rally in Bridgeport. "I never saw such a wild bunch of monkeys in any meeting that I've ever attended," Bush said looking back. At the time, he told the standing room crowd, "I must in all candor say that some of us, while we admire his objectives in his fight against Communism, we have very considerable reservations sometimes concerning the methods which he employs." That was too much for Joe's fans: "The roof went off with boos and hisses and catcalls and 'Throw him out.'" Joe, however, crossed the stage to shake hands with Bush, who won that race and launched a dynasty that would see his son and grandson make it to the White House. Over dinner that night McCarthy was even more amiable, signing autographs for fellow diners and leaning over to tell the Wall Street banker turned politician, "Now, Pres, what can I do for you? I want you to win this election . . . Do you need any money?"*

Joe campaigned in a dozen states in 1952, from New Jersey to New Mexico, but his most resounding impact came in one he pur-

---

* Bush wasn't the only Republican Joe made queasy. In Wisconsin, state senator Melvin Laird was running for Congress. "Joe comes to the Seventh District and offers Laird and those, the rest who are helping him, his support," recalls Laird friend and political adviser Bill Kraus. "And we said, 'Joe, we're really doing okay, why don't you just go elsewhere.'" Laird won that race and later served as secretary of defense under President Nixon. Author interview with Kraus.

posefully avoided and where his preferred candidate was a Democrat. During World War II, he and Jack Kennedy both served in the South Pacific, where one of McCarthy's comrades in arms says that Joe accompanied Jack on two nighttime patrols. (Kennedy's PT boat-mates say they doubt it.) There is no denying that Joe dated Kennedy sisters Patricia and Eunice in Washington when they were with Jack, and in Hyannis, where Eunice thought it fun to push Joe out of her father's boat until she learned he couldn't swim.* McCarthy also showed interest in younger sister Jean, who was impressed but felt that a twenty-year age gap was too great and worried that he "kissed very hard." Joe played shortstop for the Barefoot Boys, the Kennedy softball team, when they played their annual game against a team of Hyannis neighbors they dubbed The Pansies. (McCarthy was benched after making four errors at shortstop.) And he cracked a rib during one of the storied touch football games on the lawn in Hyannisport.

McCarthy's tightest Kennedy bond was with Papa Joe, the autocratic, magnetic, and unflinchingly family-focused patriarch, who, having seen his own political rise stymied, rechanneled his dynastic dreams into his four boys. The time he spent with McCarthy in Washington, Palm Beach, and Hyannis convinced Kennedy that the Wisconsin senator would catch on with the country. The Joes had a lot in common. Both were gruff, defiant Irishmen, each predicting he'd end up in the White House or in jail. (Kennedy was fonder of saying his second option was the shithouse.) Both started life as FDR Democrats, then grew disillusioned. Kennedy shared McCarthy's love of cocktail hour gossip and his disdain for left-wingers and the eastern establishment. As much as politics mattered to Kennedy, a man's temperament counted for more. That is why the Massachusetts magnate could number as

---

* Drew Pearson said that Adlai Stevenson, whom Joe hated, was for a time his rival for Eunice's affection. Joe and Eunice stayed close enough over the years that she was a bridesmaid at his wedding. Pearson column, January 18, 1953; and Reeves interview with Ed Nellor, June 6, 1979.

McCarthy preferred swimming pools to the ocean. In the former, he liked to play violent games of water polo, "churning across the pool like a sea-monster," said a fellow player. "Then [he] holds you at the bottom till you lose your breath and the ball at the same time." "The Private Life of Senator McCarthy."

close friends the ultraconservative Joe McCarthy and the archlib-
eral Supreme Court justice William O. Douglas, perhaps the only
man in America able to make that claim. Kennedy liked McCarthy
personally, saying he "was never a crab. If somebody was against
him, he never tried to cut his heart out. He never said that anybody
was a stinker. He was a pleasant fellow." Such stilted language was
classic Joe Kennedy. Classic, too, was his inability to see or care
about McCarthy's victims. When the senator started his anti-Communist crusade, "I thought he'd be a sensation," the elder Kennedy recalled. McCarthy back then was "the strongest man in the
United States next to Eisenhower."

A realist, Joe Kennedy understood that money remained the
coin of the American political realm the same way it had been in
the days of his businessman-politician father, and he put his fortune to work on behalf of his children. Just how much he gave Mc-
Carthy is uncertain since public reporting was not required in the
1940s and 1950s. Don Surine said it was $10,000 in 1952 alone.
Syndicated columnist Drew Pearson put it at $50,000 overall, and
Ed Nellor upped it to $100,000. Secretary of the Senate Bobby
Baker said it was five times that much, which would have made
Kennedy McCarthy's most generous benefactor. Kennedy insisted
that he gave "only a couple of thousand." Whatever the amount,
the money meant that McCarthy listened when Joe Kennedy made
it clear there was one thing he wanted most of all from him in
1952: to stay the hell out of Massachusetts. The Bay State, after all,
had enough Catholics and conservatives to make it hard-core Mc-
Carthy country, which is why even deep-blue Democrats like Tip
O'Neill and John McCormack never criticized the Wisconsin senator. Joe Kennedy understood better than any of them how a nod
by McCarthy toward his Republican colleague Henry Cabot Lodge
Jr. could on its own doom the bid by young Jack to unseat the Yankee incumbent.

Yet there was a hiccup from inside the Kennedy camp. Just
when Joe Sr. believed he had excluded McCarthy and McCarthyism from the campaign, an adviser Jack recruited to bolster
his standing with liberals proposed a newspaper advertisement
attacking both McCarthy and communism. Gardner "Pat" Jackson thought his ad was just the split-the-difference solution Jack

wanted. Jack's father thought it was insane, and when Jackson started to read the text at a campaign meeting, Joe erupted. "I can't estimate how long he poured it out on me," Jackson recalled. "It was just a stream of stuff—always referring to 'you and your sheeny friends.'" The next morning an embarrassed candidate tried to explain his father to Jackson: "I guess there isn't a motive in it which I think you'd respect, except love of family." Moments later he corrected himself: "And more often than not, I think that's just pride." Joe Kennedy denied the incident ever took place, saying that "Pat Jackson has been living off that story for years."

But a fondness for the Kennedys and their money was just half the story. The rest, as it was so often, was about settling old scores. While Lodge had backed his Wisconsin colleague during the Tydings investigation, there were rumors now that the Massachusetts Republican was plotting against McCarthy with two of Eisenhower's closest advisers. "I'm going to teach that bastard of a Lodge to suck eggs," Joe told Ray Kiermas. He did that by setting what he knew would be too high a price for his support: that Lodge would have to fully and publicly embrace McCarthy. Lodge tells a surprisingly similar version: "I asked [McCarthy] whether he would come into Massachusetts and campaign against Kennedy *without* mentioning me in any way. He told me that he couldn't do this. He would endorse me but he would say nothing against the son of Joe Kennedy. I told McCarthy 'thanks but no thanks.'" Given the narrowness of Kennedy's victory margin—3 percent, compared to Eisenhower's 9 percent landslide win in Massachusetts—McCarthy's staying away probably was as decisive as the pundits said. It was a slight Lodge wouldn't forget, and he would have an opportunity to get revenge for it.

Even as he was providing assists to candidates around the country, Joe was counting on one from General Eisenhower. The Republican nominee's coattails were sure to be long, but his loathing and fear of McCarthy predated the campaign and would last each man's lifetime. The moment of confrontation that predicted those to come happened on October 3, a month before the election and an embarrassingly late date for the national standard-bearer not to have endorsed the Wisconsin Republican. A practical man, Ike knew how much Joe could help in his bid to win Wisconsin, whose dozen electoral votes might be decisive in a close election. He'd already implicitly embraced the Red-baiting senator by adopting as his campaign formula K1C2, which stood for "Korea, Communism and Corruption."* But the former Supreme Commander of the Allied Expeditionary Force and of NATO knew how McCarthy had demeaned the patriotism of his friend and mentor George Marshall. So while he agreed to appear with McCarthy that October day on his whistle-stop through the Badger State, he was armed with a defense of Marshall meant to be read as an attack on the Wisconsin senator, and he relished delivering it, as he said, "right in McCarthy's backyard." He began with a nonspecific statement of principle that "the right to challenge a man's judgment carries with it no automatic right to question his honor." Then he got specific.

"Here I have a case in mind," the general wrote in his hand-edited draft of the speech. "Charges of disloyalty have in the past been [leveled] against General George C. Marshall. I am not now discussing any errors in judgment he may have made while serving in capacities other than military. But I was privileged throughout the years of World War II to know General Marshall personally, as Chief of Staff of the Army. I know him, as a man and a soldier, to be dedicated with singular selflessness and the profoundest patriotism to the service of America."

Eighty-eight valorous words, never uttered. Speechwriter Gabriel Hauge defended the controversial paragraph the day before it was to be delivered, when Eisenhower was in Peoria, Illinois, but Hauge's was a lonely mission. Arguing to expunge the Marshall defense were campaign manager Sherman Adams, Republican National Committee director Arthur Summerfield, and a bevy of other big shots. The future president had stood up for his pal Marshall two weeks before, they argued; no need to rub it in, on Joe's home turf, where he was popular enough to cost Ike Wisconsin.† Joe made a similar case when he flew to Peoria from Madi-

---

* The Democrats didn't have as catchy a slogan, but Stevenson, Kennedy, and a host of others made no bones about bashing Communists and insisting they, not their opponents, were the real patriots.

† General Wilton Persons, a senior Eisenhower aide, said he had long conservations with Joe about how much he resented the senator's assault on Marshall,

son in a private plane, and he continued making it the next day on Eisenhower's campaign train. The discussions left little doubt how much Ike disliked Joe, as he wouldn't let the senator ride in his compartment and banished him to the sixth car of the train, behind lesser-ranking Wisconsin Republicans. Joe, in turn, took a submissive tone with the nominee, which was the first time his buddy Raymond Dohr had seen him act that way with anyone and would be one of the last times he'd kowtow to Eisenhower. It was Adams, not McCarthy, who finally won over Eisenhower, telling him the paragraph in question was "a little gratuitous." Ike: "Take it out." The deletion was so awkward that McCarthy and Adams lied about it to reporters. Eisenhower was so abashed about having ordered it that, when Hauge asked why he did, the normally even-keeled candidate exploded, "I don't have to mention George Marshall in every speech, do I?" *New York Times* publisher Arthur Hays Sulzberger was so distraught about the expunged words, which he'd apparently written, that he wired Adams: "Do I need to tell you that I am sick at heart?"

Sulzberger wasn't the only one disheartened. Campaigning in Wisconsin five days later, the normally no-nonsense Democratic nominee, Adlai Stevenson, wisecracked, "My opponent has been worrying about my funnybone. I'm worrying about his backbone." And President Truman sounded this sober note: "[Eisenhower] ought to despise McCarthy, just as I expected him to—and just as I do. Now, in his bid for votes, he has endorsed Joe McCarthy for reelection—and humbly thanked him for riding on his train." The irony about the clumsy deletion is that it ended up being unnecessary. Ike's Wisconsin audience "was so euphoric and so enthusiastic that it cheered everything, every sentence, every pause . . . I am sure they would have cheered Eisenhower even if he had called for

"and at times I got the impression that he wished that he had not made those remarks, but he didn't see any way of withdrawing them and living with it." Persons OH, Columbia University, 1970, 25.

Eisenhower, meanwhile, used his memoir to justify his failure to take on McCarthy in Milwaukee, saying that doing it would have meant "arousing new public clamor" and "inadvertently embarrassing General Marshall." Still, the ex-president added, if he had known he'd be accused of capitulating, "I would never have acceded to the staff's arguments, logical as they sounded at the time." Eisenhower, *Mandate for Change,* 318.

Joe McCarthy's impeachment," Hauge said. "It did not affect the outcome of the election, but it did tarnish Eisenhower's image."

Joe had never liked Ike. He took swipes at Eisenhower in his 1951 Senate speech attacking General Marshall. Before the 1952 Republican convention, McCarthy passed on rumors that, as president of Columbia University, Eisenhower had coddled Communists. The morning after the party picked its nominees, Joe was asked by reporters for his reaction. His answer: "Dick Nixon will make a fine Vice-President."* But whatever doubts McCarthy had about Ike, he was rabid in his contempt for the Democratic standard-bearer, whom he called "Alger — I mean, Adlai" Stevenson.† It was guilt by Freudian slip, and was just the beginning. In October, in what a senior Stevenson aide termed "the worst night of the campaign," Joe told a nationwide TV audience that the Democrat's aides were left-wingers (half-true) and the *Daily Worker* was supporting Stevenson (untrue, and one of eighteen distortions the Democrats would document, even as Surine was claiming he'd gathered ninety pounds of dirt on the Illinois governor). Two days before the election, McCarthy charged Stevenson with "the most frantic lying spree upon which a Presidential campaign has ever embarked." And on election morning, voters awoke to Joe's charge that the Democratic slate's policies on Korea proved that the party was bent on "the decimation of our Air Force and the squandering of millions and billions of dollars." Going after Stevenson was a

---

* Joe may have helped ensure that Nixon kept his place on the GOP ticket by dispensing a bit of history-making political counsel in 1952 that historians missed. "I was told by my mother, who said she answered the call, that Nixon called my parents' house in 1952 before his Checkers speech and he was all upset — my mother always referred to him as crying or choked up — because he wanted Joe's advice on how to handle what then went on to be the Checkers speech," says Urban Van Susteren's daughter Greta, the TV news anchor. Accused of taking inappropriate campaign gifts, Nixon — in a masterly stroke that saved his spot as Ike's running mate — said there was one gift he would never give back: a black-and-white cocker spaniel named Checkers. Did Nixon reach Joe before delivering the speech, and did Joe weigh in on it? "I only assume so," says Greta, "from family folklore." Author interview with and email from Greta Van Susteren.
† Alger Hiss, the supposed Soviet spy, was one of Joe's favorite targets. McCarthy also called Stevenson "a graduate of Dean Acheson's College of Cowardly Communist Containment." Glazer, Lewis, and Tanenhaus, "'Have You No Sense of Decency?,'" *Bulletin of the American Academy*.

calculated strategy to let people back home know that he had bigger fish to fry than Fairchild. And it made McCarthy seem bolder than Eisenhower, who was reserved in his attacks on the opposition. But there was one attack line that even Joe didn't use, although he was aching to: that the Democratic nominee was a homosexual whose campaign was full of "pinks, punks, and pansies." Years later, insiders made clear why Joe held back this rare time: the Truman White House had threatened that if he aired such gossip, the Democrats would leak evidence that Ike had been planning to divorce his wife, Mamie, and marry his mistress Kay Summersby.*

Back in Wisconsin, Joe won reelection handily. But a closer look suggests it was less of a groundswell than he claimed or the public realized. Of the six Republicans running statewide, he had the sixth-best showing, winning just 54 percent of the vote — 12 percent less than the ballot-topping secretary of state and 7 percent less than Eisenhower. Rather than Ike needing Joe to win in Wisconsin, election analyst Louis Bean concluded that "but for the 1952 Eisenhower landslide, McCarthy undoubtedly would have lost." He fared worse than expected among Poles, with Fairchild drawing 75 percent of voters in the blue-collar Polish Catholic neighborhoods of Milwaukee. He also fared worse, percentagewise, than he had when he ran as an unknown six years before, and his margin of victory was 103,000 fewer votes. Familiarity with the freshman senator clearly bred disgruntlement.

Bean also examined the McCarthy influence in eleven other states where Joe campaigned that year, and again his conclusion was counterintuitive and, for Joe, crushing: "In all states where McCarthy pinpointed his charges against Democratic Senatorial candidates the Democratic candidates ran ahead of the general ticket." And while six Republicans whom he backed won, three of Joe's staunchest allies — Harry Cain of Washington, James Kem of

---

* Among the "damning" material that McCarthy was collecting on Stevenson was his having taken extended trips to Moscow when foreign visitors weren't welcome, his associations with Hiss, and his being an active member of the Unitarian Church. Among those helping him gather dirt was Howard Jarvis, who later led a tax-cutting campaign that started in California and swept the nation. Stevenson Files, series 14, MUA.

Missouri, and Zales Ecton of Montana — were broomed from office. A boost from McCarthy also was insufficient to lift William Revercomb back into his old Senate seat in West Virginia. The best explanation for those mixed results, Bean said, is that "the communist issue in the 1950 mid-term election was more pronounced than in 1952 when practically all issues played minor roles in comparison with the fact of Eisenhower's popularity . . . McCarthy apparently added little if anything to the Republican-Eisenhower sweep." The scholar's takeaway, published two years after the election, was unambiguous: McCarthy's political invincibility was a myth. But on the ground at the time, where it counted, most people still believed that Joe was driving the bulldozer.

That fear factor helps explain why the Subcommittee on Privileges and Elections waited until after the 1952 elections to unveil its report, and even then it was vintage Senate-speak. It dug deep into McCarthy's past to raise troubling questions on everything from his Lustron payments to his misuse of donations to his election and Red-hunting campaigns — but always stopped half a step shy of damning him. It zeroed in on his torment of Senate colleagues, saying he "deliberately set out to thwart any investigation" with his "charges of lack of jurisdiction, smear, and communist-inspired persecution" — but while that broke with Senate norms, it didn't break any statutes. And while it won rare bipartisan approval, with its only Republican member agreeing with the two Democrats, that came with a price. Instead of pursuing its findings to their logical conclusion, which could have included the banishment Benton had asked for, the subcommittee passed the buck to the Department of Justice, the Bureau of Internal Revenue, and the full Senate. Any chance of the Senate's acting was doomed by the congressional calendar, with the report coming out just as Senate Democrats were reluctantly yielding power, and the Republicans — with a one-vote majority — weren't about to boot one of their members.*

---

* The Eisenhower Justice Department determined there was insufficient evidence for an indictment, which is what the Truman department had decided with earlier probes. The new Republican-controlled Senate fired most subcommittee staffers, nearly every copy of its report on Joe disappeared, and the full

Joe had once again managed to duck any consequences for his actions. The subcommittee report arrived too late for Fairchild to ballyhoo its embarrassing findings or for Wisconsin voters to factor it in. Joe took his seat in the 83rd Congress unchallenged. This time, however, it was a respite, not a pardon. While it was Benton who was ousted in 1952, courtesy of Connecticut voters, he would get his revenge two years later when his dusted-off resolution provided the foundation for McCarthy's downfall.

In the meantime, Joe was uncharacteristically sentimental about what he'd managed on Election Day and where he was heading. The night after his triumph "he was damned near tears," recalled Tom Korb, who was driving the senator to the Milwaukee airport. "He kept telling us that he was unworthy of this appreciation." Was he really a senator, and how could voters have been so loyal? This was the same "sentimental slob" side that belied his image as hard-boiled and still had him choking up at the sight of the Capitol. "You know," Korb added, "all his life he wanted so much for people to like him, and when it finally happened it was almost too much for him."

Others have a different memory of the aftermath of that 1952 campaign. More even than his own win, what delighted Joe was seeing Senator Benton get beat. The election tally board at the Hotel Appleton, where the McCarthy team was celebrating, carried this pronouncement: "Benton went to hell at 8:30." And the next morning, the Appleton paper said the phrase heard most often among McCarthy partisans was "Joe won in Connecticut." His role in unseating Little Willie Benton, his second-most arch-adversary, was the perfect bookend to the comeuppance he'd delivered to the first, "Milord" Tydings.

Rules Committee never acted on the findings. Hyman, *Lives of William Benton,* 483–84.

McCarthy defenders like Stan Evans are right in pointing out the enormous discrepancy between the eight exhibit pages devoted in the final report to Benton, who was administered a light wrist-slap for a possible conflict of interest, versus the 266 pages laying out Joe's alleged fraud and deceit. But it was Joe who had trampled on Senate civilities to the point where his colleagues felt compelled to investigate, while his countercharges against the Connecticut Democrat were a concession senators had to make to give the appearance of evenhandedness. Evans, *Blacklisted,* 439.

• • •

The '52 election changed everything for Joe. It wasn't just getting to serve a second term, although that was a fine start. With the Republicans in charge of the Senate, he could for the first time claim institutional clout. The House of Representatives and White House also switched to friendly hands, giving the GOP total control for the first time since the Great Depression. In light of the waves McCarthy managed to generate as a precocious freshman from the out-of-power party, it is easy to forget that he had conducted his probes of communism as an interloper on other members' committees, or from the press conference podium. Now he'd have a panel of his own, ironically the same Government Operations Committee that owed its existence to a congressional reorganization engineered by Young Bob La Follette, and would chair as well its Permanent Subcommittee on Investigations. That meant the power to hold hearings, summon witnesses, issue subpoenas, publish findings, and raise Cain.*

The Republican senators who ran things knew well the peril that posed and thought they had it under control. Senator George Aiken gave up his seniority on the Labor and Public Welfare Committee to take a seat on Foreign Relations that would otherwise have gone to Joe. Majority leader Robert Taft handed control of the primary Communist-hunting subcommittee, Internal Security, to Senator William Jenner, and as further insurance ordered that all investigations be cleared through the Republican leadership team. "We've got McCarthy where he can't do any harm," Taft told one journalist, grinning and purring as he envisioned Joe cooped up in an out-of-the-spotlight office reviewing bureaucratic studies from the goody-two-shoes General Accounting Office.†

Joe seemed willing to go along, telling a reporter just after the

---

* Being chairman, he said, made it "12 times easier" to conduct his investigations. "Before I became chairman it was necessary to do all the investigating myself, or to hire investigators at my own expense or with the help of contributions from friends." "The Controversial Senator Contends His Tactics Are Both Practical and Fair."

† Richard Nixon said he knew early on that Joe wasn't about to go away or play nice: "As a Democratic friend put it to me, 'Joe has been a snake in the grass for us. If you're not careful he'll become a viper in your bosom.'" Nixon, *RN,* 137.

election, "It will be unnecessary for me to conduct a one-man campaign to expose Communists in government. We have a new President who doesn't want party-line thinkers or fellow travelers. He will conduct the fight." From now on, McCarthy added, he would play "an entirely different role," focusing on graft and corruption. It was a 180-degree turnaround for the senator whose very name had come to stand for exposing Communists in government — and it lasted for all of one month. By December he'd reversed again, promising "no slackening" of his crusade to weed out the Reds from the government and, echoing Revolutionary War hero Captain John Paul Jones, vowing, "We have only scratched the surface." No surprise there, editorialized the *Washington Post:* "No bear leaves a honey pot while it's still full of honey. Senator McCarthy has made a political as well as a monetary mint out of his charges of communism; no doubt he will keep on working these for all they are worth — just as long as he is allowed to do so."

Most senators focused on whatever full committee they chaired, milking any subcommittee they held on to for the money, staff, and space it brought but less concerned with its day-to-day operations. Not Joe. He knew from having served on it when his party was in the minority that the Investigations Subcommittee had the real power, with a wide-open mandate to scrutinize everything from waste to fraud in all 2,117 federal agencies and departments, military along with civilian. Communists weren't mentioned in any enabling legislation, but they weren't ruled out, which was good enough for the new chairman. "Some people don't realize it, but it could be the most powerful committee in the Senate," McCarthy said. "There won't be enough cells in Federal prisons when I get through."

Lending credence to that boast was the free hand he'd be given, at least at first, by fellow members. Two years before, he'd managed to oust the one Republican who might have raised roadblocks, Margaret Chase Smith. His GOP colleagues now included two friends, Karl Mundt of South Dakota and Everett Dirksen of Illinois, along with Michigan's Charles Potter, who'd lost both legs in the war and whose anti-Communist ardor led some to label him a junior McCarthy. The real McCarthy hadn't helped his cause by campaigning in Washington state and Missouri against two of his Democratic members, Henry Jackson and Stuart Symington, but they were freshmen in an era when most newcomers lacked guts and influence. The Democrat who did matter was the man Joe was succeeding as chairman of the full committee, John McClellan, a crusty, conservative fifty-six-year-old Arkansan who was as straitlaced as McCarthy was peacockish. Joe thought he knew just how to play him. "I went to see Senator McCarthy when he got back to town, and I said, 'Senator McClellan says that he doesn't think that he's going to stay on the committee,'" recalled Ruth Watt, the longtime chief clerk of the subcommittee. "So Senator McCarthy picked up the phone and called Senator McClellan and he said, 'John, what's going on here? I hear that you're thinking about not staying on the committee.' He said, 'You've got to stay in the committee to keep that son-of-a-bitch Joe McCarthy in line!'" McClellan did both.

The Democrats, meanwhile, had seen how Joe helped finish off their last two majority leaders, Scott Lucas and Ernest McFarland, and were on guard. McCarthy is "a Republican problem," said Lyndon Johnson, who succeeded McFarland. The wily and wise Texan cautioned liberal Democrats not to pounce until the Wisconsin lawmaker did something that offended conservatives too. "I will not," he insisted, "commit my party to some high-school debate on the subject, 'Resolved that Communism is good for the United States,' with my party taking affirmative." Drew Pearson suggested another reason LBJ was gun-shy: his Texas oilmen benefactors liked Joe, and "Lyndon feared they might put a candidate in the race against him if he bucked McCarthy . . . [I]t was this evasion that helped win for the senator from Texas the nickname of 'lyin'-down' Johnson."*

Joe was off and unbridled, with a hefty $200,000 budget (a third more than Jenner's subcommittee got), a fixed agenda (same as since Wheeling), and the focus now on assembling a staff. That mattered for any congressional panel, and more so for Joe, given his reliance on aides to back up yesterday's charges and give him fresh ones for tomorrow. Don Surine had been fine for tossing bombs, but he was not up to the painstaking work of running a subcom-

---

* Pearson's more lyrical version was "lyin-down Lyndon."

mittee.* Neither were all the scribes working out of Joe's office, no matter whose payroll they were on. The one person who could have done it all, ably, was Jean Kerr. She'd been ghostwriting everything important published under Joe's byline and orchestrating his most attention-grabbing ploys. But after Drew Pearson called her McCarthy's "gorgeous Girl Friday," she quit and went to work for the Republican National Committee. She still played an essential role behind the scenes during the senator's 1952 campaign— he called her "the indispensable half of the team"—but then she began searching for a new career. Maybe the media, she thought, as she helped launch a TV show called *Facts Forum,* financed by Texas oil tycoon and conservative benefactor H. L. Hunt.

One of the first calls Joe took in his search for a chief of staff was from the other Joe. Kennedy had already cashed in an enormous chit by getting McCarthy to steer clear of Massachusetts during Jack's campaign. Now he was back plugging the next-born he'd once described as the runt of his litter of nine—the lamest athlete, most tongue-tied, and least likely to matter. He now understood that Bobby was the most like him in everything from his capacity to hate as well as love to his hard-as-nails single-mindedness. (In Joe's case, his cause was to make money so his kids wouldn't have to; Bobby's three totems were, in order, the Kennedy family, God, and the Democratic Party.)

While Bobby Kennedy knew and respected McCarthy's ties to his family, he had attachments of his own. Their first significant encounter came in 1951, when Bobby, as a third-year law student at the University of Virginia, invited McCarthy onto campus to speak. The occasion was memorable less for the senator's fiery oration than for what happened when Bobby had him to dinner afterward. McCarthy "asked for a drink right away," recalled E. Barrett Prettyman Jr., an editor of the law review who was there that evening. "We began to ask him questions. In the beginning, he was very sure-footed in his responses, but as he began to get sloshed, he began to

* One of Surine's post-election schemes, Matusow said, was "to subpoena all of former Secretary of State Dean Acheson's files, a few days after Acheson left office. Surine said that they had a van ready to go to Acheson's home . . . His well-laid plans fell through." Ex-FBI agent Jim Juliana said Surine "saw Communists in trees." Matusow, *False Witness,* 210; and December 25, 1997, interview, JJP.

get tangled . . . He just went to pieces. And he began to *realize* he was embarrassing himself, so he would get more embarrassed, and drink more, and people began to slip out." Before the night was out, McCarthy had pawed a female guest and Bobby had helped him to bed. Prettyman was horrified, but Bobby's recollection of that first meeting with the senator was "I liked him almost immediately."

Bobby had shown where he stood on Joe's soon-to-be holy war when he defended the senator in impassioned debates with friends during his undergraduate years at Harvard in the 1940s. In a law school paper he argued that President Roosevelt had sold out US interests in his 1945 Yalta agreement with the Soviets on the configuration of postwar Europe. His first job after graduating was investigating Bolsheviks at the Internal Security Division of the Justice Department, and as his brother Jack's campaign manager he attacked Senator Lodge for being soft on communism. Now Bobby was almost as alarmed as Joe about what he saw as the "serious internal security threat to the United States," and he thought that "Joe McCarthy seemed to be the only one who was doing anything about it." The lawmaker and the newly minted lawyer both had the whatever-it-takes instincts of alley fighters, which Bobby believed they'd need in a Cold War in which the enemy fought dirty. "Joe's *methods* may be a little rough," Kennedy confided to a pair of reporters, "but, after all, his goal is to expose Communists in government, and that's a worthy goal. So why are you reporters so critical of his methods?"

There was one last reason why a job with Joe McCarthy was so appealing to Bobby Kennedy. Like so much in his life, it had to do with Joe Kennedy. Bobby knew his father admired McCarthy, and he saw the senator as a reflection of much that he loved in his dad. Working for a tough-minded jingoist like McCarthy also was Bobby's way of trying to erase the public's lingering memory of Joe Kennedy as a Nazi apologist and, as many British still saw him after his time as FDR's early wartime ambassador to the Court of St. James's, a coward. What RFK failed to see was that his father — an isolationist who believed that Communists, like fascists, could be accommodated until their regimes collapsed from within — was far less of a Cold Warrior than McCarthy was and than Bobby was becoming.

Joe McCarthy couldn't say no to Joe Kennedy; of course he would give Kennedy's son a job.* It was just a question of what position would be right for Bobby and for sticky committee politics. The Wisconsin senator had wanted from the start to hire as his chief counsel a smart lawyer and GOP activist, John Sirica, who in a later career as a federal judge would doggedly pursue the Watergate investigation that ultimately led President Nixon to resign. Sirica and McCarthy were close enough friends to double-date and keep each other company at the horse track. "Joe McCarthy offered me the job" and "I found the offer very attractive," Sirica recalled in his memoir. But he'd just taken a position at a silk-stocking Washington law firm, and his wife was opposed, so he begged off. "I have often wondered what I would have done had I been his counsel. I don't know whether I could have controlled him. Perhaps he would have listened to me. But most likely I would have gone down with him."

With Sirica and other experienced hands opting out, and Bobby Kennedy in limbo, Joe turned to another ambitious and combative young lawyer, Roy Cohn. Cohn was a Democrat with family connections, although not nearly as powerful as the Kennedys', and he had arrived at his anticommunism in part through his religion, the same way Bobby did.† But unlike Kennedy, Cohn was a top-notch student with a photographic memory so keen that, after hearing but not writing down a series of telephone numbers, he could dial them in succession. He already had helped send America's most notorious spies, Julius and Ethel Rosenberg, to the electric chair, and he had sent to prison eleven Communist operatives

---

* Kennedy would telephone often enough that it started to grate on McCarthy, at least in Roy Cohn's telling. Cohn walked in during one such chat and, even as McCarthy was reassuring Kennedy, "Sure, Joe. I see. That's a good point," he put the handset on his desk, scribbling this note to Cohn: "Remind me to check the size of his campaign contribution. I'm not sure it's worth it." Cohn, *McCarthy*, 66.
† In Cohn's case, he was out to show in the wake of the Rosenberg trials that not all Jews were Communists, while Kennedy was convinced that many of Joe's critics were more anti-Catholic than anti-McCarthy. Kennedy also occasionally echoed his father's insensitivity toward Jews, according to ex-FBI agent and later McCarthy staffer Jim Juliana, who said Bobby's reaction to the hiring of James Alderman was "Well, you've got to give the Jews something." June 10, 1998, interview, JJP.

who were conspiring to overthrow the government. One senior FBI official called him "smart beyond comprehension." There was another factor in Cohn's favor: he was Jewish. This gave McCarthy cover at a moment when he was being attacked as anti-Semitic by Drew Pearson and the Anti-Defamation League. Not giving the top job to Bobby offered McCarthy a different kind of cover, deflecting charges that the appointment was a payoff to his patron Joe Kennedy.

The McCarthy-Cohn match became so storied that a lineup of witnesses would claim to have made it. Walter Winchell said it happened one night at New York's posh Stork Club, where a pimple-faced, disheveled Cohn was a table-hopping regular: "Roy came in looking for me. I introduced Cohn to McCarthy. They became what they became." Brigid Berlin, whose father, Richard, ran the Hearst media empire, remembers it differently: "Nick [the chauffeur] had gone to pick up Roy Cohn to bring him back to dad's office . . . Dad came down with Joe. Roy was already in the car. He was on the left, in the back seat. Daddy got in and he was in the middle. Roy was on his right. He looked at Joe and he said, 'You're a crazy Irishman and this fellow, he's a crazy Jew, and I think you ought to get together.' That was the beginning." Or was J. Edgar Hoover the middleman, as a congressional pal claimed? Cohn himself said he was put in touch with the senator by Berlin, Hearst columnist George Sokolsky, and Robert Morris, a Capitol Hill staffer Joe wanted for the job but who turned it down. Their first meeting wasn't at the Stork Club or in a chauffeured car. It happened, Cohn said, in McCarthy's bedroom at the Astor Hotel, where the senator was wearing just pants, suspenders, socks, and shoes. "Joe McCarthy in hair-shirt!" Roy remembered. "McCarthy leaned through a few bodies and grabbed my hand, a big, infectious smile on his famous map. 'I wanted to see for myself,' he said, 'whether you're the genius they say you are, or if you just have good press agents.' Obviously, I was supposed to smile or laugh or something, but I blew it. I think I gave him a cold fish handshake and mumbled a few dummy things. Altogether awkward, Jeezus it was embarrassing."

McCarthy wanted both Roy and Bobby, and since he was unsure how to work it out, his solution was to make Cohn chief counsel. Ex-FBI agent Francis "Frip" Flanagan would stay on as general counsel, and Bobby would start as Flanagan's assistant, with the promise of becoming his replacement. The arrangement was confusing even to its architect, who never was one to exercise control over his staff. When reporters asked who would be doing what, McCarthy sheepishly smiled, spread his hands wide, and confessed, "I don't know." What was obvious was that Bobby was one of ten assistant counsels to the committee, earning less than half as much as Roy, who at twenty-five was the youngest chief counsel on Capitol Hill. With official lines of authority hazy, an informal hierarchy of duties and loyalties took shape. It soon became apparent, Cohn said, that Kennedy "was my enemy," with Flanagan confiding to Cohn that "first of all, he isn't crazy about Jews. Second, you're not exactly a member of the Palm Beach polo set. And thirdly, you've got the job he wanted." For his part, Cohn saw in Bobby the Irish toughs who'd prowled the streets when he was growing up in the Bronx, and he knew how to bully back. "Roy treats [Kennedy] as a gofer. Literally as a gofer," observed Washington journalist Murrey Marder. "Not as a lawyer, fellow counselor, or anything like that. As a kid. A rich bitch kid."

To some, the Cohn-Kennedy conflict seemed like an insider's game, interesting only because of the seminal figures they both became. Yet it was more than that, much more. It defined not just Joe's staff but his career and life. Instead of a man who would grow into a racial healer, a tribune for the poor, and the last progressive knight, he chose to run his subcommittee a man who would be disbarred for conduct that was ruled "unethical," "unprofessional," and "particularly reprehensible." Cohn "was super smart and super manipulative and super out for himself," said Henry Kissinger, himself a master in the exercise of political power.* Whether or

---

* The FBI, in its thirty-three-part file on Cohn, seemed to agree with Kissinger. Hoover worried about Cohn's "propensity to seize upon our production of information and run with it as his own." For him to succeed, the director said, "I would like to see someone a little older and more mature just caution Cohn to kind of watch his step and not be so flamboyant." A. H. Belmont to D. M. Ladd, October 15, 1952, and Hoover to Nichols and Tolson, November 24, 1952, pt. 19 of 33, Cohn FBI Files.

Juliana said Cohn "could have been the best thing to happen to Joe McCarthy because of the knowledge that he brought to the committee. However in my

not things would actually have been different under Kennedy, or even Sirica, is unknowable. Joe, after all, was the boss, and there never was a doubt where he was heading. There were, however, questions about tactics, ethics, and rudimentary maturity, now that he had traded in his bully pulpit for the chairman's gavel. For all his genius, Roy Cohn's answers would reinforce Joe McCarthy's worst instincts.

opinion he was one of the worst things to ever happen to Joe McCarthy because of his methods of operation . . . [H]e always cut that corner." June 10, 1998, interview, JJP.

5

BEHIND CLOSED DOORS

IT DIDN'T TAKE HIM LONG. Just two weeks into the 83rd Congress, at the very first caucus of his Permanent Subcommittee on Investigations, Chairman Joe McCarthy was wielding his new sovereignty like a shillelagh, slaying old enemies. No need to work through intermediaries now or ask voters for their blessing; a fresh term and title gave him all the levers he required to exact the revenge he craved. Nobody even had to know, unless he leaked it, once he banished the public and convened an executive session. He did that 117 times in 1953 alone, compared to the six closed-door inquiries by his predecessor the previous year. There were public hearings, too, but only 214 witnesses were summoned there, compared to 403 in secret. It was a grand inquisitor's dream.

Who better to target first than Edward Morgan, who as chief counsel authored the damning Tydings Committee report in 1950, then as a private citizen took to the Wisconsin airwaves during Joe's 1952 campaign to warn that "this junior senator of yours, instead of fighting communism, has been the voice of fascism and the secret weapon of communism in America." It was precisely the kind of vitriol that Joe was aiming at others, and it stung more than he let on. Before their split, McCarthy had steered a series of lucrative clients to Morgan. Subsequently, the senator "spread talk around Washington" that sent those cash cows scurrying to other law firms, Morgan said. "The aftermath was bloody. I don't even want to talk about it."* That was just a warm-up. Now Joe could do real damage, dragging the lawyer before his subcommittee to grill him about his ties to a shady lobbyist and logroller named Russell Duke.

Morgan, it turned out, had demonstrated bad judgment by working with Duke, who he later learned had served time for robbery, been indicted for perjury, and thrown his ex-wife down a flight of stairs. Morgan represented several clients Duke sent his way, tapping his old contacts in the government (he'd been a chief inspector at the FBI) the way too many ex-officials did and do, and earning $13,700 in fees. McCarthy's wasn't the only congressional panel interested in Duke and Morgan, but as always, Joe went further than anyone else in pursuit of his own as well as the nation's business. He seized a garage full of Duke's records, and all of Morgan's relating to Duke. He held Duke in contempt and had him arrested when he failed to show up for a later hearing, then asked the Washington, DC, Bar Association to censure Morgan. A full year later, Duke was acquitted. Morgan remained a member in good standing of the Bar Association and would be named to three presidential commissions. Lacking evidence, Joe never held the public hearings he had promised. Instead, the newly crowned chairman quietly abandoned his first big case.

Before he let go of the Morgan matter, there was one more score to settle. Three years before, Senator Wayne Morse had signed Margaret Chase Smith's Declaration of Conscience taking Joe to task. Now the famously maverick senator from Oregon found himself in McCarthy's line of fire.† Subcommittee investigators pressed Morgan and Duke on every time they'd met with, written to, or discussed Morse, zeroing in on the help Morse lent a Duke client who faced a hefty tax bill after inheriting a fortune from Chinese relatives. The testimony failed to show that Morse

---

* When he took the job as Tydings Committee counsel, Morgan said, "Joe called me to say 'Ed, if I could have named the counsel myself, I'd have chosen you.'" McCarthy Claque File, Fleming Papers.
† Morse would later demonstrate his independence by being one of two senators to oppose the blank check that Congress wrote President Lyndon Johnson to wage an undeclared war in Vietnam.

did anything beyond vigorously aiding a wealthy constituent, and Oregonians elected him to two more terms.

A major reason for holding such closed hearings, McCarthy explained, was so anyone on whom the committee had derogatory information could clear his name and keep it out of the public realm. But the cases of Morgan and Morse made plain the real reason: Joe used the sequestered hearings as dress rehearsals to gauge if the individuals he was cross-examining privately were worth trumpeting or shaming in public. One in three wasn't.

There was another way in which the early clandestine hearings set the template for Joe's two-year reign as warden of America's most notorious Star Chamber. He issued a warning cum threat to Russell Duke that he would repeat to nearly every unfriendly witness: "Time after time, witnesses have come and they have not been guilty of any criminal activity of any kind until they testify, and they make the mistake of thinking they can outsmart the committee . . . So I would suggest to you that for your own protection you either tell us the truth and nothing but the truth, or else avail yourself of the privilege of refusal to answer."

When they sought to avail themselves of that privilege, which seventy-one witnesses did in 1953, Joe branded them "Fifth Amendment Communists." He also tried to get them fired, and oftentimes succeeded. "An innocent man does not need the Fifth Amendment," he chided, never acknowledging two ironies: that an innocent man is precisely whom many jurists believe the amendment was crafted to protect, and that McCarthy himself perpetually hid behind his own Senate immunity. In fairness, the Supreme Court had given trial judges broad latitude to deny a claim of self-incrimination to protect other people, and the Justice Department said that panels like the Subcommittee on Investigations could do the same. Joe pushed that and other logic over the edge, telling witnesses they could take the Fifth only if an honest answer to whatever question he was asking—Are you a spy for the Russians? for instance—would incriminate them. (Part of the point of the Fifth is that witnesses can invoke it without having to explain why.) Those who rejected his premises and persisted in their claims were cited for contempt, their names shipped to the attorney general for possible indictment. To play by the chairman's rules, however, carried a steep toll of its own: entering a Kafkaesque universe where asserting the right against self-incrimination was itself incriminating.*

It got worse. A witness who heeded the senator's caution against taking the Fifth and answered no, he wasn't a spy, was peppered with related questions like whether he knew any foreign agents or had expressed feelings about superspies like the Rosenbergs. Any attempt then to assert a freedom from self-incrimination was swatted down, with McCarthy chiding, "You have waived the privilege, Mister," and have to answer the broader questions. (In fact answering one question did, in the eyes of the Supreme Court, mean witnesses had to answer others, but only — and this was a nuance McCarthy didn't always acknowledge — if the first response was incriminating, like admitting to being a spy.) The senator sprang his trap over and over, joyfully, threatening to prosecute anyone who failed to answer. No one said unmasking treachery would be painless.

That wasn't the only menace for people he called to testify. Keeping the hearings secret was essential, Joe told them, warning that "senators are all bound not to discuss what goes on here,

---

* Joe wasn't the only one who read a sinister meaning into a witness exercising his or her rights under the Fifth Amendment. Rather than guessing, a University of North Carolina law professor asked 120 congressional witnesses why they claimed it when asked about any subversive activities. Answers ranged from a belief that the questions infringed on their freedom of speech to fear that talking about themselves would require them to spill the beans about others. The professor said his survey, the most thorough on the topic, showed that "most witnesses who rely upon the amendment do so for reasons apart from fear of [self-] incrimination." Pollitt, "The Fifth Amendment Plea," *University of Pennsylvania Law Review.*

Concerns about self-incrimination date back to the use of torture in the Middle Ages to induce confessions. In America, one of the first to invoke the Fifth was President Ulysses S. Grant, who did so in his last year in office, when the US House was taking him to task for being away from Washington so often for frivolous purposes. Taylor, *Grand Inquest,* 196.

Joe said he understood that "heritage coming down from English law. It ought to be preserved. I'd rather see an occasional guilty man escape punishment than to compel innocent people to testify against themselves." But asked about moves to limit Fifth Amendment protections, he said the time "may come when we'll have to make such a change." "The Controversial Senator Contends His Tactics Are Both Practical and Fair."

and the witnesses are always warned, under pain of punishment, for contempt of the committee, not to divulge anything." He was right about witnesses being bound by standards. But not him. While holding executive sessions wasn't unusual for the Senate back then, with this chairman "it didn't really mean a closed session, since McCarthy allowed in various friends, hangers-on, and favored newspaper reporters," said Army general counsel John Adams, who was ushered in along with the CEO of the Hearst papers and his wife, and Jean Kerr, her mother, and her mother's friend from Connecticut. "Nor did it mean secret, because afterward McCarthy would tell the reporters waiting outside whatever he pleased. Basically, 'executive' meant that Joe could do anything he wanted."

Then there was the single damning question that became not just McCarthy's signature but a metaphor for an era of political and personal defamation: "Are you now or have you ever been a member of the Communist Party?" The first witness he asked, as if he were cautiously testing how it would play, was Malvina Kerr, a lowly personnel assistant in the State Department's Performance Measurement Branch. Her answer was a polite "no, sir," to that and to the follow-up: "Have you ever belonged to any organization that has been named by the attorney general as subversive?" The senator was uncharacteristically apologetic to Kerr, assuring her, "I did not even know your name before yesterday, and all I know about you is just from examining you today, so therefore do not misunderstand these questions as reflecting upon you."

While it was less commented on, because it seemed like he was lending witnesses a helping hand, there was another phrase Chairman McCarthy used even more: "in other words" — after which he would rephrase their testimony into something with sinister implications. If they objected, he took that as a sign they were covering up something.

We can see now that the executive sessions were an unsanitized, easy-to-understand blueprint for McCarthyism. As famously madcap as the heretical senator appeared in his public hearings, comparing open and closed sessions makes plain that the TV cameras and public galleries acted as a restraint rather than the license to grandstand that they are for most politicians. Here in private, finally, we get the real Joe — penetrating and quick-witted at moments, but more often irascible, irresponsible, and irrepressible. Nowhere was that clearer than in his efforts to unearth embarrassing revelations about events in a witness's youth, or even before she or he was born. The political beliefs of colleagues, neighbors, and family members all were fair game. Those who swore they had never joined the Communist Party or engaged in espionage were held accountable for long-forgotten petitions they'd signed or for joining organizations the attorney general would later name as Communist fronts. The point was to mark them as guilty by early indiscretion. Guilty by friendships. Or guilty by suspicious parentage. Whatever the reason, the guilt was presumed, whereas innocence had to be proven.

In the process he redefined the very notion of what a witness was. Most who were called by Joe weren't there to offer evidence that could shed light on a particular question being investigated, the way they would have been in a courtroom or before most congressional committees. More often they themselves were the subject of Joe's probe. His staff or his Underground had given him the names. He summoned them because he considered them guilty and sought to expose their wrongdoing, or the misdeeds of others. To label them witnesses sugarcoated the reality of their presence before his tribunal, as many who were blameless as well as naïve quickly learned.

His smears backfired with Vladimir Toumanoff, a more senior official in the same branch of the State Department as Malvina Kerr. The story Toumanoff told behind closed doors had a twist that Joe couldn't wait to reveal to the world — that this Foreign Service official who handled critical personnel files had been born to Russian parents on the grounds of that country's embassy in Turkey in 1923, when it was in Soviet hands. But the chairman, whose zeal had never been matched by rigor, simply hadn't probed deeply enough to get the full story in the private hearing, so he watched in horror as it spilled out in the public session. "My father and mother were titled members of the Czarist regime," Toumanoff said.

My father was an officer in the Czar's personal Imperial Guard. He fought in the White Russian Army against the Communists. He was captured by them and sentenced to death, and escaped. When the White Russian Army was defeated by the Communists, he and my mother escaped from Russia to Turkey. They were political refugees from the Communists. It is an understatement to say that my family was in no way acceptable to the Soviet[s] — My parents were in fact mortal enemies of the Soviet Government. My parents told me that I was born on the grounds of the Russian Embassy in Constantinople on April 11, 1923. I am informed that in May of 1923, the Soviet Embassy was functioning in Ankara and not in Constantinople.

McCarthy was mortified. "Several days ago, you said you did not know whether it was under Soviet control or not," the senator stammered. "Since then, you have made an investigation, and you are now convinced that at the time you were born in the Embassy it was not under Communist control. Is that correct?" Toumanoff: "There is one tiny correction in your statement, Senator, that is that I don't recall in executive session your having asked me my opinion or having made any statement concerning the acceptability of my family to the Soviets, because if you had, I am sure I would have explained this background to you."

Toumanoff, Morgan, and Morse were the lucky ones. It wasn't easy being subjected to McCarthy's third degree, yet they emerged relatively unscathed. Not so Stanley Berinsky, who was suspended from the Army Signal Corps at Fort Monmouth, not for anything he'd done but because his mother had once been a member of the Communist Party. Henry Canning Archdeacon, Donald H. Morrill, and Witulad Piekarski all worked for defense contractor General Electric, all took the Fifth Amendment when asked if they were Communists, and all were shelved at a time when, even if they were Reds, that was perfectly legal if not politically acceptable. What mattered more was that GE knew better than to cross the newly empowered senator from Wisconsin, who was so well pleased with the scalps he'd claimed that he listed many of them in the subcommittee's annual report.

Communism was the panel's most single-minded focus but not

its solitary one. Old hobgoblins reeled Joe back in, including the threat of homosexuals selling out their government to cover up their iniquity. "I am no psychiatrist or psychologist but I understand that there is considerable interdependence among people who have that particular affliction, if we can call it that, and that they do recruit, often, people of the same difficulty to work with them. So it is of interest to know who you have got in the government, whether you have got anyone else with the same difficulty in the government," the senator lectured Eric Kohler, an esteemed accountant who had served in various senior government posts and was president of the American Accounting Association. Asked by Roy Cohn — who himself had the "affliction" but wouldn't say so — whether he was attracted to other men, Kohler answered, "I am perfectly willing to admit that I am, for the purposes of your private record here." Joe: "Looking at you, I don't think anybody would suspect you." To Kohler's great relief, he was not called to testify in public.

Whether it was homosexuals he was going after or Reds, there were other ways Joe's Permanent Subcommittee on Investigations was distinct. Witnesses included luminaries like composer Aaron Copland, poet Langston Hughes, and journalist James Reston, along with government functionaries, labor organizers, and army officers. He took the hearings on the road when he could — to Albany and Houston, Boston and Los Angeles — knowing that fellow senators couldn't join and, as he would be the only senator present, there'd be nobody to question what he was doing in the subcommittee's name. His staff did much of the interrogating, and sometimes Roy Cohn ran the show without Joe. And while those who refused to answer Chairman McCarthy's sweeping questions often were threatened with contempt of Congress, every last one of those who actually were cited had their cases thrown out of court or overturned on appeal.

One last thing stood out about the hush-hush hearings: their chairman seemed to get ornerier in the afternoon hours, if the midday break had been long enough for him to enjoy the martini-lubricated lunch that was standard for many lawmakers in that era. The cause and effect is impossible to prove, but fellow subcommittee member Charles Potter was struck by how, thanks to such "liquid luncheons," Joe "always seems to make his worst mistakes in the afternoon." Reading through the 8,969 pages of transcripts, one finds the chairman's morning politesse and deftness often have melted away, replaced by late-day outbursts like this directed at John Sardella, a member of what McCarthy said was the Communist-dominated United Electrical Workers union: "I would no more give you access to confidential material than I would cut my throat." Or this to GE worker Abden Francisco: "You are under oath, and you understand if you lie you are guilty of perjury, and you will be subject to spend[ing] a long time in jail." GE shop steward William Mastriani, a third foreign-born witness of the kind the senator seemed to delight in tormenting, said that same evening that he was nervous. Joe: "Mister, you have got reason to be nervous . . . You start telling the truth, and you need not be nervous." (Addressing a witness as "Mister" was a sure sign that Joe was angry and that the witness had reason to be anxious.)

At another nighttime session, McCarthy became enraged at Benjamin Wolman, the assistant principal at Public School 3 in Brooklyn, who'd taken the Fifth Amendment, as did his wife, Diana, a high school teacher. The senator directed his staff to "transmit this testimony to the Board of Education. I assume with this testimony they will discharge this man . . . I may say, your wife's testimony is being transmitted to the Board of Education also. I assume she will be discharged also." Max Finestone, a marketing researcher, got a dismissive "Mister" and a withering lecture the afternoon he took the Fifth. "You have had an accusation against you of being a part of the Rosenberg spy ring," McCarthy said. "In view of the fact that the Rosenbergs were executed for the same crime of which you are obviously guilty, can you see any reason why you should not meet the same fate that they did?"*

There is one more reason Joe's mood might have soured as the day dragged on: pain. It wasn't just his pounding sinuses, which

---

* This time, says spy historian Harvey Klehr, McCarthy was right: "Max Finestone, it turns out, was [a] member of the Rosenberg ring." Finestone himself continued to be evasive about his role until his death in 2011, admitting to knowing some things about Rosenberg's activities but not to any wrongdoing. Email to author from Klehr; and Radosh and Usdin, "The Sobell Confession," *Washington Examiner*.

required repeated draining, or the chronic backaches that some-times became acute. The veins in his backside swelled, producing hemorrhoids uncomfortable enough to require surgical removal of the clots. It can't have helped to sit for endless hours as hearings stretched into the night.

The records of those executive sessions were sealed for fifty years, as required by a law intended in part to protect witnesses whose privacy Joe had already violated in case after case. "I just felt that it was time for the public to know the whole story," ex-plained Republican senator Susan Collins of Maine, who, along with Democrat Carl Levin of Michigan, who also had chaired Mc-Carthy's old subcommittee, in 2003 unlocked the hidden tran-scripts. Both senators had special reasons to care — Collins be-cause she held Margaret Chase Smith's seat in the Senate and saw Smith as her mentor, while Levin says his political greening began when he gathered anti-McCarthy signatures from college class-mates in 1954.

The transcriptions offer an extraordinary peek inside one of the most hyperactive and disruptive panels in the 164-year history of the US Senate, and a look at Joe McCarthy unshackled. Joe said the mayhem was unavoidable because rooting out Communists was a dirty business, requiring brass knuckles and a single-minded focus. "The [sub]committee," he added in his first report to Con-gress and the public, "has been forced by these circumstances to deal with ugly instances of fraud and subversion, and its members have found no pleasure in their exposure, nor satisfaction in their magnitude." Erwin Griswold, dean of the Harvard Law School during McCarthy's tenure and later solicitor general under Presi-dents Johnson and Nixon, rendered a different verdict on Joe's way of governing: "This has often been a one-man sub-committee, where the witness finds presiding a legislator who is judge, jury, prosecutor, castigator, and press agent, all in one."*

By the end of 1953 enough time had passed since the launch of his crusade, and enough witnesses had been grilled, that it was pos-

---

* Griswold was too polite to name Senator McCarthy specifically, but as Joe him-self might say, he more than anyone else passed the dean's walks-like-a-duck test.

sible to grade Senator McCarthy's performance. Had his hundreds of accusations held up? What about the Communist putsch he'd warned about in Wheeling? And was the newly empowered chairman of the Subcommittee on Investigations worthy of that trust — or was he the autocrat his growing legion of critics charged?

The most complete contemporaneous analysis of the McCarthy record was made by a Duke University professor of sociology, Hornell Hart. He reviewed a representative sampling of cases, painstakingly parsing the charges about lists of saboteurs and disloyalty of government loyalty boards. His "prime conclusion," Hart said, "was that Senator McCarthy's statements had been radically at variance with the facts in 50 specific instances" that he examined. Joe had claimed, for instance, to have "photostats showing that the FBI gave the State Department a detailed chart three years ago showing that there were a total of 124 Soviet agents, Communists, Communist sympathizers and suspects in the State Department," but "no such chart had ever been prepared by or received from the FBI." The senator said that "in dozens of cases . . . recommendation from Alger Hiss on the State Department employees was all that was needed to completely clear them," but "not one specific case of this kind was cited by McCarthy." Communism "is dangerous, fundamentally, because it destroys human liberties by distorting and suppressing the truth," Hart cautioned. "We must triumph by truth, integrity and fair play, not by McCarthyism."

The senator's response underlined the professor's warning. Publicly, McCarthy dismissed the study as "trash." Privately, he wrote the president of Duke, demanding to know "what, if any, action you intend to take to undo the damage done by the publication of this false and defamatory material." When he didn't hear back, he wrote again two weeks later: "Unless I hear from you on or before November 10 that you are taking steps to have retracted the false and defamatory statements made, I shall assume that the material in the publication meets with your approval." The president wrote back nine days later, saying he'd been away and assuring the senator, "I shall be glad to discuss with Professor Hart the matter you mentioned and I am confident that he will want to correct any mistakes." Hart, however, had given McCarthy a chance to comment on the report before it was released, and he knew the

senator well enough to recognize his strong-arming and his bluffing. The letters, which are in the Marquette archives, never were
made public. And not only wasn't the study redacted or retracted,
but a version published in *The New Republic* was boldly titled "Mc-
Carthyism Versus Democracy."

Fact-checking wasn't the only way to judge the senator's performance. Emmet John Hughes, an adviser to President Eisenhower and longtime foreign correspondent for *Time,* tried to
assess the political damage across the federal government and especially at the State Department. It "eludes precise measure. But
its size was not small," Hughes wrote in 1963. "Professional officers charged with conduct of America's foreign affairs felt more
than a loss of morale: they felt an estrangement from the Administration—edged with an intellectual aversion—that would endure,
subtly but stubbornly, throughout the 1950s. One career diplomat,
a distinguished veteran of a half-dozen ambassadorial posts who
had never been personally touched by any of McCarthy's thrusts,
grimly confessed to me on one occasion: 'If I had a son, I would do
everything in my power to suppress any desire he might have to
enter the Foreign Service of the United States.'"

Those who did enter that service or any other in government
were less likely to speak up for fear of standing out, Marie Jahoda,
a psychologist at New York University, said in 1955. "No longer
was appropriate behavior defined in terms of general principles
such as discretion, decorum, or responsibility. Rather federal employees said: You should not discuss the admission of Red China to
the U.N.; you should not advocate interracial equality; you should
not mix with people unless you know them very well; if you want
to read the *Nation* you should not take it to the office; if you do
bring it to the office, you should explain in considerable detail why
you have it with you; you should take certain books off your private bookshelves," according to Jahoda. Such suspicion had even
spread to the baseball diamond, which is why the Cincinnati Reds
in 1953 temporarily rebranded themselves the Redlegs.

Those were prices worth paying, given the stakes of the Cold
War, McCarthy defenders said. "It is clear that he has been guilty
of a number of exaggerations, some of them reckless," but "*Mc-
Carthy's record is nevertheless not only much better than his critics*

allege but, given his métier, extremely good," William Buckley and his brother-in-law Brent Bozell wrote in their 425-page book *McCarthy and His Enemies,* published in 1954. Fifty-three years later M. Stanton Evans argued in his 663-page book — and its title — that rather than being an architect of toxic blacklists, it was McCarthy who had been "blacklisted by history." In his year-plus as subcommittee chairman, Evans wrote, the senator "did the equivalent of perhaps a decade's work." Operating "in prosecutorial mode, he pushed the evidence hard to make an indictment and seldom erred through understatement," but "he wasn't simply inventing charges out of whole cloth."

It was a fair point. The State Department security program was lax and sometimes ineffective, and Joe's scrutiny had security officers working overtime. While there was a fear of guilt by association, there was a corresponding one of innocence by association, whereby merely being accused by McCarthy was enough for many liberals to leap to the defense of lawbreakers like Alger Hiss. Government jobs were a privilege, not a prerogative, the senator said, with the law requiring that any benefit of the doubt go to the nation's security, not the employee's rights. Still, even the FBI conceded that the Communist Party USA wasn't nearly the threat it used to be by the time Joe took over the subcommittee. In 1953 enrollment nationally was at a twenty-year low of 23,800, a third of what it had been ten years before.

Where one came down on McCarthy questions partly depended on what biases you started with. Did the fact that federal loyalty review boards cleared 90 percent of their employees, for instance, mean everything was okay, and the threat of Communists infesting the State Department was overblown? That's how liberals interpreted the numbers. Conservatives said it showed how permissive the standards and the boards were. In the electrified environment of the Cold War, Presidents Truman and Eisenhower generally sided with the latter, tightening the regulations, or at least not loosening them.

The Wisconsin senator largely ignored the arguments between his critics and boosters, offering the only justification he thought necessary in his stouthearted report to Congress and the country after his first year as chairman. He seemed to admit his job was more salesman than investigator, saying that while the FBI was "the greatest law enforcement body of all times," it needed public exposés to push other agencies to act. He confused questions he'd posed about Communist influence with having elicited confessions, and equated finding a tinge of pink in someone's deep background with having proved the person was a spy. His numbers left little doubt that the subcommittee was as frenetic as its chairman, with 546 witnesses summoned in public or private (some were under suspicion themselves, others he asked to finger or exonerate different targets), 445 preliminary inquiries (nearly one inquiry per witness called), and 157 full-fledged investigations (impressive, given that the subcommittee had just three investigators). But all that action yielded more commotion than results. He was proudest of the government and federal contract workers he'd gotten fired because they were incompetent, inefficient, undesirable, or, worst in his eyes, Fifth Amendment Communists.

One of the dozens in that last category was Doris Walters Powell, a procurement clerk in the Army Quartermaster's Office and a classic example of how McCarthy handled witnesses he didn't like. Powell, who was on maternity leave, had worked years before as a secretary at a weekly newspaper in Harlem called *The People's Voice*, when it was run by a Communist Party leader. Louis Budenz, McCarthy's favorite ex-Communist, testified that he'd met with Powell and her boss in the offices of the *Daily Worker* and felt sure "she was a comrade." Her next boss at the newspaper said she'd seemed to be working for the Communists when they were running things there, then helped him clear out the Communists when she understood he was an anti-Communist and that was the way to keep her job. Marvel Cooke, an assistant managing editor known as "Mrs. Commissar," later said that Powell was actually a "red-baiter . . . [T]hat little gal was so far away from the Communist party, the Socialist party, the Democratic party . . . She just had worked in a place where a known Communist worked."

McCarthy, meanwhile, was busy inflating Doris's invoice-processing job into one vital to the nation's security. Knowing things like how many tons of ham, Hershey's bars, or peas and corn went to a particular military base could be useful to any enemy she might conspire with, McCarthy said, so he demanded to know who'd hired her and who had given her security clearance. "It may take us a while to get the information, but I assure you we will get it." It wasn't the first or last time he would tangle with the Army, only this time the senator looked like he was playing a one-man version of the children's game telephone. The facts transformed, drama enlarged, and stakes were heightened each time he addressed a new witness or whispered about what had happened inside the sealed hearing room to reporters waiting outside. But the game was up when Powell refused to answer whether she'd been a member of the Communist Party when she worked at *The People's Voice*. (She did say she wasn't a member anymore.) No need to prove she was a spy, a security risk, or even a Communist. Claiming her constitutional right was enough for the Army to revoke her government credentials that very day, then to suspend her.*

Her nightmare didn't end there. McCarthy was leaking to the press even though he'd made witnesses promise not to. The first stories referred to her as "Miss Q," presumably for "Quartermaster," said she'd taken the Fifth, and added that he'd be "very surprised" if the Army didn't suspend her. A week later he was (mis)naming her as Dora Walters Powell and calling her "a 100 per cent Communist." Her lawyer denied that, saying she had never taken out party membership, "nor did she ever consider herself a Communist." His denials, however, were afterthoughts in the story, which gave deference to McCarthy, the self-interested leaker, and gave the lowly clerk Powell much too much credit for being in a position to wreak havoc.

McCarthy's supporters were being punished too, although not in nearly the same numbers and sometimes with reversible results. John Matson, a State Department security officer, had told Joe's subcommittee that employee security files had been purged of derogatory information in a way that let disloyal workers keep their jobs. Matson's bosses said the problem was his persecution com-

---

* Joe struck a patronizing tone with many witnesses, but especially with women and Negroes, as in Powell's case. He told her lawyer, "She is an intelligent girl. She went through high school with high scholastic standings and had several years of college." And he told her, "I know you are not as dumb as you are trying to make out." US Senate, Permanent Subcommittee on Investigations, *Executive Sessions*, 2:1631 and 1634.

plex, not their filing system, and they demoted him to what Mc-Carthy called a "beat-pounding job similar to those that erring po-licemen get." The "low-echelon switch" was something the new secretary of state, John Foster Dulles, "would probably never have heard of if McCarthy had not hit the headlines by protesting about reprisals," *Time* magazine reported, adding, "Within a few days Matson was restored to his desk job."

As for the senator's leaks about what went on behind barred doors, they were calculated and continuing. "McCarthy used to bring his witnesses out of closed hearings each day in time for the noon news and the six o'clock news," said Ben Bagdikian, a Pulitzer Prize–winning journalist and later the dean of Berkeley's Graduate School of Journalism. "He was so blunt about it that he'd cut off the witness abruptly once the deadline passed."

Reporters were perpetually pressing McCarthy to name one se-rious Communist he had outed since Wheeling. It wasn't Miss Q. Powell he thought of, or Commissar Cooke. The name he cited most often was William Remington, a former Commerce Depart-ment official who, while he had been a Communist, may or may not have been a spy. And Joe wasn't the only one claiming his hide. Remington was first exposed in 1945 by whistleblower Elizabeth Bentley, who testified that he'd been a member of her old spy nest. Roy Cohn later helped convict him for lying about his Commu-nist Party ties. Asked by a *New York Times* reporter what evidence he had to back up his smear about card-carrying Communists at the State Department, McCarthy pointed to Remington. Reminded that Remington was at Commerce, not State, Joe said Remington "was working with the State Department — and beside[s] a Com-munist is just as dangerous in the Commerce Department as the State Department . . . You ask whether I proved any man was a Communist. I've given you one who was convicted and sentenced to five years." Reminded that Remington had been revealed before McCarthy entered the fray, the senator persisted: "That's one of the old dodges — to say these are old cases . . . You said give me the name of one. I've given you the name of one."

Dodge indeed. McCarthy did turn over Remington's name to the Tydings Committee at a moment when most considered him innocent, and he raised the chilling theory that "no one will ever know how many American boys have died because William W. Remington was in charge of licensing exports of war materials to Communist countries." But the FBI had known about Remington for years. So did the Office of Naval Intelligence. Senator Homer Ferguson's Investigations Subcommittee had sounded alarms two years before, and there were stories in the *New York World-Telegram* and on *Meet the Press,* an investigation by a federal grand jury, and, eventually, an inquiry by the House Un-American Activities Committee. There also was the question of what, other than lying about his party membership, the handsome young Dartmouth and Columbia graduate was guilty of. He had served his country on wartime boards, as a presidential economic adviser, and as a senior official at the Commerce Department. His major accuser, Elizabeth Bentley, was conspiring to write her memoir with the foreman of the grand jury that was indicting Remington and had a stake in making him into a super-spy. Cohn's ambitions as a spycatcher meant that he, too, had a vested interest in seeing the case catch fire. While Remington was identified as an espionage agent in KGB files, his biographer says whatever information he passed to the Russians was done when they were our wartime ally, and he "was no pro-Soviet automaton, no slave to Party or ideology, and not even the FBI, at least privately, was willing to classify him as a Russian spy." Harvey Klehr offers a different verdict, saying history has shown "he was" a spy. Whatever the truth, Remington was imprisoned for perjury, then murdered by fellow inmates who bashed his head in with a brick stuffed inside a sock. One of the assassins confessed, "I hate Communists."

The best measure of how many real spies McCarthy turned up lay buried in the five thousand pages of decoded Soviet intelligence cables that were intercepted by the super-secret Venona Project. Parsing those messages at a former school for girls in Arlington, Virginia, American cryptographers, mathematicians, and linguists uncovered evidence that hundreds of Americans were helping the Soviets steal everything from atomic secrets to diplomatic strategies. How many of McCarthy's targets popped up on that gold-standard list? Political historian John Haynes, the ultimate Venona expert, carefully cross-checked the 159 people McCarthy named, between 1950 and 1952, as Communists, spies, security risks, or other actors in the grand conspiracy. He found seven whom Venona identified as having been involved in Soviet espionage against the United States. Another two were named as spies in the KGB archives, and a tenth was what Haynes called an "ambiguous case."

But there were caveats even with the nine Haynes says were sure things. Four had been identified as spies by Elizabeth Bentley years before McCarthy named them, which meant that while he might have been bringing them back into what he insisted was a revealing spotlight, he wasn't telling security officials or the world anything new. Drew Pearson aide David Karr had been unmasked by Congressman Martin Dies and columnist Westbrook Pegler. United Nations librarian Mary Jane Keeney was targeted by HUAC and an FBI informant, and named in two newspapers, the year before McCarthy identified her. The remaining three—Gerald and Stanley Graze, brothers who worked for the State Department and carried the Russian code names Arena and Dan, and labor lawyer and activist Franz Neumann ("Ruff")—were publicly exposed for the first time by Joe. But after he named them, as Haynes notes, they "were subsequently ignored by him and never became an issue in his debates with his critics." The same was true of Venona spies who testified before Joe's subcommittee: there were only eight of them, all already were well-known radicals or converts, and none got any special grilling or follow-up. Having bluffed so often, the Red-baiting senator apparently didn't recognize when he'd reeled in a true traitor.

Stan Evans assembled his own slightly divergent compilation of McCarthy's targets, compared it to the Venona files, and came up with a different list of confirmed spies that also numbered ten. They demonstrated that McCarthy was unmasking a real peril, Evans said, and they weren't the only proof. "If we look to other information sources—reports of the FBI, dossiers from counter-intelligence archives, sworn testimony by credible witnesses—it would be possible to identify twenty, thirty, forty, fifty, or more McCarthy targets in like manner."

Maybe. But those other sources generally weren't as reliable as Venona, and Evans was on a campaign to vindicate McCarthy. The fact is that many names on McCarthy's lists were, like Berinsky and

Powell, there because of family or work associations rather than evidence of bad behavior. Others had ties to communism, but they dated back decades and had been severed years before. Still more were gone from government service, and even from the country, by the time he fingered them. Few were proven spies, and even among them, most weren't originally unmasked by Joe or brought to justice because of him. Some — Dean Acheson, George Marshall, and Drew Pearson stand out — were named by McCarthy to make a point, not because he believed they were dangerous. Then there was luck: name enough names and some are likely to stick even if, as with librarian Keeney, he didn't know they had.

"When McCarthy was right, he was not original and was only repeating charges made years earlier by others. When he was original, he was wrong," said Haynes. While the Communist threat then was real, it was not from espionage but from political subversion of unions and other liberal institutions, added Haynes. Not only did McCarthy not grasp that distinction, but he also went to war with liberal anti-Communists who should have been his allies, like historian Arthur Schlesinger, Senator Hubert Humphrey, and labor leader Walter Reuther. As for the Venona decrypts, Haynes says they "offer no support for McCarthy's wild and irresponsible charges against the Truman and Roosevelt administrations."

Did Joe know about Venona, which was kept secret even from President Truman? There is speculation that he did, but the evidence is paper-thin. "Proving a negative is difficult, but [it] seems very, very, very unlikely," says Haynes. "First, if McCarthy had been told that the government had a secret code-breaking project that had identified hundreds of Americans, including a number of government officials, as Soviet spies or Communists, why wouldn't he announce it [to] the world and demand that the government make the information available and expose the spies? . . . Second, you can see from the comparison of the various McCarthy 'lists' with Venona that there was very little overlap between those identified in Venona and those uniquely identified by McCarthy." There are two more reasons why Joe likely didn't know, or want to know: The very existence of a brilliantly successful counterspy operation like Venona belied the thesis underlying everything he said and did — that the US government was clueless in combating

Soviet espionage. And while Venona showed how widespread actual espionage was, it also showed that the worst of the leaks had been plugged by the time Joe got involved.

Journalists who were following him in real time offered their own damning scorecards. "What is the reason that McCarthy has never as yet caught an important spy, in fact any spy?" asked Walter Lippmann, a two-time Pulitzer winner and his era's most penetrating political commentator:

> Not because he would not like to catch one if he could. Not because he has not had money, agents and investigators and what not. The reason is that McCarthy does not know, or is pretending not to know, that spies do not have red bulbs attached to their foreheads which light up and blink so that nobody shall miss seeing them. McCarthy is forever investigating people who from the point of view of an enemy intelligence service are either incapable of spying because they have no access to secrets, or are disqualified for employment as spies by the fact that they have in one way or another fastened blinking bulbs to their foreheads.

Many anti-Communist stalwarts of McCarthy's time agreed. "According to leaders of the Communist Party, McCarthy has helped them a great deal," said Herbert Philbrick, who spent nine years undercover for the FBI within the innermost Red circles. "The kinds of attacks he has made do three things that the comrades like: They add greatly to the confusion . . . making it more difficult than ever for people to discern just who is a Communist and who is not; they make the Party appear a lot stronger than it is; and they do considerable damage to some of the 'stupid liberals' whom the party hates." Whittaker Chambers, the most famous of the anti-Communist tattletales, tried to tutor McCarthy during the senator's visits to his Maryland farm, but in the end he despaired, calling McCarthy "a raven of disaster, and an irresponsible, headstrong bird, to boot." Father Leon Sullivan, a Catholic missionary, chimed in, "I would rather return to my Chinese Communist prison cell than avail myself of Senator McCarthy's 'protection.' He is as great, if not a greater threat to American freedom than the military might of the Kremlin, and believe me I do not underestimate either the Kremlin's might or its cleverness." (Joe's response was predictable — suggesting that Sullivan had received an overdose of indoctrination while he was imprisoned in China.)

One unnamed government official turned to metaphor in explaining the McCarthy phenomenon to the *New York Times:* "It all reminds me of a piece of land I once owned that contained some of the most beautiful wild roses you'd ever seen. The only trouble was that mixed in with the wild roses were masses of poison ivy. I spent many hours trying to root out the ivy without destroying the roses; but sometimes when I was hot and tired I wouldn't care too much and I'd rip out roses, ivy and all. The sad part of it is that when I got through taking out the ivy, I'm afraid there weren't any roses left. There is some Communist ivy in our country that has to be ripped out, but I hope we're not going to destroy the flower of our liberties in the effort."

Nowhere was Joe's overreaching more apparent than in the hearings the headstrong chairman held, behind locked doors, concerning the Voice of America. The agency was just what its purposeful name implied, a government-funded radio service that beamed to 300 million people, in forty-six tongues and dialects, the news, cultural offerings, and other tastes of life in the freedom-loving United States of America. It aired more hours of programming than CBS and NBC combined. Founded during World War II to counter Nazi propaganda, the Voice was recalibrated during the Cold War as a direct challenge to Radio Moscow. Home front patriots saw its broadcasts as extending hope to those enslaved behind the Iron Curtain or in a Third World tempted by Karl Marx and Joseph Stalin. To the men of the Politburo, it was the kind of disinformation they were familiar with, and they spent millions of dollars trying to jam the transmissions. There also was a schism within the Voice itself over its 1950s mission. Should it maintain its traditional objectivity, offering a contrast with Russia's warped coverage? Or was it best to fight Soviet agitprop with anti-Communist evangelism? Advocates for the latter view prevailed on the senator to launch what would become his most protracted and contentious investigation of 1953.

The probe kicked off with a headline in the *Chicago Tribune*

— "Uncover Plot in 'Voice' to Sabotage U.S." — and an accompanying story on McCarthy's "amazing evidence of a conspiracy to subvert American policy in this nation's radio propaganda broadcasts abroad." Reporter Willard Edwards laid out the background: "Some two years ago, a large number of Voice of America workers banded together in an 'American underground' to oppose the operations of the pro-communist groups. They quietly gathered records and office memoranda which showed Red influences and stored them for the day of investigation which they hoped would come." As for why the hearings needed to be secret, Edwards answered that too: the Investigations Subcommittee "had planned open hearings here after an earlier preliminary investigation had indicated communist leanings among employes [*sic*] who direct the policy of foreign broadcasts intended to fight Russia's propaganda. But the closed door questioning has developed a picture of such appalling proportions that executive sessions, beginning tomorrow in the United States courthouse, have been ordered."

It was vintage McCarthy. He had decided the verdict before calling his first witness. He picked a favored mouthpiece, old friend Edwards, to set the scene, leaking him an exclusive even as he was proclaiming the need for secrecy. And he inflated the thin evidence from dissenters and naysayers within the Voice to trumpet his tale of perfidy.

The hearings began on Friday the thirteenth of February, 1953, the day Edwards's story appeared. The kickoff witness, an ex-Voice engineer, pointed the subcommittee to two expensive radio transmitters he said had been sited where the signals would be anemic and the cost to taxpayers exorbitant. "I had done everything I thought was possible to correct this sad situation, and thought that I had reached the end of my rope, so I got out," Lewis McKesson told the panel. Joe recognized a story worth repeating, with a twist of his own trademark tall talk. "Veteran Senators, long inured to bureaucratic bungling and profligacy with Government funds, expressed amazement at some of the worst disclosures," the Wisconsin senator reported. The subcommittee found that "millions of dollars had been wasted due to such inefficiency, and that upward of $18 million more would have been squandered were it not for the hearings held." Words alone wouldn't do for this outraged chairman. He showed his clout when, four days after the hearings commenced, the government suspended construction of the two transmitting stations. The chief Voice engineer, whom Joe had placed at the center of the "colossal blunders," was removed from his post, and Secretary of State Dulles accepted the resignation of Wilson Compton, who ran the International Information Administration that ran the Voice of America.

To Joe, it wasn't enough to conclude that bad decisions had been made and money wasted. There had to be a seditious confederacy. "The subcommittee's investigation," he proclaimed in his final report, "uncovered waste and mismanagement of such magnitude as to suggest deliberate sabotage as a possible alternative to hopeless incompetence."

That judgment might have stood if not for a series of articles in the *New York World-Telegram* by Frederick Woltman, whose exposé on communism had led the Pulitzer board to award him its 1947 prize for reporting and the *Daily Worker* to dub him "Freddie the Fink." In a five-part series on the senator, his former friend looked especially hard at the Voice of America hearings, concluding that "Mr. McCarthy tried to pin a fantastic sabotage plot on Voice engineers and their superiors. What was involved was nothing more than a problem of radio transmission." To appreciate the senator's distortions, the writer suggested, consider how he treated Jerome Wiesner, head of the MIT electronics lab and future president of the university, upon whose say-so one of the radio transmitters was put in Seattle. Roy Cohn said he had interviewed Wiesner, who admitted that he, RCA, and everyone else had made a big mistake by choosing that location, although he would just as soon not formally testify to that. "But this writer recently visited Dr. Wiesner at MIT," Woltman disclosed, and the scientist had said that he and Roy "had a long, heated discussion in which [Cohn] tried hard to get me to agree that the Seattle site was inferior. I refused . . . Since I had no idea he was going to misrepresent me, I thought I had no need of coming" to testify. What did Wiesner think about McCarthy and Cohn's charge of sabotage? "I told Cohn I saw no evidence of sabotage . . . I felt at the time and still do that the sabotage charge was completely unfounded and ridiculous."

What happened with Wiesner was part of a pattern, said Woltman: McCarthy and his investigators "set out to show sabotage and subversion. Evidence to the contrary was brushed aside. The few Voice employees who fancied 'plots'—on the flimsiest pretexts—were rushed into public hearings. Responsible anti-Communist employees, who did not, were never called." Also culled from public sessions were witnesses who'd fought back effectively once the hearing room doors were shut. When Joe claimed that federal marshals had been looking for Communist organizer Elba Chase Nelson for a week, she shot back, "I beg your pardon. You are absolutely incorrect. I was home. I want to make that very clear." The chairman ordered her removed from the hearing room, saying he'd let her know when she would have to return for a public session; she never did. Nor did GE worker and self-described FBI stool pigeon Paul Hacko, who'd likewise stood up to McCarthy, telling him, "You are not going to put words in my mouth. I say this committee is illegal, and we will let the courts of the United States decide whether it is." There was one more way the McCarthy subcommittee reversed the congressional pattern. Top officials typically were summoned first to explain agency policy, then underlings testified how it was carried out. Joe preferred a prosecutor's approach of starting with disgruntled low-level staffers like McKesson, then climbing the chain of command to see who had hired and protected them. Sometimes, as with Wiesner, he never made it to the bosses.

It took an intrepid reporter like Woltman to plumb the depths of transmission tower placements and reach out to pointy-heads like Wiesner. By contrast, an imbroglio over book burning was such low-hanging fruit that less seasoned scribes here and overseas couldn't resist feasting. The US government supported libraries in some seventy-five countries intended, in part, to tell America's story to the world. As with Voice broadcasts, the information centers were at first deliberately broad-minded, which meant including books not just by controversial authors but by Communists. That was already a point of contention by the time Joe jumped in in March 1953, and he turned it into a fiasco. The basic outlines of this story were obvious at the time, but it would take half a century to open the subcommittee's doors and records, longer still to unlock the last pieces from McCarthy's archives at Marquette.

In Joe's telling, the shelves of libraries that were supposed to be promoting America were teeming with pro-USSR, anti-US literature — "well over 30,000 books either written by known Communists or Communist sympathizers, or containing obvious pro-Soviet or Communist propaganda," from "well over 300" authors with "varying Communist Party front records." A dozen of those authors were Russian spies "or connected in some manner with Soviet espionage," he added in his annual report. Fifteen were "hard core" Communist Party members, including four who had served prison time for those connections. Twenty-one were "Fifth Amendment Authors." Worse, no one took responsibility for having put the books on the shelves: "Thirty thousand or more pro-Communist books or books written by Communist sympathizers had mysteriously found their way into these libraries apparently without benefit of human intercession." The logical conclusion, the wry chairman surmised, was that "these information centers themselves had been infiltrated by crypto-Communists who would naturally push the books of Communists and their sympathizers." Another plot foiled.

McCarthy went fishing not just for the officials stocking the libraries but for the authors of their leftist tracts. First up was novelist and screenwriter Howard Fast, a Communist Party member whose writings already had been singled out by the Truman administration as propaganda and some of whose books had been discarded from the overseas libraries. Joe relished putting Fast on the spot by asking whether he was a Red, knowing he wouldn't say.* What upset this author more was the hour and manner in which he'd been summoned: "At about 1:30 [a.m.] there was a pounding on the door and a [ringing] of the bell, which woke my children and terrified them in the time honored Gestapo meth-

---

* Fast did say, years later in his memoir, "I was for many years what that old brute Senator Joseph McCarthy delighted in calling 'a card-carrying member of the Communist Party.'" Fast, *Being Red*, 1.

One of his novels, *Spartacus*, would be turned into a film by blacklisted screenwriter Dalton Trumbo. When Trumbo was given screen credit for that work in 1960, it signaled the end of the Hollywood blacklist.

ods, and I came down there, and here was this offensive character again, and this time for the first time he stated that he had
a subpoena with him." McCarthy: "Would you say they were the
GPU type tactics or NKVD type tactics also?"* Fast: "I have read
of these tactics in connection with the Gestapo. This is my choice
of description, and this action I find offensive and unworthy of any
arm of the government of the United States. I would have accepted
service very simply and directly the following morning. There was
no need to go through that procedure."

But that was the way the McCarthy subcommittee operated.
Witnesses often were ordered to appear the very next morning.
Rather than requiring members to vote on subpoenas, the way
senators were supposed to, this chairman "signed scores of blank
subpoenas which his staff members carried in their inside pockets, and issued as regularly as traffic tickets," according to John
Adams, the Army counselor. Joe did let witnesses bring lawyers —
in fact he advised it — but that was only window dressing when he
wouldn't let the attorneys speak for their client, raise objections,
or read and copy hearing transcripts. Those who watched him noticed a last quirk that set this chairman apart: his voice took on a
tremolo when he was accusing a witness, returning to a normal
register when he was done, which made him seem like two different people.

Langston Hughes, a guiding light of the Harlem Renaissance
and the civil rights revolution, brought with him a famous human rights lawyer, but he didn't need anyone to tell him not to
name names or to fight back when his patriotism was questioned.
"When I finally met my father [in Mexico] at the age of seventeen,"
the poet and playwright told an impatient subcommittee, "he said,
'Never go back to the United States. Negroes are fools to live there.'
I didn't believe that. I loved the country I had grown up in. I was
concerned with the problems and I came back here. My father
wanted me to live in Mexico or Europe. I did not. I went here and
went to college and my whole career has been built here."

---

* The GPU was the early Soviet secret police. The NKVD was the interior ministry that oversaw the gulag system of forced labor camps and, as of 1934, took over
the secret police.

Another author and activist, Sovietologist William Marx Mandel, begged the subcommittee not to let anyone know he had testified for fear it would threaten the public relations work he had to do to earn a living. McCarthy wasn't moved: "When a man comes before the committee and says, 'I will not tell whether I am a Communist or not,' he, I believe, forfeits any right or any privilege or special protection by the committee. I think he should answer all the questions. Under the circumstances, the answer will stay in the record." Mandel got his revenge when he was called to a public hearing, telling the subcommittee — and the TV cameras — "This is a book-burning! You lack only the tinder to set fire to the books as Hitler did twenty years ago, and I am going to get that across to the American people!"*

Edwin Seaver was more compliant, knowing that was what McCarthy demanded. The editor, journalist, and novelist had flirted with the left in the 1930s. He was petrified that in the maelstrom of the '50s, his employer, the Little, Brown publishing house, would fire him if it was dragged back into the discussion after having itself been accused of being a "red outfit." Seaver kept McCarthy happy by answering no when asked if he thought his books deserved to be displayed in the overseas libraries. That helped him keep his job, although his literary pals accused of him of having been a "cooperative witness" who "repudiated" his own writings. "I said such talk was nonsense," Seaver wrote in his memoir. "But no matter how much I rejected the imputation of my holier-than-thou friends, or how small I chose to think my fault was, I felt the fault was there, that it has been motivated by ignoble fear, and I have suffered in the recognition of this."

As interested as he was in making monkeys out of activist authors, Joe's real aim was to scrub the shelves of their books and to cleanse federal agencies of the officials who put them there. The Eisenhower administration had already shown its willingness to fall in line behind the crusading subcommittee chairman.

---

* What actually got across to the people of America was a different message. "All these books . . . They should be thrown on a bonfire — or sent to Russia," ex-congressman Charles Swanson railed at a battle over a textbook in Council Bluffs, Iowa. Goldman, *The Crucial Decade*, 214.

It fired hundreds of workers at the Voice and its sister agencies, replaced its director, dumped a number of foreign-language programs, shuttered several overseas libraries, and eventually took the program away from the State Department. A month after Ike assumed office, State's new leadership tightened regulations defining what books should be kept out of American-supported libraries. When McCarthy insisted it clamp down even more, the department obliged, ordering the removal of books by "any Communists, fellow travelers, *et cetera*." Nobody knew what "et cetera" meant, so librarians from Athens to Cairo improvised. Mark Twain and Nathaniel Hawthorne could stay, as could transcendentalists Ralph Waldo Emerson and Henry David Thoreau. Verboten were titles by existentialist Jean-Paul Sartre, NAACP head Walter White, best-selling detective writer Dashiell Hammett and his lover, playwright Lillian Hellman, and historian Foster Rhea Dulles, the cousin of Secretary of State John Foster Dulles and John's brother, CIA chief Allen Dulles. While most rejected books were merely discarded, Secretary Dulles admitted that some were set ablaze. "Anyone who did anything about destroying a book," a State Department spokesman prevaricated after the burnings became public and controversial, "did so under his own initiative."

The blowback was fast and frenzied. So soon after the notorious Nazi book burnings, no one had to remind Americans that the torching of titles was a scary proposition. While he'd never advocated bonfires, McCarthy's whole understanding of how overseas libraries worked was flawed, according to Dan Mabry Lacy, who used to run those libraries and, by the time he testified before the subcommittee, was running the American Book Publishers Council. They weren't infested with Communist propaganda or even with inflammatory books by the authors the senator cited, Lacy said. There were, for instance, just two stories by Dashiell Hammett, both of which "have been made into movies and sold in hundreds of thousands of copies in this country before Hammett had ever become widely known publicly as a Communist." As for Seaver, who'd been intimidated into denouncing his own writing, "the only one of his books bought in any quantity was a rather standard anthology of American humor, of selections from Mark Twain and Washington Irving, and so on." Most titles had been donated by well-wishers, during and after World War II, with the libraries having "a very limited budget" to buy more. Whatever small number of pro-Communist books were displayed had to be weighed against the 2 million volumes carried by the government-supported libraries, which included many recommended by the American Legion. "I think you see, sir," Lacy politely explained, "that there has been an overwhelming concentration on specifically anti-Communist sentiment."

Roy Cohn led the interrogation of Lacy that April Fools' Day in 1953, but he had no time to digest the new information. And no inclination. He was too busy getting ready to jet off to Europe with G. David Schine, whom the subcommittee had brought on as an unsalaried adviser. Their fact-finding mission was straightforward: to document at US overseas libraries the infestation of Communist manuscripts that Lacy said was an illusion. By the time the expedition was over, it had terminated at least one government career, provided riveting copy for reporters from across two continents, and was, as Cohn said looking back, the sole thing he would have done differently in his controversial career with Joe McCarthy. The trip was such a whirlwind — forty hours in Paris, sixteen in Bonn, nineteen in Frankfurt, sixty in Munich, forty-one in Vienna, twenty-three in Belgrade, twenty-four in Athens, twenty in Rome, and six in London — that a young Ben Bradlee dubbed it a "Paul Revere ride through Europe." In each city, Schine and Cohn ruffled the feathers of American diplomats and their host countries (the chairman of the *Financial Times* told them to butt out of Britain's affairs), staged in-and-out interviews (they would claim to have done loyalty checks on thousands), met with reporters (a hostile horde "followed us around like fireflies," Cohn said), and defined their mission variously as rooting out Communists or rooting out profligacy (or both). The most telling memories came not from what they said but from the handles journalists gave them: Abbott and Costello, distempered jackals, Laurel and Hardy, scummy snoopers, Rosencrantz and Guildenstern, junior G-men, Katzenjammer Kids, and Mc-Men. The one that stuck —

and sealed the fate of its author, Theodore Kaghan — was junketeering gumshoes.*

Joe's real intent in dispatching the two aides was for them to
come home not just with evidence of subversive literature but with
the scalp of at least one high-profile government enabler. The official all three had in mind from the start was Kaghan, acting deputy director of public affairs for the US High Commission for Occupied Germany (HICOG) and, in McCarthy's mind, the poster
child for communistically inclined American diplomats. Cohn got
right to work. Three days after arriving in Bonn, he reported back
to Washington that he was "working all day & most of the night . . .
[W]e've dug up plenty. This HICOG situation in Germany is terrible — and they are very hostile to the Senator — as is usual in a hotbed of pseudo-America . . . Theodore Kaghan (KAGHAN) is the
center of the trouble at HICOG. He is in virtual charge of 4,000
personnel in the information program. He *admitted* to me that he
had signed the Communist Party nominating petition."† Cohn instructed his staff to get "*all* the dope on him" and emphasized that
"this Kaghan business is *top priority*." Roy was working hand in
glove with R. W. Scott McLeod, the State Department's top security man, to build a case. And his letter from Bonn — marked CON-
FIDENTIAL and buried in the Marquette archives — made it clear
it wasn't just Kaghan they were after. "Tell him Scotty should fire
State Dept. Security man who cleared Kaghan in spite of his record," Cohn wrote in a message he wanted relayed immediately to
McCarthy staffer Dan O'Donnell, adding, "& express our deep appreciation to Scotty for his trouble."

Things snowballed from there. Kaghan was called to testify before the subcommittee in late April, and on his flight back to Bonn

---

* J. Edgar Hoover was wary from the start about the junket and the gumshoes.
"Should they contact you, extend usual courtesies but use caution and avoid any
disclosure of confidential files," he cabled the legal attaché in the US embassy in
Paris, asking him to pass the word to colleagues in other cities the congressional
aides would be visiting. Cable from Hoover to Roland O. L'Allier, April 3, 1953, pt.
3 of 28, MFBI.

† Kaghan said he'd signed the nomination papers for a Communist candidate because "I thought any American had the right to be on the ballot where the voter
could make his own choice," adding, "I didn't vote for him." Kaghan, "The Mc-
Carthyization of Theodore Kaghan," *The Reporter.*

he learned that the State Department "had accepted his resignation." While it wasn't his choice to go, he said, "the lack of leadership in the [State] Department, the presence in high Information
posts of people I considered incompetent, the abject submission
to McCarthy and McLeod, and the utter lack of any fight among
my old associates all contributed to my conclusion that the sooner
the separation took place between the State Department and me,
the better." Still, he couldn't resist a parting shot. Taking on Cohn,
Schine, and McCarthy "meant being a little rude, a little belligerent, and a little undiplomatic. It meant, in short, reacting like a free
and independent American citizen who has been slandered, and
not like a Foreign Service officer replying in measured tones that
would make paragraph six of a six-paragraph story," Kaghan wrote
in an article titled "The McCarthyization of Theodore Kaghan" for
The Reporter magazine. "I wrote out a couple of lines for a statement to be used if anybody asked me, and the phrase 'junketeering
gumshoes' practically wrote itself in."*

 It seemed especially apt after a cartoonish incident reported in
a Frankfurt newspaper and repeated by Drew Pearson:

> The two investigators informed the personnel of the public af-
> fairs office at the High Commission that they should be available
> Monday morning at 8 o'clock. They themselves, however, were
> delayed and arrived at the High Commission building shortly
> before 11 o'clock. Then the event occurred which still is a main
> topic of conversation. At 12:30, Mr. Schine announced that he
> put on the wrong trousers. A driver was sent to the hotel in or-
> der to pick up the right ones. Mr. Schine put them on and then

---

* One more sign of how much McCarthy hated Kaghan: while the chairman normally told witnesses he wouldn't talk about them to the press (a vow he regularly
broke), with Kaghan there wasn't even a pretense. "I noted your statement that
you assume this will not get into the public press," McCarthy said in a closed
hearing. "The committee will give you no guarantee as to what will be done with
this." The issue became moot when Kaghan testified in public the next day, and
again a week later. *Executive Sessions*, 2:1082.
 During his interrogation in Bonn, Kaghan said Cohn used what became a familiar technique: "First throw a handful of mud, then scrape some off apologeti-
cally, like a nice fellow, and then say, 'Doesn't he look dirty?'" Kaghan, "McCarthyization of Theodore Kaghan," *The Reporter*.

discovered that his notebook was missing. He rushed back to the hotel with Mr. Cohn in order to look for it. In the hotel lobby, it was observed that Mr. Schine batted Mr. Cohn over the head with a rolled-up magazine. Then both disappeared into Mr. Schine's room for five minutes. Later the chambermaid found ash trays and their contents strewn throughout the room. The furniture was completely overturned.

Schine later called the stories implying a prankish and perhaps amorous relationship with Cohn "ridiculous and untrue," adding, "Actually Mr. Cohn and I were quite serious about our work and we worked long hours with little levity." But a confidential letter he and Cohn mailed to McCarthy from Munich suggested otherwise. The two described their schoolboy-like joy in

sneaking into the Soviet Zone to visit two of their Information Centers. The most amazing thing about the one in Vienna is that they carry some American authors and, strangely, every American author they carry is named by us in our hearing as Communist . . . If we are both using these same books to help our cause, one of us is wrong, [and] you know as well as we do that the Russians don't tolerate the stupid mistakes or worse that we do . . . I will close on an incident which you will enjoy. When we were in the Soviet Information Center in the Soviet Sector of Berlin, as we were leaving they tried to sell us a Soviet propaganda book. We did not have the right kind of money with us, but Dave had a copy of "McCarthyism, The Fight For America." He held out the book and offered to trade it with the Russian official in charge of the Information Center for the book they wanted us to take. The Soviet official agreed to make the trade, took the "McCarthyism" book, and as we ran out and made a beeline for the car to get out before we were shot, we saw all the officials of the Information Center gather around and start leafing through your work.

Cohn later conceded the trip had been a "public relations disaster for Dave and me and Senator McCarthy," but said that was the fault of journalists who portrayed the well-intentioned investigators as "terrorizing good and decent State Department careerists, disrupting the diplomacy of the United States, destroying the Bill of Rights, the Declaration of Independence, while defacing Miss Liberty herself." As for the US officials they were meeting, he said most were left-leaning — making him and Schine "slightly less popular than an epidemic of smallpox" — and "a day before we arrive anywhere the State Department offices suddenly fill up with pictures of General Eisenhower. I hope they don't take them down as soon as we leave." What upset Roy most was the insinuation that he and Dave were lovers or, as he put it, "Jack and Jill," a "slander that continues" and was spread by "the sensitive liberals who decried 'McCarthyism.'" Joe never said what he thought. But the fact that he didn't discipline his aides made clear that he felt their shenanigans were at worst a tolerable evil and that, as an old prankster himself, he perhaps wished he'd been part of their high jinks. Also like them, he accused the State Department and media of misconstruing the mission.*

Public uproar over the junket and the book burnings forced the Eisenhower administration to rescind its sweeping "et cetera" order and moved the president himself to speak out against the crusading senator he'd been dodging since their ticklish campaign encounter in Wisconsin eight months before. "Don't join the book burners," Ike admonished graduating students at Dartmouth College in June 1953. "Don't be afraid to go in your library and read

---

* According to Drew Pearson, McCarthy's traveling investigators weren't just the victims of gay-bashing but were perpetrators, as they "seemed unusually preoccupied with investigating alleged homosexuals." And Richard Rovere said the pair had a homophobic joke they told when checking in at hotels: "Asking for adjoining rooms but insisting that the accommodations be separate, one or the other would explain to the generally uncomprehending room clerk, 'You see, we don't work for the State Department.'" Pearson column, June 5, 1954; and *Senator Joe McCarthy,* 202.

While they "paid superficial visits to only two of the 48 American libraries in Germany," Pearson said they "announced to the press that they had found Communist books in 'virtually every' library." Pearson, June 5, 1954.

Freda Utley, a Communist turned anti-Communist author and scholar called Cohn and Schine "unscrupulous careerists . . . So ignorant and so uninterested were they in any real effort to expose Communist influences in America that, on their notorious trip to Europe to investigate the U.S. Information Services, they managed to mix up the lists I had given them . . . presenting my compilation of anti-Communist books missing from the shelves as pro-Communist books!" Utley, *Odyssey of a Liberal,* 279.

every book, as long as that document does not offend our own ideas of decency. That should be the only censorship." He didn't mention Joe, nor did he have to. When reporters asked for the senator's reaction, he said the president "couldn't very well have been referring to me. I have burned no books." But the senator's even keel was an act, and the president's newfound nerve was short-lived. A seething Joe McCarthy pressed the White House not to broadcast Eisenhower's Dartmouth speech over the Voice of America. Five days later, Ike told reporters he wouldn't abide "any document or any other kind of thing that attempts to persuade or propagandize America into communism." Joe was delighted, praising the president for his "commendable clarification"

It wasn't only seditious authors and librarians who felt Joe's blunt instrument in the secret hearings, but everyone connected to the State Department he suspected was disloyal to America and to him. Woe to those who resisted. David Cushman Coyle, an economist and structural engineer who wrote pamphlets for State, learned the price of giving his journalist friends anti-Mc-Carthy material. First the senator leaked, from a supposed-to-be-secret hearing, material that mocked Coyle without naming him. A week later McCarthy not only named him but also released excerpts of Coyle's testimony that made him appear feckless, saying that for two years he'd reported to work in the "wrong building." The coup de grâce, Coyle told the subcommittee, came when "I was fired this morning" by State, "presumably because I had been called by Mr. McCarthy." Naphtali Lewis, a professor of classics at the City University of New York, got his own modern-day lesson on vengeance. He jousted with McCarthy over whether a Communist could be a good American — "It would seem to me," Lewis said, "that the American tradition of liberalism would permit a man to hold opinions ranging from the extreme right to the extreme left" — then was called back to a public session where the chairman announced that Lewis's State Department–sponsored Fulbright Scholarship had been canceled, adding, "I think that is an excellent idea."

Lewis fired back in a statement he filed with the committee: "Senator McCarthy has not inquired concerning my qualification as a scholar for a scholarly assignment. He appears to be interested in my Fulbright award only to the extent of inquiring into my political opinions and, what is even more astonishing, into my wife's politics, past as well as present. This inquisition, if it has its way, establishes a novel and singularly unAmerican principle; namely, that before a man is permitted to pursue a career of research — even in ancient manuscripts — he must have the stamp of approval of a congressional subcommittee."*

The hearings often seemed like a one-man show, but McCarthy had help roughing up witnesses, sometimes even from across the aisle. "You have refused to answer [which] of course makes us believe that you are a member of the Communist party," Senator Stuart Symington, a Missouri Democrat who was plotting a presidential campaign, told author Sol Auerbach. "Why do you want to take refuge behind your constitutional rights unless you are ashamed or afraid of admitting membership?" Democrat Henry Jackson of Washington likewise proved he could be as hard-shelled as his chairman. He pressed Helen Lewis, the wife of Professor Naphtali Lewis, on whether she'd ever been a Communist; when she declined to answer, Jackson applied McCarthy's duck test: "If you walk like a duck, sit like a duck, quack like a duck, must you not be a duck?" Helen: "No." The one Democrat who stood tall was John McClellan, who time and again sought to save McCarthy from himself. When the chairman was engaged in a lonely battle with the CIA, for instance, the battle-tested Arkansan told Joe in a closed session, "I think you have handled it wisely," but "they are gunning for you and shooting at you every chance they get, so keep it a committee action."

Such encounters make it apparent that his Democratic subcommittee members, like the Republicans and much of America, cut Joe major slack that first year of his chairmanship. Given how often and emphatically he was crying wolf, they assumed there must be one somewhere. They agreed with his goal of rooting out subversives even if they had no more evidence than McCarthy did of who or where they were, or whether there were additional Ju-

---

* McCarthy wanted to kill not just Lewis's Fulbright Scholarship but the whole program named after a colleague he despised, Arkansas Democrat J. William Fulbright, whom he referred to as "Senator Half-bright."

lius Rosenbergs or Alger Hisses waiting to be unmasked. And they had seen the fate that awaited anyone — especially a Democrat — who stood in Joe's path the way Senators Tydings and Benton had. So for now they let him set the subcommittee's agenda, and they joined him in treading on the freedoms of witnesses like Auerbach and the Lewises.

The kid staffers were even more obvious in their bids to echo their boss, which Joe loved. "You know many witnesses come before a committee, and they are not guilty of a crime, and then to avoid embarrassment or for reasons that they may not understand themselves, they do not tell the truth. They are entitled to refuse to answer on the grounds of self incrimination, but sometimes they do not take that privilege, and when they have left the room they are guilty of perjury. I think you should reconsider what you have said here today on matters of fact before you leave this room, because perjury is a very serious charge," David Schine said to Langston Hughes in an encounter that today reads like a farce. It wasn't just that Schine was twenty-five and Hughes fifty-two. Or that Schine was from a white family of privilege, while Hughes was descended from slaves and had been bounced as a youth from his mother to his grandmother to family friends. Hughes was a literary master, Schine an immature youth whom McCarthy hired solely because Cohn insisted.

Cohn took a similar tone when it was his turn with Hughes. "I think if you were a little more candid with some of these things, we would get along a little better," Roy said. "I am not going to sit here for six days and be kidded along. I will be very much impressed if you would give us a lot of straightforward answers. It would save us a lot of time. I know you do not want to waste it any more than we do."

That jarring juxtaposition of political helpers taking on intellectual titans was on display one night in the spring of 1953 when the McCarthy crew had dinner in the Presidential Suite of the Statler Hotel with officials from the International Information Administration. The conversation swung to the dean of American musical composers, Aaron Copland, and whether he deserved to be blacklisted for his leftist leanings. "As I sat quietly listening to the Copland colloquy, I was suddenly struck by the ludicrousness of the whole evening's performance," Information Administration aide Martin Merson recalled. "Cohn, Schine, McCarthy, [Hearst columnist George] Sokolsky, and for that matter the rest of us, meeting to discuss the manners and morals of our times. By whose appointment? By what right? What qualification did any of us have?"*

By the end there had been four months of intermittent hearings on just the libraries — ten of his witnesses, McCarthy said, were "friendly and cooperative," another twenty-three weren't, and several were "hostile and contumacious" — with more sessions on the Voice of America. Their impact was to undermine the International Information Administration at the very moment when anti-Communists were counting on it to lead the war of words against the Soviet behemoth. "Let it be stressed that the McCarthy Committee did not inquire into the Voice's competence, analyze its quality, measure its services against the best broadcasting standards, or learn whether the Voice held the attention of listeners. The committee was interested only in creating the impression that the Voice was the tool of subversives in the State Department," worried Raymond Swing, an influential journalist and commentator for the Voice who resigned to protest its failure to stand up to McCarthy. "The upshot of all the drama that has brought the Voice to public notice is an administrative order that leaves it a weaker agency, deprived of some of its best workers, divested of much of its audience, and with wounds from intrigue and slander still festering . . . Nothing has been solved, and the enfeebled organization that remains cannot serve the nation even as well as its predecessor."

The Voice wasn't the only institution left with scars. "McCarthy is bringing into disrepute one of the most vital functions of Congress. It is the power to investigate — an invaluable weapon in America's arsenal against communism," Frederick Woltman observed from his anticommunism beat at Scripps-Howard. "In the judgment of this writer, it will go down as one of the most disgraceful, scatter-brained, inept, misleading and unfair investigations in Congressional annals."

---

* Assistants to other senators, including Dirksen and Potter, also got to sit in on hearings and grill witnesses.

Eisenhower adviser Emmet John Hughes's take on the McCarthy-Cohn-Schine vendetta was more intimate. "One small personal incident, expressive of the shame of it all, still stings in my memory," Hughes remembered a decade later.

> It came with a visit to my White House office, one spring afternoon, by a crippled German friend whom I had known years earlier in Berlin. The young man had almost blown himself to pieces with a grenade during World War II — in the course of making one of the anti-Nazi underground's several vain attempts upon Hitler's life. And both anger and anguish trembled in this man's voice, as he spoke of the only matter he could discuss. "You have just sent us, you Americans, two visitors — two new-style American ambassadors I suppose you call them," he said. "Whatever fantastic harm they have done elsewhere, can you imagine their impact in Germany — and on Germans still looking a little skeptically at free government? *You* are supposed to be models for all us authoritarian-minded Germans. Tell me, my friend — *what* do I say to my German friends, when they gape at Messrs. Cohn and Schine, and then ask me: 'Is *this* what you call democracy?'"

A pair of relationships would shape Joe's life in 1953 and beyond — with the woman he at last was set to marry, and the aide he'd hired to tether his subcommittee to his crusade.

Jean and Joe's five-year courtship had been multifaceted and tempestuous — balancing work ties and romantic ones, with joyful ups, protracted downs, and halfhearted long-distance pledges of fidelity.* Finally, fresh from reelection, Joe proposed and they set a date. Some said he wanted to quiet forever the whispers that he was a homosexual; others insisted she had won him over, worn him down, or given him an ultimatum. It was all of the above. Jean didn't use the word "love" the way she had with her first fiancé, but she was ready and Joe was her man now. They'd hoped for

---

* Jean once went so far as to persuade FBI director Hoover to transfer to Alaska the agent husband of a secretary Joe found attractive. *Life and Times of Joe McCarthy,* 512.

a June wedding, but when she got sick, they set a new date that stuck, September 29, 1953, at St. Matthew's Cathedral in Washington. "I thought we could just announce our engagement and get married," Jean told journalist Victor Lasky. "But the news of their engagement leaked out the night before Jean's mother planned to announce their plans," Lasky wrote. "The next morning, pandemonium reigned at the Kerr household. Jeannie was awakened at 7 a.m. by a reporter calling to confirm the story. Before she had time to dress, reporters, photographers, TV and newsreel men were at the house."* Was she wary of tying her future to the controversial senator? "I know what I'm getting into," Jean told a friend. "I can take criticism thrown at Joe by his enemies. I'll start worrying only if some of them become his friends."

More than a thousand guests were at the wedding, led by Vice President Dick Nixon and his wife, Pat, whom he called his "Irish Gypsy." CIA director Allen Dulles was there, as was dethroned but still revered boxing champ Jack Dempsey. There was the expected parade of senators, congressmen, and Appletonians, plus the hostess from the Sulgrave Club showdown with Drew Pearson, and Joe Kennedy with three of his brood. Twenty-five hundred well-wishers, mainly female, lined the sidewalks and street on the sunny fall day. Jean wore a gown of Chantilly lace and candlelight satin, with a Mary Queen of Scots headdress, a cathedral train, and an armful of white orchids. Joe's morning coat and striped trousers were a perfect fit for Foggy Bottom, and at his side as best man was loyal brother William, a Chicago truck driver. Schubert's "Ave Maria" streamed from the organ. The senator looked more handsome than usual as he placed a thin platinum band on his bride's finger; she was as stunning as ever as she uttered, "I do." Vows freshly sealed — to cherish each other for the "whole future" with love that would "never fail" — the Reverend William Await read this missive from the Vatican: "Our Holy Father cordially imparts to Joseph R. McCarthy and Jean Kerr on the occasion of their mar-

* Jean apparently changed some of the wording of what Lasky wrote, scribbling in her edits. In one case she crossed out a sentence saying that she'd greeted the journalists "with her hair in curlers." Whatever embarrassment she was worried about with such revelations was moot, since Lasky apparently never got his article published. Academic Requests, unprocessed files, MUA.

riage his paternal apostolic blessings."* Leaving the church, Joe paused to wipe a tear from Jean's smiling eyes but brushed aside shutterbugs' pleas that he kiss her. (He saved that for the ride to the party.)†

The reception was at the Washington Club in Dupont Circle, a neoclassical mansion built by the former editor of the *Chicago Tribune*. The line of guests snaked down Connecticut Avenue, four abreast. By the end of the first hour the groom and bride had greeted 650 of them; Joe and Jean continued kissing, shaking hands, and posing for each of the remaining 350. The guests were well fed, but strangely missing was the liquor one expected at a wedding—or anywhere Joe was. One attendee asked an usher whether Wisconsin was dry. Usher: "No, it's one of the wettest States in the Union." Jean threw her bouquet from the balcony with such gusto that a photographer cracked, "That gal could play on my ball team." So many photojournalists were there that hardly any guests could see the wedding couple slice their four-tiered cake. A nervous groom whispered to columnist Frederick Othman, "People ought to elope." Friend Tom Korb eased Joe's aching back and shoulder by massaging them on the floor of an anteroom. Later, asked how he felt about marriage, the senator answered, "I approve of the aims, but not of the methods."

Their honeymoon was a sign of times to come. The plan was a month-long escape to isolated Spanish Cay in the Bahamas, where the only way to talk to the mainland was by radiophone. Just days in, a seaplane landed with a reporter and a photographer from Nassau who published a story headlined "McCarthy Seemed Willing, but Wife said 'No!'" She liked the implication that the marriage was his idea; he didn't complain even though it wasn't true. That night Joe cooked southern fried chicken for their servants,

---

* There was considerable debate over what Pope Pius XII had in mind when he sent his blessing. While it was true that this sort of Godspeed was routine, it also was true that Pius XII was avidly anti-Communist to the point of signing a decree ordering the excommunication of Catholic Communists.
† Reporters wrote about the celebrity guests who turned out for the wedding and speculated about those who didn't. The latter included powerful figures with reason to resent McCarthy, from President Eisenhower and Secretary of State Dulles to Senator William Jenner, chairman of the Subcommittee on Internal Security, whose anti-Communist turf Joe was perpetually invading.

who reciprocated by putting on a show. Just when the couple was starting to unwind, a radio message reached them from Roy Cohn, who'd been instructed to leave them alone unless it was urgent. He said it was: there was evidence the Reds had infiltrated a strategic Army base at Fort Monmouth, New Jersey. Joe told reporters that he would launch new hearings. The honeymoon was over barely ten days after it started.

Jean, as she'd said, knew what she was getting into and relished the chance not just to be beside Joe but to resume the roles she'd trained for as his most trusted ghostwriter, strategist, and confidante. The press would cast it as Gorgeous Gal Friday meets Good-Time Charlie, but she knew how essential she was to Joe's success. So did Capitol Hill insiders, who would inquire, with everything that mattered, "See what Jeannie thinks." Joe asked that more often than anyone else, trusting her instincts over his own. Yet while she wrote press releases and speeches at the office, at home she switched gears, giving the overwrought senator the orderly, snug surroundings he hadn't had since he left his parents' farm in Grand Chute.

They launched their married life in a tiny residence in Washington's 16th Street Historic District, in The Woodner Apartments, which were home to Chief Justice Earl Warren and boasted being the world's largest air-conditioned building (a sign of its size, and the novelty of AC). Next, they moved to a small white house on 3rd Street, behind the Library of Congress and a short walk from work. It stood out for its green shutters and for their gleaming new black Coupe de Ville with power steering and brakes, along with the air conditioning they'd grown accustomed to at The Woodner. When it arrived, Jean couldn't contain herself, jumping in one side of the front seat, scooting across and out the other, then repeating the feat in the back seat and clapping for joy. For Joe, it was the first car he'd owned outright and the first Cadillac he'd driven. He loved his dishwasher even better. The "first night he washed and rewashed to see how it worked," recalled Jean, who cherished that gee-whiz side of her tough-guy husband. The best reflection of how marriage had transformed their worlds can be seen by comparing her calendar entries just before their marriage with those just after. Earlier ones include annotations like "fight," "had row about my driving," and, just weeks before their wedding, "Joe called from NY. Did not take call." Later notes describe teas with Catholic bishops, cocktails with Kennedys, and a rendezvous in Beverly Hills with Hollywood's most successful producer-director ever, Cecil B. DeMille.

In Jean's telling, the newlyweds were Ozzie and Harriet, but a closer look suggests the more apt TV model was the popular game show *Strike It Rich.* In the McCarthys' case, their good fortune derived not from their Senate salaries but, in the case of their house, from Jean's mother. The $6,000 Cadillac came from more than 350 grateful admirers, most from Texas. Or at least that's the story Joe liked telling; in a more likely version, it was rich Texas businessmen who bought the car, and when Joe wrecked it by hitting a deer, they quickly purchased a replacement. The newlyweds got so many gifts, *Time* noted six months later in its profile of the senator, that their "dining room [was] stacked high with boxes, perhaps 200 of them — wedding presents that the busy McCarthys (married last September) have not got around to opening." They did manage to open the case of caviar that staffer Jim Juliana said turned up every month "from somebody." Less sensitive, the ex-FBI agent added, were the friends and wannabes who plied the vulnerable lawmaker with free drinks or tall bottles of booze.*

The worsening addiction was apparent to Senator Henry Jackson when he arrived early for an executive session and saw his chairman in the bathroom, chug-a-lugging glasses of undiluted whiskey. "Day after day," Jackson's biographers reported, "McCarthy would show up for committee hearings heavily fortified by alcohol. As his troubles grew, he fell back more and more on the liquor and his charges grew wilder, his accusations more and more irrational. He hinted that he would call former-President Truman to the witness chair." Chief clerk Ruth Watt said she thought that marrying Jean would temper Joe's personal and professional be-

---

* Juliana knew that Hoover and other FBI bosses were touchy about how many agents were leaving to work for McCarthy, so he invented a cover story about his departure: that he was going to work for his father-in-law, who ran a successful contracting and painting business in New Jersey. Juliana interview, December 25, 1997, JJP.

havior, "but I couldn't see any difference. I think she was a little hungry for publicity, too."

Watt also got an up-close look at Roy Cohn, the only person in Joe's life as chairman who competed with Jean for the senator's time and trust. Cohn was McCarthy's protégé in the use of bare knuckles and battering rams, but Roy was so bad-natured and true-believing that he was soon shepherding his mentor. His only legal experience when he began in the McCarthy office was as a prosecutor, and that's how he ran the subcommittee — treating the hearings as a grand jury, presuming even the most resolute testifier would crack under enough pressure, and seeking incriminations, not fairness. To Cohn, the ideal witness to drag from a private to a public grilling was one who'd grovel, stonewall, or otherwise ensure front-page headlines. He tipped his hand about what he'd be like outside work — and gave Jean one more reason to resent him — when he arrived late to her and Joe's wedding, after the other ushers were in place, then pushed into wedding party pictures the underling and companion he had brought along, G. David Schine.

The twenty-six-year-old Schine was everything Cohn wasn't: WASPishly handsome (his eyes glistened, Roy's were heavy-lidded), with prep school breeding (while Roy, too, went to private schools — New York's Horace Mann and Fieldston — Dave's money made things immensely easier for him at his patrician New England schools, Fessenden and Andover) and a demeanor that seemed as childlike as Roy's was razor-edged. Anyone could have foreseen the traits that would create trouble for Schine, and by extension McCarthy, by talking to Dave's former Harvard classmates, the way that college's paper did. "This big, blond sleepy-looking boy had one all-consuming interest: the life and times of G. David Schine," wrote a reporter for the *Harvard Crimson*. "He may have had a code of ethics, but it was a code we knew nothing about," one acquaintance told the paper. While still at Harvard, Schine was named vice president of the luxury hotel component of his father's $150 million chain of hostelries, broadcast outlets, theaters, and real estate holdings, and young David apparently oversaw a large part of it from his dormitory room in Adams House. "He lived in a style," the *Crimson* said, "which went out here with the era of the Gold Coast: [an] exquisitely furnished room, a valet, a big black convertible equipped with a two-way phone-radio, and a fabulous electronic piano with built-in radio and phonograph." One roommate remembered him carrying a suitcase stuffed with $1,100 in cash through Harvard Yard, "just for fun." A private secretary handled his business needs and helped with his schoolwork, attending classes for him and taking notes in shorthand. Even so, "he apparently had some difficulty with getting his work done, so much difficulty in fact that he was forced to leave college in the spring of 1946 . . . Those who knew him say his grades that first year were almost all D's and E's. Apparently they were not so bad that the college gave up on him, however, because he was readmitted in the fall of '47." Herbert Fisher, his first roommate in Adams, said, "I can't remember anyone who was disliked by so many people." It was the same thing people said about Roy.

Schine's experience in battling communism consisted entirely of a six-page pamphlet he'd published the year before called *Definition of Communism,* which was placed "as a public service" in his father's hotel rooms. Unfortunately, it hadn't been fact-checked. The date of the Russian Revolution was not 1916, as Schine wrote, but a year later; its first leader was Prince Georgy Lvov, not Alexander Kerensky; Lenin's given name was Vladimir, not Nicolai; and Lenin was credited with developments that occurred after he was dead. More fatally, Schine said that Russia had so many spies in the US government that it could "aid the Red conspiracy as the Soviet Union wishes," a charge the FBI called "too strong." Russia, the bureau added in its critique of Schine's screed, "has not been able to influence our policy as it wishes. The quoted statement should be toned down considerably." Another contemporaneous reviewer wrote, "Considering its length, *Definition of Communism* contains what may well be the greatest amount of nonsense per sentence ever passed off as serious scholarship." What counted to Cohn, however, was Schine's call for "defining and exposing the Communist plot of worldwide conquest." What counted to McCarthy was Cohn's insistence on bringing Schine on staff, unpaid but with the grand title of "chief consultant."*

---

* As a sign of how much everyone connected to Joe mattered to the FBI, it assembled a 127-page file of facts and rumors regarding Schine. Yet Hoover wasn't

If Cohn and Schine were problematic as individuals, together they were a terror. The pair spurned the cramped offices used by the rest of the staff, renting spacious quarters in a stately building and filling it with expensive furniture. Then, according to Ruth Watt, "Dave wrote a letter to the Rules Committee saying that it would be very desirous if Dave Schine could go in the senators' baths and so on, and he signed Joe McCarthy's name on it. Of course the Rules Committee turned it down flat, and Senator McCarthy knew nothing about it until later." If a hearing was about to be televised, Watt added, Schine "would call his friends in California and all over the place to tell them he was going to be on television. Then when the [phone] bill came, it was personal, I wasn't going to pay it. So Roy Cohn ended up paying." Even more unusual for subcommittee staffers was their using the Schine family's plush suite at the Waldorf Towers in midtown Manhattan as headquarters for their Voice of America probe. At the nearby Voice offices, "the expression 'going to the Waldorf' took on a very special meaning," according to an article in *The Reporter*. Policy meetings were held there every morning by officials frightened at the prospect of being nabbed by Cohn, Schine, and McCarthy, and the discussions "were often interrupted by 'loaded' questions from the floor. When the answers were not deemed satisfactory, even when clearly labeled as directives from the 'new team,' as the Eisenhower Administration was called, low-pitched voices could be heard remarking, 'The Waldorf will hear about this.'"

There were other whispers then, in Washington, New York, and even back in Wisconsin: not just that Cohn and Schine were lovers but that McCarthy made it a triangle. The boys, as everyone called the young rule-breakers, enjoyed fueling speculation by taking adjoining rooms at the Statler in Washington and in hotels across Europe. McCarthy came into the picture when he'd join

---

about to confront McCarthy with his negative findings on the young congressional aide, not in this honeymoon phase of the FBI director's relationship with the senator. So the very day when his agents filed their report outlining the errors in Schine's *Definition of Communism* and advising that it "not be praised or endorsed by the Director," Hoover wrote Schine saying, "I have read it and enjoyed it tremendously." Memos from W. C. Sullivan to J. P. Moore and Hoover to Schine, December 10, 1952, Schine FBI Files.

them on trips that were more play than work, to spots like Havana. An FBI informant, identifying himself as "Revolted Republican," dubbed the trio "the 3 dirtiest men in the U.S." They "were, indeed, a threesome: Schine's little-boy college face, Cohn plump of body, pout of sensual mouth, and McCarthy," wrote dramatist Lillian Hellman, who hated all three for how they treated her and her lover Dashiell Hammett. "Shouting at anything that came to hand," she added, the triad "rode to battle in official bulletproof armor." It was poetry and calumny, but Roy didn't back down. "As for Lillian Hellman," he countered, "what I can't stand about her is that double standard. I once saw her getting out of the elevator at the Pierre Hotel, followed by a whole set of Vuitton luggage — she must have bought out five stores. That's fine, that's her privilege, but just don't preach all this leftist propaganda."*

If anyone should have known about double standards, it was the master homophobe, Roy Cohn. He repeatedly denied any homosexual inclinations in his friend David, who was known to date starlets, showgirls, and models, and later married a former Miss Universe. As for Cohn himself, he wouldn't, then or ever, say a conclusive yes or a convincing no. He did date women in those days, including fledgling journalist Barbara Walters, and his mother ("Mutty") hoped he'd marry another girl he was seeing, a model. Others report that Roy was a regular at single-sex bars, and there's no doubt he had a crush on Schine, although it's unlikely they were lovers. He may not have worked out yet his later preference for men, or he may have been bisexual. More likely, said his biographer Nicholas von Hoffman, Roy understood that to have acknowledged he was a homosexual "would have been tanta-

---

* Another sign of Cohn's chutzpah came when, during a witness-vetting session at the Waldorf, he called the FBI's New York office "to inquire if he could borrow a stenographer this afternoon and tonight," Hoover assistant Lou Nichols reported. Nichols told the agent in charge to "courteously tell Cohn that they are running far behind in the New York office and simply do not have anyone." Nichols to Tolson, February 10, 1953, Cohn FBI Files.

For his part, Schine said, "I have some regrets over those years, and if we were to do it over again, probably a lot of mistakes that were made at the time could be avoided. I have no regret for having accepted a responsibility with a subcommittee of the United States Senate." Schine OH, January 13, 1971, Columbia University.

mount to saying he was a Communist; he would have been joining the enemy."* The senator, meanwhile, knew there were rumors about him, too, but he wasn't fazed. "Why should I get sore?" he asked Cohn. "They called Jefferson the bastard son of an Indian woman, Lincoln a lunatic and a drunk, Roosevelt a Jew-bastard, and Grover Cleveland a lecherous old man."

That was Joe at his glib best, unwilling not just to share his feelings but to probe them. The truth was that he tumbled into relationships, whether it was with Jean Kerr or Roy Cohn. He did love Jean, but he wouldn't have married her if she hadn't been so persistent and if he hadn't been so unwell and alone. And while Roy and his sidekick Dave would eventually hasten Joe's undoing, in the meantime they lifted him and his agenda to dizzying heights. "Cohn and Schine took him up the mountain and showed him all those wonderful things," Bobby Kennedy would say later. "He was on a toboggan. It was so exciting and exhilarating as he went downhill that it didn't matter to him if he hit a tree at the bottom."

While the pinstriped perverts and other security risks at the State Department were the subcommittee's primary focus that first year, it also looked into devious doings at other agencies and organizations, from the United Nations and the Internal Revenue Service to archenemy Drew Pearson's media operation. Joe was bored with anything that involved mere graft or corruption and not spies or Communists; he ceded that key part of the subcommittee's mandate to fellow members or sister committees. He also was even less interested than before in the normal business of being a senator, whether that involved responding to constituent complaints, recommending judges and postmasters, or promoting issues dear to Wisconsinites like healthy profits on their cranberry and corn crops. That was partly a function of the nearly nonstop traveling

* New York journalist Murray Kempton was aware of these and other stories about Cohn — "that he was what we used, in our coarse way, to describe as 'queer.'" He couldn't agree, Kempton added, because "of all ambulant creatures in my recollection, Roy Cohn is the last I should have thought in peril of being misled by moonlight and the rose. The deceptions of the heart are the promptings of an interior; and I learned early that Roy had no interior to speak of." Von Hoffman, *Citizen Cohn,* 189–90.

this senator did — holding hearings, delivering speeches, and campaigning for colleagues and himself — which meant less time for battles over public housing, sugar rationing, and the treatment of German war criminals. Even more, it reflected the belief that his destiny as a public servant was to spearhead the crusade against communism. While his Marquette files do show his staff attending to more prosaic affairs, they also reflect Joe's single-minded preoccupation with the business of his subcommittee and with battling conspiracies at the highest levels of the US government.

One agency that especially grabbed the chairman's attention was the Government Printing Office, which published and bound reports about routine activities of the federal bureaucracy, a small selection of which involved national security. His printing probe seemed like the clearest case yet of Joe's having made public an actual Communist who had access to some of America's top secrets. Edward Rothschild was a bookbinder the FBI had been suspicious of for more than fifteen years, convinced he was filching classified material and trying to organize a spy nest inside the agency. More troubling, an undercover agent said Rothschild's wife was a Commie too, and a party officer. And the GPO's Loyalty Board had cleared the printer despite having called none of the forty witnesses the FBI said were prepared to finger him. "To me," McCarthy said in closed-door hearings, "that seems worse than incompetence; that seems almost criminal incompetence; handling top secret material; handling Atomic Energy material; handling State Department secrets; CIA secrets; and defense secrets." So rotten was this egg that McCarthy felt obliged to leak to reporters large portions of the closeted hearings. Then he hauled Rothschild, his wife, and other witnesses before the TV cameras in a public session he promised would be "tremendously more important than the Hiss case." The proceedings did what they were intended to. The Printing Office suspended, then fired, Rothschild, who became a counterman at a delicatessen in Maryland. The GPO replaced its entire Loyalty Board, put the agency back on wartime security footing, transferred to non-sensitive posts fifteen workers under investigation, and promised that any employee who took the Fifth the way Rothschild had would likewise be shown the door. "In examining the course of this one investigation," Joe concluded in his annual report, "we see a practical demonstration of the subcommittee performing its function of discovering, exposing, and helping to correct inefficiency of the most serious kind in a governmental agency."

The real story of the GPO investigation was more subtle and less conclusive. Now that the executive session transcripts are public, it is possible to compare the testimony McCarthy leaked to the press with what actually was said. He told reporters, for instance, that Rothschild had access to "top secret" information from the Atomic Energy Commission about the A-bomb and H-bomb. The production manager at the Printing Office, however, testified that "material that emanates from Atomic Energy which is classified or restricted data, they send directly to the State [Department]," whereas nonclassified AEC documents might come to the GPO plant where he and Rothschild worked. Adolphus Spence, head of publications for the Navy, which oversaw AEC printing, was even more definitive when it was his turn behind closed doors. McCarthy: "Have you sent anything over [to GPO] that had to do with the H-bomb or H-energy?" Spence: "No, sir." Joe neglected to mention in his annual report anything about the trend of releasing bits and pieces of testimony out of context, or about ratcheting up legitimate questions to make them seem like definitive conclusions, both of which were demonstrated so clearly in the course of this one investigation.

As for Rothschild's taking the Fifth at a public hearing, that too was more complicated than Joe made out when he said to him, "Your refusal [to answer] is telling the world that you have been stealing secrets, that you are a member of the party, that you have engaged in espionage." We know now how candid Rothschild was in his closed-door testimony when he fully answered questions put to him, denying that he or his wife was or had been either a Communist or disloyal. He took the Fifth at the public session on the advice of his attorneys, one of whom explained why years later. The portions of Rothschild's testimony that McCarthy was leaking were incomplete and unfair, Stanley Frosh, Rothschild's lawyer, said in an unpublished essay. McCarthy wouldn't let them read into the public record or even see the full version, according to Frosh, so he told Rothschild that clamming up was the only way to protect himself from perjury charges. Frosh knew the fix was in when, after the closed hearing, "Mr. Cohn took me to one side and spoke. He told me that his best advice to me was to get out of this case as soon as possible. He assured me that my clients were Communists and that I was bound to be hurt."*

Was Rothschild in fact a Communist, and was he stealing state secrets? Maybe. The FBI was worried he could be, but the GPO Loyalty Board said its investigation disproved the allegations. Cleta Guess, Rothschild's assistant, testified in an executive session that she'd seen him holding a document with a secret code for the Merchant Marine, and had watched him put in his pocket material she thought was restricted. Phillip Cole, deputy director and head of security at the GPO, said the Loyalty Board had concluded that Guess's testimony was the "malicious" outgrowth of Rothschild's ruling against her in a personnel dispute and that she'd never mentioned a security code when she talked to the FBI. Whoever was right, the Loyalty Board had been playing it safe since it concluded its investigation five years before, preventing Rothschild from printing restricted material. To get access, he'd have had to swipe it from fellow printers without their or anyone else's seeing. Even then, the plant got barely any secret material, and none at all to do with the A-bomb or H-bomb. In the end, Rothschild's refusal to publicly answer the questions that he had answered in private proved reason enough for the frightened GPO chief to sack the lowly bookbinder.

Chairman Joe's sights were set well beyond Washington and the pilfering of printed secrets. He was involved in an actual international black op that seemed to be pulled from the pages of an espionage novel. In the fall of 1953, he tried to whisk away to the United States Stalin's ruthless former chief of security and deputy premier Lavrenty Beria. Joe's Marquette files lay out a heretofore largely untold connivance with Spanish dictator Francisco Franco's secret police, a wealthy exiled Nicaraguan plantation owner, the Spanish ambassador in Washington, a Soviet atomic scientist,

---

* Stanley Frosh's son Brian, now the activist attorney general of Maryland, is like the children of many who tangled with McCarthy and ended up in public careers they say are partly an act of defiance against the Wisconsin demagogue.

and Gene Fuson, a reporter at the *San Diego Union,* to spirit Beria and three other former Russian officials away from Spain, where they'd supposedly escaped. The quartet had flown out of the Soviet Union, then parachuted to safety along the Andalusian coast while their plane fell into the Mediterranean Sea, according to subcommittee counsel Frip Flanagan. He and McCarthy had prepared subpoenas for the group, and were salivating over keeping them from the State Department and creating a storm by having them testify before the subcommittee. "In accordance with your instructions, I turned over to Fuson five signed subpoenas," Flanagan wrote the senator. "I further informed [him] that if he should contact Beria or any other Soviet official, he should immediately serve them with subpoenas, and arrange to take them promptly to the nearest United States Embassy or Consulate, from where he would immediately contact me or you."

No overseas target was as tempting as Beria, keeper of confidences ranging from how the Soviets had developed their atom bomb to where moles had been planted in governments across the West. So hush-hush were the arrangements that ingenious code names were used for everything, with the Nicaraguan plantation owner dubbed Pete Smith and Beria referred to as a "shipment of colored copy paper." For his part, Joe started bragging about his catch before he'd landed him. No doubt Beria would have welcomed the escape, since in late June he'd been arrested for treason by Stalin's successors before he could flee to Spain or anywhere else, and he would soon be executed with a bullet to the head. Not for lack of trying, McCarthy's machinations came to nothing.

His foreign adventures as well as domestic ones left Joe more vulnerable than ever in terms of his own security. A couple of times he discovered that the nuts on his car wheel had been loosened. Once an armed man whose wife had lost her government job terrorized the senator's office until ex-FBI agent Surine coldcocked him. The FBI got tips about plots to murder the senator, one of which was investigated by the subcommittee in June 1953. Herbert Hawkins, a former FBI agent now working for the panel, said that when he was with the bureau, a reliable witness had told him about a conclave, in December 1952 in Pittsburgh, of local leaders of the Communist Party. "The witness," Hawkins added, "stated that instructions were given to those in attendance at that meeting that Senator McCarthy was among those listed by the party for liquidation or murder."

One of the few subcommittee investigations that held up over time and under scrutiny involved evidence that our closest allies were profiting by shipping goods to and from Red China at the very moment we were at war with China and its North Korean ally. Not coincidentally, it was sober-minded Bobby Kennedy, not tobogganer Roy Cohn, who steered that probe. Kennedy laid out names and numbers for the committee and the public: Western vessels had handled 75 percent of the China trade, or $2 billion in goods, since the outbreak of hostilities. More than half of those vessels sailed under the flag of our closest ally, Great Britain. And it was not just food and staples that were being traded. Communist troops were carried in the British ships, Kennedy said, along with strategic materials like fertilizer and petroleum. Adding to the affront, many of the ships had been purchased with mortgages subsidized by US taxpayers and intended to help our World War II allies rebuild their merchant fleets. To dig up those figures, Kennedy and his researchers worked into the nights poring over the Lloyd's of London shipping index, reviewing British parliamentary debates, and rechecking reports from the US Maritime Commission and the CIA. That kind of rigor stood out on Capitol Hill, and especially on the McCarthy-run Permanent Subcommittee on Investigations.

For once having legitimate blockbuster material to work with, Joe knew exactly what to do. "It seems just unbelievable, unheard of, in the history of the world, I believe, that a nation would have ships owned by its nationals transporting the troops to kill its own soldiers," the chairman railed. Referring to diagrams that broke down the embarrassing pattern by nation and goods, he added, "I think it would be an excellent thing if each of the mothers of the 3,700 British casualties could have a copy of that chart." But research findings were not enough. Joe wanted to show that Congress could change things even if the State Department couldn't or wouldn't. So he announced that he had personally negotiated a pact under which the Greek owners of 242 cargo vessels agreed to stop trading with Red China, North Korea, and other Communist countries. That, the senator predicted, would reduce China's seagoing commerce by as much as a third and hasten US victory in the Korean War.

The Eisenhower administration was not amused. It was one thing for the Republican senator to hold captive the foreign policy of the Democrats under President Truman, but now he was undermining his own party's standard-bearer. After months of back-and-forth with the executive branch, McCarthy told Bobby Kennedy to draft a letter asking the president just what US policy was on our allies' trading with our enemies. The senator signed it, and Bobby delivered the letter to the White House. Eisenhower faced a Hobson's choice: embarrassing the British or defying Congress and the public. Vice President Nixon came to the president's rescue, convincing McCarthy that he had fallen into a partisan trap by writing a letter originally proposed by Senator Symington, a Democrat. Then Nixon got McCarthy to withdraw the missive before it was officially received by the president. Reporters caught on, but when they asked McCarthy, he lied, saying he had never authorized the letter to be delivered. As for Bobby, he had gotten a lesson in realpolitik from the one politician he believed was for real. When a reporter demanded to know if he had been to the White House, Kennedy "appeared flustered and asked, 'Did somebody see me go in there?'"

The shipping investigation earned high marks from most journalists and other commentators, including some who offered their first — and last — words of praise for McCarthy. Drew Pearson wrote that the subcommittee "was absolutely right about probing the entire Greek shipping scandal" and should keep pressing. *New York Times* columnist Arthur Krock said the subcommittee had conducted a "Congressional investigation at the highest level, with documentation given for every statement represented as a fact and with conclusions and opinions expressed dispassionately."* Mc-

---

* Winston Churchill's cabinet felt the United States was being predictably isolationist and naïve in not acknowledging how a cutoff in trade with China could harm Hong Kong and England's other Asian outposts and push China to trade more with the Soviet bloc. Britain acknowledged there had been a tenfold jump in exports to China at the start of 1953, but it insisted the rise was temporary, overall shipments were modest, and no goods were weapons-related. America

Carthy bumped Bobby's salary from $4,952.20 to $5,334.57, a nice gesture although, even in today's dollars, the total would amount to a modest $50,000.

The subcommittee as a whole, meanwhile, was a holy mess. Chaos seemed to follow chief counsel Cohn everywhere. His desk was stacked high with open folders of scribbled notes. Phones rang but were not answered, staff filtered in and out without direction, and the confusion was obvious at hearings he oversaw. Some files, like Eleanor Roosevelt's, were just newspaper clippings, but that let Joe tell the press he had a file on her. "There was no discipline," recalled Jim Juliana, who'd come from the hyper-methodical FBI. Roy "made a lot of 'shortcuts,' if you will, was not well-organized . . . He was good for McCarthy, but he was very bad for McCarthy." Kennedy agreed: "Cohn and Schine claimed they knew from the outset what was wrong; and they were not going to allow the facts to interfere." And nobody but Schine could work with Cohn. Of the dozen staff members McCarthy had inherited, only four were still there by the end of the year—an investigator and three clerks. Of twenty-one new people he added during 1953, six didn't survive the year.

Joe had to act and finally did. On June 18 the chairman appointed to the new title of staff director Joseph Brown "Doc" Matthews Sr., better known as J.B. An ex-Communist turned investigator for HUAC and consultant to Hearst media, Matthews was the keeper of the files that McCarthy and others used to determine who was and who wasn't a Red. Joe didn't downgrade Roy's title, but he did limit his supervisory role and would later concede, "I found that a young man in charge of other young men doesn't work out too well." The fifty-nine-year-old Matthews might have been just the man had he not published an article claiming that Protestant clergy constituted "the largest single group supporting the Communist apparatus in the United States." That was too much not just for the clergy but for the three subcommittee Democrats and one Republican, Senator Potter, who demanded Matthews go. Joe at first refused, then accepted a compromise that

had to understand, the British added, how reliant their island nation was on exports. Daniel, "British Defend Stand on Trade with China," *New York Times*.

preserved the chair's right to hire and fire staff but compelled him to remove Matthews, who made it a bit easier by resigning.

That was too late, and too little, for Joe's Democratic members. In an unprecedented revolt in early July, Senators McClellan, Symington, and Jackson quit the panel and vowed to stay away until McCarthy gave them a say in how it was run. They had been put in "the impossible position of having responsibility without any voice, right or authority," the Democrats said. McCarthy wasn't buying it: "I will accept the resignations. If they don't want to take part in uncovering the graft and corruption of the old Truman-Acheson Administration, they are, of course, entitled to refuse." The mass resignations, he added, "would appear to be a continuation of the old Democratic policy of either rule or ruin."

Joe's handling of Matthews and Cohn also cost him a Kennedy. McCarthy had promised that Bobby would take over for general counsel Frip Flanagan, who'd been pushed up to the full committee, but Flanagan's powers went to Matthews instead. Kennedy would have been even more upset had he known that Jean had confided to FBI director Hoover that it would be "unfortunate" if McCarthy tapped Bobby for the post, although she didn't say why, and Hoover didn't disagree. If the motivation for Bobby's departure was obvious, the circumstances never were. He wrote, "When Cohn took complete charge of the staff in June, 1953, I left." In fact, Cohn never took complete charge. Kennedy was due to report to Matthews, then to his successor, ex–FBI agent Frank Carr. And Bobby's resignation took effect not in June but on July 31. Critics later accused Kennedy of overplaying his conflict with Cohn, understating his time with the controversial McCarthy, and trying to make it look like he walked out as a matter of conscience. Perhaps. But he did McCarthy a favor by delaying his official resignation so it would not come at a moment, in June 1953, when the subcommittee was coming unglued. Stability—or some appearance of it—was important to the chairman.

Whatever warnings he sounded about Cohn, Kennedy let McCarthy himself off the hook too easily. If Cohn was the master manipulator Bobby portrayed him as, rather than a subordinate doing McCarthy's bidding, the senator could have reined him in, and Bobby might have been able to help if he'd stayed. And whatever his reason for leaving, his timing could not have been better, since McCarthy's worst days were just ahead. FBI files hint that J. Edgar Hoover tipped off his friend Joe Kennedy to McCarthy's impending woes, and Joe persuaded Bobby it was time to go. Cohn later joked that Bobby owed him a debt of gratitude: "Would Bobby Kennedy have become a liberal icon had he been Joe McCarthy's right hand during his 'witch-hunt'"?

The Cohn-Kennedy conflict, the Matthews hiring-firing, and the departure of the Democrats were what made headlines, but Team McCarthy suffered from a more basic flaw. "McCarthy was looking for communists in the government, and he actually found quite a few. But what these hearings remind us is that all of them were small-fry labor organizers . . . He couldn't tell the difference between communists involved in espionage and government subversion and those who just organized unions," said Donald Ritchie, the former Senate historian who curated the release of the executive sessions. "In researching the fate of the witnesses who were cited for contempt, or for perjury, we found that not a single person who appeared before McCarthy's committee went to jail for accusations McCarthy brought against them. Either the Justice Department declined to prosecute or the courts threw out the cases."

For the rest of the year after the Democrats resigned, Joe operated without senators from the minority party to keep him in line. Senate Democrats, meanwhile, were playing self-indulgent games in that 83rd Congress, when Republicans were in charge for just the second time in twenty years. Nine senators died and two resigned during the two-year session, which at one point meant there were two more Democrats than Republicans. Yet the Democrats never asked for a reorganization that would have let them control committees and subcommittees. One reason was that "the Democrats didn't want to have to deal with McCarthy," says Betty Koed, the current Senate historian. McCarthy was rightfully his own party's headache, she added, and the Democrats' attitude was "let them deal with it."

6

THE BODY COUNT

ONE WAY TO MEASURE THE toll of a demagogue is by documenting the lives he cuts short. Doing that isn't easy, even with seventy years to assemble the proof, but with Joe McCarthy the evidence is not just plausible but recurring. And it starts with Raymond Kaplan.

Kaplan was an engineer at the Voice of America and the liaison with MIT on the radio transmitter project that Senator McCarthy was slamming as an instance of deliberate sabotage of America's propaganda war with the Russians. In the heat of those hearings early in 1953, Kaplan traveled to Cambridge to talk to the Voice's MIT advisers. Co-workers say it was a fraught mission for the anxious Kaplan, who, despite the fact that he was merely a middleman, had long worried that he might be dragged into the controversy over the siting of the towers. When he got to MIT, the researchers who could clear things up weren't available to meet with him. Kaplan came unglued. As he was leaving campus, Henry Burke was driving down the street in his ten-ton trailer truck. "I saw him standing on the sidewalk as if he was ready to cross," Burke told the police later. "I slowed the truck. When [I] got near him, he jumped in front of it."

Authorities retrieved from Kaplan's crushed remains a sealed note, stuffed in his pocket and addressed to his wife and son. "Dearest Lil and David," he wrote.

> I have not done anything in my job which I did not think was in the best interest of the country or of which I am ashamed

of. And the interest of my country is to fight communism hard ... Needless to say, the selection of what may turn out to be relatively poor sites for the [transmission] stations was not done deliberately ... You may hear many things about me in the press which may be stirred up. Believe me, the bad things will not be true because how could they be if in my heart I did what I thought best ... Since most of the information passed through me I guess I am the patsy for any mistakes made ...

This is not an easy thing to do but I think it is the only way. You see once the dogs are set on you, everything you have done since the beginning of time is suspect ... I have never done anything that I consider wrong but I can't take the pressure upon my shoulders any more. This is sincere, believe me darling even though the mess has made me too upset to write coherently ... You and darling David should not be made to bear any more than this act will make you do, if I don't I am afraid you too through absolutely no fault of your own will be continuously hounded for the rest of your lives. This way you may have a chance to live in some future happiness.

Nobody is sure when he penned that note, although it likely was at MIT. What is clear is that he was under stress outside work as well as in. His wife was sick. His parked car had recently been smashed by a garbage truck, and his finances were problematic. But his most plaguing fear was that, in the face of McCarthy's withering attacks, the MIT consultants wouldn't own up to the advice they'd given and the Wisconsin senator would somehow put him at the center of a far-fetched conspiracy regarding the radio towers. "I had the same pressure from McCarthy," recalls George Jacobs, Kaplan's supervisor, who had been called to testify. "My feeling was — and I think I may have even expressed it to Ray, because I know I expressed it to some of my other workers — calm down, in the end the Constitution will get [McCarthy]. He'll be trapped in his own box."

McCarthy denied blameworthiness for Raymond Kaplan's death. He took testimony in closed session from a secretary at the Voice who worked with Kaplan and said the engineer had been eager to testify about his role with the transmitters. (She also said he'd been "very upset" the day before he left for Cambridge.) McCarthy insisted he hadn't planned to call Kaplan as a witness, although he peppered the secretary with questions about whether the dead man was a Communist or had accepted gifts that amounted to bribes. As for the notion that if pressed too hard an already fragile target like Ray Kaplan might break, that was too painful to contemplate, so he didn't, telling reporters that "Mr. Kaplan had no fear of this committee whatsoever." Sinister forces, McCarthy added, likely were responsible for Kaplan's death, a suggestion belied by the Massachusetts coroner's finding that the death was a clear-cut case of suicide.

Jacobs, looking back sixty-five years later, says he has thought repeatedly about that suicide and about who, if anyone, should be held accountable. Balancing all the nuances that always are involved with someone taking his own life, his conclusion is unambiguous. "It was cause and effect all the way. If there had been no Joe McCarthy," says Jacobs, "we'd have Ray Kaplan."

If Kaplan had been the only one in the senator's sphere of influence to self-destruct, it would be tempting to call it an aberration. Or even to agree with McCarthy when he grumbled in 1953, "All right, what innocent person have I injured? I've asked that question lots of times — on forums and in speeches — and nobody ever tells me. I've never yet had anyone give me the name of a single innocent person who has been hurt by my methods. So much for that charge." Roy Cohn was equally defensive but more specific: "I keep hearing that people jumped out of windows because of Joe and because of me, too . . . It's a flat out lie and a very lousy lie, and the marvelous thing is that the liberals who float it don't think they even have to provide the names of the putative suicides."

But the deaths were confirmed as suicides, and the names were there and still are. One who was familiar to McCarthy, if not Cohn, was the man he beat back in Wisconsin on his way to a seat in the Senate. Young Bob La Follette had suffered from depression and anxiety over the years, along with physical ailments. But he'd always managed to rebound from the former, and the latter weren't more pronounced than normal when, on the morning of February

24, 1953, he left his office in downtown Washington and headed home. Quietly entering the bathroom off his second-floor bedroom, La Follette fatally shot himself through the roof of his mouth with a target pistol his father had given him as a child. With no note explaining why, there was rampant speculation. Was it worries about his declining memory or a sense he'd let himself, and his father, down by yielding the family Senate seat to McCarthy in 1946?

La Follette's son Bronson, who was seventeen in 1953, acknowledges those factors but has little doubt what pushed his father over the edge: the fear of being dragged back to Capitol Hill by McCarthy to explain what the former senator admitted was Communist influence on his staff when he chaired the Civil Liberties Committee. While Young Bob had quietly fired a senior aide he knew to be a card-carrying Communist, he always wondered whether he should have alerted the FBI. Bronson is fairly certain that, shortly before his death, his father got a phone call from McCarthy threatening to investigate those dated but still raw questions. "My dad committed suicide instead of being called before McCarthy's committee," says Bronson, who served as Wisconsin's attorney general in the 1960s. "No question at all." And it's not just a susceptible son who is saying that but La Follette's biographer. His subject confided to friends his anxieties about being called to testify, Patrick Maney says, and Bob La Follette Jr. may have been "Joe McCarthy's first victim."

Again, McCarthy wasn't buying any of that, which was no surprise to those who knew his history of denial. Joe had signaled how heedless he was of La Follette's quiet sensibilities a couple of years after their primary face-off in 1946, when La Follette was fresh from the hospital and treatment for a heart ailment. The two were seated across from each other at the Gridiron Dinner in Washington and, after shaking hands and a bit of small talk, the senator said to the ex-senator, "I hear you've had a heart attack. That means you can't run against me in 1952."

The son of another US senator likewise holds McCarthy accountable for the death of his father, Lester Hunt Sr., a Democrat from Wyoming. The episode was especially complex because it centered on the behavior of that son, Lester Jr. Buddy, as everyone calls him, was in 1953 a liberal activist and an active homosexual. On the night of June 9, he was in Lafayette Park, just north of the White House, and started flirting with a "swaggering" man he thought was trying to pick him up. It actually was an undercover cop trying to entrap him and succeeding. But a meeting between the head of the vice unit and Lester Sr.'s top aide, combined with the fact that the morals charge was just a misdemeanor and was a first offense, left everyone convinced the complaint wouldn't be prosecuted. It also let Buddy proceed to a summer internship in Cuba believing that he was in the clear and that his secret wouldn't become public and embarrass his dad.

Neither was true. The Senate was split down the middle then by party, and a close McCarthy pal — Herman Welker of Idaho — told Lester Sr. that unless he agreed to resign at the end of his term and not run again, the sex charges would be resuscitated. Hunt refused, and Welker, joined by another McCarthy ally, Styles Bridges of New Hampshire, made good on the threat. Buddy's now stale arrest was leaked to Joe's favorite paper, the *Washington Times-Herald,* and the young man was not just tried but convicted of sexual solicitation. McCarthy himself stayed behind the scenes, sort of, telling reporters he planned to probe an unnamed fellow senator who "had fixed a case." Hunt and McCarthy already were open enemies — Lester, who was a member of the Malmedy Massacre review panel that Joe had savagely attacked, publicly branded his Wisconsin colleague an "opportunist," a "liar," and a "drunk" — which was especially awkward since they were neighbors in Washington. With Welker vowing to send 25,000 fliers to Wyoming voters recounting the story of Hunt's son, the secretary of state turned governor turned senator finally ended his bid for reelection. Two weeks later Lester Sr. took the same way out that Young Bob had: alone in his office, he shot himself in the head with a .22-caliber Winchester rifle that he'd snuck in under his coat.

Again, everyone wanted to know why. Was it because Hunt was ill, which was the excuse he'd given constituents to justify why he wasn't running again, or was he mimicking his brother, who'd killed himself the same way two years before? Buddy offers a simpler and more plausible explanation: a father was shielding his child. That now ninety-plus-year-old son — who was kicked out of his Episcopal seminary after all the publicity back in 1953, became a history professor and community organizer, and married a woman named Rogene—believes McCarthy's pals and Joe, too, had done anything they could to "blackmail" his father, who ultimately buckled because "he worried thinking about me and what was going to happen to me." His mother believed that too, "although it wasn't a topic that we could handle at home as a family discussion." In 2015 Buddy formally petitioned the US attorney general to investigate the affair. Lester Sr.'s biographer made clear where he stood in the title of his book: *Dying for Joe McCarthy's Sins: The Suicide of Wyoming Senator Lester Hunt.* Buddy's daughter, meanwhile, is convinced that the public way her normally restrained grandfather killed himself—in his office, not his home—was aimed at the three Republicans who were persecuting him, and especially at McCarthy: "It was a big fuck-you . . . It was the 'this is the way I'm going to expose you.'"

Not all of McCarthy's victims were public servants. Don Hollenbeck, a CBS newscaster and McCarthy critic, stayed home one morning in June 1954 and, in the closed kitchenette of his apartment on East 48th Street, turned on but didn't light the oven and four burners, and slumped into a hassock dressed in shorts and a robe. Then he waited alone while the noxious gas filled his lungs and stopped his heart. His inclination to kill himself was fueled by alcoholism, three broken marriages, depression, severe stomach ulcers, a lack of support from his bosses at CBS, and a family history that saw his own mother slit her throat. But his biographer points to what may have been Hollenbeck's "emotional tipping point": venomous attacks by the pro-McCarthy press, which branded the reform-minded journalist "that Stalinbeck lad," and especially by columnist Jack O'Brian, who called him "a graduate of the demised pinko publication 'P.M.,'" dismissed him as a "portsided" thinker, and, after publishing a pair of anti-Hollenbeck letters, asked for more and promised to "print as many as we can. It might help."

Is it fair to hold McCarthy accountable for acolytes like O'Brian—and for the death of Don Hollenbeck? "To imply that such character assassination was solely responsible," Hollenbeck's friend and co-worker Fred Friendly wrote, "would be as reckless as the kind of journalism cited." Yet Friendly, who became president of CBS News, added that Hollenbeck "reeled under the barrage of constant blows" from McCarthy's mouthpieces, and he numbered Hollenbeck among the "casualties of the McCarthy age." Another CBS journalist and McCarthy doubter from back then, Shirley Wershba, goes further. The senator, she says, "definitely" shares responsibility for the death of Hollenbeck, who was a close enough friend that she named her son after him. "He was taking this beating [from pro-McCarthy columnists] with all else that was going on in his life. He just figured, 'Oh the hell with it.' He just turned the gas on."*

There was almost one more self-inflicted casualty, or so said professional witness and McCarthy staffer Harvey Matusow. So frazzled was he about the made-up testimony he'd given and the hyping he'd done for the senator that, he said, "I decided I would commit suicide. I made up my mind that I would hit the accelerator of that car and as I watched the speedometer climb, 90, 95, 100, I said to myself, I'll just keep this car on the road and at the first turn I come to I won't turn. I don't know how far I traveled or how long it took, but I soon hit a rabbit, killing it instantly. As I felt the thud of the rabbit going under the wheels of my car I suddenly snapped out of it." Instead, Matusow wrote a book of confession titled *False Witness*.†

It's tempting to cast the net too wide in blaming McCarthy for suicides and other deaths of those he investigated, and to trust relatives still looking for answers and retribution. But it's also too easy to excuse him, the way his defenders do, for the climate of

---

* Hollenbeck's daughter Zoe also points her finger at O'Brian, Roy Cohn, and the McCarthy reign of fear, calling that "just another nail in the coffin . . . I think [my father] just couldn't take the criticism." Author interview with Zoe Hollenbeck.

It wasn't just the targets of McCarthy's barbs who took their own lives but at least one whistleblower. Virgil Fulling was a Latin American desk chief for the Voice of America who testified before the subcommittee that some of his staff were "soft" on communism. Others strongly disagreed. Back at work, Fulling was "a broken and isolated man" who eventually committed suicide, according to the leading historian of the Voice. Heil, *Voice of America: A History*, 54–55.

† Partly on the basis of the confessions in his book, Matusow was convicted of perjury and spent nearly four years in prison. He ended up flirting with various religions and communes, spending years in self-exile in England, and marrying eleven times.

distrust stirred up by his inquisitions. McCarthy-era America "had something of the atmosphere that must have been present during the French Revolution when denunciations and trials led to the guillotine," said Lyman Kirkpatrick Jr., who watched it all as executive director of the CIA. "While there was no guillotine in Washington, there was perhaps an even worse fate in the destruction of an individual's career, and the wrecking of his life." As for his culpability, Joe himself created some of the confusion. He eagerly claimed credit, for instance, for locking up suspected spy William Remington, but not for provoking Remington's Communist-hating prison assassins.

What about Ethel Rosenberg and her husband, Julius, who were America's most famous Cold War spies and were electrocuted for leaking US atomic secrets to the Soviets? McCarthyism was going full tilt by the time of their trial in 1951, and it was more than just a historical backdrop to their prosecution. Joe's movement demonstrably influenced the couple's fate, says the Rosenbergs' son Robert Meeropol.* His father was a spy, he reasons, but his mother wasn't "involved in any active way." Even so, in the "climate that McCarthy created," neither parent could get a fair hearing. The jury was instructed not to read the newspapers, but it wasn't sequestered and thus was free to do so. So was the sentencing judge. The month of the trial Joe was everywhere in the news, with twenty-two stories in the *New York Times* alone, all contributing to the narrative of "an international Communist conspiracy that was out to destroy our way of life," says Meeropol. The "linchpin" of that thesis was that "Communist Party members Ethel and Julius Rosenberg stole the most vital secret that the world had ever known . . . and gave it to our archenemies, gave our archenemies the means to destroy us. And so it was against this atmosphere that my parents' trial took place . . . I don't want to say that [McCarthy] was solely responsible because I think there were other actors and he was just the sort of best known and most outrageous . . . It's a little more nuanced than direct cause and effect, but it's pretty damn close."

---

* Robert and his brother Michael were adopted by poet and songwriter Abel Meeropol and his wife, Anne, and took their last name.

Serious and less partial historians agree. "At a different time Ethel might have been found not guilty, or the penalty might have been far less severe. Meeropol's correct in that respect," says Barton Bernstein, a history professor at Stanford who has written books on the atom bomb and the Truman administration. Bernstein isn't ready to hold McCarthy culpable for the parade of tragedies with which he is reflexively tagged — from the death by jumping off the Swedish embassy roof of Canadian diplomat E. Herbert Norman, to the death by jumping out a Boston hotel window of Harvard literature scholar Francis Otto Matthiessen, to the death by an overdose of sleeping pills of actor Philip Loeb — but he says the senator almost certainly bears some blame for the deaths of those who took their own lives during that era of dread. That's what happens when your name is synonymous with a cause, in this case one that includes reckless accusations. It was a phenomenon Joe embraced when claiming scalps. With the Rosenbergs, that thesis gets unintentional support from an unusual quarter, Roy Cohn, one of the Justice Department prosecutors in the case. He held repeated behind-the-scenes conversations with the sentencing judge, Irving Kaufman, who was deeply concerned about public opinion when it came to Ethel, Cohn said in his memoir. They talked more about whether it was okay to execute a woman than about any swell of McCarthyism, although by that sentencing phase the judge knew that Roy was working for Joe and had fully embraced his crusade. "She's worse than Julius," Cohn remembered telling Kaufman. "She was the mastermind of this conspiracy. So unless you're willing to say that a woman is immune from the death penalty, I don't see how you can justify sparing her."*

The truth is that Ethel wasn't a mastermind, but she wasn't an innocent. What she was, as Cohn's confessions make clear, is an-

---

* Such private conversations between a judge and the lawyer from just one side of a case are called *ex parte*, and are typically prohibited. But Cohn acknowledged that "before, during, and after the trial, the prosecution team" was "in constant communication with Judge Kaufman ... without the presence of the defense lawyers ... I'm sure that readers who were not around before everybody and his brother became sensitive to the Canon of Ethics will be shocked at what I've said about my conversations with Judge Kaufman ... But this is how it was when I was a young lawyer ... I didn't make the world and I had no intention of tearing it down." Cohn and Zion, *Autobiography of Roy Cohn*, 68.

other casualty of a too real affliction that Bernstein calls McCarthyism without McCarthy.

Most of the senator's targets lived long lives, but they never forgot what it meant to be in his crosshairs. To some, that became a badge of honor. I survived not just the scourge of McCarthyism but Joe McCarthy himself, they would tell children and grandchildren, few of whom could appreciate the courage it required to take on a senator who fought like a cornered dog, snarling, clawing, and biting. The rare witness who was an actual security risk was less so afterward, just as Joe claimed, although the courts and history have generally judged them less of a threat at any point than he said they were. The rest suffered in ways the chairman and the public didn't know, because the press moved on to new targets just as quickly as Joe did.

New York attorney Abe Unger had represented leaders of the Communist Party in high-profile trials, and McCarthy wanted to know about them and him. Unger objected, testifying behind closed doors, "I know that you are going after Communists . . . You have the power to do so at present, and you seem to be exercising it for your own purposes. But the point that I make to you is that as a legal question you have no right to inquire into the political beliefs and opinions of people." Joe wouldn't have it. "This committee," he said, "has absolute jurisdiction if we wanted to go into any subversive activities on your part, in view of the fact that you are admitted to practice before a United States agency." In a later public session he banished Unger from the hearing room, and he persuaded the full Senate to cite the lawyer for contempt. Two years after his first appearance, when McCarthy had been dethroned, a US Court of Appeals said Unger was right: the beliefs of a private citizen like him were none of Joe's business.

Tangling with the senator was part of the job for a principled attorney, but not for his kids. Unger's daughter Elizabeth remembers going to school one morning, and the teacher "is holding this paper, where my father is up there with other so-called criminals . . . That was part of the [McCarthy] strategy, wasn't it? To make the rest of the world diminished and excluded. How was it possible that the Red Scare became so effectively scary?" It was traumatic for her brother Nick, too, but he says their father never saw himself as a "victim" of McCarthy. Abe "was a combatant, in a war . . . He was always interested in McCarthy-ism more than Mc-Carthy." The sad part is that Joe almost surely would have adored Elizabeth and Nick, the way he did most kids, who generally loved him back. But Joe McCarthy saw targets like Abe Unger as combatants, not as real people with small children, at least not while they were on his witness stand.

Unger wasn't the only lawyer who disdained McCarthy and who detested even more his hatchet men, especially Roy Cohn. Victor Rabinowitz, in a memoir titled *Unrepentant Leftist,* remembered one case in particular that showed how malicious Cohn could be and how free a hand McCarthy gave him. Sylvia Berke, who at one time worked for the Army Signal Corps, was subpoenaed to testify in an investigation of the corps. She was divorced, was the sole support of her five-year-old child, and had a temporary job as a clerk at the New York Board of Education, which let the child enroll in kindergarten at the school where Sylvia worked, saving her the prohibitive cost of a babysitter. She planned to take the Fifth Amendment if asked about membership in the Communist Party, as she knew she would be, even though she also knew that meant automatic dismissal by the Board of Education, which held that mere enrollment in such a "subversive" organization was proof that a person posed a danger to the city's youth. Rabinowitz agreed to ask McCarthy to excuse Berke from testifying, hoping that the senator would show compassion for her child if not for Sylvia herself.

"McCarthy's answer was typical: 'It's all right with me, but you'd better take it up with Roy,'" Rabinowitz recalled.

Roy Cohn was standing ten feet away, and when I put the problem to him, his answer was quick and peremptory. "Nonsense," he said. "We can't withdraw this subpoena. This woman possesses a great deal of information concerning subversive activity at the signal corps. She's one of the most important witnesses in this investigation." I told him that since she was going to plead the Fifth Amendment, the only result of the investigation would be that she would lose her job. It made not the slightest impression on Cohn. Of all the evil men I've encountered in six decades of law practice, Roy Cohn was the most vicious.

The truth, with Rabinowitz and others, was that Cohn got more blame than he deserved and McCarthy less, since both concurred in the hard-nosed decisions, but the senator let his assistant take the heat.

It didn't take much to get thrown out of your job in the fury of the McCarthy era. Having an affair with the leftist Lillian Hellman was enough to end the State Department career of John Melby, especially when he refused to repudiate her. Esther Brunauer's crime was, as she put it, being "in close and habitual association with my husband," a Hungarian refugee who worked for the Navy, had discontinued his associations with Communists thirty years before, and was now, in the words of former Republican senator Joe Ball of Minnesota, "the most violently anti-Communist person I know." Not that those details mattered. Stephen Brunauer was suspended, then resigned; Esther was suspended, then discharged. Charles Thayer, who held a modest posting as US consul general in Munich, was cast into McCarthy's firing line when President Eisenhower nominated Thayer's brother-in-law Charles "Chip" Bohlen to the high-profile post of ambassador to the Soviet Union. Knowing that McCarthy had a briefcase full of rumors about Thayer's homosexual and heterosexual affairs, and that the senator would use them to tarnish his brother-in-law, Thayer resigned so Bohlen could be confirmed. "It ruined [Uncle Charlie's] life," said Bohlen's daughter Avis, who later served as assistant secretary of state. "He was tapped to be the next ambassador of Yugoslavia" but instead "became the sacrificial victim."

Then there was the case of Julius Hlavaty, head of the math department at the Bronx High School of Science. The Czech émigré agreed to read, for free, a prepared script for a single uncontroversial Voice of America broadcast in 1952, which was enough to snag him in McCarthy's entanglement with the Voice. Summoned before the subcommittee, the teacher answered most questions put to him — including "Do you believe in God?" (yes) and whether he'd been a member of the Communist Party in 1949, 1950, 1951, or 1952 (no) — but not this one: Was he a Communist back in 1948?

Taking the Fifth produced the same result it had for fellow Board of Education hire Sylvia Berke: thrusting Hlavaty into the ranks of the fired and disgraced.

Sometimes when a parent was singled out for grilling or discharge, his or her children were too young to read the newspapers and understand the politics, as had been the case with Abe Unger's daughter Elizabeth. But at child's-eye level they could see a domino effect, which for John Brogan played out at his high school in Green Bay. "I opened the door and there were two boys — big, neat, decent farm kids. Without saying a word one smacked me in the face, knocked me down, blood all over my nose and everything. It was a goddamn mess!" John, who later became a banker and businessman, quickly pieced together why he'd been singled out. The boy who hit him had lost a cousin in the wrenching Korean conflict, and the night before McCarthy had gone on the airwaves bashing Commie sympathizers and naming, among others, John's dad, a prominent Democrat. Casey Murrow has similar memories from the age of eight, when he was a student at the mostly rich all-boys Buckley School in Manhattan and his father was CBS's legendary Edward R. Murrow, who'd gone after McCarthy. Casey remembers "people at school saying, 'Your dad's a Commie,' and making or creating a lot of confusion in my mind because I didn't know what a Commie looked like. I certainly didn't know if he was or wasn't one, really. So I didn't have a defense for what anybody might say to me." He learned later that there were kidnapping threats as well. "There was certainly somebody at my bus stop who showed up every day, a character with a hat pulled on over his head, and maybe that was some version of security . . . Having been a parent now for quite a while, what really astounds me is the degree to which my parents were able to keep that stuff away from me."*

David Fierst's father, Herb, also tried to shield his children from his experience of being number one on the list of alleged subver-

---

* When threatening postcards were mailed not just to their home in New York City but to their hideaway in Pawling, near the border with Connecticut, Murrow was offered protection by CBS. He declined — but he did let the network's PR people spread the word about his gun collection in the country and the handguns he kept at his apartment in the city. Sperber, *Murrow: His Life and Times*, 446.

sives that McCarthy sent to the Senate. The result wasn't just that it derailed Herb's golden boy career at the State Department before he ultimately was cleared, but that it produced a lifelong reluctance to jump too deeply into causes he supported. He'd take his children to watch civil rights marches but wouldn't let them march. "He was scared," surmises David, that "it would turn out that there really was Communist influence in the march and that he would be implicated again." What Stephen and Esther Brunauer's daughter Kathryn recalls most from that frightful era are the crank phone calls in the dark of night. "This guy said he would take us out of the neighborhood in a box. After that my parents wouldn't let me answer the phone." Crank calls came to Bob Service's home, too, and once when his straitlaced grandmother picked up, the caller accused her of being a lesbian. What really scared thirteen-year-old Bob was the thought that his family could be homeless after his dad, State Department China expert John Stewart Service, was targeted by McCarthy as one of those responsible for "losing" China to Mao's Reds and was purged from the government. John was about to rent an apartment in New York when "they found out his background," says Bob, who later followed his father into the US Foreign Service and was appointed ambassador to Paraguay. "They refused to rent to him." Haldore Hanson's wife and kids were sure they'd be safe on their farm in northern Virginia after he was drummed out of the State Department. But neighbors circulated a petition calling on the Hansons to "get out," with one saying, "That communist fella ought to be killed." Signe Hanson and her brother were sent to school overseas, "never with other Americans." The experience was so scarring, she adds, that seventy years later, "for most casual acquaintances, I lie to give myself a very boring past—farm in Virginia, etcetera. Later, I reveal my overseas background. Only recently have I begun to tell about my father's career."

Lucy Durán was far less concerned with how McCarthy's nonstop campaign against her father affected her childhood, although it did, than with the toll it took on him. Gustavo Durán, a State Department and United Nations official, was under assault from Communists who felt he'd abandoned them after he fought with the leftist government in the Spanish Civil War, and from anti-Communists who said he had been and still was a Communist.

(He vehemently denied both.) Lucy's grandfather had "blown his brains out" during the war in Spain because he thought his son Gustavo was dead. After the war, Gustavo came to America, where he was hounded by McCarthy until, in 1955, he finally was vindicated. It all left him "very bitter," says Lucy. "I think it made him feel that the so-called land of the free and home of the brave, that the slogan was bullshit." The bitterness, she adds, exacerbated a heart problem that killed her father at age sixty-two.

Chris Ghosh's childhood memories are from the other side of the political divide. His father, Stanley, was head of Voice of America's India desk and a McCarthy whistleblower who testified that Voice broadcasts weren't as anti-Communist as they should be. "I know that my dad said that there was indeed retaliation against him. He survived it. Exactly how he did it, he never explained to me." While his dad wasn't a fan of McCarthy's methods, Chris adds, "he felt the committee was onto something, there was something that was worthwhile that needed to be aired, that needed to be investigated."

Senate colleagues and their families were not immune from Joe's attacks, as he demonstrated with Lester and Buddy Hunt. Shortly before he died in 1953, old foe Charles Tobey of New Hampshire confided to a friend that McCarthy "had enlisted the aid of enemies in our state to see if they could get anything on me for his personal use." It didn't take long for critical stories about Tobey's son to appear in New Hampshire newspapers. Something similar happened with the sister of New Jersey senator Clifford Case, another McCarthy critic. The *Star-Ledger* in Newark reported that Case's sister was a mental patient and former Communist Party member. "The story was true," Case told author David Oshinsky. "I don't know how they found out about it and I never asked McCarthy if he was directly involved."

Joe was fighting to win and saw spouses as even more tempting targets than children or siblings. The always proper Secretary of State Dean Acheson maintained his wit when reporters asked about McCarthy taking a swipe at his bride, Alice, during the Tydings Committee hearings:

REPORTER: Are you aware, Mr. Secretary, that Senator Mc-

Carthy saw fit to inject Mrs. Acheson's name into the proceedings?

ACHESON: I understand that he made that contribution to the gaiety of the situation.

REPORTER: Do you have anything to say?

ACHESON: I telephoned my wife and said, "What's this you've been up to?" And she hadn't the faintest conception nor had she ever heard of the organization which Senator McCarthy accused her of belonging to. It was something like the Women's National Congress . . . We looked up this organization and found that it was a merger of many others, among them one called the Washington League of Women Shoppers. That rang a bell. She said that ten years or so ago she had paid two dollars . . . and she was given a list of stores in Washington classified as fair or unfair to their employees . . . I told her that it was charged that she was a sponsor of it. She said that was interesting and asked who were the other sponsors. So I read them to her and she said that sounded rather like the Social Register and she thought her position was going up.

Acheson's levelheadedness was especially impressive since, in the wake of McCarthy's attacks, there was an onslaught of threatening mail that required guards to be posted at his home day and night.

It was no joke when it came to longtime McCarthy enemies Margaret Chase Smith and Hank Greenspun. Denouncing Smith as a "puny politician" and a "thief" of taxpayer money, Joe helped recruit a candidate to challenge her in the 1954 Republican primary in Maine, secured backing from his wealthy Texas friends, rallied his pals in the press, and, borrowing a final page from the playbook he'd used to defeat Millard Tydings in Maryland, pretended to have had no involvement in any of it. But Smith had more support back home than Tydings ever did, and was wilier, clobbering her challenger five to one, setting a new record vote total for a Maine primary, and sending her Wisconsin colleague what she said was a clear message: "If a mere woman could beat Joe McCarthy by a 5 to 1 margin, then why should the men Senators have any further fear of him? It was as simple as that." The truth was more complicated. While she did win the primary with ease, she drew just 59 percent of the vote in the general election, down from 71 percent in 1948. Smith may have, as she claimed, "baffled, outwitted, outmaneuvered, and defeated [McCarthy] at every turn" in their long battle, but she emerged "feeling bedraggled, unappreciated, and sorely in need of a change in focus." Which was how most of Joe's victims felt.

Not Greenspun. He wrote the most inflammatory of his McCarthy-bashing columns in January 1954, predicting that "McCarthy will eventually be laid to rest at the hands of some poor innocent slob whose reputation and life he has destroyed . . . Really, I'm against Joe getting his head blown off, not because I do not believe in capital punishment or because he does not have it coming, but I would hate to see some simpleton get the chair for such a public service as getting rid of McCarthy." Joe's investigators already were quietly trying to dig up dirt on Greenspun, without success, but this new published assault offered an opening. The senator urged his friend J. Edgar Hoover to do something; the FBI chief agreed the column was "scurrilous" yet said there wasn't anything the bureau could do. Then Joe tried old friend Arthur Summerfield, former head of the Republican National Committee and now the postmaster general; the postal chief did more than McCarthy wanted—helping see that Greenspun was indicted for mailing newspapers that "contained nonmailable matter of an indecent character tending to incite murder or assassination."

The legal filing posed two problems: Making Greenspun's column part of a court case let newspapers across the country quote from it without fear of slander or other infractions. It also let Greenspun claim to have gotten Joe's goat, and he had, relishing the experience especially when the jury acquitted the publisher on its first ballot. "I had no more violated the irrelevant, seldom-invoked statute than Ernest Hemingway had in an article written for *Look* magazine," Greenspun proclaimed. "Describing his African plane crash, Hemingway had written, 'My last thoughts were how unfortunate it was that Senator McCarthy wasn't sitting beside me.'"

There was another category of victim Joe didn't like to talk about: those who'd done his bidding then become an embarrassment, like Charles Davis. The young Negro from Dallas had a tortured past as a Communist turned informer, an accused thief, and a homosexual whose preferences got him booted out of the Navy. Living as an expatriate in Europe, Davis supported himself in part by providing McCarthy with documents about the leftist leanings of American diplomats. In the end, the Swiss convicted Davis of espionage, then expelled him from the country, and McCarthy insisted under oath that he barely knew the man. The Marquette archives tell a different story, with handwritten letters from Davis to McCarthy offering his services, letters back welcoming them, and later missives showing that McCarthy was urging the US attorney in Washington to prosecute Davis for perjury. His relationship with Davis was close enough to suggest not just rotten judgment and a subsequent lack of loyalty but the fact that if anyone perjured himself, it was the senator.

Most McCarthy targets suffered what today we'd call posttraumatic stress, and some never felt safe talking about the encounter, even with their kids and spouses. Others, by contrast, chose to bear witness. *New York Post* editor James Wechsler chronicled his two days in McCarthy's hot seat in his newspaper columns and in two separate memoirs. Taken together, they offer a piercing look at the chairman and his movement. Wechsler was subpoenaed on the pretense of examining his biography of labor leader John L. Lewis, which was in America's overseas libraries. He really was there as punishment for the *Post*'s seventeen-part investigative trashing of the senator. The editor confessed his youthful flirtation with communism but said he'd become an ardent anti-Communist before Whittaker Chambers, Elizabeth Bentley, Louis Budenz, and other favored turncoats. Joe wasn't buying it, branding as "phony" Wechsler's supposed break with his Red past. "I know if I were head of the Communist party," McCarthy said, "and I had Jim Wechsler come to Moscow and I discovered this bright man, apparently a good writer, I would say, 'Mr. Wechsler, when you go back to the United States, you will state that you are breaking with the Communist party, you will make general attacks against communism, and then you will be our ringleader in trying to attack and destroy any man who tries to hurt and dig out the specific traitors who are hurting our country.' You have followed that pattern."

Wechsler was stunned by the insinuation that he was a Tro-jan horse but fascinated by Joe's brazenness in twisting logic to his ends. It was the dialectic of the demagogue. "There were mo-ments during the hearings when I caught myself watching Mc-Carthy with a kind of fascination, trying hard to look behind the masks he wears and almost forgetting that it was my life he was playing with," the newsman wrote. "Within ten minutes after the hearing had begun, I found myself in the preposterous position of denying under oath that I had inspired the long series of com-munist attacks against me, climaxed by the denunciation of the Central Committee . . . Here indeed was a daring new concept in which the existence of evidence of innocence becomes the damn-ing proof of guilt. This is the way it must feel to be committed to a madhouse through some medical mistake; everything is turned upside down."

McCarthy pushed Wechsler to name names, and he did, reluc-tantly and in a way he never lived down, although he insisted those on his list already were well known. "I know there are some former communists who have conscientiously declined to give any infor-mation about others than themselves. I confronted that problem a long time ago and the answer I reached was that there was no jus-tification for a vow of silence. The communist movement was not an amiable secret society to which one owed a personal loyalty af-ter abandoning membership." Yet even as he resented being put in that spot, the wordsmith remained transfixed by the senator and what drove him: "Throughout the interrogation the grand inquisi-tor was by turns truculent, contemptuous and bland. Yet I rarely had any feeling of authentic personal animosity. He acted like the gangster in a B-movie who faces the unpleasant necessity of rub-bing out someone who has gotten in his way . . . I am certain that he would have been happy to shake my hand and forget the whole thing if I had merely indicated that I had misjudged him and was prepared henceforth to write kinder things about him."

"Despite all I have written," Wechsler concluded,

it is not quite possible to communicate the quiet horror of exam-ination by McCarthy. I have no wounds to exhibit; I write what I please about McCarthy. I bear every external resemblance to the person I was a moment before the telephone call from Washington. But I do not commend the experience to anyone else; I fear for those who may be called before him who do not happen to be editors of newspapers and cannot fight back. And I am saddened by those in responsible positions — in Government and the press — who keep inventing reasons for avoiding a quarrel with the man.

Joe McCarthy never wrote a memoir or kept a journal, and he never responded directly to Wechsler and the others who claimed he'd wrecked their careers or ruined their lives. What he did say — in fire-eating interviews, speeches, and pamphlets — makes clear that he was so captured by his own rhetoric about waging war against a deadly conspiracy that he seldom paused to weigh the collateral damage. That would have required more reflection than he could muster, and would have been too painful. "This fight," he told the nation, "is your fight — your fight for your children and your children's children." Following his grandiloquent declarations and tracking his ferocious crusade was, as journalist George Reedy said, like watching a five-year-old with a loaded machine gun.* What Joe McCarthy wasn't is heartless, the way Roy Cohn was. Not by a mile. But like the early Bobby Kennedy, Joe believed that what mattered in a congressional hearing room wasn't heart, it was grit. And anyone he attacked deserved it, damn it.

Were his claims unfair? He asked himself that question in his polemic *McCarthyism: The Fight for America*. "This perhaps can best be answered," he instructed readers, "by asking you the question of whether it is unfair to the loyal, honest employees of a bank to expose and convict the cashier who is embezzling the bank's funds." Matter settled. As for unfounded accusations, Joe insisted he was the victim, not the perpetrator, of a "viciously intense smear attack . . . The purpose of this Communist tactic is two-fold: (1) to smear and discredit the individual so that his evi-

---

* Reedy was forever dreaming up McCarthy metaphors. Another favorite: Joe was like a baby tearing the wings from a butterfly. The baby doesn't know what he is doing. Joe, Reedy reasoned, was scary precisely because of such innocence. Reeves interview with Reedy, May 12, 1976.

dence on traitors will not be believed and (2) to discourage others from entering the fight."

Much of America believed that what counted most in making Joe McCarthy's enemies list was whether or not someone was a Communist, because that's what Joe said and what he convinced himself. The clarifying lens of history suggests otherwise. At least as vital was whether or not a suspect was what the senator considered a snob. What were the most telling indicators of snootiness? Coming from the East Coast or California was a good one, along with having gone to an Ivy League or other selective college, and being three other things that Joe wasn't: blue-blooded, bookish, and brainy. His mindset was rooted in America's long traditions of populism and nativism — anti–high culture and smooth talk, anti-homosexual, and anti-Washington and Wall Street. Most repugnant of all were those he called "twisted intellectuals." No need for Joe to fake any of this outrage, although, like most firebrands, he could ratchet up the resentment for the right audience. And no need to dwell on whether or how he damaged them.

McCarthy's "definition of the Enemy" is "opposite in all respects to the Ideal American, who is simple, straightforward, ungrammatical, loyal, and one hundred per cent male," wrote Leslie Fiedler, a literary critic who profiled the senator in 1954. "Such an Enemy need not be proven guilty; he is guilty by definition." Joe, like much of America, "distrusts equally 'red tape' and 'reds.'" No wonder, Fiedler added, that Joe's archenemy from Wheeling forward was Secretary of State Acheson, who "is the projection of all the hostilities of the mid-Western mind at bay: his waxed mustache, his cultivated accent, his personal loyalty to a traitor [Alger Hiss] who also belonged to the Harvard Club; one is never quite sure that he was not invented by a pro-McCarthy cartoonist."*

That version of populist likes and dislikes was, not coinciden-

---

* Reedy offered an even more graphic description of Acheson, calling him "cold in demeanor, aloof, icily intellectual, and afflicted with the facial expression of someone avoiding a foul smell." But he also noted that Acheson was "probably the most hard-line anti-Communist in government circles." Reedy, *From the Ward to the White House*, 166.

tally, a hand-me-down from McCarthy's old nemeses, the La Follettes. Fighting Bob and Young Bob convinced Wisconsinites that "somebody far away is screwing you over," says Wisconsin political journalist and author John Nichols. "So here comes Joe McCarthy and he says, 'There's nefarious forces out there that are really screwing you over' . . . In the Wisconsin ethic is this sense that, left to our own devices, we're better, we're more humane and more decent and better than a lot of the rest of the country." Blue-collar hyphenated Americans who'd once been derided by the puffed-up Yankees as dagos and hebes, micks and wops, had been waiting for a hero of their own and now they had him, the Irish German tail gunner from Grand Chute. "What [McCarthy] was saying to all of them," said George Reedy, "was 'Hey, Giovanelli, Pilsudski, Pat, Jacob! You are the real Americans! It's those Achesons, Marshalls, Saltonstalls, and Lattimores who are Communist traitors.' It was music to their ears."

The hunt for Communists would eventually overshadow any of McCarthy's other targets. It was a simple and shrill rallying cry, and it fit better with his patriotic aspirations than a direct appeal to hatreds. He transformed the real threat of Soviet expansion into a cause that saw a Soviet-backed subversive behind whatever problem caught his attention. But Joe was anti-elite long before he was anti-Red. It was in his hardscrabble farm breeding, and his truest believers got that because they shared it. The same way being ill-disposed toward illegal immigrants often masks fears of anyone who's different, McCarthyites didn't need to say that their real enemies were softheaded, limp-wristed liberals as well as party members.

It was no accident that the State Department was Joe's first enemy and the one he returned to most often. There were no more traitors or saboteurs in the diplomatic corps than in the military, or overseas libraries, as his own self-described housecleanings would demonstrate. But the denizens of Foggy Bottom had pedigrees less like his own and more like those of Drew Pearson, Millard Tydings, and others he despised. It was us versus them, which, as Huey Long and Father Coughlin had made clear, is an especially appealing strategy when there are more of us than them.

The only more tempting target than State was Harvard, the esteemed university that had trained a disproportionate number of those Foreign Service officers and, as an added irritation to McCarthy, had invited to be its twenty-fourth president a nettlesome McCarthy critic. Nathan Pusey was at the time president of Lawrence University, a selective, underappreciated college situated on both banks of the Fox River in downtown Appleton, Joe's hometown and epicenter of support. The senator and the academic got along fine until Pusey endorsed an anti-McCarthy tract called *The McCarthy Record,* published the summer before the 1952 election and intended to expose and defeat its subject. Joe was seething but kept quiet until the following spring, when Pusey was announced as Harvard's new head. "Perhaps the best description of Pusey is that he is a man who has considerable intellectual possibilities, but who has neither learned nor forgotten anything since he was a freshman in college. He appears to hide a combination of bigotry and intolerance behind a cloak of phoney, hypocritical liberalism," Joe said in a statement. He continued in trademark McCarthy phrasing that couched a condemnation in vindication: "I do not think that Pusey is or has been a member of the Communist Party. However, while he professes a sincere dislike for Communism, his hatred and contempt appear to be infinitely greater for those who effectively expose Communists . . . He is what could be best described as a rabid anti, anti-Communist . . . Harvard's loss is Wisconsin's gain."

Pusey quickly learned that speaking out against Joe carried a cost with the senator's supporters, as "invitations to speak stopped all at once. The Rotary Clubs, the PTAs, the Kiwanis Clubs, other colleges, commencements — they all thought I was some kind of a Communist." Likewise, McCarthy hadn't realized that Pusey, a deeply religious, staunchly Republican scholar, had built his own base in the community during his decade running the college. Several editorial boards that had resolutely backed Joe parted company here, including his own *Appleton Post-Crescent,* which argued, "In stating that 'I do not think Dr. Pusey is or has been a member of the Communist party,' McCarthy used a gutter-type approach. He could have referred as correctly to Pope or President." The president of a local paper company who'd raised money for the senator telegraphed that this assault on Pusey was "uninformed and unadvised" and was "letting down so many old friends."* Pusey himself responded in the pithy style of the English literature scholar he was, "When McCarthy's remarks about me are translated it means only: I didn't vote for him." His outspokenness against McCarthy won the heartiest accolades from the body that came first with Pusey, the Harvard Corporation, helping seal his appointment as president.

The spat with Pusey was classic McCarthy. Policy was personal for Joe, and it was the handmaiden to power. Red-baiting was a fig leaf for elite-bashing. And the cleavage that mattered most in Appleton and much of America in the mid-1900s grew out of clashing worldviews — on one side, McCarthy's working-class Irish Catholic Third Ward; on the other, Pusey and Lawrence University's Anglo-Protestant, silk-stocking First Ward. So deep were the passions stirred by this senator that there were fissures even within precincts. "Arguments about McCarthy could split families and friends, even husbands and wives," recalled John Torinus, an editor at the Green Bay and Appleton papers. "I remember at dinner parties we had to agree not to bring up the subject; it would just ruin the evening."

The battle that began in Appleton carried over to Cambridge. McCarthy sought vengeance against left-leaning faculty members at Harvard, who he said were fair game for his subcommittee, given the university's lucrative contracts with the Department of Defense. What he didn't say, but we know now from the Marquette files, is that Joe's investigators were digging up anything they could find on Reds at Harvard, with an old list from J. B. Matthews showing seventy-five or so "with front records." Caught in the crossfire were a physics professor and a social science graduate student, both of whom admitted to having been Communists, although neither still was, and both refused to name former comrades despite McCarthy's bullying. "Each time he refuses," McCarthy railed against Professor Wendell Furry, "he will be cited

---

* Never one to eat his words, or measure them, Joe shot back the next day, "Curious to know what old friends are being let down by the exposure of bigoted intolerant mudslinging enemy of mine?" O'Brien, *McCarthy and McCarthyism in Wisconsin,* 150.

for contempt. This will be another way, perhaps, of getting rid of Mr. Pusey's Fifth-Amendment Communists." As for Harvard, Joe added, "to me it is inconceivable that a university which has had the reputation of being a great university would keep this type of creature on teaching our children."

Pusey cabled his reply in November 1953:

> A member of the Communist Party is not fit to be on the faculty because he has not the necessary independence of thought and judgment. I am not aware that there is any person among the three thousand members of the Harvard faculty who is a member of the Communist Party. We deplore the use of the Fifth Amendment for the reasons set forth in the corporation's statement of May 20, 1953, but we do not regard the use of this constitutional safeguard as a confession of guilt. My information is that Dr. Furry has not been connected with the Communist Party in recent years. My information is also that Dr. Furry has never given secret material to unauthorized persons or sought to indoctrinate his students.

It was vintage doublespeak, seeming to back Furry but only so far, defending yet deploring the Fifth Amendment, and accepting McCarthy's premise on the perils of communism even as the college president sought to lash back at the senator he hated.* And it wasn't just Harvard. Columbia, when Dwight Eisenhower was its leader (1948–1953) and afterward, along with many other universities agreed that they wouldn't tolerate Communists on their faculties.

At McCarthy's insistence, Furry was indicted for contempt of Congress, although the case eventually was dropped. He was kept on by Harvard, reluctantly, and a decade later he chaired its physics department. Leon Kamin, the untenured grad student McCarthy targeted, fared less well. While he ultimately was acquitted of con-

---

* The student newspaper, the *Harvard Crimson,* was more stalwart, challenging McCarthy to "put up or shut up" about his allegations that Harvard students are "open to indoctrination by Communist professors." "Harvard Daily Tells Solon to Prove Charge," *Berkeley Daily Gazette.*

As for Pusey, his violent crackdown on students demonstrating against the Vietnam War in 1969 was a factor in his early retirement.

tempt, Harvard made clear he wasn't welcome. He found teaching jobs at Queen's and McMaster Universities in Canada, and when tensions eased a decade later, he returned to the United States, chairing the psychology departments at Princeton and Northeastern. But the scars from Harvard and McCarthy remained. "It left me unemployable in the United States" at the time, Kamin remembered in an interview shortly before he died in 2017. "They actually discussed, in the meeting of the [Harvard] governing board, whether they might be able to withhold my degree. They finally agreed that they couldn't."

With regard to McCarthy, two things stood out for Kamin half a century later. "In the middle of testimony, he would always get up and say he had to go to the men's room. And he would go down the hall to the men's room and take out this brown bag and have another shot." His alcohol consumption got so bad, said Kamin, that "my lawyer, at the trial, couldn't stand cross-examining him, because to cross-examine him as a witness you have to stand close to him, and he reeks of alcohol." Still, Kamin acknowledged that McCarthy "had a certain charm . . . Once, I was walking down the corridor and he was coming back from one of those trips to the men's room. And he threw his arm around me and said, 'How are you Leon? Don't take it personally, I've got nothing against you.' I'm proud to say that I looked at him for a minute, because I had nothing to lose, and said, 'Fuck you.'"

Harvard physicist Norman Ramsey also got to experience Joe up close, thanks to the help he was lending his colleague and neighbor Furry by, among other things, defending him on the Sunday morning NBC public affairs show *Meet the Press*. Afterward, McCarthy surprised Ramsey by calling the studio and inviting him to a dinner party. "McCarthy, as I learned in this and in subsequent encounters, was a man of extremely variable personality. He could be good old Joe, or the very nasty and cruel operator of an inquisition. This evening he was putting on the good old Joe act," said Ramsey. "I'm sure that at the time he was not only acting good old Joe, but being it." Similarly, "an argument used one minute wasn't consistent with another used even two or three minutes later, but each was spoken with a sincerity that he believed it," re-

called Ramsey. That annoyed the brilliant physicist, who was trying to apply the scientific method to this contradictory senator.

> I think he had long ago discovered that he could make much
> better speeches if he didn't bother to be accurate . . . He could
> phrase a statement, in a brilliant fashion, to leave a strong im-
> pression as to how bad someone was. If one examined each
> part of the statement, it wasn't quite incorrect, but the overall
> impression was absolutely wrong . . . Arguing with McCarthy
> was much analogous to trying to scoop a cube of water out of a
> swimming pool while trying to keep the hole left behind in a cu-
> bic shape. One could achieve his objective and still get nowhere.

Ramsey also was struck by Jean, and how different she was
from Joe. "She had no verve to her conversation, her remarks
were dull or certainly without any cleverness of expression in
contrast to his cleverness," the scientist said. "On the other hand,
she, more than he, kept her mind on the long-range objective of
the argument and would see how the overall argument was going . . . The combination of Senator and Mrs. McCarthy would
be much more likely to keep pushing him on in the direction of
something really high in politics than he would alone; he alone
would not get much beyond his current political level," thought
Ramsey.

"Pusey and I, independently, made almost the same statement
of what was really wrong with McCarthy," Ramsey concluded. "It
was not really correct, in McCarthy's case, to describe him as immoral. It's a word that had no meaning to him. The word 'amoral'
was really more appropriate . . . I consider this a worse problem
than if you were just out-and-out consciously immoral."*

Reed Harris had everything Joe could ask for in a witness — a radical youth and Ivy League pedigree, rumors of sexual indiscretion
and even incest, a link to the Red-tilted overseas libraries and the

---

* Even as he was going after Harvard and other elite schools in the East, McCarthy knew there were limits. He almost never lashed out at that bastion of liberalism in his own backyard, the University of Wisconsin–Madison, which had powerful political protectors and hundreds of thousands of loyal alumni who voted.
McCarthy and McCarthyism in Wisconsin, 200.

conspiratorial Voice of America, a surefire star for a closed-door warm-up followed by a public exorcism, and a bureaucrat low-grade enough that neither the president nor his aides would come to the rescue but high-profile enough that shooting him down would telegraph a message to Foreign Service officers here and abroad. It would be the sublime climax to the senator's long-running probe of the Voice and of State. Over time, however, Harris proved a more poignant symbol for Joe's foes than for his backers — of guilt by youthful indiscretion, senatorial misreckoning, and McCarthyism at its most cold-blooded.

The forty-three-year-old Harris was second in command at America's main propaganda arm, the International Information Administration, which oversaw everything from the VOA and foreign libraries to a motion picture service, news service, and educational exchange. That, in Joe's rendering, meant it was Harris's duty to "disseminate American ideals and objectives" and "expose Communist propaganda." But a day of private hearings and three in public early in 1953 suggested that instead of advancing freedom, Harris was undermining it, willfully. That wasn't surprising, the chairman reported, because

> instead of a background of anticommunism in this country, the testimony before the subcommittee indicated that Mr. Harris while at Columbia University had written blatantly pro-Communist material, some of which was reprinted in the *Daily Worker* . . . Mr. Harris conceded that in these years he was not opposed 'to the broad principles of Marxism,' although he opposed it from then on. But the record indicates that a number of years after this period Harris turned up as a sponsor for an activity of the American Students Union, cited as a Communist party front. And at a still later date, Harris appears as a member of the League of American Writers, cited by the Attorney General as a subversive organization.

The deeper the senator dug, the worse Harris looked. He'd been suspended from college twenty-one years earlier after sticking up for a professor ousted because he was a Marxist, condemning conditions in the college dining halls, attacking the ROTC program, and committing other excesses as editor in chief of the school newspaper.* Shortly after he left Columbia, he wrote a book, *King Football: The Vulgarization of the American College,* that accused his and other colleges of profligate spending on that sport, attacked the American Legion and organized religion, and praised Moscow for not endorsing or sponsoring football. Harris continued to show what McCarthy said was bad judgment during his seventeen years of government service — including as an editor at the New Deal's Works Progress Administration and as planning chief for the Office of War Information — most recently by shutting down the Voice's Hebrew broadcast at the very moment when it should have been exploiting the anti-Semitic purges under way in the Soviet Union. Even his clearance by the government security watchdog agency spawned doubts for McCarthy. "Mr. Harris, you repeat over and over that you have been cleared by the Civil Service Commission to do this job. Now, I am not comparing you to him," the senator said even as he was doing just that, "but understand that . . . Alger Hiss was also cleared."

The FBI was busy unearthing its own rumors on Harris — that he'd fathered an illegitimate baby when he was about twenty and the mother was still in high school, that he'd confessed to his sister that he was a Communist, and, as one informant said, that there had been "an unusual display of affection" between Harris and his sister indicative "of possible immorality." The bureau also had heard that Harris was or had been a member of a group called Little Soviets, a tidbit that came from McCarthy staffer Don Surine, with whom the FBI regularly traded gossip.

Disgruntled federal workers in the Loyal American Underground also were rifling through their files and spilling their guts, as the Marquette archives make clear. One of them had special clout: the zealous Frances Knight, an archconservative who later ran the US Passport Office for twenty-two years, denying entry to those she deemed enemies of the state. Roy Cohn and David Schine were paying special attention too. "The Reed Harris overall

---

* He was reinstated eighteen days later, when he threatened a lawsuit and students boycotted classes, but while his record was wiped clean, he was required to and did agree to withdraw from the college. Reed, "Former *Spec* Editor Awaits Degree," *Columbia Daily Spectator*.

setup in Washington," they warned the senator during their gum-shoeing trip across Europe, "adds up to just about as much confusion and waste of money as you might imagine."

In the face of that onslaught, few paid heed to Harris's pleas for clemency. "This is something that, in view of the headlines that have appeared from both the executive and public sessions of this committee, that I should not do," Harris testified, "but I will throw myself on the mercy of this committee." Words like those didn't come easily to the agitator turned diplomat, a makeover reinforced by his wire-rimmed glasses, thinning hair, and three-piece suit, along with a tightly knotted tie held in place by an elegant pin. Looking back to his college-age indiscretions, all he could say was mea culpa: "I was a young man feeling his oats. I should have had more political sense. I didn't. I have been trying to live down this particular part of my life since that time."

There was no mercy, just unrelenting pressure from McCarthy and his allies at the State Department, so Harris did the one thing he could: he quit. Even that wasn't enough. "Resigned," Joe said, was the wrong word, since Harris had been forced out by his new boss at the Information Agency, Robert Johnson, and his leaving was "the best thing that has happened there in a very long time. I only hope that a lot of Mr. Harris's close friends will follow him out." Johnson offered a markedly different slant, writing to Harris, "Frankly, I hate to see you go. Since coming on this new assignment of mine, I have learned to depend upon you." While that was true, it also was the case that no senior official at the State Department lifted a finger to help Harris, said Martin Merson, a special consultant to the agency who watched the drama unfold. "He had to fight alone."

In retrospect, it is apparent that nearly everything McCarthy said about Reed Harris was taken out of context or simply wasn't true. Harris had actually told the subcommittee, in closed testimony the public wouldn't see for another fifty years, that "I never have been; that I have never wanted to be" a Communist. "The fact that they had no scruples whatsoever, showed me very quickly what breed of cat a Communist with a capital 'C' is." His *King Football* book was the kind of exposé of commercialism on campus and in sports that today wins awards. That he published it nearly ninety years ago made him a pioneer in muckraking journalism at a time when most college papers were filled with social scorecards and news as the college administration defined it. In later life he didn't just verbally recant his youthful attraction to communism; he showed he meant it by his anti-Communist programming at the Voice. As for terminating the Hebrew-language broadcasts, Harris convincingly explained that most Israelis spoke German, English, and Slavic tongues—and that Israelis didn't need Americans lecturing them on anti-Semitism. The committee, Harris accurately testified, was "trying to turn a budgetary action into a Communist plot."

The FBI backed him up in its two full-blown inquiries, although they came a decade too late to help him with McCarthy or to reverse the damage the bureau did in real time when it spread unsubstantiated rumors. "Our investigations did not disclose that he was ever a member of the Communist Party and many of the individuals interviewed considered him loyal," it reported in 1961. Its probes did show that in the 1930s and early 1940s he'd "associated with some individuals who were known to be communists and was a member of several communist front organizations," which he admitted. But the FBI dismissed as uncorroborated the gossip about incest, pointed to inquiries by other government agencies that also cleared him, and quoted a former co-worker who knew him best as saying that Harris's "honesty, integrity and standards are so high it is hardly suitable to survive in the business world." While his thinking might make him "a little more 'liberal' than the average human being," his colleague added, that does not "mean 'radical' but means humanitarianism, and in the sense of pertaining to the welfare of human society."

CBS's Edward R. Murrow thought the Harris incident was a perfect case study—not of a conspiracy to undermine the government, as McCarthy was alleging, but of how the senator undermined the rights of witnesses and the rules of fair play. The newsman used it as the centerpiece for one of his half-hour *See It Now* broadcasts in March 1954. He especially liked the line that Harris used in striking back at McCarthy before the TV lights in his public hearing: "It is my neck, my public neck, that you are, I think, very skillfully trying to wring." Murrow, as he often did, switched near the end of the broadcast from reporter to editorialist, in this case letting McCarthy have it with double-barreled sarcasm: "Senator McCarthy succeeded in proving that Reed Harris had once written a bad book, which the American people had proved twenty-two years ago by not buying it, which is what they eventually do [with] all bad ideas. As for Reed Harris, his resignation was accepted a month later with a letter of commendation. McCarthy claimed it as a victory."

McCarthy ultimately moved on to other targets, and Murrow to other victims, but Harris couldn't put the experience behind him, as his unpublished journal entries make clear. They are part political narrative, part cry for help:

March 1, 1953, after his closed-door hearing: "What a crisis comes near the Ides of March this year! I am under the viciously one-sided 'investigation' (i.e. attack) of Senator McCarthy and his Senate Investigations Subcommittee aided by McCarthy's vicious counsel, Roy Cohn . . . I had 3 grueling hours before the Committee . . . Wildly misleading questions were asked . . . I was under great emotional tension — sometimes almost shouted my answers. The way McCarthy's questions and Cohn's made me appear, I felt like a criminal. Also, I realized what power these men exert in our present government; and when I realized with a surge of emotion that they could so paint me as to disgrace me before my children, my family, my friends — I choked up and could not speak for some moments . . . I was never so deeply, completely depressed in my life as when I finished that experience. And now I must do it again, on TV before a crowd of people!"

March 16, 1953, after his public testimony: "Perhaps it was the toughest and saddest week of my life, but in a way it was also the finest. For I was able to stand up to McCarthy, and I came out, perhaps, ahead of him . . . The whole performance was tough beyond any experience I have had . . . I objected, simply and clearly to the linkage of my name to various former government employees like Alger Hiss and Wm. Remington. I pointed out that *King Football*, which McCarthy attacked, was written 21 years ago. I tried to beat McCarthy & Cohn to the punch on various items, and succeeded . . .

"Today I had a minor operation on a finger — 'excision of cyst' — and when I was wheeled into the operating corridor the chief surgeon said 'It is not often that we get a chance to operate on an American hero (!!) One man wrote 'Thomas Jefferson would have been proud of you.'"

April 4, 1953: "I am on the edge of being either psychopath or genius . . . The editor and publisher of that excellent magazine The Reporter, came in to see me. Max Ascoli wears thick-lensed glasses, speaks precise English, but with a very heavy Italian accent. He invited me to write a piece or two about my experiences with McCarthy, probably built around the preliminary (Feb. 23rd) closed hearings. He spoke of his deep desire to see McCarthy destroyed. He said that in Italy, as Mussolini and his Fascists were climbing the political ladder, he had seen similar methods to those of McCarthy — but that *never* had he seen a more vicious & dangerous man than the Senator from Wisconsin! I will probably do his piece for him. It might help more people to understand the incredible, un moral, indecent, inhuman McCarthy technique."

April 19, 1953: "Irrevocable steps in my life history have been taken since I last wrote an entry here. I have resigned from the IIA, with an effective date of Friday 4-24-53."

A decade later, Harris received a measure of vindication. President John F. Kennedy had named McCarthy detractor Murrow to run the Information Agency, and on a steamy July day in 1961, Murrow assembled his senior staff to introduce the tall middle-aged man sitting next to him. "I'd like to welcome back Reed Harris," Murrow said in his understated baritone, "who has been on leave of absence for eight years." The men around the table were moved. As one witness recounted later, "They were old hands. They remembered. The tears started running down their faces; the McCarthy Era was over."

Harris got the job he relished but not his Columbia degree, despite efforts on his behalf in 1981 by the student newspaper, James Wechsler, the *Washington Post,* and Fred Friendly, Murrow's collaborator at CBS and a journalism professor at Columbia, who insisted that "history gave Harris a raw deal." Harris was living in a nursing home by then. He suffered from Alzheimer's disease, a heart condition, and diabetes, but he made clear how much the missing sheepskin still meant to him: "I want that diploma. Not for me, but for the young journalists of today. I want them to know that they will not be punished for speaking the truth and printing what is right." There was precedent at Columbia for leniency in such matters, including with McCarthy's favorite columnist, George Sokolsky, an early fan of the Russian Revolution who was given a diploma years after being expelled for cohabitating with a female student. More important, as Harris's son told the student paper, "if he got his degree now, it would bring a sense of completion to his life. Columbia could make an old man very happy." But the university announced that Harris was "many points away from having earned the degree," adding, "The case is closed."*

Donald Harris was a young boy when his father was forced out of his job, but he recalls the toll it took on everyone in the family. His older brother and sister "played a game where they tried to spot the FBI agents watching our house, which is not a fabrication. They actually were [watching]." In practical terms, he adds, "certainly it was a very harsh blow because the job he was in was quite good and if he had been able to stay in it we would not have had some of the economic problems that we had." Martha Tellier Harris, Donald's mother and Reed's wife, kept things together. "No one," Reed wrote in his journal, "could have carried all these strange episodes — from Columbia 1932 to McCarthy 1953

---

* Harris died in 1982 of a heart attack, "without being vindicated by Columbia," as reported in the student newspaper he loved. "It will be a black mark on the university's history." A year later the college dean unveiled an annual Reed Harris Memorial Lecture. An even better tribute came when the paper's editorial office displayed a framed copy of the front page from April 4, 1932, announcing Harris's expulsion. Katz, "Confrontation with McCarthy," *Columbia College Today*.

half as well. Matchie has been as close to an ideal partner as anyone could possibly be."

Her coping mechanisms began to fail, however, and by 1966 it
was all too much. Martha Harris took her own life one mild spring
morning at the Harris home in West Chevy Chase, at the young
age of fifty-five. Did the way McCarthy upended their life a decade
earlier play a role? Donald is reluctant to go further than facts allow, but he volunteers that "the stress that was in the house" growing out of the McCarthy encounter "may have contributed."

There's another reckoning of McCarthy victims where the count is
in the thousands, and perhaps tens or even hundreds of thousands.
They were educators and public servants, longshoremen, playwrights, social workers, college students, and other ordinary citizens the senator browbeat, generally at a distance, into a tongue-
tied silence. While it is impossible to name them all, there were so
many and their bruises lasted so long that it is here where McCarthy and McCarthyism had its most insidious effect.

The easiest way to appraise that damage is by considering the
ones whose names we do know at agencies such as the State Department, where the new high commissioner for Germany and
former Harvard president James Conant described a "state of war"
between McCarthy and the department that would "be almost
funny were it not so tragic for some people."* That tragedy was
especially apparent among Foreign Service officers specializing in
the Far East, the so-called China Hands. Republicans recognized
the political capital in dumbing down the complicated matter of
how Mao Tse-tung and his Communists triumphed over Chiang
Kai-shek's Nationalists into a simpleminded question: Who lost
China? Their answer, of course, was the Democrats, and McCarthy put faces on the diplomats he said had sold us out. The list
started with one of his earliest targets, Owen Lattimore, and included John Paton Davies Jr., John S. Service, John Carter Vin-

* Conant and McCarthy had a history of belligerence. The former ran Harvard
in the latter's post-Wheeling Red-hunting days, and the college president was
the frequent target of the senator's attacks. Email to author from Jim Hershberg.

cent, and a dozen others in the Foreign Service. All spoke Chinese, all knew the country from having served there during World War II, and, while they may have been naïve about the intentions of Mao's Reds, all three talked to both sides and told Washington about the corruption and incompetence they saw under Chiang Kai-shek and his minions. Speaking the language and knowing the customs of the country they were stationed in should have been an obvious advantage, but to Joe McCarthy that smelled of collusion. As for monitoring all sides in national conflicts, one diplomatic insider during the McCarthy era explained, "Part of our job when we go abroad is to keep in touch with the opposition party, as well as with the party in power. Sometimes — in fact, most of the time — the opposition is a left-wing group. Because they *are* the opposition, and because it isn't wise to let local officials see you talking to them, most such meetings are handled with some secrecy, usually at night. Can you imagine what some inexperienced [State Department] evaluator with no knowledge of foreign affairs would make of those nocturnal meetings a few years later?"

Dorsey Fisher did more than imagine. The Foreign Service officer was grilled by McCarthy allies in the State Department's security office about anonymous rumors of unsavory contacts. Exasperated, Fisher resigned and, months later, died of a heart attack that colleagues said was brought on by his loyalty ordeal. "What took the heart out of me above all," he wrote in a letter shortly before his death, "was to find that everything in the way of work, devotion and intelligence I had put into the service for 24 years, and the fact that office after office abroad had praised the job I'd done, was now regarded as completely irrelevant. They do not weigh against the most astonishing collection of rumors, allegations and mystifications."

CBS newsman Eric Sevareid, who'd traveled the world as a wartime correspondent, called State's China Hands "the ablest group of young diplomats I had ever seen in a single American mission abroad." But thanks in great measure to McCarthy's inquisitions, Davies and Service were fired, Vincent was forced to resign, and most of the rest were reassigned or hounded into self-censorship. Security checks like the ones Fisher was subjected to were mushrooming at the time. President Eisenhower was skeptical about adding to a discredited diplomatic corps during a season of economizing, and the prevailing attitude in the corps was, as one ex-ambassador put it, "You distrust me, I distrust you." The upshot was disturbing at a moment of international turmoil: the United States appointed no new Foreign Service officers between 1952 and 1954.*

That wreckage would remain for a generation as the Cold War heated up in places where there was at least a chance it could have been avoided. "The loss to the United States was more than the destruction of a few brilliant careers," said Haldore Hanson, a former war correspondent and State Department official who was himself a McCarthy target. "After this generation of Asian specialists was annihilated, the United States stumbled into two Asian wars — Korea and Vietnam; we can only guess how history might have been changed had these talented specialists on East Asia served out their government careers." The reverberations continued during the Foreign Service tenure of John Service's son Bob, which started in 1961 and lasted twenty-seven years. He'd learned the lessons of McCarthy to the point, he said, where "I probably kept my head down pretty much because of my father's experiences. I was probably not as bold and insightful as he was in many ways . . . He was clearly identified as a liberal person and therefore I, as his son, was thought to be one, too, so I didn't get my ambassadorship until the Democrats were back in power with Clinton."

The victims were less visible but the fallout was comparable with teachers. Afraid of calling attention to himself, ex-Communist professor of psychology Leon Kamin interrupted his groundbreaking but controversial research on race and human intelligence to work for years with rats. A famous anthropologist later confessed that as a graduate student in the '50s, he kept his books on Marxism "off my shelves and out of sight." Historian and li-

---

* Interest in working anywhere in the federal government plummeted in those years, with 14,200 college graduates taking the civil service exam for entry-level management jobs in 1950 but just 4,200 in 1954. A key reason was McCarthy's targeting of federal workers and, in response, two presidents tightening their security screenings to the point of a chokehold. Schrecker, *Many Are the Crimes*, 371.

brarian of Congress Daniel Boorstin didn't just apologize for his youthful communism; he named names. Physics grad students at the University of Chicago tried to gather signatures to get a Coke machine in their lab but couldn't persuade nervous colleagues to sign that or any other petition. And across the country, there was an academic blacklist as insidious as, if less notorious than, the one in the entertainment industry. Professors who were fired, meanwhile, took jobs at historically black colleges desperate for PhDs, scrounged for work in lower-paying professions, or headed abroad, the way Harvard's Kamin did.

As bad as the job downgrades or losses were, there were other costs that are harder to measure but also stung: students afraid of questioning the prevailing consensus, alongside professors whose fear of stirring up trouble drove them to quit their political clubs, substitute courses on art for art's sake for ones on social criticism, and avoid or restrict the kind of hell-raising that ivory towers are meant to protect. "Certainly compared to what happened in Hitler's Germany or Stalin's Russia, the political repression of the McCarthy period was indeed tame . . . Most of the victims simply lost their jobs. But mild as it was, McCarthyism worked," said Ellen Schrecker, a historian at Yeshiva University and specialist on the Red Scare. "Marxism and its practitioners were marginalized, if not completely banished from the academy. Open criticism of the political status quo disappeared. And college students became a silent generation whose most adventurous spirits sought cultural instead of political outlets . . . The academy did not fight McCarthyism. It contributed to it. The dismissals, the blacklists, and above all the almost universal acceptance of the legitimacy of what the congressional committees and other official investigators were doing conferred respectability upon the most repressive elements of the anti-Communist crusade." Joe was delighted, warning, "We cannot win the fight against Communism if Communist-minded professors are teaching your children."* But Schrecker said such

---

* The public was on McCarthy's side on the firings, according to a 1954 poll by the Ford Foundation's Fund for the Republic, which found that 89 percent of Americans believed an admitted Communist should be dismissed from a college teaching job, 68 percent from a store clerk's job, and 63 percent as a radio singer. Stouffer, *Communism, Conformity, and Civil Liberties*, 43.

thinking ensured that "for over a decade, at the height of the Cold War, meaningful dissent had been all but eliminated."

College campuses weren't the only settings where the tentacles of McCarthy and McCarthyism grabbed hold and meted out punishment. Grammar school and high school teachers in districts nationwide were fired if they were known to be members of the Communist Party, or had taken the Fifth Amendment like Sylvia Berke and Julius Hlavaty. General Electric and other defense contractors weeded out Reds from their workforces, having been pushed to do so by the senator. Vice presidents for "internal security," which were the rage in a fearful Hollywood, were recruited as well by breweries, brokerage houses, and casket makers. Leftist unions were special targets, along with writers, human service workers, and activists pushing for world peace, women's rights, workplace safety, and civil rights. Those movements were set back a decade or more, as was a hoped-for update of the New Deal that included lifesaving benefits like health care for the poor and aged. Losing one's job wasn't the only penalty for suspicious behavior. Passports were denied, professional licenses held up, public housing applications turned down, and some whose loyalty was doubted were arrested, or if they were here on a visa, they were deported. When neighbors knew or suspected something, red paint might be smeared on the house, as it was with a college professor in the South, while a burning cross was planted in the front yard of a blacklisted writer. In Houston, the police were dispatched to a restaurant after two diners were overheard "talking Communist." (They'd said unflattering things about Chinese strongman Chiang Kai-shek.)

A precise body count is difficult to pin down, but Schrecker calculates that more than ten thousand Americans lost their jobs after being singled out as Communists or for refusing to cooperate with anti-Communist probers. For each who was booted, an estimated five to ten resigned in anticipation that they might be. Two hundred political prisoners spent time in jail or INS detention centers. Calibrating fear is harder, but Columbia University researchers tried in 1955, polling 2,451 college professors. Nearly half said they were scared of the witch hunts, a tally that rose to 75 percent among those who belonged to a controversial organization or were at a campus facing a concerted crackdown. "For a few short years in the late 1940s, the American people had more political options than they would ever have again. McCarthyism destroyed those options, narrowing the range of acceptable activity and debate," said Schrecker. "From Harvard to Hollywood, moderation had become the passion of the day."

Biographer Arthur Herman lets the senator off more easily. While he is willing to go along with Schrecker's estimate of ten thousand people losing their jobs during the Red Scare, Herman says only two thousand were government workers, and McCarthy himself was responsible — even indirectly — for at most forty of them being fired. Ex-turned anti-Communist Freda Utley claimed the toll was smaller still, with "some few" government workers who were attacked by McCarthy being ousted. Most of them — although they might "pose as martyrs" — "suffered little if at all," Utley added. Thirty years later, conservative commentator Ann Coulter attempted to erase the slate entirely, contending that "McCarthy's real 'victims' were not sympathetic witnesses, frivolous Hollywood screenwriters, or irrelevant blowhard college professors. They were elite WASP establishment policy-makers."

John Haynes, however, writes that, while "McCarthy's investigations never directly affected more than a few hundred persons . . . because of their capricious manner, *fear* of his investigations affected tens and perhaps hundreds of thousands of persons. Enormous media coverage of McCarthy also inspired hundreds of local imitators." His victims who fought back were able to put their version of the facts into the record, but they couldn't compete with the headlines McCarthy generated or the damage he did. As biographers Jack Anderson and Ronald May put it, "You can't unscramble eggs."

Just how scrambled things had become was apparent in state after state, Nuremberg trials lawyer and McCarthy critic Telford Taylor said in 1955:

In Indiana, the loyalty of professional boxers is now a matter of official scrutiny, and another curious manifestation of this trend is a Massachusetts statute which forbids the appearance on educational television programs of persons who have refused "for any reason" to answer any question put to them by Congressional investigating committees. This remarkable provision bars from the television screen ex-President Truman, Supreme Court Justice Tom Clark, Generals Omar Bradley, Kirke Lawton, and Ralph Zwicker, Secretary of the Army [Robert T.] Stevens, Senator Joseph R. McCarthy, and Walter Winchell, all of whom have, for one reason or another, declined to answer certain committee questions.

"Now, there is a word which describes, better than any other, the status toward which these miscellaneous and cumulative pains and penalties are trending," added Taylor. "That word is 'outlawry.' The investigations are creating and constantly enlarging a category of citizens effectively stigmatized though never convicted of any offense, who are finding life in the United States increasingly difficult and who cannot, under twentieth century conditions, emulate that famous outlaw Robin Hood by taking to the forest to live under the greenwood tree."

(*Above left*) Joe's graduation portrait in 1930 at Little Wolf High School in Manawa, Wisconsin, where he finished four years of work in a single, breakneck year. The inscription to an unnamed friend reads, "To the best friend I ever had. Joe."
WISCONSIN HISTORICAL SOCIETY, IMAGE NO. 32008

(*Above right*) In college, Joe's boxing skills were impressive enough that he was asked to coach fellow students, working to build their confidence and giving up smoking to set an example.
DEPARTMENT OF SPECIAL COLLECTIONS AND UNIVERSITY ARCHIVES, MARQUETTE UNIVERSITY, JOSEPH MCCARTHY COLLECTION. USED BY PERMISSION OF THE DONORS.

Poster for McCarthy's 1939 campaign for circuit judge. He beat the twenty-four-year incumbent in a bare-knuckle campaign that sought to capitalize on his opponent's advanced age.
WISCONSIN HISTORICAL SOCIETY, IMAGE NO. 48258

ELECT
JOSEPH R.
McCARTHY

QUALIFIED BY GENERAL EXPERIENCE

FARM—Born and raised on a dairy farm in Town of Grand Chute, Outagamie County.

LABOR—Worked at common labor for a number of years before becoming lawyer.

BUSINESS—Operated a store at Shiocton, Outagamie County.

LAW—Had wide range of experience as trial lawyer as a member of the firm of Eberlein & McCarthy (formerly Eberlein & Larson).

CIRCUIT JUDGE
LANGLADE, OUTAGAMIE AND SHAWANO COUNTIES
ELECTION APRIL 4th
AUTHORIZED AND PAID FOR BY JOSEPH R. McCARTHY, SHAWANO, WIS.

In 1942, six months after the assault on Pearl Harbor, Joe secured a commission as a first lieutenant in the Marine Corps. He served in the Solomon Islands as an intelligence officer and sometimes tail gunner. Here, Joe is ready for action with his pith helmet. WISCONSIN HISTORICAL SOCIETY, IMAGE NO. 48965

Joe between two unidentified Marine buddies.
MARQUETTE, JOSEPH MCCARTHY COLLECTION

Captain Joseph R. McCarthy, somewhere in the South Pacific in 1943, looking fit.
WISCONSIN HISTORICAL SOCIETY, IMAGE NO. 48964

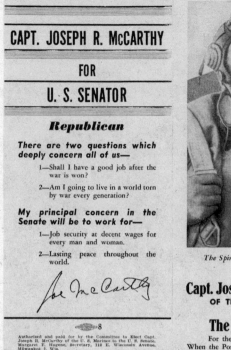

The Spirit of Our Fighting Men

ELECT

Capt. Joseph R. McCarthy
OF THE U. S. MARINES
to

The U. S. Senate
For the Term 1945 to 1951—
When the Post-War World Will Be Made

Still in the Marines, and in violation of military edicts, Joe challenged incumbent Alexander Wiley for the Republican nomination for US senator in 1944.
MARQUETTE, JOSEPH MCCARTHY COLLECTION

Joe spun his wartime exploits in that 1944 campaign to get precisely the press attention that he yearned for from his home state papers. Back on his South Pacific island, he adorned his tent and truck with "McCarthy for U.S. Senator" signs. Even with all that, McCarthy lost nearly two to one.
MARQUETTE, JOSEPH MCCARTHY COLLECTION

McCarthy posing in a Douglas SBD Bomber. By the time his resignation from the Marines took effect in March 1945, Joe, then thirty-six, had spent a full year serving his country abroad and just over twenty-nine months on active duty.
WISCONSIN HISTORICAL SOCIETY, IMAGE NO. 8005

While journalists and his political enemies questioned the legitimacy of medals Joe got for his World War II service, his wartime diaries, letters from squad mates, and Marine Corps records show he was telling the truth about this formative chapter of his biography. MARQUETTE, JOSEPH MCCARTHY COLLECTION

Joe (*left*) in uniform at the 1945 wedding of his best friend, Urban Van Susteren, at Syracuse Army Air Force Base. Helen Burke, the maid of honor, is next to McCarthy. Margery Conway Van Susteren is beside her husband.
WISCONSIN HISTORICAL SOCIETY, IMAGE NO. 47863

Distribution of campaign literature for Joe's 1946 Senate primary campaign by the Young Republicans' barnstorming Flying Badgers, who blanketed the state with his leaflets. WISCONSIN HISTORICAL SOCIETY, IMAGE NO. 48275

Robert M. La Follette Jr., the three-term Senate incumbent whom Joe beat in the Republican primary in 1946.
WISCONSIN HISTORICAL SOCIETY, IMAGE NO. 32459

Recently elected Senator Joe McCarthy tasting a favorite recipe for pheasant.
WISCONSIN HISTORICAL SOCIETY, PHOTO BY *MILWAUKEE JOURNAL SENTINEL*, IMAGE NO. 47476

Joe relaxes in front of the fireplace in a log cabin after a grueling campaign for Senate in 1946. WISCONSIN HISTORICAL SOCIETY, PHOTO BY *MILWAUKEE JOURNAL SENTINEL*, IMAGE NO. 23592

Joe loved hunting rabbits and ducks with friends in Wisconsin. MARQUETTE, JOSEPH MCCARTHY COLLECTION

In 1952, Dwight Eisenhower, who was running for president, and McCarthy, who was seeking reelection to the Senate, appeared together on the rear car of the Eisenhower Special whistle-stop train. Ike wasn't happy with Joe, but in those days he chose appeasement over confrontation. WISCONSIN HISTORICAL SOCIETY, PHOTO BY *MILWAUKEE JOURNAL SENTINEL*, IMAGE NO. 48257

Joe poses with his impressive catch in January 1953, just as he was beginning his second term in the Senate. ULLSTEIN BILD/GETTY IMAGES

Aides G. David Schine (*far right*) and Roy Cohn (*second from right*) horse around as their boss, Senator McCarthy, grills Theodore Kaghan of the US Information Agency in 1953. GEORGE SKADDING/THE LIFE PICTURE COLLECTION/GETTY IMAGES

Joe never got enough sleep at night, so he took catnaps whenever he could.

Joe marries Jean Kerr, his most trusted adviser and longtime staffer, at St. Matthew's Cathedral in Washington in September 1953, with more than a thousand guests on hand including Vice President Richard Nixon.

McCarthy and Army Secretary Robert Stevens confer at the Capitol in February 1954. AP PHOTO

Annie Lee Moss, a suspended Army Signal Corps employee, testifies in March 1954 before the Senate Investigations Subcommittee headed by McCarthy. AP PHOTO

1954 Army-McCarthy hearings. *Left to right:* G. David Schine, Senator McCarthy, and Roy Cohn. WISCONSIN HISTORICAL SOCIETY, IMAGE NO. 3614

Joe sometimes shaved twice a day to try to eliminate his five o'clock shadow, which was a particular embarrassment during the Army-McCarthy hearings.
MARQUETTE, JOSEPH MCCARTHY COLLECTION

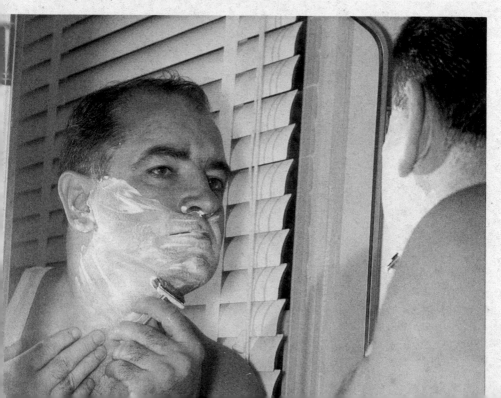

Members of United Packinghouse Workers Local 40 signing a "Joe Must Go" petition in 1954, part of an unsuccessful bid to recall Senator McCarthy.
WISCONSIN HISTORICAL SOCIETY, IMAGE NO. 67434

In October 1954, when many of his Washington supporters had abandoned the controversial senator, longtime pal J. Edgar Hoover was still sending warm notes. But behind the scenes, Hoover was cutting the FBI's ties with and leaks to McCarthy.
MARQUETTE, JOSEPH MCCARTHY COLLECTION

To Jeannie & Joe McCarthy
With all good wishes from
your friend J. Edgar Hoover
10.25.54

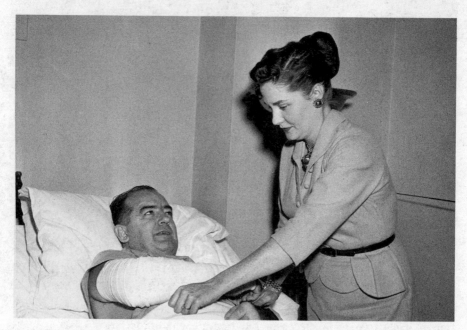

The Senate interrupted its 1954 censure deliberations when McCarthy entered the hospital with an elbow injury he said he sustained when he struck a glass tabletop while shaking hands with well-wishers. His medical records from Bethesda Naval Hospital make clear two things: His elbow really was in bad shape, requiring a plastic splint. And the Navy hospital was a safe harbor, letting him rest and rejuvenate when work left him ill or done in.
MARQUETTE, JOSEPH MCCARTHY COLLECTION

Joe consults with his friend and former aide, Bobby Kennedy, shortly after the Senate voted to condemn its renegade member.
AL MUTO/BETTMANN/GETTY IMAGES

Joe and Jean at the Gateway Hotel in Land O'Lakes, Wisconsin. A similar image appeared on the McCarthys' 1956 Christmas card. WISCONSIN HISTORICAL SOCIETY, IMAGE NO. 47592

Joe couldn't get enough of Tierney, the baby he and Jean adopted in January 1957.

Joe, Tierney, and Jean.

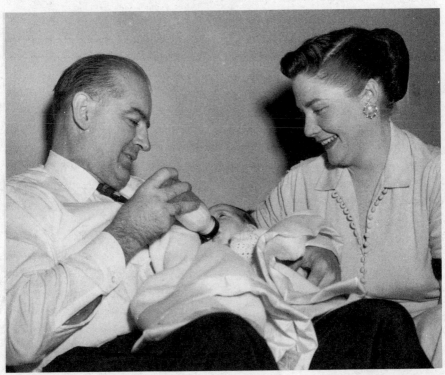

Disciples came in flocks that sunbaked Tuesday in May 1957, packing the pews at St. Mary's and spilling onto the streets outside the Irish parish where Joseph Raymond McCarthy had been baptized and, six months shy of turning forty-nine, was being eulogized.
MARQUETTE, JOSEPH MCCARTHY COLLECTION

Marine honor guard at the burial of Senator Joseph R. McCarthy. Jean McCarthy (wearing a round black hat) stands to the left of the Marines.
WISCONSIN HISTORICAL SOCIETY, IMAGE NO. 48247

7

THE ENABLERS

DWIGHT DAVID EISENHOWER WAS A MAN of inscrutable contradictions. Our thirty-fourth president loved Shakespeare almost as much as he did cowboy novels, and he listened to Beethoven's Minuet No. 2 right along with the "Battle Hymn of the Republic." At the beginning of his presidency, this avatar of the armed services threatened a nuclear strike against North Korea, although by the end he was sounding alarms about the "disastrous rise" of America's military-industrial complex. Nowhere were those dueling natures more apparent than in his mercurial and at times mystifying approach to the subject of one Senator Joe McCarthy.

While Ike detested McCarthy and all that he stood for, he vacillated between strategic retreat and frontal assault, seeming uncertain, for once, about the wisest combat strategy. It wasn't easy for a professional soldier, much less a venerated five-star general, to wage peace. At times he tried a middle course of behind-the-scenes obstruction. But during the critical first year of his administration, when the Wisconsin senator was at his reckless worst, President Eisenhower pursued a policy of appeasement that infuriated McCarthy haters as much as it delighted the senator himself.

Milton Eisenhower, Dwight's younger brother and closest confidant, saw up close how McCarthyism and McCarthy bedeviled the commander in chief. On the one hand, the president "loathed McCarthy as much as any human being could possibly loathe another, and he didn't hate many people." On the other hand, Milton knew that hating had value only if acted upon. "I wanted the President, in the strongest possible language, to repudiate him," said Milton, to "tear McCarthy to pieces." Arthur, the oldest sibling and a sober-minded banker, also pushed Little Ike to take on the Wisconsin senator, whom he called "the most dangerous menace to America." When "I think of McCarthy I automatically think of Hitler," added Arthur, knowing there was no specter more likely to rouse the former Allied supreme commander to action than that of the Nazi murderer he'd vanquished a decade earlier.

President Eisenhower listened yet only half-heard. It was true that he was privately fuming at McCarthy, who had vilified Ike's mentor, General George Marshall. But Ike, cautious by instinct and patient by habit, lectured his brothers and his aides that to Mc-Carthy, there was no such thing as bad publicity. Confronting him head-on would just guarantee him more of the spotlight and could turn him into a martyr. "I developed a practice which, so far as I know, I have never violated," the president confided. "That practice is to avoid public mention of any name *unless it can be done with favorable intent and connotation;* reserve all criticism for the private conference; speak only good in public. This is not namby-pamby. It certainly is not Pollyanna-ish. It is just sheer common sense . . . The people who want me to stand up and publicly label McCarthy with derogatory titles are the most mistaken people that are dealing with this whole problem, even though in many instances they happen to be my warm friends."

On another occasion the warrior turned politician argued, "That damn fool Truman *created* that monster. [McCarthy] didn't exist until Truman went eyeball-to-eyeball with him. Whenever a President does that with any individual he raises that individual to the President's level, and Truman was too stupid to understand that."

So instead Eisenhower waited, the way he had with D-day and other great battles during the war in Europe, convinced that Mc-Carthy would do himself in. Ike offered occasional critiques, along with a muted counterpoint to Joe's raging bravado. "I was raised in a little town of which most of you have never heard. But in the West it is a famous place. It is called Abilene, Kansas," he said in one of his veiled commentaries, broadcast over national radio and television in November 1953, and, as was his way, not naming the bullying senator. "That town had a code, and I was raised as a boy to prize that code. It was this: meet anyone face to face with whom you disagree. You could not sneak up on him from behind, or do any damage to him, without suffering the penalty of an outraged citizenry. If you met him face to face and took the same risk he did, you could get away with almost anything, as long as the bullet was in the front."

Takedowns like that were so meandering that much of America missed Ike's point, and so infrequent that Joe was undeterred. Mainly the president went on with his normal White House routine, while newspapers published so many photographs of him swinging golf clubs and casting fishing lines that the public sometimes wondered who was running the government. That uncertainty grew as reporters tried to parse his rambling, garbled answers at press conferences. Was he being rightfully circumspect or was he out of his depth? The verdict at the time was that his was a do-little presidency, a boring and safe aftermath to the wildly eventful Roosevelt and Truman tenures. Ho-hum.

Not so, a lineup of later Eisenhower biographers tells us. Neither the peace nor the prosperity of the '50s happened by chance, and the easygoing Ike was doing more than playing golf. His steadying hand was everywhere — ending the Korean War, preserving the New Deal, constructing a nationwide highway network, even undermining Jim Crow segregation. The sly presidential fox was misleading Americans on purpose, projecting a grandfatherly calm that bred public confidence and, not incidentally, helped him outmaneuver adversaries within his own political party. There was no clearer instance of that approach, the president's defenders say, than his treatment of Senator McCarthy. The seasoned general's willful silence was a calculated misdirection aimed at ensnaring the runaway senator. Eisenhower wisely "held his fire until McCarthy became open to attack by *any* right-thinking American," said Princeton professor Fred Greenstein, who came up with a name to celebrate that kind of governance by guile: the "hidden hand."

Behind the scenes, Greenstein and others argue, the president was discreetly feeding information to McCarthy's congressional foes, snubbing the senator whenever he could, and standing by high-profile appointees whom McCarthy wanted to block. A more frontal assault, Ike reasoned, would threaten his administration's sliver of a GOP majority in the Senate, where nearly a dozen lawmakers backed Joe, and would imperil its entire agenda. Predictably, little upset McCarthy more than being ignored. "Only the Senate can censure and destroy McCarthy," the clear-eyed head of state instructed his college president brother Milton. Still, it wasn't easy for a man of action to disengage totally. "What a lot of people don't know even today is that behind the scenes I was doing all I could to assist those who were wrongly accused," Ike avowed after leaving the White House. And it eventually worked, according to Eisenhower historian David Nichols, who devoted an entire book to that behind-the-scenes offensive: "Dwight Eisenhower's deceptive operation, mediated through his trusted lieutenants, 'killed' Joe McCarthy."

The hidden hand is a convincing way to unravel the riddle of Eisenhower's surprising successes with the highway program, Social Security, and perhaps civil rights, but Nichols and others are far too forgiving when it comes to Eisenhower's behavior toward McCarthy. For starters, the president did more than look the other way. As far back as the 1952 campaign, he signaled his willingness to mollify McCarthy by dropping from a speech in Wisconsin his spirited defense of George Marshall, an about-face that Ike's pal General Omar Bradley said "turned my stomach." His aides claimed Eisenhower had to back off for electoral reasons, even though he was on his way to winning thirty-nine of forty-eight states and would have won in a landslide even without McCarthy's support or Wisconsin's electoral votes. Eisenhower adviser and 1948 Republican presidential nominee Thomas Dewey had warned that McCarthy would become his "hair shirt" unless Ike hit him early and hard. Ike said he would, then didn't. Drew Pearson sounded a similar alarm but said, "It was obvious from the questions [Eisenhower] asked that he just did not understand" why the columnist was cautioning him. Instead, according to Pearson, the candidate's cowardly retrenchment on Marshall tipped off the Neanderthal wing of his party that they could "handle" him. Joe, too, smelled blood in the water, which for a shark was an invitation to bite.

Attack he did, from the instant Eisenhower moved into 1600 Pennsylvania Avenue, with the White House failing to push back. That spring, the administration let McCarthy elbow his way into US foreign policy via the crisis over Allied shipments to Red China. In June, the president stood up to the senator over the issue of book burnings, then reversed himself by saying his speech at Dartmouth College wasn't aimed at McCarthy and wouldn't be aired on Voice of America. Ike stripped nuclear scientist J. Robert Oppenheimer of his security clearance when McCarthy threatened to investigate and shunned Senator Margaret Chase Smith once she became Joe's enemy.* White House minions and even cabinet officers got the point. The secretary of state gave McCarthy the widest of berths and a say on security clearances; the attorney general brought no indictments in the wake of reports from two Senate committees lambasting McCarthy; and J. Edgar Hoover acted like he worked for the senator instead of the attorney general and president.

That message filtered down to lower rungs. "In 1953, the very thought of Joe McCarthy could shiver the White House timbers and send panic through the whole executive branch," reported journalist and author Richard Rovere:

> I remember once, in about the middle of that year, calling upon one of the President's assistants, a man who seemed to me then, as he does today, to be well above the average in courage and candor . . . At the mention of McCarthy, his whole manner and expression changed . . . "Don't ask me," he said. "For God's sake, please don't ask me to discuss this. Not now. I'll help you as much as I possibly can, I'll talk about anything else you want. Anything. Just don't press me on this" . . . I had the feeling that if I had made an issue of it, I might have persuaded him to see what he could do — in exchange for my promise not again to say

---

* McCarthy's interest in Oppenheimer was both driven and tempered by the FBI's Hoover, who didn't want Joe plowing in before evidence was assembled against the charismatic physicist, but hoped that once it was, McCarthy could help ensure that the father of the A-bomb would no longer be entrusted with America's nuclear secrets. That evidence ranged from Oppenheimer's leftist ties dating to the 1930s, to his opposition to the H-bomb. Bird, *American Prometheus*, 474, 502–3, and 546–49; and email to author from Jim Hershberg.

"McCarthy" in his presence — to get me an ambassadorship or even to declassify the recipe for the hydrogen bomb.

Even more basic to McCarthy's success, the president never challenged the senator's meat-and-potatoes premises: that merely believing in communism was dangerous, and that Soviet subversion threatened the stability and safety of America. Determined not to repeat his predecessor's presumed failure, Eisenhower outdid Harry Truman in combing the government for security risks and trying to wrest from McCarthy the mantle of top-drawer Commie-slayer. No matter that there were few if any real spies left by the time the general moved into the White House. The upshot was that the Red Scare dragged on longer than it had to. As for the constitutional protection that McCarthy undercut most often, President Eisenhower saw nothing wrong: "I must say I probably share the common reaction if a man has to go to the Fifth Amendment, there must be something he doesn't want to tell us." It was more delicate than Joe's branding witnesses Fifth Amendment Communists, but just barely.

Rather than a hidden hand guiding the country, the Eisenhower waiting game looked more like an empty glove. This ranking officer had never liked to wage war unless he was certain he would win. But holding back until the senator self-destructed meant that, in the meantime, the country would pay an unconscionable toll. The White House stayed silent while McCarthy upended Reed Harris's career and nudged his wife, Martha, toward taking her life. Similar fates befell Raymond Kaplan, Charles Thayer, Julius Hlavaty, and scores of others. It was on Eisenhower's watch, and partly thanks to his coattails, that McCarthy was elected to an office that allowed him to chair the Subcommittee on Investigations, where he was able to wreak such havoc. It wasn't just that Ike was missing in action; the commander in chief had become the senator's enabler in chief.

Editorialists understood the implications. The *New York Times* pleaded with the president "to declare open war against Senator McCarthy." Richard Strout of the *New Republic* and *Christian Science Monitor* wrote that "the man most responsible for McCarthy is Eisenhower — good idealistic, generous Ike. It was he who accepted a sordid marriage of convenience with Joe in the campaign and has played foot[s]ie with him ever since." The *Washington Post* was even more impatient: "Two years ago, in indorsing General Eisenhower for the Republican nomination, we observed: 'It is this newspaper's hope and belief that McCarthyism would disappear overnight if Eisenhower were elected.' By now we have waited some 400 nights for the President to exert the kind of leadership that would bring that happy result. Quite apart from the other considerations in a change of Administration, let us acknowledge candidly our profound disappointment."*

Alarm about the dynamic between the battle-scarred senator and the neophyte president also was spreading abroad. "In his attitude toward the G.P.U. Senator, courageous General Eisenhower appears to be downright cowardly," commented the *Arbeiter-Zeitung,* the usually sympathetic Austrian paper, likening McCarthy to the Soviet secret police. "Your president must speak up," a British letter writer echoed in the *Washington Post.* Meanwhile in Moscow, *Pravda* asserted that the US president "on the whole supported McCarthy," whom it branded a "briber, speculator and defrauder." Eisenhower's appeasement wasn't surprising, the Communist Party organ added, because "owners of American monopolies" who steered the Republican Party had always seen McCarthy as a useful weapon to grab power and batter liberals.

What could and should this president — the second in a row to be held captive by the bully from Wisconsin — have done differently?

He ought to have ordered his FBI to plug its leaks to McCarthy, the State Department to stop cowering and backpedaling, and the International Information Agency not to "deshelve" its overseas libraries. Instead, said Martin Merson, who watched it all from a senior perch at the Information Agency, "the President made the mistake in those early days of not believing enough in the people, of feeling that he had to accommodate himself to the so-called

---

* While the president and many of his aides believed that, given enough rope, Joe would "hang himself," wrote John Oakes of the *Times,* others worried, "Give him enough rope he'll hang you." Oakes, "Inquiry into McCarthy's Status," *New York Times.*

practical politicians, to make compromises, to heed the cry of expediency." But whereas Merson at least listened to the president's justifications, McCarthy target James Wechsler offered this harsher verdict: McCarthy "was not superman; he was nourished more by the weakness of those who should have resolutely challenged him — most notably Dwight D. Eisenhower — than by any mysterious resources. There must have been many moments when he shook with laughter over the conduct of those he was harassing; surely he must have enjoyed Mr. Eisenhower's austere refusal to 'indulge in personalities,' the craven formula devised early at the White House for the preservation of internal Republican peace and quiet."

Ike made another major error in trusting a middleman to broker his relations with the senator, and he compounded that misjudgment by sending his vice president. Richard Nixon was a Red-baiter himself, at least as sympathetic to McCarthy as he was to his boss the president. Even more problematic was Nixon's own overweening political ambition, which was one reason why Joe never trusted him. When the president dispatched Nixon to persuade McCarthy not to assault the Republican White House the way he had Truman's, the vice president was careful not to offend the senator or his legions of followers. Likewise, rather than pushing Ike to stand up for the Constitution or McCarthy's victims, the vice president reinforced the president's instinct to pacify. "Nixon's role in the McCarthy era was pragmatic and cynical and unprincipled," says his biographer John A. Farrell. "Nixon *above all* saw the Commie-bashing issue as an effective one for himself and Republicans and tried with all his might to keep McCarthy from alienating Ike — but only for fear of losing this trademark issue. If there was anyone outside Ike's own circle who encouraged the caution that led to the Let Him Die By His Own Hand reaction it was probably Nixon. Nixon's argument was, Let's Keep Him Alive because he's great bashing Democrats as traitors."

The truth was that at the height of McCarthy's reign of terror in 1953, Eisenhower himself was the one national figure with the patriotic service and popular following to have neutralized the out-of-control Wisconsin lawmaker. The president's monthly approval numbers that year never dropped below 61 percent and topped out at 73 percent, the kind of fawning most leaders can only dream about and that McCarthy never even approached. In 1954, and in twelve of the nineteen years between 1950 and 1968, Americans voted Eisenhower their favorite person in the world. And Ike, alone among Americans, had access to unvarnished reports from the FBI, CIA, and loyalty boards of every federal agency, laying out the limits of government treason and the breadth of McCarthy mythmaking. He had the power and knew the lies. A nation looked to him for leadership, as had his two brothers. He even had a willing adversary, because Joe always was spoiling for a fight. The one area where pollsters said Americans doubted their commander in chief was his decisiveness, qualms that an iron-fisted response to McCarthy could have put to rest. "At a time when the public would doubtless have welcomed some kind of a statement on McCarthy by the President—either pro or con—he offered nothing," said John Fenton, managing editor of the Gallup Poll. Drew Pearson still hoped he might act, telling his diary in November 1953 that "it's barely possible that Ike will now get off his fat fanny and realize that the chips are down, that he can't temporize with a would-be dictator."

Insiders were even more restless. At the same moment Pearson was venting in his journal, C. D. Jackson, Eisenhower's special assistant on the Cold War, was penning a letter to White House chief of staff Sherman Adams. "Listening to Senator McCarthy last night was an exceptionally horrible experience, because it was in effect an open declaration of war on the Republican President of the United States by a Republican Senator," Jackson wrote in response to McCarthy's national TV and radio address in which he charged that the Truman administration had "crawled with Communists" and that the Eisenhower administration was only marginally better. "I hope," Jackson added, "that this flagrant performance will at least serve to open the eyes of some of the President's advisers who seem to think that the Senator is really a good fellow at heart. They remind me of the people who kept saying for so many months that Mao Tse-Tung was just an agrarian reformer."

One more consideration weighed on the president: McCarthy's abuse of his favorite sibling, Milton. Ike likely didn't realize that the senator was trying to assemble a case linking this brother to

another of McCarthy's favorite targets, Owen Lattimore, as the
Marquette archives reveal. But he couldn't help knowing about
McCarthy's half-hour radio tirade against Milton. Joe "thought if
he attacked the President's brother, who was known to have the
President's affection, he would blast open the President's ability to
become enraged and thus cause him to depart from his firm policy," Milton said afterward. While "stopping short of calling me
a Communist" in his radio talk, McCarthy left "no doubt that he
considered me to be an evil influence in government and favoring
policies that helped the Soviet Union in the Cold War." It was the
same kind of smear Joe had spread about Ike himself before the
1952 Republican convention, and was one reason why Milton kept
pressing his brother to strike back.

The day after the broadcast, Milton attended a dinner in Wisconsin with guests including Joe and Jean.

> When [McCarthy] saw me he came over and tapped me on the
> shoulder. I stood up and deliberately turned my back to the folks
> at the table. McCarthy threw his arms around me and hugged
> me, then vigorously shook hands and said how happy he was
> to see me in Wisconsin. I refused to introduce him to anyone,
> turned back to my place, and sat down. He then proceeded to
> go round the table and speak to every one of the thirty guests,
> though he had not previously met any of them. When he came to
> [the attorney general's daughter] Ann Brownell he leaned over
> and kissed her on the cheek. This made her so ill that she left the
> table for a time to recover. This single incident is to me irrefut-
> able proof of the man's hypocrisy.*

At times Ike seemed aware of his own vacillating and doubtful
of the hidden hand strategy, as reflected in notes to himself and his

---

* More than seventy years after the fact, Ann Brownell — now Ann Sloane, who
had a long career in international development — remembers the incident differently. The senator did approach her, but on a plane rather than over dinner. "He
threw his arms around me and slobbered on my cheek," she recalls. "He may
have been heading for my mouth. I was appalled mainly by the odor of the man.
I think it was alcohol . . . I'd read about his bear-like aura and that certainly was
my experience. It was frankly disgusting." Author interview with Ann Brownell
Sloane.

counselors. "I continue to believe that the President of the United States cannot afford to name names in opposing procedures, practices and methods in our government. This applies with special force when the individual concerned enjoys the immunity of a United States Senator," he wrote in 1953 to a friend who chaired the board of General Mills.

> I do not mean that there is no possibility that I shall ever change my mind on this point. I merely mean that as of this moment, I consider that the wisest course of action is to continue to pursue a steady, positive policy in foreign relations, in legal proceedings in cleaning out the insecure and the disloyal, and in all other areas where McCarthy seems to take such a specific and personal interest. My friends on the Hill tell me that of course, among other things, [McCarthy] wants to increase his appeal as an after-dinner speaker and so raise the fees that he charges.

Other times, unable to tolerate the pain he felt biting his tongue regarding McCarthy, this thin-skinned president looked for scapegoats — Democrats, misguided staffers, or, in this case, the press. "No one has been more insistent and vociferous in urging me to challenge McCarthy than have the people who built him up, namely, writers, editors, and publishers. They have shown some of the earmarks of acting from a guilty conscience — after all, McCarthy and McCarthyism existed a long time before I came to Washington," he wrote in March 1954 to another businessman friend. "The area in which all of this really hurts is the adverse effect upon the enactment of the program of legislative action I have recommended. We have sideshows and freaks where we ought to be in the main tent with our attention on the chariot race."

Two weeks later, in March 1954, he finally said he'd had enough and would tell the world how much he loathed the Wisconsin senator. It was liberating, as his press secretary, James Hagerty, reported in his notes on that day's staff briefing, where McCarthy once again was topic number one. "I've made up my mind you can't do business with Joe and to hell with any attempt to compromise," Eisenhower told his assembled aides, not recognizing that he was echoing the sentiments of the predecessor he scorned, Harry Truman. Walking away with Hagerty, Ike added, "Jim. Lis-

ten. I'm not going to compromise my ideals and personal beliefs
for a few stinking votes. To hell with it."

At a press conference later that morning the president was
asked whether Joe had the right to cross-examine witnesses in
hearings called to investigate his own allegedly improper encounters with the U.S. Army. "In America," Ike answered, "if a man is
a party to a dispute, directly or indirectly, he does not sit in judgment on his own case." It was the president's most public and direct assault on McCarthy, but it was hardly the break that Ike had
promised barely an hour before, or that Milton Eisenhower, C. D.
Jackson, and others said was vital to curb a senator whom Jackson called "a killer abroad in the streets." Yet that too would come,
sooner and with a more crippling outcome than the senator expected.

Money was another essential enabler. And there was no shortage of cash now that Joe had so much weight to throw around in
Washington.

Texans had the most and were most openhanded. Among his
Lone Star State fans, none was more bullish, at least at first, than
Clint Murchison. A World War I veteran, Murchison owned one
of the largest independent oil companies in the nation, along with
major holdings in natural gas, banks, railroads, ranches and an
opulent resort, life insurance, and the distinguished New York
book publisher Henry Holt. He signaled his conservative politics by naming one of his firms American Liberty Oil. He reflected
his delight in what McCarthy said in Wheeling and afterward by
contributing $10,000 to Joe's effort to unseat Senator Tydings in
Maryland, donating $30,000 more to other McCarthy causes, of-
fering jobs to those Joe recommended, and letting the senator use
his private planes, swim naked in his hotel pool, and urinate outside his cabana. "I sized [McCarthy] up as the best tool in sight to
fight Communism . . . I'm for anybody who'll root out the people
who are trying to destroy the American system," Murchison said,
adding that those people included not just card-carrying Communists but "egg heads" and "longhairs."

Two fellow Texas tycoons—Dallas's H. L. Hunt and Houston's
Roy Cullen—were equally soft touches when it came to McCar-

thy. Hunt was said to be a billionaire in an age when there were very few, while in his heyday Cullen likely was the richest man in America. Both Cullen and Hunt helped pay for not just the "dump Tydings" campaign but also the efforts to dump Benton and Margaret Chase Smith. And each shared Murchison's right-wing zeal. Liberals, Socialists, and Communists constituted the Mistaken, Hunt said, and they controlled "nearly all of the big money in the United States" and could "be spoken of with complete disapproval." As for Cullen, Texas oil money chronicler Bryan Burrough called him "a Faulkneresque figure in a white summer suit, a man who detested Communists, 'pinkos,' and especially Roosevelt, [and] who preferred 'niggers and spics' and 'New York Jews' to know their place." Cullen also was the first of the big three to bring Joe to Texas, calling him "the greatest man in America" and saying, "I hope [he] keeps all the Communist spies running until they get to Moscow."

In the history of Texas, Republicans had held just two highfalutin $100-a-plate dinners, and one was to honor Joe. More than a thousand supporters turned out in Dallas to hear his familiar "Twenty Years of Treason" speech, laying out alleged Commie coddling during the Roosevelt and Truman administrations. A state that Democrats still held in their partisan grip was smitten by Wisconsin's GOP senator. The local press called him "Texas's Third Senator" because he was there so often, and because he voted the Texas line on issues affecting oil, natural gas, and other matters vital to that state and sometimes contrary to the interests of his own state. What Texans liked even more, *Fortune* magazine concluded, was McCarthy's combativeness: "The American system was being attacked by subversives; nowhere had that system reached a finer flowering than in Texas; nobody had more to lose should the attack succeed; McCarthy was determined it should not succeed. It seems to have been that simple."

But it wasn't quite. Joe's Marquette papers show that he kept a list of people who "should receive first-class treatment in case they call," and whom his staff shouldn't contact "without an okay first." All the Texas oilmen were there, from Cullen to Hunt. A back-and-forth of letters shows he had especially close ties to Murchison, his most obliging banker. The magnate tried to tone down his friend the senator, and to patch up Joe's fractured relations with President Eisenhower. "If you have erred, the error can be laid to the intensity of purpose and not to the desire to hurt any innocent people," Murchison wrote McCarthy. "I personally know that the President likes you regardless of what Milton Eisenhower, Sherman Adams, and others may think about you. I am trying to play the role of a good Samaritan who is trying to join the hands of two noble citizens. May God and others be with you, my boy, to the bitter end — including me. Sincerely, Clint."

Wealthy Wisconsinites opened their wallets too, with donations, loans, and whatever else their junior senator needed. One early donor was Frank Sensenbrenner, the millionaire head of the Kimberly-Clark paper company and president of the board of regents at the University of Wisconsin. Another was Walter Harnischfeger, a builder of prefabricated homes and patron of Germany after the war and perhaps during, who appreciated Joe's support of US homebuilders and of the Malmedy murderers. So many corporate executives liked Joe and despised unions, New Dealers, and minimum wages that they set up an operation called the McCarthy Club, which was based in Milwaukee and raised up to $100,000. Money rolled in from sources as diverse as the head of Paramount Studios and the leader of the World War II Flying Tigers squadrons. Walter Jolin, a lumber executive from Green Bay who'd known McCarthy for twenty years and was a substantial donor, said the senator wasn't shy about touching up old pals: "It always cost money to be his friend."

Whatever the cost, a Gallup poll in January 1954 found that nearly half (49 percent) of business and professional men thought well of this senator, compared to a minority (39 percent) who didn't.* The latter group included Henry Ford II, president of the Ford Motor Company. "If someone wanted to devise a deliberate policy that would torpedo the world prestige of the US and com-

---

* The news from that survey wasn't all good for McCarthy. Fifty-six percent of those businessmen registered disapproval of the senator's methods, and his 39 percent unfavorable rating among the commercial class was higher than the anti-McCarthy responses among white-collar workers (37 percent), farmers (29 percent), and manual workers (23 percent). Murphy, "McCarthy and the Businessman," *Fortune*.

pletely destroy Western unity," said the eldest grandson and name-sake of the company founder, "I can think of no better one than the attempted use of economic coercion advocated by Senator Mc-Carthy."

Joe's own finances remained as dicey as ever. How much he fleeced his political donors for his personal needs is unclear, as is whether some of his actions were illegal. Reporter Willard Edwards saw him pocket cash contributions mailed to his office, grinning as he did, likely using the money for personal expenses. McCarthy speechwriter Ed Nellor saw the same thing, although he said the senator used the money for investments. The Marquette files suggest he continued taking out loans from friends and supporters the way he had from the start, and again had trouble paying them back. The Senate had investigated him, as did the state of Wisconsin and, in 1954, the Internal Revenue Service. Joe remained defiant, telling a national television audience that he would make his financial records public only if someone produced "any evidence of wrongdoing on my part" and if other senators bared theirs, too. "There'll be no rule," he said, "that applies to McCarthy only." While he traveled a hot-tempered high road in public, backstage the senator was in cover-up mode. The papers at Marquette show letters to his brother Bill zeroing in on questionable reports Joe had filed about old loans from family members. "It is rather important," Joe wrote, "that if I deduct anything from my income tax for interest paid that it be the same figure that you charge yourself for interest received," adding, "If you could let me know this figure Bill it would make certain that both of our Income Tax Returns jibe in case of an investigation. On second thought, perhaps it might be better to just forget about any computation of interest at all, and if you think there was sufficient [money available] to take care of the notes and the interest thereon we can just forget about figuring interest entirely and let the matter drop right there." In the end, investigators did no more than slap the senator's wrist, and he defied attempts to make public more records than he had to.

While he loved gambling and put down thousands of dollars in bets at the horse track and poker table, he never lived lavishly. Just the opposite, as his clothes and homes showed. He did take money from corporations and individuals with business before his committees, although so did nearly everyone else on Capitol Hill. He also took tips on stocks, especially from the Texans, which Nellor said yielded big payouts. Richard Rovere, the journalist and biographer, concluded that McCarthy "was a Potemkin, and the followers were credulous Catherines . . . [V]ery little of the money that rolled in rolled out into the coffers of the crusade." Maybe, but Clint Murchison, who helped fill those coffers, insisted that the senator "hasn't touched a cent of it. I know, because he's always asked me to send the money to somebody else."

The most convincing portrait of his finances in those heady years, and how they affected his life at work and beyond, appeared in *Look* magazine in December 1953. "The spotlight, which always seems to be turned his way, illuminates McCarthy not as a soloist but as the leader of a potent company which has been growing steadily. The McCarthy set is a heady mixture of Texas millionaires and former corner grocers; of Catholic prelates and a campus beauty queen; of hard-working political bosses and reportorial sleuths; of hot-shot investigators and radio stars; of Wisconsin politicos and rich horsewomen; of market plungers and solid industrialists," reporter Richard Wilson wrote. "The McCarthy of today is a far cry from the one-man operator who drew these scores of people into his orbit. He is now an entity, complete with a staff of 50. He has money, powerful backers and impressive public support."

The McCarthy entity included some of the most influential people in the US government, most of whom would break with Joe when his power waned but who quietly and enthusiastically helped him scale the vertiginous heights from the Wheeling speech in 1950 to the Army-McCarthy hearings early in 1954. None was more gung-ho than the administrator of the State Department's Bureau of Inspection, Security, and Consular Affairs, Robert Walter Scott McLeod, whom Joe called Scotty.

The ex-FBI agent and onetime New Deal cheerleader was, like McCarthy, repelled by Communists and homosexuals, especially the pinstriped sort he said operated unchecked in Foggy Bottom. Nobody at the Department of State, not even Secretary John

Foster Dulles, had more day-to-day authority than McLeod, who blended the roles of top cop, mental health arbiter, adjudicator of who entered and left the country, and liaison to the FBI, CIA, and congressional bigwigs like Senator McCarthy. He used that clout, as one profiler reported, to launch "the most intensive intramural investigation undertaken in the history of our government—a 'full field' study, within the space of a year, of every single member of the [State] Department's present eleven-thousand-person complement, from ambassadors down to supply clerks, in Washington and scattered among 267 diplomatic and consular posts abroad." He weighed "such factors as a jobholder's drinking habits, sexual interests, and possible 'neurological disorders.'" Hundreds of presumed security risks left the department, with most, like Reed Harris, pushed out for long-ago leftist associations of the sort that McLeod himself harbored.* "Congress wanted heads to roll and I let 'em roll," McLeod told a journalist, adding with a grin, "Blood in the streets and all that."†

Insiders at the time suspected that McLeod and McCarthy shared information and were personally close; Scott reportedly kept an autographed picture of Joe in his office. Just how close, and how much they shared, is attested to by the Marquette records on Theodore Kaghan, the official in Germany whose scalp Joe desperately wanted. McCarthy wrote to McLeod in letters that laid out his gripes and always began "Dear Scotty." The top cop was eager to oblige. "If the Senator wants to recommend directly to Secretary to have Kaghan terminated," Joe's secretary re-

---

* In college, McLeod considered New Dealer Harry Hopkins a "deity," according to a profile in *The Reporter*. As for a Communist schoolmate, McLeod reportedly told one journalist they were roommates and another that he simply lived on the same dormitory floor, leading the *Reporter* writer to wonder "whether this derogatory information is contained in McLeod's own [security] dossier." Hale, "'Big Brother' in Foggy Bottom," *The Reporter*.

† The blood wasn't flowing just at State, or just from the hand of McLeod. "A new breed bestrode the land: the security officer," wrote Red Scare historian David Caute. "Fordham men now decided whether Harvard men were fit to work. The long shadow of the security officer fell across factories, dockyards, ships, offices. A generation of workers learned to conform or to move on. Those who moved on learned how to change their identities, to migrate, to lose their trackers, to resurface as immaculate Americans." Caute, *The Great Fear*, 12.

corded in her notes of conversations between the McCarthy office and the State Department, "McLeod will go along with that and support it; otherwise he will make the recommendation to try to get Kaghan's [resignation]." Roy Cohn, meanwhile, unofficially coordinated with McLeod during and after his junket to Germany. "Scotty says this old crowd over there is just trying to make a little trouble," Cohn wrote McCarthy about a celebrated defector they hoped would tell all to the subcommittee, to the dismay of US diplomats in Germany. McLeod "would like a letter from you asking cooperation with her in the preparation of facts for her testimony and would like that sent over to his office tomorrow . . . [H]e will then instruct immediate and full cooperation with her."

McCarthy used his ties to McLeod to go after two foes at once — *The Reporter*, which was among his most intrepid press critics, and State Department officials who read it. In the summer of 1953, he wrote Secretary Dulles asking how many subscriptions State had, how widely they were circulated, and whether the department actually recommended reading what the senator called a pro-Communist magazine. McLeod said he would investigate. Where was Dulles in this behind-the-curtain drama? Taking his lead from the president, he practiced a policy of appeasement through most of 1953, trying to avoid swipes from McCarthy and, early on, giving McLeod a free hand. "When it came to appointing ambassadors and hiring and firing Department officers," wrote Rovere, Dulles "cleared everything with McLeod, who cleared everything with McCarthy."

Joe's most consistent and valuable co-conspirator for the three years after Wheeling remained FBI director J. Edgar Hoover, who had better information to trade than even McLeod and whose power base was more solid. It was thanks to Hoover, at least as much as McCarthy's Loyal American Underground, that the senator's files included reports so super-secret that they warned, "This document contains information affecting the national defense of the United States within the meaning of the espionage laws . . . [T]he transmission or the revelation of its contents in any manner to an unauthorized person is prohibited by law." FBI agents checked scores of names submitted by the subcommittee against bureau files and turned over juicy scuttlebutt on witnesses. They squelched critical hearsay about the senator, including that he'd fathered a child out of wedlock in the late 1930s.* The director and the senator also relished dining together at Harvey's Restaurant, watching the ponies run at the Bowie Race Track, chatting when they overlapped at Clint Murchison's Hotel del Charro in La Jolla, and trading letters so warm that Joe again crossed out the greeting "Edgar" and wrote in "Boss."

But Hoover set limits. By the summer of 1953 he was hedging his support for McCarthy even as his boss, the president, was still appeasing the Wisconsin senator. The guarded FBI director saw that Joe's shoot-from-the-hip approach was threatening not just the anti-Communist crusade but the FBI's own credibility. He carefully controlled and reduced the leaks and discouraged McCarthy from hiring more of the bureau's ex-agents, as the senator's thick FBI file attests. Hoover started denying McCarthy's boasts about the closeness of their ties, which had once been a source not just of prestige but of cover, allowing him to play the good cop next to Joe's tough guy and getting Joe to smear his enemies. By the time Ike finally made his break, Edgar already had severed his ties, demonstrating the political survival instincts that let him thrive under an astonishing eight presidents.

The federal judiciary also did its part for McCarthyism. The Supreme Court, which the founders hoped would douse the inflamed passions that might sometimes prevail in the rest of the government, did just the reverse during the Red Scare. It ruled in 1951 that the state's power to quell a feared rebellion by Communists trumped free speech rights. And it generally let McCarthy assert, with some justification, clearance from the highest court

---

* An FBI source in Memphis told the bureau that the daughter, then sixteen, was living with her mother in Lowry City, Missouri. The mother was a café operator, the girl had "to give up school due to the financial condition of her mother," and the informant had written to the senator "requesting that he furnish his daughter sufficient funds on which to live and on which to attend school, but [she had] not received a reply." The source, the Memphis FBI agent in charge reported to Hoover in 1954, "talked in a[n] irrational manner and seemed to be most upset that Senator MCCARTHY is permitted to 'ride around in a Cadillac' and not take care of his daughter." The agent told the complainant "that the problem presented by her is not one coming within the investigative jurisdiction of the FBI." Memo from SAC Memphis to Hoover, March 2, 1954, pt. 7 of 28, MFBI.

in the land to investigate, sanction, and even intimidate his witnesses. The force behind those facilitations, Justice Felix Frankfurter, meant not to enable McCarthy but to keep the justices out of trouble when they were under attack, said lawyer and historian Robert Lichtman. In practice, Lichtman added, that translated into "deferring to the elective branches." That was especially unfortunate coming in an era of political repression when, as new chief justice Earl Warren observed, "it is doubtful that congress would pass the Bill of Rights if it were introduced today." The court would right those wrongs beginning in 1957, in time to quell McCarthyism but too late to curb McCarthy.

The legislative branch was even more tongue-tied. A lineup of conservative Republican senators — Styles Bridges and Barry Goldwater, William Jenner, Bourke Hickenlooper, Homer Capehart, and Joe's closest Senate friend, Herman Welker, known behind his back as "Little Joe from Idaho" — had been there for McCarthy from the start, but Democrats often were on board as well. Mississippi's James Eastland was so skillful in using the Communist cudgel against anyone agitating for civil rights that investigative journalist I. F. Stone gave him a derisive nickname of his own, the "Mississippi McCarthy." While Republican leader Robert Taft's remarks to friends showed he knew better, the sickly Ohioan continued feeding McCarthy encouragement and juicy information. James Bassett, a longtime newsman at the *Los Angeles Times,* observed the damage McCarthy was doing to Republicans from his 1954 posting as chief of PR at the Republican National Committee: "This maleficent genius of the Far Right hovered darkly over the national scene, and over Republican affairs in particular. He was a one-man civil war, setting political brother-against-brother, even pitting state-against-state."

Taft's Democratic counterpart Lyndon Johnson was equally quiescent. His longtime aide Bobby Baker recalled that, privately, Johnson "fumed and complained of the trouble McCarthy caused him. 'Joe McCarthy's just a loudmouth drunk,' he told intimates. 'Hell, he's the sorriest senator up here. Can't tie his goddamn shoes. But he's riding high now, he's got people scared to death some Communist will strangle 'em in their sleep, and anybody who takes him on before the fevers cool — well, you don't get in a pissin' contest with a polecat.'"* He sounded like Ike and with good reason. LBJ realized that McCarthy was even stronger in Texas than in the nation as a whole. So, like the president, the Democratic leader refused to sacrifice any of his stockpile of political capital to take on the bully while he ruled the playground.

The most shameless of the fence-straddlers was John Kennedy, the famously talented and ambitious Massachusetts Democrat. Kennedy knew how bonded his father and brother were to McCarthy and never forgot the quiet hand the Badger State senator had lent by staying out of the Bay State in 1952, despite an invitation from Jack's Republican opponent Henry Cabot Lodge Jr. Kennedy didn't need polls to know how warmly his fellow Catholics embraced McCarthy, and not just in Massachusetts. When constituents wrote asking where he stood on the 1953 Senate report blasting McCarthy for his dirty tricks against Maryland's Millard Tydings, Kennedy offered this coy response: "I assure you that I am giving attention to this situation, and I am hopeful that the outcome will be the one most desirable for the good of the Senate and the country." Likewise in JFK's 1960 run for president, his campaign listed ten occasions when he bucked McCarthy; in truth, few of the ten made a real difference, and none was the public break that might have earned Kennedy a spot in his own best-selling book *Profiles in Courage.* JFK biographer James MacGregor Burns explained that McCarthy was "the other type of Irishman that Kennedy tried so hard to disassociate himself with. But I don't think Kennedy was ever terribly upset by McCarthy as a moral issue . . . To a great extent Kennedy missed the moral issue of McCarthy."

There were a handful of senators who did get it, and who managed to survive electorally despite standing up to McCarthy, including George Aiken, Hubert Humphrey, Wayne Morse, Mike Mansfield, and Margaret Chase Smith. Most Republicans, however, were intimidated about speaking out against one of their party's most successful and vengeful campaigners. Most Democrats joined LBJ in rationalizing that their GOP colleagues should move

---

* McCarthy and Johnson both grew up in rural America, both liked making metaphorical references to varmints, and both were renowned tellers of tall tales.

first. A rare and noble exception was Herbert Lehman of New York, the Democrat who beat John Foster Dulles for his Senate seat, defied the Mississippi McCarthy as well as the real one from Wisconsin, and wasn't cowed by the fact that his state had nearly as many Catholics as JFK's Massachusetts. Lehman defended General Marshall and the China Hands, along with the First and Fifth Amendments. He attacked McCarthy on the Senate floor, on TV, and in newspapers and magazines. He spoke out early and never stopped even though few paid attention and McCarthy himself just laughed. "You couldn't insult him," Lehman said afterward. "I would assail him in the most scathing terms, and after the debate he would come up grinning, throw his arm around my shoulder, and inquire, 'How are you, Herb?' He seemed to have no sense of the fact that principles of right or wrong were involved."

Even for those who recognized the gravity of the situation, resisting McCarthy could be backbreakingly difficult. The exemplars within the Eisenhower administration were two men, both of whose brothers knew better but chose appeasement. John Foster Dulles's sibling Allen ran the Central Intelligence Agency, which McCarthy believed to be a security sieve and a publicity windfall. Joe had been fed documents by a triad of sources, all with transparent self-interests — Hoover's FBI, which from the start saw the CIA as a rival; an even more rivalrous anti-espionage apparatus called The Pond;* and a collection of CIA agents who'd been fired and were eager to fire back. Double agents had infiltrated the agency, the leakers said. Grants were being dispensed to pro-Communist groups, old China Hands had been hired, and, in Roy Cohn's words, "the quality of the information we were receiving was so poor that at times the CIA found out what was happening only when it read the newspapers."

The senator was especially interested in hearing from William

---

* The Pond was a super-secret federal agency founded in 1942 as part of the War Department and intended as a counterweight to the wartime Office of Strategic Services; it later became a private firm surreptitiously funded by the government and a thorn in the side of the OSS's successor, the CIA. The Pond leaked security material to McCarthy and tried to use his hatred of the CIA to build support for itself. Stout, "The Pond: Running Agents for State, War, and the CIA," https://www.cia.gov.

Bundy, a senior CIA official and the brother of McGeorge Bundy, Harvard's dean of arts and sciences. McCarthy knew that William Bundy had contributed $400 to the defense of Alger Hiss. (Before he took his CIA job, William explained to Allen Dulles that Hiss was the brother of a partner in William's firm, and the money was aimed at ensuring Alger got a fair trial.) McCarthy also charged that William Bundy had been active in a Communist front organization. (The only marginally questionable group was a public workers' union where Bundy had attended a single meeting before resigning.) Explanations notwithstanding, McCarthy thought Bundy could be his Alger Hiss — a Commie-sympathizing liberal Democrat with a brother who helped run evil Harvard,* a father who'd worked in the Roosevelt administration, and, as a bonus, a father-in-law whom McCarthy joyfully referred to as "Red" Dean Acheson. Joe handed his dozen allegations against the agency and Bundy over to Jim Juliana, his newly hired ex-FBI agent and the most competent investigator on the subcommittee staff.

Rather than backpedaling the way his brother John Foster did when McCarthy went after the State Department, Allen Dulles counterpunched. He told a meeting of six hundred CIA officials that he'd protect any of them singled out by McCarthy. No CIA officer would be allowed to testify before McCarthy's subcommittee, Allen said, and he'd fire anyone who approached McCarthy without CIA permission. His ultimate defiance was ordering Bundy to "get out of town" rather than answer McCarthy's subpoena, which the equally defiant Bundy did, vanishing with his father to a golf course outside Boston. The CIA director enlisted Vice President Nixon to rally other subcommittee Republicans into forcing their chairman to back off his probe, with Dulles agreeing in return to

* William Bundy's brother McGeorge had, in fact, helped rid the Harvard faculty of Communists and fellow travelers, including a sociology graduate student named Robert Bellah who admitted to having been a member of the Communist Party as an undergrad. McGeorge Bundy pushed Bellah not just to name names to the FBI, but to get psychiatric counseling. "What all this amounts to is a record not of Harvard's being a bulwark against McCarthyism, but of abject cowardice," Bellah, who went on to teach at Berkeley, said looking back. "Not all great American universities were so cowardly." Bellah, "McCarthyism at Harvard," *New York Review of Books*.

handle McCarthy's concerns internally and to tighten his security checks. In the end, reviews launched by the White House, the CIA, and others came up empty. So did Juliana's investigation, which lasted six months and involved nearly twenty interviews. "I recommended against going any further with the investigation," the McCarthy sleuth confided decades later. "[I suggested we] look at the budget and what they were doing with their money, rather than what they were doing operationally. And it just died. It just went away, the investigation went away."

The CIA's own secretive analysis of the face-off with McCarthy, while self-congratulatory, was on the mark: "As [a] result of Allen Dulles's fair and stout resistance to McCarthyism, morale in CIA remained very high . . . Dulles's stand vs. McCarthy won new respect for the CIA and contributed significantly to its reputation as a liberal institution . . . McCarthy [soon] backed off . . . virtually the only govt agency that had successfully resisted the attacks of the Wisc. senator."

Backing inside the Beltway wasn't enough for Joe. Washington energized his rants and tolerated his rages, but without popular support, he knew the politicians would stop appeasing and the money wouldn't matter. "For all the talk about McCarthy being a political lone wolf, he was never really alone and couldn't have achieved his peculiar success alone," said the cartoonist Herblock. "What sustained him was not so much his gullible followers and fellow-traveling demagogues as the tacit support of 'respectable' people who found it advantageous to go along with him, or at least to look the other way. They were the ones who kept him going."

Joe's list of respectable supporters started with his coreligionists. The Catholic Church in the early 1950s was ardently anti-Communist and explicitly pro–Joe McCarthy. That ardor sprang not just from political conservatism but from an eagerness to overcome anti-Catholic bias by showing that, rather than harboring a fealty to Rome and the papacy, American Catholics were true-blue patriots. An imposing 58 percent of them also were favorably inclined toward the senator, a January 1954 Gallup poll found, compared to 23 percent unfavorable and 19 percent who had no opinion. Leila Mae Edwards, wife of journalist Willard, found the same thing when she volunteered at the McCarthy office, watching as mass cards, rosaries, and crucifixes fell out of the mail.* The fact that Joe was devoted to his faith made it easy to equate Catholicism with patriotism with anticommunism with pro-McCarthyism.

A closer look at the Gallup and other surveys, however, reveals that the line wasn't quite that straight. While most Catholics were McCarthy boosters, so were most Americans; Catholics were just 8 to 10 percentage points more supportive than the rest of the population. Correspondingly, in his 1952 reelection campaign, Joe got only marginally more backing from Wisconsin Catholics than did the rest of the slate of Republicans. Nationally, his Catholic patronage was strongest among the working class, the upper crust, Republicans, Bostonians, and Irish Catholics. And while the most commanding and representative Catholic voice was the pro-McCarthy Cardinal Francis Joseph Spellman of New York, known as the American pope, liberal Catholics produced offsetting roars from the Association of Catholic Trade Unionists, the journal *Commonweal,* and, most convincingly, Bishop Bernard Sheil of Chicago. Condemning anticommunism that "feeds on the meat of suspicion and grows great on the dissension among Americans which it cynically creates and keeps alive by a mad pursuit of headlines," Sheil lashed out at the "city slicker from Appleton" who was taking us in "like country rubes."†

Old Joe Kennedy was outraged when fellow Catholics criticized McCarthy, even indirectly, which is what Monsignor John A. O'Brien of Notre Dame did alongside two other leaders of the National Conference of Christians and Jews. Kennedy complained to his friend Father John Cavanaugh, the former president of the university, "I don't think it does Notre Dame any good to have Father O'Brien signing petitions for the Christians and Jews with Notre Dame behind his name . . . I always thought that organi-

---

* What also poured in, on occasion, were razor blades. Reeves interview with Madelaine Grotnes Cocke, November 16, 1976.

† Knowing the bishop would sow confusion by mispronouncing the senator's name "McCarty," his speechwriter found other ways of referring to the senator, from citing his hometown to calling him "the junior senator from Wisconsin." Crosby, *God, Church, and Flag,* 164.

zation was completely dominated by the Jews and they just use Catholic names for the impression it makes throughout the country." Bobby Kennedy likely disagreed with his father on that anti-Jewish swipe, but he did embrace political philosopher Peter Viereck's observation that "anti-Catholicism is the anti-Semitism of the intellectuals," and he joked that the ideal headline in the Jewish-led *New York Times* would be "MORE NUNS LEAVE CHURCH."

If the Kennedys saw a conspiracy among critics of the church, an FBI source reported a plot in which "a group of Catholics in the United States led by Cardinal Spellman is at odds with the Vatican regarding various foreign issues. [The source] referred to the Cardinal's followers as a 'conspiracy' working to undermine the Eisenhower administration and to eventually bring about the election of Senator Joseph McCarthy as President. [He] claimed that McCarthy is receiving the support of many wealthy Catholics, including prominent individuals such as ex-Ambassador Joseph P. Kennedy . . . [He] stated that he was not anti-Catholic and he claimed that he has many friends who are ardent members of that church." No surprise, perhaps, that a master of conspiracy like Joe McCarthy spawned so many conspiracy rumbles.

The senator also widened the fault lines between Protestants and Catholics. Protestants presumed that Catholics supported the senator merely because he was Catholic; Catholics proposed an equally simplistic take on his Protestant detractors. The truth is that at his peak, McCarthy had the support of an impressive 49 percent of Protestants, which was just 1 point below his national rating. Jewish Americans were the one religious group that consistently and overwhelmingly rejected him, with 15 percent viewing him favorably and 71 percent unfavorably. To his credit, Joe himself never actively tried to make political hay of his Catholicism.

There was more unanimity and exuberance among the friends he kept from the political right. The anti-Communist, anti-government, anti-internationalist John Birch Society wasn't launched until a year after McCarthy's death, but Birch founder and candy mogul Robert Welch was a fan, appearing and even speaking at McCarthy rallies and applauding the senator's efforts. Joe was there alongside Russell Maguire, maker of the Thompson submachine gun, when Maguire shifted his newly purchased *American*

Mercury magazine from the mainstream to the right and into anti-Semitism. The Marquette files show that Joe even coined a pitch for the journal: "From now on the *AMERICAN MERCURY* magazine will be crusading in behalf of Americanism and sound government. I urge you and your friends to subscribe." And while Jews as a group were wary of the senator, Rabbi Benjamin Schultz never was, with Joe counting among his most trusted backers this clergyman who headed the American Jewish League Against Communism and who led a controversial push to purge Communists and fellow travelers from the government, schools, churches, and synagogues.

Others from the far right offered backing in public or behind the scenes. None did more of both than China Lobby leader and millionaire silk merchant Alfred Kohlberg, who extolled McCarthyism as "exposing disloyalty, dishonesty, and actual treason in government, and demanding that something be done about it, now, before it's too late." While journalists assumed that the quirky archconservative was one of Joe's big benefactors, Kohlberg insisted, "The amount I've contributed to him is exactly zero from beginning to end." McCarthy staffer Ed Nellor remembered differently, saying Kohlberg gave piles of money, including for elaborate Christmas parties. There was no disputing his influence, however, as he helped place the senator front and center in the debate over who lost China to the Reds (and how we could get it back). The Marquette files are filled with letters from Kohlberg offering advice on everything from exposing Owen Lattimore as a Communist to publishing a booklet of the senator's speeches.

The list of McCarthy supporters in the senator's files is illuminating, from Hollywood figures like Walt Disney, Lionel Barrymore, Hedda Hopper, and Ginger Rogers to influential lawyer and future Watergate judge John Sirica, who gave money along with moral support. James Earl Ray, who would later assassinate Martin Luther King Jr., was an ardent McCarthy booster. So were anti-abortion activist Phyllis Schlafly, anti-tax crusader Howard Jarvis, and conservative bellwether William F. Buckley Jr., all of whom began their public lives as outliers and ended in the mainstream. "The McCarthy backers of those days," says ex-congressman Toby Roth, who from 1979 to 1997 represented the Wisconsin district where Joe was born, "were the deplorables of our time." The senator himself offered clues to his personal and political passions through the organizations he joined, including the Knights of Columbus, American Legion, Navy Club, Veterans of Foreign Wars, Marquette University Alumni Association, Appleton Lodge BPO Elks, Military Order of the World Wars, Wisconsin Bar Association, and Delta Theta Phi law fraternity.

Hidden among his rightist enthusiasts were a surprising number of liberal groups, some of which offered reluctant support while others unabashedly abandoned their progressive principles. Americans for Democratic Action, the Congress of Industrial Organizations, and other reform-minded associations stood up to McCarthy mainly at the margins, writing reports, sponsoring debates, and proclaiming their opposition even as they failed to condemn his central assumption: that Communists should be purged from positions of responsibility and their freedoms limited. Many aging New Dealers felt vulnerable because of their own flirtations with communism during World War II, when it was easier to view the Soviet experiment with rose-colored glasses and when FDR's vice president, Henry Wallace, was widely viewed as a fellow traveler. Now they were circling the wagons, denying their earlier associations and, in too many cases, refusing to point fingers at McCarthy for fear he'd point back at them. "The liberal failure to defend these [civil] liberties was, given the great fears and pressures of the Cold War, explainable and even understandable," said Cold War historian Mary Sperling McAuliffe, but it "marked a loss not only for the American left, but for the nation as a whole."*

Nowhere was that failure of nerve more pronounced and the appeasement of the nation's hysteria more regrettable than within America's premier free-speech organization, the American Civil Liberties Union. During the McCarthy era, it underwent its own cold war, with McCarthy apologists doing battle with colleagues who wanted to stand foursquare against the rabble-rousing sena-

---

* There were notable exceptions to the liberal surrender. Much of organized labor and many religious leaders were firm in their opposition, as were most educators, if not their bosses. So were most of the biggest and best newspapers, along with powerful columnists like Walter Lippmann, the Alsop brothers, Marquis Childs, I. F. Stone, Mary McGrory, Murrey Marder, and Drew Pearson.

tor. The rifts meant that the group that calls itself liberty's law firm didn't defend Owen Lattimore and other McCarthy targets who sought its help. The Marquette papers include a 1953 letter to McCarthy from Irving Ferman, head of the ACLU's Washington office, railing not against the senator's smears but against the "dreadful results of the smear techniques which [have] been directed against the Senator, in his attempt to focus some of the basic issues." Ferman and others at the organization also were abetting the FBI in its Red hunts. "It was not the ACLU that existed during my tenure. It was a small, little-known, very marginal, very fragile, and tiny organization, without any of the clout it came to have in later years, or the reputation," says Ira Glasser, who helped make the group into a civil liberties powerhouse during his twenty-three years as executive director. "I always had the feeling that a lot of people at the ACLU with positions of leadership in those years felt vulnerable to what was going on during the McCarthy period."

In the final reckoning, Joe McCarthy's liberal backers and his conservative ones, along with the Texas millionaires and Presidents Truman and Eisenhower, are only partly to blame for this senator's rise and four-year reign. The enablers that mattered most of all in a democracy like America were the American people. Most who didn't adore him tolerated him, which was nearly as bad. "No demagogue is an island of mud unto himself," Herblock reminded us. "This one didn't exist without solid connections with the political mainland."

Just how those connections were forged, and where his support came from, has been debated and analyzed for three quarters of a century. Wisconsin, which bred and elected him, was no more right-wing than the rest of the nation then and may even have been less so. It never enacted the kinds of anti-subversive laws that other states had, nor did it establish special loyalty tests or publicly purge employees from the state payroll. Milwaukee, its largest city, had a Socialist mayor, and he won reelection in 1952 by a record margin even as Joe was being reelected. The same Wisconsin that gave birth to Joe McCarthy spawned Fighting Bob La Follette, Young Bob La Follette, and the Progressive Party.

McCarthy's most loyal backers there as elsewhere had less education, worked with their hands, and weren't members of unions.

Small-business owners and white-collar workers liked him too. Of course, Republicans supported him fervently, but the surprise was that Democrats were evenly split. More unexpected still was that, while Joe may have disparaged East Coasters, they were his strongest regional base. There were two wings of pro-McCarthy-ites. One was made up of conventional anti-Communists, who said his results justified his ruthlessness. The second group distrusted big institutions — government, labor, and business — as much as they hated Reds, radicals, and eggheads. To them, what mattered was Low Blow Joe's thumping for the powerless, the rougher and more relentless the better. Many of his critics, meanwhile, were less civil libertarians than snobs, recoiling from his lowbrow persona and from his Catholicism. His search for homegrown Communists resonated with the millions of Americans who were frustrated over our failure to win the war in Korea, were still angry over the United States' entry into World War II and embrace of the New Deal, and whose religion was evangelical while their wealth was newly acquired.

Add up those blocs and it is no surprise that, by January 1954, a full 50 percent of Americans felt good about the Wisconsin senator, compared to just 29 percent who were unfavorable and 21 percent with no opinion.* He was a shadow president, which didn't escape the notice of the actual president.† That is all the more remarkable since just two and a half years earlier, the same Gallup pollsters found that two out of three Americans couldn't say who

---

* A bit of bad tidings buried in the survey was that, while half of Americans liked Joe personally, just 38 percent approved of his methods, compared to 47 percent who disapproved and 15 percent with no opinion. The senator begged to differ, telling a reporter that 70 to 75 percent of their countrymen liked not just his aims but his methods, too. Fenton, *In Your Opinion*, 136; Gallup, "More Disapprove of Methods of McCarthy Than Approve," *Washington Post;* and "The Controversial Senator Contends His Tactics Are Both Practical and Fair."

† Asked whether he was tempted to make a White House bid, Joe said in 1953, "Those who have 'nominated' me for President were no friends of mine. They're the so-called liberals who are trying to make a split between McCarthy and Eisenhower ... I campaigned more for Dwight Eisenhower than perhaps any other Senator in this chamber did. I would campaign for him again ... However, when Dwight Eisenhower nominates a man I think is not suited for appointment, I will fight that nomination with all the power and strength I have." "The Controversial Senator Contends His Tactics Are Both Practical and Fair."

McCarthy was; as late as April 1953, 59 percent of respondents had no opinion of the Senate hothead. And the news in that 1954 poll got even better for the Wisconsinite: Americans picked him as their fourth-most-admired person on the planet.* Even at his lowest point in Gallup's surveys, only 51 percent of the US public viewed him unfavorably. "He never succeeded in selling more than half of Americans on his crusade," said Gallup managing editor John Fenton. "By the same token, he never completely alienated more than half by his actions. In this is the foundation of the controversy surrounding McCarthy."

Richard Rovere added intuition to the pollster's scientific take on McCarthy's support. "He built," said Rovere, "a coalition of the aggrieved — of men and women not deranged but deeply affronted by various tendencies over the preceding two or three decades: toward internationalism, and, in particular, toward closer ties with the British; toward classlessness; toward the welfare state . . . To these and many others he was a symbol of rebellion. And beyond all this, he simply persuaded a number of people that he was speaking the essential truth."

It wasn't the first time. Father Coughlin, Senator Bilbo, Governor Long, and other all-American zealots and populists had shown how many eager buyers there were for their snake oil. From Detroit to Jackson to New Orleans, long lines formed behind these Pied Pipers of unreality. Yet none of his demagogic forerunners managed to win the embrace of as wide a swath of the American public — or for as long — as Senator Joe McCarthy.

---

* The three ahead of him were President Eisenhower, ex-president Truman, and General Douglas MacArthur, with recently retired New York Yankees great Joe DiMaggio finishing fifth.

8

TOO BIG TO BULLY

IT WAS HIGH-ROLLER JOE'S GO-FOR-BROKE toss of the dice. In the fall of 1953, he put the US Army in his crosshairs. He'd picked the most stouthearted and sacrosanct institution in America to make his closing case that the government was infested with nests of Communist moles. For good measure, he was poking the war hero president in the eye — calling him a Johnny-come-lately to the home front Cold War, then slandering his faction of moderate Republicans as the party of "appeasement, retreat, and surrender." This scrappiest of lawmakers was going eyeball to eyeball with America's mighty fighting machine, and gambling that the other side would blink.

The question the country was asking was: Why would he? Many Americans readily accepted on Joe's say-so that there was a Soviet plot reaching deep into the soul of our defense forces, even though that meant admitting that they too had been duped. What would we do without Joe? Others were aghast. This was the Army, after all, which had just waged a lethal war on the Korean Peninsula against gun-toting Communists. What was the senator thinking? Half a century after the fact, records have been unlocked and memories unpacked that offer surprising answers.

His wartime diaries make clear that McCarthy had it in for the armed services going back to his World War II days as a tail gunner in the South Pacific. The military brass showed themselves to be "mental midgets," he wrote, in everything from their inter-service rivalries to the unfit-to-eat rations they fed grunts like him. That bitterness hardened when he charged (without proof) that American military investigators of the Malmedy Massacre were so hell-bent on getting confessions that they wedged burning matches under the fingernails of the accused. His self-ignited rage reached a flash point when he placed at the center of what he claimed was a vast Communist conspiracy a series of World War II generals venerated by the public, from George Marshall, orchestrator of the Allied victory, to Telford Taylor, head of American code breakers at England's Bletchley Park. The Army, Joe said, was infected, and only he was fearless enough to rip off the bandage.

McCarthy saw Ike as an equally logical target. Their 1952 campaign train showdown over Marshall erased any doubts that Eisenhower saw him as the enemy, and the loathing was mutual. Rather than scaring Joe away, the fact that the grandfatherly president was one of the few men on the planet whom Americans held in higher esteem than the Wisconsin senator made Joe even more eager to go after him. "McCarthy thought Eisenhower a lightweight," his corner man Roy Cohn explained years later. "He was contemptuous of what he saw as the President's weakness in allowing himself to be swayed and many of his policies dictated by the extreme liberals with whom he had surrounded himself. In fact, he was contemptuous of what he regarded as Eisenhower's weakness, *per se,* as a President." The skunk stalker from Grand Chute was laying a trap for Ike, unaware that the angler from Abilene was using the same Army fracas to bait Joe.

Fort Monmouth in New Jersey, McCarthy was sure, would be his grand prize. He'd already harvested the easiest pickings — the highbrowed Harvard men in Foggy Bottom, left-leaning propagandists at the Voice of America, and nosy typographers at the Government Printing Office. But he hadn't landed his own crème de la crème traitor like Julius Rosenberg or Klaus Fuchs. Until now. Fort Monmouth was the main research and training site for the Army Signal Corps, where 33,000 civilian workers helped manage the nerve center command and control operation for all the armed forces. The fort had everything Joe required: Jewish radicals schooled at the left-wing City College of New York, who made even better scapegoats than the State Department's Harvard-educated Yankees; the most tempting of targets for saboteurs bent on intercepting the military's most closely guarded secrets on tele-communications, radar, and guided missile controls, not just for the Army but for the Navy, Air Force, and Marines; and the very laboratory that had once employed über-spy Rosenberg. "'Cracking' the secrets of the Signal Corps probably would rate with any espionage ring close to having a seat at the meetings of the Joint Chiefs of Staff in their guarded Pentagon council room or attending a meeting of the National Security Council," the liberal *New York Times* warned. "It might rate even higher, because over the vast electronic network come and go 'action' messages, rather than policy statements, which directly control the nation's security, hour to hour." No wonder Joe was salivating.

The senator got his first whiff of problems in the Army and at the fort just before his wedding in September 1953. Six days of closed-door testimony revealed one worker there who admitted having gotten a Communist Party identification card, another who'd signed petitions supporting party candidates, and a third who McCarthy told reporters was "rabidly in favor of Stalin."* The headlines were screaming and Joe once again smelled blood. He demanded, and this time actually got, the scalps of the Army brass responsible. The chief of Army Intelligence and the chief of Legislative Liaison both were exiled to postings in Europe. Rather than sating Joe's appetite, such appeasement whetted it. The senator cut short his month-long honeymoon in the Bahamas when Roy Cohn called to report the latest startling developments: that the Army was suspending scientists, engineers, and technicians suspected of being security risks; that an East German defector had seen microfilm of secret documents from Monmouth; and that the fort's own commander, Major General Kirke Lawton, was reporting serious security issues. Just the stuff to rally the country.

---

* The presumed Stalin lover had been accused by his estranged wife, who said he also threatened to kill her brother. The implicated husband said he wasn't a Communist, never talked politics with his wife or anyone else, never perused leftist publications, and hadn't read the Communist nomination papers he'd signed, though he did think that the Fascists in his native Italy were okay and that the Nazis were too, because "they didn't do anything to me." After his testimony, the Army suspended him from his job as a guard at the Signal Corps. *Executive Sessions,* 2:1674–87.

Joe needn't have apologized to Jean for curtailing their honeymoon. She understood better than he did the potential in the hearings on the Army that he was promising to launch. She also saw more clearly the pitfalls. Unlike the Voice of America and the overseas libraries, his new foe was the soul of America's power structure, with both the muscle and the guts to resist his attack.

McCarthy's first challenge was the same inability to back up his charges that had plagued him at Wheeling and beyond. So he leaned on exaggeration. Signing election petitions and engaging in college-days social activism once again became the equivalent of being a card-carrying Communist Party member. Left-leaning communications clerks and dispatchers were upgraded to national security threats without convincing corroboration. "Extremely dangerous espionage" was under way at the fort, Joe warned the nation after racing home from the Bahamas, with the "strong possibility" that a Russian spy ring masterminded by Julius Rosenberg was still in place. It was true that the Army would suspend forty-two Monmouth engineers, with many stripped of their security clearances and banished to an area containing only unclassified material which everyone called the leper colony. But those actions were as much in response to McCarthy's threats as they were to solid evidence, as reflected by the facts that eleven of the forty-two were automatically reinstated when the Army failed to bring charges, twenty-three were recalled after hearings or appeals, six more were ordered back by a federal court, and even the two who were dismissed never were accused of serious breaches. "There's no espionage at Fort Monmouth," McCarthy's own espionage expert, Jim Juliana, said looking back. "Joe McCarthy should have never used that word." As for the East German, his "secret" documents were ones the United States had shared with its Russian allies during the war, and both the military and the House Un-American Activities Committee already had discounted the man's finger-pointing.* The senator did highlight real flaws in se-

---

* Juliana was the one dispatched by McCarthy to Europe to interview the defector and trace how the plans had been leaked to the Russians "by a communist at Fort Monmouth ... I mean this was the theory Cohn and McCarthy were promoting, but the facts didn't support it," Juliana revealed years later. "The facts did support that there were security risks, though. Had we stayed on that path

curity procedures at Fort Monmouth and at defense contractors like General Electric — from the casual way secret documents were sometimes handled to the loose vetting of many official promotions — but these legitimate issues were lost in the bellicosity of his inflation and invention. Also gone, yet again, was any adherence to his admonition that what was said behind closed doors should stay there, with the chairman holding press briefings after nearly every secretive session.

While he wasn't a doctor, Nobel laureate Norman Ramsey astutely diagnosed Joe's afflictions as inattention, hyperactivity, and impulsivity, which later generations would label political attention deficit disorder. The Harvard physicist attended a dinner party with the senator in Washington, and "when I told him about how his hearings at Fort Monmouth were interrupting the technical work there and causing the lab to lose good people, he admitted this, but added that his committee was doing lots of good and had exposed nine communist spies at Fort Monmouth," Ramsey recounted in an unpublished article. "Having just studied the facts, I would say that he had no proven spies but just six people who used the Fifth [Amendment] to avoid getting their friends into trouble. Surprisingly he would agree, but ten minutes later during another argument, he said again with apparent sincerity that his committee exposed ten communist spies at Ft. Monmouth. I reminded him that we had agreed there were only six and they were not proven spies. He agreed again, but later used the argument once more with a still different number."

An even bigger problem was that rather than steering the senator in ways that bolstered his effectiveness, the way Bobby Kennedy and Jim Juliana oftentimes did, his two front-and-center staffers during the Army probes — Roy Cohn and David Schine — reinforced the worst of McCarthy's tendencies. The inseparable duo also had their own agendas. Schine's was to avoid the Army altogether or, if he had to serve, to escape kitchen patrol, weekend duty, and other assignments that interfered with his social life.

---

there, had we developed a full set of facts on each one of these individuals and presented that, it would have been applauded." Juliana interview, June 10, 1998, JJP.

Cohn did the bidding of Dave, the friend he was infatuated with. Before long, the focus of the hearings shifted from McCarthy versus the Army to the Army versus Schine, Cohn, and McCarthy. Political wags called it the Battle of the Pentagon. Lillian Hellman contemptuously characterized it as the adventures of "Bonnie, Bonnie and Clyde."

The military at first fumbled its response. It mollified the senator more shamelessly than Secretary of State Dulles had and failed to point out that, given a decade of the Army and FBI probing the Signal Corps, it was the senator, not the White House, who was late to the party. But the Army eventually developed not just a backbone but an instinct for the jugular, partly because its commander in chief had finally taken charge and was crafting his own covert response. As he did, Joe's friends abandoned him, starting with J. Edgar Hoover. Lawton, the Monmouth commander, first was muzzled, then informed by doctors at Walter Reed Army Hospital that he had a dubious "circulatory ailment," and ultimately he was handed a "disability" discharge.* A similar misfortune befell Captain Benjamin Sheehan of Army Intelligence, author of one of the critical reviews of Fort Monmouth security that first drew Joe to the case, and Colonel O. J. Allen of the Signal Corps Intelligence Agency, who was investigating charges of lax security; both were reprimanded when they pushed their probes. The senator saw—too late—that while Eisenhower might indeed have behaved like a lightweight until now, the old warrior still packed a wallop when his hidden hand turned into a clenched fist. And that's what happened—finally—in the lead-up to the acclaimed Army-McCarthy hearings.

The press, which for years had played McCarthy's game of trial by headline, no longer accepted on faith that a locked brief-

---

* Before he was gagged, Lawton was a star witness for McCarthy and a big fan. The general told the senator at a closed hearing, "I have been working for the last twenty-one months trying to accomplish what is being accomplished [by you] in the last two weeks," making clear that it was pressure from Joe that had forced security upgrades. Yet when Roy Cohn pushed further, hoping Lawton would substantiate the senator's charge that there was a spy ring at the fort, the general answered, "No, sir." Was there ever one? Cohn asked. Lawton: "Not to my knowledge, no, sir." *Executive Sessions*, 3:2476–78.

case proved anything. "For over a month this vital Army Signal Corps Center has been the target of sensational accusations, implications and innuendos which portray it as a hotbed of communism and espionage," *Washington Post* reporter Murrey Marder wrote in a four-part series on McCarthy's allegations. "Nothing that can be independently ascertained from information available here or in Washington indicates that there is any known evidence to support such a conclusion." TV, meanwhile, finally showed its steel in the spring of 1954 by broadcasting nearly gavel to gavel the testimony that would unmask the grand inquisitor. Now the American public, watching from their own living rooms, could see close-up the methods of the Communist hunter they had so casually supported.

The Joe McCarthy who appeared on television screens was a menacing figure with perpetual facial stubble, a perspiration-soaked suit, and the swagger of the town rowdy. Gone was any sign of the political sorcerer who'd enchanted farm kids with his Indian wrestling and lollipops and had lit up ballrooms full of coal diggers and prayer sisters. Now, with the country bearing witness, the senator from Wisconsin ignored not just parliamentary rules but common civility—interrupting decorated Army officers mid-testimony, barreling out of the hearing room when he didn't get his way, and growling his catchphrase "point of order" so often that street urchins were mimicking him. An astounding one in two Americans was following all this on TV or radio, or in the daily papers. They could watch McCarthy's crudeness, rudeness, and cheap showmanship in action. They could see him reading when he got bored with the proceedings. This was no hero. "A decade before Marshall McLuhan coined the terms," said film historian Thomas Doherty, "the Army-McCarthy hearings showed how a hot personality melted under the glare of television while a cool one never broke a sweat."

Another way to measure Joe's seesawing fortunes was by tracking the Gallup polls. They had him at 50 percent popularity before the Army-McCarthy hearings began in April 1954, suggesting that fully half of America believed the scandalous things he was saying about the armed forces. By the time the inquiry was wrapping up in June, that believability yardstick had sunk to 34 percent, with the steepest drop among those who had supported him mainly because of his anticommunism. Suddenly, America's infatuation with the crusading senator was over, or nearly so. In retrospect, that fall from favor seems inevitable given his bad behavior and his arrogance in calling out the ultimate authority. But at the time his war with the Pentagon riveted the nation, and when the proceedings began, who would win was far from clear.

History has told us the instant when Joe conclusively lost his grip and his public was when he bushwhacked a young lawyer during the televised hearings and a shrewd barrister from Boston famously shot back, "Have you no sense of decency, sir?" But the turning point actually came a full four months earlier, when Joe was still chairing the panel rather than being probed by it, and he savaged an esteemed brigadier general and fellow Wisconsinite named Ralph Zwicker. The commander of Camp Kilmer was, like Lawton at nearby Fort Monmouth, a McCarthy ally who'd quietly slipped the senator damning evidence against his own command. Yet Zwicker knew better than Lawton how to placate his bosses and advance his career. At a closed-door session on February 18, McCarthy pressed Zwicker on how he felt about aggressively rooting out Reds from the Army, and specifically whether a general who failed to do that should himself be removed. The shrewd Kilmer commandant hedged. Zwicker: "Do you mean how I feel toward Communists?" McCarthy: "I mean exactly what I asked you, general, nothing else. And anyone with the brains of a five-year-old child can understand that question. The reporter will read it to you as often as you need to hear it so that you can answer it, and then you will answer it." Listening to the question again, Zwicker replied, "I do not think he should be removed from the military."

That was too much for the chairman. "Then, general, you should be removed from any command," McCarthy barked in his soon-to-be-famous nasal tone. "Any man who has been given the honor of being promoted to general and who says, 'I will protect another general who protected Communists,' is not fit to wear that uniform, general. I think it is a tremendous disgrace to the Army to have this sort of thing given to the public. I intend to give it to them. I have a duty to do that. I intend to repeat to the press exactly what you said. So you know that. You will be back here, general."

McCarthy's assault on Zwicker was, as fellow subcommittee member Charles Potter would say, "barbaric" and "obscene," impugning the patriotism of a hero of D-day and recipient of the Bronze Star with two oak leaf clusters, Silver Star, Legion of Merit, British Distinguished Service Order, and Croix de Guerre. Yet while Joe knew he'd gone too far — "I guess I treated Zwicker pretty rough," he told friends that night — he had excuses that few knew about at the time. His staff had interviewed Zwicker in private and become aware of the stories he could tell — and, he said, would tell — not just about the Army's generalized coddling of Communists but in dramatic particular about Irving Peress, a dentist at Camp Kilmer who'd recently been promoted to major despite suggestions of split loyalties. That, however, was before the military brass and the White House stepped in. "[If] Zwicker told the committee what he told me," said Juliana, "McCarthy's case was made." Jean agreed, concluding that the general had been ordered to shut up, and that was why Joe exploded at him. And there was more. The night before the showdown, Joe and Jean's taxi was rammed by a drunk driver in Manhattan. Her ankle was broken; he was up all night nursing her and his own bruised head and possible concussion. The next morning, Joe presided over a public hearing, raced to the hospital to visit Jeannie, had a quick and amiable sit-down with Zwicker, then was told by a spectator who'd sat behind the two-faced general at the morning session that he'd called the senator, among other things, an "SOB." By the time he gaveled the executive session to order that afternoon, Joe was famished and fortified only by his afternoon shot of bourbon. The lump on his head still ached, and he was in a mood in which, as Juliana recounted, he "wasn't going to take any poop from anybody."*

---

* While Joe and others were trying to explain his behavior, Roy Cohn refused to retrench: "Of course, [McCarthy] was right about Zwicker, just as he was right about the underlying principle . . . Zwicker brought the case to Joe. Now Zwicker had instantly turned into an ass-covering bureaucrat. Somebody, therefore, had reached Zwicker, had scared the hell out of him. What made this unacceptable to Joe — who otherwise would not have been slightly surprised — was that he couldn't blow the whistle on Zwicker. Because Joe's underground was sacred to

But all that the public saw when the Zwicker testimony was unveiled four days later was a senator who looked like a monster. "You think it is proper," McCarthy pressed the general, "to give an honorable discharge to a man known to be a Communist?" Juliana was heartbroken but not surprised. "It took 45 minutes to learn nothing new about the Major Peress case, to humiliate a war hero, to fuel political disaster and to destroy the honest commitment of Senator McCarthy to rid the United States Federal Government of Communist subversion," said McCarthy's aide and friend. "This day, one that I hope[d] fully would confirm the high expectations of many and help to correct the shortcomings in the military establishments, started the total decline of what had been a credible mission."

Outbursts like McCarthy's attack on Zwicker weren't an anomaly, and the brigadier general wasn't the only military heavyweight Joe targeted during five long months of hidden hearings that fall and winter. Now that the transcripts are public, we can see the lengths he went to, the holes into which he was digging himself, and how he arrived at that critically ruinous moment with General Zwicker.

It was a two-and-a-quarter-page FBI letter that sparked Joe's interest in the expansive Army complex in sparsely populated Monmouth County, New Jersey. In the spring of 1953, an Army intelligence officer called the subcommittee office, cloak-and-dagger style, from a pay phone, and at a secret meeting he handed the senator the letter. For the McCarthy cause, this document seemed

---

him, he had never given anybody up who provided him with information about the Communist menace, or perfidy in government, or anything else." *Autobiography of Roy Cohn*, 108.

McCarthy's boosters couldn't take back his words, but they sought to ensure that nobody would learn about them, said Army lawyer John Adams: "They tried to suppress all stenographic transcripts and 'strike from the record,' any recorded proof of the Zwicker incident." Joe didn't realize soon enough the error of his words, Adams added, and his backers didn't act fast enough, so the record was preserved. Adams, *Without Precedent*, 129.

In fairness to Zwicker, one reason he had clammed up was that his boss, the president, commanded him to. Eisenhower's executive order was aimed at protecting the privacy of security board members in the Army and elsewhere in government. Email to author from Don Ritchie.

like manna from heaven. Written by J. Edgar Hoover to Alexander Bolling, chief of Army Intelligence, it listed thirty-four scientists, engineers, and technicians who worked on radar or signals systems at Fort Monmouth and who the bureau suspected had Communist ties. McCarthy had always been mistrustful of the Army, but his evidence of wrongdoing was scattershot; here, in a letter from America's most trusted spy catcher, were the names — the actual names, his specialty! With luck, this would be the smoking gun he'd been hankering for.

The letter also was a forgery. The actual FBI document, written two and a half years earlier, ran to fifteen pages, and the juiciest parts had been condensed into the version McCarthy received. The missive was based on anonymous rumors gathered by FBI field agents, abridged to seem more like actual proof. It was signed by Hoover, but Hoover told his boss, Attorney General Herbert Brownell Jr., that he hadn't written it. Despite those attempts to make it seem as authentic and damning as possible, the memo acknowledged that with fifteen of the thirty-five men listed, there was "no derogatory" information; for the rest, the letter said further investigation was needed and asked for Bolling's help. In the time since the real FBI report was written, the Army had in fact checked out the allegations of espionage and failed to substantiate any. The abbreviated version, marked "PERSONAL AND CONFIDENTIAL," was headlined "Aaron Hyman Coleman, Espionage (R)" — Coleman was one of the Monmouth Thirty-Four, and "R" stood for Russia — but the missive became famous as the Purloined Letter.*

---

* There has been ongoing debate over who wrote the Purloined Letter. Some said it came from the FBI, and perhaps Hoover himself, which he denied and was unlikely given the phony version. Joe refused to say, insisting he'd never give up a source. Roy Cohn later identified the source only as an Army intelligence officer, although he probably was an intermediary if he existed at all. Historian Chris Lovett says it was Robert Stillmore, a low-level intelligence officer alarmed by what he saw as Soviet subversion not just in the Army but in the CIA, and who later took his concerns to Ike. Cohn, *McCarthy*, 168; Lovett, "On the Side of the Angels and the Fall of Joe McCarthy," *Emporia State Research Studies;* and emails to author from Lovett.

Cohn pointed out that the letter wasn't purloined, at least not by him, Joe, or anyone on the subcommittee staff. Cohn, *McCarthy*, 168.

Joe didn't have the original to compare it to, and didn't know at first that it had been abridged. That almost certainly wouldn't have mattered since it was precisely the kind of distortion he'd mastered after Wheeling—turning rumors into facts, pinkos into Reds, and possible security risks into proven traitors. Once again, he had flesh-and-blood witnesses to point fingers at, in the top-secret labs where Julius Rosenberg had worked and plotted. More information on the fort filtered in that summer, and on August 31, McCarthy held the first of a slow-paced series of hearings that continued until he and Jean left for the Bahamas. While he was gone, however, Cohn got wind that the Army was about to crack down, and on October 7, McCarthy pal Willard Edwards published a page-one story in the *Chicago Tribune* that kicked off with this blockbuster: "Two of the nation's top scientists, engaged in the development of America's radar secrets against enemy attack, have been suspended by the Army as security risks . . . Conditions already discovered have caused investigators to state that eventual revelations may approach those of the atomic spy case involving Julius and Ethel Rosenberg, who paid the death penalty for feeding secrets to Russia." While the first sentence was both new and largely true, the second was classic McCarthy-style hype. The story ended with the line "Sen. McCarthy, at present on a brief honeymoon in Nassau, has been kept in touch with the investigation and may cut short his vacation to return to handle the inquiry."

He did just that. Two nights later, McCarthy met Cohn in Florida to be briefed on the latest developments. Joe's view of the problems at the fort and beyond would eventually lead him to declare war on the military, but peace reigned in those early days. Army Secretary Robert Stevens rescinded an order that prohibited Monmouth employees from talking to McCarthy staff and pledged, in Edwards's words, "complete cooperation." And what few knew then was that even before those developments—the Monmouth security purges, the Edwards article, or Joe's abbreviated honeymoon—Stevens had sent the senator a telegram signaling how far he'd go in giving his backing: "SPENDING FEW DAYS VISITING IN MONTANA INCLUDING LUNCHEON WITH GOVERNOR ARONSON THURSDAY IN HELENA. HAVE JUST READ ARTICLE FRIDAYS GREAT FALLS TRIBUNE INDICATING YOU ARE DISSAT-

ISFIED WITH SOME ACTION BY FIRST ARMY HEADQUARTERS.
AM RETURNING WASHINGTON TUESDAY MORNING AND WILL
CALL YOUR OFFICE TO OFFER MY SERVICES IN TRYING TO AS-
SIST YOU TO CORRECT ANYTHING THAT MAY BE WRONG. WILL
GREATLY APPRECIATE OPPORTUNITY OF DISCUSSING MATTER
WITH YOU. YOU MAY BE SURE I WILL OPPOSE COMMUNIST
INFILTRATION OF ARMY TO LIMIT OF MY ABILITY. BEST RE-
GARDS."

John Adams, the Army and Stevens's top lawyer, tried years
later to put into context his boss's ready compliance: "It may seem
peculiar that the secretary of the army offered his services to help
a senator administer the secretary's own department. But the senator was Joe McCarthy and the year was 1953. It was not at all
unusual for Cabinet heads to stop and ask, 'What will McCarthy
do?'" Stevens's background left him particularly ill-suited to resist
such pressures. From the age of twenty-nine, when his textile titan
father died, he'd been running the giant J. P. Stevens & Company. A
rock-ribbed Yankee Republican, he spoke deliberately, was slow to
anger, and was as anti-union and anti-Communist as he was pro-
military and pro-Eisenhower. While he romanticized cowboys and
soldiers, he wasn't known for his grit. His attitude toward McCarthy, whose wedding he attended, was, from the first, one of trying
to go along and get along.

Back from his honeymoon, McCarthy turned his attention to
Coleman, the headlined figure in the FBI letter and the centerpiece of the new subcommittee hearings in the fall of 1953. The
Monmouth scientist had played a central role in designing postwar
radar defenses and would later become a laboratory section chief.
What mattered now was that in 1946, military intelligence had
discovered that Coleman had taken home forty-eight documents,
some of which were marked classified and all of which, while authorized for Coleman to take, had been handled so carelessly that
the Army reprimanded him and suspended him for ten days. Joe
was convinced that wasn't nearly enough and had a series of questions for Coleman and his bosses. Did a roommate the scientist
suspected was a Communist have access to the documents? Just
how well did Coleman know Julius Rosenberg, with whom he
had once attended a Young Communist League meeting? Would

the files, which laid out US work on sensitive radar installations, have benefited the Russians? Why hadn't Coleman locked up the documents at home when he wasn't using them, instead of leaving them lying around where, as the senator put it, they could be filched by "any one with a key to the apartment?" Why had he denied so many of these matters that he would admit to later?

The questions were legitimate, but Joe refused to accept the answers offered by Coleman and the Army. Yes, the scientist said, he attended a Communist League meeting with Rosenberg once, when the two were in college, and he dropped any contact with the League as soon as he "realized that the Communists were dominated by Moscow." He also knew Rosenberg's co-conspirator Morton Sobell in college, but hadn't known he was a Communist, had only casual contact with him afterward, and didn't know why Sobell had listed him as a job reference. There were only forty-three documents, not forty-eight, and only two still were classified. As for taking home the files, "I had just returned from the Marine Corps, and I had been away for two years, and I had been assigned an important project. I found that I was far behind in the state of the art. There were many things about which I did not know. I felt that in order to do a conscientious job, I had to catch up with what had happened in those two years," Coleman told the senator in a closed-door hearing. "So I did two things: I went to school towards trying to get my masters degree and I also worked at home trying to catch up. That was the only way I could see how to fulfill my responsibilities."

The Army had been checking out those and other concerns before Joe got involved, and as of January 1952, it had transferred Coleman to a job that involved writing nonclassified radar correspondence courses. To Joe, that wasn't enough. Coleman, he said, stole secret records (he eventually backed down from the word "stole"), violated the Espionage Act (removing documents was enough, Joe said, even without the proof he sought that Coleman had turned over the documents to an enemy agent), perjured himself (by, among other things, alleging he'd never belonged to the League), and "may have been the direct link between the laboratories and the Rosenberg spy ring" (Joe's speculation). "I may say," McCarthy added, "that I think you have given this committee about the same type of cooperation which Rosenberg gave the court in New York. I think you are evasive, lying, and doing everything you can to cover up a deliberate case on your part." Faced with that barrage from the powerful chairman, the Army buckled, ruling that Coleman was after all a security risk, and removing him from his job.

In the end Coleman, like most of Joe's targets, was vindicated. After he spent fourteen months looking for work in the private sector, and started over as a $75-a-week engineer, a court ordered the Army to reinstate the radar expert, although he opted to remain in private industry. When he finally did return to Fort Monmouth in 1973, it was to the same job, with the same "secret" clearance, issued by the same official who'd run the security program during the McCarthy investigation twenty years before.

Another of Joe's earliest and habitual marks was Carl Greenblum, an electrical engineer identified in the Purloined Letter but whom Joe didn't name after his first executive session appearance in October. He did say the witness was an "important" employee who'd originally stonewalled, but under "vigorous" cross-examination "broke down and began to cry," then admitted "he was lying the first time and now wants to tell the truth." That truth, McCarthy added, included having been "a close, personal friend of [Julius] Rosenberg. They shared an apartment at one time." The witness was so terrified "of the spy ring which is operating within Government agencies, including the Signal Corps," the senator said, that he would be placed in protective custody. After he testified again the following month, Greenblum offered reporters a decidedly different version of his earlier appearance. He had never lied, he said. He broke down because his mother had died two days earlier, he was sitting shiva,* and he'd been unprepared for McCarthy's battering. His fear, Greenblum's German-born wife added, was a natural response to having been persecuted by neighbors in the wake of McCarthy's headlines. A note pinned to his front door read, "Get out of town, you Nazis." A hammer and sickle had been

---

* Shiva is Judaism's weeklong period of mourning the loss of a family member, and traditionally involves staying at home, where relatives and friends visit to offer comfort.

painted on the back of their house. And their three-year-old son David was called a "pie" (the boy couldn't pronounce "spy") by a friend who explained "he couldn't play with him because David had a bad daddy."

What about McCarthy's most damning evidence against Greenblum—that he was Rosenberg's friend and possibly a fellow traitor? Greenblum made clear from his first appearance that it wasn't true. Rosenberg, he told the subcommittee, "was somebody who I just did not like the looks of. I hadn't liked his looks in school, and I had never had anything to do with him." As for Joe's charges that he had shared a house and a carpool with the spy, later closed-door testimony suggested that Greenblum was telling the truth. He had replaced Rosenberg in an apartment shared by Signal Corps scientists, and they apparently never overlapped in the carpool either. Fired from his Monmouth job, Greenblum sued; as with Coleman, he eventually got his job back thanks to a federal court.*

Army attorney Adams was taking in all the testimony, as the only non-staffer allowed into nearly all of the subcommittee's executive sessions on Fort Monmouth, and he was aghast at the chasm between what Joe was telling the press and what Adams was observing in the hearing room.† McCarthy intimidated the bereaved Greenblum, towering over him with his "burly" shoulders, then warning "in a thundering voice of accusation" that the engineer "was on his way to jail for perjury, maybe even for con-

---

* Nathan Sussman, another of McCarthy's 1953 witnesses in the Signal Corps probe, we now know actually was a member of the Rosenberg spy ring. But Sussman understood just how to play the probers, verifying that he'd known Rosenberg in college, naming names of others he knew to be Communists then, and generally giving the chairman what he wanted. "Amazingly, McCarthy and Cohn fell for his false claims and seeming cooperation," says spy historian Harvey Klehr. "They never asked him if he had spied!" Email to author from Klehr.

† The string of headlines growing out of the closed-door hearings included, from the *New York Times*, "M'Carthy: Certain Red Cell Is at GE," "'More Than 12' Out in Radar Spy Case," and "Top Red Agent Tied to Fort Monmouth." Other papers contributed these: "No Basis Found for Belief Monmouth Is Nest of Spies," "Army Radar Data Reported Missing," "Espionage in Signal Corps for 10 Years Is Charged," "Witness Cracks, Bares Spy Ring at Radar Center," and "McCarthy Hints of Spy Plot Hitting Whole Signal Corps." (Marder, "No Basis Found for Belief Monmouth Is Nest of Spies," *Washington Post*.)

spiracy against the U.S. government." But rather than Greenblum breaking down and needing help from a doctor and nurse, the way Joe told reporters, he "had only asked for a drink of water." As for the "protective custody" Joe supposedly offered the now cooperative witness, Adams said that "the only protective custody into which [Greenblum] had been placed was the New York subway system, which accepted his dime into the turnstile as he went to catch a train home to mourn his dead mother. I knew also that the only fear he had was of Joe McCarthy."

The Coleman and Greenblum hearings had several things in common beyond McCarthy's failure to prove the espionage he alleged. In both, the chairman went overboard. In each, as in nearly all the Monmouth sessions, he was the sole senator present. Neither of those witnesses was indicted, nor was anyone else Joe investigated in these hearings—for perjury, contempt, or anything else. There was one more thing that united Greenblum, Coleman, and the majority of McCarthy's other targets in the Army probes: they were Jewish. Forty-one of the forty-five civilians suspended at Fort Monmouth were Jews, or 95 percent, whereas just 25 percent of its overall civilian workforce was Jewish, according to the Anti-Defamation League of B'nai B'rith, which urged Secretary Stevens to do a full-fledged study of possible prejudice. The Army, in turn, tried to have it both ways, denying there was any bias even as it deflected blame onto civilian security personnel in case a problem was exposed later.

While McCarthy could claim he was merely following the Army's lead in picking his targets, several witnesses who appeared before him questioned whether the senator, too, was singling out Jews. Roy Cohn, a Jewish lawyer McCarthy hired partly in response to similar charges that had surfaced earlier in his career, answered defiantly for his boss in an exchange with Allen Lovenstein, another Jewish electrical engineer at the fort. Lovenstein: "There is an assumption that there is an anti-Semitic movement." Cohn: "Well, that is an outrageous assumption. I am a member and an officer of B'nai B'rith." Lovenstein: "I was under the same naive impression until I became aware of some facts." The Anti-Defamation League looked at those facts and traced the pattern of bias to one civilian security supervisor who it concluded "personally is an anti-Semite." Looking back, any anti-Jewish feeling at Fort Monmouth seems ironic, since it historically had hired Jewish engineers and scientists who weren't welcome at prestigious gentile-run enterprises in Manhattan and elsewhere. Another irony was that Cohen himself lamented, but never saw his own role in what he called the great anti-Semitic tradition of setting "a Jew . . . to catch a Jew."

Like so many people ordered to appear before McCarthy, the Monmouth witnesses were called to account for dumbfounding reasons. There was guilt by association with an uncle or aunt, a father-in-law, or, as in the case of suspended Bernard Lee, a sister-in-law who was a suspected Communist. ("I unfortunately cannot help it," Lee testified, "if my sister-in-law is Red. I am sorry about it.") There was guilt if you, or a friend, read *PM Magazine,* the *New York Post,* or *Consumer Reports.* (Lovenstein apologized for once having subscribed to the consumer magazine.) There was guilt by misidentification. (Private-sector workers were misidentified as working for the government, while the subcommittee and the Army mixed up Monmouth workers with the same surname often enough that Cohn joked, "Maybe they are suspending everybody with the name of Kaplan.") There was guilt by having belonged to the Young Pioneers of America when you were twelve years old and your mother signed you up. Worst of all was guilt by alma mater.* While Joe's favorite target had been Harvard, it now was the City College of New York. The school was tuition-free for students with grades good enough to win admission to its

---

* A Teamsters lawyer would keep a remarkably similar running list of ways that he said Bobby Kennedy used innuendo and affiliation to do in his clients when, as attorney general, RFK attacked the powerful truckers' union for alleged corruption: "We had guilt by association, guilt by marriage, guilt by eating in the same chophouse, guilt by the general counsel's amazement, guilt by somebody else taking the Fifth Amendment, guilt by somebody else refusing to testify. But we think the 'doozer' was the one that happened when the committee was taking testimony concerning a criminal case in which eight defendants were tried for eleven weeks; the jury was out only eight minutes and came in with a verdict of 'not guilty.' The police detective who helped prepare the case said the prosecution felt it was not a fair trial. The Committee nodded in sympathy and agreement. This is guilt by acquittal." Jacobs, "Extracurricular Activities of the McClellan Committee," *California Law Review.*

day programs, a benefit that appealed to successive waves of immigrants, including Jews. Having experienced their share of poverty and dislocation, CCNY students during the Depression and after were especially active in protesting Fascism, militarism, and limits on free speech, and especially receptive to solutions offered by the college Communists. And as Joe never tired of pointing out, it was on the CCNY campus that Julius Rosenberg became active in the Young Communist League and met at least one of his later conspirators. What he didn't point out was that the school also supported US soldiers during and after the war, and that the administration at various points tried to silence its activist faculty and students.

The Democrats, who had walked out of the subcommittee the previous summer, were back in January, enticed by the opportunity to hire their own minority counsel (they picked Bobby Kennedy) and McCarthy's promise to consult them more often regarding the way he ran the panel (an empty vow). None of the other subcommittee members, whether opposition Democrats or fellow Republicans, succeeded in restraining the chairman, or even tried. In most hearings, the only ones present other than Joe and the witness were subcommittee staffers. Roy Cohn did much of the questioning, assisted by David Schine, who, when Joe was away, enjoyed having Roy address him as "Mr. Chairman." It was like they were playing senator, with staffers for other senators sometimes joining in the charade. The real chairman's frequent guests enjoyed their peeks behind closed doors. Patricia Kennedy came with her beau and future husband, movie idol Peter Lawford, while thirteen girls from a nearby seminary were ushered into an executive session in Albany on alleged Communist infiltration of GE plants. Wisconsin governor Walter Kohler Jr. attended once with his wife after being invited to "see Joe handle a Commie." More than one witness brought his rabbi, for moral support. On occasion, Willard Edwards was let in to hearings from which the rest of the press was banished.*

The publication of these hidden hearing transcripts makes

---

* At one evening hearing in New York, Roy Cohn and David Schine brought two attractive female friends. "During a recess," John Adams recalled, "a photogra-

clear their eerie resemblance to the revenge by investigation and trial by hearing that were trademarks of Joseph Stalin's Russia, and against which Joseph McCarthy railed. Both Joes pressured witnesses to name names. Each repeated questions to the point of badgering. Targets in Washington, as in Moscow, were encouraged to repent of their past beliefs and split with impenitent family members. Jews in both settings were in the docket in disproportionate numbers. McCarthy never employed Stalin-like physical torture, but the senator had few qualms about what could only be seen as psychological torment. Victims in America had impartial courts to which they could appeal, with judges who always listened and often acted; and banishment at McCarthy's hands wasn't to Siberia, although targeted Monmouth employees found themselves working on a delicatessen truck, or as a TV repairman, or consigned to the base's colony of lepers. While some were fired from their government jobs, others resigned soon after they were subpoenaed. Workers who were suspended lost their salaries, had to dig into their own pockets to pay for lawyers, and often were charged without knowing their accusers or even the specifics of the accusations. Although he never would have accepted the Soviet comparison, Jim Juliana conceded years later that things had gotten out of control: "We moved too quickly on Peress at Fort Kilmer and General Zwicker and I was involved in that. We moved too quickly on Fort Monmouth . . . Those two cases alone, if they were handled properly by McCarthy, would have made his career."

When it came to Army brass, General Zwicker wasn't the only one or even the first to feel the chairman's wrath. Just before Zwicker testified, Joe had this to say to Lieutenant Colonel Chester T. Brown, assistant chief of staff at Camp Kilmer:

> This committee has a very difficult job, a job of digging up traitors. We have been finding some . . . with the complete wholehearted opposition of men like yourself, men who give no cooperation at all, men who like yourself are responsible for covering up the facts so that we can not find out who has been placing

pher from the Newark *News* managed to snap a picture of the girls, but Cohn ran him down and made him promise not to print the picture." *Without Precedent*, 60.

Communists in the army and keeping them there . . . I think, may I say this, that any man in the uniform of his country, who refuses to give information to a committee of the Senate which represents the American people, that that man is not fit to wear the uniform of his country. And in my opinion he is in the same category, Colonel, as the traitor whom he is protecting. I just want to make that very clear to you, so you know it will be made very clear to the people.

A few witnesses pushed back. "Now, I am going to refuse to co-operate. I have cooperated in every way, in any matter, and now at this time I use my First and Fifth Amendments," said Paul Hacko, a GE worker. McCarthy: "Look, mister, you are going to act like a gentleman." Hacko: "I am a gentleman, and I believe you are not a gentleman . . . You make me sick. I think that you are doing more harm to the government of the United States than anyone is . . . All you need is a swastika and a helmet, and you will be right in your place."

No case better captured all of those elements than that of Irving Peress, a New York dentist who was drafted into the Army in 1952, when the military was desperate for doctors and dentists. His promotion a year later from captain to major, while it seemed perfunctory, would become McCarthy's central case against the armed forces and a Cold War rallying cry. "Who promoted Per-ess?" the senator and his supporters demanded to know, the way they had asked four years before, "Who lost China?"

The Peress proceedings came to Joe's attention the way many others did, via a leak, only this one was from an unlikely source: General Zwicker, Peress's commanding officer at Camp Kilmer. "It was Zwicker who, convinced that the Army was planning a full-scale coverup of its scandalous security system, alerted McCar-thy," Roy Cohn revealed later. "He did it in a way that dramatized the sick bureaucratization of the United States Army: he had Mc-Carthy call him at a pay phone! Here was a hero of World War II, one of the top generals in the nation, afraid to talk on his own tele-phone. And the cloak-and-dagger stuff continued. After he gave Joe the brief outline of the case, I was dispatched to get fully debriefed by Zwicker's young aide. Not at Camp Kilmer. At the bar of the Sherry-Netherland Hotel in New York."*

The questions McCarthy and Cohn were asking about Peress were compelling: Why hadn't higher-ranking officers acted when the dentist twice cited his constitutional privilege in refusing to answer whether he belonged to a Communist, fascist, or other organization dedicated to overthrowing the government? Why didn't the Army court-martial him — or the Justice Department indict him for perjury — when, on a separate form, he signed an oath saying he'd never belonged to a subversive organization? Why had he been allowed to serve stateside, near his family, when he was slated to go to Japan? Why, in spite of that derogatory information and an ongoing investigation by Army Intelligence, was he bumped up to major? Why, when the Army realized all it had done wrong and Joe was hot on Peress's heels, was the dentist allowed to escape with an honorable discharge? Most important to Chairman McCarthy, what was being done with Peress's coddlers — the five officers involved in his induction, six in his promotion, and thirteen more in his discharge? Those "silent masters," Joe insisted, needed to be exposed and kicked out of the service.

They were reasonable inquiries, but again Joe seemed less interested in the answers than in scoring publicity points. The truth is that Peress, the son of a Bronx tailor, almost certainly had been a Communist in the days after he married his politically active wife, Elaine — but it's equally likely that he wasn't one years later when he was filling in his Army loyalty forms, and that he didn't believe the Communist Party was subversive. The Red Cross forwarded his request not to be shipped overseas because his wife and young daughter were ill. His promotion, meanwhile, was one

---

* Juliana said there was another general — Lawton, the commander at Fort Monmouth — who also was eager for McCarthy to investigate Peress and his situation at Camp Kilmer. Lawton's intent in leaking material on the dentist to the senator was partly to help Zwicker get rid of Peress, who both generals felt was a security risk. But Juliana said Lawton also had a self-serving purpose: "to get some of the heat off of Monmouth." Juliana interview, December 25, 1997, and book chapter "Peress Case," JJP.

Zwicker meanwhile told a McCarthy staffer that Peress had been a card-carrying Communist, as was his wife, and that she'd held party meetings in their home as recently as 1952. Unpublished manuscript, February 21, 2001, JJP.

of hundreds that were nearly automatic under a doctor and dentist draft law for which Joe had voted in the Senate. Once it launched its probe, the Army made sure that Peress didn't have access to classified material. The major was given an honorable discharge because the Army didn't believe there were grounds for military prosecution, and because it wanted Peress — and Joe's embarrassing questions about him — to go away. There was one more reason he signed off on the discharge, John Adams conceded later: fed up with McCarthy's bullying, "I just kept thinking: Fuck him; This is as far as I go."

Joe wasn't impressed and didn't go away. He continued pressing for Peress to be court-martialed by the Army, indicted by the attorney general, and recognized by the public for what he was: "the key to the deliberate Communist infiltration of our armed forces." When he was summoned to answer the senator's charges, the dentist invoked the Fifth Amendment dozens of times, but he did say that Joe called to mind this wisdom from the book of Psalms: "His mischief shall return upon his own head. And his violence shall come down upon his own pate." McCarthy predictably called Peress a Fifth Amendment Communist; Peress said anyone who took the invocation of his constitutional rights as an admission of guilt was himself a subversive.* Joe knew his critics were making fun of him, responding to his "Who promoted Peress?" with a rhetorical question of their own, "Who cares about a pink dentist?" He had a serious answer, however, buried deep in his Marquette records in a letter to Secretary Stevens. "The importance of a dentist on a Military Post is demonstrated very well by the fact that a dentist was a key contact figure in the Canadian spy case," Joe wrote. In the US military, too, there was reason to fear that "a communist could give information received from his patients to the Commu-

_____

* Fifty years later the dentist added that he'd taken the Fifth Amendment because he knew if he answered any of McCarthy's questions on his political background, he'd sacrifice his constitutional privilege and be pressed to name names, which he wouldn't do. So was he a Communist back then? a *New York Times* reporter asked him in 2005. "Not when I was in the Army, not for one minute," he answered. Before that? "I'm not going to tell you . . . I would not face a committee today, there is not that jeopardy, but I have descendants." Roberts, "The Dentist McCarthy Saw as a Threat to Security," *New York Times*.

nist Party and could condemn to death untold numbers of American young men."

A year later, the new subcommittee chairman, John McClellan, and his aide Bobby Kennedy would prove that Joe had been half-right. The Army had made errors in handling the dentist—forty-eight of them, committed by three dozen different officers. "The first error in the Peress Case was committed a month before his induction; the 48th and last error was committed a day before his discharge," explained Lionel Lokos, a self-described unreconstructed McCarthyite who wrote an entire book on the case. "Never had accident, mistake, and misjudgment meshed together so perfectly to place one Fifth Amendment Major in a charmed circle, supremely immune from the huffing and puffing of Army Intelligence, the Adjutant General, and the Army Personnel Board combined." Perhaps. But the McClellan-Kennedy report concluded that the errors were a matter of bureaucratic bungling, not sabotage. The aptest postscript on the wrangle came from Peress himself, who fifty years afterward said, "You know who promoted me? Somebody was eating lunch or making a telephone call when my promotion passed across their desk. I slipped through."

While the dentist eventually went back to filling the cavities of civilians, the firestorm he'd touched off intensified. The *New York Times* explained the raised stakes in an editorial:

> It is not a personality that is at stake, no matter how arrogant, narrow-minded and reckless that personality may be. It is the spirit of the Constitution. It is a principle in equity. We hope Secretary Stevens will make these points when he appears before the Subcommittee on Investigations on Thursday. We hope the President will back him up. We hope wise members of both houses of Congress, and of both parties, will take their stand behind the Secretary and the President. When this has been done it will be interesting to find out whether or not a specified retired Army dentist was in fact a Communist. But first things come first.

President Eisenhower was losing patience, not just with the Peress probe but with Joe McCarthy. Yet his instinct here, as when he was a general, was to try conciliating before attacking. The search for a middle ground began at the end of 1953, with Mc-Carthy hater and presidential brother Milton playing the painful role of broker over lunch with Joe's prize columnist, George So-kolsky. "It was obvious from the outset that [Milton] had been sent by the White House, if not by Ike himself," recalled Roy Cohn. "All he talked about was Joe, and finally he made the pitch. 'What can be done to work things out?' . . . But George cooled him, let them know that Joe was not in the mood for deals . . . So Milton went home empty-handed, and it really was an amateur set up." Soon after, White House troubleshooter Jack Martin made another bid, this time at a party at the home of *Washington Times-Herald* publisher Bazy McCormick Tankersley. "Jack Martin grabbed Joe and took him downstairs for a private confab. Twenty minutes later, Martin looked like the greeter at the mortuary," said Cohn, adding,

> [Joe] took me aside, and said: "This one really takes the cake. Poor Jack has to give blood to Ike or he'll be out of a job. Listen to the deal they offered: stop all public hearings and hold only executive sessions. The minutes of the executive sessions will be taken to Ike personally. He will read them closely and take what they call 'appropriate action' on the administrative level against the people named in the testimony . . . I thought about it for almost a full second before I told him no" . . . On the way home that night, Joe said his "No!" would infuriate Ike. "I guess I'll just have to lead a life deprived of tea and watercress sandwiches on the White House lawn."

The reach for détente continued into 1954, with senators, administration officials, and political pundits all floating their own proposals. Joe should fire Roy Cohn and halt his assault on the Army, friends of the military said. No, Joe's friends countered, it was the White House that needed to reverse course by firing Army counsel John Adams and hiring David Schine as deputy chief of the information agency he'd slandered. Others urged mutual disengagement, with Joe toning down his bombast in return for the executive beefing up its security checks. When nobody budged, Dick Nixon was again summoned as the man both McCarthy and Eisenhower came closest to trusting. The day the *Times* ran its "first things first" editorial, Nixon pulled together influential string pullers from the Army, the White House, and the Senate — everyone *but* Joe — to weigh in on how to handle the recalcitrant senator. It was agreed that Joe's friend and subcommittee member, the slippery Everett Dirksen, would host a bread-breaking lunch between Secretary Stevens and Senator McCarthy the next day, February 24. As his plotting session ended, the vice president cautioned the other guests, "Remember, this meeting never occurred."

The McCarthy-Stevens meal was, in Nixon's words, "one of the most controversial repasts of the 1950s." History would remember it not for its peas, French-fried potatoes, or hearts of lettuce but as "the chicken lunch" — a reference less to the fried chicken served than to the Army secretary, who emerged looking like a coward. Stevens blasted McCarthy early in the meeting: "I'm not going to have my officers browbeaten." Joe fired back: "I'm not going to sit there and see a supercilious bastard sit there and smirk." In the end, a memo of understanding clearly assigned the roles of winner and loser. Stevens agreed to root out Communists in his ranks, order testimony from every Army officer with a hand in promoting Peress, and even send Zwicker to testify again if the subcommittee wanted him. While McCarthy said he would treat military witnesses more politely, that wasn't part of the text or reporters' stories, and he'd deny any softening. "Stevens couldn't have surrendered more if he crawled on his hands and knees," Joe told one reporter. (When the remark was repeated to Stevens, the secretary first "was struck speechless," Adams said, then "he burst into tears.")* The senator kidded with Bill Lawrence of the *New York Times,* "I'm running the Army now" — would Lawrence like to be a general? Other journalists described the outcome by reaching for metaphors from the sea (a goldfish in a tank of barracuda) and from military history ("what General Burgoyne and General Cornwallis never achieved — the surrender of the American Army"). That night McCarthy hosted a party to celebrate, gloating

---

* Trying to make things right with Stevens, Joe sent him a telegram denying he'd said it and blaming *Time* magazine for "another deliberate lie" told "with the obvious hope of increasing the unpleasantness in the case." Telegram from McCarthy to Stevens, March 4, 1954, series 14, MUA.

to scribes and friends about his triumph in recasting Fighting Bob as Retreating Robert. Stevens, meanwhile, phoned the vice president just before midnight "in a highly emotional state. He said that he had decided to issue a statement the following day and then resign," Nixon recalled. "I told him to quit talking about resigning and suggested that in the morning we could talk about what kind of statement could be made."

By the next day, the initiative seemed to be shifting. The president, who at first was incensed at Stevens, redirected his rage toward McCarthy. While not acknowledging that the Army secretary's retreat was in lockstep with his own Munich-like policy of appeasement, Eisenhower told his staff there'd be no more placating. "This guy McCarthy is going to get into trouble over this. I'm not going to take this one lying down," the president vowed. "My friends tell me it won't be long in this Army stuff before McCarthy starts using my name instead of Stevens. He's ambitious. He wants to be President. He's the last guy in the world who'll ever get there, if I have anything to say." Then Ike got Stevens to issue the kind of Army-strong statement that everyone wished he had made at the chicken lunch, saying he would "never accede to the abuse of Army personnel under any circumstances," then adding, "I shall never accede to them being browbeaten or humiliated." The third and clinching blow was supposed to be the news conference Eisenhower called the next week, which drew a record-breaking 256 reporters enticed by the promise that the president would finally declare war against the senator. But as he had before and would again, Ike flinched. He apologized for "serious errors" made in the Peress case, pledged that executive branch officials would "respond cheerfully and completely" when summoned before Congress, and put the onus on Republican senators to rein in their outlaw colleague. Not only didn't he call out McCarthy; he didn't mention him by name. As the press session ended, columnist Joseph Alsop captured the dismay of his colleagues when he said to one of them, intentionally loudly, "Why the yellow son of a bitch!"

At his own news conference, Joe gave the reply he'd calibrated for the broadside he thought Ike would be aiming at him, not for the tepid statement the president actually delivered. When he realized his mistake, there was time to make only minor tweaks, and in any case he was as disinclined to back down as Eisenhower had been to stand firm. Regarding Zwicker, the senator said, "If a stupid, arrogant or witless man in a position of power appears before our committee and is found aiding the Communist party, he will be exposed." As for Eisenhower, McCarthy said, "Apparently the President and I now agree on the necessity of getting rid of Communists," implying that Ike was late to the fight. (Joe later asked that reporters delete the word "now" from his statement, explaining that it "is being given a false interpretation never intended." The *New York Times* did delete "now" from its transcript but drew even more attention to the word by running a four-paragraph news story on McCarthy's request that it be stricken.)* The senator ended on a note of defiance: "When the shouting and the tumult dies, the American people and the President will realize that this unprecedented mudslinging against the committee by extreme left-wing elements of the press and radio was caused because another Fifth Amendment Communist in government was finally dug out of the dark recesses and exposed to public view."

This was a salvo too far. Leading Republicans, including a member of the president's cabinet, called McCarthy to say they were through with him. Willard Edwards, as stalwart a friend as Joe had among the Fourth Estate, called it "the day McCarthy died." A Democratic senator irreverently inquired whether "this open declaration of war requires approval by the Senate."

Joe, Washington's most attuned politician, suddenly seemed tone-deaf. It wasn't just his failure to anticipate that the GOP wouldn't abide his eviscerating a Republican president, the party's first since Democrats had surrendered their New Deal–Fair Deal lock on the White House. He didn't appreciate that the Cold War had modestly cooled the previous summer, when the United Nations Command signed an armistice with North Korea and China, and that Americans were eager for a broader stand-down with the

---

* Also included in McCarthy's typed statement, but crossed out in pencil from the version handed to reporters, was this sentence: "Far too much wind has been blowing from high places in defense of this Fifth Amendment Communist Army officer." "McCarthy Deletes 'Now,'" *New York Times*.

Soviet bloc. He grasped too late that Ike, despite his reticence, was stronger and wilier than Harry Truman. And the senator had lost perspective, unable to see the cocoon he had built around himself, stuffed with callow yes-men like Cohn and Schine, which eventually would be the undoing of the three of them.

In the meantime, Joe faced a new and formidable foe. CBS newsman Edward R. Murrow had demonstrated his grit during World War II with live broadcasts from London during the Blitz. Back in October, Murrow's *See It Now* show had challenged the ad hominem tactic of guilt by association when he outlined "The Case Against Milo Radulovich," an Air Force Reserve lieutenant tarred as a security risk on the basis of flimsy evidence that his father and sister were Communist sympathizers. While McCarthy wasn't mentioned, no one doubted who Murrow was aiming at when he ended the telecast by editorializing, "Whatever happens in this whole area of the relationship between the individual and the state, we will do it ourselves — it cannot be blamed upon [Soviet premier Georgy] Malenkov, or Mao Tse-tung, or even our allies."* The following month the hard-hitting host, who admitted he was late to the McCarthy hunt, was back with a story about the attack on civil liberties. Called "An Argument in Indianapolis," it warned that too many Americans were being denied the rights to peaceful assembly and free speech, and implored, "Somebody certainly has to take a stand."

McCarthy's instinct was to browbeat Murrow into silence, the way he'd tried with newspaper reporters. A week before the Indianapolis broadcast, McCarthy investigator Don Surine stopped Murrow colleague Joe Wershba outside the Senate Caucus Room and presented the reporter with twenty-year-old evidence of Murrow's supposed link to a Communist front organization. "Mind you, Joe, I'm not saying Murrow is a Commie himself," Surine said, "but he's one of those goddamn anti-anti-Communists, and they're just as dangerous." The implication was clear: get your

---

* "We were looking for a Milo Radulovich long before we knew who Milo was," said Fred Friendly, Murrow's producer. "Milo Radulovich was the perfect little picture to illustrate the ravages of McCarthyism." Ranville, *To Strike at a King*, viii–ix.

boss to back off, or he'll be in our hot seat alongside Fort Monmouth and Foggy Bottom. The result was the reverse. Murrow knew how spurious McCarthy's "evidence" against him was, and the intrepid broadcaster decided this was just the time for TV to take on the racketeering senator.

He did that in March 1954, two weeks after the *Times* editorial and a week after Eisenhower's press conference. Working nearly round-the-clock for a week, and reaching into his own pocket and his producer's to pay for a promotional ad, the newsman let the senator do himself in. Clips showed Joe browbeating Reed Harris, calling the Democrats the party of treason, and referring with unbridled bravado to Adlai Stevenson as "Alger — I mean, Adlai." There was no pretense at evenhandedness, with Murrow strategically splicing in footage of McCarthy at his most vexing — giggling at his own jokes, cold-shouldering witnesses, nervously brushing a dangling cowlick back onto his balding and sweating brow, and waving documents that moderator Murrow made clear were nothing but stage props. Yet there was nothing gimmicky about the journalist's sober-minded call to action at the end of the thirty-minute broadcast. "This is no time for men who oppose Senator McCarthy's methods to keep silent — or for those who approve. We can deny our heritage and our history, but we cannot escape responsibility for the result," Murrow lectured. "We cannot defend freedom abroad by deserting it at home. The actions of the junior Senator from Wisconsin have caused alarm and dismay amongst our allies abroad and given considerable comfort to our enemies. And whose fault is that? Not really his. He didn't create this situation of fear. He merely exploited it, and rather successfully. Cassius was right: 'The fault, dear Brutus, is not in our stars, but in ourselves.'"*

No sooner had he signed off with his traditional "Good night,

---

* Field producer Joe Wershba gathered the tape that Murrow spliced together by dogging McCarthy across the country. The project was sufficiently hush-hush that Murrow gave it "a number, not a name," says Wershba's widow, Shirley. The broadcaster hoped the clips were all he'd need to tell the story, she adds, but when Surine and McCarthy came after him, Murrow "knew it was time for him to fight back with his own name. This was something that had to be done, but it was scary." Author interview with Shirley Wershba.

and good luck" than the phones started ringing. Never, CBS said, had TV ignited such a response — 12,348 calls and cables in the first twenty-four hours, running fifteen to one for Murrow, followed by nearly 100,000 letters. Among those calling and writing were Margaret Truman and her father, Harry, Groucho Marx, Albert Einstein, and Bishop Sheil of Chicago. Producer Fred Friendly called it a "contagion of courage." A month later, Joe responded on *See It Now* with a scripted speech that, while it scored rhetorical points — Murrow, he said, was "the cleverest of the jackal pack, which is always found at the throat of anyone who dares to expose individual Communists and traitors" — again lit up CBS's switchboards in the network's favor and carried none of the thump of Murrow's first punch. And Murrow got the last word. Repeatedly accused by Joe of being part of the "bleeding heart left-wing element" of radio and TV, the newsman responded, "I am somewhat left of McCarthy and Louis XIV." In his rebuttal to McCarthy's *See it Now* episode, Murrow said, "It is my devotion to the principles upon which this nation rests — justice, freedom and fairness — which sets me apart from Sen. McCarthy . . . When the record is finally written, as it will be one day, it will answer the question: Who has helped the Communist cause and who has served his country better, Senator McCarthy or I? I would like to be remembered by the answer to that question."*

Murrow's "Dear Brutus" and other scoldings were the most brazenly political use ever of national TV to attack an individual, done at a moment when networks ruled the airwaves and no anchor mattered more than Edward R. Murrow. Coming just two months after Joe's national approval ratings hit 50 percent, the broadcasts helped ensure he would climb no higher. Murrow's

---

* While Murrow is hero-worshiped today for his anti-McCarthy shows, it is fair to ask why he waited so long to go on the attack and why he signed CBS's loyalty oath. "He'd lost a sponsor, Campbell's Soup, and that may have made him circumspect," answered journalist Nicholas Lemann. Or it may be that he "sensed that, with the war being fought in Korea, the moment wasn't right for an attack on anti-Communism." No matter how late he entered the fray, however, Murrow's son Casey says he paid a price for doing it: "The McCarthy broadcasts, or all the related broadcasts, dogged my father for years after that. I think that was part of his [eventual] split with CBS." Lemann, "The Murrow Doctrine," *New Yorker;* and author interview with Casey Murrow.

broadsides did one more thing: they shored up a Vermont senator who, that very afternoon, delivered a speech to the Senate that few noticed but would later become as memorable as Murrow's. Rather than upbraiding his colleague from Grand Chute, Ralph Flanders mocked him: "The junior senator from Wisconsin interests us all, no doubt about that, but also he puzzles some of us. To what party does he belong? Is he a hidden satellite of the Democratic Party, to which he is furnishing so much material for quiet mirth? . . . One must conclude that his is a one-man party, and that its name is McCarthyism, a title which he has proudly accepted."

As withering as the back-to-back dressing-downs by Murrow and Flanders were, two days later it was a pair of little-known names — Annie Lee Moss and Gerard David Schine — that, within hours of each other, stole the headlines and shattered the senator.

Moss was the first witness at a public hearing in the Senate Office Building that chilly afternoon of March 11. The daughter of Negro tenant farmers, mother of four, and widow of a construction laborer, she worked as a low-level communications clerk at the Army Signal Corps headquarters in Washington. Now she was sitting across from five US senators in an overheated hearing room dressed in a winter coat and bejeweled white hat, with a bank of microphones in front of her, her lawyer at her side, and Annie Lee looking, as one columnist wrote, "earnest, humble, scared." Like Peress, Moss was brought to McCarthy's attention by a leaker (in this case an FBI informant) and presented as a case study of the Army cosseting Communists. (The question here was longer and less alliterative: "Who in the military, knowing that this lady was a Communist, promoted her from a waitress to a code clerk?") This time, however, it wasn't the witness who came out looking the fool; it was her interrogator and Joe's consigliere, Roy Cohn. In his haste to point fingers, Cohn said Moss had been visited by a white "Communist organizer" named Robert Hall, apparently confusing him with a black union organizer of the same name whom Moss said she did know. A reporter who recognized the slip-up tipped off Bobby Kennedy, who tipped off his Democratic bosses, who made a convincing case that Cohn was inept in mistaking Moss, a loyal American, for a subversive.* Perhaps sensing the fiasco in the making, Joe walked out of the hearing.†

The Democrats had a field day. They had recently returned from their six-month boycott of the subcommittee and were eager to show they would no longer be a rubber stamp for their out-of-control chairman. Senator Symington asked Moss if she'd heard of Karl Marx (answer, to audience applause, "Who is that?"), and said. "If you are not taken back into the Army, you come around and see me, and I am going to see that you get a job" (more applause). Senator McClellan called McCarthyism's slander by hearsay "evil." The press ate it up, especially Murrow, who devoted a *See It Now* episode to proclaiming Moss's innocence and McCarthy's guilt, with his cameraman perpetually panning to the chairman's empty seat.

The witness was, in Murrow's patronizing telling, guileless as well as simpleminded. Introducing the show as "a little picture of a little woman," the broadcaster said that "until three weeks

---

* There was one more reverberation for Bobby from the Annie Lee Moss affair. Senator Henry Jackson, one of the Democrats on the subcommittee, asked him to visit FBI headquarters and look at its file on Moss. It was Bobby's first encounter with his father's old friend J. Edgar Hoover, and neither the FBI director nor the Senate aide would forget their introduction. Hoover said the file was off-limits; Bobby persisted, knowing that the agency had been sharing information with McCarthy and Cohn. The FBI chief was sufficiently taken aback to advise his senior staff that "the attitude of Kennedy in this matter clearly shows need for absolute circumspection in any conversation with him." Bobby took notice too, later writing, "They lied to me . . . They were making information available to the committee, and they were telling me they weren't." RFK FBI File, pt. 1 of 9, 54; and RFK OH, 417, JFKL.

† McCarthy also was eager to bone up for that night's Fulton Lewis radio show, where he would blast Edward R. Murrow. As he left the hearing room, the senator said only, "I have a rather important appointment tonight, which I have to work on right now." Hearings transcript, Army Signal Corps, March 11, 1954, 447.

As for the embarrassment he suffered at the hands of mild-mannered Annie Lee Moss, McCarthy would have known more about how effective this low-key woman was as a witness — and might have decided not to summon her in public — if he'd put her through the same executive session rehearsal he did most witnesses. He didn't think he had to because Cohn already had interviewed her, and the senator apparently foresaw no problems even though Mrs. Moss had told Cohn, "I don't know anything about this Communist Party." Friedman, "Strange Career of Annie Lee Moss," *Journal of American History;* and interrogatory of Moss by Cohn, February 16, 1954, Annie Lee Moss File, PSI.

ago, Mrs. Moss probably knew very little about Senator McCarthy, General Zwicker, Mr. Cohn, or the other principals engaged in the argument in Washington," which seems unlikely, since pollsters said two thirds of Americans by then understood well who McCarthy was. "This woman, under suspicion because of charges made by Senator McCarthy and Roy Cohn, *alleged* to have *examined* and *corrected* secret and encoded overseas messages, attempted to read the uncoded words of her suspension notice," Murrow added in his voice-over. Intending to suggest that McCarthy and Cohn had overreached, he instead mocked Moss's difficulty enunciating words like "adjudication." Newspaper writers took the same tone, coincidentally besmirching Moss along with McCarthy. "I greatly doubt whether Annie Lee Moss knows she has any rights," wrote *New York Herald Tribune* columnist John Crosby. "Yet, they were being so clearly violated in front of our very eyes that she won every heart . . . The American people fought a revolution to defend, among other things, the right of Annie Lee Moss to earn a living, and Senator McCarthy now decided she had no such right."

However such racial and gender stereotyping looks today, in that era of Jim Crow bigotry and unreserved sexism, it made her sympathetic and likeable to the 3.3 million households that met her on *See It Now,* in naked contrast to her belligerent interrogator. Asked about the confusion over identities, she said, "There are three Annie Lee Mosses" in the Washington telephone directory.* What would happen if she didn't find another job soon? "I am going down to the welfare." Would she do anything to hurt her country? "No, sir." Letters flooding the offices of subcommittee senators suggested how America was responding. They blasted McCarthy for "pillorying" his witness and sent kudos to her gentlemanly defenders. Moss was "the poor soul," "a poor Negro," and "that poor old colored woman."† Senator Symington seemed to speak for ev-

---

* The Washington city directories and telephone directories from that period didn't list three Annie Lee Mosses, although they did list several women with similar names, including Mrs. Anna L. Moss, Mrs. Addie Moss, Annie Moss, and Mrs. Abbie Lee Moss. But the only one who lived at the three addresses listed in Communist Party files was the one who was testifying before the McCarthy subcommittee. "The Strange Career of Annie Lee Moss."

† Not everyone was taken with Mrs. Moss. Other letter writers said she had the

eryone when he offered this verdict to Moss: "I have been listening to you testify this afternoon, and I think you are telling the truth."

Was she telling the truth about not being a Communist? Historians have argued over that almost as much as they have about the backgrounds of Irving Peress and Alger Hiss. The FBI suspected she was a Commie as early as 1948, on the basis of party membership rolls allegedly reviewed by an informant. One federal loyalty board found "no reasonable grounds" for terminating her, while another suspended her "in the interest of national security." The secretary of defense reinstated her in 1955 to a "non-sensitive position," saying, "The record does not support a conclusion that she is actually subversive or disloyal to the United States." The subcommittee files on her, all of which are now public, likewise offer no smoking guns, just accusations and doubts, which were enough for Joe to label her guilty even before he heard her testimony. Conservatives today paint her as a full-throated Red, who perused top secrets from the CIA and military, then deceived everyone from Senator Symington to newsman Murrow; liberals see her as an agitator for civil rights with an appealing touch of pink. Ethel Payne, the first lady of the black press and Washington correspondent for the *Chicago Defender,* probably came closest to the truth when she said:

> [Moss] was a woman of limited education, she was a very humble person. The three things in her life were her son, her grandson, and her church, besides her job. And other than that, she knew little about the world outside . . . Mrs. Moss' husband was one of those who had been contacted by the communists. He was just a simple working man, but they were sending him free subscriptions to the Daily Worker, the organ of the Communist Party. And I don't know what he did with them, but when he died, they kept coming, these papers, and they piled up on her back porch, some with the wrappings still on them. She never paid any attention to it; the Bible was her thing.

"cunning" of "colored folks," and had deceived the subcommittee Democrats into thinking "there must be another ANNIE LEE MOSS hiding somewhere in the woodpile." "The Strange Career of Annie Lee Moss."

That whole debate misses the point. Senator McCarthy was, as ever, asking the wrong question. It was not whether Annie Lee Moss had ever rubbed shoulders with Reds, although she likely did, since they were more sympathetic to Negroes back then than were the FBI, paternalistic senators, or condescending broadcasters. It was whether the former dessert cook was a spy. The idea that state security was imperiled by a telegraphic typewriter operator relaying messages, most of which were encrypted — and none of which anyone suggested she had digested, not to mention filched — was even more of a stretch than a left-leaning dentist extracting secrets along with teeth. So was McCarthy's notion of a conspiracy among military brass that had planted Peress at Fort Kilmer and Moss in the Pentagon. There simply was no evidence to suggest any of this.*

The Moss mess was a setback for McCarthy, but it was of the transitory kind that Joe had dealt with before and that seldom stopped him for long. The devastating document the Army released that same afternoon — known as the Adams chronology, for its author, Army lawyer John Adams — sent the senator to the rock bottom not just of his brawl with the military but of his public career. Even as he had been waging what he said was the people's war to root out Communists from the Army, it turns out he had been fraternizing behind the scenes with key Army figures all the way up to Secretary Robert Stevens. And while he had been warning about homosexuals and Communists being subject to blackmail, the senator's senior staffers had allegedly been engaging in their own barely concealed extortion of senior officers, aimed at helping one of them wiggle out of his patriotic duty to serve in the Army they were investigating.

The case against Team McCarthy was laid out in a thirty-four-page memo that had been sitting in Adams's drawer for a week or

---

* Whereas Major Peress repeatedly took the Fifth, clerk Moss answered every question put to her. As for the documents that Moss handled on her relay machine, the Army said she never had access to the codes or code rooms and couldn't have known what was in the messages, while Moss testified there was "no way in the world" for her to know the unfiltered contents of the missives. "Mrs. Moss Ousted by the Army Again," *New York Times; Executive Sessions*, 5:xv; and hearings transcript, Army Signal Corps, March 11, 1954, 456.

so in its current form and, as an even rawer diary, for months. Or at least since January 21, when chief of staff Sherman Adams and other key Eisenhower men met in the wood-paneled office of Attorney General Herbert Brownell, and possibly as early as the previous December, when Drew Pearson first wrote about Cohn's lobbying. Having gotten wind of the Army's backroom dealings with McCarthy, Cohn, and Schine, Ike's brain trust invited John Adams to Brownell's suite to tell the full story. When they heard Adams's narrative, they had a simple and secretive instruction for the Army lawyer: write it down.* Lay out all the particulars of what the subcommittee trio was asking for and offering, in the kind of precise detail they knew would shock the press and the public. They weren't sure when they'd need it; that depended on when Eisenhower at long last was ready to reveal his hidden hand.† In the meantime, John Adams kept a journal and, on occasion, gave a peek or more to a selection of journalists, senators, Army officers, FBI agents, and White House insiders, who he presumed had then shown the president.

The chicken lunch finally made Ike fighting mad, and a week later Adams got his second order from on high: clean it up. Rework the diary into a more concise and refined chronology, he was told. That meant dropping the obscenities, along with the naming of embarrassing names and speculation about the McCarthy-Cohn-Schine relationship.‡ "I knew then that the decision had been

---

* How much he'd already written down is unclear. In his memoir and elsewhere, he at times implied that he began his record keeping after the January 21 meeting; at other times he indicated that he'd started keeping notes earlier, and took better ones once he was ordered to. That matters because his reconstruction covers a period beginning six months before that January meeting, and as he would make clear in his brief attacking McCarthy, a real-time accounting is more trustworthy than an after-the-fact one.

† At the time, White House insiders wanted their orchestrating role kept hush-hush. But in writing their memoirs years later, everyone claimed a role in having taken down McCarthy, including Nixon, Sherman Adams, and Ike adviser and UN ambassador Henry Cabot Lodge Jr., who had never forgiven Joe for not coming to Massachusetts to help in his 1952 Senate campaign against Jack Kennedy.

‡ Joe Alsop was the first journalist to whom Adams showed the unvarnished diary, and while he was sworn to secrecy then, he later wrote about what he called "the tale half told." Two thirds of what was in the original was gone from the version made public, Alsop said, including discussion of the "Nazi-like sense of

made," Adams recounted in his memoir. "The Army was going to counterattack against McCarthy, and my diary was the ammunition. Stevens and I were obviously going to lead the charge." The only one more delighted than Adams was James Hagerty, Eisenhower's press secretary, who would confide to his diary, "It's a pip . . . Should bust this thing wide open."

Defense Secretary Charles Wilson showed the mortifying report to Joe on March 10, offering him one last chance to keep it under wraps. All the senator had to do was fire Cohn, who the Army and the White House had concluded was the real troublemaker. The three Republicans on the Investigations Subcommittee had seen the report and agreed with Wilson. Fire Roy, they told Joe, and save yourself. McCarthy said he couldn't and wouldn't. Soon it was too late: by the following afternoon the administration had leaked Adams's rendering of events to every reporter who mattered in Washington.*

---

power that Cohn displayed," the implication that "Cohn possessed a peculiar power over McCarthy," and Cohn's use of "disgusting obscenities." Adams said the obscenities were primarily "the one word 'shit,' which [Cohn] had used time and time again." As to the columnist's other references to edits, said Adams, "that was pure Alsop fantasy." Alsop and Alsop, "The Tale Half Told," *New York Herald Tribune;* and *Without Precedent,* 147.

Still, Adams was distressed when, after ordering him to make the revisions, White House officials ordered him to turn over to them the originals of the diary. "Every copy I could locate was removed from my office," he said. But "nearly a year later, as I was shaking hands to say good-bye to my lawyer-colleagues in the Army counselor's office, one of them handed me an envelope as a farewell present. It contained a complete set of all the suppressed documents." *Without Precedent,* 147.

* "What did you tell him?" Cohn said he asked McCarthy after his meeting with Wilson. McCarthy: "What do you think I told him? I told him to go to hell." It was the answer Cohn wanted to hear, so Joe threw him that bone, but it was not the kind of language even a firebrand like McCarthy would have used in a private meeting with "Engine Charlie" Wilson, the secretary of defense and former CEO of General Motors. Cohn, *McCarthy,* 124.

Defense Secretary Wilson may have had another reason for the March 10 laying-down-the-law lunch with McCarthy. The president worried that McCarthy was zeroing in on Ike's decision, as a World War II general, to let former Communist Party members receive officer commissions as long as they swore they no longer were members. Rather than continuing to nervously hope the matter wouldn't be raised, Eisenhower, who felt he'd made the right choice back then, decided to use Wilson to launch his offensive against McCarthy. Author email exchange with Kai Bird; and Bird, *The Chairman,* 420–21.

By July 1953, Schine's draft status had been changed from 4-F, which meant he was medically or psychological unfit, to "qualified for military service." That sent shivers down not just the suddenly healthy spine of David Schine but those of his biggest fan, Roy Cohn, and their boss, Joe McCarthy. Cohn and McCarthy believed, with some justification, that Schine's case had come back to the attention of his draft board because of questions raised by Drew Pearson and others about how Schine had escaped conscription in the first place, which also were justified but never answered. The next day, according to the Adams chronology, McCarthy and Cohn summoned to their office Major General Miles Reber, the Army's legislative liaison. In light of Dave's education, business experience, and prior service with Army transport, Roy and Joe said, he should be given a rare commission as an officer, the way McCarthy had a decade before. The problem, the Army determined in turning them down, was that "Schine had had no previous military experience whatsoever and indeed no special training of any kind which qualified him for a commission." What about the Navy or Air Force? Cohn asked. They too said no thanks.

Yet the requests kept coming. Could the Army assign Schine to duty near New York City, so he could be available to help the subcommittee even as he was going through basic training? Could Schine be dispatched by Secretary Stevens—as a military aide or, better still, a civilian—to study pro-Communist leanings in the textbooks used at the US Military Academy at West Point? How about being assigned to the CIA? Might he be given a special pass to leave the base weekday nights and weekends? Could his basic training be limited to eight weeks instead of sixteen?

In the end, the Army stretched its rules for Schine in a way it did for no other trainee. By the conclusion of his two months' drilling at Fort Dix, subcommittee staffers had phoned base officials to make some request at least twenty-nine times, or every other day, while Schine himself got a call a day. He placed 181 calls during that time to non-subcommittee parties, and was away from the post thirty-four of his sixty-eight days there. (The average trainee was gone three or four days and didn't get any passes during his first four weeks.) The Army offered to give the private a "special room" at the base where he could write his subcommittee reports, but he and Cohn said it was vital he do that in Trenton or Manhattan. (Entrusting important work to "an inexperienced, unpaid, part-time consultant," the Army said, "defies imagination.") As for Schine's nutritional needs, "while his fellow trainees were eating simple Army meals," the Army reported, "Schine on November 30 consumed a sirloin steak smothered in french fried onions; on December 1 ordered for his party filet mignon, roast beef and squab; and on December 3 and 7 consumed a full course filet mignon dinner." On January 10, "Mr. Cohn and Mr. Schine, in the company of two young ladies . . . consumed $32.96 worth of food and $5.85 worth of liquid refreshment" at New York's Drake Hotel (a tab that would total $367 in today's dollars). Pampering like that, said General Cornelius Ryan, the base commander, made Schine "a man apart."

Cohn and McCarthy's strong-arming on Schine's behalf was unprecedented in his ten years as liaison to congressional favor seekers, Reber reported. It was especially unseemly because Schine was trying to escape military service when the US military was in its last days of a ferocious shooting war in Korea and beginning to police an uneasy armistice. The push for favors became unethical, if not criminal, because it was happening at the very moment when McCarthy and Cohn were investigating Fort Monmouth and other Army facilities. In between discussions of those probes, Cohn especially would request one after another special accommodation for Schine. And he wasn't subtle, according to Adams. When the Army attorney told Cohn that "the national interest required that no preferential treatment be given to Schine," Cohn replied that "if national interest was what the Army wanted he'd give it a little and then proceeded to outline how he would expose the Army in its worst light and show the country how shabbily it is being run." Later, told that Schine might be shipped overseas, Cohn said doing that would ensure that "Stevens is through as secretary of the army . . . We'll wreck the Army."* McCarthy, meanwhile, sensed

---

* Cohn later justified his lobbying on behalf of Schine, saying, "Did I make calls on his behalf? Certainly. More than usual? Certainly. Was I sometimes harsh in my talks with Pentagon bureaucrats? Certainly. Was I looking for 'preferential treatment' for 'my pal'? Certainly *not*. I was looking for ordinary treatment for Schine, the same treatment anybody off the street would get." It was classic Roy

the danger in Cohn's badgering but was willing to go to nearly any lengths to keep him happy. So even as he was reassuring Roy that he was doing all he could for Dave, he whispered to Senator Potter, "I don't care if they ship Schine to Siberia," and to Stevens that Schine "is a good boy, but there is nothing indispensable about him."* Joe added, in his phone chat with Stevens, that Roy "thinks Dave should be a general and work from the penthouse of the Waldorf." Then the senator begged the Army secretary not to repeat what he'd just said, for fear it might get back to Roy. Just before Christmas in 1953, McCarthy sent Stevens the kind of butt-covering letter that he himself hated receiving. "I have heard rumors to the effect that some of the members of my staff have intervened with your Department in behalf of a former staff consultant, David Schine," the senator wrote. "I have an unbreakable rule that neither I nor anyone in my behalf shall ever attempt to interfere with or influence the Army in its assignments, promotions, et cetera."

The morning after the Adams chronology was released and Annie Lee Moss testified, McCarthy dominated the newspapers in a way not even a press magnet like him had before — and that he prayed he never would again. In the *New York Times* alone, Joe was mentioned in fifteen articles, of which twelve were mainly about him, three were on the front page, and one led the newspaper. Its headline said it all: "ARMY CHARGES M'CARTHY AND COHN THREATENED IT IN TRYING TO OBTAIN PREFERRED TREATMENT FOR SCHINE." But rather than sulking, Joe and his advisers already were gathering at his home to plot their counterstrike. "We decided that as soon as the report was made public," Cohn recounted, "we would retaliate by releasing certain memoranda of our own." They did that later that day, March 12, handing out eleven memos they said they'd dictated just after their phone

---

— concede just enough to make it believable, in down-to-earth language, but *never* back down on the crucial points. It also showed how much he'd learned at Joe's side. *Autobiography of Roy Cohn*, 116.

* Potter said Joe threatened that if he kept pressing for Cohn to be fired, "'it will be [seen as] anti-Semitism, and Winchell and Sokolsky would have plenty to say about that' ... There wasn't any use protesting, although he knew that I knew that he knew it was absurd. And up to now I was one of the few human beings he had not attacked." *Days of Shame*, 21.

calls, lunches, or meetings with Stevens and Adams. Rather than the McCarthy forces trying to blackmail the Army, these documents argued, it was the Army that was coercing the senator.

"Mr. Stevens asked that we hold up our public hearings on the Army. He suggested we go after the Navy, Air Force, and the Defense Department instead," read one memo after a November 6, 1953, Pentagon lunch involving McCarthy, Stevens, and their aides. A follow-up note the next month said that Adams "had gotten specific information for us about an Air Force Base where there were a large number of homosexuals." In January, a memo from Cohn to McCarthy included this red flag about the Army lawyer's self-serving conduct: "Adams said this was the last chance for me to arrange that law partnership in New York which he wanted . . . He said he had turned down a job in industry at $17,500 and needed a guarantee of $25,000 from a law firm." The night the memos were released, the senator summoned the press to lay out his case: Private Schine was the hostage, the ransom was calling off the Fort Monmouth probe, and he, Joe McCarthy, was the real injured party. And the morning after the barrage of negative coverage, Joe was back where he felt most comfortable, on the offensive, with a front-page headline in the *New York Times* screaming, "M'CARTHY CHARGES ARMY 'BLACKMAIL.'"

As the Army-McCarthy hearings would confirm, both sides went way beyond any bounds of proper behavior in their behind-the-scenes battle. If each was accurately describing the other's misconduct, why didn't they blow the whistle at the time rather than wait until months afterward, when revealing it served their political purposes? Press reports and leaks also revealed that before any punches were thrown, the two sides were quietly coddling each other in ways that were unseemly for an American fighting force or a US senator. McCarthy and Stevens met for "refreshments" at what the secretary called "the regular place" even as the subcommittee's investigation of Stevens's Army was going full blast.* Ad-

---

* A less friendly exchange came over the phone, in February 1954, when Stevens told McCarthy that in the wake of his outburst against General Zwicker, no more Army officers would be authorized to testify until there was an understanding "as to the abuse they are going to get." McCarthy: "Just go ahead and try it, Rob-

ams and McCarthy aide Frank Carr were doing something similar, although both kept some of their tête-à-têtes secret from their bosses. Even Cohn and Stevens were conferring, with the former confiding about witnesses he hoped to interrogate and the latter signaling at least one general he planned to fire. The records raise one last question about conflicted roles: Why was a newsman like George Sokolsky of Hearst acting as the front man in McCarthy's bid to patch things up with the Army?

Those relations gave everyone involved a sense of wielding the kind of influence that mattered more than money in Washington, and that had been a driving force for Joe since his years as a power-broking circuit judge. Even as he railed at elites, when they offered him entry to their inner circle, Joe — like most demagogues — couldn't say no. In his memoir, Adams recalled the friendly days when McCarthy and Cohn hosted him at the Stork Club, ignoring the roped-off lines of chumps as they were escorted to a waiting table. He was handed hard-to-come-by tickets for fights at Madison Square Garden and Broadway musicals, and reservations were made for him at elegant hotels like the Drake. When Adams finally said no to Cohn and Schine's rising demands, however, the pushback was quick and hard, against not just him but McCarthy, who was supposed to be the boss. "We rode uptown in Cohn's car, with Cohn at the wheel, McCarthy beside him in the front seat, and [McCarthy aide Frank] Carr and I in back. As we drove, Cohn was raining systematic abuse on McCarthy, who periodically turned to me to ask if I couldn't arrange to get Dave assigned to New York," Adams wrote.

> When I finally said that I would miss my train if we continued to go in that direction, Cohn had another fit. He stopped the car in the middle lane of traffic on Park Avenue near Forty-sixth Street and said to me: "Get out and get to the train station however you can." . . . I was left standing with a suitcase in the middle of three lanes of traffic in midtown New York. Later Frank Carr told me that if I thought my departure from the automo-

---

ert. I am going to kick the brains out of anyone who protects Communists." *Without Precedent,* 129.

bile had been ignominious, I should have seen the way McCarthy had been dismissed from the car three blocks farther on, at the Waldorf.

Then secret FBI files raise equally interesting questions, starting with why, when he was originally drafted in 1951, David Schine had been deemed unfit to serve. He "was rejected on two grounds, (1) a dislocated disc in the back and (2) a schizoid personality (according to [Special Agent Supervisor Thomas] McAndrews this is a split personality but the medical dictionary describes it as a shut-in, unsocial, introspective type of personality)," a 1953 FBI report found. "The second reason for Schine's rejection does not appear in the Selective Service file but is a finding of the Surgeon General's office which conducted the physical examination at the time Schine was called up by the local draft board." Drew Pearson would reveal that second finding in a February 1954 column, but because it was either too speculative or too controversial, it generated little further discussion by the bureau or anyone else.

Cohn's military records, too, were being discussed in the corridors of the Pentagon. He received a deferment from the draft twice while seeking entrance to West Point, and a third time when he was in the National Guard. He was rejected from West Point because of a "cystic condition" in his nose, sinusitis, and "impairment of vision," although he did pass a routine pre-induction physical, which meant that the Army would have taken him even if the academy wouldn't. But again he got a deferment, this time based in part on a letter from a dean at Columbia University. All of that was in Cohn's FBI file. The press dug even deeper than the bureau, with the Scripps-Howard wire service reporting that Roy had cut nearly half of the required training drills with the National Guard. Drew Pearson and Jack Anderson claimed that his shirking was even more pervasive than that, that anyone else would have been thrown out, and that the congressman who nominated Roy for West Point was later named to the New York Supreme Court with help from Roy's father. The Army considered using this information — what Cohn's biographer would call his "slithering out of the armed service" — to embarrass the Senate aide, showing that he and Schine were dodgers of a kind. But, said Anderson, the brass worried that it could backfire, with Cohn claiming that his record was being distorted for political reasons.*

Other whisperers — at the FBI, in the Army, and down the halls of Congress — speculated on why Cohn was so loyal to Schine, and McCarthy to Cohn. Pearson thought the Cohn-Schine nexus was money, with David's magnate father J. Myer Schine funneling $50,000 or more in payments to the law firm Cohn was associated with, and Cohn in turn taking care of David (though the columnist never gathered sufficient proof to risk the libel suit he feared if he published his suspicions). Roy's biographer said Schine and Cohn each had something the other coveted: "Roy was getting in on the edges of some kind of café society life and David was getting in on the edges of governmental power." And everyone had a theory they couldn't prove that sex was at the center of things.

What was tough-guy Joe McCarthy getting in return for letting himself be dragged into mindless brawls with the Army and kicked out of cars by Roy Cohn? Schine was an indulgence he afforded Cohn, whom he admired as the one staffer who was more calculating than he was — and meaner — in charting the course of Joe's hearings and his crusade. Cohn also had contacts with Hearst CEO Richard Berlin, columnists George Sokolsky and Walter Winchell, and other captains of the Jewish and New York establishments that Roy understood as instinctively as Joe did the heartland. The senator had been justifying Roy to his right-wing friends by saying he was necessary protection against charges of anti-Semitism; in truth, Cohn was his key to a world that fascinated McCarthy, in part because it spurned him. In wrestling terms, their tag team did what neither could manage alone: Joe power slammed his opponents into submission; Roy choked, punched, and bit. Roy also stayed sober when Joe couldn't.

Whatever overseer-underling lines of authority existed at first had become blurred fifteen months later. That growing co-depen-

---

* The Army figured right. In his memoir Cohn wrote, "I know there have been imputations that I attempted to dodge the draft. I believe these stories have been planted in newspapers by persons who are attempting to stop my work." Whatever dodging there was by Cohn and Schine must have been especially galling to Ike, not just because of his time in combat, but because of his son's Army service during World War II and the Korean conflict. Cohn, *McCarthy*, 202.

dence alarmed Jean, as it did Joe's longtime friends. "If I got rid of Roy," Joe told Charlie Potter, "it would be the greatest victory the Communists have scored up to now. He's indispensable." The miscalculation was made worse by what biographer William F. Buckley Jr. called "the velocity of events." Things suddenly were happening too fast, with a face-off against the White House as well as the Army. Rather than turning to his astute wife, or to seasoned aides like Juliana, McCarthy relied more and more on the self-inflated Cohn. Joe could get away with his own recklessness and rule breaking, but not Roy's, too.*

The stories about McCarthy's bad behavior were unremitting. In the middle of hearings he'd sneak from his briefcase tumblers of straight bourbon, said Senator Everett Dirksen. At night it'd be straight vodka, according to Appleton friend Mark Catlin Jr. Add it up — the brandy in his breakfast coffee, shots mid-morning in a toilet stall, a cocktail or two at lunch, and highballs from dinner on — and he was consuming "a quart of liquor a day," Adams said. At the same time, the senator was getting even less sleep than usual, generally catnaps on the office couch or hotel room floor, and he was in and out of the hospital more than ever. His weight would rise and fall fifteen to twenty pounds in a matter of weeks, and he still ate too much beef, pork, and cheese and too little that was green or balanced. A reporter from *Time* visited the eight-room row house on Capitol Hill that Joe shared with Jean and their new Doberman pinscher. Hundreds of stacked boxes made clear they'd moved in just a month before and were too frantic to unpack. The phone rang a hundred times during the four-hour interview, and "the Senator took perhaps one call in ten, some times listening for a moment and then saying, 'The Senator is not here' . . . Several times during the evening, the Senator sank exhausted into his chair, muttering, 'I'm getting old.' He is 44." When Karl Mundt, the GOP senator from South Dakota, made a house call, he was

---

* Asked on *Meet the Press* whether he had some special hold on his boss, Roy countered, "I have no other hold on Senator McCarthy and I resent the suggestion." It was, he added, simply a matter of fealty: "No chairman ever had a more loyal staff than Senator McCarthy has on that committee and I think no staff ever had a more loyal chairman than we have in Senator McCarthy." Doherty, *Cold War, Cool Medium*, 226.

shocked to be greeted by Joe holding a .45 automatic. A Wisconsin friend "urged us to get Joe on a vacation," said Republican National Committee chairman Leonard Hall, "because he's cracking up."

Joe took solace from an anonymous quotation framed on his office wall: "Oh, God, don't let me weaken. Help me to continue on. And when I go down, let me go down like an oak tree felled by a woodsman's ax." In his home study, inspiration came in the form of a ten-foot poster of fellow desperado Jesse James, reading "Wanted Dead or Alive!"*

His staff, meanwhile, was in enough disarray that someone took it upon himself to draft a letter that everyone was asked to sign saying they believed that Cohn was loyal to McCarthy. (Bobby Kennedy, who wasn't convinced, is believed to have leaked it to the press.) In a TV address that was ostensibly a response to attacks by Adlai Stevenson on Republicans, the once supportive Vice President Nixon attacked McCarthy along with Stevenson. Domestic Communists, Nixon said, were in fact "a bunch of rats," the way Joe was charging. "But just remember this. When you go out to shoot rats, you have to shoot straight, because when you shoot wildly, it not only means that the rats may get away more easily — but you make it easier on the rats. Also you might hit someone else who is trying to shoot rats." No wonder Joe regularly referred to the vice president as "that prick Nixon."†

His speech, Nixon said in patting himself on the back, "marked the beginning of a new phase of the McCarthy episode, a phase that turned out to be the beginning of the end." He was right about the outcome if not the cause. The end game had actually begun

---

* Jean's mother was the actual owner of their new home on 3rd Street, NE, four blocks from the Senate Office Building. Mrs. Elizabeth Kerr lived in half; Jean and Joe rented the other half. Joe kept guns in that house the same way he did in his office, with his FBI files suggesting a reason. The bureau continued receiving death threats against the senator, including one saying he would "be assassinated May Day either in the Senate Hearings Hall or right outside of the Hall." *Life and Times of Joe McCarthy*, 555; and letter from Hoover to McCarthy, May 3, 1954, pt. 4 of 28, MFBI.
† A French editor offered a related metaphor for McCarthy's attack on the Army: "It is a case of burning down the barn to catch a rat." Friendly, *Due to Circumstances Beyond Our Control*, 28.

with Joe's tirade against Zwicker. "When on top of that the people not only heard but actually saw the persecution of Mrs. Moss and on top of that the extraordinary solicitude of Mr. Cohn for Mr. Schine, something happened which can best be described as the breaking of a spell," Walter Lippmann, the columnist who helped define the concept of a Cold War, wrote shortly after Moss testified and the Adams chronology was released. "The spell that has been broken is that the McCarthy activities are a rough but a necessary and salutary defense of the government, institutions, social order and the religion of the country against the Communist conspiracy and revolution. Although McCarthy says that that is what he is doing, less and less believe it."

No matter how much they trusted scribes like Lippmann, Americans needed to see for themselves. By early 1954, most had read about Joe McCarthy and caught snippets of him on Edward R. Murrow's *See It Now* broadcasts. But taking a searching look at him in action, the way tens of millions would during live TV coverage of the Army-McCarthy hearings that spring and summer, let them render judgment on whether America's most controversial political figure was a prophet or a con man. That was the privilege of democracy and the power of television.

The hearings brought into public focus the battles between the Army and the senator that had been playing out for months behind the subcommittee's closed doors and within the halls of the Pentagon and the White House. The inquiry was ordered by the Senate, with prodding from a suddenly combative president. The Permanent Subcommittee on Investigations was charged with answering two simple questions: Did Joe McCarthy and Roy Cohn pressure the Army to give Private Dave Schine special treatment? And did Army Secretary Robert Stevens and Army counsel John Adams pressure the senator to cancel his probe of the Army?

The subcommittee's three Democrats were salivating over the prospect of re-airing Joe's and the Army's humbling charges and countercharges. But it was Senator Potter of Michigan, a Republican and the swing vote on the increasingly partisan seven-man panel, who ensured that the hearings would happen. He'd had enough. When McCarthy wouldn't back off his support for Cohn,

Potter called him to account at a closed-door session just five days after the bombshell of the Adams chronology. Chairman McCarthy hesitantly agreed to yield his power and his seat temporarily, handing his gavel to Karl Mundt and his slot on the subcommittee to passionate anti-Communist Henry Dworshak, an Idaho Republican.* Other business would be put on hold, and the panel agreed to a novel set of rules for the hearings to come. There would be a two-hour session every morning, and two more hours in the afternoon. Everyone — the seven interrogating senators, three Army representatives, and Joe and his two staffers who were under investigation — would be seated along the same twenty-six-foot coffin-shaped mahogany table in the marble-walled Senate Caucus Room, with the Army and McCarthy trios changing positions on successive days to ensure equal access to the all-important television cameras. Even though Joe would himself be in what amounted to a witness box, he fought for and received the authority to question other witnesses.† A last right was granted that sounded like a technicality — being able to object on the grounds of "materiality and relevancy" — but the Wisconsin senator took it as license to filibuster by raising one point of order after another.

The hearings would rightfully be compared to a soap opera, even though there was no infidelity or seduction, the plot meandered, and the only stars were two hired-gun lawyers. Joe Welch was recruited to represent the Army by Stevens's brother, who recognized that the Boy Scout of an Army boss was "unable to defend himself" against a schoolyard bully like McCarthy.‡ Welch

---

* It wasn't actually a gavel; Mundt preferred banging a glass ashtray.
† There were six named targets in the investigation: on one side were Joe, Cohn, and Frank Carr, the ex-FBI agent and executive director of the subcommittee; the Army side included Stevens, Adams, and H. Struve Hensel, the assistant secretary of defense who was the administration's point man in preparing the Adams chronology. Near the end, Hensel and Carr were dropped from the proceedings, with each side making a concession to free one of its men and speed things up.
‡ Stevens could lay clearer claim to being a patriot than McCarthy, having served in the field artillery during World War I, manning Army headquarters during World War II, and watching three sons enter the military. Like Joe, the Army secretary "very much enjoyed a martini at lunch ... [and] he had martinis for breakfast," said Juliana. Yet Stevens "was weak and not a good match for McCarthy." Drew Pearson agreed, saying that Stevens's "motives and reactions are 100 percent right, but [his] brain is a little slow on the uptake." Juliana interview,

wasn't what he seemed. He had the air of a butter-won't-melt-in-his-mouth Brahmin. Graduating second in his class at Harvard Law, he rose quickly to senior partner at Hale and Dorr, Boston's whitest of white-shoe legal firms. But he had started out poor like Joe, on a farm in the Midwest, where, as he sweetened the story, the "maximum input of news in my early home was what was contained in a weekly newspaper, printed in Chicago, transported leisurely by rail to a little prairie town in Iowa, picked up on the occasional trips to town behind a pair of horses more noted for power than for speed, and then read by the soft yellow light of a kerosene lamp in the kitchen of a tiny farm house." Heartwarming as that picture was, Welch was a Bostonian now, albeit with quirks. He worked at a beat-up stand-up desk or lying on the couch, in an office filled with weather vanes and antique clocks. A wooden box held his supply of 150 bow ties, and the door of his office was shut most afternoons for an intra-firm game of cribbage. He thought it terrible luck for a lawyer to enter the courtroom with a two-dollar bill in his pocket, or to open his mouth unless speech was required. "I gained stature as a public speaker by a simple device of keeping still in a room where there was often accusation, charge and countercharge, and immense irrelevancy," said Welch, whose ties, tweeds, and vests gave him the air of a joyful leprechaun. "I was seen often to sit in what was actually stunned silence but was interpreted by the audience as wise restraint."

Welch's co-star and sometime antagonist was equally folkloric. Known to those following the hearings as the Terror of Tellico Plains, Ray Jenkins had been reared in the Tennessee hills, in the land of wild boars and, in the case of Tellico Plains, just 833 people. He threw a spitball so confounding that he'd thought about becoming a professional baseball player, possessed a legal mind sharp enough to pass the bar exam a year before he finished law school, and had a twang so booming that TV and radio electricians installed a special muzzle to keep his mouth two inches from the microphones. His legal philosophy, honed by representing moonshiners and husband killers, seemed just the right fit for the cur-

December 25, 1997, JJP; and Pearson, *Washington Merry-Go-Round: The Drew Pearson Diaries, 1949–1959,* 299.

rent flap: "You can always defend a man who kills a bully. You make the jury so damned mad that they want to dig up the body and kill the s.o.b. all over again." His client this time was the Subcommittee on Investigations, which meant wearing what amounted to five hats at once, none an easy fit as he tried to maintain neutrality while searching for an elusive truth. At times he defended the Army, and at other times he prosecuted it. He performed the same seesaw with McCarthy. In between, he was the arbiter on arguments over points of law and procedure. "There has been nothing like it," *Time* magazine proclaimed of the hulking counselor with a crew cut, "since Alec Guinness played eight parts in Kind Hearts and Coronets."*

Chairing the proceedings was Senator Mundt, a former schoolteacher and debating coach who wasn't eager to see his pal Joe McCarthy toppled, and wasn't adept at maintaining impartiality. (Observing his discomfort, reporters alternately called the pipe-smoking South Dakotan the "Tortured Mushroom" and the "Leaning Tower of Putty.") Other subcommittee members either relished sitting in judgment on their Wisconsin colleague or dreaded it, depending partly on their history with him. Everett Dirksen remembered how Joe helped him win election, while Henry Jackson never forgot how McCarthy campaigned against him. Stuart Symington saw the hearings as a tryout for his planned presidential bid; when Symington got overexcited, Jackson put his hand on his colleague's knee to calm him. (The press dubbed the mugging Missourian "Sanctimonious Stu," while they called the more likeable Jackson "Senator Jimmy Stewart.") John McClellan's Job-like life experience had left him with little sympathy for either the bellyaching or the draft dodging he'd heard about. The Arkansan's mother had died during his infancy, his second wife succumbed to spinal meningitis, and one son died in North Africa during World War II while a second was killed in a car accident in 1949. (Four years after the hearings, his third son would perish in a plane crash.)

The hearings officially launched on April 22, with perfect summer-like weather masking the cyclone inside the high-ceil-

* *Kind Hearts and Coronets* was a black comedy released in Britain in 1949.

inged Caucus Room that had hosted probes into such national traumas as the sinking of the *Titanic* and the surprise attack at Pearl Harbor. A crowd of four hundred filled every seat, with some lining up outside the great oak doors three hours early in hopes of snagging one of the limited spots open to the public. The rest went to celebrities, including Jean and other wives of senators, Teddy Roosevelt's daughter Alice, and four-sport sensation Babe Didrikson Zaharias. NBC, ABC, and the DuMont Television Network all broadcast the proceedings gavel to gavel, with CBS jumping in with a forty-five-minute summary at night. The TV crews were joined by fifteen cameramen from the newsreels, thirty-six photographers, and 120 reporters, which was a record for congressional coverage. Thirty wire circuits had to be installed to serve thirty-three teleprinters and eight Morse code tables. "The first sight of the hearing room was a shock to a lawyer used to the traditionally ordered interiors of courtrooms," said Welch, the Army's special counsel. "Photographers leaped up and down to get pictures. Messengers crawled beneath chairs. The cameras turned to follow the action. Senators came and went. People sat, stood and moved in every square inch of space and the whole crowded room was bathed in the bright lights of television. I took one look through the doorway and recoiled. The capitol patrolman on duty there was amused. 'Don't worry,' he said, 'in three days there won't be 20 people here.' I have often wondered why his judgment proved so wrong."

Thirty million people switched on their TV sets that first day of the clash between the senator and the Army, with 50 million more listening on the radio or following it in newspapers and magazines. That was more than for the World Series. Washing and ironing went undone. Stores and movie theaters reported slumping sales, but bars with a television set or radio began filling by mid-morning. Telephones stopped ringing even as sales of books on parliamentary procedure soared. In the one in three homes that didn't yet have a TV, people often rented one or watched with neighbors. About the only Americans who weren't glued to their sets were Vice President Nixon ("As I told a reporter, 'I just prefer professional actors to amateurs'") and perhaps President Eisenhower (whose biographer says he did watch, despite his denials).

There was, Welch observed, "something about these hearings that seemed to affect the public like a habit-forming drug."*

And they didn't tune in casually. Most who watched would remember it forever, no matter whose side they were on. It was a rare shared moment for the nation. In east Tennessee, a Knoxville TV station reversed policy and went on the air before noon, shades were drawn and the set was on in the county court office, and the Jenkins household bought its first TV to watch Ray and the others tangle. The Kornelys of Appleton also bought their first television set "just to watch the McCarthy hearings," recalls McCarthy's nephew Kelly, who wasn't quite a teenager then. Ira Glasser, who was sixteen at the time, says that "it was a seminal event for me . . . a political awakening" that would lead to a career running the American Civil Liberties Union. It also woke Carl Levin, who turned twenty during the hearings, which he watched and read about at Swarthmore College. "The country was taken by these hearings," says Levin, who would serve six terms in the Senate and chair that same Investigations Subcommittee. "We were into it, we were watching."

Such focus was more extraordinary given all that was competing for the nation's attention. The fall of Dien Bien Phu that spring signaled the end of the French era in Vietnam and the beginning of the American quagmire. *Brown v. Board of Education* banned segregated schools and loosened racial boundaries. Americans also were busy listening to "Mr. Sandman," watching *White Christmas,* and saying hello to *Annie Oakley* and good-bye to *Your Show of Shows.* Those developments were covered, but not as much as they might have been without the hearings, which consumed ten or more pages a day in the *New York Times.*

The first day set the pattern. Chairman Mundt opened by explaining the enormous stakes: "It is right and proper that each of us at this end of the committee room considers himself in a sense to be on trial." Speaking for the Democrats, Senator McClel-

---

* Popular as they were, the Army-McCarthy hearings didn't reach the record viewership of the Kefauver Crime Committee telecasts in 1951, when the topic was the proliferation of organized crime. Baker, "Inquiry's TV Rating Is Behind Kefauver's," *New York Times.*

lan added, "The charges and accusations are so diametrically in conflict, as I see it, that they cannot possibly be reconciled." It was Joe, however, who dominated the proceedings. It took just seventeen minutes for him to interrupt with his first "point of order," the phrase he would utter so often and sneeringly that it became his trademark.* Secretary Stevens and Army counselor Adams, he said, had no right to pretend they were the voice of the Army: "I may say, Mr. Chairman, that I have heard — may I have the attention of the Chair — may I say, Mr. Chairman, that I have heard from people in the military all the way down from generals, with the most upstanding combat records, down to privates recently inducted, and they indicate they are very resentful of the fact that a few Pentagon politicians, attempting to disrupt our investigations, are naming themselves the Department of the Army." That intervention, like most of his others, got nowhere with the committee, but it let Joe make his case with the TV cameras, which was his real aim. Over the course of the inaugural four-hour, eight-minute session, the Wisconsin senator clashed not just with Stevens and Adams but with subcommittee counsel Jenkins, General Miles Reber, and even his friend and acting chairman, Mundt. "While all principals to the dispute were accorded rights of cross-examination equal to subcommittee members," the *New York Times* reported, "Senator McCarthy held the microphone longer and more frequently than any other Senator, and was the only accused person who interrupted proceedings while others were talking."

That was a change in plans for Joe. For weeks he'd been saying, "This isn't my case." In the days leading up to the hearings, he was fishing in Galveston, and touching base with his Texas enablers. As late as the night before the inquiry began, during a speech in Hous-

---

* Stand-up comedians imitated his nasal tone as they shouted, "Point of order, point of order." It was the title of a best-selling vinyl spoof released that spring by radio personality Stan Freberg, and ten years later it became the title for a film on the hearings by famed documentarian Emile de Antonio. There also were parodies by the Canadian Broadcasting Corporation, *Mad Magazine,* and *The Red Skelton Show. The Crucial Decade,* 272.

Early in the hearings, a McCarthy staffer kept a written record of who used the parliamentary device, and how often, seemingly to make the point that the senator wasn't the only one. And he wasn't, although he did use it more than anyone else. Memo from Donald O'Donnell to McCarthy, April 28, 1954, series 14, MUA.

ton, he referred to "this television show of Adams versus Cohn." Once the TV cameras turned on their red lights, however, the senator couldn't resist. "It was not an Adams-Cohn show today," the *New York Times* observed. "It was McCarthy versus 'the rest' and this was so only because Mr. McCarthy made it so."*

Even as he himself stood accused, McCarthy managed from that first day to point fingers at others who weren't in the Caucus Room, or weren't part of the probe. Addressing Reber, he implied that the general was moved to testify against him by "the fact that your brother was allowed to resign when charges that he was a bad security risk were made against him as a result of the investigations of this committee." The brother was Samuel Reber, the former acting US high commissioner for Germany, who had clashed with Cohn and Schine during their junketeering investigation of overseas libraries and had paid a price. The McCarthy team quietly spread rumors that Sam Reber had engaged in homosexual activities as a Harvard undergraduate. The State Department subjected him to a polygraph and other screenings, and Sam retired from the Foreign Service in 1953 with what he hoped would be no fanfare. Miles Reber, trying to restrain himself by pounding his hand into his fist, asked for and got permission to respond to the senator's smear. "I do not know and have never heard that my brother retired as a result of any action of this committee. The answer is positively no to that question." While Joe withdrew his question, the damage had been done.

Another who found himself at the point of McCarthy's gun was Assistant Secretary of Defense H. Struve Hensel. McCarthy charged that Hensel tried to keep the subcommittee from investigating his get-rich scheme when he was a wartime official with the Navy. The senator formally dropped the charges midway through the hearings, then repeated them every chance he got in a way that Hensel convincingly argued was slander. The assistant secretary

---

* He wasn't the only one performing. What had been a one-man committee was, now that the TV cameras were there and the nation was watching, the seven-man panel it was supposed to be. And Adams-Cohn wasn't the only rebranding of the hearings that Joe would suggest. He proposed Stevens-Adams and the Cohn Mutiny, a play on *The Caine Mutiny,* a film out that year based on Herman Wouk's 1951 Pulitzer Prize–winning novel.

confronted the senator off-camera and, as Adams recounted, "Mc-Carthy responded that he had learned from an 'old Indian friend' named 'Indian Charlie,' that 'when anyone approached him in a not completely friendly fashion, [to] start kicking that person in the balls and continue to kick until there was nothing but air where the balls used to be.'"

The hearings were expected to last two weeks, and to focus on whether either the McCarthy side or the Army had strong-armed the other. Neither could answer candidly without looking culpable, so both mastered the artifice of changing the subject. Asked about his aides' misdeeds, Joe demanded to know who'd leaked such bum raps; quizzed about its pandering, the Army steered the conversation back to Cohn and Schine's bullying. The result was to drag the proceedings out for seven long weeks, by the end of which America was glassy-eyed.

The McCarthy team would be called out for its obvious and blatant lies. The two-and-a-half-page memo that had propelled its Army probes was exposed as an abbreviated fake, although it's unclear that it made much difference in the end. There also was a "doctored" photo that reminded those who knew Joe of the one that had been altered during the 1950 Maryland campaign to make it look like Senator Tydings was chumming it up with deposed Communist boss Earl Browder. The picture in question this time showed Schine and Stevens apparently enjoying each other's company at Fort Dix. In the version given to the subcommittee, the base commander was edited out in what Welch painted as a duplicitous attempt to make the relationship between the lowly private and the big boss seem cozier than it was. In fact, the Army had already done some editing of its own, erasing McCarthy staffer Frank Carr before giving the print to the McCarthy staff. While Don Surine and Jim Juliana did further pruning, Juliana said the senator had "nothing to do with the cropped picture." With and without both changes, the photo was just what Cohn said it was: evidence of Stevens and Schine posing good-naturedly when they were supposed to be feuding.

A more genuine case of trickery surrounded the eleven memoranda Joe said had been dictated in real time documenting the Army's efforts to squeeze Schine so the subcommittee would back off its probes. The memos were the foundation of the McCarthy offense, but the Army said they were constructed "not brick by brick, but all at once, when a shelter was badly needed." That mattered, it added, for two reasons. First, "the memoranda lose the probative force of documents or writings and have no greater weight than would oral testimony of the witnesses." Worse still, "those who have testified that the documents were contemporaneous have misrepresented the facts . . . casting doubt on the credibility of the witnesses themselves in all other matters." Again, anyone who'd been paying attention knew that Joe had been misrepresenting documents not just since Wheeling but as far back as his race for circuit judge. And this time Welch and the Army were right, as McCarthy confidant Willard Edwards later conceded. Correctly suspecting that the Adams chronology blended his real-time diary with his ex post facto recollections, the McCarthy team decided it, too, would "translate [its] memories into typed memos, backdated," Edwards said. "Carr, former FBI agent, advised on paper, etc. so that no check could be made to question the authenticity of these exhibits . . . There are few parallels in congressional investigating history for a hearing in which one fake memo was rebutted by a fake memo from the other side!"

Even as the subcommittee was getting into those weeds, other conflicts surfaced that were bigger than McCarthy or the Army and beyond the panel's mandate. One was the division of powers between the White House and Congress. McCarthy had been pushing those boundaries since he got to the Senate, demanding answers and witnesses from the executive branch. President Eisenhower responded by asserting executive privilege aimed at safeguarding both legitimate security secrets and political ones about his complicity in the Adams chronology.* In response, Joe went even further out on a limb, defending his right to protect the identities of leakers who defied such White House edicts. "I would like to notify those 2,000,000 Federal employees that I feel it is their duty to

---

* Seeing how easily Ike asserted that privilege might have encouraged Nixon to do the same fourteen years later during the Watergate scandal, when he tried unsuccessfully to use it to keep secret White House tape recordings whose release undermined his presidency.

give us any information which they have about graft, corruption, communism, treason," McCarthy said, "and that there is no loyalty to a superior officer which can tower above and beyond their loyalty to their country." His message was clear: while passing classified information to anyone else was espionage, it was not just okay but patriotic to pass the topmost secrets to him. "If any Administration wants to indict me for receiving and giving the American people the information about communism," Joe taunted, "they can just go right ahead and do the indicting."

The White House hit back a day later, saying the executive's responsibility "cannot be usurped by any individual who may seek to set himself above the laws of our land." The president was tougher in private, pacing behind his desk as he told his press secretary, "McCarthy is making exactly the same plea of loyalty to him that Hitler made to the German people. Both tried to set up personal loyalty within the government while both were using the pretense of fighting communism . . . This is the most disloyal act we have ever had by anyone in the government of the United States."

The president despised Joe, and the Army-McCarthy hearings offered an opportunity to bring him down. Ike knew, from his periodic secret briefings by Senator Potter, what was happening out front and in back rooms. While the Army wanted the painful hearings to end as quickly as possible, its commander in chief felt the longer they went on — and the more exposure the ungovernable senator got — the easier it would be to topple him, which was the president's goal. Democratic minority leader Lyndon Johnson wanted the same thing, as did the Republican National Committee, GOP moderates in Congress, most of the rest of the Washington establishment, and Army counselor Welch, who, by the end, seemed more concerned with the national interest than with his client's. None of that surprised Joe.

Press coverage of the high-stakes confrontation began to wane as early as day three. The subcommittee had put the networks on notice that they couldn't interrupt the hearings for commercials, which meant the loss of what NBC calculated was $50,000 a day ($472,000 today). CBS, the broadcaster that Murrow had placed ahead of the pack in its McCarthy coverage, put profits first from the start in opting for Arthur Godfrey and Art Linkletter rather than Joe McCarthy and Bob Stevens. NBC did the same after day two. That left the upstart ABC and the struggling DuMont as the only networks with beginning-to-end coverage, a decision that limited viewership, since together they had fewer than one hundred stations nationwide. But those who were able to tune in did, with the hearings spawning a 29 percent jump in morning television viewing and grabbing a 68 percent share of that audience.

What they saw didn't have the anticipated melodrama of a daytime soap, but it did have the hot-button issue of homosexuality long before that subject was acceptable to discuss on television. Adams denied the charge that he'd offered to point the senator to a homoerotic scandal in the Air Force if he went easy on the Army.* Welch, meanwhile, cynically raised the issue in the discussion of cropped pictures, asking Juliana whether he thought the photo "came from a pixie." McCarthy: "Will the counsel for my benefit define — I think he might be an expert on that — what a pixie is?" Welch: "Yes. I should say, Mr. Senator, that a pixie is a close relative of a fairy. Shall I proceed, sir? Have I enlightened you?" Spectators chuckled, knowing the gossip about Cohn's attraction to Schine, and perhaps to McCarthy. Cohn insisted afterward that "McCarthy was not offended by the remark, despite journalists' assertions that from that point on he reserved a special hatred for Mr. Welch. He told me later he thought it was funny. To me, the most significant aspect of the incident was that no one criticized the wicked and, if I may use the word in referring to Mr. Welch, indecent jab."†

Testy encounters like that were typical of the hearings' sniping and sparring. There was Joe versus Stevens, Cohn versus Ad-

---

* Adams confided later, "There actually had been a homosexual scandal brewing on an Army base in the South, and I had been scared to death that McCarthy and Co. would find out about it." *Without Precedent*, 193.

† Cohn would have had an even stronger case if he'd known about the chatter in the Army's Office of General Counsel. "There was kind of an undercurrent that Roy Cohn was gay," recalls Melvin Dow, then a young lawyer in the office. "Suspicions were stronger in the case of Roy Cohn than in the case of David Schine, and stronger in the case of Roy Cohn than of McCarthy, although I do recall [a] kind of locker room talk that McCarthy makes it hard for everybody but Jean, referring to Jean Kerr." Author interview with Dow.

ams, Democrats versus Republicans, moderate Republicans versus conservative Republicans, Jenkins versus Welch, the executive versus the legislature, and, just off-screen, Senator McCarthy versus President Eisenhower. Such backstage skirmishes have now come into clear view, with the unlocking of long-cached records. Joe was digging for any dirt he could find on the Democrats and anyone else, generals included, who stood up for the other side. He pressed the Republican National Committee to open its files in ways that made even a partisan group like that uncomfortable, and he tapped leakers, apparently including the Internal Revenue commissioner, to get sacrosanct tax returns.* With Senator Symington, McCarthy threatened to use a story from his youth of an unauthorized joyride in a neighbor's car. (Throwing his arm around his colleague, McCarthy asked with a grin, "Stole any cars lately, Stu?") Senator Jackson was convinced McCarthy "had a dossier on every member of the committee, on every member of Eisenhower's Cabinet, and even on Eisenhower himself."

Late in the hearings, when tensions between the McCarthy team and subcommittee Democrats were completely frayed, Bobby Kennedy coached Jackson on ways of ridiculing David Schine's plan for waging psychological warfare against the Communists by enlisting church leaders and Hollywood pinups. When the hearing recessed, Cohn strode up to Kennedy and, according to Bobby, threatened to "get" Jackson by revealing something he had written that was "favorably inclined toward Communists." Kennedy: "Don't you make any warnings to us about Democratic Senators." Cohn: "I'll make any warnings to you that I want to — any time, anywhere. Do you want to fight right here?" Fisticuffs were avoided,

---

* Joe was so frustrated with the RNC's failure to give him information on Senator Henry Jackson that he wrote to the committee director, "If it is true that your office has decided not to give a Republican Senator any information upon a left-wing Democrat, I would like to have that from you in writing, rather than by way of a telephone conversation from your subordinates." Those subordinates were indeed resisting the senator's entreaties, for what seemed like good reasons that their boss agreed with. "McCarthy had somehow gotten [Assistant Secretary of Defense] Hensel's income tax data, then released it contrary to all promises," RNC PR man James Bassett wrote in his memoirs. "So how *can* you trust the guy?" Letter from Joe to Leonard Hall, April 29, 1954, series 14, MUA; and Bassett, *Ugly Year, Lonely Man*, 108.

but that weekend Jackson, Bobby, and another aide worked into the nights parsing four years of official correspondence, searching for a letter that might besmirch the white knight reputation of the senator from the state of Washington. "There really was nothing to find," Jackson said. "By Monday Cohn was backing away, denying all, and McCarthy said he did 'not intend to go into any senator's background at these hearings.'"*

He made no such promises about his enemies in the Army. Joe managed to get John Adams's tax returns, or so Adams thought. He also was convinced that he was being followed and that his home phone was being tapped. So he took countermeasures. "I started leaving my cab, walking in one door and out the other of the Mayflower Hotel, and picking up a second cab," Adams said. "We took to conversing in double-talk over the phone, and during the latter days of the hearings in the evenings I usually walked to a neighborhood drugstore (but never the same one twice) to make calls." One night a legal colleague saw a G-2 Army Intelligence security man searching Adams's desk. The next day, Adams said, "I tore off a sheet of paper and wrote in red pencil: 'Fuck You G-2.' I sealed the paper in an envelope which I stamped in red letters, SECRET and put it in my top desk drawer. On the insistence of my associates, I later tore it up and put it in the 'Burn' basket, agreeing that the office already was in enough trouble."

Everyone had a different way of working out those strains. "I had never been much of a drinker, but I began drinking that spring," said Adams. "Every day when I came home, [my wife] Margaret would have two old-fashioneds waiting for me. I would gulp them down. And sometimes I would have a couple after dinner, so that I could face the night." Welch got relaxing massages before dinner. Jenkins took to settling his six-foot-three-inch,

---

* Kennedy hardly needed more reasons to despise Cohn, but he'd recently learned that Roy had tried to smear Bobby's younger brother, Ted, with unfounded rumors about Ted's association with "pinkos." Cohn had his own new gripe: Bobby had told Mary Driscoll, McCarthy's secretary, "I couldn't find Joe, but I want you to give him a message. In these hearings, I'm going to do nothing to hurt him. In fact, I'm going to protect him every way I can ... But I'm really going to get that little son-of-a-bitch Cohn." Hilty, *Brother Protector*, 88; and Roy Cohn OH, March 24, 1971, 3–4, JFKL.

195-pound frame into a hotel bathtub filled first with steaming hot water, then with ice cold.

Subcommittee Democrats fought back in a way they hadn't before their boycott, as the release of their monitored phone calls showed. Senator Symington, Joe's primary foil, quietly advised Secretary Stevens how to deal with the recalcitrant Wisconsin lawmaker. "I would never get near him if I could help it . . . This fellow might be sick, you know," said Symington, unaware that an Army stenographer was listening in and that his transcripts would later be made public. "If you are going to play with McCarthy," Symington added, "you have got to forget about any of those [Marquess of] Queensberry rules." After reading the records of those calls, McCarthy called on Symington—whom he referred to as "an alleged man"—to disqualify himself from serving on the subcommittee. "Never before in the history of this Senate," Joe said, "have we had a man who instituted the charges insist upon sitting as judge." Which of course was exactly what Joe had been doing all along.

Not all the memories from those six weeks are heavy ones. Joe sent Roy out every day for a copy of the *Washington Post*—not to read its harsh coverage but to see what *Pogo*'s Simple J. Malarkey was up to. He'd also pick up the scandal sheet *Confidential,* slipping it in between the pages of the more respectable *U.S. News & World Report*. Cohn later confided that he knew in advance about the embarrassing questions put to him because the wives of friendly senators, who were seated directly behind opposition members, peeked at the Democrats' papers and—"better than the CIA"—slipped Roy and Joe notes laying out the Dems' upcoming queries. The opposition landed its own whimsical dig when Arthur Wilson, a retired major general, mailed a check for $100 to the commander at Fort Dix to be awarded to the first noncommissioned officer to punch Private Schine in the nose.

While it wasn't meant to be funny, testimony about David Schine's conduct in the Army evoked laughter in the Caucus Room. Minutes after meeting his company commander, Schine flashed his wealth by offering the officer "a little trip to Florida." Later, that commander, Captain Joseph Miller, found Schine in the cab of a truck parked at the mess hall during a driving rainstorm while fellow trainees were taking rifle practice. Schine explained that he was "studying logistics." Miller ordered Schine to the firing range, where the private pulled the captain aside for a chat. "He thereupon told me that it was his purpose to remake the American military establishment along modern lines." As "ridiculous" incidents like that mounted, Miller's executive officer told Schine that his behavior was eroding morale among the 250 men in his company. "Private Schine said that his work [with the subcommittee] was much more important than the morale of the company," Miller testified. "Private Schine said that he wasn't worried about the morale of 250 men, he was [focused on the well-being] of 160,000,000 [American] people."*

One recurring image of the hearings was Roy leaning over Joe's shoulder and whispering in his ear, Svengali-like.† Another attention-grabber was Joe's enduring five o'clock shadow, which he knew made him seem sinister and which he tried to address by shaving twice a day during those six weeks. He also used cream-colored makeup that "gave a startling aspect to his jowls," said *New Republic* editor Michael Straight, who wrote a book about the hearings. "A roll of flesh beneath his black eyebrows came down over his upper eyelids, making slits of his eyes, and giving to his face an almost Satanic look." As for his trademark points of order, they actually kept him out of jail. It happened when he was visiting friends in Milwaukee. Finding the doors locked at his host's new home, Joe broke a window to let everyone in. The police arrived and were about to arrest him and the rest of the group, remembered Dion Henderson. When Joe said he was a senator, a disbelieving officer said that was as likely as the cop being the Prince of Wales. To prove it, Joe intoned, "Mr. Chairman . . . a point of or-

---

* Miller went on to describe unabashed bids by Schine to avoid kitchen police duty and not be required to sign out when he left the post. The pretense that Schine's time away from the base was spent toiling over subcommittee business was undermined when Welch produced receipts from nightclubs and restaurants during those leaves. "Excerpts from Transcript of 21st Day of Senate Testimony in Army-McCarthy Dispute," *New York Times*.
† That scene made Cohn so wistful that he hung a huge photograph of it on his office wall.

der." That was all it took; a minute later the policeman was asking for the senator's autograph.

Joe's days during the hearings were long ones, starting with the planning breakfast that Jean pulled together for him, Cohn, Carr, and Juliana. One plainclothes Metropolitan Police officer led the way to the hearings, while another was there for the trip home; both remained by his side in between. After an intense morning, the senator and his aides would head to the Carroll Arms for lunch. (His typically was a hamburger, washed down with tea, a milkshake, and a libation.) After more hearings, there was more strategizing with a group that sometimes included old friends from Wisconsin along with intermittent staffer David Schine. Dinner would be at home (more hamburgers and tea) or at his favorite restaurant, The Colony, where, Drew Pearson said, the group would be "whisked to a large, reserved, corner table. The management, as a 'security' measure, refuses to permit anyone to occupy the adjacent table . . . Whispered conversations follow. If a waiter approaches they stop . . . Schine demands that a table telephone be plugged in for his use . . . Main course is a huge steak, well done, partitioned into three pieces . . . They called this 'going threesies' on the steak."

Advice also poured in during the hearings from McCarthy's Texas and New York benefactors, and especially oilman Clint Murchison. Before the hearings, he had sought to mend rifts between Joe and Ike. Once the sessions started and any peace with the president was impossible, Murchison offered McCarthy this advice: "If you keep on going as you presently have gone and do not get 'snurly' with Welch, my opinion is that you are going to get back all of your public you have heretofore lost and possibly gain new admirers."

He did gain admirers, at first. He was the everyman, railing against small-minded bureaucrats and evil-intentioned traitors. His courage in taking on not just the military's mightiest brass but Boston's and east Tennessee's cagiest lawyers was inspiring. Day after tiring day he would rear back and roar, in contrast to the sickly and obsequious Stevens. "McCarthy's OK — he's got spunk," a piano tuner from East Stroudsburg, Pennsylvania, said afterward. "They've never pinned a thing on him and he's never been made a fool of." A barber in New England agreed: "He was as calm as a cucumber."

Whether he had ever been relaxed is questionable, but there is no doubt that any calm was shattered the afternoon of June 9, 1954, as the hearings reached an emotional climax. Roy Cohn was withering on the witness stand under Welch's unrelenting cross-examination, first about Roy's cavorting in Manhattan with Private Schine; then Welch demanded to know why, the first time Cohn met Stevens, "you didn't tug at his lapel and say, 'Mr. Secretary, I know something about Monmouth that won't let me sleep nights.'" Across the table, Joe was mad as a hornet as Welch continued with his taunting, and without warning the Wisconsin senator interrupted with a characteristic "Mr. Chairman, in view of that question . . ." Then out of the blue and beyond any bounds, McCarthy charged that Welch's law associate in Boston, Frederick Fisher Jr., belonged to the National Lawyers Guild "long after it had been exposed as the legal arm of the Communist party." Seemingly near tears, Welch replied, "Until this moment Senator, I think I never really gauged your cruelty or your recklessness . . . Let us not assassinate this lad further, Senator. You've done enough. Have you no sense of decency, sir? At long last, have you left no sense of decency?"

The question hung in the air of the hearing room and living rooms across America, and became the watchword of the Army-McCarthy saga. Cohn seemed to mouth the words "No! No!" as he frantically scratched out a note to his boss saying, "This is the subject which I have committed to Welch we would not go into. Please respect our agreement." Upholding his defamed associate, Welch sounded more like a preacher than a lawyer as he scolded the senator, "If there is a God in heaven it will do neither you nor your cause any good." The audience at first seemed stunned, then, defying the chairman's long-standing admonition, it burst into loud and long applause in support of Welch and Fisher. Making no attempt to gavel for silence, Mundt declared a recess. Welch followed him out of the room. McCarthy was left behind and exposed. "What did I do?" he asked his aides, his hands spread and palms turned up. "What did I do?" Of the millions who'd heard, he alone didn't know.

During the break Welch and McCarthy both dug in. The Army lawyer seemed to be wiping his eyes in the restroom. "I'm close to tears," he told reporters. "Here's a young kid with one mistake —just one mistake— and [McCarthy] tries to crucify him. I don't see how in the name of God you can fight anybody like that. I never saw such cruelty . . . such arrogance." But as McCarthy saw it, there were no bounds in his crusade against the communism conspiracy, and Welch had opened the floodgates by browbeating Cohn. "Too many people can dish it out," the senator said, "but can't take it."*

We know now there was more to the Fisher affair. McCarthy's tantrum wasn't the first revelation of the young lawyer's background, or even the second. Welch himself made it public before the hearings started, although the *New York Times* thought it unnewsworthy enough to give it two paragraphs on page twelve at the end of a related story. Four days later, in a brief filed with the subcommittee, McCarthy wrote that "a law partner of Mr. Welch has, in recent years, belonged to an organization found by the House Un-American Activities Committee to be the 'legal bulwark' of the Communist Party . . . This same law partner was selected by Mr. Welch to act as his aide in this matter, and was discharged only when his Communist-front connection became publicly known."†

---

* Was Welch's performance that day—from his "have you no sense of decency" speech, to nearly crying in front of the media—rehearsed? Adams, who wasn't a Welch fan, called him a "master actor" and said he overheard the lawyer asking a friend during the recess, "Well, how did it go?" Cohn at first agreed, calling it "an act from start to finish." But later he got to know Welch and changed his answer, saying there was no evidence that the famous remarks were prepared in advance. *Without Precedent*, 229; Cohn, *McCarthy*, 204; and Reeves interview with Cohn, April 14, 1978.

Whether the trap was pre-planned or sprung spontaneously was beside the point. What mattered is that it was laid in the open—by Welch pushing Team McCarthy beyond what he knew was McCarthy's capacity for self-restraint— and Joe fell into it.

† The Lawyers Guild was controversial, and Attorney General Brownell tried to add it to his list of subversive organizations, but he was blocked by the courts. Was the guild the legal mouthpiece of the Communist Party, as McCarthy and others charged? Some of its founders did have such ties. But the organization spent more time advocating for the New Deal and against racial segregation than pushing a Communist agenda, and most members, Fisher included, were liberal, not radical or Red.

The senator showed the discretion then not to name Fisher, even though the *New York Times* had, and had run his photo. Welch and Cohn had discussed the matter, and Cohn agreed his side wouldn't discuss Fisher during the TV hearings, in return for Welch's not bringing up Roy's draft dodging. While Joe regularly threatened to "tell the 'Fisher story,'" Fisher himself recalled, Assistant Secretary of Defense Fred Seaton had dirt on McCarthy that he thought would keep the senator quiet: "that on at least one occasion Senator McCarthy wanted a person cleared for a government post who had a Communist background and that, as a favor to McCarthy, [Seaton] had cooperated."

So why did Joe McCarthy, his generation's most masterly political tactician, break his word, risk Seaton's revenge, and, just eight days before the hearings ended, alienate much of America with his hardhearted outing of Fred Fischer? The answer is simple, said the senator's lawyer, Edward Bennett Williams: "McCarthy was a man who could never resist the temptation to touch a sign which said WET PAINT, and he had to touch this one." But Roy Cohn, one of the few people McCarthy trusted to speak for him, knew there was more to it. "Here was a man who came across, at the most important crossroad of his life, as villainy incarnate—a dictatorial, brutal, obstructive, utterly humorless bully," Cohn said. "I knew, and all of us around Joe knew, [McCarthy] was doing miserably. But we never told him . . . Would it have mattered? If we all [had] had the courage to tell him it sure would have mattered. Joe Welch certainly couldn't have done the Fred Fisher number had Joe McCarthy been even half the McCarthy we knew. It took a lot of self-destruction to get set up for that line about 'decency.' And that was the line that made the lasting impression."

That's true—if one agrees with Cohn that the real McCarthy was "a man with warmth, humor, loyalty, a man who loved people, who was forgiving almost beyond the bounds of reasonableness." A more convincing take on the man, and the "decency" moment, came from the independent, unpredictable *New York Post* columnist Murray Kempton. "Joe McCarthy was naked at that moment, and no man who ever clasped his hand and laughed with him could escape the sense that he had at that moment bathed himself in filth," Kempton wrote. "Joe McCarthy went on sneering and snarling, alone as animals are alone and unconscious that he had done an evil thing . . . You can only measure what that [audience] applause meant when you knew that two press photographers were clapping, and I have never believed before that a press photographer cared whether any subject lived or died . . . The Army, stumbling, tired and shadowed, has been handed its best witness; his name was Joseph R. McCarthy."*

Everything from then on seemed anticlimactic and a time to take stock. The notion that Joe would be done in by divulging a secret that wasn't a secret is one in a series of ironies from these hearings. The same cameras that had helped make Joe McCarthy into a national somebody now let America see how much he had overpromised and underperformed. Sensationalized allegations — of doctored photographs and purloined documents — were almost as ruinous to him as they had been to his opponents over the years. The Republican president's ablest defenders were the subcommittee Democrats. The only hero among these seven senators was the one least made for TV, the crusty Arkansan John McClellan, who came across as less partisan than his Democratic colleagues and less blinded than Joe's Republican enablers.† And Senator McCarthy, who was a legitimate war hero, was done in by two aides who, it seemed, would do anything not to serve. Most counterintuitive of all, Joe's most consequential congressional hearing centered on

---

* Fisher had a simpler explanation for McCarthy's attack on him: "The motive of the Senator in making this statement can best be illustrated in the words of a great English poet: 'A truth that's told with bad intent, Beats all the lies you can invent.'" To Defense Secretary Wilson, the perpetual back-and-forth between the senator and the Army brought to mind a more homegrown adage: "If your political opponent accuses you of being a liar, don't deny it. Accuse him of being a horse thief." Statement of Frederick G. Fisher Jr., June 10, 1954, Grinnell College Special Collections and Archives; and Lawrence, "M'Carthy Hearing Will Start Today," *New York Times*.

† While everyone from Ike to most Senate Democrats judged McClellan the hearings' only hero, that verdict wasn't unanimous. "He didn't like me from day one, not because he was soft on Communism," said Cohn. "What McClellan didn't like about me had to do with an ancient disease he had picked up. He was a Bible belt Jew hater, John McClellan was, and the more he admired my work the more he couldn't stomach the fact that here was a Jew doing it." *Autobiography of Roy Cohn*, 124–25.

G. David Schine, an unknown, unpaid, unremarkable aide whom neither side took seriously enough even to call as a witness.

There were no winners in the Army-McCarthy showdown. The Army ended up looking mealy-mouthed and two-faced, but its actions were certainly not the blackmail that McCarthy alleged. Its fault was not knowing when to say no as it dispensed one favor after another to Private Schine, and, when it finally learned, making that seem like punishment rather than a righting of the scales. Schine, Cohn, and the senator behaved still worse. Roy overtly and persistently pressured the Army to give his friend special treatment, using as his cudgel the subcommittee's hearings into vital matters of national security. Joe wouldn't admit publicly how little Schine mattered or tell Cohn that he too would be replaced if he couldn't control himself. And both the senator and his aides tried to cover up what they'd done.

The unveiling of the closed-door parts of the hearings makes clear just how eager Democrats were to keep asking questions, and how determined Republicans were to shut down the proceedings. That happened on a straight party-line vote, with the last session on June 17, which was day thirty-six. Thirty-two witnesses had spoken some 2 million words, over 187 hours, filling 7,424 pages of transcripts. Senator Mundt had planned a party, issuing "subpoenas" instead of invitations. The celebration was canceled when Senator Lester Hunt — heartbroken over the controversy roiling around his homosexual son Buddy — shot himself that same day in his Senate office, a grisly event that his descendants say was prompted by and aimed at his bitter enemy Joe McCarthy.

After seven weeks of confusing testimony, the public was "groggy, bewildered — and, above all, bored," said Gallup boss John Fenton. But while America had had enough of this Army-McCarthy show, it never tired of the underlying plot of a crusading senator waging war against his country's military. Gallup found that an astounding 78 million Americans understood the basic charges and countercharges, which was substantially more than could name their senator, their congressman, and probably Lassie the Rough Collie. Forty-five million had watched the hearings on TV, 55 million listened on the radio, and 65 million read about them. The public at first sided two to one with the Army, and it remained more sympathetic to the armed services than to McCarthy. Yet whereas only 34 percent of respondents began by agreeing that the Army had inappropriately interfered with the senator's investigations, by the end, 54 percent did.

The Army's loss wasn't Joe's gain. Seventy percent of those surveyed started out believing the senator had gone overboard; at the end, 68 percent still faulted him. His overall support nosedived — from a full half of Americans in January 1954 to merely a third as the hearings were wrapping up in June. Approval also plummeted among Catholics, his base of support. Anti-Communist backers remained steadfast, but those from the political mainstream wavered. The public verdict on the senator's performance and the Army's, Fenton pronounced, was "a plague on both your houses."*

The subcommittee said essentially the same thing when it published its findings at the end of August. The four Republicans agreed with the seventy-eight-page summary of evidence produced by Democratic counsel Bobby Kennedy. He found dereliction of duty everywhere: Cohn abusing his authority, the Army appeasing and placating the senator and his staff, Joe letting things get out of control. The question was, What to do? The Republicans recommended just procedural fixes, from never again hiring unpaid staffers, to limiting contacts between congressional staff and executive agencies like the Army. (The subcommittee did substantially tighten its rules the next year.) Democrats insisted on punitive action, especially against their errant chairman, McCarthy, calling on the Justice Department to investigate whether he'd committed the very infractions of which he'd accused so many witnesses: perjury and violation of the Espionage Act. (As with earlier requests by other committees, Justice looked into it but decided not to act.)

There was one more judgment on the senator during those turbulent months, this one by the voters of Wisconsin. A movement

* One more measure of Joe's declining clout was noted when Gallup asked whether his endorsement of a candidate would make a voter more or less likely to choose that candidate. In January 1954, 26 percent said it would make them less likely; by May, that number had soared to 43 percent. *In Your Opinion,* 142.

with the fetching title "Joe Must Go" was demanding a recall election. Leaders of labor, media, agriculture, and religion sat out the drive, believing it would fail and McCarthy would retaliate. Their constituents had more faith and courage. As time ran out that June, the must-goers had gathered a third of a million notarized signatures — 20 percent shy of what they needed, but enough to make it the largest recall bid in the nation's history and to let Joe know he was in trouble back home, too.* Leroy Gore, the small-town newspaper editor and former McCarthy booster who led the initiative, remembered afterward

> the exact moment of my conversion to anti-mccarthyism. One night I sat watching television at the home of a friend whose twelve-year-old daughter has long been a favorite of mine. Senator McCarthy was attacking one of his political foes with his customary political irresponsibility . . . "Is Mr. Truman *really* a traitor?" the little girl wanted to know. "Of course not," I assured her. "Why does Senator McCarthy say he's a traitor?" she persisted. "Politics," I explained learnedly . . . The little girl looked horrified. "You mean we run our government with lies?" . . . "O.K., Jackie," I said. "You win. Hereafter we won't defend our democracy with lies if I have anything to say about it."

Joe's war with the Army did more than stir voters and spike TV ratings; it changed the lives of nearly everyone involved. Brigadier General Zwicker was promoted to major general three years later, with Senator McCarthy one of two dissenting votes. Joe's staffers weren't so lucky, with most housecleaned out of their jobs. (Don Surine was saved when the senator put him on his office payroll, and Jim Juliana was too competent to fire.) Fred Fisher became a partner at his prestigious law firm and went on to serve as president of the Massachusetts Bar Association. John Adams lost

---

* A counterpart campus movement called itself the Robin Hood Club. Launched at the University of Wisconsin, it was spreading to other colleges by early 1954. "Members wear a white button with a green feather, signifying their opposition to all forms of totalitarianism — both communism and McCarthyism," wrote Drew Pearson. "Wearers of the green feathers call themselves Robin Hood's Merry Men. Their motto is: 'Robin Hood says they are your books. Don't let McCarthyism burn them.'" Pearson column, April 11, 1954.

his job in the spring of 1955 and had so few employment options that for three years he was what he called "a 'Fifth Street lawyer,' the Washington legal community's definition of one who practices alone near the courthouse, taking whatever cases came along . . . [I]n the first three months I grossed twenty-five dollars." Stevens survived a bit longer before returning to his family's textile empire. His departure was welcomed by the White House but was bad news for key staffers who were transferred or downgraded by the new Army secretary, a McCarthy fan. Adams wrote one in a series of reminiscences on the hearings by up-close observers; Stevens wasn't one to share memories with anyone, and certainly not to air them publicly.

David Schine served out his time in the Army, including in Alaska, which, he said, "the administration thought was a good safe place for me, because at that time it was even more remote than now, and communication was difficult." He steered clear of politics after that, marrying a former beauty queen and thriving in the hotel, music, and film worlds. Schine was executive producer of the 1971 thriller *The French Connection,* which won the Oscar for Best Picture; had a cameo on the *Batman* TV series; composed and published music; and, during a trip to Harvard for his twenty-fifth reunion, guest-conducted the *Boston Pops.* He, his wife, and one of their six children were killed in 1996 when their private plane crashed.

Roy Cohn resigned from the subcommittee a month after the hearings ended and just before he was to be fired. "I'm not sorry I left," Cohn said later, "but I have always regretted the manner of my leave-taking. I could have forced the committee to fire me . . . I should have done so . . . It bugs me to this day that I hauled off and left without making those bastards do the dirty job themselves, out in the open." He went on to serve as an attorney for the rich and an unparalleled influence peddler in Manhattan. He was tried and acquitted three times in federal court on charges including conspiracy and bribery (he blamed it on vendettas by then attorney general Bobby Kennedy and his friends), and eventually he was disbarred for conduct deemed unprofessional, unethical, and reprehensible (which he called a smear job). There has been endless speculation on Cohn's so-called "purge of the perverts" at the

State Department and beyond. Was it to camouflage his own homosexuality? Was it self-hatred, like his targeting of fellow Jews in his hunt for Reds? Cohn talked in two memoirs and elsewhere about McCarthy's motivations, but it was left to his gay lovers and others to muse about Roy's.

Robert Kennedy took Cohn's post as chief counsel when the Democrats — aided in part by the McCarthy brouhaha — took over the Senate, the House, and the Investigations Subcommittee after the November 1954 midterm elections. While he'd worked for Joe for just seven and a half months, Bobby stayed his friend till the end, making his last visit to the senator just before McCarthy died. His job with Joe not only launched Bobby's career but also injected into his life passion and direction that had been glaringly absent before then. It became, too, a paradox he couldn't escape, serving for some as a testament to his loyalty and patriotism, and for others as a measure of his youthful misdirection. Winning his own seat in the Senate, RFK ran for president in 1968 in a campaign cut short when he was gunned down at Los Angeles's Ambassador Hotel, which was owned by the Schines.

It wasn't just principals in the drama who were touched but their families. Cohn told the FBI that his controversial work with the subcommittee had given his father, Justice Albert Cohn of the New York Supreme Court, a thrombosis, and that if Roy were called before a grand jury it "would no doubt result in killing off his father." Stevens's wife had a nervous breakdown. Irving Peress returned to being a dentist, but his home was stoned, his wife was pressured to resign as editor of the PTA bulletin, and leaders of his daughter's Brownie troop were warned to beware of subversion. Jack Kennedy was perpetually asked to justify not only his ties to Joe McCarthy but Bobby's as well. And Fred Fisher's son Hamilton says, "All of our friends abandoned us, wouldn't socialize with us or return Dad's calls." Congregants at their church outside Boston wanted to "throw our family out," adds Hamilton. "People came out of their houses and shouted, 'Your dad's a communist!' and I'd shout back at them, 'My dad's not a communist!'"

The hearings' two hired-gun lawyers both became celebrities. Welch was greeted by President Eisenhower on his way out of town, and journalists and authors lined up for interviews with him. He delivered dozens of speeches from Florida to California, received a handful of honorary degrees, hosted concerts, documentaries, and TV mystery shows, and played the wise presiding judge in the 1959 film *Anatomy of a Murder*. Jenkins, meanwhile, took on a series of other high-profile cases, mostly back in Tennessee, and was recruited but declined to run for senator. In his memoir, Jenkins marveled at McCarthy's behavior during the Army-McCarthy hearings: "He succeeded in insulting every man on the 'jury' that was trying him."

The still green medium of television also cashed in, demonstrating how ably it could cover a major national controversy, while ABC used its live coverage of the hearings to begin catching up to front-runners NBC and CBS. Ronald Reagan was a winner, too, when General Electric — a focus of Joe's hearings on subversion in the defense industry — decided it needed a public relations boost and hired the actor to host a national TV (and radio) program called *General Electric Theater*. Its stars ranged from James Dean to Nancy Davis, Reagan's future wife, and within two years it was the third-most-popular show in America, reaching almost as many viewers as the Army-McCarthy hearings. Fort Monmouth, however, felt only pain. While no evidence emerged publicly of espionage, the Signal Labs quietly moved to Fort Huachuca, Arizona. "Carl Hayden, who in January 1955 became chairman of the powerful Appropriations Committee of the United States Senate, told me privately Monmouth had been moved because he and other members of the majority Democratic party were convinced security at Monmouth had been penetrated," said Joe's friend and fellow senator Barry Goldwater. "They didn't want to admit that McCarthy was right in his accusations. Their only alternative was to move the installation from New Jersey to a new location in Arizona."

As for Joe, the hearings that spring of 1954 spelled the beginning of his end. Performing on the biggest stage of his career, he flopped. He wouldn't yield when even an inch could have made him seem gracious. He took to extremes the devices of embellishment and repetition that had served him so well at Wheeling and afterward. He did finally turn around most who had dismissed him as a cynic — by now he was the truest of believers — but he exhibited the myopia of a zealot. The more his broadcast audience saw this senator toss aside not just parliamentary procedure but common courtesy, the less it listened to him. When it all got too much for Joe, he'd show his disdain by reading a newspaper or storming out of the hearing room. Pundits blamed the public's turning against him on his beard stubble, bald pate, perspiration-soaked shirt and brow, and newly flabby body, but Americans were smarter than that. His undoing was behaving like a bully.

Everyone seemed to understand that but Joe. As the hearings were wrapping up and the other principals were waxing philosophical, he was appealing for the kind of unity that he'd made impossible. He said he harbored no ill will toward the Army and counted on its assistance in future probes, failing to see that he was now Public Enemy Number One in the eyes of the military brass. He assumed the press would remain enchanted with his anti-Communist vision, not anticipating how quickly he'd fade from the headlines. As for fellow subcommittee members, the majority of whom he'd alienated beyond any chance of reestablishing trust, he pleaded for their partnership, without which, he argued, "it will be completely impossible for me as the chairman to do an effective job of digging out the communism, corruption and treason that our staff has been working on."

Yet even as he willfully plowed ahead, his doctors knew the toll the hearings and the beat-downs were taking on the senator. "For the past 18 months he has been bothered by epigastric fulness on arising in the A.M., with nausea and retching relieved by belching of large amounts of gas," they wrote in October 1954, after Joe had spent another nine days at Bethesda Naval Hospital.* "This gagging would be very distressing, leaving him perspiring and trembling at the conclusion of the episode. During the past 6 months, especially at times of mental stress and nervous tension, the symptoms have increased, with attacks of gagging and retching as often as ever[y] hour. Associated with this has been loss of appetite, dyspnea on exertion, and increased fatigability." Fatigue indeed.

---

* Doctors prescribed powerful medications — chlorpromazine, an antipsychotic, and phenobarbital, which today is mainly used to control epileptic seizures — to treat his gastric symptoms.

9

THE FALL

HIS CRUELTY, NOT HIS CRUSADE, was Joe McCarthy's undoing.

From the beginning, critics had zeroed in on his reckless methods more than his Red-purging aims. The public felt the same way, heartily embracing the senator's mission but recoiling at his meanness. So it was fitting that, the very day the Subcommittee on Investigations issued its verdicts on his ham-handed war with the Army, the full Senate launched hearings to formally censure its Wisconsin colleague for his incivility. A punishment that extreme had been meted out just five times in the chamber's 165 years, and it amounted to a political death sentence. Given how fellow senators had enabled him over the years, it was no surprise that they focused not on whether Joe was right about his conspiracy of traitors but on how contemptuous he was of them and their sacred US Senate. "You're the kid who came to the party and pee'd in the lemonade," a Senate friend told him. Even as they finally reined him in, fellow lawmakers were reluctant to utter the unspeakable word "censure," although that's what their rebuke was in practice and how history would record it. Instead, they labeled it a "condemnation."*

Joe was neither fooled nor cowed. Asked whether he felt he'd

---

* Senator Welker, a McCarthy friend, observed that "condemn" was an even stronger word than "censure," saying, "You don't censure a man to death, you condemn him to death." Leviero, "Final Vote Condemns M'Carthy, 67–22," *New York Times*.

been censured, he said with a grin, "Well, it wasn't exactly a vote of confidence." Then he added defiantly, "I'm happy to have this circus ended so I can get back to the real work of digging out communism, crime and corruption."

The self-anointed circus master was as unlikely as he was ideal for the job. Republican senator Ralph Flanders of Vermont was everything Joe wasn't—unstintingly polite, ideologically moderate, and scholarly enough to earn sixteen honorary degrees, although he hadn't had the time or money for a real one. The seventy-three-year-old machinist turned millionaire from Vermont's Northeast Kingdom was dismayed to learn during an overseas trip in 1953 that McCarthy had become the menacing face of America. Back in Washington, Flanders repeatedly took to the Senate floor not just to speak out, which was unusual for the chamber's quiet man, but to do it with McCarthy-like bite, which helped make his tongue-lashings page-one news. Describing the battle with communism as a legitimate Armageddon, Flanders asked in March 1954, "What is the part played by the Junior Senator from Wisconsin? He dons his war paint. He goes into his war dance. He emits his war-whoops. He goes forth to battle and proudly returns with the scalp of a pink Army dentist." Flanders amped up his rhetoric in a June address, comparing Joe to Dennis the Menace and Adolf Hitler, accusing him of anti-Semitism and anti-Protestantism, and insinuating that the "real heart of the mystery" of the Army-McCarthy clash "concerns the personal relationship of the Army private [Schine], the staff assistant [Cohn] and the Senator [McCarthy]."* Two weeks later the Vermont lawmaker interrupted the Army-McCarthy hearings to hand his Wisconsin colleague a letter asking him to appear on the Senate floor, where Flanders would press for McCarthy to be stripped of his committee and subcommittee chairmanships. Saying he was too busy, Joe retorted with a snicker, "They should get a man with a net and take him to a good quiet place."

Ike congratulated Flanders and liberals cheered him, but at

---

* While he was circumspect in addressing the Senate, in a later interview Flanders called the Cohn-Schine relationship "unsavory . . . I got evidence of that in Europe later . . . Anybody with half an eye could see what was going on." Flanders OH, 1967, Columbia University, 8.

first, few in the Senate paid attention. And Flanders knew it. So the paunchy, bald Vermonter was more strategic when he launched his next round on July 30, 1954. He appealed to a country still reeling from the Army hearings, offering to punish the "point of order" bully. He reeled in other lawmakers by trading his vivid metaphors for more politically palatable committee-speak, declaring McCarthy's behavior "contrary to senatorial traditions." Rather than stripping the rogue senator of power, a move that would have threatened the Senate's cherished seniority structure, he asked now for a straightforward denunciation, for which there were precedents. In urging his colleagues to act, Flanders borrowed from Joe's wordbook, saying the Wisconsinite's refusal to answer for his wrongdoing made him a "Fifth Amendment Senator" and that McCarthy "can break rules faster than we can make them."

Flanders was right and the Senate was ready. After eight years of watching him subvert their rules, senators were resolved not just to weigh the charges against their renegade colleague but to run the kind of orderly and boring hearing that he couldn't hijack. They created a special committee to hear Flanders's thirty-three charges of misconduct along with thirteen submitted by other lawmakers. The majority leader (steered by Vice President Nixon) and minority leader (the wily LBJ, who pulled his own strings) each named three members, strategically picked for their sober-mindedness and for their standing in the Senate. There were three former judges, two ex-governors, a onetime journalist, and no liberals, mavericks, or media-mugging presidential hopefuls.

The wisest choice was the chairman. Utah's Arthur Watkins was a Mormon elder and a Republican who, despite the election help he'd accepted from McCarthy, was determined not to be intimidated by him. Watkins's hearings would be public and held in the same Senate Caucus Room as the Army-McCarthy proceedings, but this time without any TV cameras, radio equipment, or newspaper photographers. Forbidden too were cigarettes, cigars, and pipes, which offended the chairman's sensibilities. Censure proponents like Flanders wouldn't be summoned as witnesses, and McCarthy's legal expenses would be paid by the committee. Those were less bids for fairness than ways of depriving Joe of the opportunity to blast another tribunal. "Let's get off the front pages," the doleful Watkins intoned, "and back among the obituaries."

Watkins made clear from the start how high the stakes were. Past censures had been for limited violations; here it was a pattern of bad behavior. "We realize the United States Senate is on trial, and we hope our conduct will be such as to maintain the American sense of fair play and the high traditions and dignity of the United States Senate under the authority given it by the Constitution," the chairman said. He also demonstrated a fortitude that few knew he possessed. From day one, his declarations that McCarthy was out of order trumped the points of order that had dominated the Army-McCarthy hearings. The soap opera had been replaced by a police procedural. "We are not going to be interrupted by these diversions and sidelines," Watkins announced in a trembling voice. "We are going straight down the line." Not used to being silenced, Joe told reporters, "This is the most unheard-of thing I have heard of."

But heard is exactly what he made himself during the two weeks that followed. "I think you certainly should not abuse the witness, no question about that, but there are times when, as you know, you must get very vigorous in your cross-examination. When you know that a witness is not telling the truth, you know he is hiding the facts, then you have got to use whatever technique you think is the best way of getting the truth," McCarthy explained in terms both crystal clear and self-serving. "Sometimes you may coax, you may beg a witness to tell the truth; you may suggest to them what the effects of perjuring themselves are . . . I think it is proper if you think it is the best way to get the facts in an important case, especially when you are dealing with treason." His interrogation of General Zwicker was the culmination of years of coaxing, and Joe not only didn't back down when given the chance but also doubled down on his implication that the decorated general was dumber than a five-year-old. The night before the hearing he and his lawyer tested on a six-year-old child the question they'd asked Zwicker — whether a general should be fired for honorably discharging a Communist dentist like Irving Peress. "Little Virginia Thompson," McCarthy recounted, "didn't have to have it reread. She answered instanter."

Even with his wit and rhetoric intact, something was missing. "During the censure hearings I detected for the first time that the mental and emotional pressures of the past several years were beginning to have a measurable effect on Senator McCarthy," said Roy Cohn.

He had been resilient under attack, buoyant, willing to fight back, at times overly belligerent and eager, and never unconfident. Now, however, with another inquiry before him, his spirit was being eroded . . . "What can I do?" he said once in his Washington home. "I'm putting in damn near every minute defending myself. I go from one of these nuisances to the next, with absolutely no time to do what we *should* be doing. I fight these things in my sleep. Hell, Roy, what's the use? Should I quit? Be a good little Administration senator? Keep my big mouth shut? Vote the way the White House wants? Stop embarrassing Ike and the gang? And pick up my little rewards — a post office here, a few roads there, and invitations to White House shindigs?"

The way he posed the questions made clear his answer: the old leatherneck would resign before he'd turn tail or knuckle under. Better disgrace than concession.

Bobby Kennedy, who still was on the subcommittee payroll, had a different take on why his ex-boss was slipping: "He was a very complicated character. His whole method of operation was complicated because he would get a guilty feeling and get hurt after he had blasted somebody. He wanted so desperately to be liked. He was so thoughtful and yet so unthoughtful in what he did to others. He was sensitive and yet insensitive. He didn't anticipate the results of what he was doing. He was very thoughtful of his friends, and yet he could be so cruel to others." Bobby, who'd also be accused of ruthlessness, wanted to believe the best of Joe as well as of himself.

The Watkins Committee didn't care about his psychological motivations; it only cared about the facts. It first reduced the forty-six charges against Senator McCarthy to five categories: contempt of a Senate subcommittee, encouraging federal workers to leak state secrets, receiving those secrets, abuse of Senate colleagues, and abuse of Zwicker. There was no need for long investigations since earlier committees had probed most of the issues, dating back to 1952. Hearings wrapped up on September 13, 1954, and two weeks later the committee released to the press its sixty-eight-page report. Senators used strong language that had some readers reaching for their dictionaries, calling McCarthy's behavior "contemptuous, contumacious and denunciatory," as well as "highly improper" and "reprehensible." They unanimously recommended that he be censured for two of the five categories: obstructing the work of the panel investigating him in 1951 and 1952, and his outburst against Zwicker. They also found "vulgar and insulting" McCarthy's reference to Senator Robert Hendrickson as "a living miracle without brains or guts." Joe responded from Bethesda Naval Hospital, where he was being treated for ongoing sinus troubles, "I do not care whether I am censured or not, but I will fight against establishing a precedent which will curb investigative power and assist any Administration in power to cover up its misdeeds."

Rather than taking up the committee's charges when they were made public, which might have been awkward for the third of its members who were up for reelection, the full Senate put off deliberations until six days after the 1954 midterm elections. It wasn't just Senate members who were worried about alienating voters who loved (or hated) Joe. A prominent gubernatorial aspirant telephoned Senator Flanders and said, "For heaven's sake don't have it before the election, because I will be dished if you do." That left Joe's fate to the lame-duck Senate, which was more inclined than ever to punish its errant colleague. The just concluded election punctured any remaining sense of McCarthy's invulnerability, which had been the key to his amassing and holding power. Democrats recaptured both houses of Congress, with help from the Army-McCarthy scandal; among Joe's allies who were beaten was Congressman Kit Clardy, who carried what by 1954 was the unfortunate nickname of Michigan's McCarthy.

Joe's supporters argued that it wasn't fair to censure him for actions involving an earlier Congress, and it wasn't prudent to limit a senator's free speech rights. He made their job harder when he blasted the select committee as the "unwitting handmaiden" of the Communist Party, referred to the proceeding as a "lynch party," and branded Chairman Watkins a "coward." Watkins defended his dignity and the Senate's in a ninety-minute speech. "I suppose I should be very indignant," he said in his tinny voice, "but in many respects I feel more sorrow than anger. [McCarthy's attack] reveals an attitude which has characterized the junior senator from Wisconsin for some time." After solemnly laying out Joe's calumnies, the Utahan echoed a question raised by Senator Sam Ervin of North Carolina: "Do we have the manhood in the Senate to stand up to a challenge of that kind?" The address was exceptional not merely for its emotion — and Joe's boycott — but because Watkins's stomach ulcer made it excruciating for him to stand and talk. When he finished, the missionary turned senator collapsed on a couch in the cloakroom.

The Senate interrupted its deliberations when McCarthy entered the hospital with an elbow injury he said he sustained when he struck a glass tabletop while shaking hands with well-wishers. There was speculation that his real affliction was the liquor he couldn't lay off and had even tried to sneak onto the ward. Drew Pearson had a third theory. Every time he'd run into political difficulty, the columnist said, the senator would retreat to his sickbed with a mysterious malady. This time "Joe McCarthy was so sick that the Senate suspended for 10 days but he was not too sick to slip out of Bethesda Naval Hospital on Nov. 25 to take a ride down Connecticut Avenue and spend the evening with friends. McCarthy was spotted at 6:50 p.m. in a big black Cadillac, with Wisconsin congressional license plates," Pearson wrote. "His wife, Jean, was at the wheel, and an unidentified man, possibly a bodyguard — for McCarthy never moves without one — was in the back seat."*

Newly unveiled records from Bethesda make two things clear. His elbow really was in bad shape, with painful swelling and a laceration, and requiring pressure dressings and a plastic splint. But those files prove Pearson right on his bigger point: that the Navy hospital was a safe harbor for Joe, one that let him rest and rejuvenate whenever work left him ill or just done in.

---

* Ed Nellor, who usually took Joe's side, also believed at least one of the senator's injuries was fake: a supposedly broken wrist. Out of the public eye, Nellor said, the senator discarded his sling and used that hand. Reeves interview with Nellor, June 6, 1979.

The Senate's medical recess offered his remaining friends there a chance to craft a compromise to forestall censure, if only he'd apologize. But Joe wouldn't have it. He saw himself as a pirate in the spirit of Blackbeard or Captain Kidd, accountable to a buccaneering code of morality, not to the rules of the Senate's polite society. Asking for forgiveness would have been admitting that his battles of the last five years were deluded, and that he was the contriver he'd started out as and that his critics still thought he was. Better to walk the plank. "When the motion to censure McCarthy was being debated on the floor, I was approached by Senator Price Daniel of Texas. The Senator told me that if I could persuade McCarthy to sign letters of apology to two members of the Senate who believed McCarthy had insulted them, the South would vote against the censure," recalled Barry Goldwater, Joe's most unabashed admirer in the Senate. "I contacted McCarthy's attorney, Edward Bennett Williams. The two of us drove out to Bethesda Hospital . . . I told Joe that if he signed one of the letters, it might be sufficient; if he signed them both, I had the word of Senator Daniel that the southern bloc would stand by him. McCarthy read the letters carefully. They were short, mild in their language, and regretted a discourtesy without really conceding any substantive error . . . [McCarthy] threw the pen across the room, started swearing at both of us, and pounded the table."

That was Joe's state of mind. His behavior from the Army-McCarthy hearings in the spring and summer of 1954 through the censure process that winter seemed truculent and self-destructive to outsiders, and even to well-wishers like Goldwater and Williams. But the Marquette archives make clear that within his insular world of true believers, the consensus was to soldier on. One letter, from a writer identifying himself only as "one of General Zwicker's officers," cheered, "More power to you in your fight against Communism and the Army brass! . . . I feel that your treatment of General Zwicker did not damage Army morale except that of General Zwicker and a few of our policy people." Other correspondents felt the same way, their missives filling three thick files. In their minds and his, Joe was the star of the kind of cliffhanger movie serial popular in his youth, where at the last second the hero saved himself from surefire disaster the way this senator had so many times before.

On the eve of the big vote, Joe and his supporters tried to make the case that the wider public loved him as much as ever. A group called Ten Million Americans Mobilizing for Justice had gathered 2,084,719 signatures. A rally at Philadelphia's Constitution Hall drew 3,500 people, with tickets reading, "Admit One Anti-Communist," and guests including the vice commander of the Wall Street American Legion who clutched an autographed picture of Roy Cohn. There was a mass meeting at Madison Square Garden, too, featuring the real Roy Cohn and Jean McCarthy. Convening for the final debate, senators found on their desks a pink rectangle with the masthead of the *Daily Worker,* nineteen pages of its anti-McCarthy editorials, and, in type big enough for reporters to make out from the galleries, the headline "Throw the Bum Out" — all Joe's idea. The League of Twenty Million Americans for the Censure of Joe McCarthy couldn't claim numbers or gimmicks like those. What it did have was an army of union, university, and other liberal groups feeding information to Flanders and buttonholing senators to support censure.

The Senate closed its case in a long session on December 2, 1954. It substituted a charge on Joe's defiant behavior toward the Watkins Committee for the earlier one on General Zwicker. At 5:03 p.m., by a margin of sixty-seven to twenty-two, it denounced its Wisconsin colleague for having treated fellow members with contempt in 1952 and again in 1954. With LBJ corralling liberals and rallying conservatives, all forty-four Democrats present voted against McCarthy. So did twenty-two of forty-four Republicans and the Senate's sole independent. Only two of the eight Catholic senators sided with their co-religionist, who himself cast a neutral ballot as "present." The only lawmakers not to vote, or to cancel their votes by pairing them with those of opposing senators who also were absent, were Republican Alexander Wiley of Wisconsin and Democrat John Kennedy of Massachusetts. Wiley was afraid of alienating McCarthy's home state fans, or angering his foes. Kennedy blamed his recent back surgery; in truth, he made no effort to pair his vote or clarify his stand for the same duck-and-run reasons as Wiley.* Despite those exceptions, "men who had feared for years to call against him the verdict of principle called against him now the verdict of expediency," wrote columnist Murray Kempton. "Even the friends of Joe McCarthy conceded that he was a dirty fellow and a bit of a fraud."

The real surprise in this historic rebuke was that it took five years for the Senate to express its outrage. Most fellow senators knew from the start that Joe was a political racketeer. Nobody was more amazed than Joe himself that simply waving his hand and pointing to a vacant briefcase could ignite a holy war. But declaring that the emperor had no clothes took a courage few had while the public still believed he was resplendent. It was only when Senator McCarthy had personally offended enough of his colleagues — and when the public, as it always does eventually, had moved on to new crusades and crusaders — that his Senate enablers cried, "Enough!" Its resolution hadn't used the word "censure," so the parliamentarian ruled that it couldn't officially be called that. Senator Herbert Lehman of New York, Joe's most idealistic and consistent critic, noted a more fatal flaw in the version that passed without the original long list of McCarthy excesses. "We have condemned the individual," Lehman said, "but we have not yet repudiated the 'ism.'" Vice President Nixon, who was presiding over the Senate and was more interested in politics than principles, concluded that "by this time the rhetoric did not matter. McCarthy had already left the chamber. For him it was all over." The public seemed to agree: 44 percent told Gallup surveyors they were for censure, with 35 percent opposed and the rest not sure. Nine in ten had followed the Army-McCarthy hearings; fewer than six in ten paid attention to the ones on censure.

Eisenhower was so delighted with the outcome that he invited Senator Watkins to the White House to thank him, knowing the gesture would make the front pages and be read by Senator McCarthy as evidence that the censure was a White House bag job, which

---

* Jim Juliana, McCarthy's friend and staffer, said Joe told him that "Jack Kennedy had no guts because he didn't vote on the censure issue." Eleanor Roosevelt and other liberal Democrats felt the same way, and some refused for that reason to back Kennedy in his presidential bid in 1960. Juliana interview, June 10, 1998, JJP.

it partly was. Joe responded in character. "It's vicious, slimy, back-door politics," he complained to Cohn. Publicly, he stretched his breach with Ike into an irreversible break. "There has been con-siderable talk about an apology to the Senate for my fight against communism. I feel rather that I should apologize to the Ameri-can people for what was an unintentional deception upon them," he told the subcommittee in what would be his last appearance as chairman. "During the Eisenhower campaign I spoke from coast to coast promising the American people that if they would elect the Eisenhower administration that they could be ensured of a vigorous, forceful fight against Communists in Government. Un-fortunately in this I was mistaken. I find that the President on one hand, congratulates the senators who hold up the work of our committee and on the other hand urges that we be patient with the Communist hoodlums who, as of this very moment are torturing and brainwashing American uniformed men in Communist dun-geons." Asked if he was angry enough to bolt the Republican Party, the senator said he had "no interest" in doing that, but added the caveat "at the present time." Having thrown down the gauntlet, he and Jean left town.

Ike got the final word. That spring, the president ended his weekly meeting with Republican legislators by asking whether they had heard the yarn going around Washington: "It's no longer McCarthyism, it's McCarthywasm."

Joe McCarthy had lost more than a censure vote. With the Dem-ocrats taking over the Senate, Joe relinquished to John McClel-lan his gavel, his staff, his budget, and the power to decide where to muckrake and whom to mow down. His assaults on the White House ensured he'd be shunned not just there but at the Army, the State Department, the FBI, and even the Post Office. Newspapers banished him to page twenty-five, next to the corset ads, or wrote him out entirely. So did his Senate colleagues. Being censured meant trading in the badge of the outlier, which he'd proudly worn from his first days in the Senate, for the stigmata of the shunned that had made him the butt of even the president's jokes.

He pretended to be unfazed, but he wasn't. "The White House was having a reception for all the senators," recalled Ruth Watt, the subcommittee's chief clerk, "and Senator McCarthy kept calling me over and saying, 'Ruthy, go ask [my secretary] Mary Driscoll if I've heard from the White House yet, if I've gotten an invitation,' which I thought was kind of sad. I'd call Mary and she'd say, 'You know very well he hasn't. He's not going to get any invitation to that party tonight' . . . It affected him greatly; I think it broke his heart, really."

Gone, too, was any chance of winning for friends and supporters the jobs senators counted on when their party occupied the White House. He withdrew his nominee for acting postmaster in Appleton when it was clear he'd be rejected. In a letter to the attorney general recommending his pal Urban Van Susteren for a federal judgeship, McCarthy added this line reflecting his desperation: "I sincerely hope that perhaps at long last it may be discovered that I actually was elected by the people of my state to represent them." Even the vice president, a supposed friend, made no pretense of solidarity anymore. At a campaign banquet for Nixon at Milwaukee's Schroeder Hotel, Joe showed up uninvited and sat down at the end of the head table, where he was informed he wasn't welcome. Curious about the home state senator getting the heave-ho, a newsman found him in a nearby alley, looking like the loneliest person on the planet and weeping like a child.

In the Senate, the snub wasn't that concerted but it was obvious. "Increasingly as McCarthy got up on the floor of the Senate to make remarks the other Senators would drift off the floor and find other interests in the cloakroom, or go to the washroom. If a group of Senators stood in the cloakroom enjoying a story and Joe joined them, the laughter quickly faded and the various Senators went on their way," recalled Arthur Watkins, who had chaired the censure hearings. "At lunch, Joe might sit at a table with former intimates and soon these would finish their bean soup and sandwich and murmur an excuse about the need to return to their offices. The merriment had long since disappeared from McCarthy's eyes, and he could be seen watching after his departing colleagues with a look of real puzzlement."

Worst was the blackout by the press. Headlines for Joe were like spinach for Popeye or long hair for Samson: without them, he wilted. Now he'd issue a release or call a press conference and nobody would stir. "It was pathetic to watch him prowling the corridors of the Capitol," said *Newsweek*'s Samuel Shaffer, "buttonholing newsmen and offering them stories they refused to file." The self-described goon squad — a dozen correspondents who had once tracked his every move — was demobilized. The few photographers who still paid attention, mainly for old times' sake, saw their pictures saved for the occasional stories that asked, "Whatever happened to Joe McCarthy?" Even the Soviet press no longer cared.

One of the most newsworthy speeches Joe had ever given was in 1955, when he told a group of supporters that the right to hold subversive opinions must be not just protected but cherished. He said reading Thomas Jefferson had persuaded him to espouse principles he'd been accused of sabotaging. That Saturday afternoon, Joe's friend Dion Henderson of the Associated Press brought the speech to Ed Bayley of the *Milwaukee Journal*. "I wrote a story that tried to put it into perspective," recalled Bayley.

> I showed how it conflicted with McCarthy's previous statements and actions and I left it to the reader to make a judgment. I put the story on the desk of the city editor, who was out to dinner, and left for the night. It didn't turn up in the paper on Sunday . . . Henderson filed a brief story on the speech on the state AP wire, and he remembers that two or three papers used part of the story on Monday. No editor saw anything unusual in it, he said. He told me later that he thought McCarthy might have changed the direction of his career if the *Journal* had run the story. I think McCarthy was just playing games with the press again, but in retrospect I wish we had published the story.

While it's impossible to know, Bayley likely was right — that Henderson was indulging in wishful thinking, and Joe was toying with a newspaper he loved sparring with, knowing it wouldn't publish what he said so he wouldn't have to explain it. What we do know is that he soon was back to his attack dog ways. He needled the Senate more than ever — to repudiate the Yalta agreement on Europe's post–World War II order, cut aid to countries doing business with China and Russia, and curb the president's "Atoms for Peace" program under which the United States would offer nuclear technology to countries committed to using it peacefully. The senator failed to see that Stalin's successor presented opportunities for détente, alleging that Nikita Khrushchev's "attack on Stalin is the Kremlin's master stroke in seeking to put a new and pleasing countenance on the World Communist movement." He charged the National Labor Relations Board with harboring a "functioning Communist cell" that posed a "grave and present threat to the security of this country," and wondered about the loyalty of employees at the Supreme Court, which was belatedly standing up against the witch hunts.*

He also sniped back at Senator Watkins. "As McCarthy would leave the Chamber to go to the Republican Senator's [sic] cloakroom, he would pass my seat. Slowing down, as he neared me on the aisle, he would lean slightly toward me and hiss: 'How is the little coward from Utah?'" the censure chairman remembered. "Months later, we met face to face as we approached the Senate's marble washroom simultaneously. He stopped and in a very respectful and friendly voice said: 'How are you, Arthur?' I returned his greeting in kind, and for a few minutes we exchanged pleasantries. I wondered what change had occurred in the man. Right after this interlude, Senator McCarthy recommenced his insolent 'greeting' as he passed my seat on the aisle."†

Many of Joe's complaints smacked of crying wolf, but some were justified and given less attention because of his diminished status. It was revealed, for instance, that his mail had been opened and inspected for three weeks in 1952, at the instigation of an overzealous staffer of a Senate subcommittee investigating him. Worse was the case of Paul Hughes, who sold Joe's enemies dirt he said he'd dug up while on the senator's payroll. But he never was a McCarthy staffer. Hughes's juicy leaks — including Joe's keeping in his basement office in the Senate an arsenal of Lugers and submachine guns, and his staff browbeating and threatening witnesses — were more fabrications. The ruse was uncovered just before the

* McCarthy actually inquired about investigating for security risks the Court's research assistants, secretaries, and other staff, according to the FBI. Memo from Nichols to Tolson, June 13, 1956, pt. 7 of 28, MFBI.
† Watkins would blame his reelection defeat in 1958 on McCarthyites' lingering hatred.

Washington Post was to run a twelve-part Hughes-inspired "exposé" that could have generated a costly libel verdict along with the embarrassment of publishing fake news.

Joe also was talking openly for the first time about running for president, something his foes had always suspected he wanted to do and his friends had hoped for. He discussed it in March 1955 with conservative columnist David Lawrence, who discouraged him, and raised it that same week with ex-publisher Bazy Miller, who offered "encouragement and delight." Clint Murchison "volunteered to have [a] team of men study [the] situation in various states," according to Joe's Marquette files.* The senator ordered Don Surine to run his own study, days after the censure vote, to see how leading Republicans felt about his challenging Eisenhower for the 1956 GOP nomination; Surine said just 3 percent of party leaders would openly back McCarthy. "It would be wrong to draw the conclusion that the incident revealed substantial presidential ambition, or anything more than a wild and momentary hope in a time of distress," Cohn said of the Surine survey. Roy was right. Being president, or even running, required a comprehensive vision that Joe never had, and a longing he lacked, especially in his post-condemnation fog. He was always more interested in being an irritant — first to President Truman, whom he'd called "viciously dangerous," and now to Ike, the subdued leader whom he'd taunt by saying, "If Eisenhower were alive . . ."

The same was true for the other career transformations he floated after the Senate made him persona non grata. Radio broadcaster Paul Harvey said Joe was contemplating publishing a newspaper, which generated a flood of encouraging letters. But he wrote back to one correspondent, "Although I have been seriously considering the idea of publishing a newspaper, I do not, at this time, have any definite plans to do so." The FBI still was keeping tabs, and one bureau source said the senator was busy writing a book on "the impact of communists and their activities around the world." The *Chicago Daily Tribune* also reported that he was about to become an author but said his topic was the origins of the war

---

* Buried in his Marquette papers is an uncashed check to the McCarthy for President Committee. Financial Records File, 1946–1957, series 20, MUA.

between Japan and China, while the *New York Times* suggested a third and more fitting subject: congressional investigations. His lack of discipline and a review of the three volumes he'd already published — the Lustron marketing manual, a rehash of his attack on George Marshall, and a pamphlet-like defense of his hunt for Communists — made the possibility of his completing an authentic book as unlikely as his winning the White House. Jean conceded as much, writing later that Joe had done "a great deal of research in preparation for writing a book but did not get to the actual writing."

Was he really thinking about abandoning the Senate and his life in politics? Maybe. A letter he wrote in April 1957 made it sound like he was gearing up for a reelection bid the next year: "It is extremely difficult to do much campaigning from Washington, and this will have to wait until I can get back to the State for the recess. However, I am planning to set up offices and an organization then, but I do not believe that active campaigning will begin until probably in the Spring of 1958." Opponents had been lining up since just after the censure to challenge him in the Republican primary (Governor Walter Kohler Jr., Lieutenant Governor Warren Knowles, and Congressman Glenn Davis), and in the general election (Judge James Doyle, Congressman Henry Reuss, State Senators Gaylord Nelson and Henry Maier, and former assemblyman William Proxmire).

But even as he was telling some friends he was running, he confided to others that he recognized the political trouble he was in back home. His rallies no longer filled the house. Other candidates did not want his help. And while he'd escaped the "Joe Must Go" drive, the burgeoning opposition was a bad omen. While he might still run, he almost wanted to be beaten, he said to one elderly companion, explaining, "Jean and I have enough money for a small cattle spread in Arizona. I might open a little law office for friends and neighbors with my books and degree right on the place." Even that modest dream was threatened when his investments in mining stocks went belly-up and a financial adviser absconded to South America with Joe's money. Yet another betrayal.

All of that might have been manageable if he'd been well. He had just turned forty-six at the time of his censure, which was young for the Senate but not for his lifestyle. He'd been in and out of Bethesda Naval Hospital for a bad back, aching elbow, wrenched knee, herniated diaphragm, painful gallstone, bleeding gums, obstructed sinuses, throbbing headaches and hemorrhoids, sore feet, and a scarred liver. His weight fluctuated by as much as forty pounds, leaving him looking obese in one newspaper photo, gaunt in the next, and pallid in both. "Some of these ailments," Cohn recounted, "were merely nuisances, some viciously painful." His bodyguard helped him upstairs, and Jean assisted everywhere else. The old catlike swiftness suddenly was gone, replaced by the lumbering movements of a senior citizen.

The pain was more than physical and the aches ran deep. That he was depressed was both obvious and understandable. Who wouldn't be, given the way he was being cold-shouldered by colleagues and so many others in Washington and Wisconsin? His brashness during the Army-McCarthy hearings had been overtaken by an unfamiliar dejection, said Madelaine Grotnes, one of his secretaries. He would enter his Senate suite through a private door, and it'd be hours before anyone even realized he was there, sitting by himself. He'd never been drawn to what he regarded as the drudgery of Senate business, missing an average of 11.7 percent of roll call votes over his career, or nearly twice the norm back then. But now he was skipping one in every four votes, and it rose to an extraordinary three out of four by the end. Cohn watched as "his sense of futility grew . . . He stayed away from his office and the Senate floor more and more often. He took to late rising and sometimes spent the day gazing into the fire in his living room and watching television soap operas. Often he would refuse telephone calls, even from close friends." And increasingly the calls were from strangers, to harass him, frequently in the middle of the night.

The truth was he didn't have many close friends left, or at least not ones he saw often. Urban Van Susteren, Tom Korb, and others from Wisconsin weren't part of his day-to-day life in Washington. Bazy Miller and her social set, along with Al Kohlberg and other true believers, were around more, but they weren't the kinds of people with whom he'd let down his guard or unveil his soul, neither of which he was inclined to do with anyone. That left Jean,

hardened ex-FBI men like Jim Juliana and Don Surine, and ten-
derfoot aides like Roy Cohn.

There were occasional ups along with the relentless downs in
the senator's life then, as Cohn observed:

> By cherry-blossom time in 1955, McCarthy seemed suddenly to
> regain much of his vitality and good spirits. But it was not to
> last. Thereafter, there were peaks and valleys — periods during
> which he would work hard, plan enthusiastically, and even per-
> form brilliantly, followed by intervals of lassitude. He would ac-
> cept invitations to make speeches and fail to show up. I recall
> an "I-Am-an-American" day in Bridgeport, where the program
> had been created around him. At three in the afternoon he sent
> word that he couldn't appear, pleading "urgent Senate business."
> When he accepted the engagement his spirits happened to be
> high, but when the day came, he was back in the doldrums and
> couldn't face the public.

Today such rises and falls might be taken as signs of bipolar disorder, or what was known as manic depression in Joe's day. So might
his chronic difficulty sleeping, love of gambling at the racetrack
and in the political arena, and difficulty focusing.*

There is one more symptom the senator exhibited that often
accompanies, and can mask, manic depression: substance abuse.
He was a drinking man in a drinking town, a deadly one-two. "I
accompanied a group of southwestern oilmen to McCarthy's office
early one afternoon some months [after the censure] to convey an
invitation that he address their convention," recalled Senator Clinton Anderson of New Mexico. "During the discussion, McCarthy,
sallow-faced and haggard, swigged from a bottle of whiskey at his
side." William Fishbait Miller, the congressional doorkeeper, said
in his 1977 memoir:

> After the collapse of his red-baiting activities, he would hang
> around the Hill bars even in the middle of the day. My friend
> Don Curry, who was working on the Hill in the 1950s, recently

---

* While the antipsychotic medication his doctors prescribed him probably was
for insomnia and anxiety, it also could have been intended to treat mania.

recalled the day he went into the old Carroll Arms Hotel lounge for a late lunch and found the old chairman already soused to the eyeballs and still ordering drinks. "He was in such bad condition," Don recalled, "that as he would pick up his drink and down it, some of it would dribble out of his mouth and down his suit . . . A couple of us simply got him out of the chair, half carried him out and put him in a cab."

An ex-FBI man who asked to go unnamed had an even more chilling recollection — of hearing from the secretary of the Senate how Joe stopped by his office for a drink, then guzzled in one gulp a glass filled to the brim with spirits. "I've been to Bethesda three times to dry out," Joe reportedly told the secretary and the two other senators who were there. "The last time the doctor said that if I had one more drop I'd die." Then he refilled the glass and drank it dry.

Physicians at Bethesda had in fact been slow to see Joe's drinking as a problem. In the 1940s they gave him whiskey, along with his sleeping pills, to help him rest during his hospital stays, and as late as 1952 they poured him a shot glass a day. They accepted his explanation that he "drinks socially," which wasn't surprising, since he was consuming less alcohol then and hiding it better. By the middle of 1956, however, he admitted to his doctors that "alcoholic intake is 3 highballs daily." New symptoms — "gross" tremors in the tongue and upper body, a foot drop that made him limp, liver damage — also pointed to alcoholism. "There is a history of heavy, excessive ethanolic intake," a note from his physician read in August, which may have been news to anyone who'd been tracking his opaquely phrased medical records. But it wasn't a revelation to the staff who monitored him during his forty-day hospitalization that August and September. "Patient appears to be under influence of alcohol . . . He is not eating & is unable to keep food down . . . Stated that he could 'use a good [shot] of bourbon,'" his nurses wrote. "Appears out of contact most of the time — thinks he is at home — then at a cocktail party . . . wants to 'go down stairs to see three people about his campaign' . . . Quiet for minutes only. Remainder of time it takes two people to keep him in bed . . . spasms of swallowing tongue . . . Pt. states headache is excruciating." A day after his discharge, a neurologist who reviewed his case wrote, "The patient has been recovering from acute hallucinosis and delirium."

He was back in the hospital in December for a twenty-day stay, and discharged on January 3, 1957, so he could attend the opening session of the Senate. Doctors were by now transparent in pinpointing his problems: "del[i]rium tremens and early alcoholic cirrhosis." His nurses, who watched him moment by moment, were clearer still: "Seems disoriented as to time & place. Wants corpsman [to] 'get me ready for my speech' . . . Patient extremely violent — kicking, hitting[,] biting etc. Making a great deal of noise." When he'd come out of it, he'd apologize, clearly embarrassed by his behavior and his incontinence. But then it would happen again. "He becomes extremely violent — 'will investigate everyone' . . . strikes everyone within range."

Once Joe was out of the hospital, Urban Van Susteren saw how fast he fell off the wagon. "Van, do you have any milk?" McCarthy would say. When Van Susteren turned his back, the senator would spike the milk with undetectable vodka. He was drinking a bottle a day by then. He sometimes imagined he was being attacked by snakes. A doctor told Van Susteren that two thirds of Joe's liver was gone, so Van confronted his friend the next morning. McCarthy became abusive, shouting, "Kiss my ass." Van Susteren slid a bottle of whiskey toward Joe and told him to drink it, ending the torment for the sake of the McCarthy family. He finally managed to get the senator to switch temporarily to beer, but even that backfired when he showed he could nearly empty a bottle in a single swig.*

Jean was panicked. She tried to stop Joe from drinking, and got Van and others to try too. She made a home for him, down to the newfangled dishwasher, the organ he bought for her birthday,

* There was speculation that McCarthy had another addiction — to the narcotics he'd been given to treat his painful conditions. Washington columnist Maxine Cheshire went so far as to claim that his habit was financed by the federal Bureau of Narcotics, which worried that if it didn't, news of his addiction might leak out and could compromise national security. It sounded like the kind of charge Joe would make, and was denied by friends of the senator. Associated Press, "Joe McCarthy Morphine Addict, Columnist Claims."

the black Doberman, and the Christmas card showing man, wife, and dog in front of the fireplace. She was his biggest backer in his campaigns against Communists and the White House, and in his bid for Senate reelection or, if he wanted, the presidency. She framed his Marine Corps medals and displayed them in a part of the house where Joe could easily see them. She persuaded any acquaintances she could—Ethel and Bobby Kennedy, Alfred Kohlberg and his wife, Jane—to visit. The only thing that worked with Joe was a baby. Neither Jean nor Joe was sure why they couldn't produce one of their own, so she enlisted Joe's friend Cardinal Spellman of New York to help them find one.*

Tierney Elizabeth was five weeks old when Joe and Jean picked her up in January 1957 at the New York Foundling Hospital and brought her home to Washington. They'd been waiting for a year for the baby, whom they named after their mothers, although final arrangements happened so fast that there was no time to get a crib. No matter, Jean stayed up most of the night ensuring Tierney didn't roll off the sofa. Joe tended to her sniffles, bought her a barrelful of toys, and cradled her often enough that Jean reminded him that infants needed sleep even if he didn't. "I don't know very much about babies," Joe told friends, "but I'm crazy about this one." The feeling apparently was mutual. Ten days after arriving at the McCarthys', baby Tierney "wrote" to Sister Bernard Marie at the Foundling Hospital:

> Mother and Dad and I are so happy about the arrangements you made. Since I have seen you last, I have acquired quite a taste for rice cereal, strained carrots, orange juice, and I even take a little scraped raw carrot in the morning to keep my eyes in good shape. My Dad massages my legs and back every night! . . . Despite all the good treatment, I do have one complaint. I get lonesome at times for a baby brother. Now that I am so well acquainted with how to take a bath (incidentally, I love taking one), change diapers, plan menus and set up schedules, how

* A fertility test at the Naval Hospital showed that Joe's "sperm count was normal." Hospital record, September 18, 1956, MBNH.

Spellman's help apparently was needed in part because Joe was older than the normal adoptive father, and sicker. Cooney, *The American Pope*, 230.

about doing me a big favor and start keeping your eyes wide open for a baby brother that I can handle.

What better way to show how much he liked being a dad than to want to do it again?

Sadly, Tierney came too late to pull Joe out of his abyss.

Everyone who ran into him that spring of 1957 had a vivid memory of how ill he was, with jaundiced skin, unsteady balance, and intermittent focus. "My last view of him was that of a drunk shuffling down a street near the Capitol," said Irish American historian George Reedy. "He was closing out the dark side of the victims of the Famine." Speechwriter Ed Nellor paid a long visit and remembered the senator seemed "dazed" and "punch-drunk." At 1:00 the next morning Nellor was roused from bed by a call from Joe asking when his ex-aide might drop by. He had forgotten! At a meeting of the Wauwatosa school board, according to a librarian for the *Milwaukee Journal,* Joe needed to be rescued from the cloakroom, where he'd become hopelessly entangled in coats and could hardly speak. When editors at the *Journal* heard about that, they assigned reporter Edwin Bayley full-time to writing McCarthy's obituary.

In his better moments, the faithfully Catholic senator seemed to be saying his good-byes and asking for a kind of redemption. "I picked up the telephone [one day] and it was Joe. It was the first time we had spoken to each other in exactly seven years — since our melee in the cloakroom of the Sulgrave Club," recalled Drew Pearson. "The following conversation took place: 'Drew, are you sitting down?' 'Yes,' I replied. 'Well, I wanted to make sure you weren't standing up or you'd faint. I just wanted to tell you that I'm putting your column today in the *Congressional Record.* As you know, I don't always agree with what you say but this column I know tells the truth' . . . We exchanged a few pleasantries and I thanked him. That was the end of the conversation . . . I couldn't help but feel sorry for him. He was a very lonesome guy."

Something similar happened to another bitter adversary, former Army lawyer John Adams. "I was sitting in my small law office near the District of Columbia courthouse," Adams said.

He wanted me to come to see him at his home . . . I decided to go . . . He poured about six ounces of Fleishman's [*sic*] gin into a glass, added a little tonic and a lump of ice, and lumbered back into the living room. He looked awful. He had lost about forty pounds, and his hands shook . . . McCarthy said that he had admired my integrity during the Army-McCarthy hearings . . . He then suggested that I now show my integrity by repudiating the Army position. He wanted me to join with him in some sort of statement which, he believed, would help him reestablish himself. He did not explain how, if one show of "integrity" repudiated another show of "integrity," either could be believed . . . "It's no good, Joe," I said. "It won't work. It's over and finished; that's all. You can't change the truth" . . . After about an hour, I got up to leave. McCarthy walked with me to the door and stood there until I reached the sidewalk. I said, "So long, Joe" to the cadaverous visage of McCarthyism, standing silently in the shadows, slowly dying.

His visit with Adams, call to Pearson, and other belated bids for forgiveness all were on his terms. There is no evidence that he was thinking about the damage he'd wrought to the system. And he was too busy feeling sorry for himself to have second thoughts about his victims, or even to acknowledge that his crusade had generated casualties.

Joe checked in to Bethesda Naval Hospital for the last time on April 28, 1957, for what was said to be treatment of an old knee injury. His room on the twelfth floor was under guard, with Jean the only one allowed in, and it was a lot more than a knee that was ailing him, as we can now see from his hospital records. Since his last admission in January, his alcohol consumption had skyrocketed from "1/5 a day of whiskey" to "4/5's a day." His food intake had plummeted from "3 well rounded meals a day" to just beef broth. In late February "he began to have severe AM nausea & vomiting" along with "watery diarrhea," his doctor wrote, and "this past 2 weeks he has been maintained on daily IV feedings — 1500–2000 cc/day — Dextrose & H2O." His liver was enlarged, his skin was jaundiced, his temperature was spiking, and he'd been sedated even before he arrived at the hospital.

Once he was admitted, doctors were by his bedside regularly and nurses were there nonstop, on "special watch," taking notes on everything that was happening in a way that made clear the Navy brass knew not just how sick the senator was but how controversial. "Patient was looking up at me and all of a sudden threw up his hands. I took them in mine, and I noticed his eyes rolled back and his face and shoulders were getting very flush. He started to gag and I then noticed patient going into what seemed like a Grand [Mal] Seizure," a nurse wrote the morning of April 29. "At first very hard jerks all over and then completely all over came to a calm, complete calm. I [immediately] got on the bed and began artificial respiration, patient started to breath[e] again." Four hours later he had another seizure and "there was difficulty in getting tongue blade in mouth." That evening, after even more convulsions, Joe "bit his tongue. He then began body tremors involving his arms, head, & the muscles of his chest, & abdomen & his legs." He was hallucinating, soiling his bedclothes, venting a pneumonia-like rattle from his chest, and excreting urine that was blood-red.

Nurses tried to make out his muttering. "I want to go home . . . [I] haven't had a drink in two or three weeks . . . only a few beers." Later, he seemed to be making a "speech" in which he "keeps addressing — 'Mr. President.'" He also talked about "going to work, his duties to investigate." What they could make out most clearly was when he "stated he had a new baby and it was his life."

The watch continued as Joe restlessly picked at his oxygen tent, then clapped his hands and began laughing. He waved his arms overhead "as if to ward off attackers, mumbling incoherently, 'Get away, get away.'" On day five, he "seemed very hot to the touch." His temperature registered 106 degrees, then an alarming 110. "Packed in ice chips," his nurse recorded at 4 p.m. "Nasal oxygen started. Color ashen." A Catholic priest delivered last rites, and at 5:45 p.m., three doctors worked in tandem to administer artificial respiration. The nurse's last entry was at 6:02 p.m. that Thursday, May 2, 1957: "Respiration ceased. Pronounced by Dr. Kenny."

Nobody who was close to him was surprised by Joe McCarthy's death. They'd known long before his last visit to the Naval Hospital that his fall from political grace had shattered his heart and that liquor was eating away at his liver. His refusal to eat —

or to stop drinking—suggested he'd lost the will to live. What is less clear is what actually killed him that perfect spring day in May. His doctors and his death certificate said it was acute hepatitis, "cause unknown." FBI files show reports of everything from bone cancer to a slow poisoning by radiated water, or arsenic, or carbon tetrachloride. Some said it was the Soviets who did him in; others blamed the CIA. At the same time, the senator's widow reportedly was telling relatives she suspected foul doings. Mary Reardon, Joe's cousin, said Jean confided to her mother that "the day that [Joe] died, [Jean] went to the hospital to pick him up, because he was feeling good, he was coming home. He had his things packed and was ready to go home. And she went to the bathroom and to finish up some things at the desk, and when she came back, there were three men leaving his room. And when she got there he was dead."

While such theories of intrigue befit the author of our grandest conspiracies, they simply aren't true. Nurses, corpsmen, or physicians were by his side continuously, making it nigh impossible for an enemy to do him harm. He didn't have cancer, and there's nothing to indicate he was poisoned by arsenic or anything else. Yet his hospital records do demonstrate one more thing: he didn't die from hepatitis. Tests showed only modest elevations of the compound bilirubin in his blood and of the time it took his blood to clot, two indications that liver disease is mild, and there's little reason to believe that his mild-to-moderate form of the disease killed him. The immediate cause of death, say four of America's most distinguished doctors who recently reviewed his files, almost certainly was the fever that spiked to deadly levels. That probably was triggered by his severe symptoms of alcohol withdrawal, with seizures and delirium tremens, which in that era were fatal for a third of patients. An infection—in his urinary tract, around a catheter in his bladder, or in his lungs—could have aggravated his DTs and contributed to his sky-high body temperature. So could his diseased liver, or even the newfangled antipsychotic medications he was taking as a sedative for agitation, which can interfere with temperature regulation and in rare cases lead to a fatal condition called neuroleptic malignant syndrome.

How could his team of esteemed Navy doctors seemingly get so wrong this final judgment on the senator from Wisconsin? If his demise was an outgrowth of his DTs, as his hospital records suggest, the medical world didn't appreciate the risk or treat it as effectively as it can today, when the mortality rate is under 5 percent. If neuroleptic syndrome played a role, his physicians wouldn't have recognized it, since the first cases were just being described in France, and the condition wouldn't be widely recognized for another two decades. If he contracted pneumonia or some other deadly infection in their hospital, they lacked the drugs and technology we now have that might have saved him. Most likely hepatitis was just the right vanilla verdict since his liver was diseased, and pointing to that—especially with the scary-sounding adjective "acute," and without the more accurate labels of alcoholic hepatitis or alcoholic cirrhosis—spared his family the pain of publicly acknowledging his chronic and perhaps suicidal drunkenness. A concerted cover-up seems improbable, since the Navy Hospital team requested an autopsy, which Jean refused.*

Tributes to the senator poured in from both sides of the McCarthy divide. The president extended "profound sympathies" to Jean over the loss of the senator who'd branded him an appeaser. William Loeb, publisher of New Hampshire's *Manchester Union Leader*, insisted Eisenhower was one of Joe's murderers, along with the Communists, Senator Ralph Flanders, and Las Vegas publisher Hank Greenspun. "Red" Dean Acheson said, "No comment at all. De mortuis nil nisi bonum (saying nothing about the dead

---

* The doctors who reviewed the hospital records were Stanley Caroff, professor of psychiatry at the University of Pennsylvania School of Medicine; Jeffrey Flier, former dean of the Harvard Medical School; Lawrence Friedman, assistant chief of medicine at Massachusetts General Hospital; and Jerome Kassirer, former editor in chief of the *New England Journal of Medicine*.

McCarthy's records show that his score on the two measures used to determine the severity of alcoholic hepatitis was "just under 20," Friedman says. "Mortality is generally associated with a value over 32." Author interview with and emails from Friedman.

As for neuroleptic malignant syndrome, Caroff, an expert on the condition, says that while "it is theoretically possible" that the particular antipsychotics McCarthy was taking "could have worsened his temperature or caused an NMS-like reaction . . . there are virtually no conclusive cases published of a link." Author interview with and emails from Caroff.

but good)." His old target Annie Lee Moss was "sorry" to hear about his death, adding, "but that's something we have all got to do sooner or later." The *New York Times* ran Joe's obituary as its lead story, along with two full pages of retrospectives, but there was no editorial. "Why dignify the bastard?" editor Charles Merz said later. "Let him pass from the scene without more attention."

Neither the Catholic Church nor the US Senate appeared to have any such qualms. Four days after Joe's death, a pontifical high requiem mass was staged at St. Matthew's Cathedral, where Jean and Joe were wed four years earlier. As two thousand mourners listened, Monsignor John J. Cartwright said McCarthy's role in raising an alarm about communism "will be more and more honored as history unfolds its record." Later that day, Joe was memorialized in the chamber of the Senate that he'd joined at the young age of thirty-eight and where, seven years later, his colleagues voted overwhelmingly to condemn him. The last senator given a Senate funeral was William Borah back in 1940, although leaders were quick to point out they'd do it for anyone whose family asked, as Jean had. "This fallen warrior through death speaketh," said Chaplain Frederick Brown Harris, "calling a nation of free men to be delivered from the complacency of a false security and from regarding those who loudly sound the trumpets of vigilance and alarm as mere disturbers of the peace." Seventy senators were on hand, along with Jean Kerr McCarthy, three of Joe's siblings, Vice President Nixon, FBI director Hoover, and Roy Cohn. Among the floral tributes was one from G. David Schine.

Joe's body was flown by military plane from Washington to Green Bay, with three of his closest Senate pals accompanying him, then it was driven to Appleton. Disciples came in flocks that sunbaked Tuesday, packing the pews at St. Mary's and spilling onto the streets outside the Irish parish where Joseph Raymond McCarthy had been baptized and, six months shy of turning forty-nine, was being eulogized. "Senator McCarthy was a dedicated man, not a fanatic," Father Adam Grill intoned. "The guidance of our beloved land is under the guidance of human beings and as human being[s] we are all fallible." Flags across the city were at half-mast, the way they had been at the White House and other public buildings in Washington, and Appleton schools and

shops were shuttered at midday. This was the last of three memorials to the fallen senator and the first in the state that had easily and repeatedly elected him. Twenty-five thousand friends and
fans from Green Bay, Neenah, and his native Grand Chute had paid
their respects at his open casket. Others were keeping vigil outside
the church alongside honor guards of military police, Boy Scouts,
and Knights of Columbus. Flying in to join them were nineteen
senators, seven congressmen, and a handful of other luminaries,
most of whom had supported Joe in his relentless assault on communism.

Joe was buried in St. Mary's nearby cemetery, at his favorite
spot on a tree-lined bluff overlooking the Fox River. As triple vol-
leys were fired by a rifle squad from the Marine Corps and Catholic War Veterans, Jean stood at attention. The casket was slowly
lowered into the ground between the graves of his parents, Timothy and Bridget, where a simple stone would read:

JOSEPH R. MCCARTHY
UNITED STATES SENATOR
NOV. 14, 1908 MAY 2, 1957

Newspapers around the world ran obituaries, and commentators weighed in from the right and left. The one who came closest to capturing the enigma of the Wisconsin senator — and the
tragedy — may have been Eric Sevareid of CBS, one of the crusading wartime correspondents dubbed "Murrow's Boys." McCarthy,
said Sevareid, "was a sudden rocket in the sky, enrapturing some,
frightening others, catching millions in a kind of spell that dis-
sipated only when the rocket itself, as a rocket must, spluttered,
went cold, and fell . . .

"If history finds that McCarthy used his strength in a wrong-
ful manner, it will find that the weakness of others was part of the
fault."

EPILOGUE

LIKE MANY MESSIANIC CAMPAIGNS IN American history, McCarthyism the movement outlived McCarthy the man. Some would even say a variant of it flourishes today.

Leading conservatives saw the Wisconsin senator's censure as an assault on both them and the anti-Communist movement, and they counterattacked with fury. A year later, William F. Buckley Jr. paid tribute to his friend in launching *National Review,* which quickly became the bible of conservatism. The John Birch Society set up shop a year after Joe's death, embracing him and his crusade. And half a century on, some on the ideological right are seeking to rehabilitate McCarthy as the victim rather than the perpetrator of a witch hunt that commentator Ann Coulter calls "the Rosetta Stone of all liberal lies." Those were just the kinds of "never surrender" messages Jean had in mind when, with help from Roy Cohn, she founded the Joseph R. McCarthy Memorial Foundation to "organize Americans to expose, combat and eliminate the Communist menace."

The senator's shadow lingered in the electoral arena too. George Wallace aped McCarthy's rabble-rousing techniques in mounting his racial backlash campaigns for the White House in the 1960s and 1970s. David Duke and Patrick Buchanan did the same a generation later. And for decades, Democrats felt the need to demonstrate they weren't as soft on communism as Joe claimed, which encouraged Jack Kennedy to launch his misadventure at the Bay of Pigs, pushed brother Bobby to spearhead a deadly campaign against Fidel Castro that intensified the Cuban Missile Crisis, and helped draw the Kennedys and Lyndon Johnson into a calamitous war in Vietnam. "Eleven years after McCarthy's censure by the Senate, Lyndon Johnson would talk to his closest political aides about the McCarthy days, of how Truman lost China and then the Congress and the White House, and how, by God, Johnson was not going to be the President who lost Vietnam and then the Congress and the White House," wrote Vietnam War historian David Halberstam.*

Joe McCarthy's most apt student was Donald Trump. Roy Cohn was the flesh-and-blood nexus between the senator and the president. An aging Cohn taught the fledgling Trump the transcendent lessons he had learned from his master, McCarthy — how to smear opponents and contrive grand conspiracies. During the 1970s, Cohn and Trump spoke as often as five times a day. "I hear Roy in the things [Trump] says quite clearly," said Peter Fraser, Cohn's lover for the last two years of his life. "If you say it aggressively and loudly enough, it's the truth."†

Trump shared even more with his mentor's mentor. Both Trump and McCarthy were geniuses at seizing upon public fears and rifts, faking evidence to support their assertions, and claiming vindication when there was none. Each railed against corrupt elites and crafted a handy scapegoat for America's troubles — in McCarthy's case, conniving Communists, in Trump's, rapacious immigrants. The president's defenders, like the senator's, said the narcissistic bully we perceived in public masked a charming and faithful friend. Both were wizards at grabbing the spotlights of their day — Joe via newspapers, magazines, pamphlets, radio, and TV; Donald on Twitter, reality TV, and cable news, and in supermarket tabloids and mass-market books. Each made his name into a ubiquitous brand. Neither had a master plan other than accumulating and holding on to power. Both shocked the world and them-

---

* These days, the dreaded label is "Socialist," which is somehow more subtle but just as damning as "Communist."

† Before special counsel Robert Mueller released his report on Russian meddling in the 2016 election, Trump tweeted, "Study the late Joseph McCarthy, because we are now in period with Mueller and his gang that make Joseph McCarthy look like a baby!" Balluck, "Trump: Mueller Makes Joseph McCarthy Look Like a 'Baby,'" *The Hill.*

selves by rising as fast and as far as they did. Trump was a dream come true for those who, for more than sixty years, had hungered to resurrect McCarthy and McCarthyism.*

But for anyone dismayed by modern-day demagoguery, the McCarthy story offers surprising and encouraging lessons. He did crush lives, yet he was done in by his own excesses. He rose to become an all-powerful senator, but most of America fell out of love with him within a few years, and only one state ever voted for him. His name, and the movement that bears it, has been vilified in the United States the way Hitler and the Nazis are in Germany and Stalin is in much of the former Soviet Union. Even a disciple like ex-President Trump has brandished the label "McCarthyism" as the nastiest thing he can say about his enemies.

A month after Joe's death, the Supreme Court handed down three sweeping decisions that repudiated most of his Red-hunting premises and bolstered the rights of congressional witnesses. Generations of schoolchildren have been taught about the evils of McCarthyism, with the 1994 edition of the National Standards for United States History mentioning it and him nineteen times, compared to a single reference to Ulysses Grant and none for Robert E. Lee, Alexander Graham Bell, Thomas Edison, Albert Einstein, and the Wright Brothers. Friends as well as foes raise his specter for movements they call sexual McCarthyism, racial McCarthyism, online McCarthyism, and Trumpism. Even the racketeer Frank Costello steered clear of McCarthy. During his deportation proceeding, he was advised to hire as his attorney Edward Bennett Williams. "Not that guy," said Costello. "Wasn't he the lawyer for McCarthy?"

The McCarthy legacy in Wisconsin was political upheaval. He became a curse to Republicans and catapulted Democrats into an era of unimaginable political dominance. "Without Joe to zero in on, we would never have pulled all our people together," said Patrick Lucey, who ran the Democratic Party there from 1957 to

---

* One area where the president and the senator parted ways was in their regard for Russia. To McCarthy, Joseph Stalin, Nikita Khrushchev, and the other Soviet leaders were never to be trusted, whereas Trump saw the newest Russian autocrat, Vladimir Putin, as a friend and fellow traveler.

1963 and served as governor in the 1970s. Others in the Badger State still debate whether their former senator was a martyr or a despot. "My mother and I didn't speak about Joe McCarthy for twenty years," says GOP activist and McCarthy critic Bill Kraus. "It split families." In Appleton, an oil painting in the public library depicts escape artist Harry Houdini, NFL halfback Rocky Bleier, and five others with ties to the community — yet the most famous son of Appleton, Joe McCarthy, was left off the canvas. A twice-life-size bronze bust of Joe was displayed for more than forty years in a place of honor in the county building where he'd held court. Boosters wanted it to stay there; critics insisted it be mothballed. The compromise was to move the statue to the county history museum, where it sits in a basement stairwell, just outside the public washroom, under a sign that reads "Why McCarthy?"*

That is a question historians have been asking for seventy years, with many seeing him as one more sprouting of America's deep-rooted demagoguery. In the summer of 1950, fifteen years after Huey Long's death, his son Russell pronounced that "the day of the demagogue is over." Even as he was saying that, Joe was proving him wrong. McCarthy repeatedly would be compared to the iconic governor known as "The Kingfish," after the smooth-talking Negro schemer in the popular *Amos 'n' Andy* radio show. Some called the Wisconsin senator a northern Huey Long; others said he was a poor man's Huey Long. Even President Eisenhower drew parallels. And it was true that both McCarthy and Long were unstoppable and charming, mastered the media, and were the kinds of senators their colleagues knew better than to tangle with.

Yet it was the differences more than the commonalities that stand out between Joe McCarthy and not just Huey Long, but most of the demagogues who came before. Whereas Long had a clear vision for the next millennium, Joe didn't know what he wanted to do the next day. He wasn't a student of history or philosophy,

* The only denominated tributes to Joe in his home state are the Joseph McCarthy Transit Center in Kenosha, McCarthy Creek Apartments in Appleton, and McCarthy Road, which runs by the old family farm in Grand Chute. In Green Bay, there was controversy over naming a street McCarthy after Packers coach Mike McCarthy, for fear it would be mistaken for Joe; to make clear the honoree, the street was named Mike McCarthy Way.

of good or evil. An adventurer rather than a strategist or a tactician, he improvised from instinct, used his fists and knuckles more than his intellect, and drew inspiration from P. T. Barnum and Jack Dempsey. Unlike with most rabble-rousers throughout history, amassing dictatorial power interested this senator less than getting a favorable boldface headline. Hitler was silver-tongued, albeit deranged; McCarthy was more prosecutor than spellbinder. He lacked Father Coughlin's anti-Semitic zeal, the racist master plans of Senators Bilbo and Tillman, and Huey Long's agenda for social reform. Joe's complete disorganization was obvious to anyone who attended his hearings, closed-door or open, and became clearer still if you pored through his professional and personal papers, or asked Jean or anyone who worked with or for him. McCarthy also was more gleeful than preceding zealots and most of his successors. "He bore far less resemblance to Huey Long," said Eisenhower adviser Emmet John Hughes, "than to Studs Lonigan," an Irish American would-be tough introduced in 1935 by novelist James T. Farrell. Will Herberg, writing in *The New Republic* in 1954, added that the senator "is *against* communism and *for* — Joe McCarthy."

That doesn't mean he wasn't as dangerous, or more so, than the more farsighted bullies who came before. If someone without a philosophy or a program could catapult to such heights of popularity, what did it say about America's capacity to be conned? Neither Coughlin nor even Huey Long had half of America on his side. Ma or Pa Ferguson couldn't rile up a mob with an empty briefcase and warmed-over accusations. The only American more recognizable from London to Lapland in the early 1950s was President Eisenhower. Today there is, thankfully, no Tillmanism, no Bilboism, nor any movement named after the fiery Louisianan who offered the audacious promise to make every man a monarch. The scars they left disappeared; Joe's haven't. Senator McCarthy was "the most gifted demagogue ever bred on these shores. No bolder seditionist ever moved among us — nor any politician with a surer, swifter access to the dark places of the American mind," said Richard Rovere, who watched in real time as Joe turned into an archetype.

In the decades since, true believers from both sides of the McCarthy divide have paid tribute to their version of his legacy at his gravesite on the anniversary of his death. Year after year, fans piled out of cars with bumper stickers reading "Joe McCarthy Was Right" and leaflets requesting information on "Who Murdered Joe McCarthy?" Foes, including poet Allen Ginsberg, held their own memorials, figuratively or literally dancing on his crypt.*

Those who were closest to the senator couldn't forget him, even when they tried. Bobby Kennedy attended McCarthy's funeral despite Jack's urging him not to and staying away himself — but at the church in Appleton, Bobby sat in the choir loft, where nobody would see him; at the graveside, he stood apart from other Washington officials; and when the service was done, he begged journalists not to mention his being there for fear of embarrassing his brother and himself. Bobby had always blamed Roy Cohn for Joe's excesses, and as JFK's attorney general, RFK would go after Cohn with a vengeance but without success. Roy, meanwhile, said looking back, "I never worked for a better man or a greater cause" than McCarthy and McCarthyism. And he correctly predicted that no matter how long he lived, his obituary would be headlined "Roy Cohn Dead; Was McCarthy Investigations Aide." When he actually died, in 1986, it was of AIDS, a disease he denied having.

CBS pulled the plug on Edward R. Murrow's *See It Now* show in 1958, in part because of lingering tensions over his anti-Mc-Carthy broadcasts, but those programs were immortalized fifty years later in the film *Good Night, and Good Luck*. Bobby Kennedy resented Murrow for his broadsides against McCarthy, but Jack hired the newscaster to run the US Information Agency. That constituted a victory for three McCarthy targets — Murrow, the USIA, and Reed Harris, whom Murrow brought back as deputy director of the agency from which McCarthy had ousted him. It was the kind of redemption enjoyed by too few of Joe's victims.

Jean tried to move on. Her first priority was keeping Tierney, whose adoption was in limbo. The Catholic Church required a six-month probation, which had two months to go when Joe died. Jean answered all the Foundling Hospital's questions. Yes, she attended

---

* In a touch McCarthy would have applauded, Appleton police recorded the license numbers of the cars at the Ginsberg memorial. "Strange Things Are Happening at McCarthy's Grave," *Appleton Post-Crescent*.

mass every Sunday and Holy Days, and received the sacraments four times a year. Yes, she and the baby had a good home (the one she shared with her aging mother) and plenty of money (nearly $10,000 a year, thanks in part to Joe's leaving her $113,000 and Fulton Lewis raising another $110,000 in a radio appeal for her and Tierney). And yes, most important, she had influential friends, including Cardinal Spellman, who once again intervened on her behalf. If all that wasn't enough, and it was, she offered this: "The one reason that has constantly been in my mind is that by causing the baby to be returned you would only prevent a child from having the honor of one day proudly proclaiming to her classmates that 'my daddy was Joseph McCarthy, Senator from Wisconsin.'" It would, over the course of Tierney's life, prove more burden than honor.

While she eventually remarried and built a new life, Jean — by then Jean Kerr Minetti — never again believed in anything or anyone the way she had in Joe. She organized his papers and left them to Marquette, but she refused to let biographers or documentarians see them.* She turned down requests for interviews, including one from the son of old pal John Wayne, who wanted to do an upbeat film on the senator. She wrote a memoir, but it never was published. She tried to console Tierney when classmates teased her about being Joe McCarthy's daughter. She survived Joe by twenty-two years, dying of a cerebral hemorrhage in 1979, at age fifty-five. Her underlying health problems were high blood pressure and, as with Joe, alcoholism.

In her last years, Jean got together regularly with cronies from her McCarthy days in what seemed like "some anti-Communist movie," according to Urban Van Susteren's daughter Greta, who lived with her in the summer of 1975 and became a close friend. "She talked about how much she hated Roy Cohn, how she blamed David Schine and Roy Cohn," Greta remembers. "Every time she got drunk there was only one topic, and that was Joe McCarthy. It was nonstop and it was endless."

---

* Herbert Hoover wanted the papers for his library at Stanford University. The Library of Congress also made a strong pitch, as did the Wisconsin Historical Society. But Joe's ties to Marquette won out. Solicitations File, 1957–58, series 24, MUA.

ACKNOWLEDGMENTS

The idea for this book came partly from my Bobby Kennedy biography, when Ethel and others told me things about Joe McCarthy that I'd never imagined. And it came from Don Ritchie, the historian emeritus of the US Senate, who organized and annotated the transcripts of McCarthy's closed-door hearings and convinced me there was not just an opportunity but a need for a new biography of the senator. Donald Trump's election as president was the clincher.

For an idea to become a book, you need an agent who believes in it, and Jill Kneerim did. She helped with my envisioning, my proposal, my landing just the right editor and publisher, my research and writing, and my fretting. That, in case you are wondering, is the definition of a crackerjack literary agent.

The only one who gave more, from start to the last word, was my wife and partner, Lisa Frusztajer.

Bruce Nichols was an editor and publisher in one, which made me doubly lucky. He asked all the right questions up front, answered the few critical ones I had mid-process, showed faith, and, most important to me, left me alone while I did my work. Then he went to work, helping me see and fill the holes in a way that I applauded. As a lifelong journalist and author, I know how rare it is to find an editor worth clapping for.

Speaking of clapping, Amanda Heller showed how much better a book can be when a copy editor has her dead-on grasp of usage, phrasing, and logic. Jennifer Freilach deftly managed the in-house production. Kudos to the designers — Brian Moore for the jacket, Margaret Rosewitz for what's inside. The marvelous Ivy Givens held my hand and answered my questions on everything from assembling photos to obtaining permissions to making changes for the paperback edition. And Deb Brody, who took over as HMH publisher and my editor when Bruce left, reunited me with a fantastic editor as well as a close friend.

Before I sent in the manuscript of this book, I had a series of amazing readers of all or parts of it. Don Ritchie, who'd done enough, did more. Historian and biographer David Nasaw took time from his deadline project to review mine. Tim Rives, deputy director of the Eisenhower Library, interrupted his house move to vet what I was saying about Ike. Few people know more about communism in America than Emory professor emeritus Harvey Klehr, and he saved me from more mistakes than I'll admit. Few know more about the Cold War than George Washington professor Jim Hershberg, and he helped me see what I'd missed. Harvard professor Fred Logevall added his input and expertise on international relations, Boston University law professor Tracey Maclin on the First Amendment, Brooklyn College professor Steve Remy on the Malmedy Massacre, Pulitzer Prize–winning biographer Kai Bird on the Bundy (and Dulles) brothers, and on Margaret Chase Smith, it was Margaret Chase Smith Library director emeritus Greg Gallant.

Friends also dug into what I had written, offering context and texture. Sally Jacobs showed, again, what a great writer, editor, and pal she is. Charles Glovsky read the complete draft and offered more careful commentary than I had a right to expect. So did Bev and Paul Jacobson.

In addition to all of that, and before it, veteran editor David Sobel took out his red pencil and, through word fixes and big picture critiques, gave me the confidence to hand out the manuscript to my other readers and hand it in to Bruce and the team at Houghton. It's the second of my books that David has helped with, and I now deem him a friend as well as an artist.

As essential as editors are, enablers matter, too, the way I saw in the Joe McCarthy story. Mine, close to home, were Alec and

Marina, Chris and Amanda. My mother, Dottie Tye, loved hearing about every step. Also there with perspective and encouragement, as always, were John Allen, George Bachrach, and Susan Centofanti, Jeff Bass, Teri Bergman, Jim Cahill, Lucy Cleland, Jerry and Susan Cohen, Hope Denekamp, Andrew Dreyfus, Kitty and Mike Dukakis, the Frusztajers — Bill, Olga, Nina, Mischa, and Edina — Judy Glasser, Suzanne and Norman Goldberg, Jessie Gottsegen, Sue and Dick Hamilton, Henry Hyde, Phil Johnston, Mike King, Bill Kovach, Ken Ludwig, Eileen McNamara, Bill and Debbie Mills, Audrey Shelto, Don Skwar, Peggy Slasman, Antonia Stephens, Don and Ariela Tye, Eileen Tye, Phil and Tamar Warburg, Richard and Peggy Wolman, and all my Health Coverage fellows and fellow Niemans.

I got to know along the way families of those who knew Joe McCarthy — of his friends and his colleagues, his victims and his detractors. All are mentioned in my bibliography, but deserving special mention are Greta and Dirk Van Susteren, who came through in ways only they and I know entirely and for which I am grateful. Same for Jim Juliana Jr. Nearly everyone I asked in Appleton, Milwaukee, and Madison helped as well, starting with Cody Splitt and Tom Nelson. Most of all, thanks to Tierney and the rest of Joe's family.

I tapped archives across the country, from the Kennedy, Eisenhower, Truman, and Lyndon Johnson presidential libraries, to the Library of Congress, Senate Historical Office, Wisconsin Historical Society, Columbia University Oral History Archives, History Museum at the Castle in Appleton, and other government, university, and private collections. No curators helped more, over a longer period, with more grace, than those at Marquette University. I am appreciative, Amy Cary and Phil Runkel. Kudos, too, to Shawn Brown at the National Committee for an Effective Congress, and Adam Berenbak, Theresa Fitzgerald, David Ferriero, and the other terrific people at the National Archives and Records Administration and the US Navy and Marine Corps, who came through just when I had given up on Joe's Bethesda Naval Hospital files, his Marine records, and endless folders from the Permanent Subcommittee on Investigations. And to Senators Susan Collins and Carl Levin, thanks for unlocking for everyone the transcripts of Senator McCarthy's executive sessions, and for explaining to me why his story has such resonance for you. I am thankful as well for the research grants I got from the Truman and Eisenhower libraries.

Every biography of a major public figure builds on the books that came before, and there were scores on McCarthy and McCarthyism. I am grateful to all those authors, and especially to David Oshinsky, who encouraged me from the start, and to Thomas Reeves, who left the transcripts of his many interviews to an archive where future biographers could utilize them.

Every book also depends on its marketing team to get anyone to pay attention, and mine had the added hurdle of the release coming at the dawn of a pandemic. You pivoted like all-stars, Michelle Triant, Gail Leondar-Wright, Michael Dudding, and Taryn Roeder.

It's impossible for me to imagine assembling a book without assistance from student researchers, and a stream of them helped with everything from library and Internet searches to transcribing interviews and planning my virtual tour. The ones who stayed longest were Aidan Calvelli, Madeleine Draper, Ben Gambuzza, Lucas Greenwalt, Martina Kunovic, John Lim, Orianne Montaubin, Steve Moray, Caleb Pennington, and Karen Yetra.

NOTES

ABBREVIATIONS

DDEL: Dwight D. Eisenhower Presidential Library
JFKL: John F. Kennedy Presidential Library
JJP: Jim Juliana papers, provided by the Juliana family
LBJL: Lyndon B. Johnson Presidential Library
MBNH: McCarthy medical records, Bethesda Naval Hospital
MFBI: McCarthy FBI records
MUA: Marquette University Archives, Joseph R. McCarthy Collection
NCEC: National Committee for an Effective Congress Archives
NPRC: National Personnel Records Center, McCarthy military records
OH: Oral history
PSI: Files of the Senate Permanent Subcommittee on Investigations, National Archives and Records Administration
WHS: Wisconsin Historical Society
See the bibliography for a full listing of books, articles, and other references cited in the endnotes and footnotes.

PREFACE

page

1   *"conspiracy so immense"*: *Congressional Record,* June 14, 1951, 6556.
     "To those of you": McCarthy speech to Diamond Jubilee Convention of the Sons of the American Revolution, May 15, 1950, Atlantic City, as

inserted into Congressional Record, May 19, 1950, 3787; and "McCarthy Says Leaders Put U.S. in Slaughter Contest," *Louisville Courier-Journal.*

3 *Candidate Trump boasted:* "Donald Trump: 'I Could . . . Shoot Somebody, and I Wouldn't Lose any Voters,'" npr.org; and letter to Gerard Arrnbert, June 14, 1954, John Foster Dulles Papers, Princeton University.

4 *These papers and others:* Russian Lessons File, series 21, MUA; Academic Requests, unprocessed files, MUA; and Ramsey, "History of Defending Professor Wendell Furry and Harvard University from Attacks by Joseph McCarthy," unpublished manuscript.

5 *Even as I was:* Author interviews with Leon Kamin and Bronson La Follette; and Harris, "Life of Sirrah," unpublished journal supplied by Donald Harris.

6 *Yet Ethel Kennedy:* Author interview with Ethel Kennedy.
Examining all the fresh: Author interview with Kelly Kornely.

John Kennedy had a higher average approval rating than Eisenhower, but also had higher disapproval ratings, and his presidency lasted barely three years compared to Ike's eight.

1. COMING ALIVE

17 *And it worked:* "Appleton Captain Has Triple Exploit While Off Duty," *Racine Journal Times;* McMillin, "Phony Heroism Is Backfiring for McCarthy," *Capital Times;* and Pearson, ABC broadcast, June 17, 1951.

18 *We know that from:* McCarthy wartime diaries, May 14, July 17, and December 26, 1943, and February 12, 1944, series 17, MUA.
Convincing backup: Letters from E. C. Willard, July 30, 1951, Duane Faw, July 24, 1951, E. G. McIntyre, August 6, 1951, and "Touty," July 26, 1951, series 17, MUA.

19 *If journalists had actually had:* "Fitness of Officers of the United States Marine Corps, 1942–1945," NPRC; "Fourth Endorsement on Maj. Joseph R. McCarthy," April 29, 1952, NPRC; and "Tail Gunner Joe," memorandum to the assistant secretary of defense from Colonel M. J. Gravel, August 16, 1976, NPRC.

21 *Grandfather Stephen Patrick McCarthy:* Thomas Reeves interview with James S. Heenan Sr., January 16, 1976, WHS.
Timothy, the third: Reeves interviews with Urban Van Susteren, January 15 and February 21, 1976, Howard Crabb, July 14, 1977, Heenan, and Stephen Timothy McCarthy, October 14, 1977.

22 *Wisconsin farm families:* Pilat and Shannon, "Smear, Inc.: The One-Man Mob of Joe McCarthy," pt. 2; Crosby, *God, Church, and Flag,* 35; and Lubell, *Revolt of the Moderates,* 64–65.
Over the decades: Anderson and May, *McCarthy: The Man, the Senator, the "Ism,"* 8–11; and Herman, *Joseph McCarthy,* 21–23.

23 *In reality:* Reeves, *The Life and Times of Joe McCarthy,* 4; and Pett, "Senator McCarthy Courageous or Arrogant?," *Portland Oregonian.*

24 *Sometimes that gumption:* Reeves interviews with Van Susteren, Ray L. Feuerstein, October 14, 1977, Heenan, and Stephen McCarthy; "Smear, Inc.," pt. 2; Castonia, "McCarthy the Man," *Appleton Post-Crescent; Life*

and Times of Joe McCarthy, 4; and Oshinsky, *A Conspiracy So Immense,*
4–6.

   In 1930, just 19.1 percent of Americans had at least a high school degree. US Census Bureau.

25 *Timothy and Bridget did dream:* Fulton Lewis broadcast, May 2, 1957, pt.
28 of 28, MFBI; and https://vault.fbi.gov.
Less than a year: Karney, "The Story of Joe McCarthy," pt. 1, *Wisconsin
State Journal;* Bayley, *Joe McCarthy and the Press,* 10; "Senator McCarthy
Courageous or Arrogant?"; *The Man, the Senator, the "Ism,"* 12–13; Alexander, "The Senate's Remarkable Upstart," *Saturday Evening Post;* and
letter from McCarthy to Major Saxon Holt Jr., June 2, 1942, NPRC.

26 *But he came away:* McCarthy to Holt; *The Man, the Senator, the "Ism,"*
14–16; "Senate's Remarkable Upstart"; *Life and Times of Joe McCarthy,*
5–6; and *Conspiracy So Immense,* 10.

27 *He was savvy:* "The Story of Joe McCarthy," pt. 1; L. D. Hershberger,
"Joe McCarthy's H.S. Record," series 23, MUA; "Youth to Complete High
School in Single Year," *Milwaukee Journal;* O'Brien, *McCarthy and Mc-
Carthyism in Wisconsin,* 8; Sanstadt, "Who Was the Real Joe McCarthy?,"
New London (WI) Press-Star; Reeves interview with Leo Hershberger,
November 9, 1975; McCarthy to Holt; "Manawa Takes Pride in McCar-
thy's High School Feat," *Appleton Post-Crescent;* Little Wolf Transcripts,
WHS; and Michael O'Brien interview with Leo Hershberger, February 3,
1977.

29 *Joe's college career:* "Manawa Takes Pride"; "Who Was the Real Joe Mc-
Carthy?"; *The Man, the Senator, the "Ism,"* 20; *Conspiracy So Immense,*
10–11; *Life and Times of Joe McCarthy,* 9–10; and Reeves interview with
Hershberger.

30 *When he landed at Marquette:* Marquette yearbook and transcripts; and
email to author from registrar's office.

   The yearbook reports that, in 1931, Joe was president of the student
branch of the American Society of Mechanical Engineers, one of the few
honors he didn't trumpet and one of his few achievements as a budding
engineer.

32 *None of that bothered:* O'Brien interview with Robert Harland, April
5, 1977; Reeves interview with Charles Hanratty, July 24, 1975; and *The
Man, the Senator, the "Ism,"* 26.
Joe juggled: McCarthy to Holt; Reeves interviews with Thomas Korb,
September 6, 1975, Hanratty, and William Lamers, June 30, 1975; Tim
McCarthy will; Joe letters to William McCarthy, September 13, 1948,
and August 21, 1956, series 20, MUA; and author interview with Jack
Pankratz.

33 *However much money:* Reeves interviews with Korb, Hanratty, and Gerald T. Flynn, October 30 and December 10, 1975.
Joe's other after-hours: O'Brien interview with Francis Reiske, April 5,
1977; Reeves interview with Korb; and *McCarthy and McCarthyism in
Wisconsin,* 16.

34 *Joe lived at:* Reeves interviews with Korb and Flynn.

Boxing offered another: "Hilltop Sport Fans Display Interest in Boxing at Show," *Marquette Tribune;* Reeves interviews with Hanratty and Adrian Delaney, August 18, 1977; Cohn, *McCarthy,* 13; *Conspiracy So Immense,* 13–14; "Senate's Remarkable Upstart"; and *McCarthy and McCarthyism in Wisconsin,* 10.

35   *McCarthy didn't expressly:* Reeves interview with Steve Swedish, May 24, 1975; and *The Man, the Senator, the "Ism,"* 27.

      Joe did take: Curran letter to Reeves, June 26, 1975.

36   *Joe's years at Marquette:* Archdiocese of Milwaukee.

      Still, we should not: Crosby, *God, Church, and Flag,* 27.

37   *Joe was reaching:* Reeves interview with Hanratty.

      The unfledged attorney's: The Man, the Senator, the "Ism," 30; and Reeves interviews with Edward J. Hart, September 19, 1975, and Karl Baldwin, November 25, 1975.

      Joe no longer: Reeves interviews with Andrew Parnell, September 4, 1976, Gus Keller, November 25, 1975, and Hart.

38   *McCarthy showed a more:* Reeves interview with Hart, October 6, 1975.

      McCarthy didn't drink: Reeves interview with Hart, September 19, 1975; "Senate's Remarkable Upstart"; *Life and Times of Joe McCarthy,* 21; *The Man, the Senator, the "Ism,"* 31; and *McCarthy and McCarthyism in Wisconsin,* 17.

      Eberlein was a seasoned: "The Story of Joe McCarthy," pt. 1; McCarthy to Holt; *The Man, the Senator, the "Ism,"* 33; and "Broken Slugs," *Waupaca County Post.*

39   *It didn't take long: The Man, the Senator, the "Ism,"* 34–35; Reeves interview with Ruth Meyer, September 3, 1976; *Conspiracy So Immense,* 19; *McCarthy and McCarthyism in Wisconsin,* 20–21; Fleming, "McCarthy War Injury?," *Milwaukee Journal;* and "Attorneys Speak at Service Clubs," *Shawano County Journal.*

      He started his own: McCarthy and McCarthyism in Wisconsin, 21 and 25; and "Jos. M'Carthy Joins Shawano Law Firm," *Shawano County Journal.*

      The *County Journal* article, timed for his arrival in Shawano, said that he'd worked for the Milwaukee firm of Breneham, Lucas, and Mc-Donough, which he hadn't. It also said that he rose higher than he had in the ranks of wrestlers and boxers. While the reporter might have done the inventing, it is more likely that Joe supplied the information. *McCarthy and McCarthyism in Wisconsin,* 25.

40   *Grover Meisner, a stalwart: McCarthy and McCarthyism in Wisconsin,* 22–23; and *Conspiracy So Immense,* 16.

41   *He was spending more time:* "Senate's Remarkable Upstart"; Reeves interview with Mae Voy, September 3, 1976; and "Jr. Woman's Club Hears Talk on 'Americanization,'" *Shawano County Journal.*

      Early in 1937: McCarthy to Holt; and *The Man, the Senator, the "Ism,"* 34.

      Joe already was: https://www.infoplease.com/us/marital-status/median-age-first-marriage-1890-2010.

42   *Joe's single-minded:* "The Circuit Judgeship," *Appleton Post-Crescent;* author interviews with Cody Splitt and Jim Long; "The Story of Joe Mc-Carthy," pt. 2; author interview with Jim Long; *The Man, the Senator, the*

"Ism," 38–41 and 69; "Senate's Remarkable Upstart"; *McCarthy and Mc-Carthyism in Wisconsin,* 29–31; Reeves interview with Van Susteren, February 5, 1977; *Life and Times of Joe McCarthy,* 27–28; "McCarthy Elected Judge to Succeed E. V. Werner," *Appleton Post-Crescent;* "Senator McCarthy Will Marry Sept. 29," *Appleton Post-Crescent;* MBNH records; *Congressional Record; Who's Who in America;* "Record Lists McCarthy Age as 48, Not 47," *Chicago Daily Tribune;* Coady, "The Wisconsin Press and Joseph McCarthy"; "Joseph R. McCarthy: A Judge and a Soldier," 1944 campaign literature; and draft card, NPRC.

It is impossible to know whether Werner supplied the wrong dates published in the *Martindale-Hubbell Law Directory,* which said he was born in 1866, and a Shawano newspaper that pegged the year as 1870. But he apparently did nothing to correct either, both of which he presumably would at least have known about. On Joe's age, the earliest mention of his being born in 1909 was in an April 5, 1939, edition of the *Green Bay Press-Gazette.* On that same date an article in the *Appleton Post-Crescent* listed his birth year as 1908.

45 *McCarthy's relentless messaging:* "McCarthy Elected Judge to Succeed E. V. Werner"; and Pearson Attorney File, Robert Fleming Papers, WHS. *Judge Joe toasted:* Email to author from William E. Raftery, National Center for State Courts; McCarthy to Holt; O'Brien interview with Robert Harland, April 5, 1977; Reeves interviews with Parnell and John Wyngaard, March 22, 1978; "Senate's Remarkable Upstart"; and Reeves interview with Van Susteren, November 25, 1975.

46 *The circuit courts played: Life and Times of Joe McCarthy* 34–35; *Conspiracy So Immense,* 24–27; *The Man, the Senator, the "Ism,"* 44–45 and 73–74; *Milwaukee Journal* editorial, September 28, 1946; Reeves interview with Van Susteren, February 21, 1976; and letters of recommendation, June 2, 1942, NPRC.

47 *The recklessness: Life and Times of Joe McCarthy,* 36; Morgan, *Reds,* 331; and *The Man, the Senator, the "Ism,"* 46.

48 *There wasn't as much: Conspiracy So Immense,* 15.
In 1942, Joe: Reeves interview with Flynn, October 30, 1975.

Not all his gambling in Wisconsin would be law-abiding, according to information provided to *Capital Times* publisher William Evjue, a McCarthy critic. In later years, Joe apparently relished sidling up to the illegal gaming tables in Vilas County, which somehow escaped the attention of state officials who were shutting down such operations elsewhere in Wisconsin.

The National Committee for an Effective Congress relished assembling that and other damning information about the senator it despised, using the same techniques of leaks and spies that Joe and his committee did. The committee was set up in 1948 by Eleanor Roosevelt to help elect progressive congressional candidates [August 13, 1947 memo from Miles McMillin to Evjue, NCEC].

49 *The case that offered: McCarthy and McCarthyism in Wisconsin,* 34–36; and *State ex rel. Department of Agriculture v. McCarthy,* 299 N.W. 58 (Wis. 1941).

50 *McCarthy's enlistment produced:* "Smear, Inc.," pt. 4; "McCarthy War Injury?"; letter from Saxon Holt Jr. to Commandant, June 4, 1942, NPRC; McCarthy to Victor O'Kelleher, May 25, 1942, series 17, MUA; Steinke, "The Rise of McCarthyism"; "State Judge on Leave Injured in Pacific," *Racine Journal Times; Life and Times of Joe McCarthy,* 49; "Senate's Remarkable Upstart"; *Conspiracy So Immense,* 33; and wartime diaries, July 21 and 23, 1943.

53 *Most maladies:* Medical records, March 3, 6, and 8, September 2, 1944, and wartime diary, February 19, 1944, NPRC and MUA.

54 *His official overseas:* Letters from Robert Barvotes, July 23, 1951, and Coop, August 7, 1951, series 17, MUA; and Reeves interview with Jerome Wander, September 9, 1977.
    In the end, did: Marine Corps Record Files, series 17, MUA; *National Enquirer* interview with Glenn Todd, unprocessed files, MUA (the *Enquirer* says that it can't pin down the date because all of its pre-2001 files were lost); and "Second Endorsement of Maj Joseph R. McCarthy," from commandant of the Marine Corps to secretary of the Navy, undated, NPRC.

56 *Others defined heroism:* Letter from Arold Murphy to McCarthy, July 6, 1942, and from Gerald Jolin to McCarthy, September 25, 1944, NPRC.
    Neither Jolin nor Murphy: Wartime diaries, May 11, July 21, and September 12, 1943, and March 24 and 25, 1944.

57 *What would become:* Wartime diaries, May 18, July 4, and August 17, 1943.
    Being overseas didn't: Wartime diaries, February 12, 1944; letter from Bob Schwartz to Robert Fleming, October 8, 1951, Fleming Papers; and Reeves interview with Wander.

58 *As his diary attested:* Wartime diary, September 5, 1943; letter from E. E. Munn to Commandant, February 11, 1944, series 17, MUA; *The Man, the Senator, the "Ism,"* 65; and Rovere, *Senator Joe McCarthy,* 98.
    More than thirty years later, Munn would tell Thomas Reeves he couldn't recall writing a letter of recommendation for Joe, and disputing some of what was attributed to him, but he added, "I have never discredited Joe since he was always an asset to the Squadron and everyone in it." Munn to Reeves, September 21, 1977.
    His Marquette archives: Stimson and Knox, "Participation of Members of the Armed Services in Political Campaigns," March 15, 1944, NPRC; Reeves interview with Leo Day, February 11, 1977; *Life and Times of Joe McCarthy,* 52–55; *Conspiracy So Immense,* 35; McCarthy Campaign Records, series 23, wartime diaries, December 26, 1943, and February 19 and March 27, 1944, series 17, and letters to Wisconsin League of Women Voters, June 22, 1944, and to Les, September 7, 1944, series 20, MUA; War Files, Fleming Papers; Wisconsin Constitution, Article 7, sec. 10; chap. 256.02(2), Wisconsin Statutes, 1943; American Bar Association Canons of Judicial Ethics, 1924; letter from Jack Canaan to William Evjue, December 1949, Evjue Papers, WHS; and "Weighed in the Balance," *Time.*

62 *That made his relations:* Hoving, "My Friend McCarthy," *The Reporter;* and "Smear, Inc.," pt. 2.

Things weren't always easy: Memo from Commanding General, First Marine Aircraft Wing, to McCarthy, July 2, 1944, NPRC.

63 *All his behind-the-scenes:* Letter from Senator Wiley to McCarthy, September 18, 1944, series 23, and letters from Jolin to McCarthy, September 1 and December 4, 1944, unprocessed files, MUA.

64 *By the end of 1944:* Letter from Arold Murphy; letter from Jolin, September 25, 1944; letter from McCarthy to Commandant, October 19, 1944, and reply from Personnel Department, November 20, 1944, NPRC; and "M'Carthy Will Resume Bench," *Milwaukee Sentinel.*
His first day back: "Man in Uniform Is on Bench," *Milwaukee Journal;* and "Resumes Judicial Duties," *Appleton Post-Crescent.*

2. SENATOR WHO?

65 *"Young Bob" defied:* Maney, "Joe McCarthy's First Victim," *Virginia Quarterly Review;* and *Wisconsin Blue Book,* 1922 and 1928.
   The second-biggest vote-getter was Young Bob's father, with 80.6 percent in 1922.

66 *But Joe was a master:* "La Follette's Folly," *The Nation.*
If the RVC: The Man, the Senator, the "Ism," 78–79; and "Senate's Remarkable Upstart."

67 *McCarthy backed up:* "Smear, Inc.," pt. 5; and "Senate's Remarkable Upstart."

68 *Round two was:* Speech to Young Republicans Convention, Eau Claire, WI, May 2, 1946, series 19, MUA; and "La Follette Opponent Sees Rough, Clean Fight," *Wisconsin State Journal.*

69 *On Memorial Day:* Speeches to unnamed audiences, May 30 and October 1, 1946, series 19, MUA; and "McCarthy Covers OPA, Labor, Bonus and Russian Questions," *Wisconsin Rapids Daily Tribune.*
He had promised: Maney, *"Young Bob" La Follette,* 290; "Insurgent's Way," *Time;* and *The Man, the Senator, the "Ism,"* 85.

70 *And the mud:* "McCarthy Flays Bob's Farm Record," *Madison Capital Times; "Young Bob" La Follette,* 290–93; "Insurgent's Way"; Johnson, *Robert M. La Follette, Jr. and the Decline of the Progressive Party in Wisconsin,* 131; and *McCarthy and McCarthyism in Wisconsin,* 65.
Once an admirer: Author interview with John Nichols.

71 *To break that hold:* Reeves interview with Ray Kiermas, March 17, 1977; and "Senate's Remarkable Upstart."
It wasn't just: Author interview with Cody Splitt; *Life and Times of Joe McCarthy,* 81; and "Senate's Remarkable Upstart."

72 *Cody Splitt:* Splitt interview.
The barnstorming: McMillin, "The Wisconsin Political Scene," *Madison Capital Times; McCarthy and McCarthyism in Wisconsin,* 71; and *Life and Times of Joe McCarthy,* 91 and 690.
Those efforts cost: Life and Times of Joe McCarthy, 66.

73 *Impressive as those: "Young Bob" La Follette,* 292–93.
Young Bob was just: "Young Bob" La Follette, 296–97; and Hyman, *The Lives of William Benton,* 365.

74 *His miserable health: "Young Bob" La Follette,* 16–18 and 25–28.

When the senator: *McCarthy and McCarthyism in Wisconsin*, 68–69; "Conference with Governor Goodland," April 19, 1946, Coleman Papers, WHS; and *"Young Bob" La Follette*, 298.

75 *There was a general:* "Questions by Hearers, Rivals Enliven Candidates' Forums," *Milwaukee Journal;* "McCarthy, McMurray Stage a Verbal 'Slugfest,'" *Milwaukee Journal; Life and Times of Joe McCarthy*, 102; and winstonchurchill.org.

76 *McMurray punched back:* "Questions by Hearers, Rivals Enliven Candidates' Forums."

77 *The Democrat was helped:* Letter from W. T. Doar to R. T. Reinholdt et al., January 10, 1949, Dempsey Papers, WHS; and "McCarthy, McMurray Stage a Verbal 'Slugfest.'"
Joe's glib answers: State of Wisconsin v. Joseph R. McCarthy, 255, Wis. 234 (1949); Bob Schwartz, "Report from Wisconsin," October 4, 1951, Fleming Papers, WHS; and Griffith, *The Politics of Fear*, 86–87.

78 *One reason why:* Letters to McCarthy from Dick Rice, September 18, 1945, and Rhyner and Zappen Law Office, August 6, 1946, MUA; letters from Shirley Foresman to Francis Reiske, August 6, 1946, and Peter H. McCarthy, July 2, 1946, MUA; and letter from McCarthy to Van Susteren, March 13, 1945, MUA.
Joe also blithely: Letters from McCarthy to "Vincent," November 9, 1945, and Van Susteren, January 9, 1946, MUA.
McCarthy got an assist: Author interview with Maney; *"Young Bob" La Follette*, 302; and Maney, "Joe McCarthy's First Victim," *Virginia Quarterly Review*.

80 *They could have gotten: The Politics of Fear*, 12; and author interview with Robert Lorge.
McCarthy was never: Conspiracy So Immense, 58–59; "Senate's Remarkable Upstart"; "Senate Newcomer," *Newsweek;* "McCarthy Proposes U.S. Draft Lewis, Miners into Army," *Washington Post;* and Loftus, "Labor Bids Made," *New York Times*.

81 *It was Joe's perfect:* Eklund, "Work Is McCarthy's Formula for Success," *Milwaukee Journal*.

82 *Press coverage didn't:* "Senate's Remarkable Upstart"; "Senate Newcomer"; "New Faces in the Senate," *Time;* and Childs, "Washington Calling: Dangerous Drift," *Washington Post*.
Nobody in the press: Harris, "The Private Life of Senator McCarthy," *American Weekly;* and Anderson, *Confessions of a Muckraker*, 177.

83 *Publicity was Joe's alpha: Congressional Record*, March 27, 1947, 2698–700; US Senate, Subcommittee on Privileges and Elections, *Investigations of Senators Joseph R. McCarthy and William Benton*, 39; Drew Pearson column, March 28, 1947; *Life and Times of Joe McCarthy*, 118–23; and "Smear, Inc.," pt. 10.

85 *Housing was his other:* Furman, "M'Carthy Pledges Housing Aid Speed," *New York Times;* von Hoffman, *History Lessons for Today's Housing Policy: The Political Processes of Making Low-Income Housing Policy*, Joint Center for Housing Studies, Harvard University; "Tobey, Beaten, Sees Threat to Wreck Inquiry," *Washington Post;* Drew Pearson column, September 7,

1947; *The Man, the Senator, the "Ism,"* 142 and 145; *Conspiracy So Immense,* 67; and "Smear, Inc.," pt. 7.

88 *That characterization:* "Smear, Inc.," pt. 8; Lustron contract, series 20, letter from Jean Kerr to Carl Strandlund, October 27, 1948, series 14, and Jean Kerr McCarthy, "The Joe McCarthy I Knew," series 24, MUA; *The Man, the Senator, the "Ism,"* 154; "McCarthy's Ideas on Housing Published by 'Prefab' Maker," *Milwaukee Journal;* http://www.ohiohistory central.org/w/Lustron_Corporation; Lustron, *How to Own Your Own Home Now;* "Lustron Check to McCarthy in Court File," *Madison Capital Times; Conspiracy So Immense,* 71; and *Investigations of Senators Joseph R. McCarthy and William Benton.*

89 *Joe's tone deafness:* Letter from McCarthy to F. J. Sensenbrenner, February 14, 1948, series 20, MUA.

90 *He also imposed:* Letter from McCarthy to Walter Schroeder, May 19, 1947, series 20, MUA.
    Financial entanglements: "Smear, Inc.," pt. 7; "The Joe McCarthy I Knew"; and McCarthy voting record, US Senate.

91 *But he reveled:* McCarthy "Dear Folks" letter to voters, March 31, 1948, series 23, MUA.

92 *Senator Joe's performance:* "Smear, Inc.," pt. 1.
    Lots of groups: Oshinsky, *Senator Joseph McCarthy and the American Labor Movement,* 82–86; Drew Pearson column, August 1, 1947; and "Who Are the Nation's Best and Worst Senators?" *Pageant,* 1949.

93 *A consensus was building:* Letters from McCarthy to Roy Matson, December 3, 1948, and to V. I. Minahan, December 2, 1948, McCarthy Files, WHS.
    The fact was that: "Work Is McCarthy's Formula for Success," *Milwaukee Journal;* and Evjue, "Joe McCarthy in Wisconsin," *The Nation.*

94 *Jean Fraser Kerr had:* "The Joe McCarthy I Knew"; Lasky, "The Gal Who Married Joe McCarthy," unprocessed files, MUA; and Reeves interview with Tom Korb.
    Korb — Joe's law school friend, now his top staffer, and eventually his best man — claimed credit for hiring Jean.

95 *Once she headed back:* "The Joe McCarthy I Knew"; and telegrams from McCarthy to Jean, April 27 and May 4, 1948, series 24, MUA.
    Jean didn't have nearly: "The Joe McCarthy I Knew"; and letter from Jean to Benjamin Semple Chase, undated, unprocessed files, MUA.
    Jean laid out: "The Joe McCarthy I Knew"; "The Gal Who Married Joe McCarthy"; and "The Private Life of Senator McCarthy."

96 *That may have been: Conspiracy So Immense,* 56.
    Another factor that: "The Joe McCarthy I Knew"; Reeves interviews with Robert Fleming, October 27, 1975, and Kiermas; "Weighed in the Balance"; Crosby, *God, Church, and Flag,* 34; "Report from Wisconsin"; and Lincoln Day speech, Tulsa, February 15, 1947, series 19, MUA.

97 *That earnestness:* Reeves interview with Agnes Buckley, September 2, 1975; author interview with Peter Voy; and Castonia, "McCarthy the Man," *Appleton Post-Crescent.*

98 *Senator McCarthy knew:* "Senate's Remarkable Upstart."

He was also palling: McCarthy letter to Hoover, June 1, 1949, series 14, MUA; Cox and Theoharis, *The Boss,* 280–81; and transcript of Hoover-McCarthy radio interview, April 6, 1949, pt. 6 of 28, MFBI.

99 *Joe acted as if:* "Senate's Remarkable Upstart"; "The Private Life of Senator McCarthy"; and *Conspiracy So Immense,* 55.

Joe made it back: Author interviews with Kelly Kornely and Vi Stoner.

100 *The paper ran: Conspiracy So Immense,* 56; will and other legal documents, Tim McCarthy, Outagamie County (WI) Courthouse; and Reeves interview with Kiermas.

Despite his air: Hospital notes, February 15, June 29, and December 21, 1948, July 25 and November 16 and 23, 1949, and March 31, 1950, MBNH; and Reeves interviews with Loyal Eddy, May 24, 1976, Delaney, Korb, and Ed Nellor, June 6, 1979.

102 *To the outside world:* "Senate's Remarkable Upstart"; and "The Private Life of Senator McCarthy."

His drinking remained: Anderson, *Outsider in the Senate,* 101–2; and McCarthy Gambling File, Fleming Papers.

103 *Samuel Shaffer, a* Newsweek: Shaffer, *On and Off the Floor,* 26.

The more famous: Reeves interview with Parnell.

The event that triggered: Remy, *The Malmedy Massacre,* 1–20; and Remy emails to author.

106 *Joe's interest in Malmedy:* McCarthy radio speech, November 13, 1945, series 19, MUA; "The Joe McCarthy I Knew"; and Reeves interview with Jean McCarthy, June 24, 1975.

With Joe, however: WHS; and *Joe McCarthy and the Press,* 9. (Riedl told Nathan Pusey, who told journalist and author Edwin Bayley.)

107 *A more troubling theory:* Reeves interviews with Urban and Margery Van Susteren, Nellor, and Keller; Adams, *Without Precedent,* 115; Acheson, *Present at the Creation,* 370; US Senate, Subcommittee of the Committee on Armed Services, Malmedy Massacre Investigation, 179 and 201; and Tuck, *McCarthyism and New York's Hearst Press,* 183.

108 *Whatever drew him:* Malmedy *Massacre Investigation,* 630–31 and 839; Van Roden, "American Atrocities in Germany," *The Progressive;* Johnson, *Raymond E. Baldwin,* 250–51; *Life and Times of Joe McCarthy,* 179; and *The Malmedy Massacre,* 4, 221–36, and 275.

112 *Joe's miscasting: The Man, the Senator, the "Ism,"* 161; "Malmedy Survivor Says McCarthy 'Dupe' of Reds in Defending SS Troops," *Madison Capital Times;* and Remy emails to author.

But Malmedy was just: Malmedy hearings, 127 and 177; and *Raymond E. Baldwin,* 251.

113 *The Malmedy hearings were: Senator Joe McCarthy,* 111–18.

3. AN ISM IS BORN

114 *The cause that would:* February 9, 1950, Lincoln Day speech, series 19, MUA; Desmond, "M'Carthy Charges Reds Holding US Offices," *Wheeling Intelligencer;* and Edwards, "Tell How Red Spies Escaped Prosecution," *Chicago Daily Tribune,* February 9, 1950.

Joe saw the speech that would define his career only after he got on the train to Wheeling, said William A. Roberts, a Washington lawyer who occasionally advised the senator. Roberts said he managed to reach Joe shortly before he delivered the address in West Virginia, and might have persuaded him to scrap it, but McCarthy already had handed out copies to reporters [August 23, 1951 NCEC interview of Roberts].

115 *Or did he?:* US Senate, *Subcommittee of the Committee on Foreign Relations, State Department Employee Loyalty Investigation;* "M'Carthy Charges Reds Holding US Offices"; Associated Press, "State Dept. Hired Reds Solon Says"; "M'Carthy Note Again Asks Reds' Ouster," *Salt Lake Tribune;* Green, "FBI 'Covers' 4400 Reds in America," *Deseret News;* Connors, "'Red' Allegation Gets Sharp Reply," *Nevada State Journal;* Connors, "McCarthy Blasts State Department," *Nevada State Journal;* "More M'Carthy Charges Made," *Nevada State Journal;* Friendly, "The Noble Crusade of Senator McCarthy," *Harper's;* Merrill, *Documentary History of the Truman Presidency,* vols. 1 and 4; and *Joe McCarthy and the Press,* 24–25.

The Marquette archives include an audio recording of Joe saying, before an unspecified audience in late 1951, that he'd used the numbers fifty-seven *and* 205 in Wheeling. He'd known then the names of fifty-seven Communists at the State Department, he explained, and called on President Truman to release the names of all 205 who were there. http://cdm16280.contentdm.oclc.org/cdm/singleitem/collection/p128701coll0/id/28/rec/2.

117 *The senator intended:* Letter to Reeves from Mrs. Garvin Tankersley, January 10, 1979, WHS; Reeves interview with Nellor, May 7, 1977; *The Boss,* 282; Abrahamsen, *Nixon vs. Nixon,* 155–56; Ybarra, *Washington Gone Crazy,* 490; and versions of Lincoln Day speech, series 19, MUA.

118 *The address was the most:* Record, 79th Cong., 2nd sess., July 26, 1946, A4891–4892; letter to Reeves from Tankersley, January 10, 1979; *Life and Times of Joe McCarthy,* 223; *Washington Gone Crazy,* 490; "The Noble Crusade of Senator McCarthy"; and *Conspiracy So Immense,* 110–11.

119 *He all but confessed:* Halberstam, *The Fifties,* 51–52; Johnson, *Age of Anxiety,* 142–44; author interview with McCulloch via Candace Akers; and *Joe McCarthy and the Press,* 36.

120 *It wasn't only that:* Anderson, *Outsider in the Senate,* 105; Wendt, *Chicago Tribune,* 703; and "The Joe McCarthy I Knew."

121 *Defiant though he was:* Nixon, *RN: The Memoirs of Richard Nixon,* 138; and Reeves interview with Robert E. Lee, March 15, 1977.

122 *The press was essential:* Chaney and Cieply, *The Hearsts,* 128; and *Confessions of a Muckraker,* 181 and 185.
Joe's most important call: Life and Times of Joe McCarthy, 245; Sullivan, *The Bureau,* 45 and 267; and Gentry, *J. Edgar Hoover,* 379.
What mattered in the end: Hyman, *The Lives of William Benton,* 422; and McCarthy Methods File, Fleming Papers.

123 *His longtime executive secretary:* Brinkley, *David Brinkley: A Memoir,* 112–13.

124 *To understand McCarthy:* Koch, "Demagogues and Democracy"; Bailey, "10 Divisive Demagogues Through History"; "The Texas Politics Proj-

ect"; Signer, *Demagogue*, 34–36; and Cooper, *The American Democrat*, 87–89.

126 *The label "demagogue"*: Williams, *Huey Long*, 748–49 and 762; White, *The Reign of Huey P. Long*, 65; and Brinkley, *Voices of Protest*.

128 *One of America's*: http://www.let.rug.nl/usa/presidents/woodrow-wil son/state-of-the-union-1915.php; *Conspiracy So Immense*, 88; and Fried, *Nightmare in Red*, 43.

129 *The anti-Communist fervor*: White, "Seeing Red."
   It was against: Ritchie, *Congress and Harry S. Truman*, 112; *The Politics of Fear*, 32–33; *Life and Times of Joe McCarthy*, 208; *Conspiracy So Immense*, 92; "Seeing Red"; and "Ex-Rep. Martin Dies, 71, Is Dead," *New York Times*.

131 *And it wasn't just Dies*: Lewy, *The Federal Loyalty-Security Program*; and Caute, *The Great Fear*, 169 and 581.

133 *As a senator*: Pells, *The Liberal Mind in a Conservative Age*, 339; *Nightmare in Red*, 7; Freeland, *The Truman Doctrine and the Origins of McCarthyism*, 6–11 and 360; Hellman, *Scoundrel Time*, 21; Griffith and Theoharis, *The Specter*, 24–62; Spillane, *The Hammer Strikes Again*, 167; "Seeing Red"; McDonald, *Feminism, the Left, and Postwar Literary Culture*, 17; and "Red Plot on Bubble Gum — Or Much Ado," *Billboard*.

134 *Were these appropriate reactions*: Neikind, "US Communists, 1950," *The Reporter*.

135 *We now know even more*: Author interview with John Earl Haynes.
   Other developments, however: Author interview with Haynes; Andrew and Mitrokhin, *The Sword and the Shield*, 165; and email to author from Harvey Klehr.

136 *Where was Joe McCarthy*: McCarthy speech of October 1, 1946, series 19, MUA.

137 *He returned to the issue*: McCarthy speeches of February 15 and March 15, 1947, and radio address, April 3, 1947, series 19, MUA.

138 *His most blistering attack*: McCarthy and McCarthyism in Wisconsin, 91–97; and *Life and Times of Joe McCarthy*, 191–97.
   Jack Anderson knew: *The Man, the Senator, the "Ism,"* 172–73; *Confessions of a Muckraker*, 181; and email to author from Don Ritchie.
   William A. Roberts described what almost certainly was that same meeting, which started in his office, continued at Georgetown University, may or may not have taken time out for dinner, and included him, McCarthy, Father Walsh, and Georgetown political science professor Charles Kraus. Joe's pension proposal, Roberts said, called for paying everyone in the country $100 a month. The senator quickly dropped that scheme in favor of a more radical Red-baiting one, and kept asking his three consultants whether anti-communism would remain a hot-button issue two years hence, when he'd be running for reelection.
   Joe also hinted that night that he was interested in running for vice president, according to Roberts [August 23, 1951 NCEC interview of Roberts].

139 *Joe's awakening*: Cahoe, "McCarthy: Old Friend Is as Loyal as Ever,"

Appleton Post-Crescent; and Fried, "The Idea of Conspiracy in McCarthy-Era Politics," *Prologue.*

140 *Joe's own take:* McCarthy, *McCarthyism: Fight for America,* 2; "The Joe McCarthy I Knew"; "Senator McCarthy Answers Some Important Questions," *Cosmopolitan;* and Cohn, *McCarthy,* 8–10.

142 *As soon as Joe landed: Life and Times of Joe McCarthy,* 237–39; Buckley and Bozell, *McCarthy and His Enemies,* 60; *Conspiracy So Immense,* 114; *Congressional Record,* February 20, 1950, 1952–81; and *State Department Employee Loyalty Investigation,* 1770–1813.

143 *Samuel Shaffer, the* Newsweek: *On and Off the Floor,* 31.
McCarthy's grandstanding: Documentary History of the Truman Presidency, 25:30–35, 44–50, and 78–82; *Life and Times of Joe McCarthy,* 285; and Evans, *Blacklisted by History,* 302–4.

144 *The FBI was in a dither:* 1950 memos in MFBI: on Reno visit, February 11, Louis Nichols to Hoover, February 21, and Alan Belmont to D. Milton Ladd, March 7, pt. 11 of 28; and Attorney General McGrath to Hoover July 25, pt. 26 of 28.
Joe's own office: Memos from Hoover to Clyde Tolson et al., July 14, 1954, and Hoover to Don Surine, March 6, 1950, Surine FBI Files; Reeves interview with Surine, July 30, 1977; *The Man, the Senator, the "Ism,"* 197–98 and 262; Wilson, "The Ring Around McCarthy," *Look;* Pearson Files, LBJL; $125K: Reeves interview with Kiermas; *Conspiracy So Immense,* 160; https://archive.org/stream/investigations1953of00unitrich/investigations1953of00unitrich_djvu.txt, 16–19; Edwards, *Just Right,* 9; Brinkley, *A Memoir,* 113; Alsop and Alsop, "Why Has Washington Gone Crazy," *Saturday Evening Post; On and Off the Floor,* 26–27; "Smear, Inc.," pt. 1.

148 *The staff's most consuming job:* Series 14 and unprocessed files, MUA; Reeves interview with Surine, July 18, 1980; *The Boss,* 285–86; Ladd to Hoover, March 3, 1950, pt. 11 of 28, MFBI; and Gentry, *J. Edgar Hoover,* 379–80.

149 *Hoover wasn't alone: New York Post* File, series 14, MUA; and Reeves interview with Nellor, May 7, 1977.
McCarthy meant it: McCarthy Tipsters File, Fleming Papers; and McCarthy letter to Pilat, April 6, 1951, series 14, MUA.

150 *His focus was* necessarily: *The Man, the Senator, the "Ism,"* 206–7; *Life and Times of Joe McCarthy,* 320; McCarthy speech at Diamond Jubilee Convention of the Sons of the American Revolution, *Congressional Record,* May 19, 1950, 3786–89; and Taylor, *Grand Inquest,* 265 and 276.

151 *After Wheeling, Joe's message:* McCarthy speech to Diamond Jubilee Convention; and *The Man, the Senator, the "Ism,"* 207.

152 *The Tydings Committee launched: Senator Joe McCarthy,* 148–49; *State Department Employee Loyalty Investigation,* 16, 26, 32, 176, 187, and 207; *Blacklisted by History,* 346–48; *McCarthy and His Enemies,* 80–81; *Conspiracy So Immense,* 121–22; White, "Miss Kenyon Cites Patriotic Record to Refute Charges," *New York Times;* "Judge Dorothy Kenyon Is Dead," *New York Times; Congressional Record,* March 30, 1950, 4380; Weigand

and Horowitz, "Dorothy Kenyon: Feminist Organizing, 1919–1963"; and Gold, "McCarthy Without Paranoia," *The Washingtonian.*

154 *Kenyon quickly fell: The Man, the Senator, the "Ism,"* 213; "Lattimore, Accused by McCarthy as Red, Calls Charges 'Moonshine,'" *Madison Capital Times;* Lattimore, *Ordeal by Slander,* 2 and 6; *State Department Employee Loyalty Investigation,* 92, 104, 204, 421, 523, 526, 559, and 1111; *Congressional Record,* March 30, 1950, 4385; Tydings, "McCarthyism: How It All Began," *The Reporter;* "Tydings on a Tear," *Newsweek;* telegram from McCarthy to Louis Budenz, April 10, 1950, series 14, MUA; *Conspiracy So Immense,* 149–50; Haynes, *Red Scare or Red Menace?,* 149–52; and Schrecker, *Many Are the Crimes,* 253.

159 *That ability to spin: Senator Joe McCarthy,* 53; Yoder, *Joe Alsop's Cold War,* 67; *Without Precedent,* 122; and Griffith, *The Waist-High Culture,* 100. *The extent to which:* Cohn, *McCarthy,* 269.
The Lattimore case marked: State Department Employee Loyalty Investigation Hearings, 880; McCarthy telegram to Alfred Kohlberg, October 30, 1951, series 14, MUA; "Recalling All Liberals to the Real Fight," *Life;* Fiedler, "McCarthy," *Encounter;* "Benton-McCarthy Feud Heralds Mud-Slinging Campaign," *Washington Star; Senator Joe McCarthy,* 8; *McCarthy and His Enemies,* 335; and Pearson column, May 6, 1950.

161 *Important critics both: RN,* 158; Hemingway letter to McCarthy, August 5, 1950; and "Mrs. Roosevelt Says M'Carthy Is Menace," *New York Times. Composer and lyricist:* Unprocessed files, MUA.

162 *What the senator's critics:* Buchanan, *Right from the Beginning,* 91.

163 *The threat, as McCarthy:* Miller, *Out of the Past,* 258–59; "Act of Humiliation," *Time; State Department Employee Loyalty Investigation Hearings,* 128–29; *Congressional Record,* February 20, 1950, 1961 and 1979; Johnson, *The Lavender Scare,* 16; *Joe McCarthy and the Press,* 163; and *Joe Alsop's Cold War,* 153–55.

165 *"It is common talk":* Reeves interview with Warren Woods, March 14, 1977; McCarthy charges against Greenspun: letter from Joe to Greenspun, October 18, 1952, University of Notre Dame Archives; Greenspun, "Where I Stand" columns, October 25, 1952, and February 3 and 5, 1954, *Las Vegas Sun;* and Dean, *Imperial Brotherhood,* 149.

166 *When the charges:* Letter from unnamed Army lieutenant, December 27, 1951, and memos from Hoover to Tolson et al., January 16, 17, and 18, 1952, and Nichols to Tolson, June 5, 1956, 2 and 28 of 28, MFBI; author interview with Robert Andrew; "Smear, Inc.," pt. 12; *Washington Gone Crazy,* 685; *J. Edgar Hoover,* 433; and Reeves interview with Van Susteren, November 25, 1975.

167 *Anti-Semitism was another:* Pogue interview with Rosenberg, December 30, 1957; Nelson, "Caught in the Web of McCarthyism," *Congress & the Presidency; The Man, the Senator, the "Ism,"* 309–10; https://archive.org/stream/AnnaRosenberg/Rosenberg%2C%20Anna%20M.-HQ-2_djvu.txt; "Gerald L. K. Smith Dead," *New York Times; Life and Times of Joe McCarthy,* 358; *Conspiracy So Immense,* 203–5; and Rose File, Fleming Papers.

Conservative radio host Fulton Lewis and Ed Nellor, who worked for Lewis and McCarthy, also apparently were key actors in the anti-Rosenberg, anti-Semitic campaign. Gerald L. K. Smith, founder of the America First Party, wrote that Lewis was "doing a magnificent job in the Rosenberg matter" and that he and Nellor should be "treated very kindly." Smith added, in his instructions to Rosenberg critic and Holocaust denier Benjamin Freedman, "Please destroy this upon reading it" [Undated letter from Smith to Freedman, NCEC].

169 *Marshall, a former five-star:* Marshall Book Papers, series 22, MUA; McCarthy, *America's Retreat from Victory,* 1; *Congressional Record,* June 14, 1951, 6556–603; Pogue, *George C. Marshall: Statesman,* 489; *The Man, the Senator, the "Ism,"* 238; *Life and Times of Joe McCarthy,* 372–74; Wilson, *General Marshall Remembered,* 354–55; "Why Not Spank Him?," *Collier's Weekly; Conspiracy So Immense,* 201; and Reeves interview with Van Susteren, November 25, 1975.

171 *McCarthy's attack on:* Pilat, *Drew Pearson,* 1; Pearson, *Washington Merry-Go-Round: Drew Pearson Diaries, 1960–1969,* xi; Ferguson, "McCarthy v. Pearson," 47; Drew Pearson columns: February 25, March 14, and April 7, 1950; Feldstein: *Poisoning the Press,* 36; Pearson File, series 14, MUA; *Confessions of a Muckraker,* 209–12; and Tim McCarthy's Estate File, Fleming Papers.

174 *Talk turned into action:* Pearson depositions, September 25 and October 4, 1951, and McCarthy deposition, October 5, 1951, *Drew Pearson v. Joseph R. McCarthy et al.,* US District Court for the District of Columbia (1951); Bachrach, "Louise Ansberry," *Washington Post; RN,* 138–39; McCarthy, "McCarthy vs. Pearson," *Saturday Evening Post;* and letter from Joe to Jean, December 16, 1950, series 24, MUA.

    McCarthy, like Pearson and many of their biographers, got mixed up on the dates of the Sulgrave confrontation, sometimes placing the dinner on December 13 and other times on the correct day, the twelfth.

    William A. Roberts, who was Pearson's attorney, speculates that the Sulgrave episode wasn't the heat-of-the-moment dust-up that McCarthy portrayed it as. Rather, said Roberts, it was a premeditated attack plotted during a meeting of McCarthy supporters in the office of Maine Senator Owen Brewster [August 23, 1951 NCEC interview of Roberts].

176 *Three days after: Confessions of a Muckraker,* 208, 217–18, and 223; *Congressional Record,* December 15, 1950, 16634–41; Haynes and Klehr, *Venona,* 245; "Arrest of Drew Pearson," series 14, MUA; Usdin, *Bureau of Spies,* 20–28; Haynes, Klehr, and Vassiliev, *Spies: The Rise and Fall of the KGB in America,* 159; emails to author from Ritchie and Klehr; McCarthy-Pearson File, Fleming Papers; *McCarthyism and New York's Hearst Press,* 87; and Thomas, *Winchell,* 227–28.

179 *Interestingly, Joe hesitated:* "Infiltration of Scientific Profession," October 20, 1950, series 19, MUA; Calaprice, *The Ultimate Quotable Einstein,* 303–5; Buder, "'Refuse to Testify,'" *New York Times;* and "Einstein Criticized," *New York Times.*

180 *Republicans were torn:* Patterson, *Mr. Republican,* 446; Wunderlin, *The Papers of Robert A. Taft;* and Rovere, "What Course for the Powerful Mr. Taft?," *New York Times.*

182 *The only Republican:* Smith, *Declaration of Conscience,* 7 and 11–21; author interview with Gregory Gallant; Reeves interview with Kiermas; and Wallace, *Politics of Conscience,* 107–10.

184 *While the Democrats: McCarthy and His Enemies,* 64; *Blacklisted by History,* 253–60; and Keith, *For Hell and a Brown Mule,* 9–14.

185 *The subcommittee's final report: Life and Times of Joe McCarthy,* 304 and 307; "Excerpts from Text of Majority Report on Charges by Senator McCarthy," *New York Times;* "Text of McCarthy Reply," *New York Times;* "Summary by Senator Lodge on Minority's Report on Communism," *New York Times; Conspiracy So Immense,* 171; McCarthy address before Midwest Council of Young Republicans, May 6, 1950, *Congressional Record;* and *Confessions of a Muckraker,* 194.

4. BULLY'S PULPIT

188 *With the who decided: The Man, the Senator, the "Ism,"* 296.

Butler actually lost the popular vote in the Republican primary but won the nomination under Maryland's arcane unit polling system. A candidate who carried a county by even one vote received all of that county's ballots at the state convention; each county was allotted the same number of ballots as it had seats in the Maryland legislature; and the convention picked the nominee, in this case Butler, who'd spent four times as much as Markey, who won the popular vote. *For Hell and a Brown Mule,* 92–93.

189 *Step one was: Conspiracy So Immense,* 175; *Life and Times of Joe McCarthy,* 336–37; *For Hell and a Brown Mule,* 93; and US Senate, Subcommittee on Privileges and Elections, *Maryland Senatorial Election of 1950,* 35.
Money has always: Maryland Senatorial Election of 1950, 3–4, 16; and "Butler Manager Is Fined $5,000," *Janesville Daily Gazette.*

The Senate subcommittee investigating Butler's campaign thought that some campaign expenditures might have been exempt under federal law, but it had enough suspicions that it sent its files to the Justice Department.

190 *Two contributions were: Maryland Senatorial Election of 1950,* 19; *Life and Times of Joe McCarthy,* 412; and Matusow, *False Witness,* 177–83.

191 *The second eye-catching:* Letter from C. W. Murchison to Fulton Lewis, October 5, 1950, unprocessed files, MUA; and *Maryland Senatorial Election of 1950,* 16.
Joe's rallying the troops: "Smear, Inc.," pt. 14; "The McCarthy Issue: Pro and Con," *U.S. News & World Report;* Maryland Campaign File, series 14, MUA; *Maryland Senatorial Election of 1950,* 1121–23; and *Life and Times of Joe McCarthy,* 340.

192 *The Butler drive: Maryland Senatorial Election of 1950,* 19, 32–33, 39, and 68.

193 *The day after: For Hell and a Brown Mule,* 87, 101, and 105.

194 *What happened in Maryland:* Maryland Senatorial Election of 1950, 2, 6, and 8–9; "The McCarthy Issue: Pro and Con"; and White, "M'Carthy's Influence Is Greater in the 82d," *New York Times.*

195 *The shadow of McCarthyism:* "The Atlantic Report on the World Today,"

Atlantic; Conspiracy So Immense, 174 and 176; "M'Carthy's Influence Is Greater in the 82d"; and *Senator Joe McCarthy,* 65.

196 *Nothing happened by accident: False Witness,* 205.

197 *Jean never saw: False Witness,* 212; Academic Requests, unprocessed files, and Pearson File, series 14, MUA; and letter from J. B. Matthews to Jean Kerr, July 19, 1951, and wire from Hoover to SAC, November 26, 1950, pt. 6 of 28, MFBI.

McCarthy nemesis Drew Pearson but was at one time close to Jean and Joe, said she was deeply in love with McCarthy from nearly the beginning, but he stalled her by saying he couldn't marry her because he was Catholic and she wasn't.

Roberts also was convinced that Jean had an abortion in Baltimore before flying off to Hawaii, probably based on reports from the detective hired by Pearson [August 23, 1951 NCEC interview of Roberts].

Rather than safeguarding: Letter from Joseph T. Logue to Hoover, December 9, 1950, and undated radiograms and telegrams to Hoover, pt. 6 of 28, MFBI; and Reeves interview of Jean, April 12, 1978.

198 *Joe kept in constant:* Memo from L. B. Nichols to Tolson, April 30, 1951, pt. 6 of 28, MFBI; McCarthy-Pearson File, Fleming Papers; letters from Joe to Jean, December 16, 1950, and January 16, 1951, series 24, MUA.

200 *Joe's own health:* Reeves interviews with Van Susteren, January 15, 1976, and Kiermas; *Life and Times of Joe McCarthy,* 319–20 and 402; *The Man, the Senator, the "Ism,"* 318; Cohn, *McCarthy,* 259; hospital notes, October 13, 1954, MBNH; and "The Private Life of Senator McCarthy."

Liquor made things: False Witness, 144–46; "The Private Life of Senator McCarthy"; *American Weekly,* August 23, 1953; Reeves interview with Loren Osman, May 20, 1975; Halberstam, *The Fifties,* 54; Wells, *The Milwaukee Journal,* 372; and *Senator Joe McCarthy,* 51–52.

202 *Joe also wanted: Senator Joe McCarthy,* 64–65.

It was an act: Miller, *Fishbait,* 128; Acheson, *Present at the Creation,* 369; Reeves interview with Frank Kelly, March 27, 1976; *Senator Joe McCarthy,* 66–67; Associated Press, "Joe McCarthy Morphine Addict, Columnist Claims"; and Reeves interview with Van Susteren, November 21, 1978.

203 *For someone who:* Fleming, "Truman Tipsy, Senator Hints," *Milwaukee Journal.*

204 *No politician: Senator Joe McCarthy,* 164; and *Joe McCarthy and the Press,* 67–69 and 87.

205 *The most surefire:* Halberstam, *The Fifties,* 55; and *Joe McCarthy and the Press,* 64 and 223–28.

206 *Joe also was: The Fifties,* 55; *Conspiracy So Immense,* 189; Reeves interview with Dion Henderson, July 20, 1977; "Reporters' Roundup," September 13, 1951; and *Joe McCarthy and the Press,* 73.

If Joe rewrote: False Witness, 155–56.

207 *Reporters who crossed:* Deaver, "A Study of Sen. Joseph R. McCarthy and 'McCarthyism's' influences upon the News Media," 191; Freedom of the Press File, Fleming Papers; *Joe McCarthy and the Press,* 94 and 135; and Wells, *The Milwaukee Journal,* 371–72.

208 *As he had with Drew:* Letter from William Evjue to John Moore, April 15, 1952, *Investigations of Senators Joseph R. McCarthy and William Benton; Joe McCarthy and the Press,* 135; and author interview with Bob Wills.

209 *The* Post-Standard: "McCarthy and the Davis Incident" and "The McCarthy Record," *Appleton Post-Crescent; Joe McCarthy and the Press,* 170 (saying the settlement was $16,500); *Life and Times of Joe McCarthy,* 369 (saying it was $12,000); and Reeves interview with Nellor.
The senator went after: "Weighed in the Balance," *Time;* "Taft and McCarthy," *Life;* letter from Luce to Joe, November 5, 1951, series 14, MUA; and Swanberg, *Luce and His Empire,* 302.

210 *While* Time *and:* "McCarthy Gets Wilder," *Milwaukee Journal; Joe McCarthy and the Press,* 148 and 151; Block, *Herblock's Here and Now,* 115; and Reeves interview with Nellor.
That was easier: Cater, "The Captive Press," *The Reporter.*
It was Joe's attack: "Smear, Inc.," pt. 1; Nissenson, *Lady Upstairs,* 154–56; and May 3, 1951, letter from Oliver Pilat to John Maragon, series 14, MUA.

211 *When the press attacked:* Carpenter, *The Inner Life of Abraham Lincoln,* 258–59; and *Joe McCarthy and the Press,* 150.

212 *Yet Joe seemed to mean:* Stuart, "The Controversial Senator Contends His Tactics Are Both Practical and Fair," *New York World-Telegram.*
Some media outlets: McCarthy and McCarthyism in Wisconsin, 119; *Senator Joe McCarthy,* 19; *Conspiracy So Immense,* 187; "New Crusade," *Pravda;* and *Joe McCarthy and the Press,* 79, 136, and 145–47.

213 *He may have believed:* Herblock File, series 14, MUA; and Black, *Walt Kelly and Pogo: The Art of the Political Swamp,* 214 and 219.

214 *With Kelly against: Joe McCarthy and the Press,* 127; and Chaney and Cieply, *The Hearsts,* 130–35.

215 *Initially one of: Joe McCarthy and the Press,* 155–56.
The European press: Servan-Schreiber, "How It Looks from Europe," *The Reporter.*

216 *In Russia:* Email to author from Vladimir Pechatnov; "Reds Say President Supports M'Carthy," *New York Times;* "Political Circus in Washington," *Izvestia;* "Total Hysteria," *Pravda;* "What the Congress," *Pravda;* correspondence between US sympathizers and the Soviet embassy in Washington, December 19, 1953–July 31, 1954, Russian State Archive of Socio-Political History, Moscow; and author interview with Sergei Khrushchev.

217 *Love him or:* "Who Are the Nation's Best and Worst Senators," *Pageant,* 1951.
The timing of the vote: Thomas, *Ike's Bluff,* 11; Benton statement, September 28, 1951, *Documentary History,* Vol. 25, 189; and https://www.youtube.com/watch?v=g0yBpRrwGOk.

219 *The subcommittee wanted: Investigations of Senators Joseph R. McCarthy and William Benton,* 82–83 and 106; *Confessions of a Muckraker,* 261 (Anderson said Buckley was drawing 30 percent disability from the Air Force as a result of his mental illness); *Life and Times of Joe McCarthy,* 395; *Senator Joe McCarthy,* 39; letter from McCarthy to Thomas Hen-

nings, September 18, 1951, series 14, MUA; Hyman, *The Lives of William Benton*, 464–65 and 484–85; tax record leak: letter from Benton to A. M. Gilbert, August 14, 1952, Benton Papers, WHS; McCarthy letter to Benton, May 7, 1952, Benton File, series 14, MUA; and Reeves interview with Van Susteren, November 25, 1975.

221 *Joe himself had nothing:* Walter Kohler OH, Columbia University, 1971, 23–24; and "How McCarthy Sold Wisconsin," *New Republic.*
The Democratic nominee: McCarthy and McCarthyism in Wisconsin, 141.

222 *Joe's base, by contrast:* Donoghue, "How Wisconsin Voted, 1848–1954"; and Oakes, "Report on McCarthy and McCarthyism."
This Senate race: McCarthy and McCarthyism in Wisconsin, 143; *Life and Times of Joe McCarthy,* 430; *False Witness,* 138–39; and "Hits Forgery of McCarthy," *Milwaukee Journal.*

224 *Aldric Revell: McCarthy and McCarthyism in Wisconsin,* 124; and Lubell, *Revolt of the Moderates,* 268.
Campaigning wasn't without: Reeves interviews with Van Susteren, November 25, 1975 and February 5, 1977; *Life and Times of Joe McCarthy,* 289; O'Brien interview with Shortridge, April 5, 1977; and Reeves interview with Gerald Lorge, March 22, 1978.
He put that outlook: Associated Press, *Nevada News Digest* transcript.

225 *Raucous tactics:* Prescott Bush OH, Columbia University, 1967.
Joe campaigned in: Blair and Blair, *Search for JFK,* 307–8; Thomas, *Robert Kennedy: His Life,* 65; "The Campaign: Pride of the Clan," *Time;* Ross, "Joseph P. Kennedy: The True Story," *New York Post;* Kennedy, *Hostage to Fortune,* 664; Pearson column, May 3, 1968; author interview with Bobby Baker; McCarthy, *The Remarkable Kennedys,* 26; Reeves interviews with Surine, Nellor (June 6, 1979), and Kiermas; and *Conspiracy So Immense,* 241–42.

228 *Even as he was:* Hughes, *The Ordeal of Power,* 42; "Sixth Draft—Communism and Freedom," Eisenhower Library; Kohler OH, 18; Adams OH, Columbia University, 1972, 67 and 69; *Life and Times of Joe McCarthy,* 437–40; Salisbury, *Without Fear or Favor,* 470; Reeves interview with Raymond Dohr, February 20, 1976; Stephen Benedict OH, Columbia University, 84; "M'Carthy Denies Swaying General," *New York Times;* Nichols, *Ike and McCarthy,* 1; Reston, "Stevenson Scores Rival on M'Carthy in Wisconsin Talks," *New York Times;* McCullough, *Truman,* 911; and unpublished memoir of Gabriel Hauge.

231 *Joe had never liked: The Man, the Senator, the "Ism,"* 355–56; *Senator Joe McCarthy,* 181; Martin, *Adlai Stevenson of Illinois,* 744; *Conspiracy So Immense,* 242–43; Johnston, "McCarthy Terms It 'Lying'" and "M'Carthy Repeats Charges," *New York Times; Life and Times of Joe McCarthy,* 444–45; Smith, *Eisenhower in War and Peace,* 546; October 10 and 27, 1952, memos from Ladd to Hoover, pt. 2 of 28, MFBI; and Adlai Stevenson File, series 14, MUA.

232 *Back in Wisconsin: Conspiracy So Immense,* 245; and Bean, *Influences in the 1954 Mid-Term Elections,* 8–36.

233 *That fear factor: Investigations of Senators Joseph R. McCarthy and William Benton,* 11 and 45.

234 *Joe had once again:* Reeves interview with Korb; *Conspiracy So Immense,* 234; and Brooker, "Joe, Tired but Happy," *Appleton Post-Crescent.*

235 *The Republican senators: Fishbait,* 423; and *Senator Joe McCarthy,* 187–88. *Joe seemed willing:* Woltman, "The McCarthy Balance Sheet," pt. 3, *New York World-Telegram;* and "Plagiarism and Trespass," *Washington Post.*

236 *Most senators focused: False Witness,* 146; *Conspiracy So Immense,* 252; and Ruth Young Watt OH, Senate Historical Office, 101.

237 *The Democrats, meanwhile: Life and Times of Joe McCarthy,* 460; and Pearson column, July 17, 1954.
Joe was off: Telegram from Joe to Jean, September 10, 1953, series 24, and Academic Requests, unprocessed files, MUA.

238 *One of the first:* Hersh, *Bobby and J. Edgar,* 128; *Robert Kennedy: His Life,* 65; Thompson and Myers, *Robert F. Kennedy: The Brother Within,* 100; author interview with Barrett Prettyman; Stein and Plimpton, *American Journey,* 50; Martin, *A Hero for Our Time,* 58; author interview with Alvin Spivak; and Sirica, *To Set the Record Straight,* 37–38.

240 *With Sirica and other:* Reeves interview with Kiermas; *Robert F. Kennedy: The Brother Within,* 109; Herman, *Joseph McCarthy,* 211; Cohn and Zion, *Autobiography of Roy Cohn,* 83–87; letter from Nichols to Tolson, January 21, 1954, pt. 19 of 33, Cohn FBI Files; Gabler, *Winchell,* 252–53; and author interviews with Brigid Berlin and Neil Gallagher.

241 *McCarthy wanted both: Autobiography of Roy Cohn,* 87–88; von Hoffman, *Citizen Cohn,* 182; Gottlieb, "New York Court Disbars Roy Cohn on Charges of Unethical Conduct," *New York Times;* and *The Real American: Joe McCarthy.*
The first payroll, for two weeks, was $220.09 for Bobby and $517.60 for Cohn. Report of Secretary of Senate, January 7, 1954.

5. BEHIND CLOSED DOORS

244 *It didn't take him:* US Senate, Permanent Subcommittee on Investigations, *Executive Sessions,* 1:xiii.
Who better to target: "Hits Forgery of McCarthy," *Milwaukee Journal;* Tydings Investigation File, Fleming Papers; Reeves interview with Edward Morgan, June 5, 1979; and *Executive Sessions,* 1:1–96.

246 *One in three:* Ritchie, "Are You Now or Have You Ever Been?" *Journal of Government Information.*
There was another: Executive Sessions, 1:xxiii and 2, and 3:2713; and emails to author from Tracey Maclin.

247 *That wasn't the only: Executive Sessions,* 1:186; and *Without Precedent,* 53 and 60.

248 *Then there was: Executive Sessions,* 1:234.
While it was less: Executive Sessions, 1:xxi.

249 *His smears backfired: Executive Sessions,* 1:248–49.

250 *Toumanoff, Morgan:* Email to author from Fraser Ottanelli.
Communism was the panel's: Executive Sessions, 1:421–22.

251 *One last thing: Conspiracy So Immense,* 465; *Executive Sessions,* 4:3032, 3533, 3487, and 3519, and 5:46–47; and hospital notes, May 4, 1949, and letter from Old Line Life Insurance Co., June 7, 1949, MBNH.

253 *The records of:* Author interviews with Susan Collins and Carl Levin.
The transcriptions: Permanent Subcommittee on Investigations Annual Report, January 25, 1954, 1; and Griswold, *The Fifth Amendment Today,* 67.

254 *The most complete:* Hart, "McCarthyism Versus Democracy," *New Republic;* and McCarthy letters to Duke president Arthur Hollis Edens, October 19 and 31, 1951, Edens's reply, November 9, 1951, and McCarthy letter to Denny Rusinow, January 31, 1952, series 14, MUA.

255 *Fact-checking wasn't:* Hughes, *Ordeal of Power,* 91; and Jahoda, "Morale in the Federal Civil Service," *Annals of the American Academy of Political and Social Science.*
Those were prices: McCarthy and His Enemies, 277; *Blacklisted by History,* 200 and 455; "Senator McCarthy Answers Some Important Questions"; and FBI, "Membership of the Communist Party, USA, 1919–1954," iii–v.

256 *The Wisconsin senator: PSI Annual Report,* 3 and 10 (546 witnesses was Joe's count in his annual report, but names compiled later by the Senate historian suggest that the subcommittee called 617 witnesses in 1953).

257 *One of the dozens: Executive Sessions,* 2:1665–66, 1709–10, and 1720; Marvel Jackson Cooke OH, Washington Press Club Foundation, August 22, 1990; Kihss, "M'Carthy 'Orders' Army Bare Files," *New York Times;* and Trussell, "Stevens Will Review McCarthy's Demand," *New York Times.*

258 *McCarthy's supporters:* Trussell, "State Department Voids Curb," *New York Times;* and "Neither Flight nor Fight," *Time.*

259 *As for the senator's leaks: Joe McCarthy and the Press,* 184.
Reporters were perpetually: Blacklisted by History, 329–30; "Reporters' Roundup," September 13, 1951; May, *Un-American Activities,* 267, 315, and 321; author interview with and emails from May; http://www.johnearl haynes.org/page62.html; and email to author from Klehr.

260 *The best measure:* johnearlhaynes.org; email to author from Louise Robbins; "M'Carthy Names 4 He Says Are Linked to Reds," *Chicago Daily Tribune;* "Subpoenaed," *Chicago Daily Tribune;* Brinkley, "Fredric March Had Tears in His Eyes on 'Daily Worker' Criticism," *Washington Post; Blacklisted by History,* 38–39; https://sites.google.com/site/ernie124102/cpusa/mccarthy; author interview with and emails from John Earl Haynes; and Haynes and Klehr, *In Denial,* 81.
    The five names that turned up on both the Venona list and the list of McCarthy's witnesses were Cedric Belfrage, Elizabeth Bentley, Virginius Frank Coe, Leonard Mins, and Nathan Silvermaster.

262 *Did Joe know:* Email to author from Haynes.

263 *Journalists who were:* Lippmann, "Today and Tomorrow: Terrorists and Spies," *Washington Post; The Man, the Senator, the "Ism,"* 244; Chambers, *Odyssey of a Friend,* 102; Drew Pearson columns, July 11 and 24, 1953; and Oakes, "Inquiry into McCarthy's Status," *New York Times.*

264 *The probe kicked off:* Edwards, "Uncover Plot in 'Voice' to Sabotage U.S.," *Chicago Tribune.*

265 *The hearings began: Executive Sessions,* 1:462; and *PSI Annual Report,* 18 and 20.

266 *That judgment might: PSI Annual Report,* 18; "The McCarthy Balance

Sheet," pt. 5; Ritchie, "The Army-McCarthy Hearings, 1954," 811; and *Executive Sessions,* 4:2752, 3569, and 3571.

268 *In Joe's telling: PSI Annual Report,* 26–28.
McCarthy went fishing: Executive Sessions, 1:495.

269 *But that was the: Without Precedent,* 67; "The Army-McCarthy Hearings, 1954," 813; and *Joe McCarthy and the Press,* 150.
Langston Hughes, a guiding light: Executive Sessions, 2:987.

270 *Another author and activist: Executive Sessions,* 2:939; and https://kpfa.org/blog/william-bill-mandel-1917-2016.
Edwin Seaver was: Seaver, *So Far So Good,* 176 and 187.
As interested as he: Life and Times of Joe McCarthy, 491; Merson, *The Private Diary of a Public Servant,* 14–15; *Executive Sessions,* 2:1052 and 1057–58; and, all from *New York Times:* "Eisenhower Backed on Book Ban Talk"; Doty, "10 Volumes Banned in Cairo"; Raymond, "Officials Act in Belgrade"; "Embassy Tales of Removals"; "Ban on Books Is Denied"; Brady, "Cloak of Secrecy in London"; "Book Burning Denied"; "Books Removed in Argentina"; "Poll of Libraries Shows Free Choice"; Sedgwick, "No Issue in Greece"; Callahan, "13 Books Removed in Karachi"; "Mark Twain Is 'Cleared' by US"; "Instructions Kept Secret"; Hill, "Librarian Opposes Controls on Ideas"; and Trussell, "Voice Must Drop Works of Leftists."

272 *Roy Cohn led: Autobiography of Roy Cohn,* 90–92; von Hoffman, *Citizen Cohn,* 170–72; "British Press Cool to M'Carthy Aides" and "British Press Pokes Fun at M'Carthy Investigators," *New York Times; Senator Joe McCarthy,* 200; letters from Cohn to Larry Lawrence, April 8, 1953, and from Cohn and Schine to McCarthy, April 13, 1953, series 14, MUA; Kaghan, "The McCarthyization of Theodore Kaghan," *The Reporter;* Pearson column, April 22, 1953; and Schine OH, Columbia University, 1971.

276 *Public uproar over:* "Eisenhower Backed on Book Ban Talk," *New York Times;* and Bird, *The Chairman,* 409.

277 *It wasn't only seditious: Executive Sessions,* 1:840–41 and 2:1235–59; and "Taft Asks Dulles Put End to 'Voice,'" *New York Times.*

278 *The hearings often seemed: Executive Sessions,* 2:919–20, 1247, and 1403.

279 *The kid staffers: Executive Sessions,* 2:982–83 and 990; and *The Private Diary of a Public Servant,* 84.

280 *By the end there:* US Senate, Permanent Subcommittee on Investigations, State Department Information Program — Information Centers, 2; and Swing, "V.O.A.: A Survey of the Wreckage," *The Reporter.*
The Voice wasn't: Woltman, "The McCarthy Balance Sheet," pt. 5.

281 *Eisenhower adviser Emmet:* Hughes, *Ordeal of Power,* 89.
Jean and Joe's: Lasky, "The Gal Who Married Joe McCarthy," unprocessed files, MUA; "McCarthy Weds Jean Kerr" and Beale, "Exclusively Yours," *Washington Evening Star;* and Reeves interview with Korb.

283 *Their honeymoon was:* Academic Requests, unprocessed files, MUA; and Cohn, *McCarthy,* 94.

284 *Jean, as she'd said:* Diaries and Appointment Books, series 24, MUA;

"A Cadillac to M'Carthy," *Kansas City Star;* "The Oak & the Ivy," *Time;* Reeves interview with Ed Nellor; and *Life and Times of Joe McCarthy,* 513.

285 *The worsening addiction:* Prochnau and Larsen, *A Certain Democrat,* 139; and Ruth Young Watt OH, 106.

286 *Watt also got an:* Citizen Cohn, 186.
The twenty-six-year-old: "Schine at Harvard," *Harvard Crimson;* Schine, *Definition of Communism;* memo from J. P. Moore to W. C. Sullivan, December 10, 1952, Schine FBI Files; and Caldwell, "Pvt. Schine's Famous Pamphlet," *New Leader.*

288 *If Cohn and Schine:* Ruth Young Watt OH, 107–8; and Horton, "Voices Within the Voice," *The Reporter.*
There were other whispers: Anonymous letter to Hoover, May 29, 1954, Schine FBI Files; Hellman, *Scoundrel Time,* 150; *Citizen Cohn,* 186, 189, and 231; Cohn, *McCarthy,* 245; and family interview of Jim Juliana, June 10, 1998, JJP.

290 *That was Joe: Robert F. Kennedy: The Brother Within,* 112.

291 *One agency that: Life and Times of Joe McCarthy,* 509–11; "Senate Probe Hints H-Bomb Red Spy Link," *Washington Post; PSI Annual Report,* 17; *Conspiracy So Immense,* 328; *Executive Sessions,* 2:1439, 1453–57, 1505, 1549, 1565, and 1568; Stanley Frosh, "The McCarthy Era Begins," undated essay provided by Frosh's children; and Huston, "Printing Official Doubts Spy Leaks," *New York Times.*

293 *Chairman Joe's sights:* Beria Case, series 14, MUA.

294 *His foreign adventures:* Reeves interview with Surine, June 8, 1977; *Executive Sessions,* 2:1374; and Reeves interview with Nellor, June 6, 1979.

295 *One of the few:* "Control of Trade with the Soviet Bloc," PSI, pt. 2, May 4 and 20, 1953, 66 and 130–40; Krock, "Large Trade with China by the U.N. Members Shown," and Trussell, "Increase in Trade with the Reds Charged by M'Carthy group," *New York Times;* Lawford, *That Shining Hour,* 45–46; *Conspiracy So Immense,* 297–98; *Life and Times of Joe McCarthy,* 488; Childs, "McCarthy Letter Contents Revealed," *Washington Post;* Pearson column, April 7, 1953; and letter from Francis Flanagan to Bobby Kennedy, April 2, 1953.

297 *The subcommittee as:* Smithsonian video interview of Juliana, September 11, 2007, JJP; Kennedy, *The Enemy Within,* 307; author interview with Don Ritchie; "Are You Now or Have You Ever Been?"; *Executive Sessions,* 2:1413; and Morris, "3 Democrats Scorn Bid from M'Carthy," *New York Times.*

298 *That was too late:* "3 Democrats Quit McCarthy's Group in Fight on Powers," *New York Times.*
Joe's handling of Matthews: Theoharis, *From the Secret Files,* 262; *Enemy Within,* 176; *Life and Times of Joe McCarthy,* 498; "Aide to McCarthy Resigns," *New York Times; Robert F. Kennedy: The Brother Within,* 112; reports of the secretary of the Senate, January 7, 1954 and January 6, 1955; Bobby Kennedy FBI Files; Hilty, *Robert Kennedy: Brother Protector,* 82; and *Autobiography of Roy Cohn,* 87.

299 *The Cohn-Kennedy conflict:* Ringle, "Tales from a Redbaiter's '50s Fishing Expedition," *Washington Post;* and "Are You Now or Have You Ever Been?"
For the rest: Author interview with Betty Koed.

6. THE BODY COUNT

300 *One way to measure:* "Voice Worker's Mystery Death Ruled Suicide," *Chicago Tribune;* "Text of Letter Left by 'Voice' Suicide," and "M'Carthy Turns Up Nothing on Kaplan," *New York Times; Executive Sessions,* 1:779–80; *Conspiracy So Immense,* 271; and author interview with Jacobs.

302 *If Kaplan had been:* Stuart, "The Controversial Senator Contends His Tactics Are Both Practical and Fair," *New York World-Telegram and Sun;* and *Autobiography of Roy Cohn,* 153.
But the deaths: Author interview with Bronson La Follette; and Maney, "Joe McCarthy's First Victim" and *"Young Bob" La Follette,* 308–9.

303 *The son of another:* McDaniel, *Dying for Joe McCarthy's Sins,* 253–55 and 280–98; Ewig, "McCarthy Era Politics: The Ordeal of Senator Lester Hunt," *Annals of Wyoming;* https://www.senate.gov/artandhistory/history/minute/Senator_Lester_Hunts_Decision.htm; author interviews with Buddy and Ellen Hunt; and https://mattachinesocietywashingtondc.files.wordpress.com/2015/11/lester-hunt-letter.pdf.

305 *Not all of McCarthy's:* Ghiglione, *CBS's Don Hollenbeck,* 222–24, and "Back to the Future," *Law and Contemporary Problems;* O'Brian, "Continuing Study of the Continuing CBS News 'Slant,'" "An Analysis of Murrow's Portsided Political Pitching," and "Letters from Readers on Slanted Newscasts," *New York Journal-American;* Friendly, *Due to Circumstances Beyond Our Control,* 64–66; and author interview with Shirley Wershba.

306 *There was almost: False Witness,* 226.
It's tempting to cast: "Ex-Law Teacher, Aide to UN's Lie, Commits Suicide," *Harvard Crimson;* and Kirkpatrick, *The Real CIA,* 138.

307 *What about Ethel:* Author interview with Bernstein; Bernstein, "The Oppenheimer Loyalty-Security Case Reconsidered," *Stanford Law Review;* and *Autobiography of Roy Cohn,* 77.

309 *New York attorney: Executive Sessions,* 3:1855 and 1861; and author interviews with Nick Unger and Elizabeth Starčević.

310 *Unger wasn't the only:* Rabinowitz, *Unrepentant Leftist,* 111–12.

311 *It didn't take much:* Newman, *The Cold War Romance of Lillian Hellman and John Melby,* 253–67; author interview with Avis Bohlen; letter from Esther Brunauer to Truman, July 9, 1952; and "Lattimore, Accused by McCarthy as Red, Calls Charges 'Moonshine,'" *Madison Capital Times.*
Then there was: Stone, *The Haunted Fifties,* 36–37; and Trussell, "'Voice' Accused of Wasting Million," *New York Times.*

312 *Sometimes when a parent:* Author interviews with John Brogan and Casey Murrow.
David Fierst's father: Author interviews with David Fierst, Kathryn Horvat, Bob Service, and Signe Hanson; Hanson, *Fifty Years Around the Third World,* 120–21; and John S. Service OH, University of California, Berkeley, 394.

313 *Lucy Durán was:* Author interview with Lucy Durán.
314 *Chris Ghosh's childhood:* Author interview with Chris Ghosh.
Senate colleagues and: Conspiracy So Immense, 317.
Joe was fighting: "The Press Meets McCarthy," *The Nation;* Acheson, *Present at the Creation,* 363; and McCullough, *Truman,* 766.
315 *It was no joke:* Childs, "Independent Lady from New England," *Washington Post; Declaration of Conscience,* 51–57; and Gallant, *Hope and Fear,* 195.
316 *Not Greenspun:* Greenspun, "McCarthy Willing to Compromise" and *Where I Stand,* 238–44 and 264; McCarthy letter to Hoover, January 13, 1954, and Hoover to McCarthy, January 14, 1954, pt. 28 of 28, MFBI; Hank Greenspun File, series 14, MUA; and Pearson column, April 22, 1954.
There was another category: Life and Times of Joe McCarthy, 365–70; and Charles Davis File, series 14, MUA.
317 *Most McCarthy targets:* "Excerpts from Testimony of Wechsler" and "Clash of M'Carthy, Wechsler Is Bared," *New York Times;* and Wechsler, *The Age of Suspicion,* 264–323.
319 *Joe McCarthy never wrote:* Reeves interview with George Reedy, May 12, 1976; and McCarthy, *McCarthyism: The Fight for America,* 7, 81, and 85.
320 *Much of America:* Fiedler, "McCarthy," *Encounter;* and Reedy, *From the Ward to the White House,* 167.
321 *The only more tempting:* Harris, "McCarthy Takes a Dim View of Pusey," *Boston Daily Globe; Joe McCarthy and the Press,* 10, 13, and 15; "McCarthy and Pusey" and "McCarthy's Attack on Dr. Pusey Termed Unfair by His Friends," *Appleton Post-Crescent;* and *McCarthy and McCarthyism in Wisconsin,* 149–50.
323 *The battle that began: Life and Times of Joe McCarthy,* 535–36; memo from Karl Baarslag to Francis Carr, November 6, 1953, series 23, and cable from Nathan Pusey to McCarthy, November 9, 1953, series 14, MUA; author interview with Leon Kamin; and Norman Ramsey OH, Columbia University, 1960, 250–64.
326 *Reed Harris had everything: PSI Annual Report,* 20; *Executive Sessions,* 1:615, 663–64, 671–75, 680, and 706; "Reed Harris Expelled," *Columbia Daily Spectator; A Conspiracy So Immense,* 275; Special Inquiry, September 1, 1950, memo from F. E. Crosby to Nichols, March 17, 1953, attachment to letter from Hoover to Harris, March 20, 1961, and report, June 29, 1961, Harris FBI Files; Cohn and Schine letter to McCarthy, April 13, 1953, series 14, MUA; "Reed Harris Quits," *New York Times; The Private Diary of a Public Servant,* 62–64; Sperber, *Murrow: His Life and Times,* 400; and http://www.plosin.com/BeatBegins/archive/Murrow540309.htm.
331 *McCarthy ultimately moved:* Harris, "Life of Sirrah."
332 *A decade later:* Katz, "Confrontation with McCarthy," pt. 2, *Columbia College Today; Murrow: His Life and Times,* 633; Earley, "5 Decades Later, Renegade Wants Diploma," *Washington Post;* Perlez, "A Degree of Indifference," *New York Daily News;* Reed, "Former *Spec* Editor Awaits Degree," *Columbia Spectator;* Harris, "Life of Sirrah"; and author interview with Donald Harris.

334 *The easiest way:* Knight, "What Price Security?," *Collier's.*

335 *CBS newsman Eric Sevareid:* Conant, *Man of the Hour,* 450–51; Kahn, *The China Hands,* 35; Schrecker, *Many Are the Crimes,* 371; "What Price Security?"; and email to author from Jack Matlock.

336 *That wreckage would: Fifty Years Around the World,* 123; and author interview with Bob Service.
   The victims were less: Schrecker, *No Ivory Tower,* 339–40 and 424; Schrecker, "Political Tests for Professors," University Loyalty Oath Symposium; Price, *Threatening Anthropology,* 29; *Many Are the Crimes,* 362–63 and 404–6; *McCarthyism: The Fight for America,* 101; Taylor, *Grand Inquest,* xiv; *Nightmare in Red,* 34; and *Senator Joe McCarthy,* 268.

338 *A precise body count: Many Are the Crimes,* 298, 363–70, and 396; Storrs, *Second Red Scare,* 2; Lazarsfeld, Felis, and Thielens, *The Academic Mind,* 35–45; Herman, *Joseph McCarthy,* 4; Utley, *Odyssey of a Liberal,* 278–79; Coulter, *Treason,* 83; Haynes, *Red Scare or Red Menace?,* 161; and *The Man, the Senator, the "Ism,"* 210.

339 *Just how scrambled: Grand Inquest,* xiv.

7. THE ENABLERS

341 *Milton Eisenhower, Dwight's:* Milton Eisenhower OH, Columbia University, 1967 and 1969; Ewald, *Who Killed Joe McCarthy?,* 66; and "Brotherly Blow," *Time.*

342 *President Eisenhower listened:* Letter from Ike to Paul Helms, March 9, 1954, DDEL; Osborne, "White House Watch: Gabbing with Harlow," *New Republic;* and Rives, "Eisenhower and the Remnants of the Western Past," *Great Plains Traverse.*

343 *Not so, a lineup:* Greenstein, *The Hidden-Hand Presidency,* 182; Eisenhower, *The President Is Calling,* 317; Eisenhower, "We Must Avoid the Perils of Extremism," *Reader's Digest; Ike and McCarthy,* xiii; Halberstam, *The Fifties,* 251; Thomas Dewey OH, Columbia University, 1974; and Pearson columns, December 1, 1953, and March 4 and June 4, 1954.

345 *Attack he did:* Bird and Sherwin, *American Prometheus,* 493; Pearson column, December 1, 1953; *Declaration of Conscience,* 58; and *Senator Joe McCarthy,* 16–17.

346 *Even more basic:* Pollitt, "The Fifth Amendment Plea," *University of Pennsylvania Law Review.*
   Editorialists understood: "The President Strikes Back," *New York Times;* Strout, "McCarthyism Revisited," *Journal of American Culture;* and "Turning the Other Cheek," *Washington Post.*

347 *Alarm about the dynamic:* "Austrian Assails McCarthy," *New York Times;* "Reds Say President Supports M'Carthy"; and "Briton Views McCarthy," *Washington Post.*
   He ought to have: The Private Diary of a Public Servant, 171; Wechsler, *Reflections of an Angry Middle-Aged Editor,* 178–79; and email to author from John Farrell.

348 *The truth was:* Fenton, *In Your Opinion,* 134; and *Drew Pearson Diaries, 1949–1959,* 285.

349 *Insiders were even:* Letter from C. D. Jackson to Sherman Adams, No-

vember 25, 1953, DDEL; and "M'Carthy Accuses Truman in Reply," *New York Times.*

One more consideration: The President Is Calling, 317–18.

350 *At times Ike:* Letters from Eisenhower to Harry Bullis, May 18, 1953, and to William E. Robinson, March 12, 1954, and Hagerty notes, March 24, 1954, DDEL; and *Ike and McCarthy,* 212.

352 *Texans had the most:* Murphy, "Texas Business and McCarthy," *Fortune; The Boss,* 298; letter from Nichols to Tolson, July 23, 1953, pt. 28 of 28, MFBI; Jones, "H. L. Hunt: Magnate with Mission," *New York Times;* and Burrough, *The Big Rich,* 20 and 222.

353 *But it wasn't quite:* Letter from Murchison to McCarthy, March 1, 1954, series 14, MUA.

354 *Wealthy Wisconsinites:* "Smear, Inc.," pt. 9; *McCarthy and McCarthyism in Wisconsin,* 69; and Reeves interview with Walter Jolin, September 2, 1976.

Whatever the cost: Murphy, "McCarthy and the Businessman," *Fortune.*

355 *Joe's own finances: Life and Times of Joe McCarthy,* 318–19; "Won't Give Democrats Names," *New York Times;* Reeves interview with Nellor, June 6, 1979; and letter from Joe to Bill McCarthy, January 4, 1956, series 20, MUA.

While he loved gambling: Senator Joe McCarthy, 144; Davis, "Joe Is Doing the Job," *New York Post;* and Reeves interview with Nellor, June 6, 1979.

356 *The most convincing:* Wilson, "The Ring Around McCarthy," *Look.*

The McCarthy entity: Hale, "'Big Brother' in Foggy Bottom," *The Reporter;* "What Price Security?"; Bach and Hale, "What He Is Speaks So Loud," *The Historian;* and Scott McLeod material and memo from Cohn to McCarthy, April 30, 1953, series 14, MUA.

358 *McCarthy used his ties:* Letter from McCarthy to State Department, July 23, 1953, and response from Scott McLeod, July 30, 1953, Dulles File, series 14, MUA; and *Senator Joe McCarthy,* 32–33.

Joe's most consistent: Human Resources Research Office Project, and letter from McCarthy to Hoover, June 1, 1949, series 14, MUA; letter from SAC-Memphis to Hoover, March 2, 1954, pt. 7 of 28, MFBI; Doherty, *Cold War, Cool Medium,* 139–40; and author interview with Ellen Schrecker.

Adding to the rumors about Joe having fathered a daughter, William A. Roberts said the mother apparently was a woman several years older than Joe whom he was involved with in the early 1930s [August 23, 1951 NCEC interview of Roberts].

359 *The federal judiciary: Dennis v. United States,* 341 U.S. 494 (1951); "Are You Now or Have You Ever Been?"; Lichtman, *The Supreme Court and McCarthy-Era Repression,* 173–74; and Warren, *The Memoirs of Earl Warren,* 178.

360 *The legislative branch:* Woods, *Black Struggle, Red Scare,* 42; Bassett, *Ugly Year, Lonely Man,* viii; Baker, *Wheeling and Dealing,* 92–94; "A Fact Sheet Detailing Kennedy's Record," letter from JFK to John E. Burchard, February 2, 1953, and James MacGregor Burns OH, 1965, JFKL; and Nevins, *Herbert H. Lehman and His Era,* 346 and 436.

362 *Even for those:* Cohn, *McCarthy,* 63.

The senator was especially: Bird, *The Color of Truth,* 163–65; Kirkpatrick, *The Real CIA,* 151–52; Smithsonian video interview, JJP; and General CIA Records, released August 21, 2006.

364 *Backing inside: Herblock's Here and Now,* 118.

Joe's list of respectable: Author interview with Lee Edwards; Edwards, *Just Right,* 9; Reeves interview with Madelaine Grotnes Cocke, November 16, 1976; De Santis, "American Catholics and McCarthyism," *Catholic Historical Review;* Crosby, *God, Church, and Flag,* 164–65 and 228–51; and *McCarthy and McCarthyism in Wisconsin,* 177.

365 *Old Joe Kennedy:* Nasaw, *The Patriarch,* 672–73; Frank Mankiewicz OH, 1969, JFKL; and author interview with Jeff Greenfield.

366 *If the Kennedys:* Memo from Hoover to attorney general, July 27, 1953, pt. 3 of 28, MFBI.

The senator also: "McCarthy's Popularity Up 16%," *Washington Post.*

There was more unanimity: Author interview with John McManus; American Mercury File, series 14, MUA; Kaplan, "Rabbi Benjamin Schultz, Crusader Against Communist Infiltration," *New York Times;* Keeley, *China Lobby Man,* 108 and 110; and Reeves interview with Nellor, June 6, 1979.

367 *The list of: Black Struggle, Red Scare,* 213; author interview with Toby Roth; and Hollywood and McCarthy Broadcast Fund Files, series 23, MUA.

368 *Hidden among:* McAuliffe, *Crisis on the Left,* 88, 147; email to author from Klehr; Walker, *In Defense of American Liberties,* 202, and email to author from Walker; author interview with Ira Glasser; and letter from Irving Ferman to McCarthy, April 20, 1953, Amerasia File, series 14, MUA.

369 *In the final reckoning: Herblock's Here and Now,* 105.

Just how those connections: McCarthy and McCarthyism in Wisconsin, 188–89.

McCarthy's most loyal: In Your Opinion, 135–36; Hofstadter, *The Paranoid Style in American Politics,* 69–72; Sokol, "Power Orientation and McCarthyism," *American Journal of Sociology;* Trow, "Right-Wing Radicalism and Political Intolerance," Columbia University; Lubell, *Revolt of the Moderates,* 268–69; *Life and Times of Joe McCarthy,* 534–35; and "McCarthy's Popularity Up 16%."

370 *Add up those blocs: In Your Opinion,* 130–31; *Life and Times of Joe McCarthy,* 534–35 and 762–63; and "McCarthy's Popularity Up 16%."

371 *Richard Rovere added: Senator Joe McCarthy,* 21.

8. TOO BIG TO BULLY

372 *It was High-Roller: Autobiography of Roy Cohn,* 111.

His wartime diaries: Wartime diaries, series 17, MUA.

373 *McCarthy saw Ike:* Cohn, *McCarthy,* 112–13.

Fort Monmouth: "Role of the Signal Corps," *New York Times.*

374 *The senator got his:* Kihss, "M'Carthy Accuses 2 Army Employees" and "Army Drops Guard Called Pro-Stalin," *New York Times.*

375 *McCarthy's first challenge:* "The Army-McCarthy Hearings, 1954," 827; Juliana interview, December 25, 1997, JJP; *Executive Sessions,* 3:2457; "Signal Corps Spying Hinted by McCarthy" and Everett, "McCarthy Names Rosenberg as 'Brain' of Radar Spy Ring," *Washington Post.*

376 *While he wasn't:* "History of Defending Professor Wendell Furry and Harvard University from Attacks by Joseph McCarthy."
An even bigger problem: Scoundrel Time, 150.

377 *The military at first: Blacklisted by History,* 503–6 and 520–21; *Autobiography of Roy Cohn,* 110; and "General Lawton at Final Review," *New York Times.*
The press, which: Marder, "No Basis Found for Belief Monmouth Is Nest of Spies," *Washington Post;* and *Cold War, Cool Medium,* 190.

378 *Another way to measure: In Your Opinion,* 136–37.

379 *History has told us: Executive Sessions,* 5:33; "Transcript of General Zwicker's Testimony Before the McCarthy Senate Subcommittee," *New York Times;* Potter, *Days of Shame,* 67; *Conspiracy So Immense,* 373–77; *Life and Times of Joe McCarthy,* 540–42; Juliana interview, December 25, 1997, and "Perjury, Not Honor" chapter, JJP; Reeves interview with Jean, March 14, 1977; and *Without Precedent,* 126–27.

381 *It was a two-and-a-quarter-page: Without Precedent,* 47–49; letter from Hoover to General Bolling, January 26, 1951, series 14, MUA; and letter from Attorney General Brownell to Senator Mundt, May 6, 1954, JFKL.

383 *Joe didn't have:* Cohn, *McCarthy,* 168–70; Edwards, "Bare Hunt for Radar Spies," *Chicago Daily Tribune;* and *Without Precedent,* 53.
He did just that: "Bare Hunt for Radar Spies"; Edwards, "M'Carthy Quits Honeymoon Key for Spy Probe," *Chicago Daily Tribune;* telegram from Stevens to McCarthy, September 4, 1953, series 14, MUA; *Without Precedent,* 47; author interviews with Phoebe and Dan Miner; email to author from Mark Stevens.

384 *Back from his honeymoon:* Knowles, "Misuse of Secrets Laid to Radar Man," *New York Times;* Kihss, "Monmouth Expert Barred in Key Job," and Kihss, "Army Acts to Oust Monmouth Expert," *New York Times; Executive Sessions,* 3:2402, 2410, 2399, 2403, and 2695; *Coleman v. Newark Morning Ledger Co.* 29 N.J. 357 (1959); and *Without Precedent,* 262.

386 *Another of Joe's earliest:* Ranzal, "Radar Witness Breaks Down," and "'Mystery Witness' Disputes M'Carthy," *New York Times; Without Precedent,* 54–56; *Executive Sessions,* 3:2563 and 2588; and "The Army-McCarthy Hearings, 1954," 818.

388 *The Coleman and Greenblum hearings: Life and Times of Joe McCarthy,* 520; and Kaplan, "Monmouth Report on Bias Revealed," *New York Times.*
While McCarthy could claim: Executive Sessions, 3:2175; "The Army-McCarthy Hearings, 1954," 817; "Monmouth Report on Bias Revealed"; and Sherrill, "King Cohn," *The Nation.*

389 *Like so many: Executive Sessions,* 3:2169–70 and 4:2886–89; "The Army-McCarthy Hearings, 1954," 817; Kihss, "Monmouth Aides Reply to Charges," *New York Times;* https://virtualny.ashp.cuny.edu/gutter/panels/panel1.html; and email to author from Sydney Van Nort.

390 *The Democrats: Without Precedent,* 53, 69, and 85; and *Grand Inquest,* 246. *The publication of:* Juliana interview, June 10, 1998, JJP; and *The Real American: Joe McCarthy.*

391 *When it came to Army: Executive Sessions,* 5:56–57.

392 *A few witnesses: Executive Sessions,* 4:3569–73.
No case better: Autobiography of Roy Cohn, 105; Lokos, *Who Promoted Peress?,* 144 and 169; McCarthy letter to Secretary Stevens, November 5, 1954, series 14, MUA; *Without Precedent,* 118–19; Roberts, "The Dentist McCarthy Saw as a Threat to Security," "2d Major Admits Error on Peress," and "Army Rebuffs McCarthy," *New York Times;* letter from Secretary Stevens to McCarthy, February 16, 1954, DDEL; and *Senator Joe McCarthy,* 39.

395 *While the dentist:* "The Real Issue," *New York Times.*
President Eisenhower was: Autobiography of Roy Cohn, 112–13.

396 *The reach for détente:* Schine OH; *Without Precedent,* 133; *RN,* 137 and 142; "McCarthy and Stevens — Behind Scenes," *Newsweek;* "The Army-McCarthy Hearings, 1954," 822; *Grand Inquest,* 121–22; and "A Surrender to Mr. McCarthy," *The Times* (London).

398 *By the next day:* Hagerty, *Diary of James C. Hagerty,* 20; *Conspiracy So Immense,* 388; "Texts of Statements by President and Senator McCarthy's Reply" and "McCarthy Deletes 'Now' in Reply to President," *New York Times;* Yoder, *Joe Alsop's Cold War,* 106; "Stevens' Statement," *Washington Post;* and Pearson column, March 7, 1954.

399 *This was a salvo: Conspiracy So Immense,* 393; and "President Chides M'Carthy on 'Fair Play' at Hearings," *New York Times.*

400 *In the meantime:* Sperber, *Murrow: His Life and Times,* 419 and 422; Wershba, "Murrow vs. McCarthy: See It Now," Kihss, "H-Bomb Held Back, M'Carthy Asserts," Adams, "Praise Pours in on Murrow Show," and Lawrence, "McCarthy Strives 'to Shatter' G.O.P.," *New York Times; Due to Circumstances Beyond Our Control,* 30–32 and 42–44; https://www.youtube.com/watch?v=MnKTgmOJr78; *Life and Times of Joe McCarthy,* 589; "Let Listeners Decide," *Washington Post;* and Murray, "Persuasive Dimensions of See It Now's 'Report,'" *Today's Speech.*

403 *Moss was the first:* Friedman, "The Strange Career of Annie Lee Moss," *Journal of American History;* PSI hearings transcript, March 11, 1954, 453 and 458–62; *Cold War, Cool Medium,* 180–81; Crosby, "The Aroma of Decency," *New York Herald Tribune; Blacklisted by History,* 528–41; Ethel Payne OH, 1987, Washington Press Club Foundation; and letter from secretary of defense to secretary of the Army, January 18, 1955, Annie Lee Moss File, PSI.

407 *The case against: Without Precedent,* 111–13, 122–23, and 141–42; Pearson column, December 22, 1953; Alsop and Alsop, "The Tale Half Told," *New York Herald Tribune;* and *Diary of James C. Hagerty,* 29.

409 *Defense Secretary Charles Wilson: Without Precedent,* 142–43; *Life and Times of Joe McCarthy,* 566–67; US Secretary of the Army, *Army-McCarthy Controversy: Brief Submitted by the Army, 1954,* 3–5, 37–40; US Senate, Special Subcommittee on Investigations, *Charges and Countercharges Involving Secretary of the Army Robert T. Stevens, John G. Adams, H. Struve*

Hensel, Senator Joe McCarthy, Roy M. Cohn, and Francis P. Carr, 103–18; *Without Precedent,* 59 and 110; and *Days of Shame,* 20.

412 *The morning after:* Cohn, *McCarthy,* 126; Lawrence, "Army Charges M'Carthy and Cohn Threatened It" and "M'Carthy Charges Army 'Blackmail,'" *New York Times;* and *Charges and Countercharges,* 110–13.

413 *As the Army-McCarthy: Charges and Countercharges,* 120–24 and 129–30; *Brief Submitted by the Army,* 30; and *Without Precedent,* 85–86 and 105.

415 *Then secret FBI:* Memo from J. P. Mohr to Tolson, May 26, 1953, Schine FBI Files; and Pearson column, February 15, 1954.
Cohn's military records: Memo from V. P. Keay to A. H. Belmont, March 26, 1954, Cohn FBI Files; *Citizen Cohn,* 73–74; and memos from Raymond Carr to Pearson, March 26, 1954, and Anderson to Pearson, June 9, 1954, Pearson Files, LBJL.

416 *Other whisperers:* Memo from Jack Anderson and FBI to Pearson, March 26, 1954, LBJL; *Citizen Cohn,* 189; Straight, *Trial by Television,* 82; Reeves interview with Buckley, May 23, 1978; and *Days of Shame,* 23.

417 *The stories about: Ugly Year, Lonely Man,* 7 and 69; *Without Precedent,* 104; "The Oak & the Ivy"; Reeves interview with Mark Catlin, August 9, 1976; and *Conspiracy So Immense,* 412–13.

418 *Joe took solace:* "The Oak & the Ivy"; and *Conspiracy So Immense,* 339.
His staff, meanwhile: RN, 146; and Reeves interview with Van Susteren, November 25, 1975.
His speech, Nixon: RN, 147; and Lippmann, "Our National Obsession," *Washington Post.*

419 *No matter how: The Real American: Joe McCarthy.*
The subcommittee's three: Executive Sessions, 5:211.

420 *The hearings would:* Author interview with Phoebe Stevens Miner; Dolan, *Hale and Dorr Backgrounds & Styles;* and "That Sly Counselor—Welch," *Newsweek.*

421 *Welch's co-star: Senator Joe McCarthy,* 208; "The Terror of Tellico Plains," *Time;* and "The Men McCarthy Made Famous," *Life.*

422 *Chairing the proceedings: Without Precedent,* 153; Goldman, *Crucial Decade,* 271; and Ognibene, *Scoop: The Life and Politics of Henry M. Jackson,* 97.
The hearings officially: Joe McCarthy and the Press, 203–4; Gauger, "Flickering Images," *The Historian;* and Welch, "The Lawyer's Afterthoughts," *Life.*

423 *Thirty million people: In Your Opinion,* 137–38; "The Lawyer's Afterthoughts"; Baker, "Inquiry's TV Rating Is Behind Kefauver's," *New York Times; RN,* 148; Thomas, *Ike's Bluff,* 135; author interviews with Carl Levin, Ira Glasser, and Kelly Kornely; and "The Terror of Tellico Plains."

424 *The first day:* Lawrence, "Stevens Swears M'Carthy Falsified," and Reston, "McCarthy Changes Plan," *New York Times;* and Diaries and Appointment Books, series 24, MUA.

426 *Even as he himself: Citizen Cohn,* 148; Dean, *Imperial Brotherhood,* 127 and 140; and "Stevens Swears M'Carthy Falsified."
Another who found: Without Precedent, 149.

427 *The McCarthy team:* Smithsonian video interview, JJP.
   A more genuine case: Brief Submitted by the Army, 42–52; *Blacklisted by History,* 629; and *Conspiracy So Immense,* 456.

428 *Even as the subcommittee:* "Dare to Indict Him Made by McCarthy," "Excerpts from Transcript of 22nd Day of Senate Hearings in Army-McCarthy Dispute," and Loftus, "White House Charges M'Carthy Bid to Get Secret Data Is Usurpation," *New York Times;* and *The Diary of James C. Hagerty,* 58.

429 *The president despised: Without Precedent,* 205.
   Press coverage of: Cold War, Cool Medium, 203; and "Flickering Images."

430 *What they saw: Life and Times of Joe McCarthy,* 603; *Conspiracy So Immense,* 427; and Cohn, *McCarthy,* 245.
   Testy encounters: Ugly Year, Lonely Man, 105–8; Pearson column, June 24, 1954; *A Certain Democrat,* 138; and *The Politics of Fear,* 257.

431 *Late in the hearings: Senator Joe McCarthy,* 194; Lawrence, "Cohn Threatens to 'Get' Senator for Gibe at Schine," *New York Times; Autobiography of Roy Cohn,* 156; and *A Certain Democrat,* 146–47.

432 *He made no such: Without Precedent,* 210–11.
   Everyone had a different: Without Precedent, 214; "Lawyer's Afterthoughts"; and "Men McCarthy Made Famous."

433 *Subcommittee Democrats:* Transcripts of calls between Senator Symington and Secretary Stevens, February 20 and 21, 1954, Army-McCarthy File, JFKL; and "Excerpts from 28th Day of Senate Testimony in Dispute Between Army and McCarthy," *New York Times.*
   Not all the memories: Black, *Walt Kelly and Pogo,* 213–14; Pearson column, May 17, 1954; *Life and Times of Joe McCarthy,* 590; and Cohn, *McCarthy,* 141–42.
   While it wasn't meant: "Excerpts from Transcript of 21st Day of Senate Testimony in Army-McCarthy Dispute," *New York Times.*

434 *One recurring image:* Falk, *Fear on Trial,* 62; Reeves interviews with Madelaine Grotnes Cocke, November 16, 1976 and Dion Henderson; and *Trial by Television,* 80 and 90.

435 *Joe's days during:* Pearson column, May 17, 1954.
   Advice also poured: Murchison letter to McCarthy, May 21, 1954, series 14, MUA.
   He did gain admirers: In Your Opinion, 136 and 140.

436 *Whether he had ever:* "Excerpts from 30th Day of Testimony in Senate Hearings on Army-McCarthy Dispute," Lawrence, "Welch Assails M'Carthy's 'Cruelty' and 'Recklessness,'" Lawrence, "M'Carthy to Shun Inquiry Till Group Asked in News 'Leak,'" and "Calls Fisher a 'Fine Kid,'" *New York Times;* Cohn, *McCarthy,* 203; *Without Precedent,* 229; *Conspiracy So Immense,* 461–64; *Autobiography of Roy Cohn,* 147–49; Statement Submitted by McCarthy to Senator Mundt, April 20, 1954; Statement of Frederick G. Fisher Jr., June 10, 1954, Grinnell College Special Collections; Williams, "The Final Irony of Joe McCarthy," *Saturday Evening Post;* Williams, *One Man's Freedom,* 61; and Kempton, *America Comes of Middle Age,* 309–11.

440 *The unveiling of:* "The Army-McCarthy Hearings, 1954," 827.

After seven weeks: In Your Opinion, 130 and 137–39; and De Santis, "American Catholics and McCarthyism," *Catholic Historical Review.*

441 The subcommittee said essentially: Charges and Countercharges, August 30, 1954.

There was one more: Thelen and Thelen, "Joe Must Go," *Wisconsin Magazine of History;* Thompson, *History of Wisconsin,* 599; and Gore, *Joe Must Go,* 27–28.

442 Joe's war with the Army: Without Precedent, 265; Pearson column, August 23, 1955; and email to author from Mark Stevens.

443 David Schine served: Schine OH. Alaska was an ironic and perhaps fitting setting for Schine, since it was where many suspected security risks — including Dashiell Hammett — were sent during World War II. Email to author from Ritchie.

Roy Cohn resigned: Autobiography of Roy Cohn, 152; and Gottlieb, "New York Court Disbars Roy Cohn," *New York Times.*

444 It wasn't just principals: Nichols to Tolson, June 24, 1954, Cohn FBI Files; Roberts, "Dr. Irving Peress, Target of McCarthy Crusade, Dies at 97," *New York Times;* Reeves interview with Surine, May 27, 1977; author interviews with Hamilton Fisher and Margaret Adams; and email to author from Mark Stevens.

The hearings' two: Jenkins, *The Terror of Tellico Plains,* 137.

445 The still green medium: Goldwater, With No Apologies, 60–61.

As for Joe: Lawrence, "M'Carthy Hearings End on 36th Day as Potter Suggests Perjury Action, Removal of Top Aides on Both Sides," *New York Times.*

446 Yet even as he: Hospital notes, October 13, 1954, MBNH.

9. THE FALL

447 From the beginning: Cohn, McCarthy, 224 (the senator was William Jenner of Indiana); and Leviero, "Final Vote Condemns M'Carthy," *New York Times.*

448 The self-anointed: Pearse, "The Case of the Unexpected Senator," *Saturday Evening Post;* Lawrence, "McCarthy Strives 'to Shatter' G.O.P.," Trussell, "Flanders Moves in Senate to Strip McCarthy of Posts," White, "Flanders Likens M'Carthy, Hitler," and Leviero, "Flanders Call M'Carthy '5th Amendment Senator,'" *New York Times;* and speech by Senator Ralph Flanders, *Congressional Record,* June 1, 1954, 7389.

449 The wisest choice: Conspiracy So Immense, 478; and "Excerpts from Transcript of First Day of Senate Hearings on Censure of McCarthy" and Leviero, "New Inquiry Is On," *New York Times.*

450 But heard is exactly: "Excerpts from Transcript of Fifth Day of Senate Hearings on Censure of McCarthy," *New York Times.*

451 Even with his wit: Cohn, McCarthy, 221.

Bobby Kennedy, who still: Robert F. Kennedy: The Brother Within, 121.

The Watkins Committee: Leviero, "Committee Urges M'Carthy Censure," and "McCarthy Comment Quoted," *New York Times.*

452 Rather than taking: Flanders OH, Columbia University, 1967, 13.

Joe's supporters argued: Leviero, "Watkins Demands Senate Enlarge M'Carthy Censure," and "Excerpts from Transcript of Fifth Day of Senate Debate on Censure of McCarthy," *New York Times;* and *Conspiracy So Immense,* 484.

453 *The Senate interrupted:* Pearson columns, November 25 and 30, 1954; and hospital notes, November 28, 1954, MBNH.

454 *The Senate's medical recess:* Thomas, *When Even Angels Wept,* 1–3; and Goldwater, *With No Apologies,* 61.
That was Joe's state: Censure File, series 14, MUA; "Joe & the Handmaidens," *Time;* and Leviero, "Session of Senate on M'Carthy Opens in Angry Wrangle," and "Petition Step off in M'Carthy Fight," *New York Times.*

455 *The Senate closed: America Comes of Middle Age,* 319–20.

456 *Its resolution hadn't used:* Fried, *Men Against McCarthy,* 310; *RN,* 149; and *In Your Opinion,* 140–41.
Eisenhower was so delighted: Cohn, *McCarthy,* 239–40; and Leviero, "M'Carthy Breaks with Eisenhower" and "Texts of Statement by McCarthy and Some Replies," *New York Times.*

457 *Ike got:* Staff notes on McCarthyism, June 21, 1955, DDEL.
He pretended to be: Ruth Young Watt OH.

458 *Gone, too, was:* Letter from Joe to Attorney General Brownell, January 17, 1955, Personal Comments File, series 14, MUA; and *Conspiracy So Immense,* 503.
In the Senate: Watkins, *Enough Rope,* 183.
Worst was the blackout: On and Off the Floor, 46; *Senator Joe McCarthy,* 240; and *Joe McCarthy and the Press,* 217–18.

459 *While it's impossible:* Senate speech, March 22, 1956, series 14, and National Labor Relations Board File, series 19, MUA; and Watkins, *Enough Rope,* 182.

460 *Many of Joe's:* US Senate, Special Committee to Investigate the Use of Mail Covers on Senator Joseph R. McCarthy or Any Other Senator, *Report;* and "The Hughes Case," *Legal Aid Review.*

461 *Joe also was talking:* Notes from March and April 1955, unprocessed files, MUA; Cohn, *McCarthy,* 254; and *Life and Times of Joe McCarthy,* 667.
The same was true: Newspaper File, series 14, and letter from Jean, July 29, 1957, series 24, MUA; memo from Nichols to Tolson, July 23, 1956, pt. 7 of 28, MFBI; "Sen. McCarthy Writes Book About Sino-Japanese War," *Chicago Daily Tribune;* and "A M'Carthy Book to Be Published," *New York Times.*

462 *Was he really:* Campaign 1958 File, series 23, MUA; *McCarthy and McCarthyism in Wisconsin,* 204–8; "The Passing of McCarthy," *Time;* and *Senator Joe McCarthy,* 245–46.
All of that might: Cohn, *McCarthy,* 260–61; and *McCarthy and McCarthyism in Wisconsin,* 203.

463 *The pain was more:* Reeves interviews with Cocke and Korb; Cohn, *McCarthy,* 254; and https://www.govtrack.us/congress/members/joseph_mccarthy/407327.

464 *There were occasional:* Cohn, *McCarthy,* 254; and: www.govtrack.
 There is one more: Cohn, *McCarthy,* 257; *Outsider in the Senate,* 106;
 Reeves interviews with Warren Knowles, May 21, 1976, and Morgan; and
 Fishbait, 175.
465 *Physicians at Bethesda:* Hospital records, May 3 and 4, 1949, February
 25, 1951, August 6 and September 18, 1956, and April 28, 1957, and nursing
 notes, August 7–13 and December 17–18, 1956, MBNH.
466 *Once Joe was out:* Reeves interviews of Van Susteren, August 9, 1976, and
 February 5, 1977; and *Life and Times of Joe McCarthy,* 669–70.
 Jean was panicked: Cohn, *McCarthy,* 261; letter from Tierney to Sister
 Bernard, January 23, 1957, Sister Bernard Marie File, series 24, MUA;
 and "I'll Miss Joe McCarthy," *Chicago Daily Tribune.*
468 *Everyone who ran:* Reedy, *From the Ward to the White House,* 167; Reeves
 interviews with Nellor, May 7, 1977, and Bayley, July 7, 1977.
 In his better moments: Drew Pearson Diaries, 1949–1959, 373 and 377; and
 Without Precedent, 258–59.
469 *Joe checked in to Bethesda:* Nurses' and doctors' notes, April 28–May 2,
 1957, MBNH.
470 *Nobody who was close:* Pts. 5 and 7 of 28, MFBI; and author interview
 with Mary Reardon.
472 *Tributes to the senator:* Lawrence, "M'Carthy Is Dead of Liver Ailment
 at the Age of 47" (he actually was forty-eight), "M'Carthy Death Shocks
 Capital," "Nixon Voices Tribute," and "Mrs. Moss Is 'Sorry,'" *New York
 Times;* and Salisbury, *Without Fear or Favor,* 470.
473 *Neither the Catholic Church:* Drury, "M'Carthy Rites Held in Capital,"
 and Morris, "Rites for McCarthy in Senate Monday," *New York Times.*
 Joe's body was flown: Johnston, "M'Carthy Buried Beside Parents," *New
 York Times.*
474 *Joe was buried:* Sevareid, "Joseph R. McCarthy," *The Reporter.*

EPILOGUE

475 *Leading conservatives:* Foundation File, series 24, MUA; Edwards, *Just
 Right,* 9, and author interview with Edwards; and Coulter, "McCarthy-
 ism: The Rosetta Stone of Liberal Lies," *Human Events.*
 The senator's shadow: Halberstam, *The Fifties,* 53.
476 *Joe McCarthy's most:* Flegenheimer and Mahler, "McCarthy Aide
 Helped Shape Young Trump," *New York Times.*
477 *A month after Joe's: Konigsberg v. State Bar of California,* 353 U.S. 252
 (1957); *Schware v. Board of Bar Examiners,* 353 U.S. 232 (1957); *Jencks v.
 United States,* 353 U.S. 657 (1957); Cheney, "The End of History," *Wall
 Street Journal;* and Thomas, *When Even Angels Wept,* 639.
 The McCarthy legacy: "Also Wons" and "Hoping Against Hope," *Time;
 McCarthy and McCarthyism in Wisconsin,* 210; author interview with Bill
 Krause; letter from Eisenhower to Swede Hazlett, July 21, 1953, DDEL;
 and Don Ritchie interview with Floyd Riddick, 1978, Senate Historical
 Office.
478 *Yet it was the differences:* Hughes, *Ordeal of Power,* 90; Herberg, "McCar-
 thy and Hitler," *New Republic;* Leslie Fiedler, "McCarthy as Populist,"

in Latham, *The Meaning of McCarthyism;* Tuck, *McCarthyism and New York's Hearst Press;* Wicker, *Shooting Star,* 189–94; *Senator Joe McCarthy,* 3 and 19–22; *Reflections of an Angry Middle-Aged Editor,* 178; and Beth, "McCarthyism," *South Atlantic Quarterly.*

479 *In the decades since:* Oshinsky, "Graying Now, McCarthyites Keep the Faith," *New York Times;* "Strange Things Are Happening at McCarthy's Grave"; and Meyer, "It Happened Here: An Appleton Exorcism," *Appleton Post-Crescent;* and Weingarten, "Joe McCarthy May Be Dead, but the Faithful in His Hometown Keep His Spirit Alive," *Chicago Tribune.*

480 *Those who were closest: Autobiography of Roy Cohn,* 81; and Krebs, "Roy Cohn, Aide to McCarthy and Fiery Lawyer, Dies at 59," *New York Times.* *Jean tried to move:* Sister Bernard Marie File, series 24, MUA; Outagamie County Probate Estate document, April 30, 1959; Reeves interview with Van Susteren, March 1, 1980; "McCarthy Without Paranoia"; and author interview with Greta Van Susteren.

BIBLIOGRAPHY

INTERVIEWS AND CORRESPONDENCE

The author interviewed or exchanged emails with the following McCarthy authors, colleagues, family, friends, victims, and others familiar with him and his work: Tyler Abell, Margaret Adams, Sam Adams, Annette Amerman, Robert Andrew, Mike Arendt, Eric Arnesen, Bobby Baker, Dan Balliet, Adam Berenbak, Brigid Berlin, Richard Berlin, Kai Bird, Avis Bohlen, John Brogan, Clifford Bunks, Jonathan Bush, Stanley Caroff, Matt Carpenter, Don Castonia, Bill Cherkasky, Susan Collins, Linda Comins, Bob Conroy, Terry Dawson, Gary Dilweg, Richard Doughty, Melvin Dow, Phyllis Dowd, Jim Doyle, Kitty Dukakis, Mike Dukakis, Lucy Durán, Lee Edwards, J. P. Facher, John A. Farrell, David Fierst, Fred Fierst, Helen Fierst, Laura Finestone, Lisa-Annette Finestone, Hamilton Fisher, Jeffrey Flier, Matt Flynn, Alex Frain, Lawrence Friedman, Brian Frosh, Neil Gallagher, Gregory Peter Gallant, Patricia Gerlach, Loren Ghiglione, Chris Ghosh, Ira Glasser, Bernadine Gomillion, George Greeley, Jeff Greenfield, Ronald Gurrera, Richard Haney, Signe Hanson, Donald Harris, John Earl Haynes, Jim Hershberg, Dick Hoffman, Joseph Hoffman, Zoe Hollenbeck, Ernest Hollings, Kathryn Horvat, Buddy Hunt, Ellen Hunt, George Jacobs, James N. Juliana, James S. Juliana, Leon Kamin, Margaret Kasschau, Jerome Kassirer, Owen Katzman, Ethel Kennedy, Sergei Khrushchev, Bob Kieve, Harvey Klehr, Ann Kloehn, Bill Kloiber, Betty Koed, Kelly Kornely, Bill Kraus, Bronson La Follette,

Kate Lardner, Carl Levin, Anthony Lewis, Dave Lindsay, Jim Long, Chris Lovett, Tracey Maclin, Robert MacNeil, Patrick Maney, Frank Mankiewicz, Neil Margetson, Jack Matlock, Frank McCulloch, Robert Meeropol, Henry Merton, Jim Meyer, Harold Michael, Dan Miner, Phoebe Stevens Miner, Judy Murphy, Casey Murrow, Tom Nelson, John Nichols, Kevin O'Melia, Itohan Omoregie, Fraser Ottanelli, Jack Pankratz, Vladimir Pechatnov, Robert Pennoyer, Vladimir Pirchadnev, E. Barrett Prettyman Jr., Dave Prosser, William E. Raftery, Mary Reardon, Margaret Reber, Peter Reiss, Steven Remy, Phyllis Richman, Don Ritchie, Louise Robbins, Toby Roth, Ellen Schrecker, Bob Service, Sue Sharko, Benjamin Sinclair, Ann Brownell Sloane, Alvin Spivak, Cody Splitt, Elizabeth Starčević, Mark Stevens, Sherm Stock, Vi Stoner, Shelly Taylor, Arthur Thompson, Kathleen Kennedy Townsend, Joe Tydings, Nick Unger, Sydney Van Nort, Dirk Van Susteren, Greta Van Susteren, Carter Vincent, Peter Voy, Sam Walker, Jeanne Weilland, Shirley Wershba, Bob Wills, Don Young, and Dave Zweifel.

BOOKS, GOVERNMENT DOCUMENTS, THESES, AND UNPUBLISHED WORKS

Abrahamsen, David. *Nixon vs. Nixon: An Emotional Tragedy.* New York: Farrar, Straus and Giroux, 1977.

Acheson, Dean. *Present at the Creation: My Years in the State Department.* New York: W. W. Norton, 1969.

——. *Sketches from Life of Men I Have Known.* New York: Harper & Brothers, 1961.

Adams, John G. *Without Precedent: The Story of the Death of McCarthyism.* New York: W. W. Norton, 1983.

Adams, Sherman. *Firsthand Report: The Story of the Eisenhower Administration.* New York: Harper & Brothers, 1961.

Allen, C. Richard, and Edwin O. Guthman, eds. *RFK: Collected Speeches.* New York: Viking, 1993.

Alwood, Edward. *Dark Days in the Newsroom: McCarthyism Aimed at the Press.* Philadelphia: Temple University Press, 2007.

American Civil Liberties Union. "The Police and the Radicals." March 1921.

Anderson, Clinton P., with Milton Viorst. *Outsider in the Senate: Senator Clinton Anderson's Memoirs.* New York: World Publishing, 1970.

Anderson, Jack, with James Boyd. *Confessions of a Muckraker: The Inside Story of Life in Washington During the Truman, Eisenhower, Kennedy and Johnson Years.* New York: Random House, 1979.

Anderson, Jack, and Ronald W. May. *McCarthy: The Man, the Senator, the "Ism."* Boston: Beacon, 1952.

Andrew, Christopher M., and Vasili Mitrokhin. *The Sword and the Shield: The Mitrokhin Archive and the Secret History of the KGB.* New York: Basic, 1999.

———. *The World Was Going Our Way: The KGB and the Battle for the Third World.* New York: Basic, 2005.

Aronson, James. *The Press and the Cold War.* New York: Monthly Review, 1970.

Baker, Bobby, with Larry L. King. *Wheeling and Dealing: Confessions of a Capitol Hill Operator.* New York: W. W. Norton, 1978.

Barson, Michael, and Steve Heller. *Red Scared! The Commie Menace in Propaganda and Popular Culture.* San Francisco: Chronicle, 2001.

Barth, Alan. *The Loyalty of Free Men.* New York: Pocket, 1951.

Bassett, James. "Ugly Year, Lonely Man: A Political Journal of 1954." Unpublished diary, 1970. Bowdoin College Special Collections & Archives.

Bayley, Edwin R. *Joe McCarthy and the Press.* Madison: University of Wisconsin Press, 1981.

Bean, Louis H. *Influences in the 1954 Mid-Term Elections: War, Jobs, Parity, McCarthy.* Washington, DC: Public Affairs Institute, 1954.

Beisner, Robert L. *Dean Acheson: A Life in the Cold War.* New York: Oxford University Press, 2006.

Belfrage, Cedric. *The American Inquisition, 1945–1960: A Profile of the "McCarthy Era."* New York: Thunder's Mouth, 1973.

Bernstein, Carl. *Loyalties: A Son's Memoir.* New York: Simon & Schuster, 1989.

Bernstein, Walter. *Inside Out: A Memoir of the Blacklist.* New York: Alfred A. Knopf, 1996.

Bird, Kai. *The Chairman: John J. McCloy: The Making of the American Establishment.* New York: Simon & Schuster, 1992.

———. *The Color of Truth: McGeorge Bundy and William Bundy: Brothers in Arms.* New York: Simon & Schuster, 1998.

Bird, Kai, and Martin J. Sherwin. *American Prometheus: The Triumph and Tragedy of J. Robert Oppenheimer.* New York: Alfred A. Knopf, 2005.

Black, James Eric. *Walt Kelly and Pogo: The Art of the Political Swamp.* Jefferson, NC: McFarland, 2015.

Blair, Joan, and Clay Blair Jr. *The Search for JFK.* New York: Berkley Publishing Corporation, 1976.

Block, Herbert. *Herblock's Here and Now.* New York: Simon & Schuster, 1955.

Bohlen, Charles L. *Witness to History, 1929–1969.* London: Weidenfeld & Nicolson, 1973.

Branch, Taylor. *Parting the Waters: Martin Luther King and the Civil Rights Movement, 1954–63.* New York: Simon & Schuster, 1988.

Breindel, Eric, and Herbert Romerstein. *The Venona Secrets: The Definitive Exposé of Soviet Espionage in America.* Washington, DC: Regnery History, 2014.

Brinkley, Alan. *Voices of Protest: Huey Long, Father Coughlin and the Great Depression*. New York: Vintage, 1982.

Brinkley, David. *David Brinkley: A Memoir*. New York: Alfred A. Knopf, 1995.

Brodie, Fawn M. *Richard Nixon: The Shaping of His Character*. New York: W. W. Norton, 1981.

Brown, Ralph S., Jr. *Loyalty and Security: Employment Tests in the United States*. New Haven, CT: Yale University Press, 1958.

Buchanan, Patrick J. *Right from the Beginning*. Boston: Little, Brown, 1988.

Buckley, William F., Jr. *The Redhunter: A Novel Based on the Life of Senator Joe McCarthy*. Boston: Little, Brown, 1999.

Buckley, William F., Jr., and Brent Bozell. *McCarthy and His Enemies: The Record and Its Meaning*. Washington, DC: Regnery Publishing, 1954.

Budenz, Louis Francis. *This Is My Story*. New York: McGraw-Hill, 1946.

Burrough, Bryan. *The Big Rich: The Rise and Fall of the Greatest Texas Oil Fortunes*. New York: Penguin, 2009.

Butler, Anne M., and Wendy Wolff. *United States Senate: Election, Expulsion and Censure Cases, 1793–1990*. Washington, DC: Government Printing Office, 1995.

Calaprice, Alice, ed. *The Ultimate Quotable Einstein*. Princeton, NJ: Princeton University Press, 2010.

Caro, Robert A. *Master of the Senate: The Years of Lyndon Johnson*. New York: Vintage, 2003.

———. *The Years of Lyndon Johnson: The Passage of Power*. New York: Alfred A. Knopf, 2012.

Carpenter, F. B. *The Inner Life of Abraham Lincoln: Six Months at the White House*. New York: Hurd and Houghton, 1866.

Cater, Douglass. *The Fourth Branch of Government*. Boston: Houghton Mifflin, 1959.

Catledge, Turner. *My Life and the Times*. New York: Harper & Row, 1971.

Caute, David. *The Great Fear: The Anti-Communist Purge Under Truman and Eisenhower*. New York: Simon & Schuster, 1978.

Chambers, Whittaker. *Odyssey of a Friend: Whittaker Chambers' Letters to William F. Buckley Jr., 1954–1961*. Edited by William F. Buckley Jr. New York: Putnam, 1956.

Chaney, Lindsay, and Michael Cieply. *The Hearsts: Family and Empire — The Later Years*. New York: Simon & Schuster, 1981.

Charles River Editors. *McCarthyism: The Controversial History of Senator Joseph McCarthy, the House Un-American Activities Committee, and the Red Scare During the Cold War*. Scotts Valley, CA: CreateSpace Independent Publishing Platform, 2015.

Coady, Sharon. "The Wisconsin Press and Joseph McCarthy: A Case Study." Master's thesis, University of Wisconsin, 1965.

Cohen, Daniel. *Joseph McCarthy: The Misuse of Political Power*. Brookfield, CT: Millbrook, 1996.

Cohn, Roy. *McCarthy*. New York: New American Library, 1968.

Cohn, Roy, and Sidney Zion. *The Autobiography of Roy Cohn*. Secaucus, NJ: Lyle Stuart, 1988.

Conant, Jennet. *Man of the Hour: James B. Conant, Warrior Scientist.* New York: Simon & Schuster, 2017.

Connell, Tula A. *Conservative Counterrevolution: Challenging Liberalism in 1950s Milwaukee.* Chicago: University of Illinois Press, 2016.

Cooney, John. *The American Pope: The Life and Times of Francis Cardinal Spellman.* New York: Times Books, 1984.

Cooper, James Fenimore. *The American Democrat.* New York: Barnes and Noble, 2004.

Coulter, Ann. *Treason: Liberal Treachery from the Cold War to the War on Terrorism.* New York: Crown Forum, 2003.

Cox, John Stuart, and Athan G. Theoharis. *The Boss: J. Edgar Hoover and the Great American Inquisition.* Philadelphia: Temple University Press, 1988.

Crabtree, Charlotte A., and Gary B. Nash, eds. *National Standards for United States History: Exploring the American Experience.* Los Angeles: National Center for History in the Schools, 1994.

Cray, Ed. *General of the Army: George C. Marshall, Soldier and Statesman.* New York: W. W. Norton, 1990.

Crosby, Donald F. *God, Church, and Flag: Sen. Joseph R. McCarthy and the Catholic Church, 1950-1957.* Chapel Hill: University of North Carolina Press, 1978.

David, Lester. *Ethel: The Story of Mrs. Robert F. Kennedy.* New York: World Publishing, 1971.

Davis, Elmer. *But We Were Born Free.* New York: Bobbs-Merrill, 1952.

Dean, Robert D. *Imperial Brotherhood: Gender and the Making of Cold War Foreign Policy.* Amherst: University of Massachusetts Press, 2001.

Deaver, Jean Franklin. "A Study of Senator Joseph R. McCarthy and 'McCarthyism' as Influences upon the News Media and the Evolution of Reportorial Method." PhD diss., University of Texas at Austin, 1969.

Decter, Moshe, and James Rorty. *McCarthy and the Communists.* Boston: Beacon, 1954.

de Toledano, Ralph. *One Man Alone: Richard Nixon.* New York: Funk and Wagnalls, 1969.

Dodd, Bella V. *School of Darkness.* New York: P. J. Kenedy, 1954.

Doherty, Thomas. *Cold War, Cool Medium: Television, McCarthyism, and American Culture.* New York: Columbia University Press, 2003.

Dolan, John A. *Hale and Dorr, Backgrounds & Styles.* Boston: Hale and Dorr, 1993.

Donoghue, James R. *How Wisconsin Voted, 1848-1972: 1974 Election Supplement.* Madison: University of Wisconsin–Extension, Institute of Governmental Affairs, 1975.

Douglas, Paul H. *In the Fullness of Time: The Memoirs of Paul H. Douglas.* New York: Harcourt Brace Jovanovich, 1971.

Edwards, Lee. *Just Right: A Life in Pursuit of Liberty.* Wilmington, DE: ISI, 2017.

Eisenhower, Dwight D. *The Eisenhower Diaries.* Edited by Robert H. Ferrell. New York: W. W. Norton, 1981.

———. *Mandate for Change, 1953-1956: The White House Years.* Garden City, NY: Doubleday, 1963.

Eisenhower, Milton S. *The President Is Calling.* Garden City, NY: Doubleday, 1974.

Epstein, Benjamin R., and Arnold Forster. *Cross-Currents: The Book That Tells How Anti-Semitism Is Used Today as a Cultural Weapon.* Garden City, NY: Doubleday, 1956.

——. *The Troublemakers: The New Anti-Defamation League Report on Intolerance in the United States.* Garden City, NY: Doubleday, 1952.

Epstein, Leon D. *Politics in Wisconsin.* Madison: University of Wisconsin Press, 1958.

Evans, Stanton M. *Blacklisted by History: The Untold Story of Senator Joseph Mc-Carthy and His Fight Against America's Enemies.* New York: Three Rivers, 2007.

Evjue, William T. *A Fighting Editor.* Madison, WI: Wells Printing, 1968.

Ewald, William Bragg, Jr. *McCarthyism and Consensus.* New York: University Press of America, 1986.

——. *Who Killed Joe McCarthy?* New York: Simon & Schuster, 1984.

Falk, John Henry. *Fear on Trial.* Austin: University of Texas Press, 1963.

Farrell, John A. *Richard Nixon: The Life.* New York: Doubleday, 2017.

Fast, Howard. *Being Red: A Memoir.* Boston: Houghton Mifflin, 1990.

Faulk, John Henry. *Fear on Trial.* Austin: University of Texas Press, 1963.

Feldman, Jay. *Manufacturing Hysteria: A History of Scapegoating, Surveillance, and Secrecy in Modern America.* New York: Random House, 2012.

Feldstein, Mark. *Poisoning the Press: Richard Nixon, Jack Anderson, and the Rise of Washington's Scandal Culture.* New York: Farrar, Straus and Giroux, 2010.

Fenton, John M. *In Your Opinion: The Managing Editor of the Gallup Poll Looks at Polls, Politics, and the People from 1945 to 1960.* Boston: Little, Brown, 1960.

Ferguson, Leroy C., and Ralph H. Smuckler. *Politics in the Press: An Analysis of Press Content in 1952 Senatorial Campaigns.* East Lansing: Governmental Research Bureau, Michigan State College, 1954.

Ferguson, Mary Jane. "McCarthy v. Pearson: Criticism or Intimidation?" Master's thesis, University of Wisconsin, 1969.

Feuerlicht, Roberta Strauss. *Joe McCarthy and McCarthyism: The Hate That Haunts America.* New York: McGraw-Hill, 1972.

Flanders, Ralph E. *Senator from Vermont.* Boston: Little, Brown, 1961.

Flarity, William P. "Recollections of Joe McCarthy." Unpublished manuscript, last modified 1966.

Flynn, John T. *The Lattimore Story: The Full Story of the Most Incredible Conspiracy of Our Time.* New York: Devin-Adair, 1962.

Ford, Sherman, Jr. *The McCarthy Menace: An Evaluation of the Facts and an Interpretation of the Evidence.* New York: William-Frederick, 1954.

Freeland, Richard M. *The Truman Doctrine and the Origins of McCarthyism: Foreign Policy, Domestic Politics, and Internal Security, 1946–1948.* New York: Alfred A. Knopf, 1975.

Fried, Albert. *McCarthyism, the Great American Red Scare: A Documentary History.* New York: Oxford University Press, 1997.

Fried, Richard M. *Men Against McCarthy.* New York: Columbia University Press, 1976.

——. *Nightmare in Red: The McCarthy Era in Perspective.* New York: Oxford University Press, 1990.

Friendly, Fred W. *Due to Circumstances Beyond Our Control . . .* New York: Random House, 1967.

Gabler, Neil. *Winchell: Gossip, Power and the Culture of Celebrity.* New York: Alfred A. Knopf, 1994.

Gallant, Gregory Peter. *Hope and Fear in Margaret Chase Smith's America: A Continuous Tangle.* Lanham, MD: Lexington, 2014.

Gentry, Curt. *J. Edgar Hoover: The Man and the Secrets.* New York: W. W. Norton, 1991.

Ghiglione, Loren. *CBS's Don Hollenbeck: An Honest Reporter in the Age of McCarthyism.* New York: Columbia University Press, 2008.

Giblin, James. *The Rise and Fall of Senator Joe McCarthy.* Boston: Clarion, 2009.

Goldbloom, Maurice J. *American Security and Freedom.* New York: American Jewish Committee, 1954.

Goldman, Eric F. *The Crucial Decade: America, 1945–1955.* New York: Alfred A. Knopf, 1956.

Goldston, Robert C. *The American Nightmare: Senator Joseph R. McCarthy and the Politics of Hate.* New York: Bobbs-Merrill, 1973.

Goldwater, Barry M. *With No Apologies: The Personal and Political Memoirs of United States Senator Barry M. Goldwater.* New York: William Morrow, 1979.

Gore, Leroy. *Joe Must Go.* New York: Julian Messner, 1954.

Greenspun, Hank. *Where I Stand: The Record of a Reckless Man.* New York: David McKay, 1966.

Greenstein, Fred I. *The Hidden-Hand Presidency: Eisenhower as Leader.* New York: Basic, 1982.

Griffith, Robert. *The Politics of Fear: Joseph R. McCarthy and the Senate.* Lexington: University Press of Kentucky, 1970.

Griffith, Robert, and Athan Theoharis, eds. *The Specter: Original Essays on the Cold War and the Origins of McCarthyism.* New York: New Viewpoints, 1974.

Griffith, Thomas. *The Waist-High Culture.* New York: Grosset and Dunlap, 1959.

Griswold, Erwin N. *The Fifth Amendment Today.* Cambridge: Harvard University Press, 1955.

Guthman, Edwin. *We Band of Brothers: A Memoir of Robert F. Kennedy.* New York: Harper and Row, 1964.

Hagerty, James C. *The Diary of James C. Hagerty: Eisenhower in Mid-Course, 1954–1955.* Bloomington: Indiana University Press, 1983.

Halberstam, David. *The Fifties.* New York: Fawcett Columbine, 1993.

——. *The Unfinished Odyssey of Robert Kennedy.* New York: Bantam, 1969.

Hanson, Haldore. *Fifty Years Around the Third World: Adventures and Reflections of an Overseas American.* Burlington, VT: Fraser Publishing, 1986.

Harris, Reed. "Life of Sirrah." Unpublished diary, courtesy of Donald Harris.

Hauge, Gabriel. Unpublished memoirs. George B. Bookman Papers, 1981–1993, Eisenhower Library.

Haynes, John Earl. *Communism and Anti-Communism in the United States: An Annotated Guide to Historical Writings.* New York: Garland, 1987.

——. *Red Scare or Red Menace? American Communism and Anticommunism in the Cold War Era.* Chicago: Ivan R. Dee, 1996.

Haynes, John Earl, and Harvey Klehr. *The American Communist Movement: Storming Heaven Itself.* New York: Twain, 1992.

——. *Early Cold War Spies: The Espionage Trials That Shaped American Politics.* New York: Cambridge University Press, 2006.

——. *In Denial: Historians, Communism and Espionage.* San Francisco: Encounter, 2003.

——. *Venona: Decoding Soviet Espionage in America.* New Haven, CT: Yale University Press, 1999.

Haynes, John Earl, Harvey Klehr, and Alexander Vassiliev. *Spies: The Rise and Fall of the KGB in America.* New Haven, CT: Yale University Press, 2010.

Heil, Alan L., Jr. *Voice of America: A History.* New York: Columbia University Press, 2003.

Hellman, Lillian. *Scoundrel Time.* Boston: Little, Brown, 1976.

Hemmer, Nicole. *Messengers of the Right: Conservative Media and the Transformation of American Politics.* Philadelphia: University of Pennsylvania Press, 2016.

Herman, Arthur. *Joseph McCarthy: Reexamining the Life and Legacy of America's Most Hated Senator.* New York: Free Press, 2000.

Herndon, Booton. *Praised and Damned: The Story of Fulton Lewis, Jr.* Boston: Little, Brown, 1954.

Hersh, Burton. *Bobby and J. Edgar: The Historic Face-Off Between the Kennedys and J. Edgar Hoover That Transformed America.* New York: Basic, 2007.

Hilty, James W. *Robert Kennedy: Brother Protector.* Philadelphia: Temple University Press, 1997.

Hirschfeld, Burt. *Freedom in Jeopardy: The Story of the McCarthy Years.* New York: Julian Messner, 1969.

Hitchcock, William I. *The Age of Eisenhower: America and the World in the 1950s.* New York: Simon & Schuster, 2018.

Hofstadter, Richard. *The Paranoid Style in American Politics.* New York: Vintage, 1952.

Hughes, Emmett John. *The Ordeal of Power: A Political Memoir of the Eisenhower Years.* New York: Atheneum, 1963.

Hyman, Sidney. *The Lives of William Benton.* Chicago: University of Chicago Press, 1969.

Ingalls, Robert P. *Point of Order: A Profile of Senator Joe McCarthy.* New York: Putnam, 1981.

Isaacson, Walter, and Evan Thomas. *The Wise Men: Six Friends and the World They Made.* New York: Simon & Schuster, 1986.

Jenkins, Ray H. *The Terror of Tellico Plains: The Memoirs of Ray H. Jenkins.* Knoxville: East Tennessee Historical Society, 1978.

Johnson, Curtiss S. *Raymond E. Baldwin: Connecticut Statesman.* Chester, CT: Pequot, 1972.

Johnson, David K. *The Lavender Scare: The Cold War Persecution of Gays and Lesbians in the Federal Government.* Chicago: University of Chicago Press, 2004.

Johnson, Haynes. *The Age of Anxiety: McCarthyism to Terrorism.* Orlando: Harcourt, 2005.

Johnson, Roger T. *Robert M. La Follette, Jr. and the Decline of the Progressive Party in Wisconsin.* Hamden, CT: Archon, 1970.

Joiner, Lynne. *Honorable Survivor: Mao's China, McCarthy's America, and the Persecution of John S. Service.* Annapolis, MD: Naval Institute Press, 2009.

Kahn, E. J., Jr. *The China Hands: America's Foreign Service Officers and What Befell Them.* New York: Viking, 1972.

Kaplan, Judy, and Linn Shapiro, eds. *Red Diapers: Growing Up in the Communist Left.* Urbana: University of Illinois Press, 1998.

Keeley, Joseph. *The China Lobby Man: The Story of Alfred Kohlberg.* New Rochelle, NY: Arlington House, 1969.

Keith, Caroline H. *For Hell and a Brown Mule: The Biography of Senator Millard E. Tydings.* New York: Madison, 1991.

Kelley, Stanley, Jr. *Professional Public Relations and Political Power.* Baltimore: Johns Hopkins University Press, 1956.

Kempton, Murray. *America Comes of Middle Age: Columns, 1950–1962.* Boston: Little, Brown, 1963.

Kennedy, Joseph P. *Hostage to Fortune: The Letters of Joseph P. Kennedy.* Edited by Amanda Smith. New York: Viking, 2001.

Kennedy, Robert F. *The Enemy Within: The McClellan Committee's Crusade Against Jimmy Hoffa and Corrupt Labor Unions.* New York: Da Capo, 1960.

———. *RFK: Collected Speeches.* Edited by Edwin O. Guthman and C. Richard Allen. New York: Viking, 1993.

Kessler, Lauren. *Clever Girl: Elizabeth Bentley, the Spy Who Ushered in the McCarthy Era.* New York: HarperCollins, 2003.

Kessler, Ronald. *The Bureau: The Secret History of the FBI.* New York: St. Martin's, 2002.

Kinzer, Stephen. *The Brothers: John Foster Dulles, Allen Dulles, and Their Secret World War.* New York: Times Books, 2013.

Kirkpatrick, Lyman B., Jr. *The Real CIA: An Insider's View of the Strengths and Weaknesses of Our Government's Most Important Agency.* New York: Macmillan, 1968.

Klehr, Harvey, and Ronald Radosh. *The Amerasia Spy Case: Prelude to McCarthyism.* Chapel Hill: University of North Carolina Press, 1996.

Klurfeld, Herman. *Behind the Lines: The World of Drew Pearson.* Englewood Cliffs, NJ: Prentice-Hall, 1968.

———. *Winchell: His Life and Times.* New York: Praeger, 1952.

Kutler, Stanley I. *The American Inquisition: Justice and Injustice in the Cold War.* New York: Hill and Wang, 1982.

Lait, Jack, and Lee Mortimer. *U.S.A. Confidential.* New York: Crown, 1952.

Lamphere, Robert J., and Tom Shachtman. *The FBI-KGB War: A Special Agent's Story.* London: W. H. Allen, 1987.

Landis, Mark. *Joseph McCarthy: The Politics of Chaos.* London: Associated University Presses, 1987.

Latham, Earl, ed. *The Meaning of McCarthyism.* Lexington, MA: D. C. Heath, 1973.

Lattimore, Owen. *Ordeal by Slander.* New York: Bantam, 1950.

Lawford, Patricia Kennedy. *That Shining Hour.* New York: Halliday Lithograph, 1969.

Laymon, Sherry. *Fearless: John L. McClellan, United States Senator.* Mustang, OK: Tate Publishing, 2011.

Lazarsfeld, Paul Felix, and Wagner Thielens Jr. *The Academic Mind: Social Scientists in a Time of Crisis.* New York: Free Press, 1958.

Lewy, Guenter. *The Federal Loyalty-Security Program: The Need for Reform.* Washington, DC: American Enterprise Institute, 1983.

Lichtman, Robert M. *The Supreme Court and McCarthy-Era Repression: One Hundred Decisions.* Urbana: University of Illinois Press, 2012.

Lichtman, Robert M., and Ronald D. Cohen. *Deadly Farce: Harvey Matusow and the Informer System in the McCarthy Era.* Chicago: University of Illinois Press, 2004.

Liman, Arthur L. *Lawyer: A Life of Counsel and Controversy.* New York: Public Affairs, 1998.

Lodge, Henry Cabot. *As It Was: An Inside View of Politics and Power in the '50s and '60s.* New York: W. W. Norton, 1976.

Lokos, Lionel. *Who Promoted Peress?* New York: The Bookmailer, 1961.

Long, Huey P. *Every Man a King: The Autobiography of Huey P. Long.* New Orleans: Da Capo, 1933.

Lubell, Samuel. *The Revolt of the Moderates.* New York: Harper & Brothers, 1956.

Lustron Corporation. *How to Own Your Own Home Now.* Columbus, OH: Lustron, 1949.

Machiavelli, Niccolò. *The Prince.* New York: St. Martin's Press, 2017.

Maney, Patrick. *"Young Bob" La Follette: A Biography of Robert M. La Follette, Jr., 1895–1953.* Columbia: University of Missouri Press, 1978.

Maraniss, David. *A Good American Family: The Red Scare and My Father.* New York: Simon & Schuster, 2019.

Marquette University Law School Announcements, 1932–33. Marquette University Law School.

Martin, John Bartlow. *Adlai Stevenson of Illinois: The Life of Adlai E. Stevenson.* Garden City, NY: Doubleday, 1976.

Martin, Ralph G. *A Hero for Our Time: An Intimate Story of the Kennedy Years.* New York: Fawcett Crest, 1983.

Matthews, J. B. *Odyssey of a Fellow Traveler.* New York: Mount Vernon, 1939.

Matusow, Harvey. *False Witness.* New York: Cameron & Kahn, 1955.

May, Gary. *China Scapegoat: The Diplomatic Ordeal of John Carter Vincent.* Prospect Heights, IL: Waveland, 1979.

——. *Un-American Activities: The Trials of William Remington.* New York: Oxford University Press, 1994.

Mazo, Earl. *Richard Nixon: A Political and Personal Portrait.* New York: Harper & Brothers, 1959.

McAuliffe, Mary Sperling. *Crisis on the Left: Cold War Politics and American Liberals, 1947–1954.* Amherst: University of Massachusetts Press, 1978.

McCarthy, Jean Kerr. "The Joe McCarthy I Knew." Unpublished memoir, Marquette University Archives.

McCarthy, Joe. *The Remarkable Kennedys: The Dramatic, Inside Story of John Fitzgerald Kennedy and His Remarkable Family.* New York: Dial, 1960.

McCarthy, Joseph. *America's Retreat from Victory: The Story of George Catlett Marshall.* New York: Devin-Adair, 1951.

——. *Major Speeches and Debates of Senator Joe McCarthy Delivered in the United States Senate, 1950–1951.* New York: Gordon Press, 1975.

——. *McCarthyism: The Fight for America.* New York: Devin-Adair, 1952.

McCullough, David. *Truman.* New York: Simon & Schuster, 1992.

McCumber, John. *Time in the Ditch: American Philosophy and the McCarthy Era.* Evanston, IL: Northwestern University Press, 2001.

McDaniel, Rodger. *Dying for Joe McCarthy's Sins: The Suicide of Wyoming Senator Lester Hunt.* Cody, WY: WordsWorth, 2013.

McDonald, Kathlene. *Feminism, the Left, and Postwar Literary Culture.* Jackson: University Press of Mississippi, 2012.

McKinley, Wayne Edwin. "A Study of the American Right: Senator Joseph McCarthy and the American Legion, 1946–1955." Master's thesis, University of Wisconsin, 1962.

McReynolds, Rosalee, and Louise Robbins. *The Librarian Spies: Philip and Mary Jane Keeney and Cold War Espionage.* Westport, CT: Praeger Security International, 2009.

Merrill, Dennis. *Documentary History of the Truman Presidency.* Vols. 1–35. Bethesda: University Publications of America, 1995–2002.

Merson, Martin. *The Private Diary of a Public Servant.* New York: Macmillan, 1955.

Miller, Merle. *The Judges and the Judged.* Garden City, NY: Doubleday, 1952.

Miller, Neil. *Out of the Past: Gay and Lesbian History from 1869 to the Present.* New York: Vintage, 1995.

Miller, William. *Fishbait: The Memoirs of the Congressional Doorkeeper.* Englewood Cliffs, NJ: Prentice-Hall, 1977.

Morgan, Ted. *Reds: McCarthyism in Twentieth-Century America.* New York: Random House, 2003.

Morris, Robert. *No Wonder We Are Losing.* New York: The Bookmailer, 1958.

Morton, Joseph. *McCarthy: The Man and the Ism.* San Francisco: Pacific Publishing Foundation, 1953.

Moynihan, Daniel Patrick. *Secrecy.* New Haven, CT: Yale University Press, 1998.

Murray, Robert K. *Red Scare: A Study in National Hysteria, 1919–1920.* Minneapolis: University of Minnesota Press, 1955.

Nasaw, David. *The Patriarch: The Remarkable Life and Turbulent Times of Joseph P. Kennedy.* New York: Penguin, 2012.

Navasky, Victor S. *Kennedy Justice.* New York: Atheneum, 1971.

——. *Naming Names.* New York: Viking, 1980.

Nesbit, Robert C. *Wisconsin: A History.* Madison: University of Wisconsin Press, 1973.

Nevins, Allan. *Herbert H. Lehman and His Era.* New York: Charles Scribner's Sons, 1963.

Newfield, Jack. *RFK: A Memoir.* New York: Thunder's Mouth, 1969.

Newman, Robert P. *The Cold War Romance of Lillian Hellman and John Melby.* Chapel Hill: University of North Carolina Press, 1989.

Newton, Jim. *Eisenhower: The White House Years.* New York: Doubleday, 2011.

Nichols, David A. *Ike and McCarthy: Dwight Eisenhower's Secret Campaign Against Joseph McCarthy.* New York: Simon & Schuster, 2017.

Nissenson, Marilyn. *The Lady Upstairs: Dorothy Schiff and the New York Post.* New York: St. Martin's, 2007.

Nixon, Richard. *RN: The Memoirs of Richard Nixon.* New York: Grossett & Dunlap, 1978.

Norris, John. *Mary McGrory: The Trailblazing Columnist Who Stood Washington on Its Head.* New York: Penguin, 2015.

O'Brien, Michael. *McCarthy and McCarthyism in Wisconsin.* Columbia: University of Missouri Press, 1980.

Ognibene, Peter J. *Scoop: The Life and Politics of Henry M. Jackson.* New York: Stein and Day, 1975.

Oshinksy, David M. *A Conspiracy So Immense: The World of Joe McCarthy.* New York: Free Press, 1983.

——. *Senator Joseph McCarthy and the American Labor Movement.* Columbia: University of Missouri Press, 1976.

Patterson, James T. *Mr. Republican: A Biography of Robert A. Taft.* Boston: Houghton Mifflin, 1972.

Pearson, Drew. *Drew Pearson Diaries, 1949–1959.* Edited by Tyler Abell. New York: Holt, Rinehart and Winston, 1974.

——. *Washington Merry-Go-Round: The Drew Pearson Diaries, 1960–1969.* Edited by Peter Hannaford. Lincoln, NE: Potomac Books, 2015.

Pells, Richard H. *The Liberal Mind in a Conservative Age: American Intellectuals in the 1940s and 1950s.* New York: Harper & Row, 1985.

Peters, J. *The Communist Party: A Manual on Organization.* New York: Workers Library, 1935.

Pilat, Oliver. *Drew Pearson: An Unauthorized Biography.* New York: Harper's Magazine Press, 1973.

Pogue, Forrest C. *George C. Marshall: Statesman, 1945–1959.* New York: Penguin, 1987.

Posner, Gerald. *Killing the Dream: James Earl Ray and the Assassination of Martin Luther King, Jr.* New York: Random House, 1998.

Potter, Charles E. *Days of Shame.* New York: Signet, 1965.

Powers, Richard Gid. *Not Without Honor: The History of American Anticommunism.* New York: Free Press, 1995.

Price, David H. *Threatening Anthropology: McCarthyism and the FBI's Surveillance of Activist Anthropologists.* Durham, NC: Duke University Press, 2004.

Prochnau, William W., and Richard W. Larsen. *A Certain Democrat: Senator Henry M. Jackson — A Political Biography.* Englewood Cliffs, NJ: Prentice-Hall, 1972

Purifoy, Lewis McCarroll. *Harry Truman's China Policy: McCarthyism and the Diplomacy of Hysteria, 1947–1951.* New York: New Viewpoints, 1976.

Rabinowitz, Victor. *Unrepentant Leftist: A Lawyer's Memoir.* Chicago: University of Illinois Press, 1996.

Ramsey, Norman F. "History of Defending Professor Wendell Furry and Harvard University from Attacks by Joseph McCarthy." Unpublished manuscript, December 7, 2009, courtesy of Margaret Ramsey Kasschau.

Ranville, Michael. *To Strike at a King: The Turning Point in the McCarthy Witch-Hunts.* Troy, MI: Momentum Books, 1997.

Reedy, George. *From the Ward to the White House: The Irish in American Politics.* New York: Charles Scribner's Sons, 1991.

Reeves, Thomas C. *The Life and Times of Joe McCarthy: A Biography.* New York: Stein and Day, 1982.

Reitman, Alan, ed. *The Pulse of Freedom: American Liberties, 1920–1970s.* New York: W. W. Norton, 1975.

Remy, Steven P. *The Malmedy Massacre: The War Crimes Trial Controversy.* Cambridge, MA: Harvard University Press, 2017.

Ribuffo, Leo P. *The Old Christian Right: The Protestant Far Right from the Great Depression to the Cold War.* Philadelphia: Temple University Press, 1983.

Ritchie, Donald A., ed. *Congress and Harry S. Truman: A Conflicted Legacy.* Vol. 7. Kirksville, MO: Truman State University Press, 2013.

Rogin, Michael Paul. *The Intellectuals and McCarthy: The Radical Specter.* Cambridge, MA: MIT Press, 1967.

Rosteck, Thomas. *See It Now Confronts McCarthyism.* Tuscaloosa: University of Alabama Press, 1994.

Rovere, Richard H. *Senator Joe McCarthy.* New York: Harcourt, Brace, 1959.

Rubin, Morris, *The McCarthy Record.* Madison: Wisconsin Citizens' Committee on McCarthy's Record, 1952.

Rumsfeld, Donald. *Known and Unknown: A Memoir.* New York: Sentinel, 2011.

Rusher, William A. *Special Counsel: An Inside Report on the Senate Investigations into Communism.* New Rochelle, NY: Arlington House, 1968.

Ryskind, Allan H. *Hollywood Traitors: Blacklisted Screenwriters — Agents of Stalin, Allies of Hitler.* Washington, DC: Regnery History, 2015.

Salisbury, Harrison E. *Without Fear or Favor: The New York Times and Its Times.* New York: Times Books, 1980.

Sayre, Nora. *Running Time: Films of the Cold War.* New York: Dial, 1978.

Schine, G. David. *Definition of Communism.* Placed in Schine Hotels, 1952.

Schlesinger, Arthur M., Jr. *Robert Kennedy and His Times.* Boston: Houghton Mifflin, 1978.

——. *A Thousand Days: John F. Kennedy in the White House.* Boston: Houghton Mifflin, 1965.

Schrecker, Ellen. *Many Are the Crimes: McCarthyism in America.* Boston: Little, Brown, 1998.

——. *No Ivory Tower: McCarthyism & the Universities.* New York: Oxford University Press, 1986.

Seaver, Edwin. *So Far, So Good: Recollections of a Life in Publishing.* Westport, CT: Lawrence Hill, 1986.

Shaffer, Samuel. *On and Off the Floor: Thirty Years as a Correspondent on Capitol Hill.* New York: Newsweek Books, 1980.

Sheehan, Neil. *A Fiery Peace in a Cold War: Bernard Schriever and the Ultimate Weapon.* New York: Vintage, 2010.

Shesol, Jeff. *Mutual Contempt: Lyndon Johnson, Robert Kennedy, and the Feud That Defined a Decade.* New York: W. W. Norton, 1997.

Signer, Michael. *Demagogue: The Fight to Save Democracy from Its Worst Enemies.* New York: Palgrave Macmillan, 2009.

Sirica, John J. *To Set the Record Straight: The Break-in, the Tapes, the Conspirators, the Pardon.* New York: W. W. Norton, 1979.

Smith, Jean Edward. *Eisenhower in War and Peace.* New York: Random House, 2012.

Smith, Margaret Chase. *Declaration of Conscience.* New York: Doubleday, 1972.

Sperber, A. M. *Murrow: His Life and Times.* New York: Fordham University Press, 1998.

Spillane, Mickey. *The Hammer Strikes Again: Five Complete Mike Hammer Novels.* New York: Avenel, 1951.

Stein, Jean. *American Journey: The Times of Robert Kennedy.* Edited by George Plimpton. New York: Harcourt, 1970.

Steinke, John. "The Rise of McCarthyism." Master's thesis, University of Wisconsin, 1960.

Stevenson, Adlai. *The Papers of Adlai E. Stevenson.* Vol. 2. *Washington to Springfield, 1941–1948.* Edited by Walter Johnson and Carol Evans. Boston: Little, Brown, 1973.

———. *The Papers of Adlai Stevenson.* Vol. 3. *Governor of Illinois, 1949–1953.* Edited by Walter Johnson and Carol Evans. Boston: Little, Brown, 1973.

Stone, I. F. *The Haunted Fifties, 1953–1963: A Nonconformist History of Our Times.* Boston: Little, Brown, 1963.

Storrs, Landon R. Y. *The Second Red Scare and the Unmaking of the New Deal Left.* Princeton, NJ: Princeton University Press, 2013.

Stouffer, Samuel A. *Communism, Conformity, and Civil Liberties: A Cross-Section of the Nation Speaks Its Mind.* Garden City, NY: Doubleday, 1955.

Straight, Michael. *After Long Silence.* New York: W. W. Norton, 1983.

———. *Trial by Television.* Boston: Beacon, 1954.

Sullivan, William C., with Bill Brown. *The Bureau: My 30 Years in Hoover's FBI.* New York: W. W. Norton, 1979.

Swanberg, W. A. *Luce and His Empire.* New York: Charles Scribner's Sons, 1972.

Tanenhaus, Sam. *Whittaker Chambers: A Biography.* New York: Random House, 1997.

Taylor, Telford. *Grand Inquest: The Story of Congressional Investigations.* New York: Simon & Schuster, 1955.

Thayer, Charles W. *Bears in the Caviar.* Montpelier, VT: Russian Life Books, 1950.

Theoharis, Athan. *Chasing Spies: How the FBI Failed in Counterintelligence but Promoted the Politics of McCarthyism in the Cold War Years.* Chicago: Ivan R. Dee, 2002.

———. *From the Secret Files of J. Edgar Hoover.* Chicago: Ivan R. Dee, 1993.

Thomas, Bob. *Winchell*. Garden City, NY: Doubleday, 1971.

Thomas, Evan. *Ike's Bluff: President Eisenhower's Secret Battle to Save the World*. New York: Little, Brown, 2012.

———. *Robert Kennedy: His Life*. New York: Simon & Schuster, 2000.

Thomas, Lately. *When Even Angels Wept: The Senator Joseph McCarthy Affair—A Story Without a Hero*. New York: William Morrow, 1973.

Thompson, Robert F., and Hortense Myers. *Robert F. Kennedy: The Brother Within*. New York: Macmillan, 1962.

Thompson, William F. *The History of Wisconsin*. Vol. 6. *Continuity and Change, 1940–1965*. Madison: State Historical Society of Wisconsin, 1988.

Trohan, Walter. *Political Animals: Memoirs of a Sentimental Cynic*. Garden City, NY: Doubleday, 1975.

Trow, Martin A. "Right-Wing Radicalism and Political Intolerance: A Study of Support for McCarthy in a New England Town." PhD diss., Columbia University, 1957.

Truman, Harry S. *Memoirs of Harry S. Truman*. Vol. 2. *Years of Trial and Hope*. New York: Doubleday, 1956.

Tuck, Jim. *McCarthyism and New York's Hearst Press: A Study of Roles in the Witch Hunt*. Lanham, MD: University Press of America, 1995.

US House of Representatives, Subcommittee of the Committee on Un-American Activities. *Communist Methods of Infiltration*. Washington, DC: Government Printing Office, 1953–54.

US Secretary of the Army. *Army-McCarthy Controversy: Brief Submitted by the Army, 1954*. College Park, MD: National Archives.

US Senate and House of Representatives. *Memorial Addresses Delivered in Congress*. New York: National Weekly, 1959.

———. *Memorial Services, Joseph Raymond McCarthy, Late Senator from Wisconsin*. Washington, DC: Government Printing Office, 1957.

US Senate, Permanent Subcommittee on Investigations. *Control of Trade with the Soviet Bloc*. Washington, DC: Government Printing Office, 1953.

———. *Executive Sessions*. https://archive.org/details/McCarthy-Hearing-Transcripts.

———. *State Department Information Program—Information Centers*. January 8, 1954.

US Senate, Special Committee to Investigate the Use of Mail Covers on Senator Joseph R. McCarthy or Any Other Senator. Report, December 3, 1954.

US Senate, Special Subcommittee on Investigations. *Charges and Countercharges Involving Secretary of the Army Robert T. Stevens, John G. Adams, H. Struve Hensel, Senator Joe McCarthy, Roy M. Cohn, and Francis P. Carr*. Washington, DC: Government Printing Office, 1954.

US Senate, Subcommittee of the Committee on Armed Services. *Malmedy Massacre Investigation*. Washington, DC: Government Printing Office, 1949.

US Senate, Subcommittee of the Committee on Foreign Relations. *State Department Employee Loyalty Investigation, 1950*. Washington, DC: Government Printing Office, 1950.

US Senate, Subcommittee on Privileges and Elections. *Investigations of Senators*

Joseph R. McCarthy and William Benton. Washington, DC: Government Printing Office, 1952.

——. *Maryland Senatorial Election of 1950.* Washington, DC: Government Printing Office, 1951.

Usdin, Steven T. *Bureau of Spies: The Secret Connections Between Espionage and Journalism in Washington.* Amherst, NY: Prometheus, 2018.

Utley, Freda. *Odyssey of a Liberal: Memoirs.* Washington, DC: Washington National Press, 1970.

von Hoffman, Alexander. *History Lessons for Today's Housing Policy: The Political Processes of Making Low-Income Housing Policy.* Cambridge: Joint Center for Housing Studies, Harvard University, August 2012.

von Hoffman, Nicholas. *Citizen Cohn: The Life and Times of Roy Cohn.* New York: Doubleday, 1988.

Walker, Samuel. *In Defense of American Liberties: A History of the ACLU.* New York: Oxford University Press, 1990.

Wallace, Patricia Ward. *Politics of Conscience: A Biography of Margaret Chase Smith.* Westport, CT: Praeger, 1995.

Wallerstein, Immanuel Maurice. "McCarthyism and the Conservative." Master's thesis, Columbia University, 1954.

Warren, Earl. *The Memoirs of Earl Warren.* Garden City, NY: Doubleday, 1977.

Watkins, Arthur V. *Enough Rope.* Englewood Cliffs, NJ: Prentice-Hall, 1969.

Webster, Margaret. *Don't Put Your Daughter on the Stage.* New York: Alfred A. Knopf, 1972.

Wechsler, James A. *The Age of Suspicion.* New York: Random House, 1953.

——. *Reflections of an Angry Middle-Aged Editor.* New York: Random House, 1960.

Weinstein, Allen, and Alexander Vassiliev. *The Haunted Wood: Soviet Espionage in America — The Stalin Era.* New York: Random House, 1999.

Wells, Robert W. *The Milwaukee Journal: An Informal Chronicle of Its First 100 Years.* Milwaukee: Milwaukee Journal, 1981.

Wendt, Lloyd. *Chicago Tribune: The Rise of a Great American Newspaper.* Chicago: Rand McNally, 1979.

White, Richard D., Jr. *Kingfish: The Reign of Huey P. Long.* New York: Random House, 2006.

White, William S. *Citadel: The Story of the U.S. Senate.* New York: Harper & Brothers, 1956.

Wicker, Tom. *Shooting Star: The Brief Arc of Joe McCarthy.* New York: Harcourt, 2006.

Williams, Edward Bennett. *One Man's Freedom.* New York: Atheneum, 1962.

Williams, Selma R. *Red-Listed: Haunted by the Washington Witch Hunt.* Reading, MA: Addison-Wesley, 1993.

Williams, T. Harry. *Huey Long: A Biography.* New York: Alfred A. Knopf, 1969.

Wilson, Rose Page. *General Marshall Remembered.* Englewood Cliffs, NJ: Prentice-Hall, 1968.

Winchell, Walter. *Winchell Exclusive.* Englewood Cliffs, NJ: Prentice-Hall, 1975.

Wisconsin Citizens' Committee on McCarthy's Record. *The McCarthy Record.* New York: Anglobooks, 1952.

Wolfe, Henry C. *The Imperial Soviets.* New York: Doubleday, Doran, 1940.

Woods, Jeff. *Black Struggle, Red Scare: Segregation and Anti-Communism in the South, 1948–1968.* Baton Rouge: Louisiana State University Press, 2004.

Wunderlin, Clarence E., Jr., ed. *The Papers of Robert A. Taft. Volume 4. 1949–1953.* Kent, OH: Kent State University Press, 2006.

Ybarra, Michael J. *Washington Gone Crazy: Senator Pat McCarran and the Great American Communist Hunt.* Hanover, NH: Steerforth, 2004.

Yoder, Edwin M. *Joe Alsop's Cold War: A Study of Journalistic Influence and Intrigue.* Chapel Hill: University of North Carolina Press, 1995.

ARTICLES

Abrams, George S. "Furry Denies All Present Ties with Any Red Group." *Harvard Crimson,* February 27, 1953.

Adams, Val. "Praise Pours in on Murrow Show." *New York Times,* March 11, 1954.

Agaston, Tom. "Says Commie Spy Network Extended into Ft. Monmouth." *Atlanta Daily World,* October 22, 1953.

Alexander, Jack. "The Senate's Remarkable Upstart." *Saturday Evening Post,* August 9, 1947.

Allen, Charles R., Jr., and Arthur J. Dlugoff. "McCarthy and Anti-Semitism: A Documented Exposé." *Jewish Life,* July 1953.

Alsop, Joseph, and Stewart Alsop. "Smearing Is Evil, but Whitewashing of Reds Is Worse." *Saturday Evening Post,* July 15, 1950.

——. "The Tale Half Told." *New York Herald Tribune,* March 15, 1954.

——. "Why Has Washington Gone Crazy?" *Saturday Evening Post,* July 29, 1950.

Alsop, Stewart. "Matter of Fact: Sen. McCarthy and His 'Big Three.'" *New York Herald Tribune,* March 5, 1950.

——. "Matter of Fact: We May as Well Confess." *New York Herald Tribune,* August 11, 1950.

American Weekly. "The Private Life of Senator McCarthy: Part 1." August 1953.

Appleton (WI) Post-Crescent. "The Circuit Judgeship." March 31, 1939.

——. "Controversial Senators." May 8, 1957.

——. "Joe Called 'Fallen Warrior' in Service of His Country." May 6, 1957.

——. "Joe McCarthy's Only Interest Was Welfare of Country, Sokolsky Says." May 6, 1957.

——. "Joe's Widow Breaks Silence, Criticizes NBC." February 14, 1977.

——. "Judge McCarthy Is Welcomed by Bar Association." January 5, 1940.

——. "Manawa Takes Pride in McCarthy's High School Feat." May 11, 1957.

——. "M'Carthy Takes Judicial Oath in Supreme Court." December 19, 1939.

——. "McCarthy and Pusey." July 6, 1953.

——. "McCarthy and the Davis Incident." Editorial. October 19, 1951.

——. "McCarthy Elected Judge to Succeed E. V. Werner." April 5, 1939.

——. "The McCarthy Record." Editorial. March 15, 1953.

——. "McCarthy's Attack on Dr. Pusey Termed Unfair by His Friends." July 1, 1953.

——. "No Reds on Faculty: Harvard." November 10, 1953.

——. "Resumes Judicial Duties." January 31, 1945.

——. "Senator McCarthy Will Marry Sept. 29." September 17, 1953.

——. "Strange Things Are Happening at McCarthy's Grave." February 21, 1968.

——. "This Picture Was Taken . . ." May 3, 1957.

——. "U.S. Marines Give Judge McCarthy Inactive Status." January 26, 1945.

Arendt, Hannah. "The Ex-Communists." *Commonweal,* March 1953.

Associated Press. "Joe McCarthy Morphine Addict, Columnist Claims." November 21, 1978.

——. "State Dept. Hired Reds Solon Says." February 11, 1950.

——. Transcript of Joe McCarthy–Hank Greenspun confrontation at War Memorial Building in Las Vegas. *Nevada News Digest,* October 13, 1952.

Atlantic. "The Atlantic Report on the World Today: Washington." July 1950.

Atlas, James. "Ways to Look at the Past (Or Did It Really Happen?)." *New York Times,* November 13, 1994.

Auletta, Ken. "Don't Mess with Roy Cohn." *Esquire,* December 1978.

Bach, Morten, and Korcaighe Hale. "'What He Is Speaks So Loud That I Can't Hear What He's Saying': R. W. Scott McLeod and the Long Shadow of Joe McCarthy." *Historian,* Spring 2010.

Bachrach, Judy. "Louise Ansberry: A Tale of Changes." *Washington Post,* February 17, 1975.

Bailey, B. C. "10 Decisive Demagogues Through History." https://listverse.com/2016/03/12/10-divisive-demagogues-throughout-history/.

Baker, Richard T. "Inquiry's TV Rating Is Behind Kefauver's." *New York Times,* April 23, 1954.

Balliet, David. "I'll Miss Joe McCarthy." *Chicago Daily Tribune,* June 30, 1957.

Balluck, Kyle. "Trump: Mueller Makes Joseph McCarthy Look Like a 'Baby.'" *The Hill,* August 19, 2018.

Baltimore Sun. "McMillan Asks How McCarthy Got His Letter." March 18, 1952.

Barbas, Samantha. "Dorothy Kenyon and the Making of Modern Legal Feminism." *Stanford Journal of Civil Rights and Liberties* 5 (2009).

Barry, Donald. "Cleared or Covered Up?" *International Journal* 66, No. 1 (2010–11).

Beale, Betty. "Exclusively Yours." *Washington Evening Star,* September 30, 1953.

Bean, Louis H. "The Myth of McCarthy's Strength." *Look,* June 1954.

Beichman, Arnold. "The Politics of Personal Self-Destruction: Stevenson and McCarthy as Anti-Leaders." *Policy Review,* February–March 2006.

Bellah, Robert H. "McCarthyism at Harvard." *New York Review of Books,* February 10, 2005.

Benton, William. "Book Ban Protested." *New York Times,* June 28, 1953.

Berinsky, Adam J., and Gabriel S. Lenz. "Red Scare? Revisiting Joe McCarthy's Influence on 1950 Elections." *Public Opinion Quarterly,* January 1, 2014.

Berkeley Daily Gazette. "Harvard Daily Tells Solon to Prove Charge." November 7, 1953.

——. "'Smelly Mess' at Harvard Charged by Sen. McCarthy." November 5, 1953.

Berkshire Eagle. "Maj. Gen. Miles Reber, 74, Witness at McCarthy Hearing." November 24, 1976.

Bernstein, Barton. "The Oppenheimer Loyalty-Security Case Reconsidered." *Stanford Law Review* 42, No. 6 (July 1990).

Beth, Loren P. "McCarthyism." *South Atlantic Quarterly,* January 1, 1956.

Billboard. "Red Plot on Bubble Gum — Or Much Ado." January 26, 1952.

Biselx, E. L. "McCarthy Is Working Hard but He Likes It." *Appleton Post-Crescent,* August 15, 1947.

Blair, William M. "Senate Studies 1952 Check Made on Mail of McCarthy." *New York Times,* December 2, 1954.

Blumenthal, Ralph. "When Suspicion of Teachers Ran Unchecked in New York." *New York Times,* June 16, 2009.

Borger, Julian. "The Spy Who Made McCarthy." *Guardian,* January 26, 1999.

Boston Daily Globe. "Fisher Defended by Newton's GOP Chairman." June 10, 1954.

——. "McCarthy, Welch Exchange on Fisher." June 10, 1954.

Boston Globe. "C. George Anastos, 76; Was Judge in Nantucket District Court." December 28, 1993.

——. "West Must Join Arms to Stop Reds — Acheson." May 31, 1950.

Brady, Thomas F. "Cloak of Secrecy in London." *New York Times,* June 22, 1953.

Breslin, Jimmy. "Ed Murrow." *New York Herald Tribune,* April 28, 1965.

Brinkley, Bill. "Fredric March Had Tears in His Eyes on 'Daily Worker' Criticism." *Washington Post,* June 9, 1949.

Brooker, Dave. "Joe, Tired but Happy, Pleased with Republican Victory, Benton's Defeat." *Appleton Post-Crescent,* November 5, 1952.

Brownfeld, Gail, and Peter Hennessy. "Britain's Cold War Security Purge: The Origins of Positive Vetting." *Historical Journal,* December 1982.

Bryan, Ferald J. "Joseph McCarthy, Robert Kennedy, and the Greek Shipping Crisis." *Presidential Studies Quarterly,* Winter 1994.

Buder, Leonard. "'Refuse to Testify,' Einstein Advises Intellectuals Called in by Congress." *New York Times,* June 12, 1953.

Bulletin of the Atomic Scientists. "Fort Monmouth One Year Later." April 1955.

Business Week. "The Greeks, the Senator, and the Slump." April 11, 1953.

Cahoe, Tom L. "McCarthy: Old Friend Is as Loyal as Ever." *Appleton Post-Crescent,* July 28, 1990.

Caldwell, H. William. "Pvt. Schine's Famous Pamphlet." *New Leader,* May 24, 1954.

Callahan, John P. "13 Books Removed in Karachi." *New York Times,* June 22, 1953.

Capital Times (Madison). "Budenz Says He 'Was Told' by Red Leaders Lattimore Was a Communist Cell Member." April 20, 1950.

——. "Lattimore, Accused by McCarthy as Red, Calls Charges 'Moonshine.'" March 27, 1953.

——. "Lustron Check to McCarthy in Court File." June 16, 1950.

——. "Malmedy Survivor Says McCarthy 'Dupe' of Reds in Defending SS Troops." February 16, 1951.

——. "M'Carthy Got $28,947 in '48: Paid No State Tax; Claims 'Losses.'" April 21, 1950.

——. "McCarthy Flays Bob's Farm Record." June 13, 1946.

——. "Top Leaders of AVC Rush to Defend Vets' Unit from 'Red' Charge." June 30, 1946.

Castonia, Don. "McCarthy the Man." *Appleton Post-Crescent,* May 1, 1977.

Cater, Douglass. "The Captive Press." *The Reporter,* June 6, 1950.

——. "Is McCarthy Slipping?" *The Reporter,* September 18, 1951.

Ceplair, Larry. "McCarthy Revisited." *Historical Journal of Film, Radio and Television,* August 2008.

Cheney, Lynne V. "The End of History." *Wall Street Journal,* October 20, 1994.

Chicago Daily Tribune. "Briton Hits Cry of M'Carthyism as Red Tactic." April 13, 1953.

——. "Lauds McCarthy in Wisconsin Legislature." May 4, 1957.

——. "M'Carthy Names 4 He Says Are Linked to Reds." February 13, 1950.

——. "M'Carthy Raps Truman Order to 7th Fleet." June 23, 1952.

——. "McCarthy and Zwicker." February 25, 1954.

——. "McCarthy 'Spy' Is Branded 'Pig' by Swiss Reds." October 16, 1951.

——. "Record Lists McCarthy Age as 48, Not 47." May 4, 1957.

——. "Senator McCarthy and the World." December 26, 1946.

——. "Sen. McCarthy Writes Book About Sino-Japanese War." September 23, 1956.

——. "State Senate Hails Service of M'Carthy." May 14, 1957.

——. "Tribute Paid to M'Carthy's Fighting Spirit." May 3, 1957.

——. "Truman Thinks Sen. Taft Won't Get Nomination." July 10, 1952.

——. "U.S. Policy Aids Reds in Korea, M'Carthy Finds." October 21, 1952.

——. "A Valiant Fighter." May 4, 1957.

Chicago Tribune. "Anna Rosenberg No. 2; May Solve Mystery." December 20, 1950.

——. "It's a Baby Girl for the McCarthy's — But by Adoption." January 14, 1957.

——. "Voice Worker's Mystery Death Ruled Suicide." March 6, 1953.

Childs, Marquis. "Attitude Toward U.S." *Washington Post,* March 4, 1954.

——. "Independent Lady from New England." *Washington Post,* August 18, 1953.

——. "McCarthy Letter Contents Revealed." *Washington Post,* June 2, 1953.

——. "Smears and Tears Plague the Senate." *Washington Post,* June 30, 1954.

——. "Washington Calling: Dangerous Drift." *Washington Post,* December 6, 1946.

Christian Science Monitor. "Letter to Wife Disclosed from 'Voice' Aide Suicide." March 7, 1953.

——. "They Just Love It." February 4, 1952.

CIO News. "HST Slaps McCarthy as Pathological Character Assassin." February 4, 1952.

Code, Dozier C. "Witch-Hunting, 1952: The Role of the Press." *Journalism Quarterly* (Los Angeles), December 1952.

Cogley, John. "The Murrow Show." *Commonweal,* March 26, 1954.

Cohen, Richard. "Trump Is Our Modern-Day McCarthy." *Washington Post,* February 5, 2018.

Collier's Weekly. "Why Not Spank Him?" August 1951.

Columbia Daily Spectator. "Reed Harris Expelled in '32 for His 'Explosive' Editorials." April 5, 1951.

——. "Steadfast Educators." November 10, 1953.

Commonweal. "The McCarthy Question." November 16, 1973.

Congressional Quarterly Almanac. "On the Record 1951." 1951.

Conklin, William R. "M'Carthy to Call Perl, Greenglass." *New York Times,* October 28, 1953.

——. "'More Than 12' Out in Radar Spy Case." *New York Times,* October 21, 1953.

Connaughton, John D. "Mr. McCarthy Commended." Letter to the editor. *New York Times,* March 12, 1954.

Connolly, Mike. "Rambling Reporter." *Hollywood Reporter,* May 1957.

Connors, Edward. "McCarthy Blasts State Department." *Nevada State Journal,* February 12, 1950.

——. "'Red' Allegation Gets Sharp Reply." *Nevada State Journal,* February 12, 1950.

Conroy, Sarah Booth. "A Career in Step with History." *Washington Post,* October 20, 1997.

Corddry, Charles. "No Argument, McCarthy and Wilson Say." *Washington Post,* March 11, 1954.

Cosmopolitan. "Senator McCarthy Answers Some Important Questions." May 1952.

Coulter, Ann. "McCarthyism: The Rosetta Stone of Liberal Lies." *Human Events,* November 7, 2007.

Crosby, John. "The Aroma of Decency." *New York Herald Tribune,* March 19, 1954.

Currivan, Gene. "Teachers Bar Reds from Their Ranks." *New York Times,* November 25, 1953.

Daily Cardinal (University of Wisconsin). "Applause, Boos Greet McCarthy's Attack on 'Clique.'" May 15, 1951.

Daniel, Barry M. "The 'Loss' of China and American Politics: The Case of John Carter Vincent." *Selected Papers in Asian Studies: Western Conference for the Association for Asian Studies,* June 2016.

Daniel, Clifton. "British Defend Stand on Trade with China." *New York Times.* May 24, 1953.

Darsey, James. "Joe McCarthy's Fantastic Moment." *Communications Monograph* 62, No. 1 (March 1995).

Davis, Alvin. "'Joe Is Doing the Job,' Says Texas 'Angel.'" *New York Post,* July 7, 1953.

Dear, Joseph A. "Comments from Nation's Capitol." *Elizabeth City (NC) Daily Advance,* February 26, 1954.

De Santis, Vincent P. "American Catholics and McCarthyism." *Catholic Historical Review* 51, No. 1 (April 1965).

Desmond, Frank. "M'Carthy Charges Reds Holding US Offices." *Wheeling Intelligencer,* February 10, 1950.

De Toledano, Nora. "Time Marches on McCarthy." *American Mercury* 74, No. 338 (February 1952).

Dorworth, Dick. "Integrity: In Praise of Rockwell Kent." *Idaho Mountain Express and Guide,* October 6–22, 2002.

Doty, Robert C. "10 Volumes Banned in Cairo." *New York Times,* June 22, 1953.

Douglas, William O. "The Black Silence of Fear." *New York Times,* January 13, 1952.

Drummey, James J. "McCarthy: The Truth, the Smear, and the Lesson." *American Opinion,* May 1964.

———. "McCarthyism: Forty Questions and Answers about Senator Joseph McCarthy." *New American,* May 11, 1987.

Drury, Allen. "M'Carthy Rites Held in Capital: 4,000 at Green Bay." *New York Times,* May 7, 1957.

Dulles, Eleanor Lansing. "Footnote to History: A Day in the Life of Senator Joe McCarthy." *World Affairs* 143, No. 2 (Fall 1980).

Dulles, John Foster. "Memorandum by the Secretary of State in the Matter of John Carter Vincent." *Foreign Service Journal* 30, No. 4 (April 1953).

Dwyer, Colin. "Donald Trump: 'I Could . . . Shoot Somebody, and I Wouldn't Lose Any Voters.'" npr.org, January 23, 2016.

Earley, Pete. "5 Decades Later, Renegade Wants Diploma." *Washington Post,* April 17, 1981.

Edwards, Willard. "Bare Hunt for Radar Spies: Army Fires 5; 30 More Face Security Quiz." *Chicago Daily Tribune,* October 7, 1953.

———. "Bare New Data in the Remington Loyalty Case." *Chicago Daily Tribune,* April 27, 1950.

———. "M'Carthy Quits Honeymoon Key for Spy Probe." *Chicago Daily Tribune,* October 10, 1953.

———. Ten-part series on communist infiltration of the U.S. government. *Chicago Daily Tribune,* February 5–14, 1950.

Egan, Charles E. "Flanders' Motion to Curb M'Carthy Hit by Knowland." *New York Times,* June 13, 1954.

Ehrmann, Peter N. "Good Ol' Joe." *Milwaukee Journal,* March 20, 1977.

Eisenhower, Dwight D. "We Must Avoid the Perils of Extremism." *Reader's Digest* 94, No. 564 (April 1969).

Eklund, Laurence C. "Joe McCarthy in Kennedy's Past." *Milwaukee Journal,* May 20, 1968.

———. "Work Is McCarthy's Formula for Success." *Milwaukee Journal,* November 10, 1946.

Elko (NV) Daily Free Press. "Why Didn't You Reprint This Editorial, Mr. Greenspun?" October 16, 1952.

Elson, John. "History, the Sequel." *Time,* November 7, 1994.

Evans, M. Stanton. "Bonus! Wall Street Journal Stonewalls on McCarthy." AnnCoulter.com, May 13, 2008.

——. "How Senate Historian Botched Data on McCarthy." *Human Events,* May 23, 2003.

——. "Mainstream Media Try to Burn a Book." Accuracy in Media, June 24, 2008.

——. "A Response to Ron Radosh by M. Stanton Evans." Ruthfullyyours.com, September 8, 2013.

Everett, Arthur. "McCarthy Names Rosenberg as 'Brain' of Radar Spy Ring." *Washington Post,* October 16, 1953.

Evjue, William T. "Joe McCarthy in Wisconsin." *The Nation,* April 5, 1952.

Ewig, Rick. "McCarthy Era Politics: The Ordeal of Senator Lester Hunt." *Annals of Wyoming* 55 (Spring 1983).

Fast, Howard. "Нас ожидает большая борьба" ["A Great Struggle Awaits Us"]. *Pravda,* December 30, 1953.

Federal Bureau of Investigation. "Membership of the Communist Party, 1919–1954." May 1955.

Feinsinger, N. P. "Divorce Law and Administration in England." *Wisconsin Law Review,* June 1, 1934.

Fellman, David. "Constitutional Law in 1956–1957." *American Political Science Review* 52, No. 1 (March 1958).

Fenton, John H. "M'Carthy: Certain Red Cell Is at G.E." *New York Times,* November 19, 1953.

Ferguson, J. D. "Letter to FM Trickey." *Milwaukee Journal,* December 14, 1953.

Fessenden, Donald. "Sears, Foe of Reds, Praised McCarthy." *Boston Herald,* April 2, 1954.

Fiedler, Leslie A. "McCarthy." *Encounter,* August 1954.

Fisher, John. "Reds Still Prey on U.S., Says McCarthy." *Chicago Daily Tribune,* January 25, 1954.

——. "2 Profs Name Fellow Reds at Harvard, M.I.T." *Chicago Tribune,* April 23, 1953.

Flegenheimer, Matt, and Jonathan Mahler. "McCarthy Aide Helped Shape Young Trump." *New York Times,* June 21, 2016.

Fleming, Dewey L. "Report Stirs McCarthy Ire." *Baltimore Sun,* August 4, 1951.

Fleming, Robert H. "McCarthy War Injury? Just Felled by a Bucket." *Milwaukee Journal,* June 8, 1952.

——. "Truman Tipsy, Senator Hints." *Milwaukee Journal,* April 12, 1951.

Folliard, Edward T. "Fair Play Plea Draws Attack on 'Army Brass.'" *Washington Post,* March 4, 1954.

——. "The Partnership of Cohn & Schine." *Washington Post and Times Herald,* March 21, 1954.

Foster, Herbert. "McCarthy, Ike Dispute McLeod Shift." *Washington Post,* March 4, 1954.

Fried, Richard M. "The Idea of Conspiracy in McCarthy-Era Politics." *Prologue,* Spring 2002.

Friedman, Andrea. "The Strange Career of Annie Lee Moss: Rethinking Race,

Gender, and McCarthyism." *Journal of American History* 94, No. 2 (September 2007).

Friendly, Alfred. "Loyalty Files Denied Probe by Truman." *Washington Post,* March 29, 1950.

———. "McCarthy to Fight Reds Despite Attacks." *Washington Post,* June 3, 1950.

———. "The Noble Crusade of Senator McCarthy." *Harper's,* August 1950.

———. "'Top Red Agent' Left U.S. Job 5 Years Ago, Tydings Asserts." *Washington Post,* March 24, 1950.

Frosh, Stanley. "The McCarthy Era Begins." Undated essay provided by Frosh's children.

Furman, Bess. "M'Carthy Pledges Housing Aid Speed." *New York Times,* September 3, 1947.

Fyodorov, D. "'Схватка' Маккарти с генералами" ["McCarthy's 'Skirmishes' with the Generals"]. *Pravda,* September 13, 1953.

Gallup, George. "McCarthy's Popularity Up 16% Since August 1953 to 50%." *Washington Post,* January 5, 1954.

———. "More Disapprove of Methods of McCarthy Than Approve." *Washington Post,* January 16, 1954.

Gauger, Michael. "Flickering Images: Live Television Coverage and Viewership of the Army-McCarthy Hearings." *Historian* 67, No. 4 (Winter 2005).

Getter, Doyle. "M'Carthy Vote on Gas Bill Upsets Wisconsin Backers." *New York Times,* February 19, 1956.

Ghiglione, Loren. "Back to the Future—Questions for the News Media from the Past." *Law and Contemporary Problems* 71 No. 4 (Fall 2008).

Gibney, Frank. "After the Ball." *Commonweal* 60 (September 3, 1954).

Gibson, James L. "Political Intolerance and Political Repression During the McCarthy Red Scare." *American Political Science Review* 82, No. 2 (June 1988).

Glazer, Nathan. "The Method of Senator McCarthy: Its Origins, Its Uses, and Its Prospects." *Commentary,* January–June 1953.

Glazer, Nathan, Anthony Lewis, and Sam Tanenhaus. "'Have You No Sense of Decency?' McCarthyism 50 Years Later." *Bulletin of the American Academy of Arts & Sciences* 57, No. 3 (Spring 2004).

Gold, Vic. "McCarthy Without Paranoia." *Washingtonian,* February 1981.

Goldstein, Richard. "John Eisenhower, Military Historian and Son of the President, Dies at 91." *New York Times,* December 23, 2013.

Gore, Leroy. "Wisconsin Doesn't Have to Wait Four Long Years." *Sauk-Prairie (WI) Star,* March 18, 1954.

Gottlieb, Martin. "New York Court Disbars Roy Cohn on Charges of Unethical Conduct." *New York Times,* June 24, 1986.

Gould, Jack. "'Bootleg' Record of Canadian Program Parodying McCarthy On Sale Here." *New York Times,* December 31, 1954.

———. "Cutting Reed Harris Off in Middle of Rebuttal to Charges in 'Voice' Inquiry Called Disgraceful." *New York Times,* March 6, 1953.

———. "Radio in Review." *New York Times,* December 31, 1954.

———. "Television in Review: Murrow Versus McCarthy." *New York Times,* March 11, 1954.

Green, Glenn M. "FBI 'Covers' 4400 Reds in America." *Deseret News,* February 12, 1950.

Green Bay Press-Gazette. "Ask Badger Plaudit for Foes of Joe." January 19, 1955.

——. "Capt. McCarthy Is the Type." March 21, 1944.

——. "Hall Seeks to Smooth Controversy on Probes." March 4, 1954.

——. "M'Carthy New Circuit Judge." April 5, 1939.

——. "McCarthy Hints Probe of F.C.C." November 29, 1952.

——. "McCarthy's Statement on Communism and the Capital Times Published in Full." November 14, 1949.

——. "Sen. McCarthy Refuses to See Journal Men." May 10, 1954.

Greenspun, Hank. "McCarthy Willing to Compromise." *Las Vegas Sun,* January 8, 1954.

——. "Secret Lives of Joe McCarthy." *Rave,* June 1954.

Greenstein, Fred I. "'The Hidden-Hand Presidency: Eisenhower as Leader,' a 1994 Perspective." *Presidential Studies Quarterly* 24, No. 2 (Spring 1994).

Grigorovich, V. "Чем расстроен сенатор Маккарти?" ["What Disturbs Senator McCarthy?"]. *Pravda,* October 19, 1953.

Grutzner, Charles. "Army Drops Clerk M'Carthy Accused." *New York Times,* September 17, 1953.

——. "Senate Red Inquiry 'Visitor' Put on Stand as Spy Suspect." *New York Times,* September 26, 1952.

Haberman, Frederick W. "Views on the Army-McCarthy Hearings." *Quarterly Journal of Speech* 41 (February 1955).

Hale, William Harlan. "'Big Brother' in Foggy Bottom." *The Reporter,* August 17, 1954.

Hance, Donna. "Judge Werner Dies Suddenly." *Wittenberg (WI) Enterprise,* May 4, 1944.

Hand, Learned. "A Plea for the Freedom of Dissent." *New York Times,* February 6, 1955.

Hansler, Jennifer. "Trump Compares Mueller Probe to McCarthyism." CNN, August 19, 2018.

Harris, Eleanor. "The Private Life of Senator McCarthy." *American Weekly,* August 16, 1953.

Harris, John. "McCarthy Cruel, Reckless — Welch: Attack on Associate Fires Lawyer's Wrath." *Boston Globe,* June 10, 1954.

——. "McCarthy Takes a Dim View of Pusey." *Boston Daily Globe,* July 1, 1953.

Hart, Hornell. "McCarthyism Versus Democracy." *New Republic,* February 25, 1952.

Harvard Crimson. "Ex–Law Teacher, Aide to UN's Lie, Commits Suicide." November 14, 1952.

——. "F. O. Matthiessen Plunges to Death from Hotel Window." April 1, 1950.

——. "Furry, Kamin Set to Testify for McCarthy." January 15, 1954.

——. "Furry to Testify Before McCarthy, TV on Friday." January 14, 1954.

——. "Schine at Harvard: Boy with the Baton." May 7, 1954.

——. "Wendell Furry." January 22, 1954.

Havemann, Ernest. "War and Politics." *Life,* August 28, 1950.

Haynes, John Earl. "McCarthy, According to Evans (and Novak)." *Washington Decoded,* December 11, 2007.

———. "Was Harry Hawkins a Soviet Spy?" *Front Page Magazine,* August 15, 2013.

Hearst, William Randolph, Jr. "McCarthy's Death Saddens Millions." *Milwaukee Sentinel,* May 5, 1957.

Hennessy, Peter, and Gail Brownfeld. "Britain's Cold War Security Purge." *Historical Journal* 24, No. 4 (December 1982).

Herberg, Will. "McCarthy and Hitler: A Delusive Parallel." *New Republic,* August 23, 1954.

Hercher, Wilmot. "Note to Wife Indicates 'Voice' Engineer Took His Life for Fear of Being Made a Scapegoat for Any Mistakes." *Washington Post,* March 7, 1953.

Hess, Karl, III. "UN as a Red Weapon." *Pathfinder,* September 21, 1949.

Hickok, Dan. "M'Carthy Had Meteoric Rise." *Green Bay Press-Gazette,* April 7, 1939.

Hill, Gladwin. "Librarian Opposes Controls on Ideas." *New York Times,* June 23, 1953.

History Is Now. "A Rocky Relationship—Eleanor Roosevelt and Senator John F. Kennedy." January 2017.

Hohmann, James. "The Daily 202: Koch Network Warns of 'McCarthyism 2.0' in Conservative Efforts to Harass Professors." *Washington Post,* August 1, 2018.

Hollywood Reporter. "Rambling Reporter." May 1957.

Hook, Sydney. "The Fifth Amendment—A Moral Issue." *New York Times,* November 1, 1953.

Horton, Philip. "Voices Within the Voice." *The Reporter,* July 21, 1953.

Hovey, Graham. "Both McCarthy and His Foes Get Jolt." *Washington Post,* October 14, 1951.

———. "How McCarthy Sold Wisconsin." *New Republic,* September 1952.

Hoving, John. "My Friend McCarthy." *The Reporter,* April 25, 1950.

Howard, Robert. "Truman Offer 'Phony,' Says Sen. McCarthy." *Chicago Daily Tribune,* July 7, 1950.

Hulten, Charles M. "The Impact of Senator Joseph McCarthy on the Press of the United States." *International Communication Gazette,* February 1958.

Human Events. "'Liberals' and Communists." June 3, 1953.

Huston, Luther A. "Printing Official Doubts Spy Leaks." *New York Times,* August 22, 1953.

———. "U.S. Printing Aide Silent at Inquiry." *New York Times,* August 19, 1953.

Ickes, Harold L. "McCarthy Strips Himself." *New Republic,* August 7, 1950.

———. "Not Guilty—You're Fired!" November 5, 1951.

Israels, Josef, II. "Mrs. Fix-It." *Saturday Evening Post,* October 16, 1943.

Izvestia. "Политический цирк в Вашингтоне" ["Political Circus in Washington"]. March 26, 1950.

———. "Министерство юстиции США прекратило расследование махинаций Маккарти" ["U.S. Department of Justice Halts Investigation of McCarthy's Machinations"]. October 24, 1953.

Jacobs, Paul. "Extracurricular Activities of the McClellan Committee." *California Law Review* 51, No. 2 (May 1963).

Jahoda, Marie. "Morale in the Federal Civil Service." *Annals of the American Academy of Political and Social Science* 300, No. 1 (July 1, 1955).

Janesville (WI) Daily Gazette. "Butler Manager Is Fined $5,000." June 5, 1951.

Jensen, Elizabeth. "Remembering a Forgotten Newsman." *New York Times,* October 18, 2008.

Johnson, Gerald. "Murrow, McCarthy and the 'Booboisie.'" *New Republic,* April 19, 1954.

Johnston, Richard J. H. "M'Carthy Buried Beside Parents." *New York Times,* May 8, 1957.

––––––. "M'Carthy Repeats Charges: He Says Stevenson Is in Intrigue to Hand U.S. Over to Reds." *New York Times,* November 4, 1952.

––––––. "McCarthy Terms It 'Lying.'" *New York Times,* November 3, 1952.

Jones, David R. "H. L. Hunt: Magnate with Mission." *New York Times,* August 17, 1964.

Kaghan, Theodore. "The McCarthyization of Theodore Kaghan." *The Reporter,* July 21, 1953.

Kanady, Jonathan. "Kohler Blocks Smear Move by McCarthy Foes." *Chicago Daily Tribune,* July 20, 1951.

Kansas City Star. "A Cadillac to McCarthy." August 1, 1953.

Kaplan, Morris. "Monmouth Report on Bias Revealed." *New York Times,* August 27, 1954.

––––––. "Rabbi Benjamin Schultz, Crusader Against Communist Infiltration." *New York Times,* April 25, 1978.

Karney, Rex. "The Story of Joe McCarthy." Five-part series. *Wisconsin State Journal,* July 16–20, 1946.

Katz, James C. "Confrontation with McCarthy." *Columbia College Today,* Fall 1983.

Kelso, John. "Chairman of Past Red Probes Became Top Target of Smears." *Boston Post,* April 4, 1954.

––––––. "Robert Kennedy, Senator's Brother, Factor in Greek Ship Agreement." *Boston Sunday Post,* April 12, 1953.

Kennedy, Paul P. "Loyalty Case Won by Mrs. Keyserling." *New York Times,* January 10, 1953.

Kessler, Ronald. "The Real Story on Joe McCarthy." *Newsmax,* April 7, 2008.

Kihss, Peter. "Army Acts to Oust Monmouth Expert." *New York Times,* June 6, 1954.

––––––. "Army Drops Guard Called Pro-Stalin." *New York Times,* September 3, 1953.

––––––. "H-Bomb Held Back, M'Carthy Asserts." *New York Times,* April 7, 1954.

––––––. "M'Carthy Accuses 2 Army Employees." *New York Times,* September 1, 1953.

––––––. "M'Carthy 'Orders' Army Bare Files." *New York Times,* September 2, 1953.

––––––. "Monmouth Aides Reply to Charges." *New York Times,* January 13, 1954.

––––––. "Monmouth Expert Barred in Key Job." *New York Times,* January 12, 1954.

———. "Monmouth Security Woes Antedate McCarthy Visits." *New York Times,* January 11, 1954.

———. "Witness Is Silent on Current Spying." *New York Times,* November 25, 1953.

Kinsler, Jeffrey S. "Joseph McCarthy the Law Student." *Marquette Law Review* 85, No. 2 (Winter 2001).

Kirby, Alec. "A Major Contender: Harold Stassen and the Politics of American Presidential Nominations." *Minnesota History Magazine* 55, No. 4 (Winter 1996–97).

Knight, Charlotte. "What Price Security?" *Collier's,* July 9, 1954.

Knowles, Clayton. "Misuse of Secrets Laid to Radar Man." *New York Times,* December 10, 1953.

Koch, Cynthia M. "Demagogues and Democracy." Franklin Delano Roosevelt Foundation, Harvard College, February 10, 2018.

Kokomo Tribune. "Sen. McCarthy Hurls Charge at Acheson." June 9, 1950.

Krajicek, David J. "Journalist Went Out in Front-Page Fashion with Murder-Suicide." *New York Daily News,* April 23, 2016.

Krebs, Albin. "Roy Cohn, Aide to McCarthy and Fiery Lawyer, Dies at 59." *New York Times,* August 3, 1986.

Krock, Arthur. "In the Nation: Some Damage to the G.O.P. Is Now Inevitable." *New York Times,* August 6, 1954.

———. "Large Trade with China by the U.N. Members Shown." *New York Times,* July 19, 1953.

Kruse, Michael. "Trump's Strange Tweet About Joseph McCarthy." *Politico,* August 19, 2018.

Lambert, Bruce. "Doxey Wilkerson Is Dead at 88; Educator and Advocate for Rights." *New York Times,* June 18, 1993.

Lasky, Victor. "The Gal Who Married Joe McCarthy." Unpublished article, Marquette University Archives.

Lawrence, David. "McCarthy Seen Leaving a Legacy of Controversy." *New York Herald Tribune,* May 6, 1957.

Lawrence, W. H. "Army Charges M'Carthy and Cohn Threatened It in Trying to Obtain Preferred Treatment for Schine." *New York Times,* March 12, 1954.

———. "Cohn Threatens to 'Get' Senator for Gibe at Schine." *New York Times,* June 12, 1954.

———. "M'Carthy Charges Army 'Blackmail,' Says Stevens Sought Deal with Him." *New York Times,* March 13, 1954.

———. "M'Carthy Hearing Will Start Today." *New York Times,* April 22, 1954.

———. "M'Carthy Hearings End on 36th Day as Potter Suggests Perjury Action, Removal of Top Aides on Both Sides." *New York Times,* June 18, 1954.

———. "M'Carthy Is Dead of Liver Ailment at the Age of 47." *New York Times,* May 3, 1957.

———. "M'Carthy on Defensive in His Biggest Fight." *New York Times,* March 14, 1954.

———. "M'Carthy Strives 'to Shatter' G.O.P., Flanders Asserts." *New York Times,* March 10, 1954.

——. "M'Carthy to Shun Inquiry Till Group Acts in News 'Leak.'" *New York Times,* April 16, 1954.

——. "M'Carthy, Wilson in Accord on Reds." *New York Times,* March 11, 1954.

——. "McCarthy Hearing Off a Week as Eisenhower Bars Report." *New York Times,* May 18, 1954.

——. "Mundt Will Direct Senate Unit Study of M'Carthy Fight." *New York Times,* March 17, 1954.

——. "Nixon Says 'Questionable Methods' and 'Reckless Talk' of Red Hunters Are Diversion from G.O.P. Program." *New York Times,* March 14, 1954.

——. "President Opposes M'Carthy as Judge in His Own Dispute." *New York Times,* March 25, 1954.

——. "Senators Seek to Determine Just What Work Schine Did." *New York Times,* May 29, 1954.

——. "Stevens a Target." *New York Times,* March 12, 1954.

——. "Stevenson Defends Truman, Accusing G.O.P. of 'Slander.'" *New York Times,* November 25, 1953.

——. "Stevens Swears M'Carthy Falsified, Lays 'Perversion of Power' to Him." *New York Times,* April 23, 1954.

——. "U.S. Public Affairs Officer in Germany Was Target of McCarthy Inquiry." *New York Times,* May 12, 1953.

——. "Welch Assails M'Carthy's 'Cruelty' and 'Recklessness' in Attack on Aide." *New York Times,* June 10, 1954.

Legal Aid Review. "The Hughes Case." Spring 1956.

Lemann, Nicholas. "The Murrow Doctrine: Why the Life and Times of the Broadcast Pioneer Still Matter." *New Yorker,* January 2006.

Leslie, Larry Z. "Newspaper Photo Coverage of Censure of McCarthy." *Journalism Quarterly* 63 (Winter 1986).

Leviero, Anthony. "Committee Urges M'Carthy Censure." *New York Times,* September 28, 1954.

——. "Each Side Limited: Wisconsinite on Floor, Rues Some Language Stands on Views." *New York Times,* November 30, 1954.

——. "Eisenhower Backed on Book Ban Talk." *New York Times,* June 17, 1953.

——. "Final Vote Condemns M'Carthy, 67–22." *New York Times,* December 3, 1954.

——. "Flanders Calls M'Carthy '5th Amendment Senator' as Censure Debate Opens." *New York Times,* July 31, 1954.

——. "M'Carthy Breaks with Eisenhower." *New York Times,* December 8, 1954.

——. "M'Carthy Defends His 'Right' to Use Secret Document." *New York Times,* September 12, 1954.

——. "New Inquiry Is On." *New York Times,* September 1, 1954.

——. "President Implies M'Carthy Is Peril to Unity of G.O.P." *New York Times,* March 11, 1954.

——. "Session of Senate on M'Carthy Opens in Angry Wrangle." *New York Times,* November 9, 1954.

——. "6 Senators Named as a Select Panel in M'Carthy Case." *New York Times,* August 6, 1954.

——. "Streibert Named Information Chief." *New York Times,* July 31, 1953.

——. "Watkins Demands Senate Enlarge M'Carthy Censure." *New York Times,* November 17, 1954.

Levinson, Francis. "'Aunt Anna' Captures Pentagon." *New York Times,* March 18, 1951.

Lichtman, Robert M. "Louis Budenz, the FBI, and the 'List of 400 Concealed Communists': An Extended Tale of McCarthy-Era Informing." *American Communist History* 3, No. 1 (June 2004).

Lichtman, Robert M., and Ronald D. Cohen. "Harvey Matusow, the FBI, and the Justice Department: Becoming a Government Informer-Witness in the McCarthy Era." *American Communist History* 1 (June 2002).

Life. "The Battle of Loyalties." April 10, 1950.

——. "The Men McCarthy Made Famous." May 17, 1954.

——. "A Mobilization for McCarthy." November 1954.

——. "A Pretty Researcher Marries Her Boss." October 12, 1953.

——. "Recalling All Liberals to the Real Fight." September 8, 1952.

——. "Taft and McCarthy." October 1, 1951.

Lippmann, Walter. "Our National Obsession." *Washington Post,* March 25, 1954.

——. "A Review of the Brownell-Truman-McCarthy Episode." *Louisville Times,* December 22, 1953.

——. "Today and Tomorrow: Terrorists and Spies." *Washington Post.* March 4, 1954.

——. "Today and Tomorrow: The McCarthy-Stevens Affair." *Washington Post,* March 1, 1954.

Lissner, Will. "Columbia Is Dropping Dr. Weltfish, Leftists." *New York Times,* April 1, 1953.

Loeb, William. "MURDERED!" *Manchester Union Leader,* May 3, 1957.

Loftus, Joseph A. "Labor Bids Made." *New York Times,* December 6, 1946.

——. "White House Charges M'Carthy Bid to Get Secret Data Is Usurpation; Hearing in Turmoil over Schine File." *New York Times,* May 29, 1954.

Long Beach Press. "Harvard Chief Takes Issue with McCarthy." November 10, 1953.

Los Angeles Times. "Army Denies Whitewash in Loyalty Quiz Row." September 9, 1953.

——. "Cohn Offers to Resign as McCarthy Counsel." July 20, 1954.

——. "Ralph Zwicker; Former General Felt Wrath of McCarthy." August 12, 1991.

——. "Republican Blocked as Red Inquiry Aide." April 13, 1950.

——. "Truman Gets New Blast by M'Carthy." July 13, 1950.

——. "Why Communism Is an Issue." October 15, 1952.

Louisville Courier-Journal. "McCarthy Says Leaders Put U.S. in Slaughter Contest." June 17, 1951.

Lovett, Christopher C. "On the Side of the Angels and the Fall of Joe McCarthy." *Emporia State Research Studies* 51, No. 1 (2016).

Lyon, Peyton V. "The Loyalties of E. Herbert Norman." *Labour/LeTravail* 28 (Fall 1991).

Lyons, Shante J. "The Sociopolitical Ideology of a Communist Educator: Doxey A. Wilkerson." *Journal of Philosophy and History of Education* 64, No. 1 (2014).

Mad. "What's My Line?" November 1954.

Makow, Henry. "The Communist Jews Behind Sen. Joseph McCarthy." henryma kow.com, January 8, 2016.

Manawa (WI) Advocate. "Chain Store Manager Enters Freshman Class." September 12, 1929.

Maney, Patrick. "Joe McCarthy's First Victim." *Virginia Quarterly Review* 77, No. 3 (2001).

——. "Morris H. Rubin: Memoirs of a Progressive Editor." *The Old Northwest,* Summer 1986.

Manly, Chesly. "Sulzbergerism." *American Mercury,* July 1979.

Mannes, Marya. "Channels: Comments on TV." *The Reporter,* March 31, 1953.

——. "The People vs. McCarthy." *The Reporter,* April 27, 1954.

March, James G. "McCarthy Can Still Be Beaten." *The Reporter,* October 28, 1952.

Marder, Murrey. "Attorney for Newest McCarthy Target Says Loyalty Board Cleared GPO Client." *Washington Post,* August 13, 1953.

——. "The Fort Monmouth Story." *Bulletin of Atomic Scientists,* January 1, 1954.

——. "Many Scientists Fear Probes Will Affect National Defense." *Washington Post,* November 12, 1953.

——. "No Basis Found for Belief Monmouth Is Nest of Spies." *Washington Post,* November 9, 1953.

——. "Pearson Says McCarthy Threatened to Maim Him." *Washington Post,* October 5, 1951.

——. "Senator's Account of Dispute Branded 'Fantastic' at Pentagon." *Washington Post,* March 13, 1954.

——. "Stevens Promises McCarthy to Review Army Ban on Data." *Washington Post,* September 9, 1953.

Marquette Tribune. "Boxer Completes Prep Studies in One Year." March 26, 1931.

——. "Campus News in Pictures." October 30, 1930.

——. "Gridders Open Early Season." March 26, 1931.

——. "Hilltop Sport Fans Display Interest in Boxing at Show." March 26, 1931.

Maurer, Herrymon. "Lessons of the Anna M. Rosenberg Hearings: Where Congressional Investigations Go Wrong." *Commentary,* May 1, 1951.

May, Ronald. "Is the Press Unfair to McCarthy?" *New Republic,* April 20, 1953.

McCarthy, Joe. "McCarthy vs. Pearson." *Saturday Evening Post,* January 12, 1957.

McElheny, Victor K. "Committee Asks Funds to Aid Furry Defense." *Harvard Crimson,* January 22, 1955.

McElligott, Francis L. "Hilltop Sport Mirror: Cagers Still at It, When a Judge Errs, Tierney for Sisk." *Marquette Tribune,* March 26, 1931.

McKinley, James C., Jr. "Conservatives on Texas Panel Carry the Day on Curriculum Change." *New York Times,* March 13, 2010.

McMahon, Patrick. "Ships and Greeks — and Senator Joe McCarthy." *American Mercury,* July 1953.

McManus, John F. "The Birch Log: Another Look at 'McCarthyism.'" *New American,* November 1987.

——. "Remembering Joseph McCarthy." *New American,* September 1995.

——. "Review of *Blacklisted by History.*" *New American,* March 2008.

McMillin, Miles. "Phony Heroism Is Backfiring for McCarthy." *Capital Times,* August 4, 1952.

——. "The Wisconsin Political Scene." *Capital Times,* August 25, 1946.

——. "Wisconsin Weighs M'Carthy: 'Rush It Out in the Open Air.'" *New York Times,* May 7, 1950.

Meyer, Jim. "It Happened Here: An Appleton Exorcism." *Appleton Post-Crescent —The Scene,* December 1999.

Millis, Walter. "Serious Situation at Fort Monmouth." *St. Petersburg Times,* December 8, 1953.

Milwaukee Journal. "A Divorce Day for McCarthy." September 29, 1946.

——. "Hits Forgery of McCarthy." November 3, 1952.

——. "Man in Uniform Is on Bench, and It's No Court-Martial." August 12, 1942.

——. "McCarthy Gets Wilder." September 15, 1950.

——. "McCarthy, McMurray Stage a Verbal 'Slugfest.'" October 23, 1946.

——. "McCarthy's Ideas on Housing Published by 'Prefab' Maker." March 1, 1949.

——. "Questions by Hearers, Rivals Enliven Candidates' Forums." October 17, 1946.

——. "Senate Prepares Rites for McCarthy." May 3, 1957.

——. "Youth to Complete High School in Single Year." March 16, 1930.

Milwaukee Sentinel. "M'Carthy Will Resume Bench." January 28, 1945.

Morgan, Ted. "Judge Joe: How the Youngest Judge in Wisconsin's History Became the Country's Most Notorious Senator." *Legal Affairs,* November–December 2003.

Morris, John D. "McCarthy Target Is Appointed as Top Assistant to Murrow." *New York Times,* July 16, 1961.

——. "Rites for McCarthy in Senate Monday." *New York Times,* May 4, 1957.

——. "3 Democrats Scorn Bid from M'Carthy." *New York Times,* July 19, 1953.

Morris, Robert. "Counsel for the Minority: A Report on the Tydings Investigation." *The Freeman,* October 30, 1950.

Moser, William R. "Populism, a Wisconsin Heritage: Its Effect on Judicial Accountability in the State." *Marquette University Law Review* 66, No. 1 (Fall 1982).

Moynihan, Michael C. "McCarthy and His Friends: The Unconvincing Rehabilitation of Tail Gunner Joe." *Reason,* March 2008.

Murphy, Charles J. V. "McCarthy and the Businessman." *Fortune,* April 1954.

——. "Texas Business and McCarthy." *Fortune,* May 1954.

Murray, Michael D. "Persuasive Dimensions of See It Now's 'Report on Senator Joseph R. McCarthy.'" *Today's Speech,* Fall 1975.

Murrow, Edward R. "See It Now: A Report on Senator Joseph R. McCarthy." CBS, March 9, 1954.

Mutual Broadcasting System. "Reporters' Roundup." September 13, 1951.

Narvaez, Alphonse A. "Frederick G. Fisher, 68; Was a McCarthy Target." *New York Times,* May 27, 1989.

The Nation. "The Bohlen Affair." April 4, 1953.

——. "La Follette's Folly." August 14, 1946.

——. "The Press Meets McCarthy." May 9, 1953.

——. "Sen. McCarthy." May 1957.

——. "The Shame of the Senate." January 1953.

——. "The Washington Front." July 8, 1950.

Neikind, Claire. "United States Communists, 1950: Their Numbers and Influence Seem on the Wane." *The Reporter,* June 6, 1950.

Nelson, Anna Kasten. "Anna M. Rosenberg, an 'Honorary Man.'" *Journal of Military History* 68, No. 1 (January 2004).

——. "Caught in the Web of McCarthyism: Anna M. Rosenberg and the Senate Armed Services Committee." *Congress & the Presidency* 30, No. 2 (2003).

Nevada State Journal. "More M'Carthy Charges Made." February 15, 1950.

Newcomb, James. "Joe Buried Beside Father, Mother on Bluff Above Gently Turning Fox." *Appleton Post-Crescent,* May 8, 1957.

——. "Joe Served Altar and Flag, Pastor Says at Funeral Rites." *Appleton Post-Crescent,* May 7, 1957.

New Republic. "The Menace of McCarthyism." April 6, 1953.

——. "Official Senate Report: The Financial Affairs of McCarthy." March 30, 1953.

——. "Washington Wire." July 31, 1950.

Newsweek. "Again, Who's Lying?" May 1, 1950.

——. "Jessup Backfire." October 22, 1951.

——. "McCarthy and Greek Ships: 'Undermining' or 'Constructive.'" April 13, 1952.

——. "McCarthy and Stevens — Behind Scenes." March 8, 1954.

——. "Red Books Abroad." April 6, 1953.

——. "The Scorched Air: Murrow Versus Senator McCarthy." March 22, 1954.

——. "Senate Newcomer." December 16, 1946.

——. "That Sly Counselor — Welch." June 7, 1954.

——. "Trap for McCarthy." April 3, 1950.

——. "Tydings on a Tear." July 31, 1950.

——. "The Voice on TV." March 9, 1953.

——. "War on McCarthy." May 15, 1950.

New York Daily News. "Cohn, in 'Hate Clash,' Comes Near to Blows." June 12, 1954.

New Yorker. "Home-Town Paper." May 1944.

New York Herald Tribune. "Churchill's Memoirs: To Be Published in US." May 15, 1947.

——. "Philbrick Calls Arrested Reds 'Fall Guys' for Real 'Pro' Elite." February 1, 1952.

——. "Rabbi Blames McCarthyism in College Raids." May 25, 1952.

New York Post. "McCarthy's Death Expected to Bring Special Election." May 3, 1957.

New York Times. "A. A. Kimball Named to Reed Harris Post." April 22, 1953.

——. "Acheson Clever Witness, Senator McCarthy Says." June 2, 1951.

——. "Aide Denies General Bowed to M'Carthy." October 6, 1952.

——. "Aide of M'Carthy Scored on Charge." April 9, 1955.

——. "Aide to M'Carthy Resigns." August 1, 1953.

——. "Army Disclaims Any Red Coddling in Case of Peress." November 4, 1954.

——. "Army Drops Race Equality Book; Denies May's Stand Was Reason." March 6, 1944.

——. "Army Rebuffs McCarthy, Won't Open Files on Major." February 20, 1954.

——. "Austrian Assails McCarthy." April 15, 1953.

——. "Ban on Books Is Denied." June 28, 1953.

——. "Book Burning Denied." June 17, 1953.

——. "Books Removed in Argentina." June 22, 1953.

——. "British Deny Ships Carried Red Troops." June 18, 1953.

——. "British Press Cool to M'Carthy Aides." April 18, 1953.

——. "British Press Pokes Fun at M'Carthy Investigators." April 26, 1953.

——. "Calls Fisher a 'Fine Kid.'" June 10, 1954.

——. "Civil Defense Aide Is Linked to Reds." November 25, 1953.

——. "Clash of M'Carthy, Wechsler Is Bared." May 8, 1953.

——. "Code on Inquiries Given to Senate." March 11, 1954.

——. "Cohn Says He Won't Quit." June 14, 1954.

——. "Communist Party Losses." March 26, 1952.

——. "Coolidge Action Cited." March 23, 1954.

——. "Dare to Indict Him Made by McCarthy: M'Carthy Defies Security Ruling." May 28, 1954.

——. "Death Ruled Suicide." June 3, 1953.

——. "Director of Staff Leaves McCarthy Subcommittee." October 5, 1954.

——. "Don Hollenbeck Is Suicide by Gas." June 23, 1954.

——. "Doodles by a Man Watching Inquiry." May 8, 1954.

——. "Dr. Jessup vs. Mr. M'Carthy." October 4, 1951.

——. "Einstein Criticized: M'Carthy Says Giver of Such Advice Is 'Enemy of America.'" June 14, 1953.

——. "Eisenhower and M'Carthy." March 4, 1954.

——. "Eisenhower and Truman Miss Broadcast." November 25, 1953.

——. "Eisenhower Urged to Act." October 30, 1952.

——. "Embassy Tales of Removals." June 23, 1953.

——. "Excerpts from Testimony of Wechsler Before McCarthy Inquiry." May 8, 1953.

——. "Excerpts from Text of Majority Report on Charges by Senator McCarthy." July 18, 1950.

——. "Excerpts from 30th Day of Testimony in Senate Hearings on Army-McCarthy Dispute." June 10, 1954.

——. "Excerpts from Transcript of Fifth Day of Senate Debate on Censure of McCarthy." November 17, 1954.

——. "Excerpts from Transcript of Fifth Day of Senate Hearings on Censure of McCarthy." September 9, 1954.

——. "Excerpts from Transcript of First Day of Senate Hearings on Censure of McCarthy." September 1, 1954.

——. "Excerpts from Transcript of 21st Day of Senate Testimony in Army-McCarthy Dispute." May 27, 1954.

——. "Excerpts from Transcript of 22nd Day of Senate Hearings in Army-McCarthy Dispute." May 28, 1954.

——. "Excerpts from Transcript of 23rd Day of Testimony in Army-McCarthy Dispute." May 29, 1954.

——. "Excerpts from 28th Day of Senate Testimony in Dispute Between Army and McCarthy." June 8, 1954.

——. "Ex-Envoy Lane Calls M'Carthy a Patriot." August 28, 1952.

——. "Ex-Rep. Martin Dies, 71, Is Dead; Led Un-American Activities Unit." November 15, 1972.

——. "'Fear and Smear,' Truman Says." October 29, 1952.

——. "5 Ex-Envoys Decry Attack on Corps." January 17, 1954.

——. "Flanders, Mild Vermonter of 73, Cast in the Role of Giant Killer." July 31, 1954.

——. "Flanders Supported: Frelinghuysen Backs His Attack on Senator McCarthy." March 13, 1954.

——. "Former U.S. Aide Indicted as Red." December 1, 1953.

——. "General Electric Victory in Ousters." December 31, 1954.

——. "General Lawton at Final Review." August 29, 1954.

——. "Gen. Lawton Slated to Quit as Brigadier." May 29, 1954.

——. "Gerald L. K. Smith Dead; Anti-Communist Crusader." April 16, 1976.

——. "G.O.P. Caucus in Avon, Conn., to Choose Eisenhower or McCarthy as Party Leader." March 12, 1954.

——. "Hearings Start on Coast." August 22, 1953.

——. "Herbert Backs M'Carthy." September 18, 1953.

——. "Huber in Phone Calls: Missing Witness Tells Wife He Is Going Away for Month." April 27, 1950.

——. "Inquiry Heads Criticized." December 14, 1953.

——. "Instructions Kept Secret: Mexico Embassy Aides Bar Data on Books Removed from Library." June 17, 1953.

——. "Judge Dorothy Kenyon Is Dead; Champion of Social Reform, 83." February 14, 1972.

——. "Justice Douglas Hits 'Witchhunt.'" November 25, 1953.

——. "Karl Baarslag, Author and Ex-Congress Aide." January 14, 1984.

——. "Lattimore Says U.S. Is Right to Aid Korea." August 1, 1950.

——. "Lawton Account Was Given to Senate." April 29, 1954.

——. "Lawton in Medical Test." July 24, 1954.

——. "Lehman Deluged with Stamps." June 21, 1953.

——. "Leroy Gore, Editor, Is Dead in Wisconsin." April 14, 1977.

——. "Librarians in Convention." June 22, 1953.

——. "Listed by M'Carthy, Economist Replies." August 17, 1951.

——. "Mark Twain Is 'Cleared' by U.S. in Memo to Library in the Hague." June 23, 1953.

——. "M'Carthy Accuses Official on Ships." May 5, 1953.

——. "M'Carthy Accuses Truman in Reply." November 25, 1953.

——. "M'Carthy Assails Time Magazine." January 29, 1952.

——. "M'Carthy at White House: He Gets 'Hello There' Greeting from President Eisenhower." July 11, 1953.

——. "A M'Carthy Book to Be Published." May 5, 1957.

——. "M'Carthy Critic Supported Here." April 10, 1954.

——. "M'Carthy Death Shocks Capital." May 3, 1957.

——. "M'Carthy Denies Swaying General." October 5, 1952.

——. "M'Carthy 'Extremes' Deplored by Priest." April 2, 1950.

——. "M'Carthy Gives Hug to Critical Senator." March 11, 1954.

——. "M'Carthy in Brawl with Drew Pearson." December 14, 1950.

——. "M'Carthy Inquiry Stirs Libel Action." October 14, 1954.

——. "M'Carthy Puts Off Allen Dulles Test." July 11, 1953.

——. "M'Carthys in Cab Crash." February 18, 1954.

——. "M'Carthy Turns Up Nothing on Kaplan." March 8, 1953.

——. "M'Carthy Victory Expected by G.O.P." September 7, 1952.

——. "McCarthy Accuses Symington of 'Plot.'" April 16, 1954.

——. "McCarthy Act on 'Cover.'" January 16, 1955.

——. "McCarthy Aide Ordered to Guard Duty at Kilmer." March 11, 1954.

——. "McCarthy Appeals to Democrats." February 7, 1954.

——. "McCarthy Assailed in London." February 28, 1954.

——. "McCarthy Charge Ridiculed." March 22, 1953.

——. "McCarthy Comment Quoted." September 28, 1954.

——. "McCarthy Criticizes Shuster." March 22, 1953.

——. "McCarthy Deletes 'Now' in Reply to President." March 4, 1954.

——. "McCarthy Noncommittal." April 10, 1954.

——. "McCarthy Promises Names." August 9, 1951.

——. "McCarthy's Finances Under Revenue Study." June 9, 1954.

——. "McCarthy's Surge to National Prominence Sparked by Timely Attacks on Reds in '50." May 3, 1957.

——. "McCarthy Target Ousted." November 21, 1952.

——. "McCarthy Tried to Avoid Trial of Editorial Critic, U.S. Says." April 10, 1954.

——. "McCarthy v. Army." February 21, 1954.

——. "Mitchell Opens Drive." March 8, 1954.

——. "M.I.T. Role Clarified on 'Voice' Stations." March 11, 1953.

——. "Mrs. Moss Is 'Sorry.'" May 3, 1957.

——. "Mrs. Moss Ousted by the Army Again." August 5, 1954.

——. "Mrs. Roosevelt Says M'Carthy Is Menace." September 21, 1951.

——. "'Mystery Witness' Disputes M'Carthy." November 17, 1953.

——. "Navy Suspends Explosives Expert; State Department Then Bars Wife." April 11, 1951.

——. "Networks Are Praised: Trade Journal Hails the Denial of Time to McCarthy." March 13, 1954.

——. "New Spy Evidence in M'Carthy Case." October 18, 1951.

——. "Nixon Plea Halted Letter on Vessels." May 26, 1953.

——. "Nixon Voices Tribute." May 3, 1957.

——. "No Fees for Senator." March 17, 1954.

——. "'None of My Business.'" March 17, 1955.

——. "Outcome 'Shocks' Stevens." February 25, 1954.

——. "Pearson Sues M'Carthy." March 3, 1951.

——. "Petition Step off in M'Carthy Fight." December 3, 1954.

——. "Poll of Libraries Shows Free Choice." June 16, 1953.

——. "President Chides M'Carthy on 'Fair Play' at Hearings." March 4, 1954.

——. "The President Strikes Back." July 11, 1953.

——. "Publisher Is Indicted: Herman Greenspun Accused on McCarthy Editorial." April 9, 1954.

——. "The Real Issue." February 23, 1954.

——. "Reds Say President Supports M'Carthy." March 11, 1954.

——. "Reed Harris Quits as 'Voice' Official." April 15, 1953.

——. "Role of the Signal Corps." October 18, 1953.

——. "Schine Bound for Alaska." October 5, 1954.

——. "2d Major Admits Error on Peress." March 17, 1955.

——. "Sees McCarthy 'Afraid.'" February 25, 1954.

——. "Senate Ouster Urged." February 28, 1954.

——. "Senator Attacks: Hits Back at Stevenson, Murrow, and Flanders in Radio Broadcast." March 12, 1954.

——. "Senator McCarthy Again." August 12, 1951.

——. "Senator McCarthy Is Accused." December 16, 1948.

——. "Senator Plans a Fight." March 9, 1954.

——. "Senator 'Sick of Chatter.'" March 15, 1954.

——. "Senator's Tactics Assailed." January 31, 1954.

——. "Spellman Rebukes Inquiries' Critics." October 25, 1953.

——. "Spy Inquiry Resumed in City by M'Carthy." November 17, 1953.

——. "Station Drops Program as 'Strictly Political.'" March 12, 1954.

——. "Straws in the Wind." March 11, 1954.

——. "Summary by Senator Lodge on Minority's Report on Communism." July 18, 1950.

——. "Surrender to M'Carthy." February 26, 1954.

——. "Taft Asks Dulles Put End to 'Voice.'" March 16, 1953.

——. "Teacher's Suicide Is Laid to Inquiry." December 25, 1948.

——. "Texans Give McCarthy Cadillac for His Deeds." October 22, 1953.

——. "Text of Letter Left by 'Voice' Suicide." March 7, 1953.

——. "Text of McCarthy Reply." July 18, 1950.

——. "Text of Memorandum Issued by McCarthy in Reply to Army Report." March 13, 1954.

——. "Text of Nixon Reply to Stevenson Attack on the Administration." March 14, 1954.

——. "Text of Senator McCarthy's Speech Accusing Truman of Aiding Suspected Red Agents." November 25, 1953.

——. "Text of Stevens-McCarthy Exchange." March 14, 1954.

——. "Texts of Statement by McCarthy and Some Replies." December 8, 1954.

——. "Texts of Statements by President and Senator McCarthy's Reply." March 4, 1954.

——. "3 Democrats Quit McCarthy's Group in Fight on Powers." July 11, 1953.

——. "Time Advertisers Get McCarthy Plea." June 17, 1952.

——. "Top Red Agent Tied to Fort Monmouth." November 7, 1953.

——. "Transcript of General Zwicker's Testimony Before the McCarthy Senate Subcommittee." February 23, 1954.

——. "Tribute to Hendrickson." August 20, 1954.

——. "Truman Aide Says He Quit Left Links." February 28, 1950.

——. "Turn of Tide?" March 14, 1954.

——. "'20 Years of Treason' Charged." February 6, 1954.

——. "2 Draft Delays for Cohn Recited." March 20, 1954.

——. "2 Sue to Enjoin M'Carthy." December 9, 1953.

——. "U.S. Quashes Case M'Carthy Caused." May 26, 1954.

——. "A Victory for Common Sense." July 17, 1953.

——. "White's Book Restored." July 13, 1953.

——. "Wilson Blames Stevens." March 5, 1954.

——. "Winchell Denies He Knows Source of M'Carthy Data." September 8, 1954.

——. "'Witch Hunt' Talk Decried by Jansen." December 28, 1948.

——. "Witness in Albany Assails M'Carthy." November 14, 1953.

——. "Won't Give Democrats Names." November 8, 1954.

——. "World News Summarized." March 27, 1950.

Nobel, Martin S. Letter to the editor. *Washington Post,* March 13, 1954.

Novak, Robert D. "McCarthy = Bad: But the Truth Is More Complicated." *Weekly Standard,* November 2007.

Oakes, John B. "Inquiry into McCarthy's Status." *New York Times,* April 12, 1953.

——. "Report on McCarthy and McCarthyism." *New York Times Magazine,* November 2, 1952.

O'Brian, Jack. "An Analysis of Murrow's Portsided Political Pitching." *New York Journal-American,* March 10, 1954.

——. "Berle, Silvers, Bergen, First in Anti-Red Line." *New York Journal-American,* April 30, 1954.

——. "Commie Phone Plot Exposed in Two Minutes." *New York Journal-American,* June 28, 1954.

——. "Continuing Study of the Continuing CBS News 'Slant.'" *New York Journal-American,* June 23, 1954.

——. "Gonna Wash That Color Right Out of Our Set." *New York Journal-American,* May 26, 1954.

——. "Letters from Readers on Slanted Newscasts." *New York Journal-American,* June 14, 1954.

O'Brien, Michael. "The Anti-McCarthy Campaign in Wisconsin, 1951–1952." *Wisconsin Magazine of History* 56, No. 2 (1972–1973).

——. "Young Joe McCarthy, 1908–1944." *Wisconsin Magazine of History* 63, No. 3 (Spring 1980).

O'Connor, John E. "Edward R. Murrow's Report on Senator McCarthy: Image as Artifact." *Film & History* 16, No. 3 (September 1986).

O'Donnell, James P. "Professor in a Hot Spot." *Saturday Evening Post,* December 5, 1953.

Osborne, John. "White House Watch: Gabbing with Harlow." *New Republic,* May 13, 1978.

Oshinksy, David. "Graying Now, McCarthyites Keep the Faith." *New York Times,* June 1, 2002.

——. "In the Heart of the Heart of Conspiracy." *New York Times,* January 27, 2008.

Pageant. "Who Are the Nation's Best and Worst Senators?" October 1949.

——. "Who Are the Nation's Best and Worst Senators?" September 1951.

Parke, Richard H. "McCarthy Says Leaders Put U.S. in Slaughter Contest." Louisville *Courier-Journal,* June 17, 1951.

Payne, Ethel. "Moss Case Flops; Exit McCarthy." *Chicago Defender,* March 20, 1954.

Pearse, Ben. "The Case of the Unexpected Senator." *Saturday Evening Post,* July 31, 1954.

Pearson, Drew. ABC broadcast, June 17, 1951. National Personnel Records Center, Joseph R. McCarthy files.

——. "Confession of an S.O.B." *Saturday Evening Post,* November 3, 1956.

——. "Washington Merry-Go-Round" syndicated columns: March 28, April 11, August 1, October 21, and November 20, 1947. December 1, 1948. August 28, 1949. February 18 and 25, March 14, April 7, 13, 19, 20, and 21, May 4, 6, 7, and 20, June 2, 9, 19, 20, 21, and 25, July 9, 11, and 23, November 5 and 28, and December 3 and 22, 1950. January 3, 6, 15, 17, 21, and 27, May 5, 20, and 29, June 19 and 28, July 7 and 11, and November 26, 1951. January 11, 27, and 28, February 6 and 12, June 10, August 28, September 8, October 20 and 28, November 2 and 23, and December 14, 19, and 29, 1952. January 1, 2, 3, 7, 8, 9, 18, and 19, March 2, April 2, 3, 7, 10, 17, and 22, June 25 and 28, July 11, 17, 22, and 24, August 16, 21, and 25, September 4 and 10, October 5, 11, and 29, November 18, December 1, 7, 8, 10, 13, 19, and 30, 1953. January 1, 4, and 25, February 15 and 25, March 2, 3, 4, 7, 10, 13, 17, 19, 25, 26, 27, and 31, April 1, 4, 5, 11, 14, 16, 19, 20, 22, 24, and 29, May 1, 6, 11, 13, 14, 15, 17, 19, 20, 24, 25, and 31, June 4, 5, 14, 15, 18, 22, 23, and 24, July 2, 13, 17, 24, 25, and 30, August 1, 8, 11, and 13, September 10, 12, 17, 20, 23, and 28, October 2, 24, and 28, November 8, 10, 17, 19, and 30, and December 3, 9, 11, 12, and 15, 1954. January 11 and 28, February 4, 5, 6, 8, 15, and 18, June 28, and August 23, 1955. February 15, March 9, May 7, June 4, November 2, and December 7 and 28, 1956. January 10 and 14, February 2, and April 25, 1957. March 27, 1958. April 18, 1960. February 14, 1961.

Pedrick, Willard H. "Senator McCarthy and the Law of Libel: A Study of Two Campaign Speeches." *Northwestern University Law Review* 48, No. 2 (May–June 1953).

Perlez, Jane. "A Degree of Indifference." *New York Daily News,* May 18, 1981.

Persia, Jorge de. "Gustavo Duran: Memory of a Multifaceted Spanish." *Residencia Magazine,* June 1997.

Pett, Saul. "Senator McCarthy Courageous or Arrogant?" *Oregonian,* April 11, 1954.

Phillips, Wayne. "Harassing Feared by 'Voice' Suicide." *New York Times,* March 7, 1953.

Pilat, Oliver, and William V. Shannon. "Smear, Inc.: The One-Man Mob of Joe McCarthy." Seventeen-part series. *New York Post,* September 4–23, 1951.

Pollitt, Daniel. "The Fifth Amendment Plea Before Congressional Committees Investigating Subversion." *University of Pennsylvania Law Review* 106 (June 1958).

Popham, John N. "Stevens Decries 'Irresponsibility.'" *New York Times,* March 20, 1954.

Porter, Russell. "6 G.E. Men Balk M'Carthy Inquiry." *New York Times,* February 20, 1954.

Potter, Philip. "Democrats Urge Nonpartisan Probe of Disloyalty Charges." *Baltimore Sun,* May 26, 1950.

——. "Hobbs Would Welcome New Amerasia Inquiry." *Baltimore Sun,* May 23, 1950.

——. "McGrath Talk Under Attack." *Baltimore Sun,* May 25, 1950.

——. "Not Worried by McCarthy, Lucas Says." *Baltimore Sun,* May 17, 1950.

——. "Probe Delays 3 Major Bills, Tydings Hints." *Baltimore Sun,* May 19, 1950.

——. "7 GOP Senators Repudiate McCarthy Tactics." *Baltimore Sun,* June 2, 1950.

——. "Ship Data Seizure Denied by U.S. Aide." *Baltimore Sun,* June 1, 1950.

——. "Truman Again Under Attack by McCarthy." *Baltimore Sun,* June 3, 1950.

——. "Tydings Sifts Amerasia File." *Baltimore Sun,* May 24, 1950.

Pravda. "Изъятие книг из американских библиотек за границей" ["Confiscation of Books from Overseas American Libraries"]. June 24, 1953.

——. "Газета 'Дейли уоркер' о покровителях сенатора Маккарти" ["'Daily Worker' on Senator McCarthy's Patrons"]. January 12, 1954.

——. "Новый поход на гражданские права в США" ["New Crusade on Civil Rights in USA"]. January 6, 1953.

——. "Общественный суд в Нью-Йорке над сенатором Маккарти" ["Public Trial of Senator McCarthy in New York"]. January 8, 1954.

——. "Мошеннические проделки сенатор Маккарти" ["Senator McCarthy's Frauds"]. January 14, 1953.

——. "Тотальная Истерия" ["Total Hysteria"]. May 12, 1950.

——. "Что показал конгресс британских тред-юнионов" ["What the Congress of British Trade Unions Showed"]. September 15, 1953.

Prendergast, William B. "State Legislatures and Communism: The Current Scene." *American Political Science Review* 44, No. 3 (September 1950).

Price, David H. "Anthropologists on Trial: The Lessons of McCarthyism." *Annual Meeting of the American Anthropological Association,* November 1997.

The Progressive. "McCarthyism in Action." April 1954.

Punnett, Ian. "Would Eye Lie to You? Reexamining CBS' Reported Phone Response to 'Murrow Versus McCarthy.'" *Southwestern Mass Communication Journal* 30, No. 2 (Spring 2015).

Pusey, Nathan Marsh. "Pusey: McCarthy Should Be Forgotten." *Appleton Post-Crescent,* May 3, 1992.

Racine Journal Times. "Appleton Captain Has Triple Exploit While Off Duty." January 1, 1944.

——. "State Judge on Leave Injured in the Pacific." July 9, 1943.

——. "Vote Taft 'Best Senator' and Bricker 'Worst' — Both from Ohio." September 4, 1949.

Radosh, Ronald. "The Enemy Within." *National Review,* December 17, 2007.

——. "What Conservatives Need to Know About Joe McCarthy." *Free Republic,* September 30, 2009.

Radosh, Ronald, and Steven Usdin. "The Sobell Confession." *Washington Examiner,* August 19, 2019.

Ranzal, Edward. "Radar Witness Breaks Down; Will Tell All About Spy Ring." *New York Times,* October 17, 1953.

Raymond, Jack. "Officials Act in Belgrade." *New York Times,* June 22, 1953.

Reed, Ted. "Former *Spec* Editor Awaits Degree." *Columbia Daily Spectator,* March 27, 1981.

Reeves, Thomas C. "McCarthyism: Interpretations Since Hofstadter." *Wisconsin Magazine of History* 60, No. 1 (Autumn 1976).

Reston, James. "Censure Held Unlikely." *New York Times,* July 31, 1954.

——. "McCarthy Changes Plan." *New York Times,* April 23, 1954.

——. "Stevenson Scores Rival on M'Carthy in Wisconsin Talks." *New York Times,* October 9, 1952.

Rhinelander (WI) Daily News. "Look What the Milwaukee Journal Says About McCarthy." November 2, 1946.

Rich, Frank. "The Original Donald Trump." *New York Magazine,* April 30–May 13, 2018.

Ringle, Ken. "Tales from a Redbaiter's '50s Fishing Expedition." *Washington Post,* May 6, 2003.

Ritchie, Donald A. "Are You Now or Have You Ever Been? Opening the Records of the McCarthy Investigation." *Journal of Government Information* 30 (2004).

——. "The Army-McCarthy Hearings, 1954." In *Congress Investigates: A Critical and Documentary History.* Edited by Roger A. Bruns, David L. Hostetter, and Raymond W. Smock. New York: Facts on File, 2011.

Rives, Tim. "Eisenhower and the Remnants of the Western Past." *Great Plains Traverse,* May 17, 2018.

Roberts, Chalmers M. "McCarthy Feuds with Priest over TV 'Smear.'" *Washington Post,* January 4, 1953.

——. "'Opened' Mail to Benton Stirs Hearing." *Washington Post,* September 4, 1952.

Roberts, Sam. "The Dentist McCarthy Saw as a Threat to Security." *New York Times,* April 4, 2005.

———. "Dr. Irving Peress, Target of McCarthy Crusade, Dies at 97." *New York Times,* November 18, 2014.

Roosevelt, Eleanor. "Excerpt, 'On My Own.'" *Saturday Evening Post,* March 8, 1958.

———. "Stevenson, Truman and Kennedy." *Saturday Evening Post,* March 8, 1958.

Ross, Irwin. "Joseph P. Kennedy: The True Story." *New York Post,* January 9–13, 1961.

Rovere, Richard H. "The Adventures of Cohn and Schine." *The Reporter,* July 21, 1953.

———. "Letter from Washington." *New Yorker,* April 1950, and March and June 1954.

———. "What Course for the Powerful Mr. Taft?" *New York Times,* March 22, 1953.

Rubin, Morris, ed. "McCarthy: A Documented Record." *The Progressive,* April 1954.

Rushmore, Howard. "The Gentleman from Indiana: A Profile of William E Jenner." *American Mercury,* April 1956.

———. "McCarthy Held Back Hot Ammo." *New York Journal-American,* June 19, 1954.

———. "Mr. Anti-Communist." *American Mercury,* May 1953.

———. "Pekin Farm Boy." *American Mercury,* July 1953.

———. "The Senator from Moscow (Idaho)." *American Mercury,* July 1955.

———. "Young Mr. Cohn." *American Mercury,* February 1953.

Salt Lake Tribune. "M'Carthy Note Again Asks Reds' Ouster." February 12, 1950.

Sanstadt, Joan. "Who Was the Real Joe McCarthy?" *New London (WI) Press-Star,* February 9, 1977.

Saunders, D. A. "The Dies Committee: First Phase." *Public Opinion Quarterly* 3, No. 2 (April 1939).

Schlesinger, Arthur M., Jr. "McCarthy Is Threatening Us Again." *Saturday Evening Post,* August 13, 1966.

Schmidt, Dana Adams. "M'Carthy Called Feared in Europe." *New York Times,* June 14, 1954.

———. "One Book Banned in Tel Aviv." *New York Times,* June 22, 1953.

Schrecker, Ellen. "Political Tests for Professors: Academic Freedom During the McCarthy Years." University Loyalty Oath Symposium, October 7, 1999.

Scruton, Roger. "McCarthy Was Right on the Red Menace." *Los Angeles Times,* December 27, 1990.

Sedgwick, A. C. "No Issue in Greece." *New York Times,* June 22, 1953.

Seldes, Gilbert. "Murrow, McCarthy and the Empty Formula." *Saturday Review,* April 24, 1954.

Servan-Schreiber, Jean-Jacques. "How It Looks from Europe." *The Reporter,* June 6, 1950.

Service, John. "Foreign Service Reporting." *Foreign Service Journal,* March 1973.

Sevareid, Eric. "Joseph R. McCarthy." *The Reporter,* May 16, 1957.

Shafer, Jack. "Week Four: The President Summons the Ghost of Roy Cohn." *Politico,* June 17, 2017.

Shannon, David. "Was McCarthy a Political Heir of LaFollette?" *Wisconsin Magazine of History* 45 (Autumn 1961).

Shapiro, Walter. "Opinion: Red-Scare Henchman a Role Model for Russia-Challenged President." *Roll Call,* May 16, 2017.

Shawano (WI) County Journal. "Attorneys Speak at Service Clubs." April 8, 1937.

———. "Jos. M'Carthy Joins Shawano Law Firm." February 13, 1936.

———. "Jr. Woman's Club Hears Talk on 'Americanization.'" April 14, 1938.

Sheboygan (WI) Press. "Judge McCarthy 'Holds Court' in Dilapidated Jungle Shack." November 15, 1943.

———. "No Violation, Is Bar Reply of McCarthy." January 7, 1949.

Sherrill, Robert. "King Cohn." *The Nation,* August 12, 2009.

Ship, Reuben. *The Investigator.* Canadian Broadcasting Corporation, May 30, 1954.

Shipp, E. R. "Prof. Gene Weltfish Dead at 78." *New York Times,* August 5, 1980.

Simkin, John. "Howard Rushmore." *Spartacus Educational,* September 1997.

Sing, Kenneth S. W. "Stephen Brunauer, 1903–1986." *Langmuir* 3, No. 1 (January 1, 1987).

Sitov, V. I. "Сенатор и классики" ["The Senator and the Classics"]. *Pravda,* August 24, 1953.

Sniegoski, Stephen J. "Joseph R. McCarthy and the Historians: Of Myth and Reality." *Unz Review,* March 1, 1985.

Sokol, Robert. "Power Orientation and McCarthyism." *American Journal of Sociology* 73, No. 4 (January 1968).

Spannaus, Edward. "It Didn't Start with Joe McCarthy." *Executive Intelligence Review,* December 9, 2005.

Starnes, Richard. "End of a Nightmare." *Washington Daily News,* July 18, 1961.

Steele, Jack. "Fighting Kennedy Succeeds Cohn on 'McCarthy' Staff." *New York World-Telegram and Sun,* January 18, 1955.

———. "Order: Bohlen." *Washington Daily News,* September 22, 1959.

Steinberg, Alfred. "McCarran: Lone Wolf of the Senate." *Harper's Magazine,* November 1950.

Stevens, David. "Letter from Wisconsin: McCarthy on the Home Front." *Pacific Spectator,* Winter 1950.

Stokes, Dillard. "Country Facing Cold and Costly Fight to Finish over Court Power." *Washington Post,* December 4, 1946.

Stone, Geoffrey R. "Free Speech in the Age of McCarthy: A Cautionary Tale." *California Law Review* 93, No. 5 (October 2005).

Stout, David. "L. Brent Bozell, 71, a Champion of Conservatism." *New York Times,* April 19, 1997.

Stout, Mark. "The Pond: Running Agents for State, War, and the CIA." CIA Center for the Study of Intelligence, April 14, 2007.

Strout, Lawrence N. "McCarthyism Revisited: TRB's Story." *Journal of American Culture* 22 (Summer 1999).

Stuart, Roger. "The Controversial Senator Contends His Tactics Are Both Practical and Fair." *New York World-Telegram and Sun,* June 13, 1953.

Sullivan, Patricia. "Richard J. O'Melia, 88: Lawyer and Aeronautics Board Member." *Washington Post,* November 2, 2005.

Swing, Raymond. "V.O.A.: A Survey of the Wreckage." *The Reporter,* July 21, 1953.

Tagge, George. "Political Outlook." *Chicago Daily Tribune,* May 4, 1957.

Tanenhaus, Sam. "Review of *Joseph McCarthy: Reexamining the Life and Legacy of America's Most Hated Senator,* by Arthur Herman." *New York Review of Books,* November 30, 2000.

Tankersley, Ruth McCormick. "'Love Outlives Hate.'" *Chicago Daily Tribune,* May 4, 1957.

Taylor, Telford. "Struggle for Control Seen." Letter to the editor. *New York Times,* March 4, 1954.

"The Texas Politics Project." https://texaspolitics.utexas.edu/archive/html/exec/governors/15.html.

Thelen, David P., and Esther S. Thelen. "Joe Must Go: The Movement to Recall Senator Joseph R. McCarthy." *Wisconsin Magazine of History* 49 (Spring 1966).

Theoharis, Athan. "Deep Throat in the FBI's History of Hiding Its Own Leaks." *History News Network,* July 11, 2005.

Thomas, Norman. "Review of *American Security and Freedom,* by Maurice J. Goldbloom." *New York Times,* January 9, 1955.

Time. "Act of Humiliation." March 13, 1950.

——. "Also Wons." August 7, 1950.

——. "Brotherly Blow." August 3, 1953.

——. "Busy Man." October 8, 1951.

——. "The Campaign: Pride of the Clan." July 11, 1960.

——. "A Fool or a Knave." April 17, 1950.

——. "Hoping Against Hope." April 10, 1950.

——. "Insurgent's Way." March 9, 1953.

——. "Joe & the Handmaidens." November 22, 1954.

——. "Joe and the Law." March 15, 1954.

——. "The Man in the Window." January 3, 1949.

——. "The Man with the Popular Mind." November 20, 1964.

——. "Neither Flight nor Fight." March 9, 1953.

——. "New Faces in the Senate." November 18, 1946.

——. "The Oak and the Ivy." March 8, 1954.

——. "The Passing of McCarthy." May 13, 1957.

——. "The Press: The Fetish of Objectivity." May 4, 1953.

——. "Rushmore v. Cohn." November 1, 1954.

——. "Russian for 'Hello.'" May 16, 1949.

——. "The Scoop That Wasn't." January 30, 1956.

——. "The Self-Inflated Target." March 22, 1954.

——. "The Senate." November 13, 1950.

——. "The Senate's Most Expendable." March 20, 1950.

——. "The Senate's Most Valuable Ten." April 3, 1950.

——. "Sen. Joseph McCarthy Launches New Attack on Time." Press release. June 16, 1952.

——. "The Terror of Tellico Plains." May 17, 1954.

——. "Weighed in the Balance." October 22, 1951.

——. "Words from a Quiet Man." March 22, 1954.

The Times (London). "Communism in U.S. Army: Senator McCarthy's Allegations." February 2, 1954.

——. "A Surrender to Mr. McCarthy." February 25, 1954.

The Times of India. "No Need to Invite Ike to Britain." May 21, 1953.

Trohan, Walter. "McCarthyism: Security Is the Real Issue." *Chicago Daily Tribune,* April 4, 1954.

——. "The Tragedy of George Marshall." *American Mercury,* March 1951.

Trussell, C. P. "Bolters Spurn McCarthy Plea for Return to Inquiry Group." *New York Times,* July 17, 1953.

——. "15 in Red Inquiry Shifted as Risks." *New York Times,* August 30, 1953.

——. "Flanders Moves in Senate to Strip McCarthy of Posts." *New York Times,* June 12, 1954.

——. "Increase in Trade with Reds Charged by M'Carthy Group." *New York Times,* July 19, 1953.

——. "Kaghan Tells McCarthy Unit He Has Fought Reds Decade." *New York Times,* April 27, 1953.

——. "McCarthy Puts Dulles on Spot." *Boston Herald,* May 5, 1953.

——. "M'Clellan to Bar One-Man Hearings in Hunt for Reds." *New York Times,* January 1, 1955.

——. "100 British Vessels Cited in Red Trade." *New York Times,* May 21, 1953.

——. "President May Take a Hand If Inquiries Imperil Amity." *New York Times,* May 6, 1953.

——. "Printer Is Quoted on Access to Data." *New York Times,* August 13, 1953.

——. "State Department Voids Curb in McCarthy Study of 'Voice.'" *New York Times,* February 21, 1953.

——. "Stevens Will Review McCarthy's Demand." *New York Times,* September 9, 1953.

——. "US Confirms Word British Ships Transported Red Chinese Troops." *New York Times,* May 29, 1953.

——. "'Voice' Accused of Wasting Million in Constructing First Ship Station." *New York Times,* March 14, 1953.

——. "'Voice' Aide Sees McCarthy Aiming at 'My Public Neck.'" *New York Times,* May 4, 1953.

——. "Voice Must Drop Works of Leftists." *New York Times,* February 20, 1953.

Tydings, Millard G. "McCarthyism: How It All Began." *The Reporter,* August 19, 1952.

United Press International. "McCarthy Pressured on Behalf of Former Aide, Army Says." April 22, 1951.

U.S. News and World Report. "Ike vs. McCarthy—Another Round." March 1954.

——. "Investigators—Politicians—TV Actors." June 4, 1954.

——. "The McCarthy Issue: Pro and Con." September 7, 1951.

——. "Voice of America: The Problem." March 27, 1953.

——. "What Bohlen Can Do in Moscow." April 3, 1953.

US Senate Historical Office. "Ruth Young Watt, Chief Clerk, Permanent Subcommittee on Investigations, 1948–1979." July 19, 1979.

Van Roden, Judge Edward L. "American Atrocities in Germany." *The Progressive,* February 1949.

Variety. "DC Hearings TV's Biggest Soaper; GOP Tries Scalpel on Hottest Show." May 1954.

Vincent, John Carter. Letter to the editor. *Foreign Service Journal* 31, No. 12 (December 1954).

Walker, Franklin V. "Again the Fury." *Harvard Crimson,* January 25, 1954.

Walsh, Warren B. "What the American People Think of Russia." *Public Opinion Quarterly* 8, No. 4 (Winter 1944–45).

Walz, Jay. "Joint Chiefs of Staff Confer as MacArthur Issue Flares." *New York Times,* April 9, 1951.

Washington Evening Star. "McCarthy Weds Jean Kerr." September 29, 1953.

Washington Post. "Coddling the Coddler." March 13, 1954.

——. "Donald Surine, Investigator Under Sen. McCarthy, Dies." January 29, 1992.

——. "FBI Files." March 29, 1950.

——. "Institute Aids in Exchange of Students." March 13, 1954.

——. "Let Listeners Decide, Says Murrow." March 13, 1954.

——. "Loyalty Held Encouraging by Zwicker." March 13, 1954.

——. "Martha Tellier Harris, Aided Civic Campaigns." April 25, 1966.

——. "McCarthy Juggled Facts, Hanson Says." March 29, 1950.

——. "McCarthy Letter Contents Revealed." June 2, 1953.

——. "McCarthy-Pearson Mix It Up." December 14, 1950.

——. "McCarthy Proposes U.S. Draft Lewis, Miners into Army." December 4, 1946.

——. "McCarthy 'Set Price' for Lustron Booklet." May 14, 1952.

——. "More Disapprove of Methods of McCarthy Than Approve." January 16, 1954.

——. "Murrow Report Hailed by Radio-TV Magazine." March 13, 1954.

——. "Nixon Will Not 'Dodge Issues.'" March 13, 1954.

——. "Piltdown Man." July 10, 1952.

——. "Plagiarism and Trespass." January 7, 1954.

——. "Publisher Sues McCarthy for Million." October 5, 1954.

——. "Senate Probe Hints H-Bomb Red Spy Link." August 22, 1953.

——. "Sen. M'Carthy, AEC Differ over Secrets." August 14, 1953.

——. "Signal Corps Spying Hinted by McCarthy." October 13, 1953.

——. "Stevens Hints He'll Stick by Data Refusal." September 17, 1953.

——. "Stevens' Statement." February 26, 1954.

——. "Suicide Cleared by McCarthy of Wrongdoing as Voice Aide." March 8, 1953.

——. "They Can't Do This to Lewis, Miners Feel." December 4, 1946.

——. "Tobey, Beaten, Sees Threat to Wreck Inquiry." August 20, 1947.

——. "'Top Agent's' File May Pace Loyalty Probe." March 23, 1950.

——. "Truman Declines to Comment on Strike." December 4, 1946.

——. "Turning the Other Cheek." March 4, 1954.

Washington Star. "Benton-McCarthy Feud Heralds Mud-Slinging Campaign." May 18, 1952.

Waukesha (WI) Daily Freeman. "Sen. Taft Called 'Best' and Bricker 'Worst' by Capital Newsmen." September 3, 1949.

Waupaca (WI) County Post. "Broken Slugs." February 20, 1936.

——. "Joseph R. McCarthy Attorney-at-Law." February 20, 1936.

——. "McCarthy Will Join Eberlein." February 13, 1936.

Weaver, Warren, Jr. "Cohn Service Record Investigated by the New York National Guard." *New York Times,* March 24, 1954.

——. "Red Agents at G.E., M'Carthy Is Told." *New York Times,* November 13, 1953.

Weigand, Kate, and Daniel Horowitz. "Dorothy Kenyon: Feminist Organizing, 1919–1963." *Journal of Women's History* 14, No. 2 (Summer 2002).

Weingarten, Paul. "Joe McCarthy May Be Dead, but the Faithful in His Hometown Keep His Spirit Alive." *Chicago Tribune,* May 16, 1978.

Welch, Joseph N. "The Lawyer's Afterthoughts." *Life,* July 26, 1954.

Wershba, Joseph. "Murrow vs. McCarthy: See It Now." *New York Times Magazine,* March 4, 1979.

West, Rebecca. "As a Briton Looks at McCarthyism." *U.S. News and World Report,* May 22, 1953.

White, John Kenneth. "Seeing Red: The Cold War and American Public Opinion." National Archives Conference on the Cold War. September 26, 1998.

White, Theodore H. "The Army at Bay." *The Reporter,* March 30, 1954.

White, William S. "F.B.I. Shows Data on Alleged Top Spy to Senate Inquiry." *New York Times,* March 24, 1950.

——. "Flanders Likens M'Carthy, Hitler." *New York Times,* June 2, 1954.

——. "Grand Jury on McCarthy Has Senate's Full Support." *New York Times,* August 6, 1954.

——. "M'Arthur Hearing to Be Opened May 3 by Senate Group." *New York Times,* April 25, 1951.

——. "M'Carthy's Influence Is Greater in the 82d." *New York Times,* January 7, 1951.

——. "McCarthy Strikes at Allen Dulles." *New York Times,* July 10, 1953.

——. "Miss Kenyon Cites Patriotic Record to Refute Charges." *New York Times,* March 15, 1950.

——. "Never Condoned Disloyalty, Says Acheson of Hiss Stand." *New York Times,* March 1, 1950.

——. "New M'Carthy Fire Is Aimed at 'Mr. X.'" *New York Times,* July 26, 1950.

——. "Red Charges by M'Carthy Ruled False." *New York Times,* July 18, 1950.

——. "Study of McCarthy Is Set on 'Coercion.'" *New York Times,* February 22, 1952.

——. "What Motivates Joseph McCarthy." *New York Times,* March 21, 1954.

Whitman, Alden. "John Carter Vincent Dies; Specialist on China Policy." *New York Times,* December 5, 1972.

Wiebe, G. D. "The Army-McCarthy Hearings and the Public Conscience." *Public Opinion Quarterly* 22, No. 4 (Winter 1958–1959).

Williams, Edward Bennett. "The Final Irony of Joe McCarthy." *Saturday Evening Post,* June 9, 1962.

Willingham, John. "The Texas State Board of Education and the Vindication of Joe McCarthy." History News Network, April 5, 2010.

Wilson, H. H. "The Senate Sellout." *The Nation,* January 24, 1953.

Wilson, Richard. "The Ring Around McCarthy." *Look,* December 1, 1953.

Wisconsin Rapids Daily Tribune. "McCarthy Covers OPA, Labor, Bonus and Russian Questions." June 20, 1946.

Wisconsin State Journal. "Babcock to Leave for Capital January 18." December 22, 1946.

———. "La Follette Opponent Sees Rough, Clean Fight." March 18, 1946.

———. "Sen. McCarthy Joins Milwaukee Law Firm." August 12, 1949.

———. "Sen. McCarthy's War Record — The Truth." August 27, 1952.

Woltman, Frederick. "The McCarthy Balance Sheet." Five-part series. *New York World-Telegram,* July 12–16, 1954.

Wood, Percy. "McCarthy and Jenner Back Woman Who Told on Reds." *Chicago Daily Tribune,* November 7, 1952.

Wyngaard, John. "Joe McCarthy Continues to Hold Limelight." *Marshfield (WI) News-Herald,* May 4, 1944.

———. "Madison." *Green Bay Press-Gazette,* May 2, 1944.

———. "McCarthy Outlines His Views on World Affairs." *Appleton Post-Crescent,* November 15, 1946.

———. "Political Lines Finally Straightened Out Clearly in Wisconsin Campaign." *Janesville Daily Gazette,* August 26, 1946.

———. "Under the Capitol Dome." *Appleton Post-Crescent,* May 2, June 8 and 26, July 27, August 7 and 18, and October 6, 1944.

———. "Young GOP to Hear McCarthy on U.S. Policy." *Appleton Post-Crescent,* April 27, 1946.

Yee, H. N. "After McCarthy Era, Harvard Shelves the Red Scare." *Harvard Crimson,* June 3, 2006.

YouTube. "Edward R. Murrow: A Report on Senator Joseph R. McCarthy." November 10, 2014.

INDEX

Aab, Helmuth, 54
Abu Ghraib/whistleblowers, 111
academics/teachers and McCarthyism,
    336–39, 337n
Acheson, Dean
  Alice (wife) and, 314–15
  death/joke, 159
  descriptions, 314–15, 320, 320n
  McCarthy and, 115, 169, 171, 182, 188,
      203, 204, 231n, 238n, 262, 298,
      314–15, 320, 321, 363, 472–73
  McCarthy's death and, 472–73
Adams chronology
  copy of chronology and, 408–9n
  Eisenhower/officials and, 408, 428
  firing Cohn and, 409, 412n, 419–20
  McCarthy and team response/threats,
      412–13, 412n
  McCarthy team/Army officials behind
      the scenes, 407–8, 420
  significance/effects, 407, 409, 419
  writing of, 408, 408n, 428
Adams, John
  Army investigations/hearings and,
      269, 381n, 384, 387–88, 390–91n,
      396, 397, 407
  Army-McCarthy hearings and, 419,
      420nn, 425, 430, 430n, 432, 469
  following Army-McCarthy hearings,
      442–43
  McCarthy relationship, 248, 414
  on McCarthy's alcohol consumption,
      417

Margaret (wife), 432
  post-censure McCarthy and, 468–69
Adams, Sherman, 229, 230, 349, 354,
    408nn
Aiken, George, 183n, 235, 361
alcohol and McCarthy
  amounts, 417, 465, 469
  Army investigations/hearings and,
      380, 417
  Army-McCarthy hearings and, 435
  as circuit judge, 47–48
  death and, 469–72
  during McCarthyism era/hearings,
      200–202, 206, 215nn, 251–52,
      285–86, 325, 416
  Jean McCarthy and, 466, 481
  as Marine, 52, 58, 59n
  Marquette University/Law School, 34
  post-censure, 452, 464–67, 468, 469
  reputation, 102, 163, 350
  Senate censure and, 453
All the King's Men (Warren), 126
Allen, O. J., 377
Allen, Robert, 178
Alsop, Joseph, 165, 173–74, 398, 408–9n
Alsop, Joseph/Stewart, 147, 159, 368n
Amerasia "spies," 135, 136
America Firsters/Party, 41, 76, 91, 107,
    125–26, 500–501n
American Action, 76–77
American Bar Association ethics, 77
American Civil Liberties Union, 368–69,
    424

American Jewish League Against Communism, 367
American Liberty Oil, 352
American Mercury magazine, 366–67
America's Retreat from Victory: The Story of George Catlett Marshall (McCarthy), 171
Amin, Idi, 124
Amos 'n' Andy, 33, 478
Anatomy of a Murder (film), 445
Anderson, Clinton, 84, 102, 103, 120–21, 464
Anderson, Jack
  background, 22–23, 83
  Hoover-McCarthy relationship questions, 198
  McCarthy biography, 22–23, 23n, 47, 83, 138–39, 223n, 339
  as McCarthy friend, 22–23, 82–83, 83n
  McCarthyism, 122, 155, 155n, 157n, 187
  Pearson and, 22–23, 82, 155, 173, 177, 415
Andrew, Christopher, 136
Annie Oakley, 424
Anti-Defamation League, 169n, 178–79n, 241, 388–89
anti-Semitism
  Army investigations/hearings, Fort Monmouth and, 388–89, 391
  Cohn and, 412n, 416
  Malmedy Massacre hearings/McCarthy and, 107–8, 107n-nn
  McCarthyism and, 167–69, 169n, 180, 241, 448
Appleton Post-Crescent, 45, 90, 107, 322
Archdeacon, Henry Canning, 250
Army investigations/hearings
  Cohn, Roy/Schine, G. David and, 376–77, 390, 390–91n, 396
  Eisenhower and, 372, 373, 377, 381n, 395–400
  errors made, 389, 395, 397, 398
  McCarthy description/behavior, 378, 379, 380, 380–81n, 381, 385–86, 387–88
  McCarthy's reasons for investigating, 372–73
  middle ground attempts and, 395–99
  misconduct on both sides, 413

  not recognizing real spies, 387n
  polls on McCarthy, 378–79
  press and, 377–78, 383, 387nn
  television and, 378
  turning point/Zwicker, 379–81, 418–19
  witnesses pushing back, 392
  See also specific individuals
Army investigations/hearings, Fort Monmouth
  Army-McCarthy hearings and, 411, 413, 436, 445
  Cohn's warning, 284, 383
  consequences to witnesses (summary), 391
  FBI letter/writer, 381–83, 382n
  guests of McCarthy, 390
  Jews/anti-Semitism and, 388–89, 391
  "leaks," 375n, 376, 393n
  lies/lack of evidence, 374n, 375–76, 377–78, 383, 386–88, 387n, 400, 401, 404n, 406, 407
  McCarthy's views on, 373–74
  reasons for calling witnesses, 389–90
  role of fort, 373
  Rosenberg and, 374, 375
  Stalin comparisons, 390–91
Army-McCarthy hearings
  advice to McCarthy, 435
  beginning/time frame, 422–23, 427, 440
  broadcasters' coverage/lost revenue and, 429–30
  description, 424–40
  "doctored" photo and, 427, 439
  Eisenhower and, 419, 423, 429, 439nn
  era/other events, 424
  findings/remedies, 441
  "have you no sense of decency" and, 3, 14, 379, 436, 437n
  hearing room description/history, 422–23
  homosexuality issue and, 430
  imagery (summary), 434
  McCarthy behavior and, 420, 420n, 425–27, 425n, 426n, 428–29, 431, 431n, 436–37, 438–39, 445–46
  McCarthy daily routine, 435
  McCarthy description, 434, 446
  McCarthy following, 445–46

McCarthy tricks and, 427–28, 439

methods for easing tensions, 432–33

players/families' lives following, 442–46

"point of order"/McCarthy and imitations, 420, 425, 425n, 434–35, 449, 450

public/celebrities at, 423

public following, 423, 424, 440–41

public views of McCarthy and, 14, 435–36, 441, 442

purpose/questions to be answered, 419

recall election (McCarthy), 441–42

rules, 420

Schine's military special treatment and, 13, 419, 427, 431, 433–34, 434n, 440

tax returns and, 431, 431n, 432

television/significance and, 419, 420, 423, 424, 425, 426n

those under investigation, 420, 420nn

See also specific individuals

Arrowsmith, Marvin, 207, 210

Arundel, Russell, 84, 84n, 85nn

Aschenbrenner, Ed, 40

Ascoli, Max, 332

Associated Press, 120, 205, 206, 207, 459

Association of Catholic Trade Unionists, 365

atomic bombs and Soviet Union, 114

Attlee, Clement, 137

Auerbach, Sol, 278

Await, William, Reverend, 282–83

Babcock, Charles, 166–67, 178n

Bagdikian, Ben, 259

Baker, Bobby, 227, 360

Baldwin, Raymond, 106, 106n, 109, 110, 113

Ball, Joe, 311

Baltimore Sun, 205, 206, 207

Barkley, Alben, 204n

Barnum, P. T., 479

Barrymore, Lionel, 367

Baruch, Bernard, 184

Barvoets, Robert ("Ric"), 54

baseball fundraiser/donkeys, 38

Bassett, James, 360, 431n

Battle of the Bulge, 104

Bay of Pigs, 475–76

Bayley, Edwin, 26, 107n, 205, 207–8, 212, 223n, 459, 468

Bean, Louis, 232

Bellah, Robert, 363n

Bentley, Alvin, 190

Bentley, Arvilla ("Billie"), 190, 190–91n, 197

Bentley, Elizabeth, 135, 259, 260, 261, 317

Benton, William

election (1952) and, 234

fear factor and, 233

investigation into McCarthy, 218–21, 234n

investigative tactics (Benton/McCarthy), 218–21, 234n

La Follette ("Young Bob") and, 74

lawsuit, 220–21

Beria, Lavrenty

McCarthy's plan, 293–94

position in Stalin's regime/information, 293, 294

Berinsky, Stanley, 250, 261–62

Berke, Sylvia/child, 310–11, 312, 338

Berlin, Brigid, 241

Berlin, Richard, 215, 241, 416

Bernstein, Barton, 308, 309

Bilbo, Theodore, 125, 371, 479

blacklisting, 133–34, 133–34n, 158, 256, 268n, 279, 337, 338

Bleier, Rocky, 478

Block, Herb/Herblock, 159, 159n, 210, 213, 364, 369

body count of McCarthyism

difficulties in determining, 1, 300, 338–40

See also specific individuals/entities

Bohlen, Charles ("Chip") and Avis (daughter), 311

Bolling, Alexander, 382

Bolshevik Revolution, 127, 129

books and McCarthyism. *See* libraries/"book-burning" and McCarthyism

boxing and McCarthy

lessons from father, 24

Marquette University/Law School, 32, 34–35, 40, 71

boxing and McCarthy (*cont.*)
  in politics, 75, 81, 150, 157, 339
  teaching, 28, 38
Boyle, William, Jr., 144
Bozell, Brent, 142, 160, 255–56
Bradlee, Ben, 272
Bradley, Omar, 170, 340, 344
Bridges, Styles, 110, 304, 360
Brinkley, David, 123–24, 124n
Brissone, Marie, 33
Brogan, John, 312
Brooks, Walter, Mrs., 92
Browder, Earl, 122, 192, 427
Brown, Chester T., 391–92
Brown v. Board of Education, 424
Brownell, Ann, 350, 350n
Brownell, Herbert, 382, 408, 437nn
Brunauer, Esther, 151, 311
Brunauer, Kathryn, 313
Brunauer, Stephen, 151, 311
Buchanan, Patrick, 475
Buckley, Agnes, 98
Buckley, Daniel, 219
Buckley, William F., Jr., 142, 160, 255–56,
  367, 417, 475
Budenz, Louis
  behavior problems, 157n
  McCarthyism, 156–57, 158n, 184, 257,
  317
Bundy, McGeorge, 363, 363n
Bundy, William
  background, 362–63
  as McCarthy target, 363, 363n
Burke, Henry, 300
Burns, James MacGregor, 361
Burrough, Bryan, 353
Bush, Prescott
  description/descendants, 225
  McCarthy/McCarthyism and, 225
Butler, John Marshall campaign/election
  (against Tydings)
  aftermath/McCarthy and, 193–94n,
  194–95, 197, 198n, 223
  background, 189
  framing Tydings, 192, 192n, 209, 427
  kidnapping incident, 192–93
  money and, 189–91, 353, 502n
  overview/McCarthy and tactics, 13,
  189–95, 192n, 193–94n, 209, 315,
  502n

Byers, Robert, Sr., 219
Byrd, Harry F., 110
Byrnes, James, 118, 119
Byrnes, Mildred, 33

Cahoe, Tom L., 139
Cain, Harry, 232–33
Capehart, Homer, 360
Capital Times, 17, 93, 138, 206, 208, 223n,
  224
Capone, Al, 23, 60n, 146n, 173, 173n
Capone mob, 146nn
Capone, Ralph ("Bottles"), 60n, 173nn
Carr, Frank
  Army-McCarthy investigations/hear-
  ings, 413–15, 420nn, 427, 428, 435
  background/McCarthy position, 298
Carter, Douglass, 210, 211
Case, Clifford/sister, 314
Casey, Pat, 54
Cashway grocery chain, 26–27, 28
Castro, Fidel, 475–76
Catholic Church and communism, 36, 76
Catholic support for McCarthy, 364–66
Cattau, Louis, 40
Caute, David, 357nn
Cavanaugh, John, Father, 365
CCNY (City College of New York), 373,
  389–90
censure of McCarthy. *See* Senate censure
  of McCarthy
Chambers, Whittaker, 135, 156, 263, 317
Chaney, Lindsay, 215
Chaplin, Charlie, 153, 214n
Charlie and the Chocolate Factory (Dahl),
  132
Chase, Benjamin Semple, 95
Cheshire, Maxine, 466n
Chiang Kai-shek, 131, 156n, 158, 210, 334,
  335, 338
Chicago (Daily) Tribune, 44, 76, 81–82n,
  114, 121, 146, 154, 163nn, 191, 206,
  207–8, 214, 215, 264–65, 283, 383,
  461–62
Chicago Defender, 406
Childs, Marquis, 82, 124–25n, 368n
Christian Science Monitor, 346
chronology of McCarthy, 11–14
Chudakoff, Les, 107
Church of Jesus Christ Christian, 168

Churchill, Winston
  communism and, 76
  Dahl and, 132
  McCarthy/McCarthyism and, 161,
    161nn, 170, 217
  memoirs and, 88
  US shipping investigation/China and,
    296–97n
Cieply, Michael, 215
circuit courts
  divorce counsel, 46n
  importance, 46
  McCarthy as judge, 45–47
City College of New York (CCNY), 373,
  389–90
Clark, Tom, 340
Clardy, Kit, 452
Cleon of Athens, 124
Clinton, Bill, 336
Close, Upton, 107, 107nn
Cohn, Albert, 444
Cohn, Roy
  Adams chronology and, 409,
    409n
  Army investigations/hearings and,
    284, 373, 374, 377n, 380n, 382n,
    383, 388, 389, 393, 396, 403, 408,
    409, 439–40
  Army-McCarthy hearings and, 419,
    420nn, 431–32, 434, 434n, 436,
    437, 437n, 438
  background/descriptions, 9, 107n,
    133n, 141, 158, 240, 286, 287, 289n,
    290n, 297, 310–11, 319, 408–9n
  beginning of McCarthy work, 240–43,
    240n
  Bobby Kennedy and, 242, 298, 299,
    418, 431–32, 432n, 444, 480
  death/cause, 480
  as disorganized, 297
  on Eisenhower, 373
  following Army-McCarthy hearings,
    443–44
  homosexuality and, 167, 289–90, 290n,
    430, 430n
  Jean Kerr McCarthy and, 481
  as Jew/cover for McCarthy, 240n, 241,
    388, 389, 416, 439nn
  Joseph R. McCarthy Memorial Foun-
    dation, 475

Julius/Ethel Rosenberg and, 240, 308,
    308n
  lobbying for Schine (military), 410–12,
    411–12n, 427–28, 448
  on McCarthy censure/post-censure,
    451, 455, 461, 463, 464
  on McCarthy/health issues, 463
  McCarthy match/origins and, 241
  McCarthy relationship/speculation,
    408–9n, 414–15, 416–17, 417n
  McCarthyism, 251, 260, 266, 272–76,
    274n, 279, 284, 293, 295, 297, 298,
    362
  McCarthy's Senate memorial, 473
  military records questions, 415–16,
    416n
  responsibility for harm/denying re-
    sponsibility and, 302, 306n, 308n
  significance to McCarthy, 286
  tactics, 274n
  Trump and, 9, 476
Cohn, Roy/Schine, G. David
  Army investigations/hearings and,
    376–77, 390, 390–91n, 396
  behavior together/description, 288–89,
    290, 297, 390, 390–91n, 400
  European tour/McCarthyism, 272–76,
    274n, 276n, 281, 426
  Harris case and, 328–29, 331, 332
  Jean Kerr McCarthy and, 481
  Kerr/McCarthy wedding and, 286
  loyalty between/questions, 416
  reinforcing worst in McCarthy, 376–77
  relationship, 287, 377, 410–12, 411–12n,
    448n
  rumors on homosexual relationship,
    274–76, 276n, 288–89, 430n
  rumors on homosexual relationship
    with McCarthy, 288–89
  Schine hiring by McCarthy and, 279,
    416
  Voice of America investigations head-
    quarters, 288
Cole, Phillip, 293
Coleman, Aaron Hyman
  Army investigations/hearings, 382,
    384–86
  Julius Rosenberg and, 385
  previous checks/job change, 385
  vindication/consequences, 386

Coleman, Thomas ("Boss"), 67, 68, 69, 72, 75, 91, 221, 287
Collier's, 171
Collins, Susan, 253, 485
Commonweal, 365
communism/anticommunism and McCarthy's beginnings
  banned books, 36
  campaign for senator (1946) and, 75n, 76–77
  Catholic Church and, 36
  during 1940s, 136–41
  public housing and, 87, 137
  roots of/personal explanation, 136–41, 141n
  See also McCarthyism
communism/anticommunism (US)
  America's history of anticommunism, 127–29
  children and, 114, 134
  Cold War era and, 136
  communism as non-threat (1940s) overview, 135–36
  communism threat (1940s) overview, 134–35
  FBI (1940s) and, 131
  Hollywood and, 133–34, 133–34n
  legislation (1930s–1940s), 131
  Loyalty Order beginnings, 132–33
  spies, 132, 135, 136
  "subversive" organizations, 130, 132–33
  Venona Project, 135, 260–61, 262–63
  World War II and, 131–32
  See also specific committees; specific individuals
Communist Party USA, 117, 122, 127, 134–35, 136, 256
Compton, Wilson, 266
Conant, James, 124–25n, 334, 334n
Confidential (scandal sheet), 433
Congress of Industrial Organizations, 134, 368
Congressional Directory, 44n, 50
Congressional Record, 44, 171, 214, 468
Cooke, Marvel, 257
Cooper, James Fenimore, 125
Copland, Aaron, 251, 279–80
Cosmopolitan, 140
Costello, Frank, 179n, 477

Coughlin, Charles, Father, 2, 9, 126, 321, 371, 479
Coulter, Ann, 339, 475
Counihan, Maybelle, 41–42, 52, 53n
Coyle, David Cushman, 277
Cromwell, "Dirty Helen," 32
Crosby, Donald, Father, 36–37, 97
Crosby, John, 405
Cuban Missile Crisis, 475–76
Cullen, Roy, 352–53
Curley, James Michael, 2, 9
Curran, Charles, 35, 36
Curry, Don, 464

Dahl, Roald, 132
Daily Worker, 39, 76, 157, 159, 214, 216, 225, 231, 257, 266, 327, 406, 455
Daniel, Price, 454
Davies, John Paton, 334–35
Davis, Charles, 209, 316–17
Davis, Glenn, 462
Davis, Nancy, 445
Day, Leo, 59
de Antonio, Emile, 425n
de Toledano, Ralph, 187n
Dean, James, 445
death (McCarthy)
  death/cause of death, 14, 470–72, 472n
  funeral/burial, 473–74
  gravesite, 479–80, 480n
  requiem mass, 473
  Senate memorial/attendees, 473
  tributes, 472–74
Deatherage, George E., 125–26
Declaration of Conscience, 183, 194n, 245
demagogue
  examples/descriptions, 1–2, 8–9, 124–27, 222
  McCarthyism and, 124
  See also specific individuals
DeMille, Cecil B., 223, 285
Dempsey, Jack, 282, 479
Denver Post, 213
Desmond, Frank, 117
DeSola, Ralph, 168
DeSpain, Val B., 19
Dewey, Thomas, 91, 92, 344
Dies Committee. *See* Un-American Activities Committee (HUAC)

Dies, Martin
  communist lists/demanding resigna-
    tions, 130–31, 261
  position/description, 130
Dietrich, Marlene, 105
DiMaggio, Joe, 371n
Dirksen, Everett, 195, 236, 280n, 397, 417,
  422
Disney, Walt, 367
Doar, W. T., 77
Dohr, Raymond, 230
Douglas, Paul, 63n, 183–84, 204n
Douglas, William O., 227
Doyle, James, 462
Drew Pearson Comments, 172
Dreyfus, Alfred/symbol, 169, 169nn
Driscoll, Mary Brinkley, 123, 124n, 148,
  432n, 458
duck test, 138, 153, 253n, 278
Duke, David, 2, 475
Duke, Russell, 245, 246
Dulles, Allen
  CIA and, 362, 363–64
  McCarthy and, 7, 163nn, 164n, 271,
    282
  standing up to McCarthy, 363–64
Dulles, Foster Rhea, 271
Dulles, John Foster
  authority and, 356–57
  McCarthy and, 7, 259, 266, 271, 358,
    362, 363
  Voice of America and, 266
Durán, Gustavo
  background, 151–52, 313–14
  McCarthyism/effects, 151–52,
    313–14
Durán, Lucy, 313, 314
Dworshak, Henry, 420
Dying for Joe McCarthy's Sins: The Sui-
    cide of Wyoming Senator Lester
    Hunt, 305

Eastland, James, 360, 362
Eberlein, Mike
  circuit judge office and, 42
  McCarthy and, 12, 38–39, 41, 42, 98
  on McCarthy's business sense, 41
Ecton, Zales, 232–33
Eddy, Loyal, 67, 101
Edwards, Leila Mae, 364–65

Edwards, Willard, 118, 119n, 121, 146, 154,
  206, 210, 214–16, 265, 355, 364,
  383, 390, 399, 428
Einstein, Albert
  background, 179
  McCarthy and, 179–80, 402
Eisenhower, Arthur, 124n, 342, 349
Eisenhower, Dwight
  Anna Rosenberg and, 167–68
  anticommunism and, 139n, 256, 296,
    346
  approval ratings, 348–49, 488n
  books/libraries and, 276–77
  Cohn/Schine military status and, 416n
  foreign service corps and, 311, 336
  Korean War, 218
  Mamie (wife), 232
  as president (overview), 343
  reputation/description, 217, 227, 232,
    341, 342–43, 348–49, 371n
  Truman and, 351–52
Eisenhower, Dwight/McCarthy
  Army as target and, 13
  Army investigations/hearings and,
    372, 373, 377, 381n, 395–400
  Army-McCarthy hearings and, 419,
    423, 429, 439nn
  Eisenhower blaming Truman, 342
  Eisenhower vacillating and, 341–46,
    347n, 350–52, 398
  Eisenhower worries/World War II
    decision and, 409n
  as "enabler in chief," 346
  executive privilege and, 428, 428n, 429
  "hidden hand" and, 343, 344, 346, 377
  libraries/"book-burning" and, 276–77
  Marshall and, 229–31, 230n, 342, 344,
    373
  McCarthy attacks (Army investiga-
    tions/hearings), 399–400, 399n
  McCarthy's death and, 472
  middle ground attempts (Army inves-
    tigations/hearings), 395–99
  Nixon as middleman, 348
  pressing Eisenhower to act on Mc-
    Carthy and, 7, 341–42, 346–47,
    349, 350, 352
  relationship, 6, 13, 54, 228, 231, 233,
    233–34n, 270–71, 276–77, 341–52,
    359, 369, 370nn, 429

Eisenhower, Dwight/McCarthy (*cont.*)
  Senate censure of McCarthy and, 448,
    456–57
  suggestions on handling McCarthy,
    347–49
Eisenhower, Milton
  Army-McCarthy investigations/hear-
    ings compromise attempt, 386
  as McCarthy target, 349–50
  pressing brother to take on McCarthy,
    7, 341, 341–42, 344, 349, 350, 352,
    354
elevator shoes, 53, 100
elites and McCarthy
  definition (McCarthy's definition), 320
  elites' activities and, 414
  elites as "the enemy" and, 320–21, 323,
    370, 414
  State Department as first enemy and,
    321
  See also specific individuals/entities
Ellender, Allen, 86
Ervin, Sam, 453

Facts Forum (TV show), 238
Fairchild, Thomas
  description, 221
  Senate campaign (1952)/McCarthy,
    221–22, 221nn, 231–32, 234
False Witness (Matusow), 306, 306nn
Farrakhan, Louis, 2
Farrell, James T., 479
Farrell, John A., 348
Fast, Howard, 268–69, 268n
Faw, Duane, 19
fear and McCarthyism (summary),
    338–39, 401
Fedder, William, 192–93
federal government officials
  as McCarthy enablers (overview),
    356–64
  See also specific individuals/entities
federal judiciary enabling McCarthy
    (overview), 359–60
Fenton, John, 349, 371, 440, 441
Ferguson, Homer, 260
Ferguson, J. Donald, 208
Ferguson, Ma/Pa, 125, 126, 479
Ferman, Irving, 369
Fiedler, Leslie, 320

Fierst, David
  Herbert (father), 312–13
  McCarthyism/effects, 312–13
Fierst, Herbert, 155n
Fifth Amendment, 157n, 246–47, 247n,
    250, 252, 257, 258, 268, 291,
    292–93, 310, 312, 324, 338, 346,
    362, 376, 389n, 392, 394, 394n,
    395, 399, 399n, 407n, 449
films and McCarthy, 214n
Financial Times, 272
Finestone, Max, 252, 252n
Fischetti, Charlie, 173nn
Fisher, Dorsey
  death, 335
  McCarthyism, 335–36
Fisher, Frederick, Jr.
  accusations already revealed, 437, 438
  family following Army-McCarthy
    hearings, 444
  following Army-McCarthy hearings,
    442
  Lawyers Guild, 436, 437nn
  McCarthy accusations against/Army-
    McCarthy hearings, 436, 437,
    439n
  Welch and, 436
Fisher, Hamilton, 444
Fisher, Herbert, 287
Flanagan, Francis ("Frip"), 241–42, 294,
    298
Flanders, Ralph, 124n, 403, 448–49,
    448n, 452, 455, 472
Fleming, Robert, 146n, 149, 199, 208, 219n
Flynn, Gerald T./Mary, 33
Foraker, Clyde, 89
Ford, Henry, II, 354–55
foreign service/"China Hands," 334–36,
    362
Foresman, Shirley, 78
Forrestal, James, 140
Forster, Arnold, 169n, 178–79n
Fort Monmouth, New Jersey
  following Army-McCarthy, 445
  See also Army investigations/hearings,
    Fort Monmouth
Fortune, 353
Francisco, Abden, 252
Franco, Francisco, 293
Frankfurter, Felix, 360

Freberg, Stan, 425n
French Connection, The (film), 443
Friendly, Alfred, 210
Friendly, Fred, 305–6, 333, 400n, 402
Frosh, Brian, 293n
Frosh, Stanley, 292–93, 293n
Fuchs, Klaus, 114, 373
Fulbright, J. William, 278n
Fulbright Scholarships, 277–78, 278n
Fulling, Virgil, 306n
Furry, Wendell
  background, 323
  McCarthy/McCarthyism and, 323–24,
    325
Fuson, Gene, 293–94

gambling and McCarthy
  cheating and, 37
  illegal gambling, 491n
  image and, 33-34, 163, 185, 202
  importance, 37, 464
  law education/work and, 37, 47–49
  as Marine, 57, 57–58n
  Marquette University/Law School,
    33–34
  McCarthyism era and, 201, 355
  as senator, 98, 98n, 102–3, 163, 240
Gandhi, Mahatma, 35
Gandy, Helen, 163nn
Garvey, Marcus, 125
General Electric/workers, 250, 252, 267,
    338, 376, 445
Genghis Khan, 6, 92n, 104, 212, 213
German American Bund, 125–26, 130
Ghosh, Chris, 314
Ghosh, Stanley, 314
Gillette, Guy, 219
Ginsberg, Allen, 480, 480n
Glasser, Ira, 369, 424
Goebbels, Joseph, 212
Goldwater, Barry, 71n, 360, 445, 454
Good Night, and Good Luck (film),
    480
Goodland, Walter, 75
Goodman, Benny, 33
Gore, Leroy, 442
Government Printing Office/secrets, 13,
    291–93, 373
GPU, 269, 269n
Graham, Philip, 103

Grand Chute, 6, 11, 21, 21n, 22, 63, 284,
    321, 373, 403, 474, 478n
Grant, Ulysses S., 247n, 477
Grapes of Wrath (Steinbeck), 66
gravesite (McCarthy), 479–80, 480n
Graze, Gerald/Stanley, 261
Green Bay Press-Gazette, 90
Green, Edith, 39, 43
Greenblum, Carl
  Army-McCarthy hearings/McCarthy
    attacks, 386–88
  background/position, 386
  family consequences/hearings, 386–87
  "protective custody" and, 386, 388
Greenspun, Hank
  McCarthy attacks on, 224–25, 316
  as McCarthy critic, 165–66, 167, 173,
    197n, 224–25, 315, 316, 472
Greenstein, Fred, 343–44
Griffith, Thomas, 159
Grill, Adam, Father, 473
Griswold, Erwin, 253, 253n
Grotnes, Madelaine, 463
Guess, Cleta, 293

Hacko, Paul, 267, 392
Hagerty, James, 351–52, 409
Halberstam, David, 201, 476
Hall, Robert, 403
Hammett, Dashiell, 271, 289
Hanes, John W., Jr., 96
Hanratty, Charles, 32, 33, 35n, 37
Hanson, Haldore
  McCarthyism/effects, 151, 313, 336
  wife/children McCarthyism effects,
    313
Hanson, Signe, 313
Harding, Warren, 129
Harland, Robert, 46
Harnischfeger, Walter, 108, 354
Harris, Donald, 333, 334
Harris, Frederick Brown, Chaplain, 473
Harris, Martha Tellier, 333–34, 346
Harris, Reed
  background, 5, 326–28
  Columbia degree and, 333, 333n
  description, 330
  family and, 333–34
  FBI and, 330, 333
  journal entries, 5, 331–32, 333–34

Harris, Reed (*cont.*)
later years/death, 333, 333n
McCarthyism/lies and, 326–31
Murrow and, 330–31, 332, 401, 480
resignation, 329, 332, 333, 346, 357
VOA/International Information Administration, 326–27, 328, 332
Hart, Edward, 38, 40–41, 201
Hart, Hornell, 254–55
Harvard Crimson, 286, 324n
Harvard University
as McCarthy target, 4, 321–26, 324, 324n, 325, 326n, 334n, 339, 357nn, 363, 363n, 373, 389
See also specific individuals
Harvey, Paul, 461
Hatch Act (1939), 131
Hauge, Gabriel, 229, 230–31
"have you no sense of decency" and McCarthyism, 3, 14, 379, 436, 437n
Hayden, Carl, 445
Hayes, Helen, 214n
Haynes, John Earl, 135, 136, 260–61, 339
health issues (McCarthy)
addiction and, 203, 466n
asthma/smokers and, 101
Bethesda Naval Hospital summary, 463
as day progressed, 252–53
death/cause of death, 14, 470–72, 472n
diagnoses of McCarthy, 203, 376
early 1950s/diet and, 200, 200n, 417
fake injuries and, 453n
mania/bipolar disorder and, 464, 464n
Marine injury/lies, 20, 51–53, 52–53n, 58, 62
Marines and, 53–54, 53n, 101
medications, 464n, 466n, 471
physical/mental issues (post-censure), 14, 462–67, 467n, 468–70
rib cage surgery/consequences, 101–2
Senate censure and, 453–54
summary (1948), 100–101
timing/refuge and, 453, 453n
weight and, 417, 446, 463
See also alcohol and McCarthy
Hearst, William Randolph, Jr., 122, 215
Heil, Julius, 68
Hellman, Lillian, 271, 289, 311, 377

Hemingway, Ernest, 161, 316
Henderson, Dion, 167nn, 206, 434–35, 459
Hendrickson, Robert, 183n, 194n, 452
Hennings, Thomas/wife, 219
Henry Holt book publisher, 352
Hensel, H. Struve, 420nn, 426, 431n
Herberg, Will, 479
Herman, Arthur, 23, 339
Hershberger, Leo
Little Wolf High School and, 27, 28, 30
McCarthy and, 28, 29, 30
Hickenlooper, Bourke, 154, 360
Hiss, Alger, 114, 118, 121, 135, 155, 231nn, 232n, 254, 256, 320, 328, 331, 363, 406
Hitler, Adolf, 73, 104, 105, 110, 124, 124–25n, 127, 135, 180, 212, 216, 217, 221n, 270, 281, 337, 342, 429, 448, 477, 479
Hlavaty, Julius, 311–12, 338, 346
Hollenbeck, Don
background/issues, 305
as McCarthy critic, 305
suicide/McCarthyism and, 305–6, 306n
Zoe (daughter), 306n
Hollywood and anti-communism, 133–34, 133–34n, 162n, 223, 268n, 338, 339, 367
Holt, Saxon W., Jr., 51, 62
homosexuals and McCarthyism, 163–67, 163n, 164–65n, 232, 251, 276n, 303–5, 311, 317, 356, 407, 413, 426, 430, 430n, 440
Hoover, Herbert, 31n, 86, 481n
Hoover, J. Edgar
abandoning McCarthy, 377
Army investigations/hearings and, 382, 382n
Bobby Kennedy and, 404n
Cohn and, 241, 242n
communists/political dissidents and, 128–29, 134–36, 186
declining support for McCarthy/political survival and, 359
homosexuality rumors and, 166-67
Jean Kerr/McCarthy and, 197–98, 281n, 298
Joe Kennedy and, 299

Lavender Scare and, 163n, 166
McCarthy and, 122, 133n, 144, 145, 148, 149, 152, 158, 163n, 273n, 285n, 287–88n, 316, 345, 345n, 358-59, 473
McCarthy relationship, 98–99, 98–99n, 358–59
McCarthy's Senate memorial, 473
Hopkins, Harry, 130, 357n
Hopper, Hedda, 367
Houdini, Harry, 478
Hoyt, Palmer, 213
HUAC. *See* Un-American Activities Committee (HUAC)
Hughes, Emmet John, 281, 479
Hughes, Langston, 251, 269, 279
Hughes, Paul/fake news, 460–61
Humphrey, Hubert, 124–25n, 262, 361
Hunt, H. L., 238, 352–53
Hunt, Lester, Jr. ("Buddy")
background, 303–5
father's suicide and, 303, 304–5, 440
Hunt, Lester, Sr.
McCarthyism/son and, 106, 304, 305, 314
suicide/McCarthyism blackmail and, 303, 304–5, 440
Hurleigh, Bob, 223nnn

Ickes, Harold, 130
Immell, Ralph, 74–75
immunity of senators/representatives, 154, 176–77, 220, 246, 351
Irish Potato Famine, 21
"Iron Curtain" term, 76

Jackson, C. D., 349, 352
Jackson, Gardner "Pat," 227–28
Jackson, Henry, 236–37, 278, 285, 298, 404n, 422, 431–32, 431n
Jacobs, George, 301, 302
Jacoby, Oswald, 102
Jahoda, Marie, 255
James, Jesse, 418
Jarvis, Howard, 232n, 367
Jefferson, Thomas, 121, 290, 332, 459
Jenkins, Ray
Army-McCarthy hearings/role and, 421, 422, 424, 425, 431, 432–33
background/description, 421–22

following Army-McCarthy hearings, 445
Jenner, William, 170n, 235, 237, 283nn, 360
Jewish Americans and McCarthy (overview/statistics), 366, 367
John Birch Society, 366, 475
John Reed Club, 168
Johnson, Andrew, 125
Johnson, Lyndon
background/description, 361n
Baldwin/Malmedy hearings, 110
McCarthy/censure and, 237, 360–61, 429, 449, 455
presidential election and, 71n
Vietnam and, 245nn, 476
Johnson, Robert, 329
Johnston, Richard, 213
Jolin, Gerald, 56, 60, 63, 63nn
Jolin, Walter, 38, 354
Jones, John Paul, 236
Jonkel, Jon M., 189, 190, 191, 194
Joseph R. McCarthy Memorial Foundation, 475
Judgment at Nuremberg (film), 105
Juliana, James
after McCarthy's death, 5
Army investigations and, 375, 375–76n, 380, 381, 391, 393n, 420nnn, 427, 430
on Bobby Kennedy, 240nn
on Cohn, 242–43n, 297
on Hoover, 285n
McCarthy/McCarthy censure and, 285, 363, 364, 375, 375–76n, 417, 427, 435, 442, 456n, 463–64
on Surine, 145n, 238n
Julius Caesar, 124
Juneau, Mary Louise, 41

K1C2, 229
Kaghan, Theodore
on Cohn/Schine/McCarthy, 272–73, 274
HICOG and, 273
McCarthyism/consequences, 273–74, 273nn, 274n, 357–58
Kamin, Leon, 5, 324–25, 336

Kaplan, Raymond
    suicide/note and blame, 300–302, 346
    Voice of America and, 300–302
Karr, David, 178, 178n, 261
Kaufman, Irving, 308, 308n
Keeney, Mary Jane, 261, 262
Kefauver Crime Committee telecasts,
        424n
Kefauver, Estes, 106, 109, 110
Keith, Caroline, 193
Kelly, Walt, 213–14, 214n, 215
Kem, James, 232–33
Kempton, Murray, 290n, 438–39, 456
Kennedy, Bobby
    anti-Catholicism and, 366
    Army-McCarthy hearings/findings,
        431–32, 441
    Army-McCarthy investigations/hear-
        ings and, 390, 395, 403, 404n
    Cohn and, 242, 298, 299, 418, 431–32,
        432n, 444, 480
    description, 319
    following Army-McCarthy hearings,
        444
    Hoover and, 404n
    Jack (brother) and, 239, 475–76
    Jews and, 240nn
    leaving McCarthy (1953), 298–99
    on McCarthy, 451
    McCarthy and, 6, 238–42, 290, 390,
        451, 467
    1960s and, 7–8
    shipping investigation/China, 295–97
    truckers' union attacks/strategy, 389n
Kennedy, Ethel, 6, 467
Kennedy, Eunice, 226, 226n
Kennedy family and McCarthy, 226–28
Kennedy, Jean, 226
Kennedy, Joe
    Catholics criticizing McCarthy and,
        365–66
    description/views, 227–28, 239
    Hoover and, 299
    McCarthy/Bobby and, 238–40, 240n,
        241, 299
    McCarthy/money and, 226–28, 241
    McCarthy/wedding and, 282
Kennedy, John
    anticommunism actions, 475–76
    background, 79n

    Bobby (brother) and, 239, 475–76
    campaign/Lodge and, 227, 361, 408n
    McCarthy/censure and, 225–26,
        227–28, 282, 361, 444, 455–56,
        456n
    ratings, 488n
Kennedy, Patricia, 226, 390
Kennedy, Ted, 432n
Kenyon, Dorothy
    defense, 154
    McCarthyism and, 153–54, 158, 160,
        184, 185, 185n
Kerley, Lawrence, 214
Kerr, Elizabeth, 418n
Kerr, Jean Fraser
    background, 88, 94–95
    description/personality traits, 94, 96,
        282n
    education/political beliefs, 94, 94nn
    engagement to Chase, 95
    Hawaii trip/injury, 197–99, 197n, 198n,
        199n
    insurance (injury) and, 199–200n
    investigations on, 220
    Lustron Corporation and, 88, 95, 209
    McCarthy meeting/relationship,
        94–96, 96n, 113n, 167, 176, 177n,
        197n, 198–99, 238, 281, 281n, 503n
    McCarthyism, 248
    RNC/media work, 238
    wedding, reception, honeymoon, 13,
        281–84, 283nn
    working for/defending McCarthy, 88,
        89n, 106, 121, 140, 146–47, 148,
        170–71, 189, 191–92, 282
    See also McCarthy, Jean Kerr
Kerr, Malvina, 248, 249
Kerr, Robert, 102, 103
Khrushchev, Nikita, 217, 460, 477n
Khrushchev, Sergei, 217
Kidney, John ("Jocko"), 58
Kiermas, Ray/Dolores, 94n, 99, 146, 228
Kimball, Penn, 60, 60–61n
Kimberly-Clark paper company, 354
King Football: The Vulgarization of the
        American College (Harris), 328,
        329, 331–32
King, Martin Luther, Jr., 367
Kirkpatrick, Lyman, Jr., 307
Kissinger, Henry, 242, 242n

Klehr, Harvey, 135, 252n, 260, 387n
Knight, Frances, 328
Knights of the White Camellia, 125–26
Know-Nothing Party, 125
Knowland, William, 82, 110
Knowles, Warren, 462
Knox, Frank, 58–59
Koed, Betty, 299
Kohlberg, Alfred, 133–34n, 156n, 367, 463, 467
Kohlberg, Jane, 467
Kohler, Eric, 251
Kohler, Walter, Jr., 68, 221, 390, 462
Korb, Thomas, 33, 34, 90, 101–2, 107n, 195–96n, 234, 283, 463, 495n
Korean War, 168, 183n, 218, 224, 295, 296, 312, 336, 343, 370, 372, 411, 416n
Kornely, Kelly, 100
Kornely, Olive, 100
    See also McCarthy, Olive ("Sis")
Kraus, Bill, 225n, 478
Ku Klux Klan, 2, 122, 130, 168
Kuhn, Fritz Julius, 126

La Follette, Bronson, 5–6, 303
La Follette, Philip, 65, 91
La Follette, Robert ("Young Bob")
    activities as senator/investigating committee, 65–66, 73–74, 74n, 235
    becoming US senator (1925), 65
    campaign for senator (1946) and, 12, 66–67, 68–75, 75n, 76, 77, 80
    communism and, 78–79
    descriptions, 113, 321
    fans/critics, 66
    McCarthy's hearings/suicide and, 5–6, 302–3, 369
    Midwest base relationship and, 59, 73, 193
    reelection/record (1928), 66
    time as US senator, 66
La Follette, Robert, Sr., 65, 321, 369
La Follettes, Wisconsin
    status/reputation, 65
    See also specific individuals
Lacy, Dan Mabry, 271, 272
Laird, Melvin, 225n
Land, Edwin, 80
Landon, Alf, 39
Landry, Robert, 139–40

Larrabee, Charles H., 45
Las Vegas Sun, 165, 224
Lasky, Victor, 198n, 282, 282n
Lattimore, Owen
    background, 155
    McCarthyism and, 155–58, 155n, 156n, 159, 160–61, 169, 184, 185, 185n, 192, 210, 212–13, 334–35, 349–50, 367, 369
Lavender Scare, 163–67, 163n, 164–65n
law education/work and McCarthy
    abuse of judicial power and, 49, 49n, 77–78, 138
    circuit judge campaign/office and, 42–49
    Eberlein firm/life and, 38–42
    first law practice/life, 12, 37–38
    gambling and, 37
    Marquette University Law School, 11, 29, 30–37
    Quaker Dairy case, 48–49, 49n, 77
    quitting law firm (1951), 146n
    swearing in as lawyer, 37
    Waupaca newspaper/lies, 490n
    women/image and, 37
Lawrence, Bill, 397
Lawrence, David, 461
Lawton, Kirke
    investigations/consequences, 340
    position, 374
    security issues/McCarthy and, 374, 377, 377n, 379, 393n
Lawyers Guild, 436, 437nn
Lee, Bernard, 389
Lee List, 119, 142, 153, 155n
Lee, Robert E. (ex-FBI agent), 119, 119n, 121–22, 142, 144
legislative branch (US) and McCarthy
    overview, 360–62
    those standing up to McCarthy, 361–62
    See also specific individuals
Legislative Reorganization Act (1946), 73–74, 74n
Lehman, Herbert
    background, 362
    McCarthy/censure and, 362, 456
Lemann, Nicholas, 402n
Lerner, Max, 189
Leslie, Edgar, 161–62
Levin, Carl, 253, 424

Levin, Lewis Charles, 125
Lewis, Fulton, 25, 146n, 191, 214–15, 220, 223, 223nnn, 404n, 481, 500–501n
Lewis, Helen, 278, 279
Lewis, John L., 80–81, 82, 317
Lewis, Naphtali, 277–78, 278n, 279
libraries/"book-burning" and McCarthyism
 Cohn/Schine European tour and consequences, 272–76, 274n, 276n, 281, 426
 Eisenhower on, 276–77
 "handles" given Cohn/Schine, 272–73
 McCarthyism investigations/lies, 272–76, 345
 Voice of America/investigations and, 267–72, 270n, 326–27
Lichtman, Robert, 360
Life, 182n, 209, 210n
Limelight (film), 214n
Lincoln, Abraham quote, 211–12
Lincoln Day Dinner description, 114n
Lincoln Day Dinner McCarthy speech
 allegations and lies, 12, 114, 115–20, 123, 496–97n
 writers and, 117–18
Lippmann, Walter, 263, 368n, 419
Little Wolf High School/McCarthy
 activities and, 28–29
 IQ test, 28n
 pace through, 11, 27–30, 29–30n, 31, 45
 record, 28
Lodge, Henry Cabot, Jr., 186, 227, 228, 239, 361, 408nn
Loeb, Philip, 308
Loeb, William, 472
Lokos, Lionel, 395
Long, Huey ("The Kingfish"), 2, 126–27, 172, 321, 371, 478, 479
Long, Russell, 478
Longworth, Alice Roosevelt, 202–3, 423
Look magazine/funds, 145–46n, 214, 316, 356
Lorge, Gerald/Robert, 50n
Los Angeles Times, 360
Lovenstein, Allen, 388, 389
Lovett, Chris, 382n
Loyal American Underground, 149, 220, 249, 328, 358, 380–81n

Loyalty Order/Board, 132–33, 136, 154, 186, 256, 291, 293, 349
Lubell, Samuel, 224
Lucas, Scott, 143, 152, 162, 195, 207, 237
Luce, Henry, 182n, 209–10, 210n
Lucey, Patrick, 477–78
Lustron Corporation, 88–89, 94, 95, 209, 219, 233, 462

MacArthur, Douglas
 divorce, 92
 FDR and, 127
 McCarthy on, 91–92, 92n, 213
 popularity, 371n
 presidential race (1948), 91
 Truman and, 171–72, 203–4
Machiavelli, 195, 195n
Mack, Walter, Jr., 84–85, 85n
Maguire, Russell, 366–67
Maier, Henry, 462
Malcolm X, 124
Malenkov, Georgy, 400
Malmedy Massacre
 alternative story/German prisoners, 105
 Army's commission on, 105–6
 description, 103–4
 SS regiment/individuals and, 104–5, 104n
 war crimes trial/charges, 104–5, 105n
Malmedy Massacre hearings
 conclusions, 111
 Senate's investigatory subcommittee, 106, 109–11, 304
 vote of confidence in Baldwin, 110
Malmedy Massacre hearings/McCarthy
 allegations/US military and, 12, 69, 105, 106, 106n, 108–9, 108n, 110, 373
 anti-Semitism and, 107–8, 168–69
 attacking others behavior, 109–10, 304
 German roots/McCarthy and Wisconsin citizens, 106, 107, 354
 lack of evidence and, 106, 109, 113, 372–73
 legacy, 111–12
 as "observer," 106, 108–9
 polygraph bluff/leaving proceedings, 109–10
 possible reasons he championed cause, 103, 106–8, 372–73

press and, 110
tactics/lessons learned by McCarthy, 112–13, 185
Manchester Union Leader, 472
Mandel, William Marx, 270
Maney, Patrick, 303
Mansfield, Mike, 361
Mao Tse-tung, 114, 134, 158, 313, 334, 349, 400
Mapes, Charlie, 120
Mapes hotel/bar, 120
Marder, Murrey, 210, 242, 368n, 378
Marines/McCarthy
  circuit judge position and, 49–50, 56
  commission vs. private, 12, 50–51, 62, 69, 70
  corps as enabler, 62
  diaries, 18, 56–57, 58, 60, 106
  health issues/complaints, 53–54, 53n, 101
  image/publicity, 50–51, 51n, 58
  injury/lies, 20, 51–53, 52–53n, 58, 62, 101
  leave/resignation, 64
  lifestyle/money and, 58, 59, 62
  logbooks/missions, 19, 54–56, 55n
  McCarthy rescuing Marines (1949), 63n
  McCarthy's version/real version, 17–20, 30, 50–52, 51n, 54–57, 60–61n, 62, 69, 70
  medals/awards, 18, 19–20, 54, 55, 55n
  military dislike beginnings, 57, 372–73
  political campaign/US senator (1944) and, 12, 17, 20, 58–63
  ratings by superiors, 19–20
  reserve status file card, 54n
Markey, D. John, 189, 502n
Marquette Tribune, 29–30n, 34
Marquette University
  description, 29
  Golden Jubilee, 29
Marquette University/Law School and McCarthy
  age/records, 30, 31
  alcohol and, 34
  boxing, 34–35
  card games, 33–34, 33nn
  debate club presidential run, 35
  engineering, 31, 32, 489n
  freshman class presidential run, 35–36, 35n
  gambling, 33–34
  high school/pace and, 29–30n, 31
  Jesuits and, 29, 36–37
  jobs, 32
  money/loans and, 32–33
  national/world politics and, 35
  overview, 11, 29, 30–37
  pace, 31–32
  religion and, 36
  smoking and, 34
  studies and, 32
  switch to law and, 31, 31nn
  women, 33
Marshall, George
  Anna Rosenberg and, 168
  background/status, 169, 170
  Lehman and, 362
  McCarthyism/consequences and, 13, 169–71, 188, 211, 229, 229–30n, 231, 262, 342, 373
  resignation, 171
Marshall Plan, 131–32
Martin, Jack, 396
Marx, Groucho, 402
Marx, Karl, 173n, 264, 404
Mastriani, William, 252
Matson, John, 259–60
Matthews, Joseph Brown ("J.B."/"Doc"), 133–34n, 297–98
Matthiessen, Francis Otto, 308
Matusow, Harvey
  life after McCarthyism, 306nn
  McCarthy/McCarthyism and, 190, 196–97, 201, 206–7, 223, 238n, 306
May, Ronald, 23, 23n, 47, 223n
Maybank, Burnet, 92
Mayer, Louis B., 223
McAuliffe, Mary Sperling, 368
McCarran, Pat, 133n
McCarran rider, 131
McCarthy and His Enemies (Buckley and Bozell), 255–56
McCarthy, Anna Mae, 24, 25n, 26
McCarthy, Bill, 25n, 32, 33n, 355
McCarthy, Bridget ("Bid")
  children's activities/careers and, 25, 25n, 26, 27, 32
  death/grave, 100, 474

McCarthy, Bridget ("Bid") (*cont.*)
  description/beliefs, 22, 36
  marriage/child raising, 11, 21, 22
  parents, 21–22
McCarthy, Charlie (dummy), 161
McCarthy Clubs, 72, 195–96n, 354
McCarthy, Eugene, 146n
McCarthy, Howard, 22, 24, 25n, 59–60n
McCarthy, Jean Kerr
  alcoholism and, 481, 481n
  Army investigations and, 375, 380
  Army-McCarthy hearings and, 423
  Cohn relationship with husband and,
    416–17
  death/cause, 481
  description, 5, 326, 417
  donation of husband's papers, 4, 481
  following Joe McCarthy's death,
    480–81
  husband's death, memorials, burial,
    471, 472, 473, 474
  husband's work and, 284
  Joseph R. McCarthy Memorial Foun-
    dation, 475
  post-censure of husband and, 462,
    463–64
  remarriage, 481
  Senate censure of husband and, 455
  See also Kerr, Jean Fraser
McCarthy, Jean Kerr/McCarthy, Joe
  accident/injuries during Army hear-
    ings, 380
  adopting baby, 14, 467–68, 467n
  dinner in Wisconsin (1952), 350
  evening with friends/supposed hospi-
    talization and, 453
  honeymoon and, 283–84, 374, 375, 383
  house owned by Elizabeth Kerr,
    417–18, 418n
  lifestyle/money and, 284–85
  McCarthy's censure/post-censure and,
    453, 457, 462, 466–67
  quotation/poster in house, 418
  residences, 284
  wedding, reception, honeymoon, 13,
    281–84, 283nn
McCarthy, Joe
  ancestors overview, 21–22
  anti-Semitism and, 107, 167–69, 169n,
    180, 224, 500–501n

Catholic faith, 36, 96–97, 503n
children and, 6, 97–98, 310
chronology, 11–14
comparisons/tyrants, 124, 124–25n,
  168, 195, 212, 221nn, 319, 319n, 429,
  448, 475, 476–77, 478–79
descriptions/personality traits, 1–2, 3,
  3–4, 6, 17, 18, 20–21, 20n, 31, 33,
  34, 36, 37, 40–41, 46, 47–48, 50,
  56, 67, 78, 79–80, 86, 91, 92, 93, 96,
  102, 103, 106n, 109, 110, 120–21,
  124, 124n, 147n, 160, 169, 188n,
  201, 203, 204n, 234, 263–64, 290,
  319, 325–26
homosexuality rumors and, 165–67,
  167nn, 197n, 281, 288–89, 290,
  430n
image importance, 195, 195n, 196–97,
  202
1950s and, 7–8
organizations joined, 368
personal financial problems (1954),
  355–56
perspiring, 202n
reputation/lore overview, 1–9
ridicule and, 213–14
rumors of daughter and, 358–59, 359n,
  513n
"swimming" and, 226, 226n
threats to, 294–95, 418
McCarthy, Joe/childhood and youth
  biographers on, 22–23
  birth, 11, 22
  Cashway grocery store and, 26–27,
    28
  childhood description,
    23–25
  economic situation, 11, 22
  education, 25, 27–29
  Joe's description, 23–25, 27
  Little Wolf High School/pace through,
    11, 27–29
  Marquette University Law School, 11,
    29, 30–37
  poultry business, 11, 25–26
  reading and, 24, 24n
  religion and, 22
  siblings and, 11, 22, 23
  Underhill School/pace through, 11,
    11n, 25

McCarthy, Joe post-censure
  back to attacks, 457–62, 460n
  presidential run and, 461
  press and, 458–59
  shunning of, 457–58
  writing and, 461–62
McCarthy, Mary Ellen, 25n
McCarthy, Olive ("Sis"), 24, 25n, 27, 60
  See also Kornely, Olive
McCarthy Record, The (Rubin), 322
McCarthy, Stephen Patrick, 21
McCarthy, Steve, 24, 25n
McCarthy, Tierney Elizabeth, 14, 467–68,
  480-81
McCarthy, Timothy
  beliefs/alcohol and, 22, 36
  children's activities/careers and, 25,
  25n, 27
  description/traits, 21, 22
  finances/taxes, 59–60n, 100
  grave, 474
  illnesses/death, 100
  inheritance and, 21
  marriage/child raising and, 11,
  21–22
McCarthyism
  acceptance, 337–38, 337n
  analogies/comparisons, 123n, 172–73,
  173n
  background/America's history of anticommunism, 127–29
  behavior of McCarthy and, 248–49,
  251–53, 258n, 285–86
  congressional reorganization (1953)
  and, 235–37
  congressional support/"kid" staffers,
  278–81
  critics, 143–44, 150–51, 152, 160, 160n,
  161, 161n, 165, 171
  Democratic senators' resignations
  (1953), 298, 299
  evidence and, 151–52, 153, 154, 155–56,
  181, 182
  "executive" meaning, 248
  federal government workers and, 336,
  336n
  first-victim claims, 113, 113n
  guilt/innocence and, 249
  Hart (Duke University) performance
  study and, 254–55

as helping communism, 263, 280, 402
informants/tips and, 148, 149–50, 168
lawyers with witnesses, 269
leaks by McCarthy, 258, 259, 264–65,
  274n, 277, 292, 304
legacy in Wisconsin, 477–78,
  478n
legacy (overview), 475–78
lies and, 12, 114, 115–20, 123, 142, 143,
  152–53, 154, 155n, 158–59, 160,
  170, 181
Lincoln Day Dinner speech/allega-
  tions and lies, 12, 114, 115–20, 123,
  496–97n
list numbers confusion/origins, 116–17,
  118–19, 119n, 142, 497n
listening devices/countermeasures,
  147, 147–48n
lives cut short/denial of responsibility
  (examples), 300–309, 306n
lives harmed/family examples, 309–19,
  326–34, 333n
luminary examples, 251
McCarthy becoming chair of Committee on Government Operations,
  13, 235
McCarthy believing in, 162
McCarthy on, 319–20
McCarthy's early reaction, 123–24
McCarthy's lack of knowledge and,
  115, 122, 123, 271, 299
McCarthy's senator duties and, 290–91
motive, 123–24, 141–42, 142n, 162
name of movement possibilities, 133n,
  160
name origins/definitions, 159–61, 160n,
  161n, 169
naming names/consequences, 151–52,
  153–61, 153n, 155n, 159n
nickname (McCarthy), 147
officials' reactions to (early), 116,
  142–44
original list (State Department communists) and lies/confusion,
  115–17, 118–19, 119n
penalties overview, 338
press/deadlines and, 115–18, 119–20,
  119n, 122, 152–53, 154, 204–5, 259
question/phrase use and consequences, 248, 252

McCarthyism (*cont.*)
  questioning and lies/consequences,
      244–46, 248–50, 251, 252–53, 255,
      257–59, 264–71, 291–93, 326
  records sealed/opening (2003) and,
      253
  report by McCarthy (1953), 256–57
  Republicans' views, 180–84, 228, 228
  "results" and, 259–64
  roots of McCarthy anticommunism/
      dinner story, 138–39, 498n
  secrecy/reasons and, 244, 246, 247–49,
      253, 274n, 277
  "spies" and, 115, 117, 142, 143, 155, 155n
  staff after Army-McCarthy hearings,
      442
  staff (early work) and, 144–48
  staff issues (1953), 297–99
  staff set up and, 237–43
  State Department effects and, 255
  State Department response, 116,
      142–43
  stump speech/performance, 150, 151
  supporters, 123, 143, 149, 150, 151, 160,
      161–62, 162n, 187, 207–8, 214–15
  tactics, 117, 123, 143, 160, 168–69,
      169nnn, 268–69, 292
  taking "show on the road"/reasons,
      251
  threats to accused/consequences,
      246–47, 247n, 312, 313, 315
  today's verdict on, 253
  turning against (beginnings), 418–19
  "witness" meaning, 249
  See also Army investigations/hearings;
      specific individuals/entities; Tyd-
      ings Committee
McCarthyism: The Fight for America
    (McCarthy), 140, 275, 319
McClellan, John
  Army-McCarthy hearings, 422,
      424–25, 439, 439nn
  background, 422
  description, 237
  following Senate censure, 457
  McCarthy and, 176, 278, 298, 395, 404
McCormack, John, 227
McCormick, Robert, 76, 189, 191, 215,
    215n
McCulloch, Frank, 120

McFarland, Ernest, 237
McGrath, J. Howard, 143, 148
McGrory, Mary, 368n
McIntyre, E. G., 19
McKesson, Lewis, 265, 267
McLeod, Robert Walker Scott
  Cohn and, 273, 358
  Kaghan/other investigations and, 273,
      357–58
  McCarthy and, 356, 357–58
  position/background, 273, 356–57,
      357n
McLuhan, Marshall, 378
McMahon, Brien, 143, 152, 225
McMillin, Miles, 207–8, 223n
McMurray, Howard
  description/personality traits, 73, 113,
      137
  US Senator campaign/election (1946),
      12, 73, 75–76, 75n, 77, 79, 137
Meeropol, Abel/Anne, 307n
Meeropol (Rosenberg), Michael, 307n
Meeropol (Rosenberg), Robert, 307–8,
    307n
Meet the Press, 4, 150, 199, 260, 325, 417n
Mein Kampf (Hitler), 107-8
Meisner, Grover, 40
Melby, John, 311
Memphis Commercial Appeal, 206
Mercury-Chronicle (Manhattan, KS), 212
Merson, Martin, 279-80, 329, 347–48
Merz, Charles, 473
midterm elections (1954), 452, 457
Miller, Joseph, 433–34, 434n
Miller, Ruth McCormick ("Bazy"), 167,
    189, 199, 461, 463
  See also Tankersley, Bazy McCormick
Miller, Steve, 195–96n
Miller, William Fishbait, 464
Milloy, James, 145–46n
Milwaukee Journal, 28, 47, 51n, 77, 81, 87,
    93, 107n, 119n, 120, 146n, 149, 205,
    207–9, 208n, 210, 212–13, 223n,
    459, 468
Minahan, Victor, 89–90
Mitrokhin, Vasili, 136
money enabling McCarthy
  lifestyle and, 355
  McCarthy pocketing donation money,
      355–56

overview, 351–56
personal financial problems, 355
Morgan, Edward, 223, 244–46, 245n, 250
Morrill, Donald H., 250
Morris, Robert, 189, 241
Morse, Wayne
　McCarthy/McCarthyism and, 183n, 245–46, 250, 361
　political background, 245–46, 245n
Moss, Annie Lee
　Army-McCarthy investigations/hearings and response, 403–7, 404n, 405–6n, 407n, 412, 419
　background/description, 403, 404–5, 406
　error by McCarthy/Cohn and, 403–4, 404nn, 405, 406
　hearings as breaking McCarthyism spell, 419
　McCarthy's death and, 473
　racism/sexism towards, 405
Mueller, Robert, 476n
Mundt, Karl
　Army-McCarthy hearings and, 420, 420n, 422, 424, 425, 436, 440
　background/description, 422
　McCarthy and, 236, 417–18, 422
Murchison, Clint
　background/money, 352
　McCarthy and, 191, 352, 353–54, 356, 435, 461
Murphy, Arold F., 56
Murrow, Casey, 312, 402n
Murrow, Edward R.
　delay in going after McCarthy and, 402n
　going after McCarthy/effects, 7, 13, 312, 400–403, 404, 404nn, 405
　Harris and, 330–31, 332, 480
　McCarthy's response, 400–401, 402, 404nn
　tape criticizing McCarthy/response from listeners, 401–2, 401n
　threats/damage to, 312, 312n, 402n, 480
Mussolini, Benito, 8, 217, 332
My Son John (film), 214n

Nation, The, 66–67, 255
National Review, 475

Nellor, Ed
　anti-Semitic campaign, 500–501n
　background/journalism, 20n, 118, 145–46n
　McCarthy/McCarthyism and, 20n, 118, 145–46n, 147–48n, 149, 161n, 214, 227, 355, 356, 367, 453n, 468
Nelson, Elba Chase, 267
Nelson, Gaylord, 462
Neumann, Franz ("Ruff"), 261
New Deal/critics, 8, 12, 39, 62, 65, 66, 70, 73, 76, 86, 91, 130, 131, 152, 193, 328, 338, 343, 354, 356, 368, 370, 399, 437n
New Republic, The, 159, 255, 346, 434, 479
New York Herald Tribune, 405
New York Journal-American, 214
New York Post, 75n, 91, 149, 207, 211, 317, 389, 438
New York Times, 81, 164, 164n, 195, 195n, 196, 207, 213, 222, 230, 259, 264, 296, 307, 346, 347n, 366, 374, 387nn, 394n, 395, 396, 397, 399, 401, 412, 413, 424, 425, 426, 437, 438, 462, 473
New York World-Telegram, 260, 266
New Yorker, 113
Newsweek, 82, 103, 143, 459
Nichols, David, 344
Nichols, John, 321
Nichols, Lou, 148, 198, 289n
Nimitz, Chester, 55n
Nixon, Pat, 282
Nixon, Richard
　ambitions, 348
　Army-McCarthy hearings and, 423
　attacking McCarthy, 418
　beginning political office and, 79n
　campaigning, 458
　Checkers speech, 231
　communism and, 118, 121, 348
　executive privilege/tapes and, 428n
　McCarthy and, 161, 175, 183, 231, 231n, 235n, 282, 296, 348, 363, 396–97, 398, 408nn, 418, 473
　McCarthy censure and, 449, 456
　McCarthy-Pearson fight and, 175
　vice-presidency and, 231, 348, 396–97, 398
NKVD, 269, 269n

Norman, E. Herbert, 308
nuclear bombs
    H-bomb, 114
    Soviet Union, 114
    threat affects, 114–15
Nuremberg trials, 168, 339

Oakes, John, 222, 347n
O'Brian, Jack, 305, 306n
O'Brien, John A., Monsignor, 365
O'Brien, Michael, 40
O'Brien, Pat, 102
O'Donnell, Dan, 273
Older, Andrew, 177–78
Olsen, Edward, 120
O'Malley, Walter, 145
O'Neal, Bill, 58
O'Neill, Tip, 227
Oppenheimer, J. Robert, 345, 345n
Oshinsky, David, 314
Osman, Loren, 201–2
Othman, Frederick, 283

Pageant (magazine), 93, 217
Palmer, A. Mitchell, 128–29
Palmer Raids, 128–29
Pankratz, Hugo, 33
Pankratz, Jack, 33
Paramount Pictures, 214n
Parker, Cedric, 138, 173–74
Parnell, Andrew, 37, 46, 103
Paul VI, Pope, 36
Payne, Ethel, 406
Pearl Harbor attack, 12, 50, 66, 158,
    423
Pearson, Drew
    Anderson and, 22–23, 82, 138, 155, 173,
        177
    background/status, 172, 173–74
    on Cohn/Schine relationship, 416
    on Robin Hood Club, 442n
    on Schine, 415
    staff/communists and, 177–78
    story on Soviet spies, 174n
Pearson, Drew/McCarthy
    Adam Hats and, 177, 177n, 178–79,
        178–79n
    Cohn and, 408
    on McCarthy illnesses timing,
        453
    on McCarthy/McCarthyism, 226n, 227,
        237, 238, 241, 261, 274–75, 276n,
        290, 296, 410, 420nnn, 435
    McCarthy physical attacks, 13, 174–76,
        175–76n, 177n, 179, 282, 501n
    McCarthy's speech attacks, 176–78
    McCarthy's watch and, 175–76,
        175–76n
    Pearson's lawsuit and, 179
    post-censure, 468
    relationship with McCarthy, 18, 19,
        59–60nn, 92–93, 124nn, 145, 146n,
        155, 155n, 156, 172–79, 178n, 197,
        199, 208, 219, 262, 368n, 469, 503n
    relationship switch, 173
    rumors of McCarthy's homosexuality
        and, 165–66
    warning Eisenhower, 344, 349
Pearson, Luvie, 174
Pegler, Westbrook, 183, 223, 223nnn, 261
Peiper, Joachim, 111, 111n
Pelley, William Dudley, 107, 107n, 125
People's Voice, The, 257, 258
Pepper, Claude ("Red"), 69, 196, 207
Peress, Irving
    Army-McCarthy investigations/hear-
        ings, 380, 381, 391, 392, 393, 407n
    background, 393
    case errors made, 395, 397, 398
    consequences of hearings, 395, 450
    Elaine (wife), 393, 393n, 444
    family following investigations/hear-
        ings, 444
    Fifth Amendment and, 394, 394n
    position/promotion, 380, 393–94, 397
    Zwicker and, 392–93, 393n
Perkins, Frances, 130
Perl, William, 109
Permanent Subcommittee on Investiga-
    tions, 13, 235, 236, 244, 246, 251,
    254, 265, 295, 331, 346, 395, 409,
    419, 422, 424, 444, 447
Persons, Wilton, 229–30n
Piekarski, Witulad, 250
Pilat, Oliver, 149–50, 207
Pius, XII, Pope, 282–83, 283n
PM Magazine, 389
Pogo cartoon (Kelly), 213–14, 214n, 215,
    433
politics and McCarthy

campaigning for others and, 195–97,
    196n
campaigning vs. legal work, 41
circuit judge campaign and, 12, 42–45
Democratic Party and, 39, 40
direct mail use, 43
district attorney run (1936), 12, 39–40
elites and, 70
family loan investigations, 221n
lessons learned from first campaign/
    race, 40
lessons learned/tactics, 40, 42–45
money/loans and, 43
Republican Party switch, 12, 62, 62n,
    67–68n
siblings and, 43
See also specific offices/events
politics and McCarthy/campaign for
    senator (1944)
as Marine/military ban and, 12, 17, 20,
    58–63
money/family and, 59, 59–60n, 100
Wisconsin Constitution violation and,
    61
politics and McCarthy/campaign for
    senator (1946)
communism and, 75n, 76–77
description/lore of one day's cam-
    paigning, 72
direct mail/workers, 71
general election vote count, 79
isolationism and, 69
Joe's background problems and, 77–78
money, 72–73
Robert La Follette Jr./primary and, 12,
    66–67, 68–75, 75n
running while judge and, 77–78
speeches/views, 68–69, 70
strategies/deceit, 66–79, 67–68n
using military background, 79–80, 79n
Young Republicans and, 67, 67n, 69, 72
politics and McCarthy/Senate campaign
    and election (1952)
base and, 217–18, 222, 224
campaign/helping others and others
    helping, 221–24, 223nnn, 224–25,
    228, 230, 231, 231n, 232–33
Democratic nominee, 221–22
Kennedys and, 225–28
money and, 223

press and, 223, 223n, 224
primary, 221
results, 217, 224, 232
threats/precautions, 224
See also Benton, William
politics and McCarthy/senator (before
    McCarthyism)
actions overview, 90–91
bigotry, 93
committees and, 92, 92nn
confidential information for reporters,
    82–83
consensus/views on (end of 1948),
    92–93
description, 80–81
ethics and, 80–81, 82–83, 84–85, 85n,
    86–87, 88–90
everyman image, 98
FBI relationship, 98–99, 98–99n
financial connections/corporations,
    84–85, 87–89, 87–88n
financial problems/strategies, 89–91
foreign policy ignorance and, 81,
    81–82n, 91, 115
health issues, 100–102
housing/making money, 12, 85–89,
    87–88n, 92, 137, 209
on Lewis/mine workers, 80–81
personal housing situation, 99
presidential candidates (1948) and,
    91–92
press/reporters and, 80–83
relationship with children, 97–98
Russia/Russian language, 81, 81n
sugar production/control, 83–85, 85n
trips back to Wisconsin, 99–100
See also specific events/individuals
politics, Wisconsin
Appleton, 71n
La Follettes and, 65
Republican party and, 79
strains, 70–71
See also specific individuals
polls on McCarthy, 217, 337n, 338–39,
    354, 354n, 364–65, 370–71, 370n,
    378–79, 404, 441, 456
"Pond, The," 362, 362n
Post-Standard, 209, 210
posttraumatic stress of McCarthy targets,
    317

Potter, Charles
  Army-McCarthy hearings and, 419–20, 429
  background, 236
  McCarthy and, 123n, 236, 251–52, 280n, 297, 380, 412, 412n, 417
Potter, Phil, 207
Powell, Doris Walters, 257–58, 258n, 261–62
Pravda, 212, 347
presidency, McCarthy running, 461, 461n, 467
press/McCarthy
  criticism/consequences, 207–12, 208n, 210n-nn
  European press (overview), 216
  following Senate censure, 457, 458–59
  Hearst press and, 214, 215, 215nn
  McCarthyism (overview), 115–18, 119–20, 119n, 122, 152–53, 154, 204–17, 208n, 210n-nn, 214n
  Malmedy Massacre hearings and, 110
  manipulating/handling press, 82, 204–5
  politics and McCarthy (before McCarthyism) and, 80–83
  press tactics, 212–13
  publicity and McCarthy, 213
  Russian/Soviet press (overview), 216–17
  signals use, 206
  "spies in State Department" and, 205
  supporting (overview), 214–15
  wire services and, 204–5
  See also specific entities/individuals
Prettyman, E. Barrett, Jr., 238–39
Profiles in Courage (JFK), 361
Progressive (magazine), 78-79, 109
Progressive Party/Progressivism, Wisconsin, 65, 66, 70, 79, 369
Prohibition, 34
Proxmire, William, 462
Pulitzer, Joseph, 210n
Pusey, Nathan
  background/description, 322
  on McCarthy, 326
  McCarthy conflict, 322–24, 323n
  Vietnam War demonstrations and, 324n
Putin, Vladimir, 8, 477n

Quaker Dairy case, 48–49, 49n, 77

Rabinowitz, Victor, 310–11
Racine Journal Times, 17
racism, 71n, 405
Radulovich, Milo, 400, 400n
Rafferty, Joseph, 191n
Ramsey, Norman
  background, 325
  on McCarthy/Jean, 4–5, 325–26, 376
Ray, James Earl, 367
Reagan, Ronald, 445
Reber, Miles, 410, 411, 425, 426
Reber, Samuel, 426
Red Channels, 133–34, 133–34n
Red China beginnings, 114
Red Scare. *See* McCarthyism
Reedy, George, 175–76n, 205, 319, 319n, 320n, 321, 468
Reiske, Francis, 33–34
Remington, William
  background, 259
  communism and, 259–60
  murder, 260, 307
Remy, Steven, 106n, 111-12
Reno Gazette, 120
Reporter (magazine), 216, 274, 288, 332, 357n, 358
Reporter (magazine) as target, 358
Reston, James, 251
Reuss, Henry, 462
Reuther, Walter, 262
Revell, Aldric, 224
Riedl, John, 107
Ringler, Paul, 120
Roberts, Chester, 47
Roberts, Glenn, 73
Robin Hood Club, 442n
Robinson, Edward G., 133–34n
Robinson, Jackie, 80
Rogers, Ginger, 367
Roosevelt, Alice, 202–3, 423
Roosevelt, Eleanor, 124nn, 128, 161, 297, 456n, 491n
Roosevelt, Franklin D.
  anarchists' bombs and, 128
  Chiang Kai-shek and, 158
  Coughlin and, 126
  on Dies, 130
  Einstein and, 179

Kennedy, Joe and, 239
on Long/MacArthur, 127
McCarthy and, 39, 91, 170, 353
New Deal and, 65, 130
Robert La Follette Jr. and, 66
Tydings and, 189
Rosenberg, Anna
background/status, 167–68
description, 168
enemies, 168
McCarthyism and, 167, 168–69, 184, 500-01
Rosenberg, Julius/Ethel
alleged spy ring members, 384, 385, 386, 387, 387n-nn
Cohn/Judge Kaufman private conversations and, 308, 308n
Ethel's guilt and, 307–9
Julius's background, 383, 387, 390
sons, 307–8, 308n
spy case/execution, 3, 136, 186, 240, 240nn, 252, 252n, 307–9, 308n, 375, 383, 387
Rosenberry, Marvin, 49, 77–78
Roth, Toby, 367–68
Rothschild, Edward/wife, 291–93
Rountree, Martha, 167, 199
Rovere, Richard, 113, 142n, 159, 202, 203, 212, 276n, 345–46, 356, 358, 371, 479
Rushmore, Howard, 214–15
Ruth, Babe, 31n
Ryan, Cornelius, 411

St. Louis Post-Dispatch, 210nn, 219–20
Saltonstall, Leverett, 171
San Diego Union, 294
Saturday Evening Post, 43, 52, 72, 147, 165, 175
Schine, G. David
Army-McCarthy hearings/planning and, 435, 439–40
background/description, 279, 286–87
Definition of Communism/problems, 287, 287–88n
draft/McCarthy and Cohn lobbying for, 408, 410–12, 411–12n, 427–28, 448
following Army-McCarthy hearings, 443

military special treatment, 410–12, 519n
military special treatment/Army-McCarthy hearings and, 13, 419, 427, 431, 433–34, 434n, 440
military status questions, 415, 416n
position/McCarthyism, 272, 279, 289n
See also Cohn, Roy/Schine, G. David
Schine, J. Myer, 416
Schlafly, Phyllis, 367
Schlesinger, Arthur, 262
Schmitt, Leonard, 221
Schrecker, Ellen, 337–38, 339
Schroeder, Walter, 90
Schuh, Matt, 84
Schultz, Benjamin, Rabbi, 367
Schuman, Frederick, 151–52
Seaton, Fred, 438
Seaver, Edwin, 270, 271-72
security, "internal security," 338
"security officer," 357
See It Now (Murrow), 330, 400, 402, 404, 405, 419, 480
Seeger, Pete, 133–34n
Seib, Charles, 205
Senate censure of McCarthy
apology and, 454
background, 447–51
censure vs. condemnation, 447n
charges' categories/investigations and, 451–52
committee to hear charges/rules, 449–50
Eisenhower on, 456-57
hearings end/midterm elections and (1954), 452
McCarthy health issues/hospitalization and, 453–54
McCarthy responses, 447–48, 450–51, 454, 456-57, 456n, 460
McCarthy supporters on, 452–53, 454–55
Nixon and, 449, 456
outcome/vote and, 14, 455–57
Sensenbrenner, Frank, 89–90, 146, 354
Sentinel, 208–9
Service, John Stewart
Bob (son), 313, 336
as McCarthy target/consequences, 313, 334-35, 336

Sevareid, Eric
    background, 474
    on China Hands, 335
    on McCarthy, 474
sexism, 405
Shaffer, Samuel, 103, 143, 459
Shapley, Harlow, 151–52
Shawano County Journal, 39
Sheehan, Benjamin, 377
Sheil, Bernard, Bishop, 365, 365nn,
    402
shipping investigation/China, 295–97,
    296–97n, 345
Shortridge, Albert, 224
Silver Shirt Legion, 107nn, 125
Sirica, John, 240, 242-43, 367
Sloane, Ann Brownell, 350, 350n
Smathers, George, 195–96
Smith Act (1940), 131
Smith, Gerald L. K., Reverend, 107,
    125–26, 168, 500–501n
Smith, Margaret Chase
    criticism of McCarthy/consequences,
        182–83, 184, 194n, 219, 236,
        315–16, 345, 353, 361
    Declaration of Conscience, 183, 183n,
        194n, 245
    legacy, 253
    primary challenge/McCarthy (1954),
        315–16
    relationship with McCarthyism
        (early), 182
    Tydings Committee final report and,
        186
Sobell, Morton, 385
Social Security, 66, 146, 222, 344
Society of Jesus, 29
Sokolsky, George
    Army-McCarthy investigations/hear-
        ings and, 396
    background, 214–15, 333
    Cohn and, 241, 416
    McCarthy and, 220, 223nnn, 280, 396,
        412n, 414
Spellman, Francis Joseph, Cardinal, 365,
    366, 467, 467n, 481
Spence, Adolphus, 292
Spillane, Mickey, 134
Splitt, Cody, 42, 72

Stalin, Joseph, 35, 81, 81n, 91, 110, 127, 131,
    137, 158, 180, 187, 212, 222, 264,
    293, 294, 337, 374, 374n, 391, 460,
    477, 477n
Star-Ledger (Newark), 314
Stassen, Harold, 91, 95, 95n, 181
Stegle, Johnnie, 104
Stein, Sol, 160n
Steinman, Louise Tinsley, 174
Stevens, Robert
    Army investigations/hearings and,
        340, 383–84, 394–95, 397–98, 407,
        409, 410, 411-14, 413-14n
    Army-McCarthy hearings and, 419,
        420, 420nn, 425, 426n, 427, 430,
        433, 435, 436
    background, 384, 420nnn
    following Army-McCarthy hearings,
        443
    hearings anti-Semitism issue and, 388
    McCarthy-Stevens meal/conse-
        quences, 397–98, 397n, 408
    wife following Army-McCarthy hear-
        ings, 444
Stevenson, Adlai
    Eunice Kennedy and, 226n
    McCarthy and, 231–32, 231n, 232n,
        401, 418
    presidential run, 218, 230
Stillmore, Robert, 382n
Stimson, Henry, 58–59
Stoffel, Margaret, 21
Stone, I. F., 360, 368n
Straight, Michael, 434
Strandlund, Carl, 88–89
Strout, Richard, 346–47
Students for McCarthy clubs, 166
Subcommittee on Privileges and Elec-
    tions, 218–21, 233
    See also Benton, William
subpoenas, blank, 269
Sullivan, Leon, Father, 263–64
Sullivan, William C., 122
Sulzberger, Arthur Hays, 230
Summerfield, Arthur, 229
Summersby, Kay, 232
sundown towns, 71n
support for McCarthy
    Catholics, 364–66, 366n

description of supporters, 369, 371
overview, 364–71
Wisconsin and, 369
See also specific entities/individuals
Supreme Court (US) enabling McCarthy
    (overview), 246, 359–60
Surine, Don
Butler campaign and, 192, 193
FBI background/description, 145,
    145n, 146
McCarthy and, 145, 170–71, 220, 227,
    237–38, 238n, 294, 400, 401n, 427,
    442, 461, 463–64
Murrow and, 400
Stevenson and, 231
trading information with FBI, 148, 328
Truman administration and, 147–48n
Sussman, Nathan, 387n
Swanberg, W. A., 209–10
Swanson, Charles, 270n
Swedish, Steve, 35
Swift, Wesley, 168
Swing, Raymond, 280
Symington, Stuart
Army-McCarthy hearings and, 422,
    431, 433
McCarthy/McCarthyism and,
    236–37, 278, 296, 298, 404, 405–6

Taft-Ellender-Wagner bill, 86
Taft-Hartley law, 90
Taft, Robert, 82, 86, 91, 92, 95n, 181–82,
    182n, 210n, 235, 360
Tames, George, 164–65n
Tankersley, Bazy McCormick, 396
Taylor, Telford, 150–51, 339–40
teachers/academics and McCarthyism,
    336–39, 337n
television
Army-McCarthy hearings and, 378,
    419, 420, 423, 424, 425, 426, 426n,
    429-30
following Army-McCarthy hearings,
    445
See also specific individuals/shows
Texans and money enabling McCarthy
    (overview), 352–54
Thayer, Charles, 311, 346
Thorpe, Elliott, 158

Tierney, Bridget, 21–22
See also McCarthy, Bridget ("Bid")
Tillman, "Pitchfork Ben," 125, 126, 479
Time, 82, 159, 207, 209–10, 255, 259, 285,
    397n, 417, 422
Titanic sinking investigation, 423
Tobey, Charles, 84, 85, 86–87, 91, 183n,
    314
Todd, Glenn, 55, 55n
Toumanoff, Vladimir/parents, 249–50
Trohan, Walter, 163nn
Truman, Bess, 204n
Truman Doctrine, 131–32
Truman, Harry
Eisenhower and, 54, 256, 343, 346,
    351–52, 400
H-bomb, 114
as lame duck, 218
loyalty screenings, 132-33, 132n, 136
MacArthur and, 171–72, 203–4
McCarthy and, 19–20, 54, 69, 80, 84,
    87, 92, 137, 169, 175n, 179, 181, 181n,
    184, 203–4, 204n, 230, 232, 233n,
    296, 349, 353, 356, 369, 402, 461
McCarthyism/HUAC and, 116, 130,
    139–40, 142–43, 144, 156, 170, 210,
    256, 340
Margaret Chase Smith and, 184
Marshall and, 171
Murrow and, 402
Pearson and, 176, 179
popularity, 193, 371n
Rosenberg, Anna and, 167-68
sugar production/control, 84
World War II issues and, 131–32
Truman, Margaret, 402
Trumbo, Dalton, 268n
Trump, Donald J.
McCarthy similarities/differences, 2, 3,
    8–9, 210, 476–77, 476nn, 477n
"Twenty Years of Treason" speech (Mc-
    Carthy), 353
Tydings Committee
final report, 12–13, 185–86, 189, 215,
    244
hearings/cases, 152–62, 155n, 157n,
    184–85, 185n, 259–60, 314
McCarthy's response/status and,
    186–87

Tydings, Millard
  background/description, 188
  position/reputation, 143, 152
Tydings, Millard/McCarthy
  criticism and, 143–44, 152, 155, 184–85,
    188, 279
  obsession/revenge, 188–89, 188n, 361
  See also Butler, John Marshall cam-
    paign/election (against Tydings);
    Tydings Committee

Un-American Activities Committee
    (HUAC)
  activities, 130
  beginnings, 129–30
  Benton and, 220
  Dies on role, 130
  legislation, 131
Underhill School, 11, 11n, 25, 27, 29
Unger, Abe
  background/McCarthy and, 309–10
  Elizabeth/Nick (children) and McCar-
    thyism, 309–10, 312
United Electrical Workers union, 252
University of Wisconsin, Madison, 74,
    213, 326n, 354, 442n
US Chamber of Commerce, 76, 134
US High Commission for Occupied Ger-
    many (HICOG), 273
U.S. News & World Report, 433
USO tours, 105
Utley, Freda, 276n, 339

Van Susteren, Dirk, 98, 201n
Van Susteren, Greta, 46n, 231n, 481
Van Susteren, Urban
  circuit judge/divorce counsel, 46n, 47
  McCarthy and, 24n, 46, 46n, 47, 50n,
    52, 78, 99–100, 108, 157, 167, 171,
    188n, 201, 203, 220–21, 224, 458,
    463, 466
Vander Beke, George E., 30n
Vatican, 126, 282, 366
Venona counterintelligence project, 135,
    260–61, 262–63
Viereck, Peter, 366
Vietnam War, 154, 245nn, 324n, 336, 424,
    476
Vincent, John Carter, 209, 334–35

Voice of America/investigations
  Cohn/Schine headquarters for, 288
  description/mission and, 264
  Hebrew language broadcasts, 328, 330
  libraries/"book-burning" and, 267–72,
    270n, 326–27
  McCarthyism/consequences, 3, 5, 13,
    264–71, 270n, 277, 280,
    300–302, 306n, 311–12, 314, 373
  standing up to investigation, 266–67
  towers/transmitters and, 265–66, 267,
    300, 302
  See also specific individuals
von Hoffman, Nicholas, 289
Voy, Mae, 41
Voy, Peter, 98

Wagner, Robert, 86
Walker, Robert, 214n
Wall Street Journal, 206
Wallace, George, 2, 9, 71n, 475
Wallace, Henry, 131, 368
Walsh, Edmund, Father, 138, 139, 139n
Walters, Barbara, 289
Walters, Jim, 117
Wander, Jerome, 54
Warren, Earl, 284, 360
Warren, Robert Penn, 126
Washington Post, 81, 82, 103, 159, 199,
    205, 210, 236, 333, 347, 378, 433,
    460–61
Washington Times-Herald, 117, 167, 189,
    206, 214, 304, 396
Watergate, 172, 210, 240, 367, 428n
Waters, Agnes, 108
Waters, George, 118, 214
Watkins, Arthur, 176n, 449–50, 452–53,
    456–57, 458, 460, 460nn
Watt, Ruth, 237, 285–86, 288, 457–58
Wayne, John/son, 162, 162n, 481
Webster's Dictionary, 159
Wechsler, James
  Communist Party and, 211, 317
  on Eisenhower enabling Eisenhower,
    348
  Harris, 333
  McCarthy/McCarthyism and, 211,
    317–19, 348
  wife and, 211

Weir, Bill, 54
Welch, Joe
    Army-McCarthy hearings and, 3, 14,
        379, 420–21, 423, 424, 429, 430,
        436–37, 437n, 438
    background/description, 421
    following Army-McCarthy hearings,
        444–45
Welch, Robert, 366
Welker, Herman, 304, 360, 447n
Wendt, Francis, 87, 87n
Werner, A. J., 45
Werner, Edgar, 42–45, 47, 113, 491n
Werner, Francis, 47, 48
Wershba, Joe, 400, 401n
Wershba, Shirley, 306, 401n
Wherry, Kenneth, 156
White Christmas (film), 424
White, William, 196
Who's Who in America, 44
Wiesner, Jerome
    McCarthyism and, 266–67
    position, 266
Wiley, Alexander, 12, 59, 62, 63, 67nn, 93,
        455–56
Willard, E. C., 19
Williams, Edward Bennett, 438, 454, 477
Wills, Bob, 208–9
Wills, Garry, 133
Wilson, Arthur, 433
Wilson, Charles, 409, 409n, 439n
Wilson, Richard, 356
Wilson, Woodrow
    anticommunism, 128–29
    Palmer Raids and, 128–29
Winchell, Walter, 179, 179n, 241, 340,
        412n, 416
Wisconsin State Journal, 93
Wolman, Benjamin/Diana, 252

Woltman, Frederick
    background, 266
    standing up to McCarthyism, 266–67,
        280
women/girls and McCarthy
    engagements, 41–42
    as Marine, 57–58
    Marquette University/Law School/law
        work, 33, 37
    rumors/young girls, 163nn
    as senator, 94, 94n, 96
    while dating Kerr, 167, 199
    See also specific individuals
Woods, Warren, 199
World War II
    spies in America, 132
    Truman and, 131–32
    See also Marines/McCarthy; specific
        individuals
Wyngaard, John, 63–64n

Yalta agreement, 91, 222, 239, 459
Yeager, Chuck, 80
Young Republicans, 67, 67n, 69, 72
Your Show of Shows (TV show),
        424

Zaharias, Babe Didrikson, 423
Zeidler, Carl, 50, 50n, 59
Zeke (dog), 100
Zwicker, Ralph
    after Army-McCarthy hearings,
        442
    hearings/McCarthy attacks and
        consequences, 340, 379–80, 381,
        380–81n, 391, 413–14n, 418–19,
        450
    Peress and, 392–93, 393n
    position/rank, 379